Best Hi in Switze the Valais, Bel..... .u.., the Engadine and Davos

Diane Greer

Boot Jockey Press
New York

Best Hiking in Switzerland
in the Valais, Bernese Alps,
the Engadine and Davos

1st Edition, April 2021
ISBN: 978-0-9974780-5-1

All photos and original maps by the author
Cover photo: Hohbalm Trail (Hike 2)
Back Cover Photo: Fuorcla Surlej to Pontresina via Coaz Hut (Hike 78)

Your Safety is Your Responsibility

The author assumes no responsibility for the safety of users of this guide. Outdoor recreational activities involve a certain degree of risk and are by their very nature potentially hazardous. It is not within the scope of this guide to allow for disclosure of all potential hazards and risks involved in outdoor activities. All participants in such activities must assume the responsibility of their own actions and safety.

Furthermore, the author has done her best to make sure the information in this guide is as accurate and useful as possible. However, things can change, trails get rerouted, road conditions change, regulations are modified, etc. Hikers using the information in this guide should make allowances for the possibility that it may not be correct.

Even the best guide and maps can't replace good judgment and common sense. Be prepared and cautious. You will have a safer and more enjoyable trip.

Table of Contents

Accommodations
Transportation
Discount Cards
Food
Hiking in Switzerland
Weather
Hours
Holidays
Languages
Currency
Public Toilets

Best Hiking in Switzerland

An opinionated guide to the best hikes in Switzerland's top hiking areas: the Valais, the Bernese Alps, the Engadine and Davos.

Introduction

Switzerland boasts a stunning collection of majestic, glacier-clad peaks soaring above idyllic valleys cloaked in emerald green meadows and lovely forests. Mountainous terrain covers 60% of the country that is approximately the size of Vermont and New Hampshire combined, with 377 peaks over 10,000-ft.

An extensive network of well-marked and maintained trails allows hiker's easy access to this amazing alpine scenery. Over 40,000 miles of trails reach virtually every corner of the country. Each day hikers can select a different trail traveling through this alpine wonderland and then return to comfortable lodging in the evening. Walks range from easy to strenuous, accommodating casual strollers to serious hikers.

Day hikers will delight in the variety of base camps, ranging from villages and small towns to world class resorts, each with great trail systems containing more than enough hiking for a weeklong vacation. The country's excellent trail network connects the various base camps creating sensational point-to-point multi-day hiking trips. Hikers can opt to walk an entire route or selected sections of a route to fit their schedule.

Hikers will not only revel in the dramatic scenery but also the cultural diversity of this tiny country. Each region features interesting architecture, cuisine and customs. Cross Meidpass and go from French speaking Valais in Zinal to the German traditions of the Wallis in Gruben. In the Engadine Romansh, an ancient Latin based language native to the region, is spoken, taught in schools and seen on signage in towns and along the trail. Traditional homes in the villages are decorated with Sgraffiti, a 17th century technique that paints or etches designs into wet plaster.

A unique aspect of hiking through Switzerland is the melding of the spectacular scenery with the culture. While hiking it is typical to see small farms with pastures grazed by cows wearing large bells set against a backdrop of soaring peaks and stunning glaciers. Villages with traditional homes decorated with colorful flower boxes are linked by farm roads and trails, forming high routes with stunning views of the alpine scenery. Many trails follow ancient routes up into the mountains and over scenic passes. These paths traditionally used to move herds to high pastures or travel between villages are still used for these purposes today and now shared with hikers.

Linking the villages, towns and cities, along with providing access to trailheads, is one of the world's best transportation systems. Forget renting a car. Trains, buses, cable cars and gondolas with well-timed connections will whisk you your destination. Discount travel cards, reducing transportation costs, are available for trips lasting from a weekend to a year.

The wide variety of accommodations permits individual travelers, families or groups of friends to create a trip to fit a range of budgets. Options vary from dormitories in huts and hostels to high end hotels. In between are village inns, small hotels and apartment rentals.

See the appendices at the back of the book for more detailed information on accommodations, transportation, languages and other travel basics to help you plan the perfect trip to Switzerland.

About this Guide

This book is an opinionated guide to what I believe are the best hikes in Switzerland's best hiking areas: the Valais, the Bernese Alps, the Uri and Glarus Alps and Eastern Switzerland encompassing the Engadine and nearby Davos. The trails in this book, best hiked between July and mid-September, appeal to day hikers who like to go high and walk 5.0 to 12 miles/day. Elevation gains range from negligible to over 4,000-ft. Many of the trails offer intermediate turnaround points for hikers seeking shorter days. All the trails include detailed trail description with ratings, elevation profiles, maps and photographs. A companion website, hikingwalking.com, includes interactive maps and large photo galleries for each of the hikes in the book.

Also included in this guide is information about hiking the most scenic sections of the Hiker's Haute Route in the Valais and the Alpine Pass Route in the Bernese Alps. The selected segments are easily integrated into a one to two week itinerary so that you can walk a portion of the point-to-point route in addition to spending some time day hiking in one or several of the base camps along the way.

The book is divided into sections for each of the regions. Within each region hikes are grouped by base camps; the best village, town or resort nearest the trailheads. For the Valais and Bernese Alps a section is included covering the multi-day hiking opportunities.

The final section of the book includes practical information about accommodations, transportation and other basic travel topics to help you plan your trip along with tips on traveling in Switzerland on a budget.

I love feedback and would like to hear your opinion on how to improve the guide and the website. Obviously the selection of the best hikes is subjective, based on my personal opinion. Send an email (bootjockey@hikingwalking.com) or post a comment on the website about the book, the pros and cons of a particular hike or if you believe other hikes should be included in the "best of" list.

About the Ratings

All the hikes in this guide are recommended. That being said I want to make it easier for hikers to differentiate between trails. As such, hikes within a region are rated in relation to other hikes in the area. That does not mean that a hike rated as three stars is not worth doing. It just means if you only have a few days in a given area you might want to consider tackling the higher rated hikes first.

Switzerland Locator Map

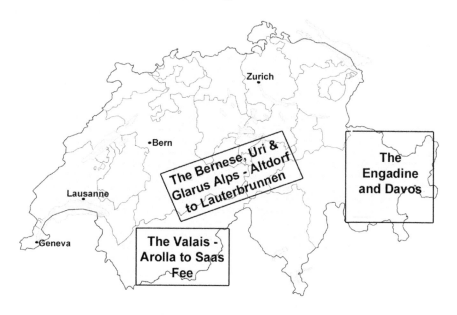

The Valais
Best Hiking Trails between Arolla and Saas Fee

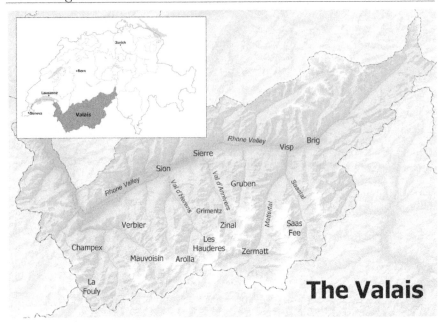

Online Valais Map: www.hikingwalking.com/valais-map

Located in the southwestern part of Switzerland, the canton of the Valais is home to some of the most dramatic scenery in Switzerland. The long, glaciated Rhone Valley charts a southwesterly course through the heart of the Valais, cutting a deep, broad trench between two major mountain ranges. The Pennine Alps extend south from the Rhone, with the range's spine running along the Valais' southern boundary on the Swiss-Italian border. Rimming the valley and the Valais to the north are the Bernese Alps.

Major side valleys branch southward from the Rhone Valley, penetrating deep into the Pennine Alps. These narrow, glaciated valleys are walled by high ridges punctuated by impressive peaks. At the head of the valleys stunning cirques, anchored by some of the country's highest summits, tower above the Swiss-Italian border. The area is home to fifty peaks over 4,000-meters (13,120-ft.), including the Grand Combin, Dent d'Herens, the Matterhorn, the Breithorn, Liskamm, Monte Rosa and the Dom.

The high peaks ringing the valleys are clad in sparkling glacier, emerald green meadows and lovely forests. Towns, villages and world-class resorts, such as Zermatt and Saas Fee, are set amid the valley floors and on sunny benches along the lower slopes. Smaller villages and farms (alps) cling to the steep hillsides.

Some of the finest hiking in Switzerland is found in the Pennine Alps of the Valais. Outstanding hiking areas are located around Zermatt in the

4

Mattertal (Matter Valley), Saas Fee in the Saastal, Gruben in the Turtmanntal, Zinal in the Val de Zinal, Les Hauderes in the Val d'Herens and Arolla in the Val d'Arolla. An excellent network of trails surrounds each base camp providing plenty of opportunities for hikers to explore the high country, climb to panoramic passes and travel through the scenic valleys. The trails, in turn, are interlinked into a regional network creating opportunities to hike between locations. The most famous of these trails, the Walker's Haute Route, travels through some of the best scenery in the Valais.

The Valais is blessed with the driest and sunniest climate in the Swiss Alps. It typically rains less here than in the Bernese Alps to the north or the Engadine to the east. This is not to say it does not rain in the Valais. I have certainly experienced extended periods of bad weather in the region.

In the event of a rainy day or if you simply want to take a day off consider a trip to the Rhone Valley. Frequently scheduled buses or trains run from the various hiking centers down to the large towns and cities in the Rhone, making for easy day trips. In the introduction to each of the base camps there is a section offering suggestions for nearby day trips to the Rhone Valley and other rainy day destinations.

French and German are the main languages in the Valais, although most people running hotels, restaurants or providing other tourist services also speak English. French is the dominate language in the western part of the Valais while German is spoken in the east with the dividing line on the ridge separating the Anniviers and Turtmann valleys. Hikers cross this divide using either the Meidpass or Forcletta Pass when traveling between Zinal, the Hotel Weisshorn or St. Luc and Gruben.

Zermatt
Location: The Mattertal Valley in the Valais

At the head of the Mattertal (Matter Valley), one of the major valleys extending south into the Pennine Alps, is Zermatt -- a year-round resort popular with skiers, mountaineers, hikers and tourists. Zermatt is best known for the Matterhorn, the iconic, pyramid-shaped peak that stands alone on the horizon at the head of the valley. Visitors from all over the world flock to Zermatt to view this majestic summit.

However the Matterhorn is just one of the many impressive peaks towering above the area. Zermatt is set amid the largest group of 4,000-meter (13,120-ft.) peaks in Switzerland. An impressive wall of jagged, glacier-clad summits, including Dent Blanche, the Ober Gabelhorn, Zinalrothorn and the Weisshorn, rim the valley to the west while the Taschhorn, Dom and Rimpfischhorn soar above the valley to the east. Monte Rosa's huge glacier-clad massif, with 22 peaks over 13,000-ft., towers above the valley to the southeast while the famed Matterhorn dominates the view to the southwest.

About Zermatt

The car-free village of Zermatt is centered along the main street (Bahnhofstrasse) running southwest between the Bahnhof (train station) and the Church. The main section of the village extends east to the two streets paralleling either side of the Matter Vispa River. Numerous side streets connect the main thoroughfares.

The Bahnhofstrasse and nearby side streets are filled with upscale boutiques selling pricey goods and gifts along with restaurants, bars, bakeries and specialty food stores. It is also home to numerous hotels, inns and vacation apartments. Neighborhoods are located to the northeast, east and south of the center, with various types of accommodations, restaurants, bars, bakeries and every other service a tourist could desire.

The Tourist Information Center (www.zermatt.ch/en) is located near the Bahnhof on the southwest side of the parking area reserved for electric taxis. Outdoor equipment and clothing stores are found along Bahnhofstrasse and the side streets. In generals these shops are expensive.

There are two supermarkets in the village; the Coop across from the Bahnhof and the Migros on Hofmattstrasse. Smaller convenience stores (Denner, Pam and Spar) along with family run shops, are located in the neighborhoods around the village.

The Gornergrat Cog Railway to the popular Gornergrat overlook is located across from the Bahnhof. To the east, across the river, the valley station for the funicular to Sunnegga connects with the gondola and cable car to the Unterrothorn. The Matterhorn Glacier Paradise lift system to the Klein Matterhorn and Schwarzee are reached by heading southwest along the east side of the river to the Schluhmatten neighborhood. The 0.9 mile walk takes about 20 minutes.

During the day the center of the village is very crowded with visitors staying in the area along with day-trippers coming up from the Rhone Valley. Most come to see the Matterhorn and ride the lifts to viewpoints at the Klein Matterhorn, Gornergrat and Sunnegga. Hikers will find the crowds dissipate as you gain distance and elevation from the center of Zermatt. In my opinion Zermatt's incredible trail system more than compensates for dealing with the crowded tourist areas.

To avoid the tourist, stay off Bahnhofstrasse and stick to the side streets. Get an Ortsplan (village street map) from the tourist center to learn the back streets to the places you wish to reach. I recommend staying in the neighborhoods outside the center where accommodations tend to be quieter and less expensive. Tasch and Randa, down valley from Zermatt, are also good places to look for more reasonably priced lodging.

Hiking around Zermatt

There are five major hiking areas in Zermatt. Starting on the west side of town a trail ascends the Thrift Gorge to the Trift Hotel (Hike 1), situated in alpine meadows beneath a stunning cirque of summits and glistening glaciers. From Trift my favorite hike climbs to the Hohbalm Plateau (Hike 2), with stunning views of the Matterhorn and breathtaking panoramas of the high peaks surrounding Zermatt.

South of Zermatt at the confluence of three glacial valleys is more great hiking. From the Hohbalm a trail drops down to the Zmutt Valley, the long glacial valley extending west from the confluence. This highly scenic valley lies beneath the north facing slopes of the Matterhorn. Trails extend up both side of the Zmutt Valley (Hike 6) and eventually connect to ascend the north side of the Zmutt Valley to Schonbiel Hut (Hike 4).

The Matterhorn Plateau, situated high above the south side of the Zmutt Valley near the foot of the Matterhorn's northeast ridge, offers up-close views of the iconic peak and the superb vistas of the area's glacier-clad mountains. The Schwarzee gondola provides fast and easy access to the plateau. From the plateau a hike climbs to Hornli Hut (Hike 5), situated directly beneath the Hornligrat, the most popular climbing route to the Matterhorn's summit. A second trail descends from Schwarzee along the Matterhorn's north face to the floor of the Zmutt Valley where it connects with trails returning to Zermatt or climbing to Schonbiel Hut (Hike 3).

The Findel Valley extends east from the confluence, with trails ascending the valley to the Findel Glacier (Hike 8) and climbing to the Sunnegga and the Oberrothorn (Hike 7) above the north side of the valley. The area's extensive trail network offers a wide variety of options from an easy stroll to a lake to a strenuous climb to the summit of the Oberrothorn. A funicular, gondola and cable car facilitate access to the trail system.

The Gorner Valley, stretching southeast from the confluence, is home to the Gorner Glacier, the second largest glacial system in the Alps. Towering above this spectacle of ice are the Monte Rosa, Liskamm and Breithorn massifs and nearby summits. Between the Gorner Valley and the Findel Valley to the north is the Riffelberg Plateau and Gornergrat (Gorner Ridge). The area's trail network includes paths climbing to the popular Gornergrat Overlook (Hike 9), the Gorner Glacier Viewpoint (Hike 10) and several intermediate destinations. When used in conjunction with the Gornergrat Cog Railway a variety of point-to-point and loop hiking options provide splendid views of the Monte Rosa massif and its glaciers, the Gorner Glacier, the Matterhorn and the high peaks surrounding Zermatt.

Getting to Zermatt

From Zurich Airport or Bahnhof (train station), take the train to Visp. In Visp exit the train station and walk a short distance to the separate loading platform for the Matterhorn Gotthard Bahn to Zermatt. The scenic ride heads up the deep cleft of the Mattertal with fine views of the surrounding peaks. The trip takes about two and a half hours from Zurich.

From the Geneva Airport or Gare (train station), take the train to Visp and then follow the directions above. The ride should take about three and 30 minutes.

Check the SBB website (sbb.ch/en) /SBB app for directions from other parts of the country.

Zermatt is a car free town. Anyone driving up the Mattertal will have to park at the large car park in Tasch and then take the train to Zermatt. It is possible to take an electric taxi or ride the electric bus to get around town. The taxis are helpful upon arrival if your accommodations are not near the train station and you have a lot of luggage.

Nearby Attractions & Rainy Day Activities

The Matterhorn Glacier Paradise atop the Klein Matterhorn – Ride gondolas and a cable car to the highest station in Europe (12,740-ft.) with a spectacular, 360-degree viewing platform boasting vistas stretching from Monte Rosa to the Matterhorn and as far as Mont Blanc to the west and the

Bernese Alps to the north. The facility includes an Ice Palace, restaurant, gift store, skiing (all year round) and other activities.

Ride the Gornergrat Cog Railway to Gornergrat and enjoy the 360-degree overlook with fantastic views of Monte Rosa and the Gorner Glacier, the second largest glacier system in the Alps. Views encompass the Matterhorn, the high peaks surrounding Zermatt and beyond.

Ride the underground Funicular to Sunnegga, set atop a sunny bench with terrific views of the Matterhorn. Children will enjoy the nearby playground and small lake. Extend the trip by walking to or taking the gondola and cable car to the top of the Rothorn with more great views. A trail network connects the various areas.

Gorner Glacier Gorge – See Hike 11c - Glacier Garden.

The Matterhorn Museum - This interesting museum covers the history of the first assent of the Matterhorn along with the development of Zermatt. The museum is located on Bahnhofstrasse and Kirchstrasse.

The Stockalper Palace in Brig - Take the train to Visp and then change to the train to Brig. The castle of Kaspar Stockalper, an early capitalist, is the largest building in 17th century Switzerland. Tour the castle and the adjoining home to learn about the building and its builder, who monetized the use of Simplon Pass to make his fortune. The entry fee includes an exhibit on Simplon Pass. After touring the castle wander through the old part of Brig and enjoy lunch at one of the City's many restaurants.

If it is not raining heavily, take a short walk. **Walk to Zmutt** (see Hike 6 – Zmutt Loop) or explore the neighbors to the south of the Zermatt center including Winkelmatten and Moos. There are also walks that head down the Mattertal along the west side of the Matter Vispa River to Tasch. Stop by the Zermatt Tourist Office, near the train station, for more ideas.

Good Things to Know about Zermatt

- Zermatt is in the German part of the Wallis (Valais). People who deal with tourist typically speak German, French and English.
- There is one campground in Zermatt, to the north of the train station. It is not recommended. If you need to camp check out the facilities down valley in Tasch or Randa.
- There are two hostels in Zermatt: the Zermatt Youth Hostel and the Matterhorn Hostel.
- There are no laundromats (waschsalons) in Zermatt. There are two laundry services, Doli (in a basement on Seilerwiessenstrasse across from the tennis courts) and Womy (in the same building as the Coop).
- There are numerous huts and mountain lodges in the Mattertal. Reservations are required.

Maps: Zermatt Trail Maps

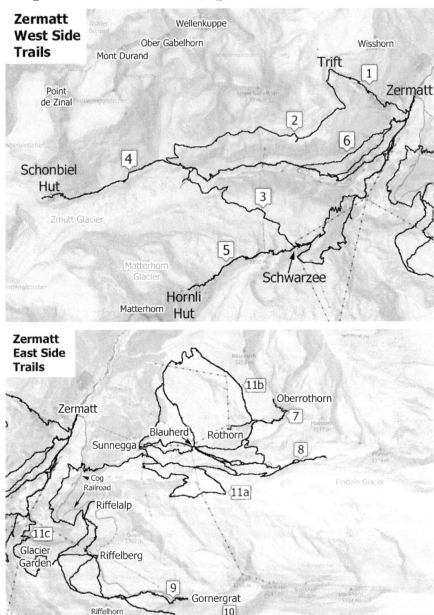

Zermatt West Side Trails

Glacier Durand
Wellenkuppe
Ober Gabelhorn
Mont Durand
Wisshorn
Trift
1
Zermatt
Point de Zinal
Unter Gabelhorn 3396 m
2
6
4
Schonbiel Hut
Zmutt Glacier
3
5
Matterhorn Glacier
Schwarzee
Hornli Hut
Matterhorn

Zermatt East Side Trails

11b
Oberrothorn
Zermatt
7
Blauherd
Rothorn
Sunnegga
8
Cog Railroad
11a
Findeln Glacier
Riffelalp
11c
Glacier Garden
Riffelberg
9
Gornergrat
Riffelhorn
10
Gorner Glacier Viewpoint
Gornergletscher Glacier

1. Trift ★★★★☆
Distance: 4.5 miles (RT)
Near Zermatt in the Valais

This lovely hike climbs steeply up the beautiful Trift Gorge beside a cascading stream, traveling through lovely wildflower-filled meadows to the basin at head of the gorge surrounded by a gorgeous cirque of rugged peaks adorn with glaciers.

Distance: 4.5 miles (RT)
Elevation: 5,325-ft. at Trailhead
7,667-ft. at Trift
Elevation Gain: 2,342-ft. to Trift

Difficulty: moderately strenuous
Basecamp: Zermatt
Zermatt West Map: See page 10
Online Map/Photos:
www.hikingwalking.com/thrift

Why Hike the Trift Gorge

Starting in downtown Zermatt, the trail ascends steeply through forest and then meadows awash in wildflowers up the Trift Gorge alongside the rushing Triftbach (Trift stream). After gaining over 2,300-ft. in 2.25 mile the trail reaches the Hotel du Trift, a restored Victorian building, situated in a lovely alpine valley surrounded by a stunning cirque of high peaks and glaciers.

Trift is the perfect place for a lazy afternoon. Eat lunch at the hotel or enjoy a picnic in the meadows above the hotel while gazing at the Zinalrothorn, Trifthorn, Wellenkuppe, Ober Gabelhorn, Mittel Gabelhorn and Unter Gabelhorn. The Trift and Gabelhorn glaciers along with numerous snow fields adorn the flanks of the peaks. Turn around for equally impressive views of the Monte Rosa massif rising above Gornergrat and the Findel valley to the east.

While many of the hillsides around Zermatt are bristling with ski apparatus, the Trift Gorge is devoid of such equipment and remains wonderfully wild with meadows boasting an impressive display of wildflowers. As an added bonus signs along the way identify the flowers and describe their unique habitat. Keep an eye out for the elusive Edelweiss, with its delicate white petals.

The hike is a good workout and a nice way to acclimatize. It is also a good option for families looking for a more challenging hike. The valley is the jumping off point for a number of longer hikes including my favorite destination, the Hohbalm.

Trailhead to Trift

The Trift hike begins at the corner of Chrum and Bahnhofstrasse (the main street), a quarter mile south of the train station (Bahnhof), in Zermatt. (See directions below.) Start walking uphill on Chrum, a narrow alley. Signs a short distance up the alley indicate you are on Chrum and point toward the Trift, Alterhaupt, Hohbalm and Arbenbach trails.

Bear left where the alley splits and about 500-ft. further along turn left onto Triftweg, a paved walkway. (Look for a blue metal Triftweg sign embedded in the stone wall along the right side of the pavement.) The steep walkway initially climbs south but soon curves to the right (north/northwest) at the corner of the Omnia Hotel. Past the hotel the path turns into a dirt track ascending steeply through meadows with nice view of Zermatt.

The trail now climbs toward the Trift Gorge, the obvious cleft in the hillside carved by the waters of the Triftbach. Pass trail junctions at 0.3 miles and 0.5 miles. At each intersection continue in the direction of Trift and Alterhaupt (Edelweiss).

After a slight bit of downhill cross the Triftbach on a good wooden bridge and then ascend to join a track coming up from town. Turn right at the signed junction toward Alterhaupt (Edelweiss), Trift and the Hohbalmen, a popular viewpoint on the Hohbalm plateau.

Follow the trail as it climbs switchbacks through a forest of larch and fir trees, leaving the river briefly to circumvent a large rock outcropping. Arrive at the Alterhaupt (6,345-ft.) and the Cafe Edelweiss at 0.9 miles. This beautiful overlook enjoys bird's-eye views of Zermatt and nice vistas of the Mattertal (Matter Valley) along with the Dom (14,911-ft.) and the Taschhorn (14,733-ft.) to the northeast.

Just beyond the restaurant the track splits. The trail to the left signed for Hohbalmen (2-hr) and Arbenbach (3-hr 40-min) is a shorter and steeper route to the Hohbalm plateau that is not recommended since it misses some spectacular scenery. Our trail toward Trift (1-hr 10-min) and the Wisshorn (3-hr 10-min) continues straight ahead up the gorge, ascending slightly before dropping gently down to the river (Triftbach).

When the trail reaches the river it resumes its ascent up the gorge, crossing a bridge to the right (north) side of the Triftbach at 1.5 miles. As you climb, periodically turn around for good views of the Oberrothorn and the Monte Rosa massif across the Mattertal to the southeast.

During late July and early August the meadows along the gorge feature an impressive display of wildflowers. Signs along the way identify the flowers and describe their unique habitat. Keep an eye out for the elusive Edelweiss with its delicate white petals.

Not far beyond the bridge views open to the Wellenkuppe's (12,805-ft.) snow covered summit rising above the head of the Trift Valley. With each step the views improve and soon the pyramid-shaped Ober Gabelhorn (13,330-ft.) joins the scene followed by the rugged crags of the Unter Gabelhorn (11,125-ft.).

Reach the Hotel du Trift (7,667-ft.) at 2.25 miles. The hotel, situated in a lovely alpine basin at the head of the gorge, is surrounded by a stunning cirque of high peaks and glaciers. Views (from right to left) encompass the Zinalrothorn (13,848-ft.), Trifthorn (12,230-ft.), Wellenkuppe, Ober Gabelhorn, Mittel Gabelhorn and Unter Gabelhorn. The Trift and Gabelhorn glaciers along with numerous snow fields adorn the flanks of the peaks. Turn around for equally impressive views of the Monte Rosa massif rising above Gornergrat (Gorner Ridge) to the southeast.

This is a great spot for a long break. The Trift Hotel provides 30 dormitory spaces and 9 private rooms along with beverages, snacks and meals. Picnic tables in front of the hotel offer front row seats to the panorama of peaks rising above the valley. Alternately, find a nice spot in the meadows to the west of the hotel to enjoy a picnic lunch and the terrific views.

The valley is the jumping off point for a number of longer hikes. Just beyond the hotel is a trail junction with signs point right toward the Wisshorn (2-hr) and the routes to the Rothhornhutte (2-hr 30-min), Platthorn (3-hr 05-m) and Mettelhorn (3-hr 40-min). A sign points left to the Hohbalm (1-hr 05min) and Schonbielhutte (4-hr 10-min) trail. We will leave these hikes for another day.

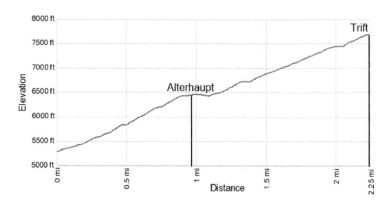

Trailhead Directions

From the Zermatt Bahnhof (train station): Walk south on Bahnhofstrasse, the main street, for 0.25 miles and turn right on Chrum, a small alley. Chrum is the first street on the right after the Mont Cervin Hotel (left).

From the Church in Zermatt: From the south end of town, walk to the church at the corner of Kirchstrasse and Bahnhofstrasse. Walk 0.15 miles (820-ft.) north on Bahnhofstrasse and turn left on Chrum, a small alley. Chrum is the first street on the left after the Hotel Monte Rosa.

Note: The Unique Hotel Post is located across from Chrum street. Gees Cockoo Club, with Grampi's on the second floor, is located at the southeast corner of Bahnhofstrasse and Chrum.

As you head up the alley you will see signs indicating you are on Chrum and pointing toward the trails to Trift, Alterhaupt, Hohbalm and Arbenbach. At 0.1 miles the alley splits. Bear left at the split and about 500-ft. further along turn left onto Triftweg, a paved walkway, marked with a blue metal sign embedded in the stone wall running along the right side of the street. Follow the hiking directions above.

2. Hohbalm ★★★★★
Distance: 7.6 - 12.3 miles (loop)
Near Zermatt in the Valais

Our favorite hike in Zermatt features magical views of the majestic Matterhorn and stunning panoramas of the 4,000-meter peaks towering above the Zermatt area.

Distance: Distance: 2.3 miles (one way) to Trift
3.8 miles (one way) to Hohbalm Viewpoint
12.3 miles (loop)
Elevation: 5,325-ft. at Trailhead
7,667-ft. at Trift
8,750-ft. at Hohbalm Viewpoint
Maximum elevation: 9,016-ft.

Elevation Gain: 2,352-ft. to Trift
3,425-ft. to Hohbalm Viewpoint
3,690-ft. for the Loop
Difficulty: strenuous
Basecamp: Zermatt
Zermatt West Map: See page 10
Online Map/Photos:
www.hikingwalking.com/hohbalm

Why Hike the Hohbalm Trail

My favorite hike in Zermatt never ceases to surprise and delight me. The first leg of the hike climbs the beautiful Trift Gorge beside a gushing stream, traveling through pretty meadows sprinkled with wildflowers to the head of the gorge surrounded by a gorgeous cirque of rugged peaks and glaciers.

The subsequent climb to the high plateau above Trift is rewarded with an extraordinary moment when you crest the plateau and the Matterhorn burst onto the scene. Soon the distinct east and north faces of this majestic peak are in full view.

As the trail wanders across the plateau's grassy meadows hikers are treated to phenomenal views of the 4,000-meter peaks surrounding the Zermatt area. The Mischabel Range, punctuated by the Dom and Taschhorn, dominate the view the northeast. A massive wall of mountains clad in glaciers, including the Breithorn, Pollux, Castor, Lyskamm and the Monte Rosa massif, fill the skyline to the southeast. To the east the Findel glacier spills down the slopes Cima di Jazzi on the Swiss/Italian border, between the Strahlhorn and Rimpfishhorn, to the north, and the Stockhorn, to the south.

The Hohbalmen (Hohbalm Viewpoint), the plateau's popular overlook, boasts breathtaking panoramic views of the high peaks and is a good turn around point for parties looking for a shorter day. We recommend a longer and more challenging hike that continues across the plateau. This trail traverses high above the Zmutt Valley with more magical vistas of the Matterhorn along with great views of the Tiefmatten and Stockji glaciers spilling down the cirque at the head of the valley.

The trail then drops down the Arben Valley accompanied by nice views to the Arben Glacier nestled beneath the Ober Gabelhorn and Mont Durand. The final segment of the hike descends through pretty meadows along the north side of the Zmutt Valley, with fine views of the Findel Glacier, Riffelalp and Gornergrat areas, to Zermatt.

While most of the hillsides around Zermatt are bristling with ski apparatus, the Trift gorge and Hohbalm plateau are devoid of such equipment and remain wonderfully wild, adding to the pleasure of this scenic hike. Be forewarned that this is a long hike gaining over 3,500-ft. in altitude. Pick a day full promise and get an early start so you can take your time enjoying this glorious hike.

Trailhead to First Viewpoint

Distance from Trailhead: 2.25 miles (one way)
Elevation at Viewpoint: 7,667-ft.
Elevation Gain: 2,352-ft.

The Hohbalm hike begins at the corner of Chrum and Bahnhofstrasse (the main street), a quarter mile south of the train station (Bahnhof), in

Zermatt. (See trailhead directions below.) Start walking uphill on Chrum, a narrow alley. Signs a short distance up the alley indicate you are on Chrum and point toward the Trift, Alterhaupt, Hohbalm and Arbenbach trails.

Bear left where the alley splits and about 500-ft. further along turn left onto Triftweg, a paved walkway. (Look for a blue metal Triftweg sign embedded in the stone wall along the right side of the pavement.) The steep walkway initially climbs south but soon curves to the right (north / northwest) at the corner of the Omnia Hotel. Past the hotel the path turns into a dirt track ascending through meadows with nice views of Zermatt.

The trail now climbs to the Trift Hotel. For a detailed description of this section of the trail see the first segment of Hike 1 - the Trift Trail.

The Trift Hotel and the beautiful alpine basin to the west is a great spot for a break and to contemplate the next phase of your ascent to the Hohbalm. The hotel offers 30 dormitory spaces and 9 private rooms along with beverages, snacks and meals. Picnic tables in front of the hotel offer a front row seat to the panorama of peaks rising above the valley. Alternately, find a nice spot in the meadows to the west of the hotel to enjoy a snack and the terrific views before continuing the hike.

Trift Hotel to Hohbalm Viewpoint

Segment Stat: 1.5 miles (one-way) and 1,073-ft. of elevation gain from Trift to the Viewpoint
Trailhead to Hohbalm Viewpoint: 3.8 miles (one way)
Maximum Elevation: 8,750-ft.
Elevation Gain/Loss to Hohbalm Viewpoint: 3,425-ft.

Just beyond the hotel signs point right to the trail leading to the Wisshorn (2-hr) and the routes to the Rothhornhutte (2-hr 30-min), Platthorn (3-hr 5-m) and Mettelhorn (3-hr 40-min). Another group of signs point left toward the Hohbalmen (1-hr 5-min) and Schonbielhutte (4-hr 10-min). To your left the Hohbalm trail is clearly visible climbing the steep grassy hillside forming the valley's south wall.

To continue the hike turn left (west) toward the Hohbalmen. The trail wanders through the meadow, crossing the nascent Thriftbach on a wood bridge. Beyond the bridge the path curves to the left (south) and begins a moderately steep ascending angling up the valley's south wall.

As you climb enjoy ever improving views of the cirque at the head of the Trift valley. To the northeast the Dom, Taschhorn and Alphubel soar above the Mattertal.

At 3.25 miles the grade abates as the trail curves to the right (west). As you crest the hill, reaching the high alpine meadows of the Hohbalm plateau, the Matterhorn burst onto the scene. No matter how many times I hike this trail I'm still surprised and delighted by the view.

The worst of the climb is now over and it is time to enjoy the fruits of your hard work. The Hohbalm plateau, located 3,400-ft. above the Zermatt valley, offers phenomenal views in all directions. To the south the Matterhorn's distinct east and north faces command your attention. A massive wall of 4,000 meter peaks, including the Breithorn (13,665-ft.), Pollux (13,425-ft.), Castor (13,864-ft.), Lyskamm (14,852-ft.) and the Monte Rosa massif (15,203-ft.) fill the skyline to the southeast. To the east the Oberrothorn towers above the Findel Valley. The Mischabel Range, with the Dom and the Taschhorn, dominate the view the northeast.

These marvelous views, from different perspectives, will be your constant companion for the next 2.8 miles as the trail traverses the Hohbalm plateau, a broad shoulder extending from the Unter Gabelhorn's southeast ridge. Follow the trail as it heads southwest, gently ascending broad grassy slopes dotted with tiny wildflowers.

Views soon open to the Findel Glacier to the east. The glacier starts on the slopes of the Cima di Jazzi (12,477-ft.) on the Swiss-Italian border and flows west between the Strahlhorn and Rimpfishhorn, to the north, and the Stockhorn, to the south.

At 3.8 miles reach a trail junction at Hohbalmen, a wonderful viewpoint (8,750-ft.). Here a signs point left (southeast) to Alterhaupt (1-hr 05-min) and Zermatt (1-hr 45-min) and straight ahead (southwest) toward Arbenbach (1-hr 40-min) and Schonbielhutte (3-hr). The junction is a popular lunch spot and a good place to turn around if you want a shorter hike.

If you decide to turn around at this point there are two options. We recommend simply retracing your steps to Zermatt via the Trift Gorge for a very satisfying 7.6 mile day. Alternatively you can take the trail to the left towards Alterhaupt. The narrow path drops very steeply to Alterhaupt where it rejoins the trail down the Trift Gorge to Zermatt for a 6.5 mile round trip hike.

Completing the Loop

Segment Stat: 8.5 miles (one-way) and 226-ft./-3,691-ft. elevation gain/loss back to the trailhead from the viewpoint
Total Distance to Complete the Loop: 12.3 miles (loop)
Maximum Elevation: 9,016-ft.
Elevation Gain for the Loop: 3,691-ft.

If time, energy and the weather permit we recommend crossing the Hohbalm plateau toward Arbenbach and Schonbielhutte (Schonbiel Hut). Beyond the viewpoint the trail follows a gentle ascending traverse toward the Matterhorn, gradually bearing right (west/southwest) along a narrow shoulder below the Unter Gabelhorn.

This portion of the trail offers numerous lunch spots with stunning, front row seats with views of the Matterhorn. The Findel Glacier and its surrounding peaks fill the skyline to the east while the snowcapped peaks between Monte Rosa and the Breithorn dominate the view to the southeast. At 4.2 miles the trail curves to the right (west) around a grassy outcropping and views open to the Tiefmatten and Stockji glaciers spilling down the cirque at the head of the Zmutt Valley.

At 5.0 miles the path heads west along grassy slopes beneath the south face of the Unter Gabelhorn, crossing occasional rock slides and avalanche chutes. The trail is narrow in spots and may feel a bit exposed but is quite safe.

Reach the high point of the trail (9,015-ft.) at 5.8 miles. The trail initially descends west on moderately easy grades for 0.2 miles to a broad grassy knoll directly across from the Matterhorn's north face, another great overlook. Past the overlook, the path drops on moderately steep grades toward the Arben Valley. Along the way views open to the Arben Glacier nestled beneath the Ober Gabelhorn and Mont Durand rimming the head of the Arben Valley.

At 6.6 miles the trail turns to the left (south) and steeply descends the east side of the Arben valley on long switchbacks with wonderful views of the Matterhorn and the peaks rising above the head of the Zmutt Valley. Reach the junction with the trail branching right (west/southwest) to Schonbielhutte at 7.2 miles. We turn left (east) toward Chalbermatten, Zmutt, Furi and Zermatt.

The trail descends on moderately-easy grades for a short distance along the left side of a small stream before curving around and dropping down a gully on a series of tight, moderately steep switchbacks, passing a photogenic waterfall at 7.4 miles.

At the bottom of the falls the trail briefly travels beside cliffs along the valley's north wall before arriving at a trail detour. (The original trail was wiped out by a rockfall and the area is still unstable.) Turn right (southeast) at the detour and follow the rerouted trail as it descends through larch trees, passing a somewhat confusing sign for a route to Zermatt and Furi branching off to the right. Ignore this trail and continue straight ahead in the direction of Chalbermatten, Zmutt and Zermatt.

At 8.0 miles reach a bridge crossing the Zmuttbach (Zmutt River). Do not cross the bridge but instead go left (east/northeast), following the trail as it drops around the bottom of the landslide and then climbs steep, dusty switchbacks to the continuation of the main trail at 8.5 miles.

A good path now descends steadily, heading east through meadows to Chalbermatten (6,906-ft.), the site of a defunct restaurant, at 9.0 miles. The Findel Glacier, Riffelalp and Gornergrat dominate the view to the east.

Beyond Chalbermatten the trail continues it moderate descent, passing above the Zmutt reservoir and then traveling through pastures to Zmutt at 10.2 miles. The small village is a popular lunch spot and a favorite destination for tourist seeking a short walk from Zermatt. (See Hike 6 - Zmutt Loop hike for more information.)

The remainder of the hike follows a popular trail descending along a wide, pleasant track that pass some old buildings and grain storehouses. At

10.6 miles the trail drops steeply down a few switchbacks and then curves left (northeast) as it heads back to Zermatt.

Reach the south end of Zermatt at 11.9 miles. From here you can either hop on an electric shuttle bus (fee required) or walk 0.4 miles through town to the start of the trail for a 12.3 miles hike. (When in doubt, follow signs pointing to the Zermatt Bahnhof.)

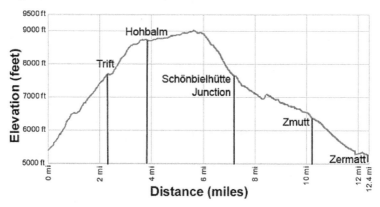

Trailhead Directions

From the Zermatt Bahnhof (train station): See Hike 1.
From the Church in Zermatt: See Hike 1

3. Schwarzsee to Zermatt ★★★★
Distance: 5.6 - 7.3 miles (one way)
Near Zermatt in the Valais

The Matterhorn is the star of the show on this scenic hike starting at Schwarzsee, a popular viewpoint atop the Matterhorn Plateau. Competing for your attention are splendid views of the high peaks rimming the Zmutt valley along with more distance views of the Findel and Monte Rosa areas.

Distance: 5.6 - 7.3 miles (one way)

Elevation: 8,490-ft. at Schwarzsee

Maximum elevation: 8,490-ft. at Schwarzsee

Elevation Gain: -3,190-ft.

Difficulty: moderate

Basecamp: Zermatt

Zermatt West Map: See page 10

Online Map/Photos: www.hikingwalking.com/schwarzee

Why Hike from Schwarzsee to Zermatt

Breathtaking views of the Matterhorn are your constant companion along much of this scenic hike. Starting at Schwarzsee atop the Matterhorn Plateau, the trail descends through meadows along the south side of the Zmutt Valley accompanied by impressive views of the Matterhorn's north face. The Ober Gabelhorn and Dent Blanche fill the skyline across the valley to the north.

The hike reaches the floor of the Zmutt Valley and then crosses to the north side of the valley at the site of the Grande Dixence Hydroelectric project, set amid the glacial debris left by the receding Zmutt Glacier. It is not a pretty sight by happily the views of the Matterhorn and the high peaks forming the cirque at the head of the Zmutt valley will divert your attention.

On the north side of the valley the trail descends through pretty meadows with fine views of the Matterhorn and, in the distance to the east, Monte Rosa and the high peaks towering above the Findel Glacier. The final leg of the hike travels through Zmutt, a lovely little village of wood houses, and then passes historic grain storehouses and small Alps on its way back to Zermatt.

The trail can be shortened by returning along the south side of the Zmutt Valley. It is also possible to walk to Schwarzsee instead of taking the gondola. Walking to the Matterhorn Plateau will add 4.0 to 5.0 miles to the hike depending on the route.

Schwarzsee to Stefelalp Restaurant

Note: This hike starts on the Matterhorn Plateau at Schwarzsee, reached by taking the Matterhorn Paradise/Schwarzsee Gondola. If you walk from Zermatt to Schwarzsee add four to five miles (depending on the route) and 3,100-ft. in elevation gain to the hike. (See trailhead directions below.)

Schwarzsee (8,490-ft.), a popular viewpoint, is located on the Matterhorn plateau beneath the Matterhorn's northeast ridge known as the Hornligrat - considered to be the easiest route to the summit. From the viewpoint visitors are treated to expansive views of the Matterhorn's east and north faces. Hornlihutte, the base camp for climbers tackling the Hornligrat, is clearly visible at the base of the ridge.

The viewpoint also enjoys panoramic views of Monte Rosa (15,203-ft.), Lyskamm (14,852-ft.-meters) and Breithorn (13,665-ft.) to the southeast. The Mischabel Range, with its two highest peaks -- the Dom (14,911-ft.) and Taschhorn (14,733-ft.), along with the Findel Glacier dominate the view the northeast while Dent Blanche (14,291-ft.) and the Ober Gabelhorn (13,330-ft.) massif fill the skyline to the northwest.

When you are done taking in the views find the signpost near the Hotel Schwarzsee (accommodations / restaurant) where markers point to broad track descending northwest across the plateau toward Stafelalp (25-min), Schonbielhutte (3-hr 20-min) and the Matterhorn Trail. Follow the track as it drops through meadows, passing a pretty little chapel near a tarn. Herds of blacknose sheep are often seen grazing in the meadows.

After walking 0.75 miles stunning views open to the Matterhorn's sheer north face and the Matterhorn glacier. This view, from different perspectives, will be your constant companion for much of the hike. Across the valley the Ober Gabelhorn massif and Dent Blanche dominate the view. As you continue descending views of the peaks and glaciers at the head of the Zmutt Valley join the scene.

Reach the signed junction at Stafelalp (7,900-ft.) after walking 1.2 miles. Just beyond the sign take the trail branches right (northwest) toward the Matterhorn Trail and Schonbielhutte, which descends on moderate grades through Obere Stafelalp's meadows adorn with shrubs and wildflowers.

The meadows soon give way to a scattered forest of larch and pine trees as the trail passes a small pond at 1.5 miles. Beyond the pond the grade steepens. Clearings now offer views of the settling ponds and buildings on the valley floor that form part of the Grande Dixence hydroelectric system.

The trail soon crosses a stream and then descends to the Stefelalp Restaurant (7,214-ft.) at 2.0 miles. Near the restaurant signs points left (west) toward Arbenbach / Schonbielhutte and right (east) to Zmutt and Zermatt.

Return via the South Side of the Zmutt Valley

The trail to the right, along the south side of the Zmutt Valley, is the shortest route back to Zermatt (south end of town). The path travels on service roads and trails above the south side of the Zmuttbach (Zmutt River). Openings in the trees and intermittent meadow offer nice views of the Ober Gabelhorn massif rising above the north side of the valley. Total distance for this option is 5.6 miles.

Along the way it is possible to cross the dam over the Zmuttbach and then descend through Zmutt on the way back to Zermatt (south end of town). This option also results in a 5.6 mile hike. Add 0.8 miles to the hike if you are walking all the way back to the Bahnhof (train station) at the north end of Zermatt. (Note: Watch for mountain bikes along the service roads.)

Return via the North Side of the Zmutt Valley

My advice is to turn left at the junction toward Arbenbach and Schonbielhutte and return to Zermatt via the north side of the valley. The trail, which is longer and includes an additional 300-ft. in elevation gain, is more scenic with great views of the Matterhorn in addition to the high peaks towering above the Findel Glacier and the Gornergrat area.

After turning left at the junction the trail descends on a broad track to a junction with a dirt road at 2.2 miles. Turn left onto the dirt road in the direction of Arbenbach and Schonbielhutte. The Matterhorn's north face now towers overhead. Several waterfalls, fed by glacial meltwater, tumble down crevasses in the cliff face below the Matterhorn Glacier. Straight ahead to the west are nice views of the peaks and glaciers at the head of the valley.

At 2.5 miles turn right at a junction on the track heading toward the hydroelectric project. The turn is marked by two yellow arrows with hiker icons. Our path now leads through an unattractive area housing hydroelectric buildings and equipment along with settling ponds amid the gravelly remains of the receding Zmutt Glacier. Signs near the buildings describe the immense Grande Dixence hydroelectric project.

The area around the hydro project is an unfortunately an eyesore. Divert your attention from the man-made structures by turning around for more great views of the Matterhorn. To the east the Oberrothorn, Rimpfishhorn, Strahlhorn and Adlerhorn tower above the Findel Glacier while Monte Rosa rises beyond the Matterhorn Plateau. Across the valley a pretty waterfall tumbles down a rock outcropping. The trail to Schonbielhutte climbs switchbacks up the right side of the falls.

A short distance beyond the hydroelectric building cross a bridge and follow the track as it skirts the right (east) side of a large settling pond. Just beyond the settling pond turn right (east) on a track marked with a yellow slash on a rock. This trail will cross a bridge and reach a signed junction at 3.0 miles. Turn right at the junction toward Chalbermatten, Zmutt and Zermatt. The trail to the left leads to Schonbielhutte and Arbenbach.

You are now on a new trail that detours around a rock slide. Follow the path as it heads southeast, descending through larch trees. At 3.3 miles reach a bridge crossing the Zmuttbach (Zmutt River). Do not cross the bridge but instead go left (east/northeast), following the trail as it drops around the bottom of the slide and then climbs up steep, dusty switchbacks to the continuation of the main trail at 3.8 miles.

A good path now descends steadily east through meadows to Chalbermatten (6,906-ft.), the site of an old restaurant, at 4.2 miles. The Findel Glacier, Riffelalp and Gornergrat dominate the view to the east.

Beyond Chalbermatten the trail continues it moderate descent, passing above the Zmutt reservoir and then traveling through pastures to Zmutt at 5.6 miles. The small village is a popular lunch spot and a favorite destination for tourist seeking a short walk from Zermatt. (See the Hike 6 - Zmutt Loop hike for more information)

The rest of the hike is on a popular trail that descends along a wide, pleasant track, passing some old buildings and grain storehouses. At 6.0 miles the trail drops steeply down a few switchbacks and then curves left (northeast) as it heads back to Zermatt.

Reach the south end of Zermatt at 7.3 miles. From here you can either hop on an electric shuttle bus (fee required) or walk 0.8 miles back through town to the start of the hike for a total distance of 8.1 mile. (When in doubt, follow signs pointing to the Zermatt Bahnhof.)

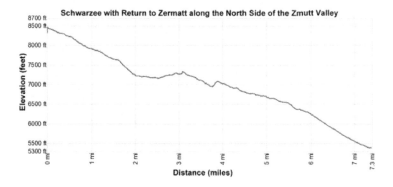

Trailhead Directions

Walking Directions from the Zermatt Bahnhof (train station) to the Schwarzsee Lift Station: Walk south/southwest on Bahnhofstrasse, the town's main street, for 0.3 miles and then turn left onto Kirchstrasse (Church Street). You will pass the Matterhorn Museum on the left just before the turn. The Pfarrkirche St. Mauritius (church) is located on the southeast corner of Bahnhofstrasse and Kirchstrasse.)

Walk down Kirchstrasse for 0.1 miles, crossing the bridge over the river, and then turn right on Schluhmattstrasse (Schluhmatt Street), the first street past the river. Follow Schluhmattstrasse for 0.4 miles to the Matterhorn Glacier Paradise/Schwarzsee Gondola Station. Purchase a one-way ticket to Schwarzsee. For more information see the Schwarzsee Information on the Matterhorn Paradise website. Note: The gondola passes through Furi, where hikers exit for the Gletschergarten hike, before continuing on to Schwarzsee.

Hiking to Schwarzsee: Walking from the lift station to Schwarzsee adds 4.0- to 5.0-miles (depending on the route) and over 3,100-ft. in elevation gain to the hike. To walk from the bottom of the Schwarzsee lift station, follow the yellow trail signs for Blatten, Zum See, Furi and Schwarzsee. The trail ascends through trees and meadows to Schwarzsee on the Matterhorn plateau. The section of the trail from Zermatt to Furi walks under or near the gondola. Beyond Furi, a mid-station for the gondola, the route enjoys some nice views of the Gorner Glacier Garden area.

4. Schonbiel Hut (Schonbielhutte) ★★★★★
Distance: 13.7 miles (round trip)
Near Zermatt in the Valais

Two great trails with terrific views of the Matterhorn are combined to create a fantastic hike to Schonbiel Hut, sitting atop a scenic overlook at the head of the Zmutt Valley.

Distance: 2.0 miles(one way) to Stafelalp
6.4 miles (one way) to Schonbiel Hut
13.7 miles (round trip) to Zermatt
Elevation: 8,490-ft. at Schwarzsee
8,490-ft. at Stafelalp
8,916-ft. at Schonbiel Hut
5,325-ft. at Zermatt
Elevation Gain: -1,276-ft. to Stafelalp
1,800-ft. to Schonbiel Hut
-3,591-ft. to Zermatt

Difficulty: strenuous
Basecamp: Zermatt
Zermatt West Map: See page 10
Online Map/Photos:
www.hikingwalking.com/schonbiel

Why Hike to Schonbielhutte

Most people walk to Schonbielhutte on the 14.6 mile out-and-back trail that passes through Zmutt and Chalbermatten. My recommended route to the hut starts at Schwarzsee and combines two great trails, the Matterhorn and Schonbielhutte trails, for a fantastic point-to-point hike with stunning views of the Matterhorn, Dent Blanche and the Ober Gabelhorn massif.

The day starts with a gondola ride to Schwarzsee, a popular overlook with amazing views of the Matterhorn and the high peaks surrounding the Zermatt valley. From the viewpoint the hike follows the Mattherhorn trail as it descends through the beautiful meadows of Obere Stafelalp accompanied by impressive views of the Matterhorn's sheer north face along with the Ober Gabelhorn massif and Dent Blanche.

From Obere Stafelalp the trail drops to and cross the floor of the Zmutt Valley at the site of a Grande Dixence hydroelectric facility. Settling ponds and a few buildings placed amid the gravelly terrain left by the receding Zmutt Glacier are unfortunate eyesores along an otherwise scenic hike.

Beyond the hydro facility the path connects with the Schonbielhutte (Schonbiel Hut) trail on the north side of the Zmutt valley. The trail now ascends switchbacks beside a photogenic waterfall and then travels beside or atop of the Zmutt Glacier's northern lateral moraine. This delightful portion of the walk enjoys magnificent views of the Matterhorn's north face and the peaks and glaciers ringing the head of the Zmutt valley.

A steep climb leads to Schonbielhutte, sitting atop a grassy plateau with breathtaking views of the Matterhorn's north and west faces and Dent d'Herens. To the west the Tiefmatten, Stockji and Schonbiel glaciers tumble down the cirque ringing the head of the valley, combining to form the Zmutt Glacier, a massive river of ice flowing along the Zmutt Valley floor.

The return to Zermatt is via the Schonbielhutte trail, which travels through pretty meadows, mixed larch and pine forest and alpine pastures on the north side of the valley to the small hamlet at Zmutt before reaching the southern outskirts of Zermatt.

This is a long hike with a good amount of altitude gain and loss. Get an early start and pick a day that promises good weather for this beautiful hike with breathtaking, ever changing views of the majestic Matterhorn.

Schwarzsee to the Stafelalp Restaurant

Distance from Schwarzsee: 2.0 miles (one way)
Elevation at Stafelalp Restaurant: 8,490-ft.
Elevation Loss to Stafelalp Restaurant: -1,276-ft.

Note: This description of the Schonbielhutte (Schonbiel Hut) trail starts on the Matterhorn Plateau at Schwarzsee, reached by taking the Matterhorn Paradise / Schwarzsee Gondola. If you choose to walk from Zermatt to Schwarzsee add four to five miles (depending on the route) and 3,100-ft. in elevation gain to the hike. (See the trailhead directions.)

Most people walk to Schonbielhutte via a 14.6 mile out-and-back trail that passes through Zmutt and Chalbermatten. My recommended route to the hut starts at Schwarzsee and combines two great trails, the Matterhorn and Schonbielhutte trails, for a fantastic point-to-point hike with stunning views of the Matterhorn, Dent Blanche and the Ober Gabelhorn massif.

Schwarzsee (8,490-ft.), a popular viewpoint, is located on the Matterhorn plateau beneath the Matterhorn's northeast ridge known as the Hornligrat – considered to be the easiest route to the summit. From the viewpoint visitors are treated to expansive views of the Matterhorn's east and north faces. Hornlihutte, the base camp for climbers tackling the Hornligrat, is clearly visible at the base of the ridge.

The viewpoint also enjoys panoramic views of Monte Rosa (15,203-ft.), Lyskamm (14,852-ft.) and the Breithorn (13,665-ft.) to the southeast. The Mischabel Range, with its two highest peaks -- the Dom (14,911-ft.) and

Taschhorn (14,733-ft.), along with the Findel Glacier dominate the view the northeast while Dent Blanche (14,291-ft.) and the Ober Gabelhorn (13,330-ft.) massif fill the skyline to the northwest.

When you are done taking in the views find the signpost near the Hotel Schwarzsee (accommodations and restaurant) where markers point to broad track descending northwest across the plateau toward Stafelalp (25-min), Schonbielhutte (3-hr 20-min) and the Matterhorn Trail. For a detailed description of this section of the trail see the first segment of Hike 5 - the Schwarzsee to Zermatt trail.

Stafelalp to Schonbielhutte

Segment Stat: 4.4 miles (one way) from Stafelalp to Schonbielhutte
Total Distance to Schonbielhutte: 6.4 miles (one way)
Elevation at Schonbielhutte: 8,916-ft.
Elevation Gain to Schonbielhutte: 1,800-ft.

Near the restaurant signs points left (west) toward Arbenbach and Schonbielhutte and right (east) to Zmutt and Zermatt. Turn left and descend along a broad track to a junction with a dirt road at 2.2 miles. Turn left onto the dirt road in the direction of Arbenbach and Schonbielhutte. The Matterhorn's north face now towers overhead. Several waterfalls, fed by glacial melt, tumble down crevasses in the cliff face below the Matterhorn Glacier. Straight ahead to the west are nice views of the peaks and glaciers at the head of the valley.

At 2.5 miles reach a junction and turn right on the road that heads toward the hydroelectric project. The turn is marked with two small yellow signs. Our path now leads through an unattractive area housing hydroelectric buildings and equipment along with settling ponds amid the gravelly remains of the receding Zmutt Glacier. Signs near the buildings describe the immense Grande Dixence hydroelectric project.

The area around the hydro project is an unfortunately an eyesore. Divert your attention from the man-made structures by turning around for more great views of the Matterhorn. To the east the Oberrothorn, Rimpfishhorn, Strahlhorn and Adlerhorn rise above the Findel Glacier. Across the valley a pretty waterfall tumbles down a rock outcropping. The trail to Schonbielhutte climbs switchbacks up the right side of the falls.

A short distance beyond the hydro plant cross a bridge and follow the road as it skirts the right (east) side of a large settling pond. Just beyond the settling pond turn right (east) on a road, which may be unmarked. This trail will cross a bridge and reach a signed junction with the Schonbielhutte trail at 3.0 miles. Turn left in the direction of Schonbielhutte and Arbenbach.

The trail now travels beside a rock face and then climbs moderately steep switchbacks up the right (east) side of a gully across from a photogenic waterfall. At the top of the switchbacks the path crosses the gully and then climbs to a bench beside the north lateral moraine of the Zmutt Glacier.

Follow the trail as it heads west ascending through meadows on easy grades, paralleling the stream and moraine wall to your left.

Reach the junction with the Hohbalm Trail branching to the right (north) at 3.8 miles. Continue straight ahead toward Schonbielhutte. Be sure to turn around at this point for nice views of Monte Rosa and Lyskamm rising beyond the Matterhorn plateau.

Soon the trail crosses a bridge over a stream at the mouth of the Arben Valley. The Ober Gabelhorn towers above the head of the valley. Just beyond the bridge reach a junction for the route to Platten splitting off to the right (north). We proceed straight ahead in the direction of the Schonbielhutte (1-hr 20-min).

The moderate ascent up the valley is delightful, traveling through rocky meadows sprinkled with wildflowers. Views soon open to waterfalls cascading off the rock face below the Hohwang Glacier, spilling down the north side of the valley between the Pointe de Zinal and Mont Durand. The Matterhorn's north face looms above the valley to the south while straight ahead the cirque of mountains adorned with glaciers at the head of the Zmutt valley become more impressive with each step.

Reach a junction at 5.0 where an old trail, blocked by rocks, climbs along the top of the glacial moraine. (This trail is no longer safe due to extensive eroding of the moraine wall.) Bear right on the new trail, marked with a rusty metal sign, which travels beside a small pond and then climbs moderately steep grades up the trough between the moraine wall and the sheer south face of the Gemsspitz.

For a brief period the moraine wall blocks views to the south. Soon the trail climbs out of the trough and moves to the top of the moraine wall, which is now wider and safe for travel. Views open to the Zmutt Glacier's massive river of ice, masked with rock debris and pitted with crevasses, covering the valley floor. Dent d' Herens, Tete de Valpelline and Tete Blanche, draped with glaciers, ring the head of the valley. Schonbiel Hut is now clearly visible on the hill above the trail.

At 5.7 miles the trail swings off the moraine wall and starts a steep ascent up a long series of switchbacks to Schonbielhutte. (Note: You may see two trails at the bottom of the switchbacks. The correct trail is the one branching to the right. Red arrows on the rocks will keep you on track.) Take a rest as you climb to enjoy the views.

Reach Schonbielhutte (8,840-ft.) at 6.2 miles after gaining 500-ft. The hut, providing dormitory accommodations and refreshments, sits atop a small grassy plateau overlooking the Zmutt Glacier. From the hut's sun terrace enjoy stunning 270-degree views that encompass the Findel Glacier, the Monte Rosa massif, the Matterhorn's north and west faces and Dent d'Herens. At the head of the valley the Tiefmatten, Stockji and Schonbiel glaciers combine with the Zmutt Glacier to form the massive river of ice, covered in huge boulder and rock debris, flowing along the valley floor.

After enjoying the views from the hut, travel around the front of the hut and follow a use trail that leads west to the end of the plateau (an additional 0.2 miles). Here a marvelous overlook offers front row seats to the glaciers tumbling down the valleys between Dent d'Herens, Tete de Valpelline, Tete Blanche, Wandfluehorn, Dent Blanche and Pte de Zinal. Directly in front of you a glacier hangs from cliff face. Occasionally chunks of the glacier breakoff and crash to the valley floor.

Schonbielhutte to Zermatt

Segment Stat: 7.3 miles (one-way) from Schonbielhutte to Zermatt
Total Distance for hike: 13.7 miles (one-way)
Elevation at Zermatt: 5,325-ft.
Elevation Loss from Schonbielhutte to Zermatt: -3,591-ft.

When you are done taking in the views, return to Zermatt by reversing the route to the point directly below the waterfall, about 3.0 miles from the viewpoint and 9.4 miles from the start. Do not cross the valley near the hydro facility but instead continue along the north side of the valley following signs toward Zmutt.

At the bottom of the falls the trail briefly travels beside cliffs along the valley's north wall before arriving at a trail detour. (The original trail was wiped out by a rockfall and the area is still unstable.) Turn right (southeast) at the detour and follow the rerouted trail as it descends through larch trees, passing a sign for a route to Zermatt and Furi branching off to the right. Ignore this trail and continue straight ahead in the direction of Chalbermatten, Zmutt and Zermatt.

At 9.8 miles reach a bridge crossing the Zmuttbach (Zmutt River). Do not cross the bridge but instead go left (east/northeast), following the trail as it drops around the bottom of the landslide and then climbs up steep, dusty switchbacks to the continuation of the main trail at 10.3 miles.

A good path now descends steadily east through meadows to Chalbermatten (6,906-ft.), the site of an old restaurant, at 10.8 miles. The Findel Glacier, Riffelalp and Gornergrat dominate the view to the east.

Beyond Chalbermatten the trail continues it moderate descending traverse, passing above the Zmutt reservoir and then traveling through pastures to Zmutt at 12.0 miles. The small village is a popular lunch spot and a favorite destination for tourist seeking a short walk from Zermatt.

The rest of the hike is on a popular trail that descends along a wide, pleasant track, passing some old buildings and grain storehouses. At 12.4 miles the trail drops steeply down a few switchbacks and then curves left (northeast) as it heads back to Zermatt.

Reach the south end of Zermatt at 13.7 miles. From here you can either hop on an electric shuttle bus (fee required) or walk 0.8 miles back through town to the start of the hike for a total distance of 14.5 miles. (When in doubt, follow signs pointing to the Zermatt Bahnhof.)

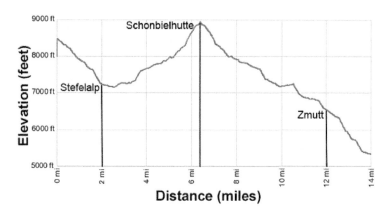

Distance (miles)

Trailhead Directions

Walking Directions from the Zermatt Bahnhof (train station) to the Schwarzsee Lift Station: See Hike 3.

Hiking to Schwarzsee: See Hike 3.

5. Hornli Hut (Hornlihutte)★★★★★

Distance: 5.6 - 10.5 miles (round trip)

Near Zermatt in the Valais

The short, steep hike to Hornlihutte offers a unique, up-close opportunity to experience the iconic Matterhorn from the base of the most popular climber's route to the summit.

Distance: 5.6 -10.5 miles (round trip)
Elevation: 8,490-ft. at Schwarzsee
Maximum elevation: 10,695-ft.
Elevation Gain: 2,205-ft.

Difficulty: strenuous
Basecamp: Zermatt
Zermatt West Map: See page 10
Online Map/Photos:
www.hikingwalking.com/hornli

Why to Hornlihutte

People flock to Zermatt to see the Matterhorn, probably the most photographed mountain in the world. Excellent overlooks along many of Zermatt's popular hiking trails showcase the iconic peak from multiple perspectives.

But if you really want an up close and personal experience with the mountain there is no better hike than the trail to Hornlihutte (Hornli Hut). After viewing the Matterhorn from afar it is truly amazing to stand directly beneath this majestic peak and gaze up at its north and east faces soaring above the hut. With binoculars it is possible to watch climbers tackling the Matterhorn's northeast ridge known as the Hornligrat – considered the easiest and most popular route to the summit.

Beside the spectacular views of the Matterhorn, the area around the hut offers marvelous views of the high peaks surrounding Zermatt. Across the valley to the north a wall of 4,000-meter peaks, from Dent Blanche to the Weisshorn, fill the skyline. The Mischabel Range towers above Zermatt to the northeast. To the southeast an incredible spectacle of peaks and glaciers along the Swiss-Italian border, including Monte Rosa, Lyskamm and the Breithorn, dominate the view. Nearer at hand to the west is the Matterhorn Glacier, clinging to the ledges along the peak's north face.

Be forewarned that Hornlihutte trail is a very popular and quite crowded. I advise getting an early start to avoid the worst of the crowds and to get the best views of the peak. The Matterhorn is famous for its banner cloud, which is more likely to form and grow larger as the day progresses.

Do not take the trail to Hornlihutte in bad weather or if bad weather is imminent. Most of the trail is quite exposed and the steep sections of the trail can be problematic without the proper equipment when covered with ice or slick snow.

Hornlihutte with Return to Schwarzsee or Zermatt

Note: This description of the Hornlihutte (Hornli Hut) trail starts atop the Matterhorn Plateau at Schwarzsee, reached by taking the Matterhorn Paradise / Schwarzsee Gondola. If you choose to walk from Zermatt to Schwarzsee add four to five miles (depending on the route) and 3,100-ft. in elevation gain to the hike. (See the directions to the trailhead for more information.)

Schwarzsee (8,490-ft.), a popular viewpoint, sits beneath the Matterhorn's northeast ridge known as the Hornligrat – considered to be the easiest route to the summit. Looking up from the viewpoint visitors are treated to expansive views of the Matterhorn's east and north faces. Hornlihutte, the base camp for climbers tacking the Hornligrat, is clearly visible at the base of the ridge.

The viewpoint also enjoys panoramic views of Monte Rosa (15,203-ft.), Lyskamm (14,852-ft.) and the Breithorn (13,665-ft.) to the southeast. The

Mischabel Range, with its two highest peaks -- the Dom (14,911-ft.) and the Taschhorn (14,733-ft.), along with the Findel Glacier fill the skyline to the northeast while Dent Blanche (14,291-ft.) and the Ober Gabelhorn (13,330-ft/4,063-meters) massif dominate the view to the northwest. These marvelous views will only get better on your climb to the hut.

When you are done taking in the views find the trail signs near the Hotel Schwarzsee. Walk southwest on the broad track toward Hirli (40-min), Hornlihutte (2-hr 10-min) and Trockener Steg (2-hr 15-min). The trail ascends a grassy bench on moderate grades, curving around and above Schwarzsee Lake and its pretty little chapel.

The grade abates briefly as the path crosses a bench and a small gully before resuming its steep ascent on switchbacks up the hillside. As you crest the hill the rocky meadows give way to talus slopes.

The trail now heads west, passing under a ski lift at 0.9 miles and then ascends along a cliff face beneath Hirli (9,478-ft.), the rocky knob at the end of the Matterhorn's east ridge. Past the junction with the trail to Trockener Steg, metal stairs and cantilevered walkways bolted to the sheer rock face provide safe passage for hikers where the trail has eroded and fallen away.

Back on solid ground the trail climbs moderately steep switchbacks up a rocky cliff face to the top of the ridge at 1.4 miles. Atop the ridge, follow the trail ascending southwest on moderately grades for half a mile. Along the way pass a trail branching right and dropping down to Stafelalp and Zermatt.

At 1.9 miles the trail starts ascending very steep switchbacks up a knife edge ridge to the hut, gaining more than 1,000-ft. over 0.8 miles. Fixed ropes along the way provide a level of security on extremely steep and/or exposed trail segments that could be problematic when covered with snow and ice.

Reach the recently rebuilt Hornlihutte (10,695-ft.) at 2.7 miles. After viewing the Matterhorn from afar it is truly amazing to stand this close to the majestic peak soaring above the hut. For even better views walk a short distance up the ridge beyond the hut to where the climbing route starts. With binoculars it is possible to see climbers on the Hornligrat ridge.

The hut and the shelf where it resides offer marvelous views of the surrounding summits. Across the valley to the north a wall of 4,000-meter peaks, from Dent Blanche to the Weisshorn, fill the skyline. The Mischabel Range rises above Zermatt to the northeast. To the southeast an incredible spectacle of peaks and glaciers along the Swiss-Italian border, including Monte Rosa, Lyskamm and the Breithorn, command your attention. Nearer at hand to the west is the Matterhorn Glacier, clinging to the rugged slopes along the peak's north face.

After enjoying the views, retrace your steps to Schwarzsee. Here you can either ride the gondola back to Zermatt for a 5.6 mile round-trip hike or walk back to Zermatt. To hike back to Zermatt find the signpost near the Schwarzsee Hotel. Here signs point to two routes descending to Zermatt. The trail leading to Hermettji, Furi and Zermatt is, in my opinion, the nicest. Another route drops down to Zermatt via Furgg and Furi.

From Schwarzsee both the trails head east on a broad track through meadows for 0.3 miles to a junction where the tracks diverge. The trail to Furgg turns right (south), descending on a dirt road to Furi. The trail to Hermetje continues straight ahead on a descending traverse through meadows and then switchbacks down steep forested slopes to Furi. I prefer this option since it has better views and keeps you off the roads. The trail to Furgg is not quite as steep but requires you to watch for bikes whizzing down the road.

From Furi, follow the signs toward Zum See, a small hamlet with traditional wooden structures and a small chapel. Beyond Zum See the path crosses a bridge to the west bank of the Zmuttbach and then follows the well beaten path back to the Schwarzsee lift station in Zermatt. Total hiking distance from Schwarzsee to Zermatt is 4.4 to 4.9 miles depending on the route. Total round trip distance from Schwarzsee to Hornlihutte to Zermatt is 10.0 to 10.5 miles, again based on the route.

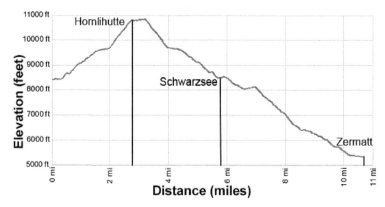

Trailhead Directions

Walking Directions from the Zermatt Bahnhof (train station) to the Schwarzsee Lift Station: See Hike 3.

Hiking to Schwarzsee: See Hike 3.

6. Zmutt Loop ★★★★☆
Distance: 5.8 miles (loop)

Near Zermatt in the Valais

Pretty meadows, larch forests and nice views of the Matterhorn make this trail a good option for families and hikers looking for a pleasant half day walk.

Distance: 5.8 miles (loop)
Elevation: 5,295-ft. at Trailhead
Maximum elevation: 6,970-ft.
Elevation Gain: 1,675-ft.
Difficulty: easy-moderate

Basecamp: Zermatt
Zermatt West Map: See page 10
Online Map/Photos:
www.hikingwalking.com/zmutt

Why Hike the Zmutt Loop Trail

Zmutt (6,352-ft.), a tiny 500-year old hamlet southwest of Zermatt, is a photogenic spot with traditional wood houses set amid pretty meadows. It is a favorite lunch destination for tourist looking for an easy, scenic walk. Several paths lead to the village. Most people walk along the low route that heads south on Zermatt's main street, Bahnhofstrasse, along the west side of the Zmutt River.

A more scenic and energetic alternative is the high route to Zmutt. This trail travels through beautiful meadows, passes the hamlets of Herbrigg and Hubel and offers good views of the Matterhorn, the Breithorn, the highest peak in the Mischabel range – the Taschhorn and Dom, along with the summits rising above the Findel Glacier.

Typically walkers complete the loop by returning to Zermatt via the popular low path. Hikers looking for more solitude on the return journey can take a slightly longer and a little more difficult mid-level path that travels above the low route.

The Zmutt Loop hike offers a good workout and is a nice way to acclimatize if you've just arrived in Switzerland. It is a good option for families or parties looking for a half day outing before catching a train. It is also a good choice for days with less than optimal weather or when the high country is shrouded in clouds.

The Zmutt Loop

This description of the Zmutt Loop trail assumes hikers walk in a counter-clockwise direction taking the high path to Zmutt and returning via the low or mid-level path. From the Bahnhof (train station) in Zermatt, walk south on Bahnhofstrasse (the main street) for 0.4 miles. After passing the Matterhorn Museum and a church (both on your left) the road soon curves to the right. The first street to the right after the curve is Schalpmattgasse. Bear right (west) onto Schalpmattgasse toward Hubel, Alterhaupt and Chalbermatten. Ignore the other signs at the intersection pointing straight ahead (south) to Zmutt. This is the low route that can be used on the return leg. (See trailhead directions below.)

Walk up Schalpmattgasse for 0.1 miles and turn right (north) on the alleyway signed for Hubel and Zmutt. The turn is between an old wood granary (on a cement base) and the Chalet Talina. Soon the paved road curves to the left and turns into a trail, ascending through pastures on steep switchbacks.

Reach a junction at 0.8 miles and turn left (south/southwest) in the direction of Hubel and Zmutt. The path now climbs the grassy hillside, passing through a small grove of larch trees, to Herbrigg (5,758-ft.) at 1.0 mile. The small hamlet, with its traditional Walser-style wood homes, barns and granaries, enjoys nice views of the high peaks of the Mischabel Range to the northeast along with bird's-eye views of Zermatt. The summit of the Matterhorn peeks above the hillside to the southwest.

At the junction in the middle of Herbrigg, take the trail branching right (west) toward Hubel and Zmutt. The trail bearing left will be our return route via the mid-level path. Beyond Herbrigg the track ascends steep grassy slopes sprinkled with wildflowers and larches. As you climb, the Breithorn and the Klein Matterhorn, a distinctively shaped knob, appear above the hillside across the valley.

Pass a group of old stone buildings at 1.3 miles and then reach Hubel (6,385-ft.), a scattered collection of old wood and stone structures, at 1.5 miles. Here a signed trail heads right (north), climbing toward Alterhaupt and Trift. We continue straight ahead to Zmutt.

The trail now ascends on moderate grades along a beautiful meadow-clad bench beneath the steep walls of the Hohbalm plateau. The distinctively-shaped Matterhorn, partially hidden by the steep slopes, rises to the southwest. Nice views extend east up the Findel Valley toward the Strahlhorn and Rimpfishhorn. Nearer at hand, small shrubs, wildflowers and scattered larches add interest to the walk.

At 1.7 miles reach a "Y" intersection. Here a trail branching left (south) descends to Zmutt in 0.75 miles. This is the traditional high route to Zmutt. If time and energy permit, I suggest taking the trail branching to the right, the continuation of the walk along the high bench. This option adds 0.9 miles and 370-ft. in elevation gain to the hike but the extra effort is well rewarded with great views.

To extend the walk, continue ascending along the bench. As you climb enjoy ever improving views of the Matterhorn, the Findel Glacier area (to the east), the Breithorn and Klein Matterhorn (to the southeast) and the Mischabel Range (behind you).

At 2.1 miles the trail curves to the west revealing the peaks and glaciers at the head of the Zmutt Valley. The full extent of the Matterhorn's east and north face, along with the Matterhorn glacier, are now in view.

Reach the high point of the hike (6,970-ft.) at 2.2 miles. Here hikers have a bird's-eye view of Zmutt, 600-ft. below. Across the valley the majestic Matterhorn dominates the view. To the southeast Monte Rosa, Lyskamm and the Breithorn rise above the Gorner Valley. The Strahlhorn, Rimpfishhorn and Findel Glacier fill the horizon to the east. Above the trail steep meadows lead to the towering south wall of the Hohbalm plateau.

The meadows around the high point are a great place to take a break and enjoy the terrific views. When you finally pull yourself away, follow the trail as it descends from the bench on moderate grades toward the Zmutt Dam. The arch dam, finished in 1964, stores water from the Zmutt Glacier and is part of the Grande Dixence hydroelectric project.

Arrive at the signed junction below the dam at 2.75 miles and turn left (southeast) toward Zmutt on a pleasant trail traveling through pastures on moderate to easy grades. At 3.0 miles turn right (south) on a trail dropping steeply down to the tiny hamlet of Zmutt (6,350-ft.) at 3.1 miles. The path now passes through a cluster of restaurants, typically packed with people, and turns left (southeast) toward Zermatt.

Beyond Zmutt a broad track, popular with tourists, returns to Zermatt via the Zmutt low route (see directions below) in 2.4 miles. Hikers looking for more solitude on the return journey can take a slightly longer trail (2.7 miles) that travels above the main track on a "mid-level" route.

To reach the mid-level route back to Zermatt follow the broad track down from Zmutt for 0.2 miles (3.3 miles from the start) to a signed junction amid a few buildings. Here signs point straight ahead toward Zum See, Blatten and Zermatt. We turn left (north) on an alternate route also signed for Zermatt.

Follow the trail along the east side of a building to a "Y" intersection. Take the trail branching to the right (northeast). Walk a very short distance on the trail to a second "Y" intersection. The trail to the left climbs to Hubel and the high route. Our trail branches right (east) toward Zermatt Kirche (Church) and the Zermatt Bahnhof.

Initially the trail travels through meadows and a small cluster of houses with nice views of the Oberrothorn, Strahlhorn and Rimpfishhorn. Not far beyond the houses the trail enters the trees and at 3.8 miles starts descending steeply along a forested hillside. At 4.3 miles the trees give way to steep meadows with views of the Oberrothorn and the high peaks of the Mischabel range.

The descent ends at 4.5 miles. The trail now climbs a short distance on moderate grades before crossing a grassy bowl to Herbrigg at 4.8 miles. From Herbrigg, retrace your steps back to Zermatt. Remember to turn right at 5.0 miles where signs point downhill toward Zermatt.

Reach Schalpmattgasse at 5.2 miles and turn left (east), walking a short distance to Oberdorfstrasse where you turn left (northeast) again. The street soon passes the church, where the street name changes to Bahnhofstrasse, and then heads to the train station at 5.8 miles.

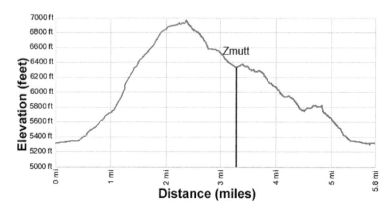

Trailhead Directions

From the Zermatt Bahnhof (train station): Walk south on Bahnhofstrasse, the town's main street, for 0.4 miles. Pass the Matterhorn Museum and the Pfarrkirche St. Mauritius (church) on the left. Just beyond the church the road curves to the right. The first road/walkway to the right is Schalpmattgasse. (Look for a blue street sign on the Chalet Adlerhost.) Signs at the corner point right (west) toward Hubel, Alterhaupt and Chalbermatten. This is the high route. Signs pointing straight ahead (south) to Zmutt direct you to the low route. (Note: At the church the street name changes from Bahnhofstrasse to Oberdorfstrasse.)

Low Route - From the Zermatt Bahnhof (train station): Walk south on Bahnhofstrasse, the town's main street. As you walk down the main street you will pass the Matterhorn Museum and the Pfarrkirche St. Mauritius (church) on the left. Soon the road curves to the right and its name changes to Oberdorfstrasse. Along the way signs point straight ahead to Zmutt.

After walking 0.75 miles, reach a large paved area with a taxi stand and bus stop where the walkway splits. Take the broad track branching right, signed for Zmuttweg and Edelweissweg. Hiking signs point to Zmutt and Schonbielhutte. The broad walkway now climbs through meadows and forested hillsides along the right (northwest) side of the Zmuttbach (Zmutt River). Signs along the way direct you to Zmutt. Reach the small hamlet in about an hour and 10 minutes after walking 2.4 miles and gaining 1,055-ft. (If you are not acclimated the walk will take longer.).

7. Oberrothorn ★★★★☆
Distance: 3.8 - 9.1 miles (round trip)
Near Zermatt in the Valais

This short, easy loop hike explores the basin below a huge amphitheater of eroded cliffs rising above the eastern side of Ouray and features scenic viewpoints to appreciate the formation along with the peaks rising to the south and west of town.

Distance: 3.8 miles (round trip) Rothorn - Oberrothorn
5.4 miles (round trip) Blauherd - Oberrothorn
8.3 miles (one-way) Rothorn - Oberrothorn - Sunnegga
9.1 miles (one-way) Blauherd - Oberrothorn - Sunnegga
Elevation: 8,453-ft. at Blauherd
10,162-ft. at Rothorn
11,190-ft. at Oberrothorn
7,217-ft. at Sunneggal

Elevation Gain: 1,400-ft. to Rothorn
2,755-ft. to Blauherd
-3,973-ft. to Sunnegga
Difficulty: strenuous
Basecamp: Zermatt
Zermatt East Map: See page 10
Online Map/Photos:
www.hikingwalking.com/oberrothorn

Why Hike to the Oberrothorn

Hikers climbing the strenuous trail to the top of the Oberrothorn (11,200-ft.) are rewarded with stunning, panoramic views of the 4,000-meter peaks surrounding the Zermatt area. From the summit enjoy glorious views of the Ober Gabelhorn-Weisshorn Group towering above the west side of the valley. The Mischabel Range dominates the view to the north while an incredible spectacle of peaks and glaciers, stretching from the Monte Rosa to the Breithorn massifs, fill the skyline to the south. The star of the show, the majestic Matterhorn, stands alone at the head of the valley.

Ski lifts facilitate the climb to the top while a good network of hiking trails allow parties to create interesting loop hikes incorporating a trip to the summit with visits to other scenic areas around the Oberrothorn massif. This hike rides the funicular to Sunnegga and then takes the gondola to Blauherd. From Blauherd it is 2.7 miles to the summit.

The Blauherd gondola connects with the Rothorn cable car that whisks hikers to the summit of the Unterrothorn, where a trail ascends the Oberrothorn in 1.9 miles. This description includes information on walking from the Blauherd and the Rothorn lift stations to the summit of the Oberrothorn. These relatively quick climbs to the summit are followed by a long descent that visits the Stellisee, the pretty meadows along the west facing slopes of the Unterrothorn and the small village of Tufteren.

Hikers looking for a more challenging day opt for the 7.4 mile (round-trip) hike from Sunnegga to the Oberrothorn that gains over 3,970-ft. The initial segment of this walk, from Sunnegga to the Blauherd lift station, is very steep and travels under or near the Blauherd gondola lines. My preference is to skip this segment and instead use the lifts to get to the summit early and then enjoy a leisurely day descending to Sunnegga.

The trail to the summit climbs through a barren landscape of rock and scree, with some exposure. It should not be attempted if the trail is covered with ice or slick snow unless parties are properly equipped. The hike is not recommended for families with small children or anyone with a fear of heights.

For the best views I strongly recommend getting an early start. Clouds can obscure views of the high peaks in the afternoon. The summit also gets quite crowded on a beautiful day given the easy access offered by the lifts.

The presence of the lifts and ski equipment along some trail segments certainly detract from the hike. While not optimal, it is easy to quickly pass through these eyesores and avoid trail segments traveling directly beneath the lift lines. I believe the fabulous views are adequate compensation for these blemishes upon an otherwise scenic landscape.

From Rothorn to Oberrothorn

Distance: 3.8 miles (round trip) Rothorn to Oberrothorn
8.3 miles (point-to-point) Rothorn - Oberrothorn - Sunnegga
Elevation: 10,162-ft. at Rothorn
Elevation at the Oberrothorn: 11,190-ft.
Elevation at the Sunnegga: 7,217-ft.
Elevation Gain: 1,400-ft./-3,973-ft.

To start the hike from the top of the Rothorn cable car, follow the directions (below) to the Sunnegga Funicular in Zermatt. Get a ticket from

Zermatt to the Rothorn station and a return ticket from Sunnegga to Zermatt. (Other options are available.)

Take the funicular to Sunnegga, a popular overlook with panoramic views of the Matterhorn, and then catch the gondola to Blauherd. Upon exiting the Blauherd gondola follow the signs to the Rothorn cable car, which ends atop the Unterrothorn (10,180-ft.).

The lifts are timed to facilitate transfers without long waits. Both Sunnegga and Blauherd (8,435-ft.) are popular viewpoints. My advice is to take a short break between rides to take in the morning views.

At the top of the Unterrothorn enjoy wonderful views of the Matterhorn to the southwest. Across the Zermatt valley a massive wall of 4,000-meter peaks, including the Ober Gabelhorn massif, the Wellenkuppe, the Zinalrothorn and the Weisshorn, fill the skyline. To the south, Monte Rosa and Lyskamm form the backdrop for the long ridge running between Gornergrat and Hohtalli. Signboards near the lift station help you identify the peaks.

From the signpost near the cable car station, descend east on a broad rutted path in the direction of Furggli, Fluhalp and the Oberrothorn. Reach a junction on the saddle on the ridge between the Unterrothorn and the Oberrothorn at 0.5 miles after losing 400-ft. Here a sign points left (north) to Tufterchumme (See Hike 11b - Tufternkumme). We continue straight ahead toward the Oberrothorn, reaching a junction at Furggli (9,970-ft.) at 0.6 miles. Here a broad track branches right to Blauherd, Stellisee and Sunnegga. We head east toward the Oberrothorn.

Skip down to the section entitled, "Hiking to the Summit," to continue the description.

From Blauherd to the Oberrothorn

Distance from Trailhead: 5.4 miles (round-trip) Blauherd to Oberrothorn
9.1 miles (point-to-point) Blauherd - Oberrothorn - Sunnegga
Elevation: 8,453-ft. at Blauherd
Elevation at the Oberrothorn: 11,190-ft.
Elevation at the Sunnegga: 7,217-ft.
Elevation Gain/Loss: 2,755-ft./-3,973-ft.

Start the day by riding the funicular to Sunnegga, a popular overlook with panoramic views of the Matterhorn, and then catch the gondola to Blauherd (8,435-ft.). You can purchase a ticket from Zermatt to Blauherd and a return ticket from Sunnegga to Zermatt. Other options are available. (See the trailhead directions below.)

At the top of the Blauherd lift enjoy wonderful views of the Matterhorn to the southwest. Across the Zermatt valley a massive wall of 4,000-meter peaks, including the Ober Gabelhorn massif, the Wellenkuppe, the Zinalrothorn and the Weisshorn, fill the skyline. To the south, the Monte

Rosa massif and Lyskamm form the backdrop for the long ridge running between Gornergrat and Hohtalli.

From the signpost near the gondola station, walk east on a broad track ascending toward the Unterrothorn (1-hr 40-min) and Oberrothorn (3-hr 10-min). The trail curves around the base of the Unterrothorn, reaching a junction at 0.8 miles. Along the way the path enjoys great views of the Matterhorn and Monte Rosa-Breithorn group.

At the junction, turn left (north) on a dirt road climbing steeply toward the Unterrothorn and Oberrothorn. As you climb, watch for a trail branching left (north) off the road at 1.0 mile. Take the trail, which ascends through meadows paralleling the road. (It is best to leave the road since it is used by mountain bikers that fly down the hill from the Rothorn lift.)

Reach a junction at Furggli (9,970-ft.), a saddle on the ridge between the Unterrothorn and the Oberrothorn, at 1.4 miles. Turn right (east) toward the Oberrothorn. Ignore the trail to the left that climbs to the Rothorn cable car station on the summit of the Unterrothorn.

Hiking to the Oberrothorn Summit

(The description below includes two mileage numbers for each point along the trail. The first is the distance from the Rothorn lift and the second is the distance from the Blauherd lift.)

From Furggli, the trail heads east, ascending the south face of the Oberrothorn on moderate grades. At 0.8 miles/1.6 miles the grade steepens as the path turns left (northeast) and starts climbing a series of switchbacks up rocky slopes littered with shale.

As you climb, enjoy marvelous views south to the glaciated chain of 13,000-ft. (4,000-meter) peaks forming the border between Switzerland and Italy, including Monte Rosa, Lyskamm, Castor, Pollux and the Breithorn. Bookending the western end of the visible chain is the distinctive pyramid-shaped Matterhorn. To the southeast the Findel Glacier flows down the slopes of the Cima di Jazzi (12,477-ft.) between the Strahlhorn and Rimpfishhorn, to the north, and the Stockhorn, to the south.

At 1.2 miles/2.0 miles fix ropes offer a level of security where a section of exposed trail climbs very steeply around a rock outcropping. The trail should not present any problems to experienced hikers unless it is covered with snow and/or ice.

Reach a ridge extending southeast at 1.4 miles/2.2 miles. Take a short detour to an overlook at the edge of the ridge for terrific views of the Mischabel Range, including the Strahlhorn, Rimpfischhorn and the Allalinhorn. The trail now turns northwest, climbing up the ridge on steep switchbacks.

Attain the south ridge of the Oberrothorn at 1.7 miles/2.5 miles. Follow the trail as it heads north on an ascending traverse along the west side of the ridge, reaching the top of the Oberrothorn (11,200-ft.) at 1.9 miles/2.8 miles. Use caution if snow is present atop the peak.

From the summit, marvelous panoramic views extend in all directions. Across the valley to the west Dent Blanche, the Ober Gabelhorn massif, the Zinalrothorn and the Weisshorn tower above the Zermatt Valley. Looking north, the Dom, Taschhorn and Alphubel dominate the view. To the east, glaciers cling to the flanks of the Rimpfischhorn, Strahlhorn and Adlerhorn. An incredible spectacle of peaks and glaciers along the Swiss-Italian border, including Monte Rosa, Lyskamm and the Breithorn, fill the skyline to the south while the majestic Matterhorn stands alone at the head of the valley.

Oberrothorn to Sunnegga

Segment Stat: 3.8 - 6.4 miles (one-way)
Total Distance: 5.7 - 9.1 miles (one-way)
Elevation at Sunnegga: 7,217-ft.
Elevation Loss to Sunnegga: :-3,973-ft.

When you are done enjoying the views head back down the trail. At 3.2 miles/4.0 miles (1.3 miles from the summit), reach a signpost at Furggli. Here you have a choice of heading to the Rothorn cable car (a 3.8 mile/4.6 mile hike) and taking the lifts back to Sunnegga, walking down to Blauherd or walking all the way back to Sunnegga. If it is a nice day, I recommend walking to Sunnegga.

To walk to Sunnegga, turn left (south/southwest) at the signpost in the direction of Fluealp, Blauherd and Sunnegga. Descend steeply down a dirt road for a short distance, watching for a trail breaking off to the right. Take the trail, which parallels the road, descending through meadows. (It is best to leave the road since it is used by mountain bikers that fly down the hill from the Rothorn lift.)

Reach at junction at 3.8 miles/4.6 miles. The trail branching right (west) to Blauherd (25-min) and Sunnegga (1h 10min) is the fastest route. This path curves around the base of the Unterrothorn, reaching Blauherd in 0.9 miles. Along the way enjoy great views of the Matterhorn and Monte Rosa-Breithorn group.

The trail to the left (south/southwest), signed for the Stellisee (50min), Sunnegga (1-hr 55-min) and Fluealp, is longer but offers the opportunity to visit the Stellisee, a small lake famous with photographers for its wonderful views of the Matterhorn perfectly reflected on the lake's crystalline waters.

If you are not in a hurry and are enjoying the hike, turn left toward the Stellisee. Travel along the ski area service road for 0.2 miles and then take the trail branching right, which zig-zags down rocky meadows to rejoin the road at 4.3 miles/5.1 miles.

Upon reaching the road ignore the trail directly across the way pointing toward Flue and Fluealp. Instead turn right (south) onto the broad track heading toward the Stellisee and Sunnegga. As you descend the Berghaus Flue at Fluehalp is visible to the southeast.

At 4.4 miles/5.2 miles watch for an unmarked trail (a short-cut) that heads right (east) through meadows and an old rock slide toward the Stellisee. Take this trail. If you miss the turn you will reach a road where you should turn right (east) toward the lake.

Arrive at the east end of the Stellisee at 4.8 miles/5.6 miles. Views of the Matterhorn from the mirror-like surface of the lake are sublime. The lake is a great spot for a picnic and to soak in the sun while gazing at the Matterhorn.

When you are ready to move on, walk along the north side of the lake to a signpost at the west end of the lake at 5.0 miles/5.8 miles. Here you have several options. The shortest is to walk to Blauherd and take the gondola back to Sunnegga. From Blauherd there three options for walking back Sunnegga. Looking at the map you will see other options that take you past the Leisee, a popular tarn.

At the west end of the Stellisee turn right (northwest) toward Blauherd. The path climbs on gentle grades to the top station for the Blauherd gondola (8,435-ft.), at 5.7 miles/6.5 miles. The walk features nice views of the Matterhorn and the Findel Glacier area (behind you to the east).

At Blauherd either take the gondola to Sunnegga or hike down to Sunnegga. If you decide to hike there are three options. Along the south side of the gondola/lift station, a trail drops steeply down the hillside and then descends through meadows to the south of the gondola, arriving in Sunnegga after 1.4 miles for a total hiking distance of 7.1 miles/7.9 miles. A road, which departs from the north side of the gondola/lift station, parallels the route of the gondola slightly to the north of the lift line, dropping on steep grades to Sunnegga in 1.2 miles for a 6.9 mile/7.7 mile hike.

For hikers looking for a longer, more scenic and less traveled route, I recommend taking a side trip to Tufteren and then head back to Sunnegga. From the signpost near the lift station, walk northwest on a broad track toward Tufteren and Zermatt. Shortly after passing under a chair lift the track reverts to a trail that descends through beautiful wildflower-filled meadows strewn with large boulders. The Weisshorn, Zinalrothorn and Ober Gabelhorn group along with the Matterhorn dominate the views along this scenic trail.

At 7.1 miles/7.9 miles arrive at a junction. The trail heading right previously lead to Ober Sattla, a lovely viewpoint above Tasch, that is now closed due to a landslide. We turn left (southwest) toward Tufteren and Sunnegga.

Reach Tufteren (7,267-ft.), a small village of wooden houses and barns set amid lovely meadow high above the Zermatt Valley, at 7.3 miles/8.1 miles. A few restaurants serve refreshments from sun terraces with great views of the Matterhorn. Here signs point left to the track heading south toward Sunnegga.

The rest of the walk is mostly level, following a broad, dirt track lined with larches growing amid pretty meadows. Openings in the trees offer nice views of the Matterhorn. As you near Sunnegga you may run into some mountain bikes.

Bear left at a junction at 8.2 miles toward Sunnegga. In a short distance you will see doorways that lead to the funicular station. Total hiking distance, including the side trip to Tufteren, is 8.3 miles/9.1 miles.

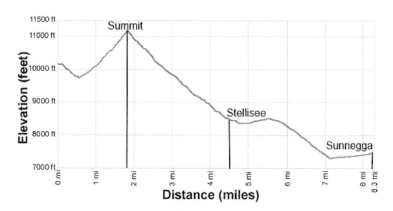

Trailhead Directions

Walking from the Zermatt Bahnhof (train station) to the Sunnegga Funicular: The Gornergrat Cog Railway station is located across the street from the Zermatt train station. On the south side of the Gornergrat Station is Getwingstrasse (Getwing Street), which runs east. Find Getwingstrasse and walk east along the street for 0.2 miles (300-meters). The street will curve to the southeast and cross the Vispa River.

On the other side of the river turn left (east/northeast) on Vispastrasse (also labeled as Rechte Uferstrasse on some maps). Walk about 0.1 miles, following the street as it curves to the north/northeast. The Sunnegga Funicular Station is on the right side of the road at Vispastrasse 34.

After obtaining funicular tickets, walk through a long underground tunnel to get to the base of the funicular. The schedule for the funicular is found on the Matterhorn Paradise time table page. Select the Sunnegga – Rothorn option.

Note: At the top of the funicular take the gondola to Blauherd. (Exit the funicular building and follow the signs to the Blauherd gondola.) At Blauherd you catch the cable car to Rothorn. Round-trip tickets are available for a variety of ride combinations. For example you can purchase tickets from Zermatt to Rothorn going up and from Sunnegga to Zermatt going down.

8. Findel Glacier Viewpoint ⭐⭐⭐⭐⭐
Distance: 5.4 - 8.3 miles (round trip)
Near Zermatt in the Valais

This moderately-easy trail leads to a peaceful overlook with wonderful views of the Findel Glacier flowing down the slopes of the Cima di Jazzi. Along the way hikers enjoy splendid views of the Matterhorn.

Distance: Distance: 5.4 miles (round trip) to Findel Glacier Viewpoint
8.3 miles (round trip) Blauherd - Viewpoint - Zermatt
Elevation: 8,457-ft. at Blauherd
9,217-ft. at Findel Glacier Viewpoint
5,490-ft. at Zermatt

Elevation Gain: 892-ft. to Findel Glacier Viewpoint
-3,727-ft. back to Zermatt
Difficulty: moderately-easy
Basecamp: Zermatt
Zermatt East Map: See page 10
Online Map/Photos:
www.hikingwalking.com/findel

Why Hike to the Findel Glacier Viewpoint

This hike leads to a lovely overlook with captivating views of the Findel Glacier, a massive river of ice spilling down the slopes Strahlhorn and Cima di Jazzi on the Swiss-Italian border. Terrific views of the iconic Matterhorn are your constant companion during much of the moderately-easy hike.

The day starts by taking the funicular to Sunnegga followed by scenic gondola ride to Blauherd. Here the hike descends east through meadows to the Stellisee, a beautiful lake which perfectly reflects the Matterhorn on its mirror-like surface.

Beyond the Stellisee, the trail ascends rocky meadows beside the Findel Glacier's northern lateral moraine. Before reaching the viewpoint, side trails allow hikers to climb up and walk along the knife-edge crest of the moraine wall with great views of the Findel Glacier and the deep, rugged trench dug by the receding river of ice. A final steep haul leads to a grassy knoll overlooking the huge icefield flowing in motionless waves down the flanks of the Cima Di Jazzi to the valley floor. To the west the Matterhorn, Dent Blanche and Ober Gabelhorn massif dominate the skyline.

On a sunny day the overlook is a great spot for a picnic. Not many people travel this far up the valley so you are likely to experience a level of solitude not found at the other viewpoints around the Zermatt valley.

The area's good trail system allows hikers to return to Blauherd gondola or walk down to Sunnegga and catch the funicular back to Zermatt. Energetic parties looking for a longer day can follow one of several trails descending steeply through meadows and larch forests to Winkelmatten, a neighborhood at the south end of Zermatt.

To the Findel Glacier Viewpoint

Distance from Trailhead: 2.7 miles (one-way)
Elevation at Junction: 9,217-ft.
Elevation Gain: 892-ft.

The day starts by taking the funicular to Sunnegga, a popular overlook with panoramic views of the Matterhorn, and then riding the gondola to Blauherd (8,435-ft.). (See trailhead directions below.)

At Blauherd enjoy great views of the Matterhorn to the southwest. Across the valley to the west a massive wall of 4,000-meter peaks, including the Ober Gabelhorn massif, the Wellenkuppe, the Zinalrothorn and the Weisshorn, fill the skyline. To the south the top of the Breithorn massif rises above the Gornergrat ridge.

After taking in the views find the trail signpost and head southeast on the broad track toward the Stellisee and Fluealp. After walking about 0.1 miles watch for a trail branching left and climbing above the road. Follow the trail as it descends on gentle grades to the Stellisee. Soon nice views open east to the Findel Glacier pouring down the slopes of the Cima di Jazzi (12,477-ft.) between the Strahlhorn and Rimpfishhorn, to the north, and the Stockhorn, to the south.

Reach the west end of the Stellisee at 0.7 miles. The small lake is famous with photographers for its wonderful views of the Matterhorn perfectly reflected on the lake's clear waters. After enjoying the views from the lake, walk around the south side of the lake to a dirt track. Turn left (east) on a track ascending on easy grades toward Flue and Fluhalp.

At 1.1 miles a trail, marked by a wood sign leaning against a rock, branches left from the road toward Fluealp. You can either stay on the road or take this trail through meadows and an old rock slide. (I personally prefer the trail.) In the distance you will see the Berghaus at Fluhalp.

Ascend through rocky meadow on moderate grades toward the Berghaus. Be sure to turn around for nice views of the Matterhorn and the Ober Gabelhorn massif rising above the Hohbalm plateau.

Cross a broad track descending from the Oberrothorn at 1.3 miles and arrive at the Berghaus Fluhalp (lodging and refreshments), at 1.4 miles. The trail curves around the west side of the Berghaus and rejoins the track.

Turn left (east) and walk along the track for a short distance to an intersection. Here the road turns north toward the hotel. Bear right (south/southeast) on a trail that descends gently across rocky meadows toward the north moraine wall of the Findel Glacier. At 1.6 miles the trail reaches a path, which I call the Findel Viewpoint trail, paralleling the base of the wall. Turn left on the Findel Viewpoint trail and follow the path as it ascends east/northeast through lovely meadows between the grassy slopes of the moraine wall and the rugged cliffs of the Oberrothorn massif.

At 1.75 miles a use/social trail climbs to the top of the moraine wall, revealing the huge river of ice flowing down the flanks of the Cima de Jazzi, a snow-clad flat-topped peak on the Swiss–Italian border. The Adlerhorn and Strahlhorn tower above the glacier to the north.

The use trail travels along the top of the moraine for 0.3 miles. Hikers uncomfortable walking on the moraine crest should drop back down to the Viewpoint trail and continue ascending northeast through the meadows. (Note: The condition of the moraine changes every year. Use your judgment and descend when the crest becomes too eroded and dangerous to follow.)

At 2.1 miles reach a section of the moraine wall that has collapsed, forcing the use/social trail to descend to the meadows and the Viewpoint Trail. The Viewpoint trail now ascends on easy grades up the slopes to the north of the moraine, passing two small ponds. Just beyond the second pond the the trail climbs steeply up the hillside to a grassy knoll at 2.7 miles. Leave the trail here and walk to the edge of the knoll where marvelous views open to the Findel Glacier, a vast sea of ice pouring down the valley. The overlook features bird's-eye view of the deep trench carved by the glacier and the knife edge wall of the moraine. In the distance, the majestic Matterhorn towers above the Zermatt valley.

On a sunny day this is a great spot for a picnic. Not very many people hike this far up the valley, so you are likely to have a level of solitude not found at many of the viewpoints around Zermatt area.

(Note: The trail continues climbing and soon becomes a route that crosses a rugged saddle between the Spitzi Flue and the Pfulwe. Beyond the saddle a route descends to Tasch.)

Back to Blauherd, Sunnegga or Zermatt

Segment Stat: 2.7 miles back to Blauherd
3.6 miles (one-way) back to Sunnegga
5.6 miles (one-way) back to Zermatt
Total Distance: 5.4 miles (round-trip) to Blauherd
6.3 miles (one way) from Blauherd - Findel Viewpoint - Sunnegga
8.3 miles (one way) from Blauherd - Findel Viewpoint - Zermatt

Maximum Elevation: 9,217-ft.
Ending Elevation at Blauherd: 8,457-ft.
Ending Elevation at Sunnegga: 7,217-ft.
Ending Elevation in Zermatt: 5,490-ft.
Elevation Gain/Loss: -892-ft. to Blauherd
-2,000-ft. to Sunnegga
-3,727-ft. to Zermatt

When you are ready to head back, either retrace your steps to Blauherd, walk back to Sunnegga or hike all the way down to Zermatt. If time, energy and the weather permit, I recommend walking back to Zermatt.

To walk back to Sunnegga or Zermatt, descend the steep hillside to the use/social trail climbing atop the moraine. Here you have a choice. Either continue on the trail traveling through meadows beside the moraine, passing the turnoff to the Berghaus, or climb back atop the moraine. If you climb the moraine you should be able to continue along the use/social trail for 0.6 miles before you are again forced to climb down to the meadow (Viewpoint) trail at 4.0 miles (1.3 miles from the knoll).

In the meadows continue west on the Viewpoint trail, descending on moderate grades toward the Leisee, Winkelmatten and Zermatt. Ignore any trails branching right or left. At 5.9 miles the grade abates as it approaches the Leisee (7,320-ft.), a small lake just below Sunnegga. The lake, at 6.1 miles, is a popular spot with families and features a playground and barbeque area along with stunning views of the Matterhorn.

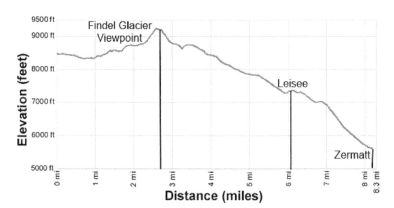

From the lake a trail climbs a short distance to Sunnegga where the funicular back to Zermatt. Total hiking distance for this option is 6.3 miles.

Alternatively a number of walking paths descend steeply through meadows and larch forests to Winkelmatten, a neighborhood at the south end of Zermatt, losing over 1,800-ft. in 2.2 miles, for an 8.3 mile hike. If you are interested in stopping for refreshments on the hike down, take the path back to Zermatt that pass through Eggen and Findeln. Restaurants in both village feature sun terraces with pretty views of the Matterhorn.

Trailhead Directions

Walking from the Zermatt Bahnhof (train station) to the Sunnegga Funicular: See Hike 7.

9. Gornergrat Loop ★★★★★
Distance: 7.0 - 8.5 mile (loop)
Near Zermatt in the Valais

Great views accompany almost every step of this hike leading to Gornergrat, a glorious overlook with panoramic views of 20 peaks over 13,000-ft. (4,000-meters) high.

Distance: 7.0 - 8.5 mile (loop)
Elevation: 7,134-ft. at Riffelalp
10,138-ft. at Gornergrat
7,134-ft. return to Riffelalp from
Gornergrat via Riffelberg
Elevation Gain: 3,004-ft.

Difficulty: moderate-strenuous
Basecamp: Zermatt
Zermatt East Map: See page 10
Online Map/Photos:
www.hikingwalking.com/gornergrat

Why Hike the Gornergrat Loop

Gornergrat is one of the finest overlooks in Zermatt with glorious, panoramic views of 20 peaks over 13,000-ft. (4,000-meters) high. A network of scenic hiking trails climbs the Riffelalp plateau and the Gornergrat ridge to the viewpoint. This loop hikes combines a short ride on the Gornergrat Cog railway with, in my opinion, the most scenic trails to create an unforgettable hike that will have you constantly reaching for your camera.

The hike, starting in Riffelalp, ascends the steep slopes below the Riffelberg plateau accompanied by great views of the iconic Matterhorn towering above the head of the Zermatt Valley. To the northwest a massive wall of 4,000-meter peaks, including Dent Blanche, the Ober Gabelhorn massif, the Zinalrothorn and the Weisshorn, fill the skyline. The Taschhorn and the Dom form a backdrop for the Oberrothorn to the northeast.

As the trail crests and then curves around the south side of the Riffelberg plateau views open to Monte Rosa, Liskamm, Castor, Pollux and the Breithorn massifs, clad in glistening glaciers. Soon the path passes the Riffelsee with more great views of the Matterhorn reflected in its mirror-like surface. Beyond the Riffelsee the trail climbs steeply up the ridge to the summit of Gornergrat, where you'll find a railway station, hotel and restaurants.

The lookout above the complex offers superb 360-degree vistas of the high peaks and glaciers showcased on the ascent from Riffelalp. Below the viewpoint are breathtaking, bird's-eye views of the Gorner Glacier, the second largest glacier system in the Alps. Tributary glaciers flowing down the slopes of Monte Rosa and nearby peaks join this massive river of ice flowing west from the Monte Rosa massif. Signs at the viewpoint help you to identify the summits and glaciers.

The return journey from Gornergrat drops down the ridge and then crosses the Riffelberg plateau, with more wonderful views of the peaks to the north and west. A scenic trail, with wide-ranging views of the valley, descends steeply from Riffelberg to Riffelalp where hikers jump on a return train to Zermatt.

The hike can be shortened by riding the cog railway all the way to Gornergrat and walking down or by taking the train to Riffelberg or Rotenboden, which reduce the distance and elevation gain required to reach Gornergrat. Energetic parties may opt to walk all the way back to Zermatt along pleasant, forested tracks dropping down steep switchbacks to Winkelmatten, a neighborhood at the south end of Zermatt.

It is best to get an early start on the hike. In the afternoon the Gornergrat viewpoint can get quite windy and the peaks are more likely to be obscured in clouds.

To Gornergrat

Distance from Riffelalp: 4.4 miles (one-way)
Elevation at Gornergrat: 10,138-ft.
Elevation Gain: 3,004-ft.

The 15 minute train ride from Zermatt to the Riffelalp Train Station ascends along the east side of Zermatt, crosses a bridge with views of a waterfall above Winkelmatten and then switchbacks up forested hillsides to Riffelalp, with some nice views of the Matterhorn along the way.

At the Riffelalp Train Station (7,254-ft.) look for signs on the west side of the building pointing toward a broad trail heading west to Riffelalp (10-min), Riffelberg (1-hr 10-min), Rotenboden (2-hr) and Gornergrat (2-hr 50-min). The trail curves to the southwest on easy grades, paralleling a small cog railway transporting luggage and people to the Riffelalp Hotel. Arrive at the Riffelalp Hotel and Restaurant in 0.25 miles.

Continue along the broad track through the hotel complex, enjoying beautiful views of the Matterhorn's east and north faces. At 0.3 miles reach a junction with signs pointing right (southwest) to the road that drops to Winkelmatten and Zermatt and left (southeast) toward a trail heading to Gagenhaupt, Rotenboden, Gornergrat, Gletschergarten and Furi. Turn left and walk along the trail for 0.2 miles, passing a tennis court and chapel, to a second junction where the trail to Furi and the Gletschergarten continues straight ahead. Bear left (south) on the path toward Gagenhaupt, Rotenboden and Gornergrat.

Follow the trail as it curves to the southwest on easy grades and soon starts ascending steep slopes clad in rocky meadows and scattered larches beneath the Riffelberg plateau. Occasional switchbacks facilitate the moderately-steep climb. Along the way enjoy great views of the Matterhorn towering above the Matterhorn Plateau. A massive wall of 4,000-meter peaks, including Dent Blanche, the Ober Gabelhorn massif, the Zinalrothorn and the Weisshorn, fill the skyline to the northwest while the Taschhorn and the Dom form a backdrop for the Oberrothorn to the northeast. As the trail gains altitude hikers are treated to bird's-eye views of Riffelalp and Zermatt. In the distance, to the north, are the peaks rising above the Rhone Valley.

At 1.3 miles the grade eases as the trail curves to the south and soon reaches a junction with a trail branching right (southwest) toward the Gletschergarten, Furi and Zermatt. Another trail takes off uphill to the northeast toward Riffelberg. Our path continues straight ahead to Gagenhaupt, Rotenboden and Gornergrat.

The path now veers to the southeast, climbing on moderate grades through pretty meadows. Views open to the Klein Matterhorn and the Breithorn massif. The pyramid-shaped Matterhorn is particularly lovely from this angle.

At 1.9 miles the trail curves to the east and ascends a shallow valley formed by the Riffelhorn's eastern ridge and the Riffelberg plateau (to the north). The Riffelhorn (9,603-ft.), a small, triangular-shaped peak rising to the south of the Riffelberg plateau, is a favorite place for climbers to train before tackling the big peaks.

Arrive at Gagenhaupt (8,412-ft.) at 2.0 miles. Here a trail branches to the left (northwest) toward Riffelberg. We continue straight ahead, climbing the small valley toward the Riffelsee, Rotenboden and Gornergrat. As you ascend turn around for nice views of the Matterhorn, Dent Blanche, the Ober Gabelhorn massif and Wellenkuppe.

More signposts are passed at 2.3 and 2.5 miles. As before, ignore the trails to the left toward Riffelberg and continue straight ahead toward the Riffelsee and Rotenboden. After the second signpost the grade abates as the trail approaches a small tarn and then reaches the Riffelsee, a small alpine lake cradled beneath the Riffelhorn, at 2.7 miles. On calm mornings the tarn and the popular lake are a photographer's delight, with the Matterhorn perfectly reflected in the still waters.

Beyond the Riffelsee the trail climbs toward Rotenboden. Wonderful views open to the snow-covered summits of the Monte Rosa, Liskamm and the Breithorn. Glaciers cascade down the flanks of the peaks.

Reach the turnoff to the Rotenboden Train Station on the Gornergrat line at 3.0 miles. To the left (north) is a trail ascending to the railway. To the right (south) a trail drops down to the Gornergletscher (Gorner Glacier) viewpoint (Hike 10) and the route to Monte Rosa Hut. Continue straight ahead toward Gornergrat.

The trail now climbs steeply up a rocky hillside beside the Gornergrat Railway. Marvelous views of Monte Rosa, Liskamm, Castor, Pollux and the Breithorn, along with the glaciers spilling down the mountains, will help take you mind off the steep ascent. Behind you are glorious views of the Matterhorn. It is unfortunate that the railway is so close to this section of the trail but you will likely to be riveted to the views of the mountains and glaciers to the south, ignoring the presence of the tracks and the occasional passing train.

At 3.7 miles the grade eases as the trail contours around a small bowl. Here views open north to the Taschhorn, Dom, Rimpfischhorn and Strahlhorn in the Mischabel Range. In the distance are the peaks rising above the Rhone Valley.

Beyond the bowl, the trail makes its final short, steep ascent to the Gornergrat rail station and hotel complex at 4.3 miles. The complex, set atop the Gornergrat summit (10,138-ft.), is located along a ridge separating the Findel and Gorner Glaciers. The complex includes a hotel, restaurants and observatories (not open to the public).

Ascend a short distance behind the complex to an overlook, at 4.4 miles, for the best views. Here a stunning 360-degree panorama encompasses 20 peaks over 13,000-ft. (4,000-meters) high. To the south are breathtaking views of Monte Rosa, Liskamm, Castor, Pollux and the Breithorn, covered in snow and ice. The Monte Rosa, Grenz, Zwillings and Schwarzee glaciers pour off the flanks of the peaks and down the valleys to combine with the Gorner Glacier, flowing to the north of Monte Rosa, to form the second largest glacial system in the Alps.

Dominating the skyline to the west is the majestic Matterhorn. To the northwest are glorious views of Dent Blanche, the Ober Gabelhorn massif, the Zinalrothorn and the Weisshorn towering above the Zermatt valley. To the northeast, the distinctive jagged peaks of the Mischabel Range rise beyond the Oberrothorn.

On a nice day it is delightful to sit in the sun on the benches around the overlook and soak in the scene. Be sure to take warm clothes. It can get quite windy at the viewpoint.

Back to Riffelalp via Riffelberg

Segment Stat: 4.1 miles (one-way)
Total Distance: 8.5 miles (loop)
Ending Elevation: 7,134-ft.
Elevation Gain/Loss: -3,004-ft.

When you finally pull yourself away from the Gornergrat Viewpoint, retrace your steps back to Rotenboden junction (5.8 miles), the Riffelsee and the tarn to a sign post at 6.3 miles. Turn right (north) and head toward Riffelberg.

The trail now descends on moderately-steep grades across the rocky meadows of the Riffelberg plateau, accompanied by lovely views of the peaks surrounding the Zermatt valley. Reach Riffelberg (8,471-ft.) at 7.0 miles. Here you can either catch the train back to Zermatt or continue walking to Riffelalp.

To continue to Riffelalp, find the sign post near the train station pointing left (west) toward Riffelalp, Winkelmatten and Zermatt. Walk west, curving around the south side of the Hotel Restaurant Riffelberg (pink Victorian building with red shutters). Here a trail drops steeply down the grassy slopes forming the west wall of the Riffelberg plateau.

The descent, facilitated by switchbacks, offers bird's-eye views of Riffelalp and Zermatt. Initially the trail heads west but soon swings around to the north/northwest as it drops down the steep slopes. Near the bottom of the descent the path crosses a small stream, turns to the west and then meets a dirt road above Riffelalp.

Travel down the dirt road for a short distance to a signpost. To the left (southwest) is the road descending to Winkelmatten and Zermatt. We turn right (northeast), walk by the Riffelalp Hotel and Restaurant (8.25 miles) and then continue along the broad track that leads back to the train station at 8.5 miles.

Hop on the next train to Zermatt or cross the tracks and take the trail, which drops down through larch and pine trees, to Winkelmatten in 2.2 miles for a total round-trip hiking distance of 10.7 miles. Add 0.6 miles if walking to the Zermatt Bahnhof. (See the trailhead directions below for information on walking to Winkelmatten and Zermatt.)

Shorter Hikes to/from Gornergrat

The Gornergrat hike can be shortened by riding the cog railway all the way to Gornergrat and walking down or by taking the train to Riffelberg or Rotenboden, which reduce the distance and elevation gain required to reach Gornergrat. Energetic parties may opt to walk all the way back to Zermatt along pleasant, forested tracks dropping down steep switchbacks to Winkelmatten, a neighborhood at the south end of Zermatt. (See trailhead directions below.)

Rotenboden (9,236-ft.) to Gornergrat (10,138-ft.): 1.6 miles (one-way)/3.2 miles (round trip) with 902-ft. in elevation gain.

Riffelberg (8,471-ft.) to Gornergrat (10,138-ft.): 2.6 miles (one-way)/5.2 miles (round trip) with 1,667-ft. in elevation gain.

Gornergrat (10,138-ft.) to Riffelalp (7,134-ft.) via Riffelberg: 4.1 miles (one-way) with a 3,004-ft. elevation loss. To walk all the way back to the Zermatt Bahnhof (5,490-ft.) is 6.9 miles (one-way) with an additional 1,644-ft. in elevation loss.

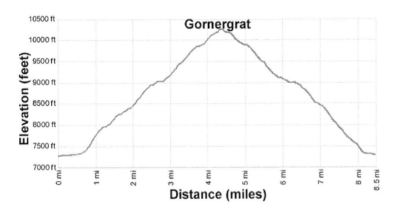

Trailhead Directions

Walking Directions from the Zermatt Bahnhof (train station): The Gornergrat Cog Railway is located directly across the street from the Zermatt Bahnhof. In the height of the summer the trains run from 7 am until 8 pm. There are also some special sunrise trains that start as early as 5 am (advanced booking required). Check at the station or the main tourist office for current schedule.

It takes 15 minutes to reach Riffelalp, 23 minutes to Riffelberg and 33 minutes to Gornergrat. During the height of the day the trains get crowded and you may need to wait to board a train. It is best to get an early start and beat the crowds.

Walking from the Zermatt Bahnhof (train station) to Riffelalp: The hike to Riffelalp is about 2.8 miles (depending on route) and gains 1,930-ft. Walk south/southwest on Bahnhofstrasse, the town's main street for 0.3 miles and then turn left onto Kirchstrasse (Church Street). You will pass the Matterhorn Museum just before the turn. The Pfarrkirche St. Mauritius (church) is located on the southeast corner of Bahnhofstrasse and Kirchstrasse.

Walk down Kirchstrasse for 0.15 miles, crossing the bridge and turn right on Steinmattstrasse (Steinmatt Street), the second street past the river. The Hotel Bellerive is at the northeast corner and the Hotel Julen at the southeast. Signs at the corner now point toward Winkelmatten.

Follow Steinmattstrasse for 0.2 miles as it ascends along a narrow street and then climbs steps. At the top of the steps continue along Staldenstrasse for 0.3 miles to the small church at the center of Winkelmatten, essentially a suburb of Zermatt.

Head around the front of the church and follow the signs pointing southeast toward Riffelalp. After crossing a bridge you will see signs pointing to two routes heading to Riffelalp. One continues along the road, ascending long switchbacks. The other turns left and climbs steeply up a forested trail. The road ends at the Riffelalp Hotel while the trail ascends to the Riffelalp train station and then follows a broad track to the hotel (see above).

I prefer the trail. Note: Both trails travel through forest with occasional glimpses of the surrounding peaks. My advice is to take the train and save your time and energy for wandering the broad open meadows between Riffelalp and Gornergrat.

10. Gorner Glacier Viewpoint ★★★★★
Distance: 7.8 - 8.6 miles (round trip)
Near Zermatt in the Valais

This delightful hike leads to an overlook with front row seats to the amazing spectacle of massive rivers of ice flowing down the flanks of 4,000-meter peaks, joining with the Gorner Glacier to form the second largest glacial system in the Alps.

Distance: 3.9 miles (one way) to Gorner Glacier Viewpoint
8.6 miles (round trip) to back to Riffelalp
Elevation: 8,471-ft. at Riffelberg
8,670-ft. at Gorner Glacier Viewpoint
7,254-ft. at Riffelalp
Elevation Gain: 782-ft. to Gorner Glacier Viewpoint
-2,000-ft. back to Riffelalp

Difficulty: moderate
Basecamp: Zermatt
Zermatt East Map: See page 10
Online Map/Photos:
www.hikingwalking.com/gorner-glacier

Why Hike to the Gorner Glacier Viewpoint

The Gornergletscher (Gorner Glacier) viewpoint offers a unique opportunity to get up close and personal with the second largest glacial system in the Alps. The lookout, perched atop a grassy knoll on a moraine wall, offers bird's-eye view of the convergence of two massive rivers of ice, the Gorner and Grenz Glaciers, spilling down the flanks of Monte Rosa.

Towering above this spectacle of ice are the Monte Rosa, Liskamm and Breithorn massifs along with Castor, Pollux and the Klein Matterhorn, capped in snow and ice. The tributaries of the Gorner Glacier; the Grenz, Monte Rosa, Zwillings and Schwarzee glaciers, spill down the slopes of these peaks, combining with the Gorner Glacier to form an imposing glacial river flowing in motionless waves down the Gorner Valley.

Further down the valley the Breithorn, Triftji, and Unterer Theodul glaciers, former tributaries of the Gorner Glacier, no longer reach the valley floor but instead hang from the flanks of the Breithorn and Klein Matterhorn. Completing the scene the majestic Matterhorn stands alone, rising to the west of the Gorner Valley.

The hike to the viewpoint, starting at Riffelberg, is filled with scenic delights. The Gornergrat Cog Railway and an extensive network of trails allow hikers to tailor their day and modify itineraries on the fly. This description includes return routes to Riffelberg, Riffelalp (recommended) and Zermatt.

Get an early start on this hike. In the afternoon clouds often move in, covering the tops of the peaks and obstructing the views.

To the Gorner Glacier Viewpoint

Distance from Trailhead: 3.9 miles (one way)
Elevation: 8,670-ft.
Elevation Gain: 782-ft.

From the train station in Riffelberg (8,471-ft.), walk a short distance along the west side of the railroad tracks to a "Y" intersection. Here two trails lead to Rotenboden where we pick up the trail to the Gornergletscher (Gorner Glacier) viewpoint. Take the trail branching right (southwest) in the direction of Gagenhaupt (20-min), Riffelsee (1-hr 10-min) and Rotenboden (1-hr 20-min). While this route is 0.8 miles longer, in my opinion it is more scenic. The trail to the left (south), heads over the plateau to Rotenboden (45-min) and Gornergrat (1-hr 40-min).

Follow the trail through meadows with great views of the massive wall of 4,000-meter peaks, including Dent Blanche, the Ober Gabelhorn massif, the Zinalrothorn and the Weisshorn, towering above the Zermatt valley to the northwest. The Matterhorn dominates the skyline to the south.

After passing a pretty little stone chapel with a slate roof at 0.3 miles, the trail continues southwest, ascending the undulating plateau on moderate grades. Ahead the tops of the Klein Matterhorn and Breithorn appear above the plateau. At 0.8 miles the trail curves to the south/southeast as it drops into a shallow valley formed by the Riffelhorn's eastern ridge and the Riffelberg plateau (to the north). The Riffelhorn (9,603-ft.), a small, triangular-shaped peak rising to the south of the Riffelberg plateau, is a favorite place for climbers to train before tackling the big peaks.

Arrive at Gagenhaupt (8,412-ft.) at 1.0 mile where our path joins a trail coming up from Riffelalp. Continue straight ahead, climbing up the valley on moderate to moderately-steep grades toward the Riffelsee, Rotenboden and Gornergrat. Turn around occasionally for nice views of the Matterhorn, Dent Blanche, the Ober Gabelhorn massif and the Wellenkuppe.

Pass trail junctions at 1.3 and 1.5 miles, ignoring the paths branching left toward Riffelberg. Our route is straight ahead toward the Riffelsee and Rotenboden. After the second signpost the grade abates as the trail travels by a small tarn and then reaches the popular Riffelsee, a small alpine lake cradled beneath the Riffelhorn, at 1.8 miles. On calm mornings the tarn and the lake are a photographer's delight, with the Matterhorn perfectly reflected in the still waters.

The trail now ascends above the north side of the lake to a junction. Ignore trails climbing uphill toward the Rotenboden train station or ascending east toward Gornergrat. Instead head southeast on the trail toward the Gornergletscher that curves above the east end of the lake and then travels on easy grades toward the edge of the plateau. Along the way pass a signed junction with a path ascending to the Rotenboden train station. We continue straight ahead toward the Monte Rosa Hut and the Gornergletscher.

At 2.3 miles the trail reaches the edge of the plateau and curves left (east). Here we enjoy marvelous panoramic views. Monte Rosa, Liskamm, Castor, Pollux and the Breithorn, covered in snow and ice, dominate the view across the valley. Glaciers, including the Monte Rosa, Grenz, Zwillings and Schwarze, pour off the flanks of the peaks and combine with the Gorner Glacier, flowing down the west side of Monte Rosa, in the Gorner Valley.

Initially the trail ascends 120-ft. to a rock outcropping at 2.5 miles before descending on moderate grades along the south facing slopes of the Gornergrat ridge, accompanied by amazing views of the spectacle of rock and ice across the valley. Along the way pass a route at 3.3 miles that ascends on very steep grades to Gornergrat. (This is a route, not a trail, and is only recommended for experienced, sure-footed hikers.)

At 3.5 miles the grade abates as the trail travels along the Gorner glacier's north lateral moraine to the Gornergletscher viewpoint (8,670-ft.) at 3.9 miles, losing over 550-ft. from the plateau. The glacier viewpoint, atop a grassy knoll, offers splendid views of the massive Gorner glacier spilling down the west facing flanks of Monte Rosa to the valley floor where it flows west to a point just below the Klein Matterhorn. The Monte Rosa, Grenz, Zwillings and Schwarze glaciers flow into and combine with the Gorner

Glacier to form the second largest glacial system in the Alps, after the Aletsch Glacier. Further down the valley the Breithorn, Triftji, and Unterer Theodul glaciers, former tributaries of the Gorner Glacier, no longer reach the valley floor but instead hang from flanks of the Breithorn and Klein Matterhorn.

The Monte Rosa, Liskamm and Breithorn massifs, along with Castor, Pollux, the Klein Matterhorn tower above the sea of ice. Across the valley on a low ridge to the west of the Grenz Glacier is the new hi-tech glass and aluminum clad Monte Rosa Hut. A pair of binoculars will help you to spot the hut perched atop the bare rock on the rugged ridge.

A route, using ladders to drop down to the Gorner glacier, crosses the glacier and then climbs 1,200-ft. to the hut. Only properly equipped, experienced parties should venture out onto the ice. Over the past decade melting has created major crevasses in the ice flow. Hikers interested in trekking to the hut should inquire about guides at the Zermatt Tourism Office near the train station.

From the Viewpoint to Riffelalp

Segment Stat: 4.7 miles (one-way)
Total Distance: 8.6 miles (round trip)
Ending Elevation: 7,254-ft.
Elevation Gain/Loss: 564-ft./-2,000-ft.

When you are done enjoying the views, retrace your steps to the Riffelsee (9,087-ft.) at 6.0 miles. Follow the signs pointing west toward Gagenhaupt, Riffelberg and Riffelalp. Reach a junction at 6.3 miles and turn right (northwest) toward Riffelberg. This path descends across the Riffelberg plateau for 0.7 miles to Riffelberg for a total round trip hiking distance of 7.0 miles.

To return to Riffelberg along the original route or walk to Riffelalp, at the junction at 6.3 miles, continue straight toward Gagenhaupt, Riffelberg and Riffelalp. Ignore a second sign pointing left to Riffelberg at 6.5 miles. Follow the trail as it drops down the narrow valley between the Riffelberg plateau and the Riffelhorn's eastern ridge.

Reach Gagenhaupt junction at 6.9 miles. To return on the original route, take the trail branching right (northwest) and climbing the hillside to the Riffelberg plateau. From the signpost back to Riffelberg is 0.9 miles for a total hiking distance of 7.8 miles.

Alternatively, if time and energy permit, continue straight ahead toward Riffelalp and Zermatt. Soon the trail curves northwest and then north/northeast on a descending traverse down the steep slopes beneath the Riffelberg plateau, passing through rocky meadows that are soon populated with scattered larches. Occasional switchbacks facilitate the moderately-steep descent. Ignore any signs pointing toward the Gletschergarten, Furi and Zermatt.

Along his section of the hike enjoy great views of the Matterhorn towering above the Matterhorn Plateau. Dent Blanche, the Ober Gabelhorn massif, the Zinalrothorn and the Weisshorn, fill the skyline to the northwest while the Taschhorn and the Dom form a backdrop to the Oberrothorn to the northeast. As you descend, views open to Furi, Riffelalp and Zermatt.

At 8.3 miles, just above Riffelalp, our trail joins with a path coming up from the Gletschergarten. Soon the trail breaks out of the trees, passes a small chapel and a tennis court to meet a road in the Riffelalp Resort complex (7,454-ft.) at 8.5 miles. Here signs point right (northeast) toward the Riffelalp train station and a trail back to Winkelmatten and Zermatt.

To take the train back to Zermatt, turn right (northeast) and walk through the resort complex on a broad track. Beyond the hotel continue along the track, which parallels the course of a small cog railway used to transport luggage and passengers to the resort. Arrive at the Riffelalp Train Station (7,254-ft.) at 8.6 miles where you can hop on a train back to Zermatt.

To walk back to Zermatt from Riffelalp follow the signs pointing towards Winkelmatten (a suburb of Zermatt) and Zermatt. The trail descends on moderately-steep grades through forests and meadows, passing a few chalets along the way. Intermittent openings in the trees offer nice views of the Matterhorn. Reach the small church in the middle of Winkelmatten at 10.8 miles. In Winkelmatten follow the signs back to Zermatt and the Zermatt train station. Walking all the way to the Zermatt Bahnhof (train station) will add another 0.6 miles to the day.

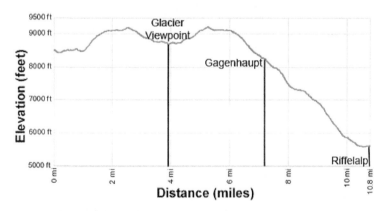

Trailhead Directions

Walking Directions from the Zermatt Bahnhof (train station) to the Gornergrat Cog Railway: See Hike 9.

11. Other Trails in Zermatt
Near Zermatt in the Valais

11a) Five Lakes Trail

This great family walk visits five pretty lakes: the Stellisee, Grindjisee, Grunsee, Moosjisee and the Leisee. Each lake has its own unique personality and views.

Distance: 5.7 miles (point to point)
Elevation at Blauherd: 8,457-ft.
Minimum Elevation: 7,000-ft.
Elevation at Sunnegga: 7,217-ft.
Elevation Loss/Gain: -1,457-ft./217-ft.
Difficulty: moderate-easy
Base camp: Zermatt
Map: Zermatt East Map (See page 10)

Start the day by taking the funicular to Sunnegga and then ride the gondola to Blauherd. Signs outside the gondola station point to the 5-Seenweg (5 Lake Trail) and the Stellisee. Follow a broad track and then a trail descending to the Stellisee. Walk to the east end of the lake for postcard vistas of the Matterhorn perfectly reflected in the lake's still waters.

Return to the west end of the Stellisee and follow the 5-Seenweg signs downhill to the Grindjisee, surround by larches and meadows. From here the trail descends through clusters of trees and crosses a small stream to the Grunsee, set amid a rugged landscape with fine views of the Ober Gabelhorn-Weisshorn Group towering above the west side of the Zermatt valley. This lake is a good place for a swim.

From the Grunsee the 5-Seenweg trail soon enters the trees and then descends a short series of steep switchbacks. At the bottom of the switchbacks the path passes a waterfall and crosses a bridge before turning west to the Moosjisee.

The Moosjisee's turquoise waters are fed by glacial melt and provide a pretty foreground for the Matterhorn. From here the trail climbs to the Leisee, a popular swimming hole with a playground. Lovely views from the lake encompass the Matterhorn, Ober Gabelhorn and Zinalrothorn. Finish the hike by walking uphill to the Sunnegga station where the funicular returns hikers to Zermatt. See the Findel Glacier hike for directions to Sunnegga and the Blauherd.

11b) Tufterchumme

Enjoy solitude and good views on this hike descending the wild and seldom traveled Tufterchumme Valley to the village of Tufteren and then follow an easy, scenic walk back to Sunnegga.

Distance: 4.75 miles from the Rothorn / 5.75 miles from Blauherd
Starting Elevation: 10,162-ft. at Rothorn / 8,453-ft. at Blauherd
Elevation at Tufterchumme Junction: 9,792-ft.
Elevation at Sunnegga: 7,217-ft.
Elevation Loss from Rothorn to Sunnegga: -2,945-ft.
Elevation Gain/Loss from Blauherd to Sunnegga: 1,339-ft./-2,575-ft.
Difficulty: moderate
Base camp: Zermatt
Map: Zermatt East Map (See page 10)

Ride the funicular to Sunnegga and then the gondola to Blauherd. Hike east toward the Unterrothorn and Oberrothorn, ascending on a trail that curves around the base of the Unterrothorn and then turns north, climbing steeply to the junction at Furggli (9,970-ft.), a saddle on the ridge between the Unterrothorn and the Oberrothorn. Turn left and walk a short distance to the Tufterchumme (Tufternkumme) junction at 1.5 miles.

Alternatively, from Blauherd ride the cable car to the Rothorn station and then descend to the Tufterchumme junction at 0.5 miles.

The trail now descends north/northwest along the east side of the wild and rugged Tufterchumme Valley, situated between the Oberrothorn and Unterrothorn. As you descend enjoy ever improving views of the Weisshorn and nearby peaks. At the foot of the valley the path swings to the southwest and descends to meet a track heading toward the village of Tufteren. Upon reaching the village, turn left on the broad track toward Sunnegga. The pretty track is lined with larches growing amid meadows. Openings in the trees offer fine views of the Ober Gabelhorn-Weisshorn Group and the Matterhorn. At Sunnegga, ride the funicular back to Zermatt.

See the Oberrothorn hike for detailed hiking directions from Blauherd or the Rothorn stations to the Tufterchumme junction along with directions to the Sunnegga funicular and the lifts.

11c) Glacier Garden

The Dossen Gletschergarten (Glacier Garden), located at the foot of the Gorner Glacier, is the largest glacier garden in Switzerland. This is a great family hike, showcasing the effects of a receding glacier on the landscape.

Distance: 1.8 miles (round-trip) or 3.9 miles (one-way)
Elevation at Riffelberg: 8,471-ft.
Elevation at Furi: 6,109-ft.
Elevation Gain: -2,362-ft
Difficulty: easy to moderate
Base camp: Zermatt
Map: Zermatt East Map (See page 10)

There are two ways to hike to the Glacier Garden. The first starts at Riffelberg, reached by the Gornergrat Cog Railway. This trail descends over 1,600-ft. on steep to moderately-steep switchbacks into the Gorner Glacier valley accompanied by great views of the Matterhorn, the peak rising above the west side of Zermatt and the Zermatt valley. In the valley the path descends along cliffs, traveling through an area scoured by the receding Gorner Glacier and now populated with larches.

Soon you reach the Glacier Garden, where meltwater from the glacier has polished large rock slabs and carved potholes and crevasses in the glacier bed. Rock sculpted into fanciful shapes will delight hikers young and old. A new section of the garden, added in 2012, has wooden pathways and stairs that climb along rock polished smooth by the glacier and shaped by meltwater. This section of the trail then travels over rock and scree before crossing a swing bridge over the river and ending in Furi. Total distant for this walk is 3.9 miles.

The path also passes through the Giltstein Quarry, where soap stone was extracted for the production of dishes. The trail includes a playground and picnic area set amid a forest of larches and stone pines.

Families with young children will want to opt for the 1.8 mile round trip hike from Furi that passes through the garden but avoids the steep descent from Riffelberg. This trail can be done as an out-and-back hike or a circular walk that travels over the swing bridge.

See the Gornergrat hike for directions to Riffelberg. For the directions to Furi see the Schwarzsee hike.

Saas Fee

Location: The Saastal Valley in the Valais

Saas Fee (5,900-ft.) lies cradled in a sunny bowl beneath a dramatic glacial cirque of 4,000-meter (13,120-ft.) summits in a shallow valley along the west side of the Saastal (Saas Valley). The Fee Glacier clings to the flanks of the high peaks while waterfalls, fed by glacial meltwater, gush down the mountainsides to the valley floor.

These magnificent peaks are part of the Mischabel Range in the Pennine Alp, a massive wall of jagged summits separating Sass Fee from Zermatt, to the west in the Mattertal. The range includes 11 peaks over 4,000-meters including the Dom, the highest mountain entirely within Switzerland.

Saas Fee is smaller, quieter and less well known than Zermatt, with a atmosphere that preserves the feel of a mountain village. Traditional timber chalets and some granaries are still seen in the village. Here you will not find the throngs of tourists jostling for views of the Matterhorn. Instead people come here for hiking, climbing and year-round skiing.

About Saas Fee

The center of Saas Fee is located in the southwest part of the village along Obere Dorfstrasse and its adjacent side streets. The Bus Terminal and Post Office are located at Postplatz, situated at the northeast end of Obere Dorfstrasse. Like Zermatt, cars are not permitted in Saas Fee. Anyone driving to Saas Fee must leave their vehicle in the Parkhaus, a multilevel parking garage at the entrance to the village.

The Tourist Information Office (www.saas-fee.ch/en/summer) is located on the northwest side of the Postplatz. Two grocery stores; the Coop and Migros, are situated on side streets to the east of Dorfstrasse around the intersection of Wang and Blomattenstrasse. Smaller groceries, convenience stores, bakeries, butchers and cheese shops are located in the center and surrounding neighborhoods.

The center is home to plenty of restaurants, hotels, inns, vacation apartments and shops to satisfy the needs of most tourists. Various neighborhoods located to the north, west and southeast of the center offer a good selection of accommodations and vacation apartments.

Four lifts in Saas Fee are open in the summer: the Hannig gondola goes to Hannig Alp, the gondola to Spielboden links to the cable car to Langfluh, the Plattjen gondola provdes service to the Plattjen ski area and the Felskinn/Metroalpin system uses a gondola to reach Felskin and then an underground funicular to access the Mittelallalin ski area.

Summer skiing is popular in Saas Fee. It's typical to see groups of young people from international ski teams carrying ski equipment to the Metroalpin Lift taking them to the year-round slopes beneath the Allalinhorn.

During the summer in Saas Grund, the village below Saas Fee on the floor of the Saastal, the Saas Grund-Kreuzboden gondola whisks hikers to Kreuzboden. A second gondola takes visitors to Hohsaas for up-close views of the Trift Glacier. At Saas Almagell, up valley from Saas Grund, chairlifts take hikers to Furggstalden and Heidbodme. At the foot of the Saastal, a two stage cable car takes visitors and hikers to Gspon.

Hiking around Saas Fee

There is no shortage of scenic trails showcasing the Saastal and Saas Fee's superb mountain scenery. Convenient, frequently schedule buses along with lifts in Saas Fee and the villages along the valley floor facilitate access to the trails.

The Saastal is home to several excellent hohenwegs (high level routes) with spectacular, non-stop views of the Weissmies Range, rimming the east side of the valley, and the Mischabel Range, lining the valley to the west. The most challenging hike, the Saas Fee Hohenweg (Hike 15), starts in Grachen at the foot of the Mattertal and then swings around into the Saastal where the path travels to Saas Fee along the valley's steep western slopes beneath the summits of the Mischabel Range. The walk is accompanied by great views of the Bernese Alps and the Weissmies Range.

The Mischabel Range is the star of the show on the Gspon Hohenweg (Hike 16). This trail starts on the eastern slopes of the Saastal at Gspon and then traverses along the west facing slopes of the Weissmies Range to Kreuzboden. The Hohenweg Kreuzboden (Hike 17) continues up the west side of the valley to Almagelleralp, with more great views of the Mischabel Range along with the summits towering above the Mattmark area at the head of the valley.

In Saas Fee the Gemsweg, circles the valley from Hannig Alp (Hike 12) to Plattjen (Hike 13) with breathtaking views of the glacier clad peaks towering above the village. Viewpoints at Mellig and Gibidum (Hike 14) serve up more great views of the Saas Fee area. Trails also climb to Britannia Hut (Hike 21b), set amid glaciers at the southeast edge of the Mischabel Range.

Starting from Saas Almagell the Antrona Pass trail offers hikers a chance to get off the beaten path, ascending through beautiful meadows beneath the rugged peaks rimming the untamed Furgg valley to the pass on the Swiss-Italian border. Hikes at the head of the Sasstal in the Mattmark area circle the reservoir and climb to panoramic passes. A demanding hike over Jazzilucke Pass (Hike 20) links with the trails to Antrona Pass.

Getting to Saas Fee

From the Zurich Airport or Zurich Bahnhof (train station) take the train to Visp. In Visp, walk outside the train station to the bus terminal and board the bus to Saas Fee for a scenic ride up the Saastal. The trip takes three hours and nine minutes.

From the Geneva Airport or Gare (train station), take the train to Visp and then follow the directions above. The ride should take about three hours and 33 minutes.

Check the SBB website (sbb.ch/en) /SBB app for directions from other parts of the country.

Saas Fee is a car free town. Anyone driving up the Saastal to Saas Fee must park in the multilevel garage outside the village entrance. Lodging operators typically arrange for an electric taxi to pick people up at the bus station or garage so visitors don't need to carry luggage through town.

Nearby Attractions & Rainy Day Activities

Take the Alpin Express to Felskinn and then the Metro Alpin funicular to Mittelallalin where you will find a revolving restaurant with 360-degree panoramic views of the summits soaring above the upper Saastal Valley, an ice cave and summer skiing. Note: This is an expensive outing.

Families will enjoy taking the **gondola to Spielboden** to visit the friend community of marmots in the rocky meadows below the lift station. Continue the trip by taking the cable car to Langfluh for front seat views of the Saas Fee Glacier. See the Saas Fee website for lift schedules and prices.

The Hohsaas lift system from Saas Grund to Kreuzboden and then Hohsaas ends at a 10,200-ft. overlook with stunning views of the Mischabel Range and the glaciers spilling down between the Weissmies and the Lagginhorn.

The Saaser Museum at Dorfstrasse 6 in Saas Fee encompasses four floors of exhibits covering the history of Saas Fee and the Saastal.

On a rainy day head down to Saas Grund and take a delightful stroll on the **Saas Valley Riverbank Trail** along the Saaser Vispa River. The trail heads down valley to Saas Balen and up valley to Saas Almagell. Alternatively, head northeast through Saas Fee to the Carl Zuckmayer trail that travels through larch forests and meadows with nice views of the Saas Fee. The Tourist Office can provide a list of other easy, forested tracks for a rainy day excursion.

Another option on a rainy day is a visit to the **Stockalper Palace in Brig.** From Saas Fee take the bus to Visp and then change for the train to Brig. The castle of Kaspar Stockalper, an early capitalist, is the largest building in 17th century Switzerland. Tour the castle and the adjoining home to learn about the building and its builder, who monetized the use of Simplon Pass to make his fortune. The entry fee includes an exhibit on Simplon Pass. After touring the castle wander through the old part of Brig and enjoy lunch at one of the City's many restaurants.

Good Things to Know about Saas Fee

- Saas Fee is in the German part of the Wallis (Valais). People dealing with tourist typically speak German, French and English.

- In the summer the Saastal Card, available when staying at participating hotels, inns and vacation apartments, offers free rides on all lifts, except the Metro Alpin, and all bus rides in the upper Saas Valley. Bicycles and dogs are not free. See the card information for more details.

- There are no campgrounds in Saas Fee. If you need to camp check out the facilities in Saas Grund.

- The Wellness Hostel 4000 is located near the bus station. It is a very nice but more expensive than most hostels.

- There are no laundromats or laundry services in Saas Fee. Some hotels offer laundry services and some holiday apartments allow visitors to use the building's washing machines.

- There are four huts in the Saastal: the Weissmies Hut beneath the ridge between the Wessmies and the Lagginhorn, the Almageller Hut situated beneath Zwischbergen Pass, Britannia Hut at the northeast end of the Mischabel Range, and the Mischabel Hut on a ridge extending east from the Lenzspitze.

Maps: Saas Fee Area Trails and Hohenweg Trails in the Saas Valley

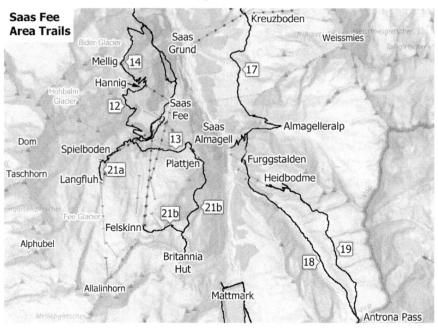

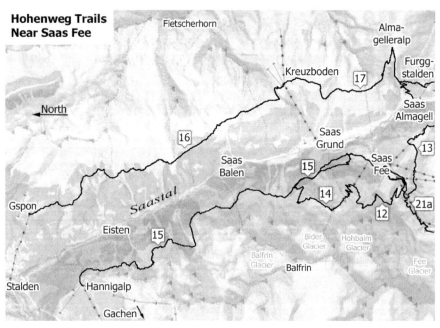

12. Hannig to Saas Fee (Gemsweg Part 1)

★★★★☆

Distance: 4.0 miles (one way)

Near Saas Fee in the Valais

Few trails in the Saas Fee area feature the scenic bang for the miles hiked as the Gemsweg (Chamois Path) from Hannig to Saas Fee. A glacial lake, glistening waterfalls and ever changing views of the high peaks towering above Saas Fee are just a few of the highlights along this delightful trail.

Distance: 4.0 miles (one way)
Elevation: 7,684-ft. at Hannig
Ending Elevation: 5,880-ft.
Elevation Gain: -1,804-ft.
Difficulty: moderate

Basecamp: Sass Fee
Saas Fee Map: See page 66
Online Map/Photos:
www.hikingwalking.com/hannig

Why Hike the Gemsweg from Hannig to Saas Fee

This short hike features birds-eye-views of the stunning glacial cirque surrounding Saas Fee and the peaks towering above the east side of the Saas Valley. Starting in Hannig, reach by a gondola from Saas Fee, the trail curves around the west and south slopes above Saas Fee, traveling through meadows dotted with wildflowers, crossing glacial streams and then dropping to a glacial lake below a pretty waterfall.

Every step of the way is filled with captivating views. Numerous spots along the trail beckon hikers to take a break and soak in the scene. This is the perfect half day walk.

The trail, when combined with Hike 13 from Plattjen to Saas Fee, forms the Gemsweg (Chamois Path), a 5.6 mile trail following a 180-degree arc around the lower slopes of the cirque surrounding Saas Fee. From the glacial lake the second half of the hike travels by waterfalls and crosses the Fee-Vispa River before climbing steeply through larches, low shrubs and then meadows to Plattjen, where a gondola descends to Saas Fee. Hikers are rewarded for their efforts with great views of the Mischabel Range and the Saas Fee glacial cirque.

Alternatively, take the gondola to Hannig and start your day with a round-trip hike visiting two lofty overlooks, Mellig and Gibidum (see hike 14), with stunning panoramic views. Upon returning to Hannig, take the Gemsweg to the glacier lake and then back to Saas Fee for a 7.6 mile day.

However you incorporate the trail into your itinerary, you will have a wonderful day.

Hannig to Saas Fee (Gemsweg Part 1)

Take the gondola to Hannigalp (7,677-ft.). (See trailhead directions below.) From overlooks near the lift station enjoy wonderful views of the 13,000-ft. (4,000-meter) peaks defining the glacial cirque surrounding Saas Fee. To the south the Fee Glacier clings to the flanks of the Allalinhorn and Alphubel while waterfalls, fed by glacial meltwater, gush down the mountainsides to the valley. The Taschhorn, Dom and Lenzspitze tower above overlook to the southwest while the Fletschhorn, Lagginhorn and Weissmies fill the skyline above the Kreuzboden area to the northeast.

When you are ready to start hiking find the trail signs behind the lift station. Walk southwest in the direction of the Gletschergrotte (1-hr 30-min) and Plattjen (3-hr 20-min). The trail is also referred to as the Gemsweg or Weg von Saas Fee – the Saas Fee trail.

The trail descends on gentle grades, passing above Hannigalp's restaurant and playground. Near the play area are the first of several signs along the trail explaining the history and geology of the Saas Fee area.

At 0.1 miles reach a trail junction. The path to the left (south) drops to Haldenwald and Saas Fee. Continue straight ahead in the direction of the Gletschergrotte and Plattjen, traveling through pretty meadows with splendid views to the glacial cirque towering above Saas Fee.

Follow the trail as it curves to the right (northwest) into a shallow side valley. Here views open the tongue of the Hohbalm Glacier, a hanging glacier spilling down the flanks of a cirque formed by Lenzspitze, the Nadelhorn and the Ulrichshorn.

The trail now drops steeply and crosses a small stream. Beyond the stream the trail climbs gentle slopes heading south/southwest and soon crests a minor ridge at Spissen at 0.7 miles. Here a trail branches right toward the Mischabel Hut. Continue on the main trail that curves right (west) as it drops into a gully and crosses a bridge over a gushing stream carrying meltwater from the Hohbalm Glacier. A use trail, branching to the right after the bridge, climbs steeply toward the Mischabel Hut. Continue along the main trail toward the Gletschergrotte.

The trail now turns south/southeast, descending on moderately-steep grades before climbing slightly to crest a minor ridge at Trift (7,260-ft.) at 1.2 miles. From this vantage point enjoy fine views of the peaks towering above the east side of the Saas Valley including the Fletschhorn, Lagginhorn and

Weissmies. Views extend up the length of the Almageller Valley to the Portjenhorn. The Almagellerhorn rises along the south side of the valley.

At Trift a path heads west, climbing steep switchbacks to the Mischabel Hut. We turn left (east) toward the Gletschergrotte, dropping down a series of short, steep switchbacks, passing some beautiful old larch trees.

Reach a junction at 1.6 miles with a trail that continues descending switchbacks toward Saas Fee. Our trail turns right (southwest) toward the Gletschergrotte, descending on easy grades along a rugged hillside. To the south, glistening waterfalls fed by meltwater from the Fee Glacier cascade down the steep slopes beneath the Allalinhorn and Alphubel.

Cross the temporary bridge over a stream rushing down a cleft in the rocky cliffs above the trail at 1.9 miles. Beyond the crossing enjoy beautiful bird's-eye views of Saas Fee.

At 2.1 miles the trail turns left (east) and travels through larch trees along the north side of a lateral moraine. Soon the trail swings to the right (south) and climbs to an overlook atop the moraine. Here the Alphubel, Taschhorn and the Fee Glacier form the backdrop for a waterfall, fed by glacial meltwater, cascading down a rugged gorge. Below, a glacial lake lies nestle in a bowl.

The trail now descends along the crest of the moraine for a quarter mile. At 2.6 miles reach an intersection. Here you have a choice. The Weg von Saas Fee turns left (north) and drops down to the open pastures to the south Saas Fee. Broad walkways lead through the pasture back to the main street in Sass Fee at 3.7 miles. Another path heads southeast toward Spielboden and Langfluh (Langflue). I recommend turning right (west) toward the Gletschergrotte and Plattjen.

Follow the trail as it descends along the south face of the moraine wall to the floor of the gorge. Here the trail turns south and cross bridges over braided streams emanating from the waterfall. Beyond the second bridge reach a junction at 2.9 miles. Here you can either return to Saas Fee or continue the hike along the Gemsweg to Plattjen. For more information on Plattjen trail, see the hiking description for Plattjen to Saas Fee.

To return to Saas Fee, travel along the trail as it heads southeast, skirting the right (south) side of the lake at the foot of the glacier gorge. Ignore signs pointing to the Gletschergrotte, Spielboden or Langfluh. Instead walk in the direction of Saas Fee.

Cross a bridge over the lake's outlet stream at 3.1 miles. Past this point the trail descends on moderate grades beside the stream. At 3.25 miles the trail curves to the left (northeast/north) around the base of a hill and heads toward the large open pastures to the south of Saas Fee. Arrive at the pastures at 3.7 miles. Here broad walkways lead northeast toward Saas Fee, reaching the edge of town at 4.0 miles.

For a longer, more challenging hike, combine this hike the reverse of the Plattjen to Saas Fee hike.

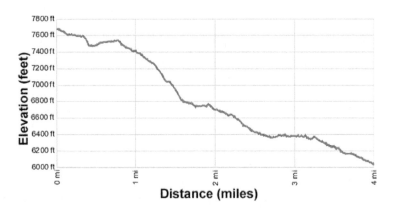

Distance (miles)

Trailhead Directions

To the Hannig Gondola in Saas Fee: This hike starts by taking the Hannig Gondola to Hannigalp. From the Saas Fee Bus Terminal at the Post Platz, head west/northwest on Obere Dorfstrasse to a "T" intersection. Turn right on Bielmattstrasse. Follow Bielmattstrasse for one block and turn left on Bielmattweg. (The Hotel Garni Domino Gabriel Bumann is at the corner.) Follow Bielmattweg to the "T" intersection and take a right on Hannigstrasse. Walk a little over 100-ft. up the street to the Hannig gondola station. There are trail signs along the route directing you to the lift.

13. Plattjen to Saas Fee (Gemsweg Part 2)

★★★★☆

Distance: 3.9 miles (one way)

Near Saas Fee in the Valais

Great views of the Mischabel peaks towering above Saas Fee and the Saas Valley are the highlights of this short trail descending from Plattjen to Saas Fee along the Gemsweg.

Distance: 3.9 miles (one way)
Elevation: 8,447-ft. at Plattjen
Maximum elevation: 5,854-ft.
Elevation Gain: -2,593-ft.
Difficulty: moderate

Basecamp: Sass Fee
Saas Fee Map: See page 66
Online Map/Photos:
www.hikingwalking.com/plattjen

Why Hike from Plattjen to Saas Fee (Gemsweg Part 2)

This short hike offers terrific views of the 13,000-ft. (4,000-meter) peaks of the Mischabel Range, the Hohbalm and Fee Glaciers and the Saas Valley. Starting in Plattjen, reached by a gondola from Saas Fee, the trail drops down rocky meadows and then travels through low-lying shrubs and larch forests as it curves around the east and south slopes above Saas Fee.

This splendid half day hike, accompanied by terrific views, can be extended when combined with the reverse of Hike 12 from Hannig to Saas Fee. The resulting 5.6 miles hike, called the Gemsweg, essentially follows a 180-degree arc around the lower slopes of the cirque surrounding Saas Fee.

The second half of the hike to Hannig travels by a glacial lake fed by a beautiful waterfall, climbs a moraine wall and then ascends through pretty meadows along the steep slopes above the west side of Saas Fee. Along the way the trail enjoys bird's-eye views of the stunning glacial cirque surrounding Saas Fee and the peaks rising along the east side of the Saas Valley. At Hannigalp a gondola descends to Sass Fee. For more information see the Hannig to Saas Fee hike.

Whether you just take the trail from Plattjen to Saas Fee or combine the hike with the Hannig Trail (Hike 12), you are guaranteed a great walk.

Plattjen to Saas Fee

Take the gondola from Saas Fee to Plattjen. (See trailhead directions below.) Upon exiting the lift walk behind the restaurant, heading southeast on a track that ascends a short distance to an overlook with wonderful panoramic views. Looking west from the overlook a wall of 13,000-ft. (4,000-meter) peaks in the Mischabel Range, including the Taschhorn, Dom and Lenzspitze, dominate the view. To the east the peaks rising along the Saastal (Saas Valley) fill the skyline. To the north views extend up the Saas Valley to the distinctively shaped Bietschhorn (the triangular peak) and nearby summits of the Bernese Alps.

To start the hike, return to the sign post behind the lift station. Here the Gemsweg heads west in the direction of the Plattjen Berghaus (20-min), Gletschergrotte (1-hr 15-min), Hannig (3-hr 5-min) and Saas Fee (1-hr 30-min). Soon the trail turns northwest and descends through rocky meadows on a series of moderately-steep switchbacks with terrific views of the Mischabel Range. After walking about 0.4 miles take a detour to the ridge to the right (east) of the trail for stunning views of the Saastal.

Reach the Plattjen Berghaus and the Restaurant V at 0.7 miles. Beyond the Berghaus, the trail descends a series of tight, steep switchbacks that end at 0.9 miles. From this vantage point enjoy lovely views of Saas Fee and the Saastal Valley.

The trail now curves to the left (west/southwest) and reaches a trail junction at 1.1 miles. Ignore the broad track to the right which makes a "U" turn and drops down to Saas Almagell and instead continue straight ahead. A short distance beyond pass a trail branching right (northwest) that descends steep switchbacks to Saas Fee. We continue heading southwest, passing to the right of a small cement building with signs pointing straight ahead toward the Gemsweg (Gletschergrotte, Thrift and Hannig).

Follow the trail as it descends on moderate grades through pretty meadows sprinkled with wildflowers. Along the way enjoy fine views of the the Mischabel Range towering over the west side of Saas Fee and the Saas Valley to the north. Below are good bird's-eye views of Saas Fee.

Soon the meadows give way to low lying shrubs and scattered larches. At 1.6 miles the path starts dropping down a series of steep switchbacks beneath sheer rock slopes, passing a few pretty waterfalls. Fixed ropes along sections of the trail provide a level of security on steep sections that could be problematic if wet or covered with ice. As you descend, pass a trail junction where you continue straight ahead on the Gemsweg.

The grade abates as the path enters a larch forest at 2.1 miles. The easy walking is short lived. Soon the trail drops steeply down a wooded hillside and curves to the right (northwest) as it crosses a bridge over a raging torrent of meltwater from the Fee Glacier. On the other side of the bridge the trail ascends a forested hillside, crosses a ski run and then reenters the trees, traveling through an undulating landscape.

Cross a bridge over another stream at 2.7 miles. Beyond the second bridge the trail reaches an area where several gravel roads converge. These roads are used by mountain bikes and are best avoided when possible. My advice is to travel along the road heading toward the Café Gletschergrotte for a short distance. Before arriving at the café reach a junction where you turn right on a trail toward Saas Fee (35-min).

There are now several routes heading back to Saas Fee. The best option is to watch for a trail to the left that drops down to a glacial lake. Reach at "T" intersection near the lake and turn right, following the trail as it crosses the lake's outlet stream and then curves around the base of a small hill to the pastures to the south of Saas Fee. In the pastures broad walkways lead back the main street in Saas Fee at 3.9 miles.

If you miss the turn for the trail heading down to the lake, the trail you are on soon rejoins the road where it crosses the stream. Follow the road as it drops down to the pastures to the south of Saas Fee. Here broad walkways head northeast toward the town, meeting the main street at 3.9 miles.

For a more challenging hike combine this hike with the reverse of the Hannig to Saas Fee hike. To continue the hike to Hannig, follow the signs near the Café Gletschergrotte pointing to Hannig along the Gemsweg trail.

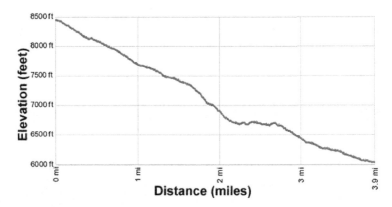

Trailhead Directions

From the Saas Fee Bus Terminal to the Plattjen Gondola: Walk southwest along the Postplatz, past the Post Office. Take Stadelweg, the street heading southwest that drops steeply down the hill, passing some old wood building along the way. Signs point to the Alpin Express and the gondola to Plattjen.

At the "Y" intersection, bear left (south) on Panoramastrasse (Panorama Street). Follow the road as it crosses the bridge over the Fee-Vispa River and then curves to the southwest, skirting the west side of the Alpin Express Station.

Beyond the lift, the road joins with Mischiweg Strasse, which dead ends at Gletscherstrasse (Glacier Street). Turn left on Gletscherstrasse and travel along the road a short distance to the Plattjen lift Station. Sign along the way pointing to the Plattjen lift should keep you on track.

14. Mellig, Gibidum and the Bider Glacier

★★★★☆

Distance: 2.7 - 6.4 miles (loop)

Near Saas Fee in the Valais

Two lofty overlooks offer impressive bird's-eye views of the glacial cirque surrounding Saas Fee, the Hohbalm Glacier and the Fletschhorn-Weissmies group. The return to Saas Fee features views of the Bider Glacier and a walk through a pretty forest.

Distance: 2.7 - 6.4 miles (loop)
Elevation: 7,685-ft. at Hannig
Maximum elevation: 9,027-ft.
Elevation Gain: 1,342-ft.

Difficulty: moderate-strenuous
Basecamp: Sass Fee
Saas Fee Map: See page 66
Online Map/Photos:
www.hikingwalking.com/mellig

Why Hike to Mellig, Gibidum and the Bider Glacier

This hike visits two lofty viewpoints, Mellig and Gibidum, high above the northwest side of Saas Fee. The overlooks feature panoramic views of the dramatic cirque of 13,000-ft. (4,000-meter) peaks, adorn with glaciers and waterfalls, towering above the village. Above the viewpoints, the Hohbalm Glacier spills down the rugged flanks of the cirque formed by Lenzspitze, the Nadelhorn and Ulrichshorn. Across the Saas Valley to the east, the Fletschhorn, Lagginhorn and Weissmies dominate the view while distant views extend north to the Bernese Alps rising above the Rhone Valley.

Beyond the overlooks the trail drops down to Balmiboden, enjoying fine views of the Bidergletscher (Bider Glacier) cradled along the slopes of the Gemshorn and the southeast face of Balfrin. The trail then turns southeast, descending along forested slopes to Saas Fee.

Shorter versions of the hike visit one or both of the viewpoints before returning the Hannigalp. These options are great, albeit steep, hikes for anyone looking for a nice half day walk.

(Note: Mellig is spelled as Mallig on some maps. You may also see Gibidum spelled as Gebidum. For purposes of this description, I have used the spellings on the trail signs.)

Hannig to Mellig, Gibidum and the Bider Glacier

Take the gondola to Hannigalp (7,677-ft.). (See trailhead directions below.) From the overlook near the lift station enjoy wonderful views of the 13,000-ft. (4,000-meter) peaks defining the glacial cirque surrounding Saas Fee. To the south the Fee Glacier clings to the flanks of the Allalinhorn and Alphubel while waterfalls, fed by glacial meltwater, gush down the mountainsides. The Taschhorn, Dom and Lenzspitze tower overhead. To the northeast, the Fletschhorn, Lagginhorn and Weissmies fill the skyline above the Kreuzboden area.

Start the hike at the signpost behind the lift station. Head right (north/northwest) toward Mellig (1-hr), ascending moderately-steep switchbacks up a wide dirt/gravel road. As you climb enjoy ever improving views of the peaks surrounding Saas Fee. To the south views extend up the Almageller and Furgg Valleys.

At 0.9 miles the road ends and a trail branches right (north/northwest), ascending a series of steep, tight switchbacks through rocky meadows. Views soon open to the Hohbalm Glacier spilling down the flanks of a cirque formed by Lenzspitze, the Nadelhorn and the Ulrichshorn.

The grade eases at 1.25 miles and reaches Mellig (8,858-ft.) at 1.35 miles. This vantage point offers stunning view of the glacial cirque surrounding Saas Fee and the Hohbalm Glacier. To the north are distant views of the Bernese Alps rising above the Rhone Valley. If you are lucky you may spot ibex climbing the steep rocky slopes near the viewpoint.

Many people turn around at this point and return to Hannig for a 2.7 mile round-trip hike. From Hannig extend the hike by walking back to Saas Fee via the Gemsweg (Hike 12 from Hannig to the Gletschergrotte) for a 6.7 mile hike. I suggest leaving the Gemsweg for another day and continuing on to Gibidum, another great overlook.

To reach Gibidum, follow the trail as it descends along the rocky spine of a ridge extending northwest from Mellig and then drops down to and crosses a grassy saddle. From the saddle the path climbs very steeply to Gibidum (9,039-ft.) at 1.8 miles. The lofty overlook features panoramic views extending from the Furgg Valley in the southeast to the peaks rising above the Rhone Valley to the north. Across the valley to the east the Fletschhorn, Lagginhorn and Weissmies dominate the view while the Saas Fee glacial cirque fills the skyline to the south. Above the viewpoint to the southwest, the Hohbalm Glacier spills down rugged slopes.

This is another turn around point. Return to Hannig for a 3.6 mile hike or combine the hike to Gibidum with the Gemsweg from Hannig to the Gletschergrotte (Hike 12) for a 7.6 miles hike. If you have time to do the

Gemsweg another day I suggest continuing the hike to Balmiboden and then back to Saas Fee.

To continue the hike, walk northeast in the direction of Balmiboden (1-hr 5-min) and Saas Fee (2-hr 10-min). The trail drops steeply down the rocky slope below the lookout and then descends on moderate grades across a broad grassy ridge.

At 2.2 miles the grade steepens as the trail descends rocky meadows on switchbacks. Soon views open northwest to the tip of the Bidergletscher (Bider Glacier). Along the way enjoy every improving views of the glacier, cradled along the slopes of the Gemshorn and the southeast face of Balfrin.

The trail curves to the east at 3.0 miles and descends on moderate grades along rugged slopes clad in meadows and low-lying shrubs, crossing a few boulder fields along the way. Be sure to turn around for views of Balfrin rising above the Bidergletscher. At 3.4 miles the trail curves to the northwest and then drops down a series steep switchbacks.

The grade eases as the trail reaches Balmiboden (6,955-ft.) at 3.7 miles. Turn right (southeast) toward Saas Fee (1-rh 5-min). The trail now descends on moderate grades and soon enters the forest. Openings in the trees offer nice view of the peaks rising along the east side of the Saastal (Saas Valley).

At 4.2 miles reach a junction at Senggboden. Bear right toward Saas Fee. At a clearing a short distance beyond arrive at a second sign for Senggboden that points straight ahead to Saas Fee.

After a short uphill stint the trail drops steeply through trees. At the next junction there are two routes listed to Saas Fee. Either way will get you back to Saas Fee. This hike takes the trail toward Melchboden and Saas Fee. (See the directions below for the alternate route.)

The trail now heads south ascending on easy grades through forest, reaching a gravel road at 4.8 miles. Descend along the road on moderate grades. At 5.2 miles the road curves east/northeast, passes a small pond and then arrives at Melchboden at 5.3 miles.

Beyond Melchboden, the track turns south/southeast and drops to a "Y" intersection on the outskirts of Saas Fee. Turn right on the Carl Zuckmayer Weg trail that passes between two houses on the northern edge of Saas Fee. Several walkways now head south toward downtown Saas Fee. When in doubt, walk in the direction of the signs pointing toward Dorfzentrum (town center) or the Tourist Information Bureau, which is located near the bus station. Reach the center of Saas Fee at 6.4 miles.

Alternate Route Back

Instead of taking the route marked for Melchboden/Saas Fee, continue straight ahead following the sign listing only Saas Fee. At Barenfalle (6,178-ft.), stay on the trail toward Saas Fee Post (30-min), which crosses a dirt road and then continues downhill, skirting a horse corral to join a broad dirt track. This track eventually turns into a wide dirt lane which goes by several exercise stations before coming to houses on the outskirts of Saas Fee.

At a "Y" intersection take the walkway marked as Carl Zuckmayer Weg that passes between two houses on the northern edge of Saas Fee. Walkways now head south toward downtown Saas Fee. When in doubt, walk in the direction of the signs pointing toward Dorfzentrum or the Tourist Information Bureau, which is located near the bus station. Reach the center of Saas Fee after walking 6.4 miles

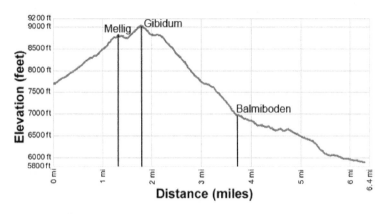

Trailhead Directions

To the Hannig Gondola in Saas Fee: See Hike 12.

15. Grachen to Saas Fee (Hohenweg Saas Fee)
★★★★★
Distance: 10.8 miles (one way)
Near Saas Fee in the Valais

The Saas Fee Hohenweg is one of the classic hikes in the Valais. The challenging trail follows a high route along the west side of the Saastal with stunning, nonstop views of the glacier-clad peaks towering above the Saas Valley and the Bernese Alps to the north.

Distance: 10.8 miles (one way)
Elevation: 6,973-ft. at Hannigalp
Maximum elevation: 7,945-ft.
Elevation Gain: 1,980-ft.
Difficulty: strenuous

Basecamp: Sass Fee
Hohenweg Saas Fee Map: See page **Error! Bookmark not defined.**
Online Map/Photos:
www.hikingwalking.com/grachen

Why Hike Grachen to Saas Fee (Hohenweg Saas Fee)

The Saas Fee Hohenweg starts in Grachen, a resort perched on the sunny eastern slopes above the foot of the Mattertal (Matter Valley) beneath the northern most peaks of the Mischabel Range. Here a gondola whisks hikers to Hannigalp. After exiting the gondola we follow a trail that curves around the head of the Mattertal valley, accompanied by great views of the Bernese Alps rising above the Rhone Valley.

Soon the trail veers to the south and enters the Saastal, traveling along the valley's steep western slopes beneath the summits of the Mischabel Range. The Fletschhorn, Lagginhorn and Weissmies, rising along the east side of the valley, dominate the magnificent panorama. Views of these peaks will only get better as you progress up the valley.

The overlook at Rote Biel, reached after walking about an hour and a half, features wonderful views of Balfrin, the Lammerhorn and the Bigerhorn towering over the Balfrin Valley, a small side valley. The Balfrin Glacier spills down the flanks of the peaks.

After dropping into the Balfrin Valley the trail climbs to Bockwang, crosses a large rockslide and then travels to another great overlook at Lammugrabe, with fine views of the Almagellerhorn, Stellihorn and the Egginer to the south. Across the valley the Fletschhorn-Weissmies group fills the skyline.

Beyond Lammugrabe the path descends along Balfrin's western flanks, with terrific views of the Bidergletscher (Bider Glacier). Waterfalls, fed by meltwater, spill down the sides of the mountain. A culvert, tunneling under the main torrent of meltwater from the glacier, provides safe passage under the falls. Past the falls, the trail descends down forested slopes to Saas Fee.

This is a very long and demanding walk with lots of ups and downs making it much more difficult than the distance and simple elevation gains and losses may suggest. In places the trail is quite narrow, clinging to the steep slopes. Fixed ropes and chains provide a level of security along steep and exposed sections of the route. This is definitely not a trail for people with a fear of heights.

This hike can be done in reverse from Saas Fee to Grachen but includes an additional 1,000-ft in elevation gain. My recommendation is to do the hike in the Grachen to Saas Fee direction.

Note that there are no places to obtain food and drink along the route. Once on the trail there are very few places to "escape" to the valley if the weather turns foul. So pick a beautiful day, set out early, take plenty of food and water and enjoy this glorious high walk along the Saastal. It is one you will remember for a long time.

Grachen to Saas Fee along the Hohenweg Saas Fee

Note: Due to the up and down nature of the trail, the elevation gain and loss is much greater than it appears by simply looking at the trailhead elevation and the high point on the hike.

In Grachen take the Hannigbahn lift, a gondola located a short distance to the northeast of the post office bus stop, to Hannigalp (6,960-ft.). (See trailhead directions below.) Given the length and strenuous nature of this walk it is definitely worth the cost of the lift to avoid the 1.5 mile hike to Hannigalp, which climbs 1,640-ft. through forest with limited views. Hikers taking the lift will also get an earlier start on what will be a long day.

At the top of the lift enjoy nice views of the Weisshorn to the southwest and the Beitschhorn, the prominent pyramid-shaped peak, in the Bernese Alps to the north. Find the signpost near the lift station and walk northeast on a broad track signed for Sass Fee (6-hr 35-min). The trail ascends a hillside on moderate grades, passes a small chapel and then curves to the east, entering a wooded area of larches and pines.

As the path rounds the head of the valley it curves to the south and briefly descends as it starts up the Saastal (Saas Valley). Openings in the trees reveal nice views of the peaks towering above the Rhone Valley to the north. To the southeast, the Fletschhorn, Lagginhorn and Weissmies, rising along the east side of the Saastal, dominate the view.

Signs along the path point toward Saas Fee or Hohenweg Saas Fee. Ignore trails branching right to Furggen / Wannehorn and left to a picnic table.

At 0.5 miles the trail starts a steep ascent. Over the course of the hike the trail will rise and fall to circumvent rock outcroppings and other obstacles, finding the path of least resistance as it traverses ridges and valleys along the valley's steep hillsides.

Near the top of the climb the trail passes a second trail branching right to Fruggen / Wannehorn. Continue straight ahead toward Stock and Saas Fee. The grade abates at 0.9 miles and the trail now travels through an undulating landscape with great views of the Fletschhorn, Lagginhorn and Weissmies.

Near a gate at 1.4 miles fixed ropes provide handholds along an exposed section of the trail. Past the gate care should be used as the trail crosses a small rock slide.

Beyond the slide the narrow path, clinging to the hillside, climbs and descends steeply as it travels around two ridges beneath the Wannehorn. Fixed ropes and metal handrails attached to the rock face along sections of the rocky trail offer a level of security, especially if ice is present on the path. A short tunnel at 1.7 miles allows hikers to bypass a rock outcropping.

Reach Stock (7,775-ft.), a grassy overlook with wonderful views of the peaks towering above the Saastal, at 2.0 miles. A bench at the viewpoint provides a comfortable spot to rest and enjoy the panorama.

Beyond Stock the path drops steeply down a grassy hillside and then climb again as it passes beneath the Distelhorn. Soon the trail curves to the east, navigating a rocky cirque below the southeast ridge of the Seetalhorn. Exercise caution crossing an avalanche chute at 2.6 miles that is often wet and muddy.

As the trail crosses the Seetalhorn's southeast ridge the grade eases and fine views reopen to the Saastal and the peaks towering above the Rhone Valley to the north. The path now descends on moderate grades through lovely meadows clinging to the steep hillside.

Reach Rote Biel (7,480-ft.), a popular overlook, at 3.6 miles. Here a sign (Schweibbach 20-min / Saas Fee 3-hr 40-min) points toward the continuation of our trail. Near the sign you may see vestiges of an old trail climbing the hillside. This trail, previously known as the Hohenweg Seetal, is now closed.

A short distance past the sign is a grassy knoll with wonderful views of Balfrin, the Lammerhorn and the Bigerhorn massif towering over the Balfrin Valley, a small side valley. The Balfrin Glacier spills down the flanks of the peaks while the tip of the Farichhorn rises above the head of the valley. Senggchuppa, the Fletschhorn, the Lagginhorn and the Weissmies fill the skyline to the southeast.

Beyond the overlook the trail descends southwest through larch and pine trees, crossing a few boulder fields along the way. The path loses almost 600-ft. as it drops to the floor of the Balfrin valley where it crosses a bridge over the Schweibbach stream.

Past the bridge the trail turns left (east) and ascends the slopes along the south side of the Balfrin valley on moderate grades that grow steeper as the path gains altitude. At 5.0 miles the trail enters the trees and curves to the south around the end of a ridge, returning to the Saastal Valley. For the next half mile the trail dips up and down as it travels beside a rock face high above the valley.

At 5.5 miles start a very steep climb up rocky meadows on an open slope with far reaching views of the Saas Valley and the peaks to the north. Reach Bockwang (7,411-ft.) at 5.9 miles where red and white blazes mark the best route through large rock slabs.

The trail drops briefly and then ascends across a large rockslide. Pay careful attention to the red/white blazes on the rocks to find the easiest route through the boulders.

Beyond the boulder field the narrow path climbs along a rock face. Fixed metal pipes and ropes bolted to the wall provide handholds along exposed section of the trail. A metal ladder at 6.3 miles facilitates the climb over a man-made rock wall intended to block livestock.

The trail now descends as it crosses a few small rockslides before curving around the end of a ridge to a great viewpoint at Lammugrabe (7,533-ft.) at 6.8 miles. From the overlook enjoy fine views of the Almagellerhorn, Stellihorn and the Egginer to the south. Saas Grund sprawls along the valley floor while Saas Fee lies nestled in a hanging valley along the west side of the valley. The Fletschhorn, Lagginhorn and Weissmies tower above the valley to the east. Signs at the overlook point toward Stafelalpji (25-min) and Saas Fee (2-hr).

The trail now drops through trees that give way to meadows where views open to the Bidergletscher (Bider Glacier) clinging to the western flanks of the Balfin. Cascades of melt water spill down the rocky hillside below the glacier.

Reach Stefelalpji (7,130-ft.) at 7.5 miles. Ignore signs pointing left (downhill) toward Bideralp, Saas Balen, Saas Grund and Saas Fee. Instead, continue straight ahead toward Balmiboden (30-min) and Saas Fee (1-hr 35-min).

After a brief ascent the trail resumes its descent, crossing several streams carrying glacial meltwater. At 7.9 miles the path reaches a large culvert going under a torrent of meltwater from the Bidergletscher. The trail actually goes through two culverts to safely bypass this obstacle. Signs nearby explain the construction of the culverts.

Shortly after passing through the culverts the trail enters the woods and starts descending toward Saas Fee, reaching Balmiboden (6,955-ft.) at 8.25 miles. Ignore the signs pointing toward Hannigbahn / Gibidum and Mellig. Instead continue in the direction of Saas Fee (1-hr 5-min).

Bear right toward Saas Fee at Senggboden, a small clearing at 8.7 miles. Soon you reach a second sign for Senggboden. We continue straight ahead to Saas Fee.

After a short uphill stint the trail drops steeply through trees. At the next sign there are two routes listed to Saas Fee. Avoid the route pointing right toward Hohnegg/Melchboden/Saas Fee and instead continue straight ahead following the sign only listing Saas Fee.

At Barenfalle (6,178-ft.), follow the trail toward the Saas Fee Post (30-min), which crosses a dirt road and then continues downhill, skirting a horse corral to join a broad dirt track. This track eventually turns into a wide dirt lane which goes by several exercise stations before coming to houses on the outskirts of Saas Fee.

At a "Y" intersection take the walkway marked as Carl Zuckmayer Weg that passes between two houses on the northern edge of Saas Fee. Walkways now head south toward downtown Saas Fee. When in doubt, walk in the direction of the signs pointing toward Dorfzentrum or the Tourist Information Bureau, which is located near the bus station. Reach the center of Saas Fee after walking 10.8 miles.

This hike can be done in reverse from Saas Fee to Grachen but includes an additional 1,000-ft in elevation gain. My recommendation is to do the hike in the Grachen to Saas Fee direction.

Note that there are no places to obtain food and drink along the route. Once on the trail there are very few places to "escape" to the valley if the weather turns foul. So pick a beautiful day, set out early, take plenty of food and water and enjoy this glorious high walk along the Saastal. It is one you will remember for a long time.

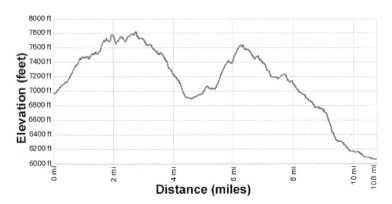

Trailhead Directions

From the Post Office in Grachen: Walk to the front of the post office/Kiosk. With your back to the post office, turn right on the main street (Dorfweg) and walk a very short distance to a "Y" intersection. Bear right (east/northeast) up Barglistrasse. A sign at the corner points right toward the cable car station. You will be walking between the Haus Allain/Woodstock Restaurant (on the left) and the north side of the post office (on the right). Walk up the street for one block and turn right (south) on Spieli Strasse. The cable car station is clearly visible ahead. Walk up the street a short distance to the Hannig Cable Car Station on the left (north) side of the street. Signposts along the way will direct you to the Hannig lift.

From Saas Fee: Take Post Buses and a train to Grachen. From Saas Fee, board an early morning bus headed for Brig and get off at the Stalden-Saas Bahnhof (train station). At the train station catch a train heading for Zermatt and get off at the St. Niklaus station. At the St. Niklaus train station take the Post bus to Grachen, getting off at the Grachen Post stop. The entire trip takes 1-hour 40-minutes. You can buy a combined ticket to cover all the transportation at the bus station in Saas Fee. In Grachen, follow the directions above.

See the SBB website/SBB app for the schedule. Note: Grachen is spelled with an umlaut over the "a". On the SBB site enter Graechen. When you see the list of destinations select Grächen, post.

From St. Niklaus: Take the Post Bus to Grachen, getting off at the Grachen Post stop. In Grachen, follow the directions above.

From Zermatt: Take the train to St. Niklaus. Trains run every half hour and the trip takes about 36 minutes. In St. Niklaus catch the Post Bus to Grachen and get off at the Grachen Post stop. In Grachen, follow the directions above.

Note: Train and bus schedules are available online at the SBB website or the SBB app. Grachen is spelled with an umlaut over the "a". On the SBB site enter Graechen. When you see the list of destinations select Grächen, post.

16. Gspon to Kreuzboden (Gspon Hohenweg)

★★★★★
Distance: 8.6 miles (one way)
Near Saas Fee in the Valais

The Gspon Hohenweg is another of the great high routes in the Saas Valley. This scenic trail, traversing high above the east side of the valley, features wonderful, panoramic views of the 13,000-ft. (4,000-meter) peaks of the Mischabel Range.

Distance: 8.6 miles (one way)
Elevation: 6,260-ft. at Gspon
Maximum elevation: 8,110-ft.
Elevation Gain: 1,850-ft.
Difficulty: moderate-strenuous

Basecamp: Sass Fee
Hohenweg Saas Fee Map: See page **Error! Bookmark not defined.**
Online Map/Photos: www.hikingwalking.com/gspon

Why Hike from Gspon to Kreuzboden (Gspon Hohenweg)

The panoramic Gspon Hohenweg traverses high above the east side of the Saastal (Saas Valley) with splendid views of the Mischabel Range. The range, separating the Saas Valley from the Mattertal – with Zermatt at it head, is a magnificent wall of mountains with twelve peaks over 13,000-ft. (4,000-meters) high including the Dom – the highest mountain entirely in Switzerland.

Starting in Gspon, a sun-drenched hamlet on the high slopes near the foot of the Saas Valley, the trail travels south/southeast through meadows and forest high above the valley floor with ever evolving views of the Mischabel Range. Initially the Seetalhorn, Bigerhorn and Balfrin dominate the view. Halfway along the route the jagged profiles of the Taschhorn, Dom and Lenzspitze join the stunning scene.

Soon views open to the southwest where the massive Fee Glacier spills down the slopes between the Allalinhorn and Alphubel. These peaks, along with the Taschhorn, Dom and Lenzspitze, form an amazing cirque of 4,000-meter summits surrounding Saas Fee. Huge glaciers cling to the flanks of the peaks while waterfalls, fed by glacial meltwater, gush down the mountainsides.

The trail ends at Kreuzboden where a scenic gondola whisks hikers down to the Saas Gund for a bus ride back to Saas Fee. Purists can walk down to Saas Grund along a very steep trail plunging over 2,700-ft. to the valley floor.

This walk is a slightly easier and shorter alternative to the challenging Saas Fee Hohenweg (Hike 15) across the valley, making it a good option for parties looking for a great hike with lovely views.

The trail can be walked in either direction, I recommend walking up valley from Gspon to Kreuzboden for the best views.

Gspon to Kreuzboden along the Gspon Hohenweg

Take the bus from Saas Fee to the Stalden Bahnhof and then ride the two stage cable car to Gspon. (See trailhead directions below.) In Gspon (6,217-ft.) find the trail signs outside the lift station. Walk south/southeast along the cobbled track descending through the village toward Chrizbode (alternative spelling for Kreuzboden). Along the way enjoy fine views of the Mischabel Range, including the Balfrin, Lammerhorn, Bigerhorn and Seetalhorn, towering above the west side of the Saastal (Saas Valley). The Bernese Oberland peaks, including the distinctive triangular-shaped Bietschhorn, rise above the Rhone Valley to the north/northwest.

Reach at "Y" intersection at Ze Hiischinu (6,070-ft.) at 0.2 miles. Bear left on the dirt road in the direction of Chrizbode (Kreuzboden). The path branching to the right drops to Stalden. Beyond the intersection the road ascends through pastures on easy to moderate grades along the east side of the valley and soon enters the trees. After walking a little over a mile the trees thin and give way to meadows with nice views of the peaks across the valley.

At 1.7 miles arrive at Oberfinilu (6,690-ft.) where the trail splits. Bear left on the narrow track toward Chrizbode (Kreuzboden) that ascends through a small alp with a pretty little chapel and then enters the trees. After passing a trail branching left toward Richtung the ascent continues on moderate to steep grades. Note the trail signs now point you toward Kreuzboden (the alternative spelling).

At 2.4 miles the trail starts traveling through an area scarred by landslides. Beyond the last slide the path climbs through trees up a rocky hillside to Schwarzwald (7,218-ft.) at 3.0 miles. Here a small alp/cafe is set amid lovely meadows with wonderful views of the Balfrin massif and the Mischabel Range. In the distance, a portion of the glacial cirque rising above Saas Fee is visible.

Beyond the meadows the trail briefly reenters the trees before descending rocky meadows to cross a stream at 3.4 miles. The path now ascends through trees, dipping in and out of minor gullies with small streams.

Reach a pasture at 3.9 miles with more great views across the valley. The trail ascends across the pasture, passing an old stone building and the remains of holding pens, before dropping down soggy slopes on moderately steep grades to cross a wood bridge over the Mattwaldbach (stream).

Past the bridge the trail climbs a series of switchbacks through a wooded area and then ascends a rockslide to emerge on a large, beautiful meadow at 4.7 miles. The meadows feature breathtaking views of the Mischabel Range. The Lammerhorn and Balfrin are now joined by the jagged profiles of the Taschhorn, Dom and Lenzspitze, the tallest peaks in the range. Further to the southwest the massive Fee Glacier spills down the slopes of the Allalinhorn and Alphubel. To the north are splendid views of the Bietschhorn.

The meadow is a great place for a picnic or to simply take a break and soak in the scene. When you are ready to continue, follow the trail as it wanders southeast across the meadows on easy grades and then travels through a forest of old larch and pine trees. Openings in the trees offer ever improving views of the Mischabel Range. In the distance Saas Grund sprawls along the valley floor while Saas Fee lies nestled in a hanging valley along the west side of the valley.

At 5.1 miles the path climbs briefly and then descends on moderate grades to a trail junction at Linde Bode (7,310-ft.) at 5.5 miles. Here a trail branches to the right (south) toward Saas-Balen and Saas Grund. We continue toward Kreuzboden, descending through meadows and then trees to a gravel road at 5.6 miles.

Follow the gravel road as it ascends southeast on easy grades, reaching a signed "Y" intersection at 6.0 miles. The trail to the left ascends toward Gletscher Seewjine and Sattel. We bear right toward Kreuzboden. Looking south, views open to the Mattmark area and the Schwarzberg Glacier at the head of the Saas Valley.

A short distance past the junction, reach Hoferalpi (7,415-ft.) where more signs point toward Kreuzboden. Soon the road passes to the right (south) of an alp with a restaurant. Shortly beyond the alp the trail dips into ravine, crosses a bridge over the Fellbach carrying glacial meltwater and then climbs out of the ravine. Past the ravine the path ascends steeply through pretty meadows to the tiny hamlet of Gruebe (7,546-ft.) at 6.5 miles.

The steep ascent through rocky meadows continues past Gruebe. Stunning views of the amazing cirque of 4,000-meter peaks, including the Allalinhorn, Alphubel, Taschhorn, Dom and Lenzspitze, surrounding the Saas Fee valley will help take your mind off the stiff climb. Huge glaciers cling to the flanks of the peaks while waterfalls fed by glacial meltwater gush down the mountainsides.

At 7.0 miles the grade abates as the trail reaches the massive boulder field along the southwest flanks for the Jegihorn. Trail crews have done an exceptional job of plotting a course through the rock. Grand views of the Mischabel range make it hard to keep your eyes on the trail.

Finally the rocks end and you arrive at Hannig (8,022-ft.), a popular viewpoint, at 8.0 miles. Here the trail turns left (northeast) and descends to Kreuzboden on moderate grades. Along the way enjoy views of the Lagginhorn and Weissmies towering above the Kreuzboden valley.

Reach the gondola at Kreuzboden (7,874-ft.) at 8.7 miles. Near the lift station is a playground, a small lake and a restaurant with a sun terrace offering sweeping views of the Mischabel Range. From Kreuzboden take the Kreuzboden Gondola down to Saas Grund and then catch a bus back to Saas Fee.

Alternatively, you can walk back to Saas Grund via Triftalp on a trail descending extremely steep switchbacks down a rugged hillside, losing 2,760-ft over 2.8 miles. My advice is to take the gondola and save your knees.

This walk is an easier and shorter alternative to the challenging Saas Fee Hohenweg (Hike 15) across the valley, making it a good option for parties looking for a great hike with lovely views.

The trail can be walked in either direction, I recommend walking up valley, from Gspon to Kreuzboden, for the best views.

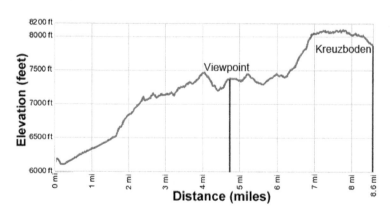

Trailhead Directions

From the Saas Fee Bus Terminal to Gspon: Take the bus bound for Brig and get off at the Stalden Bahnhof (train station). The ride takes 32 minutes. Walk across the train tracks to the Stalden-Gspon Luftseilbahn (Cable Car) station and buy a one-way ticket to Gspon. The two stage cable car requires a change of cars at Stalden Reid. Note that the first stage of the cable car stops at a mid-station. Stay put until you get to Stalden Reid where you change to the cable car bound for Gspon. It is a very short walk to the connecting cable car so there is no need to rush while changing cars.

Schedules are posted at the bus stops and at the SBB website/app.

Returning to Saas Fee from Saas Grund: The valley station for the Kreuzboden Gondola is in Saas Grund. To return to Saas Fee, walk west from the gondola station to the main road. Cross the road and turn left to reach the post bus stop (between the Hotel Bergheimat and the Alpen-Perle) A post bus schedule marks the stop. Catch the bus heading to Saas Fee.

17. Kreuzboden to Saas Almagell (Hohenweg Kreuzboden) ★★★★☆

Distance: 6.0 - 6.3 miles (one way)

Near Saas Fee in the Valais

This scenic walk, with panoramic views of the Mischabel Range, traverses high above the east side of the Saas Valley before entering the beautiful Almageller Valley. End the hike by descending to Saas Almagell or take the challenging Adventure Trail to Furggstalden.

Distance: 6.0 - 6.3 miles (one way)

Elevation: 7,872-ft. at Trailhead

Maximum elevation: 8,302-ft.

Elevation Gain: 430-ft.

Difficulty: moderate

Basecamp: Sass Fee

Hohenweg Saas Fee Map: See page **Error! Bookmark not defined.**

Online Map/Photos: www.hikingwalking.com/kreuzboden

Why Hike from Kreuzboden to Saas Almagell (Hohenweg Kreuzboden)

Hohenweg Kreuzboden, aka Hohenweg Almagelleralp, is a panoramic high route in the Saas Valley. The scenic trail traverses the flower-speckled meadows and rugged slopes between the Lagginhorn and Weissmies with splendid views of the Mischabel Range soaring above Saas Fee. As the hike progresses, views open to the Mattmark Dam and the summits ringing the head of the Saas Valley.

Halfway through the hike the trail curves southeast, entering the Almageller Valley. The Portjenhorn and Pizzo d'Andolla rise above the head of the valley while the Almagellerhorn dominates the view to the south. The trail now descends pretty meadows to Almagelleralp on the valley floor. Here hikers will find many lovely spots for a picnic while enjoying the beautiful views.

Parties can opt to continue the hike to Saas Almagell by following a trail dropping steeply through a pretty larch forest or take the challenging Adventure Trail, featuring a 60-meter long swing bridge, to Furggstalden. At Furggstalden a chairlift whisks hikers down to Saas Almagell.

The Adventure Trail is not recommended for small children or anyone with a fear of heights. Sections of the trail are narrow, steep and exposed. Hikers need to scale metal ladders, descend rungs bolted to a cliff face and climb around minor obstacles. The trail is great fun but should only be undertaken by surefooted parties prepared for the challenge.

Kreuzboden to Saas Almagell or Furggstalden via the Hohenweg Kreuzboden

Take the bus to Saas Grund and then ride the gondola to Kreuzboden (7,874-ft.). (See trailhead directions below.) Outside the lift station trail signs point east to a gravel road heading for Almagelleralp (2-hr 45-min) and Saas Almagell (3-hr 45-min). The road/trail to Almagelleralp coincides with the first section of the Alpenblumen-Promenade (Alpine Flower Trail), with signs along the path identifying some of the 240 species of wildflowers found in the area.

The gravel path curves around the back of the gondola station and quickly turns into a dirt trail heading south/southeast. Soon the trail crosses a wood bridge over a stream fed by meltwater from the Trift Glacier. Beyond the bridge the path ascends on easy to moderate grades through pretty meadows sprinkled with wildflowers along the Weissmies west facing slopes.

To the west/southwest, across the Saastal (Saas Valley), enjoy wonderful views of the 13,000-ft. (4,000-meter) peaks of the Mischabel Range including the Allalinhorn, Alphubel, Taschhorn, Dom and Lenzspitze. The massive Fee Glacier glaciers cling to the flanks of the peaks between the Allalinhorn and Lenzspitze while waterfalls, fed by glacial meltwater, gush down the mountainsides. To the west then Hohbalm and Bider Glaciers spill down the slopes between Lenzspitze and Balfrin. In the distance to the north are views of the Bernese Alps.

At 0.6 miles the trail crosses a wood/metal bridge over a small stream. Soon the meadows give way to a rocky landscape strewn with large boulders. At 1.0 mile the trail curves to the west and starts climbing through rockslides. As you ascend the rugged landscape views open behind you to the Lagginhorn and the Fletschhorn rising above Kreuzboden.

Soon the grade abates and the trail descends gently as it curves to the south around the end of a ridge extending west from the Trifthorn. From this vantage point enjoy wonderful views of the 13,000-ft. summits defining the glacial cirque surrounding Saas Fee. In the distance to the south views open to the Mattmark Dam and the peaks rimming the head of the Saastal.

Beyond the viewpoint the trail descends on moderate grades along a steep hillside, threading its way through snow fencing installed to control avalanches. Metal and rope fencing offers a level of security along a steep, narrow section of the trail with some exposure. This section of the trail should not present any problems unless it is covered with ice or slick snow.

Reach a dirt road and trail junction at 1.7 miles. The road descending on switchbacks down the hillside to the right (west) leads to Furrwald and Saas Grund on the valley floor. We continue straight ahead (south) on the dirt road heading toward Almagelleralp (1-hr 50-min) and Saas Almagell (2-hr 50-min). The road now ascends on easy to moderate grades along the west facing slopes of the Trifthorn, accompanied by excellent views of Saas Fee and the Mischabel Range.

At 2.0 miles the grade abates and the road reverts to a trail that descends south across the hillside on gentle grades. Go through a metal gate at 2.4 miles and then follow the trail as it crosses a few landslides. To the south enjoy ever improving views of the Mattmark area at the head of the Saas Valley.

At 2.7 miles the path briefly climbs to avoid an old landslide and then continues descending as it curves to the southeast into the Almagellertal (Almageller Valley). Here views open to the Portjenhorn and Pizzo d'Andolla towering above the ridge at the head of the valley. The rugged Almagellerhorn looms above the south side of the Almageller Valley.

The trail now descends on moderately steep grades through rocky meadows along the north side of the valley. Near the valley floor the path travels by a few beautiful old larch trees. At a junction at 3.8 miles continue toward Almagelleralp. The trail will actually pass above the Almagelleralp's three story stone structure and then drop down to the valley floor at 4.2 miles. Here signs point east toward Zwischbergen Pass and the Almagell Hut. To find a nice place for a picnic turn left (east) and walk a short distance up the valley to a spot with good views. Along the way pass Almagelleralp where you will find a small restaurant.

When you are ready to continue the hike, follow the trail heading down valley (west) on moderate grades through boulder strewn pastures along the right (north) side of the Leebach, the stream draining the Almageller Valley. Reach a junction at 5.0 miles and turn left (south) toward Furggstalden and Saas Almagell on a trail that crosses a wood bridge over the stream.

Travel through a larch forest for 0.1 miles to a second junction. Here you have two options. The trail branching to the right (southwest) drops down steep switchbacks to Saas Almagell. The path continuing straight ahead (south) toward Furggstalden travels along an "Adventure Trail," a challenging route with a ~200-ft. (60-meter) long swing bridge. At Furggstalden a chairlift and a trail descend to Saas Almagell.

The Adventure Trail is not recommended for small children or anyone with a fear of heights. Sections of the trail travel along narrow boards attached to steep slopes, climb down metal steps bolted to a cliff face and cross rockslides. This trail is definitely not for the faint of heart. (The online photo gallery includes pictures of trail.) If you are not tired and up for the challenge then take the Adventure Trail and have a great time.

If you have any doubts about the Adventure Trail, turn right at the junction on the path towards Saas Almagell. This trail descends step switchbacks through a larch forest, reaching the Saas Almagell Post bus stop at 6.3 miles. The "Adventure Trail" arrives at Furggstalden at 6.0 miles. At Furggstalden take the chairlift down the Saas Almagell and then walk to the post bus stop. Signs point the way.

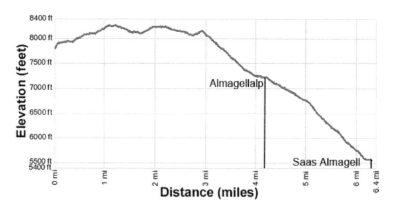

Trailhead Directions

From the Saas Fee Bus Terminal to Kreuzboden: At the Saas Fee bus terminal, purchase a ticket for Saas Grund Bergbahnen. Get on a bus bound for Brig and get off at the Saas Grund Bergbahnen stop. The ride takes 10 minutes. From the bus stop walk east to the bottom of the Kreuzboden Gondola Station and purchase a one-way ticket to Kreuzboden. See the Kreuzboden Gondola site for schedules and fares.

Bus schedules are posted at the bus stops and are also available online at the SBB website or the SBB app.

Return to Saas Fee from Saas Almagell: Get on a bus bound for either Saas Fee or Saas Grund. If you are on a Saas Grund bus, change at Saas Grund for a bus going to Saas Free. (During busy times in the summer you may not need to change buses – always check the front of the bus to see its ultimate destination.)

Return to Saas Fee from Furggstalden: Take the Furggstalden chair lift down to Saas Almagell and then follow the signs to the post bus stop. Get on a bus bound for either Saas Fee or Saas Grund. If you are on a Saas Grund bus, change at Saas Grund for a bus going to Saas Free. (During busy times in the summer you may not need to change buses – always check the front of the bus to see its ultimate destination.) For more information on the lifts see the Saas Fee Lift Schedule and look at the section labeled Saas-Almagell.

Maps: Mattmark Area Trails

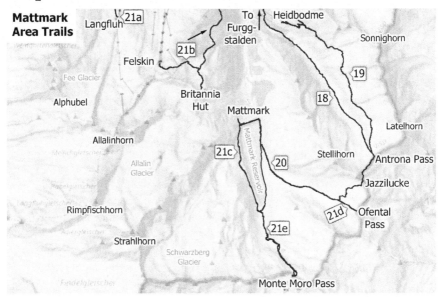

18. Antrona Pass from Furggstalden ★★★★★
Distance: 10.4 miles (round trip)
Near Saas Fee in the Valais

A lovely walk up a pretty valley leads to a remote and wild saddle on the Swiss-Italian border, offering a degree of solitude not found on many hikes around the Saas Fee area.

Distance: 10.4 miles (round trip)
Elevation: 6,250-ft. at Trailhead
Maximum elevation: 9,320-ft.
Elevation Gain: 3,070-ft.
Difficulty: moderate strenuous

Basecamp: Sass Fee
Mattmark/Saas Fee Map: See page 91
Online Map/Photos:
www.hikingwalking.com/antrona

Why Hike to Antrona Pass from Furggstalden

Antrona Pass, on the Swiss-Italian border, was once an important medieval trade route that fell into disuse after a massive landslide in 1642 almost wiped out the village of Antronapianna on the Italian side. Today the pass offers a pleasant refuge from the crowded viewpoints around the Saas Valley. Here there are no ski lifts, huts or cafes. Instead the pass retains a remote, wild feeling with extended views of the Furgg Valley in Switzerland and high peaks to the south side rimming the Troncone Valley in Italy.

Two trails lead to Antrona Pass. This hike, starting in Furggstalden, follows an ascending traverse along the Furggtal (Furgg Valley), a long, broad U-shaped valley clad in pretty meadows sprinkled with wildflowers. Waterfalls, fed by glacial meltwater, spill down the valley's rugged cliffs. Near the head of the valley the path climbs steep, rocky slopes, travels along an old moraine wall and then weaves its way up and around large rock slabs to the pass.

This hike is truly off the beaten path. You may see a few other parties but typically it's a peaceful walk, giving you the sense of having the valley to yourself. It is also a good workout, gaining a little over 3,000-ft in 5.2 miles.

The alternate route starts at Heidbodme, a scenic overlook with panoramic views of the peaks rising along the west side of the Saastal. This trail follows a high route along the Furgg Valley's steep northeastern slopes. Although the trail starts 1,400-ft. higher than the valley route, it can feel almost as strenuous due to the steep ascents and elevation losses required to circumvent ridges and landslides along the route. Sections of this trail are exposed and only recommended for sure-footed hikers with a head for heights. For more information see the Hike 19 - Antrona Pass via Heidbodme.

A great option is the use the two hikes to form a loop that takes the high trail out and the valley trail back, or vice versa. Be sure to check the times the last lift down from from Heidbodme and Furggstalden. It is a long and very steep walk down to Saas Almagell if you miss the last lift down.

I strongly recommend getting an early start for this hike. Warm air rising from the Troncone Valley in Italy often causes mist/clouds to form around the pass by mid-day, obscuring the views into Italy.

Antrona Pass from the Furggstalden Lift

Take the bus to Saas Almagell and then ride the chairlift to Furggstalden (6,234-ft.). (See the trailhead directions below.) At the top of the lift walk north toward Antrona Pass (4-hr). The trail passes a house and storage shed before turning turn right (east) at the signed junction toward Antrona Pass. Ascend steeply up a hill past a small restaurant and then follow the trail as it curves to the right (southeast) and enters the trees.

At 0.4 miles turn right (south) on a broad dirt track. (There is a yellow arrow on the hydro plant (left) pointing right toward the track). Walk a short distance and then take the trail branching left that ascends above the track. Continue along the trail, passing a junction on the right where the road ends at the trail.

Soon the trail curves to the left (southeast) into the Furgg Valley. Along the way enjoy views of the Strahlhorn, Fluchthorn and Allalin Glacier to the southwest. The Mittaghorn and Egginer rise to the west.

In the valley the trail rises gently as it travels through pastures, staying to the left (north/northeast) of the Furggbach, the stream draining the valley. The trail will remain on the north/northeast side of the stream for the entire hike.

Reach Furggalp (6,808-ft.) at 1.0 mile. Beyond the Alp the ascent steepens as the trail passes beneath talus slopes and travels by a small hydroelectric intake facility. Past the hydro facility the trail ascends on moderate grades through meadows, passing a pretty waterfall cascading down a rocky cleft at 2.4 miles. As you head up the valley more waterfalls, fed by glacial meltwater, are seen spilling down the rugged cliffs along the west side of the valley.

Pass the remains of some old stone walls at 2.8 miles. A short distance beyond the trail ascends a low hill where the trail fades a bit as it climbs through rocky meadows and travels by a second hydroelectric intake facility. Crest the hill and follow the trail as it winds through beautiful emerald green meadows sprinkled with wildflowers, crossing a small stream at 3.2 miles. In the distance, the low saddle on the ridge at the head of the valley is Antrona Pass.

Soon the grade steepens as the trail climbs through rocky meadows beneath talus slopes. This section of the hike enjoys great views of the Stellihorn towering above the west side of the valley. Waterfalls, felt by glacial meltwater, spill down the sides of the valley.

At 3.9 miles the trail starts a steep climb up a rocky slope. Rock cairns and red/white blazes on the rocks will keep you on track.

At the top of the slope the trail takes a jog to the right along the former rocky bed of the Furggen Glacier. Soon the trail climbs a dirt hill and then begins a very steep ascent along the remains of the glacier's lateral moraine along the left (east) side of the valley. The grade abates as you top the moraine wall at 4.9 miles. Here views open to a landscape of huge polished rock slabs. The pass is now in sight on the ridge.

Follow the trail, marked by red/white blazes, as it weaves its way up and around the large rock slabs. The markings can be hard to follow, especially if portions of the route are covered in snow. If this is the case, follow the footsteps in the snow or plot your own course to the ridge.

Reach Antrona Pass (9,311-ft.), located on the Swiss-Italian border, at 5.2 miles. The pass enjoys nice views of the peaks lining the east side of the valley and the Stellihorn to the west. To the southeast is Italy where views extend to the peaks forming the south wall of the Troncone Valley. Looking down you will see the Lago del Cingino (Lake Cingino).

From the pass a trail descends toward Antronapianna in Italy, a multi-day excursion. The trail to Jazzilucke (Jazzilicke) climbs south/southwest along the ridge on a challenging trail that leads to the Mattmark area. For more information on this hike see Hike 20 - Mattmark – Antrona.

When you are done enjoying the views retrace your steps to the Furggstalden lift for a 10.4 mile round trip hike. Alternatively, return via the new trail to Heidbodme which travels along the valley's northeast slopes, rising and falling to circumvent landslides and avoid crossing steep ridges. Over the 5.2 miles the trail loses a little over 2,000-ft. and climbs about 500-ft. At Heidbodme there is a chair lift that descends to the Furggstalden area. Total round trip hiking distance if you are returning via Heidbodme is also 10.4 miles.

If you are tired and/or pressed for time the route to Furggstalden is the best bet. If you have the time and energy then select the trail to Heidbodme, which has the best views. For more information see Hike 19 - Antrona Pass via Heidbodme.

Note: If returning via the Heidbodme chair lift, at the bottom of the lift you need to walk north for 0.25 miles to the Furggstalden chair lift and take the lift down to Saas Almagell. (See the trailhead directions below.)

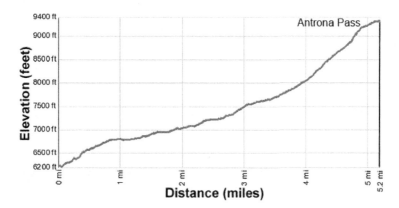

Trailhead Directions

From Saas Fee to Furggstalden: Obtain a bus ticket from Saas Fee to Saas Almagell Dorfplatz. In Saas Fee, take the bus heading toward Brig. Change at Saas Grund for the bus going to Mattmark or Saas Almagell Sportsplatz (south up the valley). Get off the bus at the Saas Almagell Post (Dorfplatz). Follow the signs to the Furggstalden Sesselbahn (chair lift). Make note of the time when the last ride descends to the valley. For more information on the lifts see the Saas Fee Lift Schedule and look at the section labeled Saas-Almagell.

Bus schedules are posted at the bus stops and are also available online at the SBB website or the SBB app.

Return Directions from Heidbodme (Saas Almagell) to Saas Fee: At Heidbodme, purchase a ticket for the two stage lift to Saas Almagell. Take the Heidbodme Sesselbahn (chair lift) and then walk north, following the signs to the Furggstalden Sesselbahn (chair left) in Furggstalden. The walk is a little over a quarter mile.

Take the Furggstalden lift down to Saas Almagell and then follow the signs to the postbus stop. Get on a bus bound for either Saas Fee or Saas Grund. If you are on a Saas Grund bus, change at Saas Grund for a bus going to Saas Fee. (During busy times in the summer you may not need to change buses – always check the front of the bus to see its ultimate destination.) For more information on the lifts see the Saas Fee Lift Schedule and look at the section labeled Saas-Almagell.

19. Antrona Pass via Heidbodme ★★★★☆
Distance: 10.4 miles (round trip)

Near Saas Fee in the Valais

This trail starts at the scenic overlook at Heidbodme, with panoramic views of the peaks towering above the Saastal. The path then travels on a high route along the eastern slopes of the Furgg Valley to Antrona Pass, a remote and wild saddle on the Swiss-Italian border.

Distance: 10.4 miles (round trip)
Elevation: 7,685-ft. at Trailhead
Maximum elevation: 9,311-ft.
Elevation Gain: 2,126-ft.
Difficulty: strenuous

Basecamp: Sass Fee
Mattmark/Saas Fee Map: See page 91
Online Map/Photos:
www.hikingwalking.com/heidbodme

Why Hike to Antrona Pass via Heidbodme

Antrona Pass, on the Swiss-Italian border, was once an important medieval trade route that fell into disuse after a massive landslide in 1642 almost wiped out the village of Antronapianna on the Italian side. Today the pass offers a pleasant refuge from the crowded viewpoints around the Saas Valley. Here there are no ski lifts, huts or cafes. Instead the pass retains a remote, wild feeling with extended views of the Furgg Valley in Switzerland and the high peaks along the south side of the Troncone Valley in Italy.

Two trails lead to Antrona Pass. This hike starts at Heidbodme, a scenic overlook with panoramic views of the peaks rising along the west side of the Saastal, including the Strahlhorn and Rimpfischhorn towering to the west of the Mattmark area and the peaks forming the cirque around Saas Fee, the Allalinhorn, Alphubel, Taschhorn, Dom and Lenzspitze. Directly across the valley the Mittaghorn and Egginer rise to the south of the Plattjen area. The viewpoint, which features a restaurant, small pond and play area, is popular with families.

From Heidbodme, the trail follows a high route along the Furgg Valley's steep eastern slopes, rising and falling to circumvent ridges and landslides in-route. Several lookouts along the trail offer great views of the peaks towering above Saas Fee. As the trail nears the head of the valley high meadows give way to rocky slopes. The final push to the pass navigates a landscape of large rock slabs.

Once you leave the Heidbodme area, the walk offers a degree of solitude not available on many of the trails around Saas Fee. You may see a few other parties but typically it's a peaceful walk, giving you the sense of having the valley to yourself.

The alternate route, starting in Furggstalden, follows an ascending traverse along the floor of the Furggtal (Furgg Valley), a long, broad U-shaped valley clad in pretty meadows sprinkled with wildflowers. Waterfalls, fed by glacial meltwater, spill down the valley's rugged cliffs. For more information see Hike 18 - Antrona Pass via Furggstalden.

A great option is the use the two hikes to form a loop that takes the high trail out and the valley trail back, or vice versa. Be sure to check the times of the last lift down from Heidbodme and Furggstalden. It is a long and very steep walk down to Saas Almagell if you miss the last lift.

Please note that although the Heidbodme trail starts 1,400-ft. higher than the valley route, it can feel almost as strenuous due to the steep ascents and descents required to circumvent obstacles along the route. Sections of this trail are prone to rock slides and may be exposed and/or covered in loose rock. This trail is best suited for sure-footed hikers with a head for heights.

I strongly recommend getting an early start for this hike. Warm air rising from the Troncone Valley in Italy often causes mist/clouds to form around the pass by mid-day, obscuring the views into Italy.

Heidbodme to Antrona Pass

Take the bus to Saas Almagell Dorftplatz and then the two stage chairlift to Heidbodme. (See the trailhead directions below.) Before starting the hike, take some time at Heidbodme (7,698-ft.) to enjoy the wonderful views of the peaks rising along the west side of the Saastal (Saas Valley). Notable peaks include the Strahlhorn and Rimpfischhorn towering to the west of the Mattmark area and the peaks forming the cirque around Saas Fee, the Allalinhorn, Alphubel, Taschhorn, Dom and Lenzspitze. Directly across the valley are the Mittaghorn and Egginer rising to the south of the Plattjen area.

From the top of the Heidbodme chairlift walk east toward Antrona Pass. Soon the trail starts climbing a series of steep switchbacks along the south facing slopes of the Almagellerhorn. At the 1.0 mile mark, ignore the trail branching left to the Panoramaplatz (panoramic viewpoint). Continue climbing toward Ougschtchumme (40-min) and Antrona Pass (2-hr 40-min).

At 1.3 miles the trail drops steeply for a short distance to cross a gully then resumes its steep climb, reaching Ougschtchumme (8,967-ft.) at 1.9 miles. Ougschtchumme enjoys wonderful views of the Nollenhorn and Stellihorn towering over the southwest side of the Furggtal (Furgg Valley).

The low saddle at the head of the valley is Antrona Pass. The peaks rising along the Saas Fee and the upper Saas Valley fill the skyline to the west/southwest.

Past the viewpoint the grade eases as the trail crosses an avalanche chute, curves around a crag and then traverses the steep slopes beneath the Sonnighorn. At 2.9 miles reach the signpost for Beerterrigg (9,186-ft.). A short distance beyond the sign the trail descends a flight of steep log steps and then continues its descent, on easy to moderate grades, through rocky meadows.

At 3.6 miles the trail curves around a ridge and then climbs a hillside on moderately steep grades, crossing a few rock slides along the way. At 3.9 miles the grade abates and the path now ascends on easy to moderate grades.

Soon the meadows give way to rocky slopes sprinkled with small tufts of grass. Red and white blazed rocks and occasional metal posts mark the trail. Along the way the trail crosses a few streams and travels through moist areas of flattened rocks interspersed with mounds of moss.

At 4.7 miles the path starts climbing on moderate grades up a rocky hillside, weaving its way up and around large rock slabs. Red/white blazes will keep you on track. The markings can be hard to follow, especially if portions of the trail are covered in snow. If this is the case, follow the footsteps in the snow or plot your own course to the ridge.

At 5.1 miles pass a large boulder with an arrow point left toward Furggu (Furggstalden) and right toward Heidbodme. A final short climb up rocky slopes brings you to Antrona Pass (9,311-ft.), on the Swiss/Italian border, at 5.2 miles. The pass enjoys nice views of the peaks rimming east side of the valley and the Stellihorn to the west. To the southeast is Italy where views extend to the peaks forming the southern wall of the Troncone Valley. Looking down you will see the Lago del Cingino (Lake Cingino).

From the pass a trail descends toward Antronapiana in Italy, a multi-day excursion. The trail to Jazzilucke (Jazzilicke) climbs south/southwest along the ridge on a challenging route that leads to the Mattmark area. For more information see Hike 20 - Mattmark to Antrona via the Jazzilucke hike.

When you are done enjoying the views retrace your steps to the Heidbodme lift for a 10.4 mile round trip hike. Alternatively, take the trail to Furggstalden which drops to the valley floor and then descends through pretty meadows, losing over 3,000-ft in 5.2 miles for a 10.4 mile hike.

If you are tired and/or pressed for time the route to Furggstalden is the best bet. For more information see Hike 18 - Antrona Pass via Furggstalden. If you have the time and energy then return via Heidbodme, which has the best views.

Trailhead Directions

From Saas Fee to Heidbodme: Obtain a bus ticket from Saas Fee to Saas Almagell Dorfplatz. In Saas Fee take the bus heading toward Brig. Change at Saas Grund for the bus going to Mattmark or Saas Almagell Sportsplatz (south up the valley). Get off the bus at the Saas Almagell Dorfplatz. Follow the signs to the Furggstalden Sesselbahn (chair lift). Make note of the time when the last ride descends to the valley.

At the top of the Furggstalden lift find the trail heading southwest to the bottom of the Heidbodme Sesselbahn (chair lift). The 0.25 miles walk loses about 200-ft. At Heidbodme purchase a ticket and take the lift to the top station.

Bus schedules are posted at the bus stops and are also available online at the SBB website or the SBB app.

Note: Purchasing round-trip tickets for lifts is typically cheaper than purchasing two one-way tickets. For more information on the chairlifts see the Saas Fee Lift Schedule and look at the section labeled Saas-Almagell.

Return Directions from Heidbodme (Saas Almagell) to Saas Fee: At Heidbodme, purchase a ticket for the two stage lift to Saas Almagell. Take the Heidbodme Sesselbahn (chair lift) and then walk northeast, following the signs to the Furggstalden Sesselbahn (chair left) in Furggstalden. The walk is a little over a quarter mile. Take the Furggstalden lift down to Saas Almagell and then follow the signs to the postbus stop.

Get on a bus bound for either Saas Fee or Saas Grund. If you are on a Saas Grund bus, change at Saas Grund for a bus going to Saas Fee. (During busy times in the summer extra buses are run that do not follow the typical routes. Always check the front of the bus to see its ultimate destination.)

For more information on the chairlifts see the Saas Fee Lift Schedule and look at the section labeled Saas-Almagell.

20. Mattmark to Heidbodme via Jazzilucke

★★★★★

Distance: 9.6 (round-trip) - 10.8 miles (one way)

Near Saas Fee in the Valais

A great hike traversing two beautiful valleys connected by a challenging, exposed trail traveling between the Jazzilucke and Antrona passes on the Swiss-Italian border.

Distance: 4.8 miles (one way)/9.6 miles (round-trip) to Jazzilucke
5.6 miles (one way) to Antrona Pass
10.8 miles (one way) to Heidbodme
Elevation: 7,193-ft. at Mattmark
10,129-ft. at Jazzilucke
9,311-ft. at Antrona Pass
7,698-ft. at Heidbodme
Elevation Gain: 2,936-ft. to Jazzilucke
-818-ft. to Antrona Pass
-2,000-ft. to Heidbodme

Difficulty: strenuous-difficult
Basecamp: Sass Fee
Mattmark/Saas Fee Map: See page 91
Online Map/Photos: www.hikingwalking.com/mattmark

Why Hike Mattmark to Heidbodme via Jazzilucke

This challenging hike ascends the beautiful Ofen Valley accompanied by panoramic views of the peaks surrounding the Mattmark Dam and beyond. At Jazzilucke, the high point of the hike, a narrow, exposed trail travels along ledges clinging to the sheer east face of the Jazzihorn before climbing rocky slopes to the peak's eastern ridge.

The trail then descends along the ridge crest to Antrona Pass, located on the saddle between the Jazzihorn and Latelhorn. Antrona Pass, once an important medieval trade route, is a wild and remote spot with views extending down the Furgg Valley in Switzerland and southeast to the high peaks rimming the Troncone Valley in Italy.

Beyond the pass the trail follows an undulating high route traversing the Furggtal's steep eastern slopes. This trail segment enjoys extended views of the 13,000-ft. (4,000-meter) peaks rising above Saas Fee. The trail ends at Heidbodme, a scenic overlook with panoramic views of the peaks towering above the Saastal (Saas Valley).

This trail is recommended for experienced hikers with a good head for heights. Sections of the trail between Jazzilucke to Antrona Pass are exposed. Don't hike this trail during bad weather or if the weather is taking a turn for the worse. The trail should also be avoided if covered by ice or slick snow.

I strongly recommend getting an early start for this hike. Warm air rising from the Troncone Valley in Italy often causes mist/clouds to form along the east face of the Jazzihorn and around Antrona pass by mid-day, enveloping the exposed section of the trail and obscuring views into Italy.

Although this trail can be hiked in either direction, I recommend starting at Mattmark and walking in a counter-clockwise direction to reach Jazzilucke and the traverse to Antrona Pass, the most challenging part of the hike, earlier in the day. (See the trailhead directions below.)

Before starting the hike, be sure to check the times for the last chairlifts down from Heidbodme and Furggstalden. It is a long and very steep walk down to Saas Almagell if you miss the last lift. An alternative and easier route, descending from Antrona along the floor of the Furgg Valley to Furggstalden, is a recommended alternative for hikers who are tired or pressed for time.

Mattmark to Jazzilucke

Distance from Trailhead: 4.8 miles (one way)/9.6 miles (round-trip)
Elevation at Jazzilucke: 10,129-ft.
Elevation Gain: 2,936-ft.

Note: This trail can be hiked in either direction. I recommend walking counter-clockwise from Mattmark to Antrona. This will allow you to get to Jazzilucke (alternative spelling – Jatzilicku) and the most challenging part of the hike earlier in the day. (See the trailhead directions below.)

From the bus stop at the Mattmark Dam, climb the trail to the top of the dam and then walk east on the paved road atop the dam. Along the way enjoy nice views of Monte Moro and the Rothorn rising above the head of the valley. The large expanse of ice visible to the southwest is the Schwarzberg Glacier.

Reach the end of the dam at 0.6 miles. Turn right (south) toward Jazzilucke (3-hr 10-min), Antrona Pass (4-hr 10-min), Heidbodme (6-hr 40-min) and Saas Almagell (8-hr 10-min) on a good gravel trail heading south along the east side of the reservoir.

At 1.2 miles reach a junction and turn left (southeast) toward Jazzilucke. The trail climbs up tight, steep switchbacks and then ascends through a rock slide. Beyond the slide the trail continues its steep ascent through meadows, passing a waterfall in-route.

As you climb enjoy ever improving views of the peaks lining the Swiss-Italian border to the south. To the west/southwest the Schwarzberghorn, Strahlhorn and Fluchthorn along with the Schwarzberg Glacier dominate the view.

At 1.5 miles pass a trail branching right toward Dischtealp, located at the head of the dam. Continue straight ahead toward Jazzilucke.

The grade eases at 2.0 miles as the trail curves left (southeast) and enters the Ofental (Ofen Valley), a wide "U" shaped valley clad in pretty meadows. Turn around for great views of the Egginer, Allalinhorn, Taschhorn and the Dom, along with the Strahlhorn and the Fluchthorn to the west of the dam. These views will be with you almost all the way up the valley.

As you ascend the valley pass a second trail branching right toward Dischtealp at 2.3 miles. At 2.7 miles reach a marked junction at Ofutal (8,300-ft.). The trail to the right (south/southwest) leads to Monte Moro Pass on the Swiss-Italian border. Continue straight ahead toward Jazzilucke.

Beyond the junction the trail climbs steeply up a low rise, essentially a stair-step in the valley, and then continues ascending the valley on easy to moderate grades. At 3.3 miles the grade steepens as the trail curves to the northeast, climbing up the valley's south facing slopes toward Jazzilucke Pass. The south face of the Stellihorn towers overhead. To the south are good views of the Spechhorn and the Ofental Glacier.

Reach a trail junction at 3.75 miles. The trail straight ahead leads to Ofental Pass, a small saddle on the ridge at the head of the Ofen Valley. Turn left toward Jazzilucke and Antrona Pass. The trail now climbs steep switchbacks on a diagonal, heading northeast along the south face of the Jazzihorn. Red and white blazed rocks keep you on track.

The rocky meadows soon give way to scree covered slopes and views open to the saddle on the ridge to the right (east) of the Jazzihorn, this is our destination. The final push to the pass is very steep, zigzagging up through boulders and loose rock to Jazzilucke/Passo di Cingino (10,108-ft.), atop the ridge on the Swiss-Italian border, at 4.8 miles.

From Jazzilucke the Schwarzberghorn, Strahlhorn, Rimpfischhorn and, in the distance, the Monte Rosa massif dominates the view to the west/southwest. On the Italian (east) side of the pass, sheer rugged slopes drop to a deep valley. The peaks forming the south wall of a large cirque fill the skyline across the valley. On a clear day views extend north toward the Latelhorn rising above Furggtal Valley.

Jazzilucke is a excellent destination and a good turn around point for hikers who are not comfortable on exposed trails or anyone with a fear of heights. It is also a good turn around point if the weather is taking a turn for the worse. Simply retrace your steps to the trailhead at Mattmark Dam for a very scenic and satisfying 9.6 mile round-trip hike.

If the weather is good, I recommend sure-footed hikers with the time and energy continue to Antrona Pass.

Jazzilucke to Antrona Pass

Segment Stat: 0.8 miles (one-way) Jazzilucke to Antrona Pass
Total Distance to Antrona Pass: 5.6 miles (one way)
Maximum Elevation: 9,311-ft.
Elevation Gain/Loss: -818-ft.

A sign at the pass points north to Antrona Pass (1-hr), Heidbodme (3-hr 30-min) and Saas Almagell (5-hr). Note: The route between Jazzilucke and Antrona is not recommended for anyone with a fear of heights. It should never be attempted in bad weather or if the trail is covered by ice or snow.

To continue to Antrona Pass, follow the trail as it weaves through large boulders to the east side of the ridge. Here a narrow, exposed trail travels along ledges, clinging to the sheer east face of the Jazzihorn. Fixed ropes and fencing provide a level of security as you navigate the challenging trail. Soon the trail climbs a little and then crosses a boulder field marked with blazes, arrows and metal posts. It is easy to get off track if you are not paying attention. At the end of the boulder field the trail crosses a gully that is often covered in snow. A rope strung across the gully provides a handhold to facilitate the slippery traverse.

Beyond the gully the rocky trail ascends along a bench to the Jazzihorn's east ridge. The low point on this ridge, extending between the Jazzihorn and the Latelhorn is Antrona Pass. At 5.1 miles the trail starts descending along the ridge crest to Antrona Pass, climbing down rocky slopes and around huge rocky slabs. Red and white markers along with metal posts mark the way.

At 5.5 miles, a descending traverse along a narrow, winding path on the east side of the ridge goes by old stone buildings without roofs. Pass the buildings the trail reaches Antrona Pass (9,311-ft.) at 5.6 miles. The pass was formerly used by mule trains going between Italy and Switzerland. The buildings are believed to be either stables or salt storage sheds.

From the pass enjoy fine views of the peaks forming the ridge along the east side of the Furgg Valley and the Stellihorn to the west. To the southeast views extend to the peaks rimming the south wall of the Troncone Valley in Italy. Beneath the Italian side of the pass the Lago del Cingino (Lake Cingino) lies in a rugged bowl.

Antrona Pass to Heidbodme

Segment Stat: 5.3 miles (one-way) from Antrona Pass to Heidbodme
Total Distance: 10.8 miles (one way)
Ending Elevation: 7,698-ft.
Elevation Gain/Loss: -2,000-ft.

After taking a break, follow the trail dropping down the west side of the pass toward Furggstalden and Heidbodme. At 5.8 miles reach at large boulder with an arrow point left toward Furggu (Furggstalden) and right toward Heidbodme. The trail from Antrona to Furggstalden drops to the valley floor and then descends through pretty meadows, losing over 3,000-ft in 5.2 miles. See Hike 18 - Antrona Pass trail description for more information.

The new trail from Antrona to Heidbodme (Hike 19) travels along the valley's northwest wall, rising and falling to circumvent ridges and landslides. Sections of the trail are prone to rock slides and may be exposed and/or covered in loose rock. Over the 5.2 miles the trail loses a little over 2,000-ft. and climbs about 500-ft. At Heidbodme there is a chair lift that descends to the Furggstalden area where you catch a second chair lift to Saas Almagell.

If you are tired and/or pressed for time the route to Furggstalden is the best bet. If you have the time and energy then select the trail to Heidbodme, which has the best views but involves some climbing and sections of exposed trail, which makes it more strenuous and difficult. For more information see Hike 18 -Antrona Pass via Furggstalden and Hike 19 - Antrona Pass via Heidbodme hikes. The mileage and elevation profile for this hike assumes you return via Heidbodme.

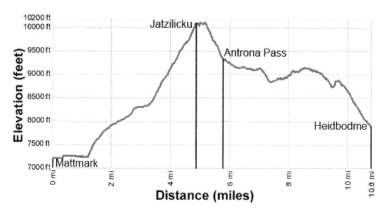

Trailhead Directions

From Saas Fee to Mattmark: Obtain a bus ticket from Saas Fee to Mattmark, a large dam at the head of the Saastal Valley. Take the bus heading toward Sass Grund/Brig. At Saas Grund, change for the bus heading south toward Mattmark and get off at the last stop at the dam. Bus schedules are posted at the bus stops and are also available online at the SBB website or the SBB app.

Return directions from Furggstalden (Saas Almagell) to Saas Fee: Take the Furggstalden lift down to Saas Almagell and then follow the signs to the post bus stop. Get on a bus bound for either Saas Fee or Saas Grund. If you are on a Saas Grund bus, change at Saas Grund for a bus going to

Saas Fee. (During busy times in the summer extra buses are run that do not follow the typical routes. Always check the front of the bus to see its ultimate destination.) For more information on the chairlift see the Saas Fee Lift Schedule and look at the section labeled Saas-Almagell.

Return directions from Heidbodme (Saas Almagell) to Saas Fee: See Hike 19.

21. Other Trails in Saas Fee
Near Saas Fee in the Valais

21a) Spielboden and Langfluh

An easy ascent through pastures and larch forest leads to a steep climb to Spielboden and the amazing overlook at Langfluh. The hike is accompanied by terrific views of the Taschhorn, Dom and the Fee Glacier. A colony of Marmots adds some entertainment along the way.

- **Distance:** 3.6 miles (one-way) / 7.2 miles (round-trip) Saas Fee to Langfluh
  1.2 miles / 2.4 miles (round trip) Spielboden to Langfluh
- **Elevation at Saas Fee:** 5,880-ft.
  Elevation at Spielboden:8,050-ft.
  Elevation at Langfluh: 9,416-ft.
- **Elevation Gain from Spielboden to Langfluh**: 1,366-ft.
  Elevation Gain from Saas Fee to Langfluh: 3,536-ft.
- **Difficulty:** moderately-strenuous to strenuous (depending on direction hiked)
- **Base camp**: Saas Fee
- **Saas Fee Area Map:** See Page 66

Langfluh (9,416-ft.) is a dramatic overlook set atop a ridge between two tongues of the Fee Glacier. Viewpoints around the overlook feature impressive, up-close views of the seracs and deep crevasses in this massive river of ice. The high peaks of the Mischabel range tower above the overlook to the west.

Many hikers ride the Spielboden/Langfluh lifts to the overlook and then walk down the steep trail. For a shorter walk start or end the hike at Spielboden, where a friendly colony of marmots greets hikers.

The walk up from Saas Fee starts in the pastures to the south of the village and then ascends through larch forests to Gletscheralp. Beyond the alp the trail climbs steeply through meadows to Spielboden where a rugged path climbs on steep grades to the overlook. Along the way enjoy great views of Saas Fee, the high peaks of the Mischabel range and the summits rising above the Kreuzboden area to the northeast.

Follow the directions to the bottom station for the Plattjen lift (see Hike 13 - Plattjen to Saas Fee trail). The bottom station for the Spielboden gondola is located in an adjacent building. At Spielboden a short walk leads to the cable car ascending to Langfluh.

21b) Britannia Hut

There are two ways to get to Britannia Hut. The shorter route starts at Felskinn while the longer trail begins at Plattjen. The hut enjoys panoramic views of the Allalinhorn, Rimpfischhorn and the high peaks and glaciers surrounding Mattmark.

- **Distance:** 3.6 miles (round-trip) from Felskinn
  4.6 miles (one-way) Felskinn - Britannia Hut - Plattjen
  5.6 miles (round trip) from Plattjen
- **Elevation at Felskinn:** 9,806-ft.
  Elevation at Plattjen: 8,447-ft.
  Elevation at Britannia Hut 9,941-ft.
- **Elevation Gain/Loss - Felskinn to Britannia Hut:** 600-ft. / -560-ft.
  Elevation Gain/Loss - Plattjen to Britannia Hut: 1,644-ft./-150-ft.
- **Difficulty:** moderate from Felskinn / strenuous from Plattjen
- **Base camp:** Saas Fee
- **Saas Fee Area Map:** See Page 66

From Felskinn: Ride the Alpin Express lift to Felskinn. Exit the lift and follow the signs marking the trail ascending across the Chessjen Glacier to Egginerjoch Pass (9,803-ft.). The walk is accompanied by stunning views of the Fee Glacier and the high peaks of the Mischabel Range, including the Dom. From the pass the trail descends to a rugged bowl and then climbs a detached section of the Chessjen Glacier to the hut. The route across the glacier is well marked and typically safe. Check at the Saas Fee tourist center for the current condition of the crossing. At times the glacier is covered with meltwater and is very slick, requiring microspikes for a safe passage.

To reach the Alpin Express walk southwest along the Postplatz, past the Post Office. Take Stadelweg, the street heading southwest that drops steeply down the hill, passing some old wood granaries and other buildings along the way. Signs point to the Alpin Express and the gondola to Plattjen. At the "Y" intersection, bear left (south) on Panoramastrasse (Panorama Street). Follow the road as it crosses the bridge over the Fee-Vispa River and then curves to the southwest. The Alpin Express Station is on the east side of the street.

From Plattjen: Ride the lift to Plattjen. (See Hike 13 - Plattjen hike for directions to the Plattjen lift.) Walk behind the lift and then head south toward Britannia Hut. The trail ascends along the steep east facing slopes of Mittaghorn and Egginer high above the Saas Valley. Exposed sections of the trail are protected by cables affixed to the cliff face. Great views encompass the high peaks towering above the south side of the Saastal (Saas Valley) and the summits lining the Almageller and Furgg Valleys extending southeast from the Saastal. The glacier clad mountains ringing the Mattmark area fill the skyline to the south.

At 1.3 miles crest the ridge extending east from the Egginer. From the ridge crest the trail descends briefly before climbing steeply along the base of the Egginer's southeast facing slopes. The grade abates as the trail enter a rugged bowl and passes the junction with the trail to Felskinn at 2.2 miles. Our path now climbs the Chessjen Glacier to the hut. Check at the tourist office for current conditions. Meltwater running across the ice can create very slick conditions.

Britannia Hut, built and 1912 and renovated in 1997, enjoys panoramic views of the Allalinhorn, Rimpfischhorn and the Strahlhorn along with the Hohlaub and Allalin Glaciers to the south/southwest. The Stellihorn and Spechhorn rise above the Mattmark Reservoir to the southeast. The Egginer and Mittaghorn dominate the view to the north while the high peaks rimming the Saas Valley, including the Lagginhorn and Weissmies, fill the skyline to the northeast.

21c) Mattmark Circuit

This scenic walk around the Mattmark Reservoir features fine views of the high peaks and glaciers rimming the head of the Saas Valley.

- **Distance:** 5.0 mile (loop)
- **Elevation at Mattmark:** 7,193-ft.
- **Elevation Gain/Loss:** approx. 500-ft.
- **Difficulty:** easy
- **Base camp:** Saas Fee
- **Mattmark Area Map:** See page 91

Take the bus to Mattmark, Europe's largest earthen dam. (See Hike 20 - Mattmark to Heidbodme trail for directions to the dam.) From the bus stop take the trail to the top of the dam. Here great views extend up the length of the reservoir to Monte Moro at the head of the valley. The saddle to the east of the peak is Monte Moro Pass.

The circuit around Mattmark can be walked in either direction. For this description we head up the west side of the lake on a broad track and soon pass through a tunnel. At 0.5 miles, cross a bridge spanning a stream with a pretty waterfall. Past the falls, bear left at the next junction and reach a second tunnel. Bear left, taking the trail circumventing the tunnel. Views east across the reservoir stretch up the Ofen Valley to Ofen Pass. The Stellihorn and Spechhorn tower above the valley.

At 1.0 mile cross a bridge beneath a photogenic waterfall and then continue to Distelalp (7,297-ft.) at the head of the reservoir. Beyond Distelalp cross a bridge over the nascent Saaser-Vispa River at 2.25 miles.

On the east side of the bridge pass a junction with the trail climbing south toward Monte Moro Pass. Our path now swings around the head of the valley and heads north along the east side of the reservoir. The walk back to the dam is accompanied by fine views of the high peaks, including the Allalin, Rimpfischhorn and Strahlhorn towering above the reservoir to the west. The Allalin and Schwarzberg Glaciers spill down the sloped beneath the summits.

Reach the east end of the dam at 4.5 miles. Here a trail drops down to Saas Almagell. Turn left, walk across the dam and then descend to the bus stop at 5.0 miles. (There is a restaurant adjacent to the bus stop.)

21d) Mattmark to Ofental Pass

This hike starts at the Mattmark dam and then climbs the lovely Ofental (Ofen Valley) to Ofental Pass (9,298-ft.) on the Swiss-Italian border. Along the way enjoy fine views of the peak rising above the Mattmark Reservoir, the Ofen Valley and the Valle d'Antrona in Italy.

- **Distance:** 8.5 miles (one-way)
- **Elevation at Mattmark:** 7,193-ft.
  Elevation at Ofental Pass: 9,298-ft.
- **Elevation Gain:** 2,105-ft
- **Difficulty:** moderately-strenuous
- **Base camp:** Saas Fee
- **Mattmark Area Map:** See page 91

From the bus stop at the Mattmark Dam, walk across the dam and then a short distance south along the east side of the reservoir to the trail branching left up the Ofental (Ofen Valley). Ascend the valley to the junction with Jazzilucke at 3.75 miles. See Hike 20 - Mattmark the Heidbodme trail description for more trail details and trailhead directions.

At the junction the trail to Jazzilucke branches left. We continue straight ahead, ascending through rocky meadows toward Ofental Pass. At times the trail fades in the meadows. Soon the ascent steeps as the path climbs scree covered slopes, passing a small tarn along the way. Reach Ofental Pass at 4.25 miles

At the pass, views open to the peaks rimming the south side of the Valle d'Antrona in Italy. Behind you are good views down the Ofen Valley. The Alphubel, Taschhorn and Dom rise in the distance to the west. A metal sided bivouac sits on the Italian side of the pass. When you are done enjoying the views, retrace your steps to the bus stop at the Mattmark Dam.

21e) Mattmark to Monte Moro Pass

The trail to Monte Moro Pass (9,409-ft.), an ancient trade route between Switzerland and Italy, features terrific views of the high peaks rimming the upper Saastal (Saas Valley). At the pass views open to Monte Rosa (14,938-ft.) to the southwest and the Valle Anzasca in Italy.

- **Distance:** 9.2 miles (round-trip)
- **Elevation at Mattmark:** 7,193-ft.
  Elevation at Monte Moro Pass: 9,409-ft.
- **Elevation Gain:** 2,216-ft
- **Difficulty:** moderately-strenuous
- **Base camp:** Saas Fee
- **Mattmark Area Map:** See page 91

Take the bus to Mattmark, Europe's largest earthen dam. (See Hike 20 - Mattmark to Heidbodme trail for directions to the dam.) At the dam follow the directions in Hike 21c - Mattmark Circuit (above) to Distelalp (7,297-ft.) at the head of the Mattmark reservoir. Cross the bridge over the nascent Saaser-Vispa River at 2.25 miles and then turn right on the trail climbing to Monte Moro Pass.

Ascend on moderate to moderately-steep grades through rocky meadows, crossing back to the west side of the Saaser-Vispa at 2.9 miles. Reach a junction at Talliboden 1t 3.5 miles. Here a trail branches left toward Ofental Pass. We bear right on the trail toward Monte Moro, which now climbs on steeper grades straight up a rocky hillside. Sections of the trail climb stone staircases. Near the pass the terrain becomes more rugged, forcing the trail to climb up rock slabs and cross boulder fields to reach Monte Moro Pass at 4.6 miles.

As you crest the pass the east face of the Monte Rosa massif springs into view to the southwest. Below you is the a small tarn, the Rifugio Oberto-Maroli and a cable car whisking hikers down to Macugnaga, Italy (3,921-ft.). The peaks rimming the south side of the Valle Anzasca dominate the view to the south. Up the ridge to the west is the gold statue of the Blessed Virgin.

When you are done taking in the views retrace your steps to the dam. Cover some new ground by walking back along the east side of the dam. This alternate route will add 0.5 miles to the hike.

Zinal and Grimentz
Location: The Val d'Anniviers in the Valais

The Val d'Anniviers extends south into the Pennine Alps from the Rhone Valley. After 12 miles the valley splits into the Val de Zinal (Zinal Valley), to the southeast, and the Val de Moiry (Moiry Valley), to the southwest. At the head of the Val de Zinal is a magnificent cirque of ice-clad summits over 13,000-ft. high, including the Zinalrothorn, Ober Gabelhorn, Dent Blanche and the Grand Cornier. A smaller but equally dramatic cirque rims the Zinal Valley's eastern lobe, anchored by the Weisshorn (13,848-ft.). Near the foot of the valley lies Zinal, a small village with an excellent network of trails ascending through picturesque meadows and scree covered slopes with magical views of the soaring peaks and glistening glaciers.

Grimentz, a pretty village, lies at the foot of the Val de Moiry. From Grimentz, a road ascends the valley to the dam at the foot of the Moiry Reservoir and then traverses along the reservoir's eastern shore to the foot of the Moiry Glacier. The glacier spills down the slopes of the cirque anchored by the Grand Cornier, Les Bouquetins and Point de Bricola. Paths, circling the reservoir and the slopes above, lead to the glacial basin and the trail to the Cabane de Moiry overlooking its namesake glacier.

About Zinal and Grimentz

Most hikers visit Grimentz and/or Zinal when hiking the Walker's Haute Route between Les Hauderes and Gruben. Very few take the time to explore all the scenic delights the Zinal Valley has to offer. That is a shame because the stunning views from the trails around Zinal are some of the best in the Pennine Alps.

Being off the main tourist circuit has its benefits. Zinal remains relatively unspoiled, with the main part of the villages filled with traditional wood chalets along with a few preserved granaries. New developments have been kept, for the most part, along the perimeter. The atmosphere is laid back and relaxing. Sorebois, the town's ski area, is located above the west side of the village and accessible via the Sorbois Cable Car. In the summer the cable car provides access to trails in the area.

The center of town runs along the main street, Route de Cinque 4000, from the valley station of the Sorebois cable car to the tennis court/ice skating rink, and along the Route de Vieux Zinal, which parallels the Cinque 4000 to the east. On the west side of the main street are two groceries, the Marche les Rochers and Supermarche Forum. A good bakery is located on the east side of the street. The center includes several restaurants, bars, sporting goods stores and general merchandise shops.

There are a range of hotels, small inns and a good selection of vacation apartments. The Auberge Alpina/Zinal is a hostel that offers rooms and dormitory accommodations. Relais de la Tzoucdana, at the south end of the village, runs a campsite (with showers) and a gite with a cafe, small dormitory and two guest rooms.

The Tourist Office (zinal.ch/en), on the east side of the main street across from the bus stop/post office, is very helpful. They have a good selection of maps and information about the trail conditions. Another good resource is the Val d'Anniviers website.

Grimentz, a charming village at the foot of the Val de Moiry, offers a variety of accommodations along with restaurants, a Coop supermarket, two bakeries, sporting goods stores, shops and a tourist office. If time permits, it is worth walking around the village to see the traditional buildings decorated with beautiful window boxes.

Hiking around Zinal

Unlike Zermatt and Saas Fee the slopes and mountains above the Zinal Valley, with the exception of Sorebois, are not accessible via lifts. Therefore hikes to high overlooks and huts around the valley require steep ascents. Happily, the incredible scenery will take your mind off the climb.

One of the best and most challenging hikes in the area heads south up the Zinal valley, ascending very steeply to the Cabane du Grand Mountet (Hike 26) set beneath the spectacular cirque soaring above the head of the valley. An easier walk to the Cabane de Petite Mountet (Hike 23) is much shorter and features fine views of the valley.

The walks to Cabane Arpitetta (Hike 25) and Roc de la Vache (Hike 24) are steep but repay the effort with terrific views of the Weisshorn along with the high peaks towering above the Zinal Area. For an easier day visit the Arpitetta Lake. Another long, steep hike climbs to Forcletta Pass (Hike 31), an alternative crossing on the Walker's Haute Route that can also be done as an out-and-back hike from Zinal.

A bus ride to St. Luc followed by a funicular ride leads to one of my favorite Hohenwegs (high routes), the traverse from St. Luc to Zinal (Hike 30). This trail features magnificent views of the glacier-clad peaks gracing the skyline at the head of the Zinal Valley along with panoramic vistas of the rugged mountains towering above the Rhone and Anniviers valleys. Another option from St. Luc is an out and back hike to Meidpass (Hike 32), a high pass on the Walker's Haute Route with views of the peaks rising above the Turtmanntal (Turtmann Valley).

Take the Cable Car to Sorbois and then follow the trail over the Col de Sorbois (Hike 27), a pass on the ridge separating the Val de Zinal from the Val de Moiry. Drop down the west side of the Col to reach the Haut Tour de Lac 2500, a high route that leads to the head of the Lac de Moiry (Moiry Lake) and connects with the trail climbing to the Cabane de Moiry (Moiry Hut). For an easier day simply descend to the dam at the foot of the lake.

From Zinal take the bus to the Moiry Dam where an easy, scenic trail travels around the large lake (Hike 33b). Alternatively, follow a segment of the Haute Route by ascending from the dam to the Lac des Autannes and then the Col de Torrent (Hike 33c), the pass between Les Hauderes and Grimentz. From the pass stunning views encompass the summits rising above the valleys to the west, including the Grand Combin and Mont Blanc de Cheilon. Alternatively, stay on the bus to the head of the Lac de Moiry where a scenic trail ascend to the Cabane de Moiry (Hike 28) accompanied by terrific views of the Moiry Glacier and the surrounding peaks.

Getting to Zinal

Take the train to Sierre/Siders Gare (train station), a stop on the main line along the Rhone Valley. Follow the signs to the bus stop, located on the south side of the tracks, and board a bus headed to Vissoie Poste. At Vissoie Poste change to the bus headed to Zinal, Centre (the center of Zinal). The ride should take just over an hour. The connections in Vissoie are fast, ranging from a 2 - 7 minute wait. Don't panic if you have a short connection time. The buses park next to each other and the drivers wait for everyone to change buses. They also wait if one of the buses is running a little late.

If you prefer to stay in Grimentz, at Vissoie Poste board a bus heading to Grimentz and get off at the stop recommended by your hotel, probably Place du Meleze or Tele (lift station).

Nearby Attractions & Rainy Day Activities

If the weather precludes hiking in the high country, **hike the Zinal Valley Loop** (Hike 22) or walk around the Lac de Moiry (Hike 33b). You can also walk from Zinal to Grimentz and then explore around the village. Stop at the Tourist Office for maps and more ideas.

Tours are available of the **Mine De Cuivre de la Lee**, an old copper mine. Ask at the Zinal Tourist Office for more information.

There is a lot to do on a rainy day in **Sion**. Simply take the bus to Sierre/Siders Gare and then the train to Sion (total time one hour and 30 minutes). The Chateau de Tourbillon, a castle built in the 1300's for the Bishop of Sion, and the Valere Basilica, a 13th century church, are set atop two adjacent hills on the east side of the city. The town is also home to interesting art, history and nature museums. Another enjoyable option is to walk around the old town. See the Sion Tourism Site for more options.

Good Things to Know about Zinal

- Saas Fee is in the French part of the Valais. People in the Tourist office and hotels typically speak French, German and English.

- Holiday apartments are usually rented from Saturday to Saturday in Zinal.

- There are four huts in the Zinal Valley, the Cabane de Tracuit on a high pass between Les Diablons and Tete Milon, the Cabane d'Arpitetta beneath the slopes of the Weisshorn, Cabane du Grand Mountet to the south of Le Mammouth ridge beneath the cirque at the head of the Zinal Valley and Cabane du Petite Mountet set atop a lateral moraine beneath the northeast slopes of the Pigne de la Le.

- The only hut in the Val de Moir is the Cabane de Moiry situated on a rocky knoll along the east side of the Moiry Glacier.

Map of Zinal and the Lac de Moiry

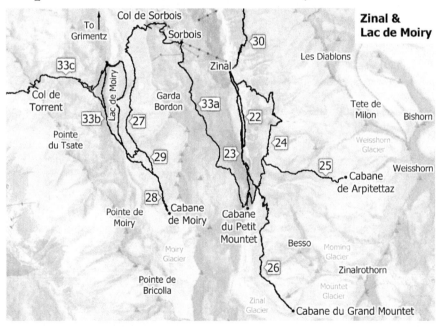

22. Zinal Valley Loop ★★★★★
Distance: 3.6 - 3.8 mile (loop)
Near Zinal in the Valais

The pleasant Valley Loop hike, starting in the center of Zinal, travels on a wide path along the west side of the Navisence River, crosses two bridges and then returns to via the east side of the river. This is a great walk for families with small children and a good option on a rainy day.

Distance: 3.6 - 3.8 mile (loop)
Elevation: 5,450-ft.
Maximum elevation: 5,700-ft.
Elevation Gain: 250-ft.
Difficulty: easy

Basecamp: Zinal
Zinal Map: See page 113
Online Map/Photos:
www.hikingwalking.com/zinal-loop

Description of the Zinal Valley Loop

Note: the mileage for this hike is measured starting at the tennis courts and ice skating rink in Zinal. The hike from this start/end point is 3.6 miles. If starting from the post office/bus stop, add 0.3 miles (round trip) to the hike.

In Zinal walk south along Rue des Cinque 4000, the town's main street, to the parking lot at the south end of the village. Turn right into the parking lot and then cross the wood bridge over the Navisence River. On the west side of the river turn left (south) on the broad track signed for Petit Mountet and Grand Mountet. The track now travels through pastures on easy grades with nice views of Besso (12,001-ft.) towering above the east side of the valley.

At 1.7 miles reach a junction and turn left (east) toward Lac Arpitetta and the Arpitetta Hut. Follow the trail down to the river. The river here is braided into two channels, separated by a small island. Cross the first channel on a wood bridge, walk a short distance across the island and then cross a second wood bridge over the main channel to the east side of the river.

On the east side of the river, turn left (north) and follow a broad track back to the parking lot and village. Along the way you will find some picnic tables and a few spots to sit along the river. Before reaching the car park pass a restaurant on the right.

Hike Variations

If you want a longer walk along the river, from the post office walk south along Rue des Cinque 4000 and then turn right (west) on the narrow road between the Hotel Europe and the Restaurant La Ferme. Follow the road as it drops down to the Navisence River. Cross the river on the La Barmette Bridge and then turn left (south). Walk south (up valley) along the west side of the river. You can walk as far as the bridge at the car park at the south end of the village or walk all the way to bridge near the La Arpitettaz junction (described above) and then follow the trail back along the east side of the river. Total distance for this variation is 3.8 miles.

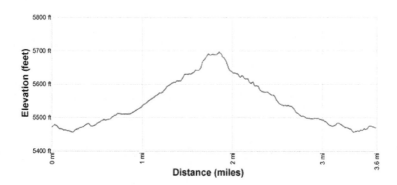

Trailhead Directions

Directions in Zinal: From the Post Office/Bus stop in Zinal, walk south along Rue des Cinque 4000 (the town's main street). The mileage in this description starts the hike a few blocks beyond, near the tennis courts and ice skating rink. Add 0.3 miles (round trip) to the hike if starting from the bus stop.

From Grimentz to Zinal: From Grimentz, board the bus to Zinal and get off at the post office. If possible catch a direct bus to Zinal. Otherwise, take the Vissoie Bus to Vissoie where you will need to change for a bus headed up the valley to Zinal. The direct buses take 15 minutes. If you need to change in Vissoie the ride takes 58 minutes or longer.

Buses make several stops in Grimentz. Schedules are posted at the bus stops and are available online at the SBB website and the SBB app.

23. Cabane du Petit Mountet ★★★★

Distance: 6.6 - 8.0 miles

Near Zinal in the Valais

This trail offers a good perspective of the Zinal Valley, ascending through forests and meadows before climbing the slopes of an old moraine to the Cabane du Peitit Mountet. The hut features fine views of the Zinal Glacier and the ice-clad peaks rimming the upper Zinal Valley.

Distance: 6.6 - 8.0 miles
Elevation: 5,450-ft.
Maximum elevation: 7,028-ft.
Elevation Gain: 1,578-ft.
Difficulty: moderate

Basecamp: Zinal
Zinal Map: See page 113
Online Map/Photos:
www.hikingwalking.com/petit-mountet

Zinal to the Cabane du Petit Mountet

This hike starts on Zinal's (5,479-ft.) main street. (See trailhead directions below.) Walk south (up valley) along the main street to a car park at 0.6 miles. Turn right (west) and cross the wood bridge over the La Navisence River, the river draining the Zinal Valley. On the west side of the river turn left (south) and continue walking up the Zinal valley toward the Petite Mountet (1-hr 50-min) and Grand Mountet (4-hr 10-min). The broad track ascends through pastures on easy grades with nice views of Besso (12,001-ft.) towering above the east side of the valley.

Pass a junction at 1.7 miles with a route branching left toward Lac Arpitetta and the Arpitetta Hut. Our track continues south and soon starts ascending on moderately-steep grades through meadows and scattered trees.

At 2.2 miles the trail travels by a pretty waterfall and then climbs a switchback. Soon the path reaches a junction at Le Vichiesso (6,109-ft.). Here a path branches right toward the Petit Mountet (45-min). This is a shorter, steeper trail to the hut that we will take on the return leg. For now, stay on the main track toward Petit Mountet (1-hr), Grand Mountet (3-hr 20-min) and the Arpitetta Hut.

The grade eases as the trail passes a small building at 2.5 miles. La Navisence tumbles down the rocky riverbed below the trail.

Reach a junction at 2.9 miles. Continue straight ahead toward the Petit Mountet. The trail to the left (east) crosses the river and heads toward the Grand Mountet. To the east are great views of a waterfall cascading down rocky slopes beneath the Pointe de Arpitetta.

The trail now climbs on moderate to moderately-steep grades up a brushy hillside atop the remains of any old lateral moraine. The Navisence River rushes down a rock streambed beside the trail. At 3.3 miles the grade steepens as the trail climbs switchbacks up the hill. As you climb enjoy ever improving views of the Pointe de Zinal, a triangular peak, at the head of the valley. Besso and the Grand Cornier tower above the massive trench dug by the retreating Zinal Glacier. As you gain altitude Mont Durand joins the scene. To the east are fine views of the Pointe de Arpitetta, the Weisshorn and neighboring giants rimming the eastern wall of the Zinal Valley.

Reach the Cabane du Petit Mountet (7,028-ft.) at 4.0 miles. The cabane, sitting atop the eroding moraine, features great views of the glaciers clinging to the peaks at the head of the valley. The Zinal Glacier, covered by debris, flows down the valley floor. Besso looms above the valley to the east while the Grand Cornier dominates the view to the west. The Navisence flows along the valley floor, littered with debris from the retreating glacier.

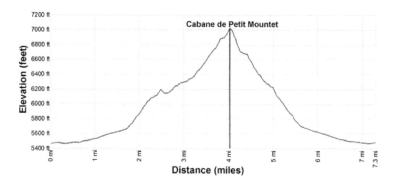

The Cabane offers drinks, meals and dormitory accommodations. From the Cabane it is possible to walk a short distance along the moraine crest to an overlook for more panoramic views. Don't go beyond the sign marking the end of the overlook. The moraine is extremely eroded, unstable and not safe for travel beyond the sign.

When you are done admiring the views, retrace your steps to the trailhead for an 8.0 mile round trip hike. Alternatively, take the shorter, steeper trail back. To find the alternative trail, walk a short distance down the hill from the hut. At the first switchback (hairpin curves where the main trail turns right) take the narrow trail, signed for Zinal, straight ahead (north). The rocky trail descends through bushy meadows on steep to moderately-steep grades to the junction we passed on the trip up the valley, shaving 0.7

miles off the return journey. At 5.1 miles the alternate trail rejoins the broad track heading back to Zinal for a 7.3 mile hike.

This is a good hike for families or hikers trying to acclimate. The trail is also a good option when the weather precludes travel in the high country.

Trailhead Directions

Directions in Zinal: See Hike 22.
From Grimentz to Zinal: See Hike 22.

24. Roc de la Vache ★★★★★
Distance: 8.2 miles (loop)
Near Zinal in the Valais

This steep hike leads to Roc de la Vache, a panoramic overlook high above the east side of the Zinal Valley.

Distance: 4.1 miles (one-way) to Lac d'Arpitetta
8.2 miles (loop) to Roc de la Vache
Elevation: 5,480-ft. at Zinal
7,375-ft. at Lac d'Arpitetta
8,468-ft. at Roc de la Vache
Elevation Gain: 1,895-ft. to Lac d'Arpitetta
2,988-ft. to Roc de la Vache

Difficulty: strenuous
Basecamp: Zinal
Zinal Map: See page 113
Online Map/Photos:
www.hikingwalking.com/roc

Why Hike to Roc de la Vache

A steep hike through varied terrain leads to Roc de la Vache, a popular viewpoint offering a superb perspective of the Zinal area. Starting in Zinal, the trail travels up the Zinal Valley along La Navisence River with fine view of Besso rising to the east. Near the Petite Mountet hut the trail crosses the

La Navisence River to the east side of the Zinal valley and then crosses the Torrent de l'Arpitetta to the north side of the Arpitetta Valley.

The path now climbs steeply up the valley's north slopes. Along the way a recommended detour leads to the Lac d'Arpitetta with wonderful views of the cirque at the head of the Arpitetta valley. To the south the high peaks rising along the west side of the Zinal Valley dominate the view.

Beyond the lake the trail ascends steeply up the slopes beneath the Pointe d'Arpitetta to Roc de la Vache. Terrific panoramic views from the overlook extend south to Besso and the Pigne de la Le guarding the entrance to the head of the Zinal valley. The Grand Cornier, Dent Blanche and the Pointe de Zinal, adorn with glaciers, tower above the head of the Zinal valley. The Zinalrothorn, Moming massif and the Moming glacier dominate the view to the southeast while to the east the Tete de Milon and the Pointe d'Arpitetta frame the Weisshorn at the head of the Arpitetta Valley. Zinal lays 3,000-ft. below on the valley floor while to the north views extend up the Val de Anniviers to the Bernese Alps.

Past the viewpoint the trail descends on steep to very steep grades to Zinal accompanied by nice views of the Torrent du Barme and the peaks towering above the west side of Zinal.

The loop can be hiked in either direction. The climb is not quite as steep in the counter-clockwise direction. Another option is to hike to the Roc de la Vache viewpoint after visiting the Cabane Arpitettaz (Hike 25).

From Zinal to Lac d'Arpitetta

- **Distance from Trailhead:** 4.1 miles (one way)
- **Elevation at Lac d'Arpitetta:** 7,375-ft.
- **Elevation Gain:** 1,895-ft.

Note: This hike can be done in either direction. The description below describes the hike in the counter-clockwise direction, which is not quite as steep. Hiking the trail clockwise is steeper but you are facing up valley, which means the views to the head of the valley are in front of you. I've done the hike in both directions. My favorite option is to hike to the Roc de la Vache viewpoint after visiting the Cabane Arpitettaz (Hike 25).

This hike starts on Zinal's (5,479-ft.) main street. (See trailhead directions below.) Walk south (up valley) along the main street to a car park at 0.6 miles. Turn right (west) and cross the wood bridge over the La Navisence River, the river draining the Zinal Valley. On the west side of the river turn left (south) and continue walking up the Zinal valley toward the Petite Mountet (1-hr 50-min) and Grand Mountet (4-hr 10-min). The broad track ascends through pastures on easy grades with nice views of Besso towering above the east side of the valley.

Pass a junction at 1.7 miles with a route branching left toward Lac Arpitetta and the Arpitettaz Hut. We continue heading south on the track, which starts ascending on moderately-steep grades up a wooded hillside along the west side of the valley.

At 2.2 miles the trail travels by a pretty waterfall and then climbs a switchback. Soon the path reaches a junction at Le Vichiesso (6,109-ft.). Here a trail branches right toward the Petite Mountet (45-min). We continue along the main track toward Petite Mountet (1-hr), Roc de la Vache (2-hr 30-min), Grand Mountet (3-hr 20-min) and Arpitettaz Hut.

The grade eases at 2.5 miles as the trail ascends along the hillside. La Navisence tumbles down the rocky riverbed below the trail. Reach a junction at 2.9 miles and turn left (east) on the trail toward the Roc de la Vache, Grand Mountet and Arpitettaz. The trail to the right leads to the Petite Mountet Hut.

Our trail drops down to and crosses La Navisence River on a bridge. On the east side of the river is a "Y" intersection. Here we turn left toward Arpitettaz (Hike 25) and Roc de la Vache. The trail to the right heads to Cabane du Grand Mountet (Hike 26).

Follow the trail a short distance as it curves to the right (east) and crosses a bridge over the Torrent de l'Arpitetta, a glacial stream draining the Arpitetta Valley, at 3.1 miles. On the north side of the stream the trail climbs steep switchbacks up a wooded hillside on the north side of the Arpitetta Valley.

At 3.5 miles the trees give way to grassy slopes and pastures of Le Chiesso, a small alp. From the Alp fine views open to Pigne de la Le, the Grand Cornier, Dent Blanche and Pointe de Zinal rising along the west side of the Zinal Valley. Besso, Blanc de Moming and Pointe Sud de Moming tower above the southeast side of the Arpitetta valley.

Beyond the Alp the trail climbs a long, steep switchback through low-lying shrubs and scattered trees, passing a junction with a route branching left that descends to Zinal. At 3.9 miles the trail curves to the right and reaches a "Y" intersection at Lac Arpitetta (7,375-ft.). (The lake is actually a short distance beyond the sign.) The trail to the left climbs to Roc de la Vache (1-hr 10-min) while the trail to the right (southeast) heads toward the Arpitettaz Hut (1-hr 40-min). At this point I suggest a detour to the Lac d'Arpitetta, which will add a quarter of a mile to the hike.

To visit the lake, turn right toward the Arpitettaz Hut and ascend along a gully with nice views of Besso. Reach Lac d'Arpitetta, a popular picnic spot, at 4.1 miles. The small lake boasts terrific views of the Weisshorn, Schalihorn, Pointe Sud de Moming, the Zinalrothorn, Blanc de Moming and Besso, forming the east and south sides of the beautiful glacial cirque at the head of the Arpitetta valley. The Pigne de la Le, Bouquetins, Grand Cornier, Dent Blanche and the Pointe de Zinal fill the skyline to the south.

To Roc de la Vache and back to Zinal

- **Segment Stat:** 4.1 miles (one-way) Lac d'Arpitetta - Roc de La Vache - Zinal
- **Total Distance:** 8.2 miles (loop)
- **Maximum Elevation:** 8,468-ft.
- **Elevation Gain/Loss:** 2,988-ft.

After soaking in the views continue along the trail as it heads east for about 300-ft. to a junction. Take the trail branching left toward Roc de la Vache (45-min) and the Cabane de Tracuit (2-hr 30-min), which ascends on moderate grades for 0.25 miles to join the main trail to Roc de la Vache. Turn right and follow the main trail as it ascends on very steep grades up the grassy slopes beneath the west face of Pointe d'Arpitetta. Along the way enjoy fine views of the Zinal Valley to the south and the Arpitetta valley to the southeast.

Reach Roc de la Vache (8,468-ft.) at 5.0 miles after gaining over 1,000-ft. from the lake. The viewpoint offers a superb perspective of the Zinal area. To the north Zinal lies cradled 3,000-ft. below on the valley floor while further to the north views extend down the Val de Anniviers to the Bernese Alps rising beyond the Rhone Valley. Across the valley to the west are the rugged profiles of the Garde de Bordon and Corne de Sorebois.

To the south Besso and the Pigne de la Le guard the entrance to the head of the Zinal valley. The Grand Cornier, Dent Blanche and the Pointe de Zinal, adorn with glaciers, tower above the west side of valley. The Zinalrothorn, Moming massif and the Moming glacier dominate to the view to the southeast while Tete de Milon and the Pointe d'Arpitetta frame the Weisshorn at the head of the Arpitetta Valley.

After enjoying the views, descend northeast on the trail toward Zinal. The path drops into a grassy bowl and crosses the Torrent du Barme, a stream draining the slopes below Tete de Milon and the Diablon des Dames, at 5.2 miles. Beyond the stream the trail turns left (northwest) and descends to a junction at 5.3 miles. Here a trail branches right (northeast) toward the Cabane de Tracuit, located on the ridge between Tete de Milon and the Diablon des Dames. We continue straight ahead toward Zinal on a path dropping down very steep switchbacks along the north side of a Torrent du Barme.

At 5.7 miles the trail turns right (north) away from the stream and continues its steep descent down long switchbacks accompanied by fine views of the peaks rising along the west side of the Zinal Valley. To the north are distant views of the Bernese Alps.

At 6.3 miles pass a junction with the Sentier des Arolles trail. We turn left and descend on switchbacks toward Zinal. Look up to see the Torrent du Barme plunging down the steep hillside as you descend.

The trail drops on very steep grades through pastures, passing a small Alp at 6.8 miles. Beyond the Alp descend a wide track on very steep switchbacks along the south side of a deep gully channeling the Torrent de Tracuit. Drop down to and cross the gully at 7.4 miles. On the north side of the stream the track skirts the east side of a large bowl and soon reaches a junction with Tracuit Street in Zinal. Follow the street as it switchbacks down the hillside on moderate grades, passing chalets and the Reka Zinal resort.

Reach a junction at 7.8 miles with Peterey Street and turn right (north/northwest). Follow Peterey Street to the center of Zinal at 8.2 miles. The post bus stop is on the left (west) side of the main street (one block to the west of Peterey Street) in the northern part of the village.

Walking in the Reverse Direction: If walking the route in the reverse direction, head south along the main street from the post office. Near the south end of the tennis courts, located on the right (west) side of the street, turn left on a side street. At the next street turn right (south) and walk south for about 0.3 miles to the corner of Peterey and Tracuit Street. Turn left onto Tracuit and follow the signs toward Roc de la Vache (4-hr) and Cabane Tracuit (5-hr).

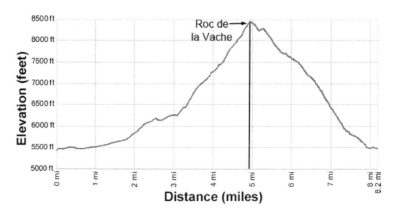

Trailhead Directions

Directions in Zinal: See Hike 22.
From Grimentz to Zinal: See Hike 22.

25. Cabane Arpitetta ★★★★☆
Distance: 12.6 miles (round trip)
Near Zinal in the Valais

The long and strenuous climb to the Cabane Arpitetta features wonderful views of the glacial cirque at the head of the Arpitetta valley, dominated by the Weisshorn, Zinalrothorn, Moming massif and the Moming glacier.

Distance: 12.6 miles (round trip)
Elevation: 5,480-ft. at Zinal
Maximum elevation: 9,140-ft. at Cabane Arpitetta
Elevation Gain: 3,660-ft.

Difficulty: strenuous
Basecamp: Zinal
Zinal Map: See page 113
Online Map/Photos:
www.hikingwalking.com/arpitetta

Why Hike to the Cabane Arpitettaz

This great hike ascends the Arpitetta Valley to the Cabane Arpitetta, situated at the base of the Weisshorn's west face. Hikers making the steep climb to the hut are rewarded with glorious views of the large glacial cirque at the head of the Arpitetta Valley, dominated by the Weisshorn and Schalihorn to the east and the Zinalrothorn, Moming massif and Besso to the south. Two massive glaciers, the Moming and the Weisshorn spill down the flanks of the cirque.

Starting in Zinal, the trail travels up the Zinal Valley along La Navisence River with fine view of Besso rising to the east. Near the Petite Mountet hut the trail crosses the La Navisence to the east side of the Zinal Valley and then crosses the Torrent de l'Arpitetta to the north side of the Arpitetta Valley.

Beyond the crossings the path climbs steeply to Lac d'Arpitetta with wonderful views of the Weisshorn, Schalihorn, Pointe Sud de Moming, the Zinalrothorn, Blanc de Moming and Besso, in the Arpitetta valley. To the south are views of the Pigne de la Le, the Grand Cornier, Dent Blanche and Pointe de Zinal towering above the west side of the Zinal Valley.

Beyond the lake the trail climbs up the north side of the valley on moderate to very steep grades beneath the south facing flanks of the Pointe d'Arpitetta. A final steep climb through rocky meadows leads to the hut with stunning panoramic views of the Weisshorn and nearby peaks forming the splendid cirque towering above the head of the valley. The massive Moming glacier tumbles down the flanks of the peaks to the south. The amphitheater is bookended by Besso to the southwest and the Pointe d'Arpitetta to the northwest.

This is a long, strenuous hike best undertaken by hikers who are well acclimated and fit. The hike can be extended by returning to Zinal via Roc de la Vache (Hike 24).

Trailhead to Cabane Arpitetta

Note: On maps and literature you may see the name of the hut as Cabane Arpitettaz and Cabane Arpitetta (with no "z").

This hike starts on Zinal's (5,479-ft.) main street. (See trailhead directions below.) Walk south (toward the head of the valley) along the main street to a car park at 0.6 miles. Turn right (west) and cross the wood bridge over the La Navisence River, the river draining the Zinal Valley. On the west side of the river turn left (south) and continue walking up the Zinal valley toward the Petite Mountet (1-hr 50-min) and Grand Mountet (4-hr 10-min). The broad track ascends through pastures on easy grades with nice views of Besso towering above the east side of the valley.

Pass a junction at 1.7 miles with a route branching left toward Lac Arpitetta and the Arpitetta Hut. We continue heading south on the track, which starts ascending on moderately-steep grades up a wooded hillside along the west side of the valley.

At 2.2 miles the trail travels by a pretty waterfall and then climbs a switchback. Soon the path reaches a junction at Le Vichiesso (6,109-ft.). Here a trail branches right toward the Petite Mountet (45-min). We stay on the main track toward Petite Mountet (1-hr), Grand Mountet (3-hr 20-min) and the Arpitetta Hut.

The grade eases at 2.5 miles as the trail ascends along the hillside. La Navisence tumbles down the rocky riverbed below the trail. Reach a junction at 2.9 miles and turn left (east) on the trail toward the Grand Mountet and Arpitetta. The trail to the right leads to the Petite Mountet Hut.

Our trail drops down to and crosses La Navisence on a bridge. The Grand Cornier dominates the view to the south. On the east side of the river is a "Y" intersection. We turn left toward Arpitetta and Roc de la Vache (Hike 24). The trail to the right heads to Cabane du Grand Mountet (Hike 26).

Follow the trail a short distance as it curves to the right (east) and crosses a bridge over the Torrent de l'Arpitetta, a glacial stream draining the Arpitetta Valley, at 3.1 miles. On the north side of the stream the trail climbs steep switchbacks up a wooded hillside at the foot of the Arpitetta Valley.

At 3.5 miles the trees give way to grassy slopes and pastures of Le Chiesso, a small Alp. From the Alp fine views open Pigne de la Le, the Grand Cornier, Dent Blanche and Pointe de Zinal rising along the west side of the Zinal Valley. Besso, the Blanc de Moming and Pointe Sud de Moming tower above the south side of the Arpitetta valley.

Beyond the alp the trail climbs a long, steep switchback through low-lying shrubs and scattered trees, passing a junction with a route branching left that descends to Zinal. At 3.9 miles the trail curves to the right and reaches a "Y" intersection at Lac Arpitetta (7,375-ft.). (The lake is actually a short distance beyond the sign.) The trail to the left climbs to Roc de la Vache (1-hr 10-min). We turn right (southeast) toward the Arpitetta Hut (1-hr 40-min) on a trail ascending along a gully with nice views of Besso.

Reach Lac d'Arpitetta, a popular picnic spot, at 4.1 miles. The small lake boasts terrific views of the Weisshorn, Schalihorn, Pointe Sud de Moming, the Zinalrothorn, Blanc de Moming and Besso, forming part of the beautiful glacial cirque at the head of the Arpitetta Vvalley. To the south views encompass the Pigne de la Le, Bouquetins, Grand Cornier, Dent Blanche and the Pointe de Zinal in the Zinal Valley.

After soaking in the views continue along the trail as it heads east through pastures, passing a second trail branching left toward Roc de la Vache. Beyond the junction the trail heads east, crosses the lake's inlet stream and then ascends on moderate grades high above the north side of the Arpitetta Valley. As you climb enjoy every improving views of the Moming glacier spills down the flanks of the Moming massif. Waterfalls, fed by glacial meltwater, tumbled down the rugged slopes beneath the glacier.

At 4.5 miles the trail rounds a minor ridge and the Weisshorn and Schalihorn join the scene. Turn around occasionally for nice views of the La Le meadows, nestled in a bowl beneath the Pigne de la Le and the Garde de Bordon to the west.

At 4.8 mile the trail starts ascending steep switchback along the south facing flanks of Pointe d'Arpitetta. The grade abates briefly at 5.3 miles as the trail contours along the steep hillside and crosses several streams. Soon the trail resumes its steep ascent through rocky meadows and scree covered slopes. Temporary bridges facilitate the crossing of gushing streams carrying glacial meltwater at 5.8 and 5.9 miles.

Beyond the last stream the trail climbs steep switchback through rocky meadows with glorious views of the Moming massif, the Moming Glacier and Besso to the south. The Weisshorn soars above the head of the valley to the east. Reach the Cabane Arpitetta (9,140-ft.), a nice old stone hut situated at the foot of the Weisshorn's west facing slopes, at 6.3 miles.

From the hut stunning, panoramic views extend west to Besso and the Pointe d'Arpitetta bookending the foot of the Arpitetta Valley. The Moming massif fills the skyline to the south with the tip of the Zinalrothorn peeking above the ice covered peaks. The Moming glacier spills down the flanks of the massif to a huge bowl and then cascades over the lip of the bowl down the rugged slopes across from the hut. The Weisshorn dominates the views to the east. A small section of the Weisshorn glacier is visible to the north of the hut, below the Tete de Milon. Unfortunately a high moraine wall limits the views of the glacier to the east.

When you are done taking in the views retrace your steps to Zinal. Energetic parties should consider returning to Zinal via the Roc de la Vache trail (Hike 24). This option adds over 1,300-ft of elevation gain and 0.4 miles to the return journey to Zinal.

Note: A guardian is present at the hut during the summer months. Hiker with reservations can stay overnight but no meals are served. Be sure to pack water, lunch and plenty of snacks for your day hike and all the food you will need if you plan to spend the night at the hut.

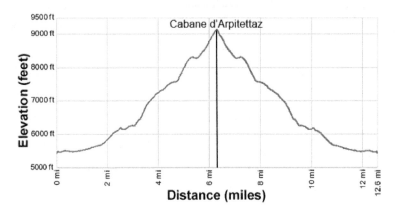

Trailhead Directions

Directions in Zinal: See Hike 22.
From Grimentz to Zinal: See Hike 22.

26. Cabane du Grand Mountet ☆☆☆☆☆
Distance: 12.2 - 14.1 miles (round trip)

Near Zinal in the Valais

Magnificent views of one of the most stunning glacial cirques in the Pennine Alps is the reward for hikers completing this long and very strenuous hike to the Cabane du Grand Mountet at the head of the Zinal Valley.

Distance: 12.2 miles (round trip) to the Rocky Knoll
14.1 miles (round trip) to Cabane du Grand Mountet
Elevation: 5,480-ft. at the Trailhead
9,284-ft. at the Rocky Knoll
9,520-ft. at Cabane du Grand Mountet
Elevation Gain: 3,804-ft. to the Rocky Knoll
4,040-ft. to Cabane du Grand Mountet

Difficulty: strenuous-difficult
Basecamp: Zinal
Zinal Map: See page 113
Online Map/Photos:
www.hikingwalking.com/grand-mountet

Why Hike to the Cabane du Grand Mountet

At the head of the Zinal Valley is one of the most dramatic cirques in the Pennine Alps. A massive wall of high peaks including the Zinalrothorn, Ober Gabelhorn, Mont Durand, the Pointe de Zinal, Dent Blanche and the Grand Cornier tower above the head of the valley. Three large glaciers, the Grand Cornier, Durand and Mountet, tumble down the flanks of the peak and join to form the Zinal Glacier, a massive river of ice flowing along the valley floor. Smaller glaciers hang from ledges, glistening in the sun.

The Cabane du Grand Mountet lies at the base of this magnificent amphitheater, offering front row seats to a spectacular landscape of rock and ice. The long and strenuous trail to the hut permits day hikers entry into this splendid realm.

Starting in Zinal, the trail travels up the Zinal Valley along the La Navisence River with fine view of Besso rising to the east. Near the Petite

Mountet hut the trail crosses the Navisence to the east side of the valley. Here views open to the Grand Cornier.

Now the real work begins as the trail climbs steeply up the east side of the valley and then follows an ascending traverse across steep slopes beneath Besso's west face. As the trail progresses up the valley Dent Blanche and the Pointe de Zinal join the scene.

At 5.6 miles the trail starts an extremely steep climb, aided by switchbacks, up the rocky flanks of Besso's northwest ridge. Fix chains offer handholds and a level of security as you haul yourself up rocky, exposed and extremely steep sections of the trail. After an exhausting climb the trail crosses Besso's northwest ridge and views open to Mont Durand, the Ober Gabelhorn and the Wellenkuppe.

After crossing a boulder field the trail arrives at a rocky knoll, featuring stunning views of the ice-clad peaks stretching from the Grand Cornier to the Wellenkuppe, at 6.1 miles. Below the knoll the Zinal Glacier flows along the valley floor. This is a good turnaround point for many hikers.

Parties with the stamina, along with good weather, can continue ascending across boulder fields to the hut. Beyond the hut a use/social trail ascends to the crest of the moraine along the west side of the Mountet Glacier for breathtaking 270-degree views of the entire cirque, which now includes the Zinalrothorn and the Trifthorn. From this vantage point you are surrounded by towering mountains and rivers of ice flowing down the flanks of the rugged peaks and along the valley floor.

The day hike to the hut is only recommended for strong, well acclimated hikers. Pick a clear day, get a very early start and take plenty of food and drink. The hike will take longer than you expect. An overnight visit to the hut is a more viable proposition for many hikers and allows extra time to explore this amazing landscape.

To the Rocky Knoll

- **Distance from Trailhead:** 12.2 miles (round trip)
- **Elevation** 9,284-ft.
- **Elevation Gain:** 3,804-ft.

Walk south, up the valley, on Zinal's (5,479-ft) main street along the left (east) side of La Navisence, the river draining the Zinal Valley. Reach a car park at 0.6 miles and turn right (west), crossing the wood bridge over the river. On the west side of the river turn left (south) and continue walking up the Zinal valley toward the Petite Mountet (1-hr 50-min) and Grand Mountet (4-hr 10-min). The broad track travels through pastures on easy grades with nice views of Besso towering above the east side of the valley.

Pass a junction at 1.7 miles with a route branching left toward Lac Arpitetta and the Arpitetta Hut. Our track continues south and soon starts ascending on moderately-steep grades up a wooded hillside along the west side of the valley.

At 2.2 miles the trail travels by a pretty waterfall and then climbs a switchback. Soon the path reaches a junction at Le Vichiesso (6,109-ft.). Here a trail branches right toward the Petite Mountet (45-min). We continue on the main track toward Petite Mountet (1-hr), Grand Mountet (3-hr 20-min) and the Arpitetta Hut.

The grade eases at 2.5 miles as the trail ascends the hillside. La Navisence tumbles down the rocky riverbed below the trail. Reach a junction at 2.9 miles and turn left (east) on the trail toward the Grand Mountet. The trail to the right leads to the Petite Mountet Hut.

Our trail drops down to and crosses La Navisence on a bridge. On the east side of the river is a "Y" intersection. We turn right toward the Grand Mountet. The trail to the left heads to the Arpitetta Hut (Hike 25) and Roc de la Vache (Hike 24).

Follow the trail as it travels southeast through thick willows and then ascends steep switchbacks up the east side of the valley. As you climb, scattered trees soon give way to shrubs and rocky meadows. At 3.4 miles the trail briefly climbs along the remains of an old moraine wall, with nice views of the Grand Cornier, before continuing its stiff climb up the hillside on steep to very steep switchbacks. As you gain height, enjoy nice views to the north of the Garde de Bordon rising above the west side of Zinal. Pique de la Le, the Bouquetins and the Grand Cornier fill the skyline to the southwest.

At 4.4 miles the grade abates briefly as the trail contours through rocky meadows beneath the west face of Besso. To the north views open to Point Arpitetta and Les Diablons rising above the east side of the Zinal Valley. Soon the trail resumes its steep ascent. To the south Dent Blanche and the Pointe de Zinal enter the scene.

At 5.25 the trail drops down to and crosses a man-made, partially covered bridge providing safe passage across an avalanche chute. The descent to the bridge is quite steep. Use caution if the trail or bridge is wet.

Follow the trail as it climbs out of the chute and then travels on easy grades for a short distance. At 5.6 miles the path starts an extremely steep ascent, aided by switchbacks, up the rocky flanks of Besso's northwest ridge. Fixed chains provide a level of security and handholds to facilitate the climb up rocky, exposed and very steep sections of the trail. This is an extremely tiring section of the path. Take your time.

As you crest the ridge at 5.9 miles enjoy splendid views across the valley to the south/southwest of the Grand Cornier, Dent Blanche and the Pointe de Zinal. The Bouquetins, Grand Cornier and Durand glaciers spills down the flanks of the rugged peaks to join the Zinal Glacier, flowing along the valley floor. To the southeast views open to Mont Durand, the Ober Gabelhorn and the Wellenkuppe. These peaks along with the Zinalrothorn, still hidden from view, form the spectacular glacial cirque at the head of the valley.

Beyond the ridge crest the trail curves to the southeast as it climbs steeply through a boulder field. Red/white blazed rocks will keep you on track. The grade abates at 6.1 miles as the path ascends on easy to moderate grades to a rocky knoll (9,284-ft.). Along the way pass a wood sign indicating that the Cabane Grand Mountet is still 30 minutes away.

The knoll is a fabulous place to take a break and soak in the stunning views stretching from the ice-shrouded peaks of the Wellenkuppe and Ober Gabelhorn to the Grand Cornier. Glaciers, clinging to the flanks of the rugged peaks, glisten in the sun. Below you the Zinal Glacier, a massive river of ice flows down the valley. Besso rises above the trail to the northeast.

For many hikers the knoll is a good destination for a day hike. If you are tired or it's getting late in the day or if the weather is taking a turn for the worse you should turn around at this point. The final mile to the hut crosses boulder fields and will take much longer than 30 minutes for hikers that are not adept at walking through piles of rock.

To Cabane du Grand Mountet

- **Segment Stat:** 0.95 miles (one-way) from the Rocky Knoll to the Cabane du Grant Mountet
- **Total Distance:** 14.1 miles (round trip)
- **Maximum Elevation:** 9,520-ft.
- **Elevation Gain/Loss:** 4,040-ft.

To continue to the hut, follow the trail as it ascends through the boulder fields on easy to moderate grades. Look ahead to find the next red/white markers to stay on route. In some areas that trail is clear, in other places you will need to take your time and scan for markers.

At 6.7 miles the trail skirts the southwest end of the Le Mammouth ridge, a massive granite fin protruding from the Dome that has been blocking views to the east. Beyond Le Mammouth, views open to the top of Zinalrothorn and the Trifthorn to the east/southeast. Directly across the valley are terrific views of Dent Blanche, towering above the valley, and the Durand and Grand Cornier glacier flowing around Roc Noir, a horn rising in front of the Pointe de Zinal.

The hike now gets easier. Reach the Cabane du Grand Mountet (9,459-ft.), with incredible views of the glacial cirque ringing the head of the valley, at 6.9 miles. The hut, offering dormitory accommodations and meals, is a base camp for climbers tackling the high peaks and hikers wishing to spend more time exploring this amazing place.

For the best views continue beyond the hut and climb to the crest of the Mountet Glacier's northwest moraine wall at 7.05 miles. From atop the wall enjoy breathtaking views of the Mountet Glacier spilling down the flanks of the Zinalrothorn. The ice and snow-cloaked Wellenkuppe and Ober Gabelhorn rise to the south of the Zinalrothorn. To the south huge sheets of ice pour down the flanks of Mont Durand, Pointe de Zinal and Dent Blanche.

Hikers staying overnight will want to follow the use trail as it climbs along the crest of the moraine wall for ever improving views of the high peaks. At some point day hikers will need to pull themselves away from the glorious scene and retrace their steps to the trailhead.

Whether this trail is done as a day hike or an overnight excursion you will arrive back in Zinal tired but elated after tackling this very strenuous hike to a very special place in the Pennine Alps.

Note: The day hike to the hut is only recommended for strong, well acclimated hikers. Pick a clear day, get a very early start and take plenty of food and water. The hike will take longer than you expect. An overnight visit to the hut is a more viable proposition for many hikers and allows extra time to explore this amazing landscape.

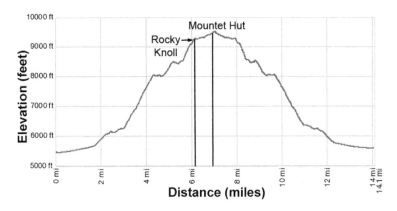

Trailhead Directions

Directions in Zinal: See Hike 22.
From Grimentz to Zinal: See Hike 22.

27. Sorebois to Lac de Moiry via Col de Sorebois

★★★★☆

Distance: Distance: 5.6 - 8.9 miles (one way)

Near Zinal in the Valais

Climb to the Col de Sorebois and then travel high above the Lac de Moiry to the Moiry Glacier. The walk is accompanied by fine views of the peaks towering above the Zinal, Moiry and Arolla valleys. Extend the hike by visiting the Moiry Hut or walking back along the lake to the dam.

Distance: Distance: 5.6 miles (one way) to Moiry Glacier over the Col du Sorebois
8.9 miles (one way) to Lac de Moiry Barrage (Dam)
Elevation: 8,000-ft. at Sorebois
9,374-ft. at the Col du Sorebois
8,452-ft. at High Point above Lac de Moiry
7,723-ft. at the Foot of the Moiry Glacier
7,380-ft. at the Moiry Barrage (Dam)

Elevation Gain: 2,000-ft. to Moiry Glacier over the Col du Sorebois
-343-ft. to Lac de Moiry Barrage (Dam).
Difficulty: moderate
Basecamp: Zinal
Zinal Map: See page 113
Online Map/Photos:
www.hikingwalking.com/sorebois

Why Hike from Sorebois to Lac de Moiry via Col de Sorebois

This hike crosses the ridge separating the Zinal and the Moiry valleys at the Col du Sorebois, a scenic pass with panoramic views of the peaks towering above the east side of the Zinal Valley, the rugged summits rising to the west of the Lac de Moiry and, in the distance, the high-peaks soaring above Arolla.

The ascent to the pass travels through the pastures of the Sorebois ski area marred with ski apparatus. After crossing the Col du Sorebois the trail drops steeply into the Val de Moiry and then traverses the steep slopes on the east side of the valley, high above the Lac de Moiry. This segment is accompanied by views of the ridge, punctuated with minor summits, along the west side of the Moiry valley. For much of the traverse the glacier-clad peaks at the head of the valley are hidden by the slopes of the west face of the Garde de Bordon protruding into the valley.

As the trail approaches the head of the valley grand views open to the Moiry Glacier, spilling down the slopes of the Grand Cornier. Near the head of the valley the trail drops down to the valley floor. The hike can be cut short at this point by taking the bus back to Grimentz and Zinal.

At the head of the valley hikers can opt to visit the Moiry Hut (Hike 28) with splendid views of the Moiry Glacier. This side trip climbs over 1,300-ft. on a 4.0 mile round-trip hike to the hut. Alternatively, hikers can walk to the Barrage de Moiry (dam) on a pleasant trail traveling along the west side of the lake. At the dam, regularly scheduled buses return to Grimentz and Zinal.

Sorebois to the Moiry Glacier via Col du Sorebois

- **Distance from Trailhead:** 5.6 miles (one way)
- **Elevation at at the Col du Sorebois:** 9,374-ft.
- **Elevation Gain:** 2,000-ft.

Take the cable car from Zinal to Sorebois (8,000-ft.) situated high above the west side of the Zinal valley. (See trailhead directions below.) Exit the lift and find the trail signs behind the lift station. Walk west on a dirt road toward the Corne de Sorebois (1-h4 20-min) and the Lac de Moiry (2-hr 20-min), ascending on moderate grades through pastures marred with ski apparatus. As you ascend enjoy great views of the high peaks towering above the east side of the Zinal valley including the Weisshorn, Schalihorn, Zinalrothorn, Besso and Ober Gabelhorn.

After a half mile the trail curves to the right (north). Soon views open south to the Garde de Bordon towering along the ridge separating Zinal Valley from the Val de Moiry (Moiry Valley). The grade steepens as the trail climbs to the top of a ridge extending east from the Corne de Sorebois at 1.2 miles. From atop the ridge, views stretch north up the Val d'Anniviers to the Bernese Alps.

The trail now turns left (west) and climbs steeply along the south face of the ridge, slightly below the ridge crest. Soon the path curves to the left (southwest), ascending along the east facing slopes below the Corne de Sorebois to the Col de Sorebois (9,301-ft.) at 1.8 miles.

The pass, on the ridge separate the Val de Moriy from the Val de Zinal, enjoys fine views of the Weisshorn, Zinalrothorn and Ober Gabelhorn to the southeast. In the distance to the southwest, summits in the valleys to the west, including the Bouquetins, Aiguille de la Tsa, Dents de Veisivi, Pigne d'Arolla, Mont Blanc de Cheillon, the Grand Combin and Aiguilles Rouges d'Arolla, rise beyond the ridge separating the Val de Moriy from Val de Herens. Below the pass the Lac de Moiry sprawls along the floor of the Val de Moiry. Sasseneire, Sex de Marinda and Bec de Bosson fill the skyline to the west. Garde de Bordon rises along the ridge to the south of the Col. Unfortunately views of the peaks rising at the head of the Val de Moiry are mostly blocked by a ridge of the Garde de Bordon extending into the Moiry valley.

Hikers with the time and energy can make the short side trip to the summit of the Corne de Sorebois (9,574-ft.), which features terrific 360-degree views that include the Bernese Alps to the north.

From the pass the trail drops down the west side of the ridge on steep switchback to a trail junction at 3.1 miles, losing 1,500-ft. from the Col. At the junction turn left on the trail called the Haut Tour de Lac 2500, which heads south toward the Moiry Glacier (2-hr 30-min) and the Cabane de Moiry (4-hr). The trail branching right descends on steep switchbacks to the dam (barrage) at the foot of the Lac de Moiry where buses return to Grimentz and Zinal.

Our path ascends along the eastern slopes of the Val de Moiry high above the lake. At 4.0 miles the grade abates as the trail contours along the hillside. After a half mile of easy walking the trail briefly climbs up a gully beside a stream to avoid an eroded section of the hillside. Soon the trail crosses the stream and reaches the high point along the trail before dropping a short distance down the slope.

The path now traverses the west facing slopes of the Garde de Bordon, curving to the southwest and then south. To southwest are nice views of the Pointes de Mourti, Pointe de Moiry and Couronne de Breona.

At 5.0 miles the path rounds a minor ridge and curves to the southeast. The Moiry Glacier, flowing down the north face of the Grand Cornier at the head of the valley, springs into view. The tip of Dent Blanche rises beyond the Grand Cornier. Pigne de la Le towers above the glacier to the east.

Reach a "Y" intersection (8,235-ft.) at 5.6 miles. The path branching left contours along the hillside and soon joins the trail ascending to the Cabane de Moiry in 0.8 miles. Take the trail to the right that drops down steep switchbacks to the Lac de Chateaupre, the lake near the foot of the Moiry Glacier. From the lake views extend southeast to the Moiry Glacier along with the Pointes de Mourti and Pointe de Moiry, rising to the west of the river of ice.

After enjoying the views, turnaround and head north to the Moiry Glacier parking lot. Here buses return to the dam (barrage) at the foot of Lac de Moiry, Grimentz and Zinal. Alternatively, hikers can opt to walk back to the dam on the trail along the west side of the lake.

See the description of Hike 28 to the Cabane de Moiry for more information on visiting this scenic hut with terrific views of the Moiry Glacier.

From Moiry Glacier to Lac de Moiry Barrage (Dam)

- **Segment Stat:** 3.3 miles (one-way) from the Moiry Glacier to the Moiry Barrage
- **Total Distance:** 8.9 miles (one way)
- **Ending Elevation:** 7,780-ft. at the Moiry Barrage
- **Elevation Gain/Loss:** -343-ft.

To return to the Moiry dam along the west side of the lake, walk north/northwest from the Moiry Glacier parking lot for 0.2 miles to a trail junction on the west side of the road at 6.25 miles. Take the trail branching left (northwest) that drops steeply through meadows and then travels on easy grades along the right (east) side of the outlet stream for Lac de Chateaupre. Along the way pass a trail branching right and climbing to the road.

Rock hop across the stream at 6.6 miles and then follow the trail as it cuts across meadows to the southwest end of the Lac de Moiry at 6.9 miles. Nice views extend north across the aquamarine lake to Sasseneire rising to the west above the dam. Turn around for fine views of the Moiry Glacier. The tip of the Grand Cornier peeks above the ice sheet.

The trail now drops down to the lake and heads north, traveling along the west side of the lake shore on easy grades. Turn around occasionally for views of the glacier. Soon you will see the tip of Dent Blanche appear to the south of the Grand Cornier.

A rocky outcropping near the foot of the lake forces the trail to climb to meet a road at 8.4 miles. After walking a short distance along the road the trail drops down to the west end of the Barrage de Moiry (7,380-ft.) at 8.5 miles. Here signs point north to a trail dropping steeply down to Grimentz (1-hr 40-min), losing over 2,250-ft. in 3.8 miles.

We turn right (east) and walk cross the top of the dam on a wide paved road. Along the way enjoy fine views that stretch up the length of the lake to the Moiry Glacier. Reach the cafe and bus stop at the east end of the dam at 8.9 miles. During the summer regularly scheduled buses depart for Grimentz and Zinal. Buses also travel south to the Glacier Parking area at the head of Lac Moiry

Note: This hike can be done in either direction. I prefer starting the hike at Sorebois so that I get over the Col de Sorebois in the morning when skies are typically clear. Clouds are more likely to obscure views of the glacier and surrounding peaks in the afternoon.

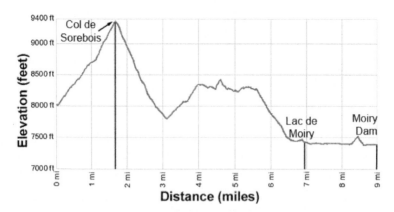

Trailhead Directions

From Zinal to the Sorebois Cable Car: From the post office in Zinal, walk north along the main street for a short distance to the Zinal Telepherique (Cable Car station) and take the cable car to Sorebois.

From Grimentz to the Sorebois Cable Car: From Grimentz, board the bus to Zinal and get off at the Zinal post office stop. From the post office, walk north along the main street for a short distance to the Zinal Telepherique (Cable Car station) and take the cable car to Sorebois

If possible catch a direct bus to Zinal. Otherwise, take the Vissoie Bus to Vissoie where you will need to change for a bus headed up valley to Zinal. The direct buses take 15 minutes. If you need to change in Vissoie the ride will take 58 minutes.

Buses make several stops in Grimentz. Schedules are posted at the bus stops and are available online at the SBB website and the SBB app.

From the Moiry Barrage to Grimentz or Zinal: At the dam, board a bus headed toward Zinal or Vissoie. There are several stops in Grimentz, about a 20 minute ride from the dam. If you are headed to Zinal, the best bet is to catch a bus heading directly to Zinal. Otherwise, take the Vissoie Bus to Vissoie where you will need to change for a bus headed up valley to Zinal. The direct buses take a little over a half hour. If you need to change the ride will take an hour and 15 minute or more, depending on the time of day. Schedules are posted at the bus stop by the dam and are available online at the SBB website and the SBB app.

28. Cabane de Moiry★★★★★
Distance: Distance: 4.0 - 6.7 miles (one way)
Near Zinal in the Valais

This short hike leads to the Moiry Hut with stunning bird's-eye-views of the Moiry Glacier. Extend the hike with a scenic walk along the west side of the Lac de Moiry to the Moiry Barrage (dam) at the foot of the lake.

Distance: Distance: 4.0 miles (round trip) to Cabane de Moiry 6.7 miles (complete hike) to Lac de Moiry Barrage
Elevation: 7,723-ft. at Trailhead 9,300-ft. at Cabane de Moiry 7,380-ft. at Lac de Moiry Barrage
Elevation Gain: 1,577-ft. to Cabane de Moiry -343-ft. to Lac de Moiry Barrage

Difficulty: moderately-strenuous
Basecamp: Zinal
Zinal Map: See page 113
Online Map/Photos: www.hikingwalking.com/cabane-moiry

Why Hike to Cabane de Moiry

Situated atop a rocky knoll along the west side of the Moiry Glacier, the Moiry Hut overlooks an incredible river of ice spilling down the north face of the Grand Cornier. Overlooks around the hut offer panoramic vistas of this amazing spectacle of ice, covered with seracs and crevasses.

The short, steep hike to the hut ascends through rocky meadows and then climbs steeply up hillsides clad in rock and boulder fields. Fine views along the trail encompass the Couronne de Breona, Pointes de Mourti and Pointe de Moiry towering above the west side of the valley. To the north, Pointe du Tsate and Sasseneire rise above the west side of the Lac de Moiry.

Extend the hike with a return trip along the west side of the Lac de Moiry to the Moiry Barrage (Dam). Alternately, this hike can be combined with the hike over the Col de Sorebois (Hike 29).

To Cabane de Moiry

- **Distance from Trailhead:** 4.0 miles (round trip)
- **Elevation at Cabane de Moiry:** 9,300-ft.
- **Elevation Gain:** 1,577-ft.

Take the postbus to Moiry Glacier. The bus stop is located beyond the head of the Lac de Moiry, a dammed reservoir to the south of Grimentz, and just before the tiny Lac de Chateaupre near the foot of the Moiry Glacier.

Walk a short distance south from the parking lot. Soon you will see signs pointing left (southeast) toward a broad track heading to the Cabane de Moiry (1-hr 25-min). Follow the trail as it skirts the north side of the Lac de Chateaupre, ascending through rocky meadows on easy grades. Views extend southeast to the Moiry Glacier along with the Pointes de Mourti and Pointe de Moiry, rising to the west of the river of ice.

At 0.3 miles the grade steepens as the path climbs the hillside along the east side of the glacier. Pass a junction at 0.6 miles with a trail, the Haut Tour de Lac 2500m, branching to the left toward Barrage de Moiry, Sorebois and Zinal. We continue straight ahead toward the Moiry Hut.

Beyond the junction the grade eases as the trail ascends atop the lateral moraine running along the east side of the glacier. At 0.8 miles the trail curves to the south, moving off the moraine crest to travel up a rocky gully to the left (east) of the moraine. Use trails split off from the main track and climb to viewpoints along the moraine.

At 1.3 miles the trail climbs a series of very steep switchbacks up a rocky hillside, gaining 800-ft. in a half mile. Turn around and look northwest for nice views of the Pointe du Tsate and Sasseneire rising above the west side of the Lac de Moiry. Directly across the valley is the Couronne de Breona.

The grade abates at 1.8 miles and soon reaches the Cabane de Moiry (9,268-ft.), an old stone hut with a modern copper-clad addition, at 1.9 miles. From the hut enjoy splendid, bird's-eye-views of the Moiry glacier.

For the best views follow a use trail which goes around the east side of the hut and then climbs to a rocky overlook (9,300-ft.) at 2.0 miles. To the north the glacier, covered with a morass of seracs and crevasses, spills down a steep incline. Pointes de Mourti, Tsa de l'Ano and Points de Moiry tower above the valley to the west. Pigne de la Le dominates the view to the south.

When you are done taking in the views, retrace your steps to the bus stop at the foot of the glacier for a 4.0 miles round trip hike.

From the Foot of the Glacier to Lac de Moiry Barrage

- **Segment Stat:** 2.7 miles (one-way) to the Moiry Barrage
- **Total Distance:** 6.7 miles (round trip)
- **Ending Elevation:** 7,380-ft.
- **Elevation Gain/Loss to the Dam:** -343-ft.

The hike can be extended by walking to Zinal on the Haut Tour de Lac 2500m, which climbs to the Col de Sorebois and then descends to the cable car station at Sorebois, or walking to the foot of the Lac de Moiry along the west side of the lake. See Hike 29 Moiry to Sorebois for information on the first option.

To return to the Moiry Barrage from the Moiry Glacier bus stop, walk north/northwest toward the Lac de Moiry for 0.2 miles to a trail junction on the west side of the road. Take the trail branching left (northwest) that drops steeply through meadows and then travels on easy grades along the right (east) side of the outlet stream for Lac de Chateaupre. Along the way pass a trail branching right and climbing to the road.

Rock hop across the stream at 4.4 miles and then follow the trail as it cuts across meadows to the southwest end of the Lac de Moiry at 4.6 miles. Nice views extend north across the aquamarine lake to Sasseneire rising to the west above the dam. Turn around for fine views of the Moiry Glacier. The tip of the Grand Cornier peeks above the ice sheet.

The trail now drops down to the lake and heads north, traveling along the west side of the lake on easy grades. Turn around occasionally for views of the glacier. Soon you will see the tip of Dent Blanche appear to the south of the Grand Cornier.

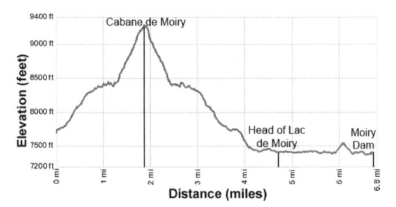

A rocky outcropping at the foot of the lake forces the trail to climb to meet a road at 6.2 miles. After walking a short distance along the road the trail drops down to the west end of the Barrage de Moiry (7,380-ft.) at 6.3 miles. Here signs point north to a trail dropping steeply down to Grimentz (1-hr 40-min), losing over 2,250-ft. in 3.8 miles.

We turn right (east) and cross the top of the dam on a wide paved road. Reach the cafe and bus stop at the eastern end of the barrage at 6.7 miles. During the summer regularly scheduled buses depart for Grimentz and Zinal. Buses also travel south Moiry Glacier parking area.

Note: This hike can be done in either direction. I prefer to hike to the Cabane de Moiry in the morning when skies are typically clear. Clouds are more likely to obscure views of the glacier and surrounding peaks in the afternoon.

Trailhead Directions

From Zinal to the Moiry Glacier: From the post office in Zinal, board bus #455 bound for Moiry Glacier. The bus ride takes 42 minutes. Note: The bus will stop at Moiry Barrage at the foot of the dam. Stay on the bus and get off at the last stop at the Moiry Glacier.

From Grimentz to the Moiry Glacier: From the post office in Grimentz, board bus #455 bound for the Moiry Glacier. The bus ride takes 29 minutes. Note: The bus will stop at Moiry Barrage at the foot of the dam. Stay on the bus and get off at the last stop at Moiry Glacier.

From the Moiry Barrage to Grimentz or Zinal: At the dam, board a bus headed toward Zinal or Vissoie. There are several stops in Grimentz, about a 20 minute ride from the dam. If you are headed to Zinal, the best bet is to catch a bus going directly to Zinal. Otherwise, take the Vissoie Bus to Vissoie where you will need to change for a bus headed up valley to Zinal. The direct buses take a little over a half hour. If you need to change the ride will take an hour and 15 minute or more, depending on the time of day.

Schedules are posted at the bus stops in Zinal, Grimentz and at the dam. Alternatively, check the SBB website or the SBB app for current schedules.

29. Cabane de Moiry to Zinal via Col de Sorebois ★★★★
Distance: 7.5 - 9.9 miles (one way)
Near Zinal in the Valais

This hike, part of the Haute Route, also makes for a great point to point day hike with lovely views of the Zinal and Moiry Valleys along with dramatic up-close views of the Moiry Glacier. The hike can be walked in either direction.

Distance: 7.5 - 9.9 miles (one way)
Elevation: 9,268-ft. at Cabane de Moiry
9,374-ft. at the Col du Sorebois
8,000-ft. at Sorebois
Elevation Gain: 1,574-ft. to Sorebois

Difficulty: moderate-strenuous
Basecamp: Zinal
Zinal Map: See page 113
Online Map/Photos:
www.hikingwalking.com/moiry-sorebois

Why Hike from Cabane de Moiry to Zinal via Col de Sorebois

This pleasant hike, part of the Walker's Haute Route, descends from the Cabane de Moiry and then travels along a high route above the Lac de Moiry with fine views of the Moiry Valley. As you near the dam at the foot of the lake the trail climbs steep switchbacks to the Col de Sorebois, a scenic crossing on the ridge separating the Val de Moiry from the Val de Zinal.

The pass enjoys stunning views of the glacier-clad Weisshorn, Zinalrothorn, Besso and Ober Gabelhorn soaring above the east side of Zinal. To west/southwest the high peaks towering above Grimentz and the Moiry Valley form the backdrop for distance views of the summits rising in the Arolla and Herens valleys including, Bouquetins, Aiguille de la Tsa, Dents de Veisivi, Pigne d'Arolla, Mont Blanc de Cheillon, Grand Combin and Aiguilles Rouges d'Arolla.

Descend from the Col to the ski area at Sorebois where a gondola and trails descend to Zinal. Several escape routes permit hikers to take a bus to either Grimentz or Zinal if the weather takes a turn for the worse, making travel over the Col problematic.

This walk is part of the Walker's Haute Route. It also makes a great day hike, which can be walked in either direction. Total mileage for the day hike is 9.7 miles, which includes the round-trip hike to the Cabane de Moiry.

Cabane de Moiry to Sorebois via the Col de Sorebois

- **Distance from Trailhead:** 7.5 miles
- **Elevation at the Cabane de Moiry:** 9,268-ft.
  Low Point on the Hike: 7,800-ft.
  Col de Sorebois: 9,374-ft.
  Sorebois: 8,000-ft.
  Zinal: 5,450-ft.
- **Elevation Gain/Loss to Sorebois:** 1,574-ft. / -2,834-ft.
  Gain/Loss to Zinal: 1,574-ft. / -5,392-ft.

This description assumes you spent the night at the Cabane de Moiry. Day hikers will need to first climb to the hut, which adds 1.9 miles and 1,534-ft. in elevation to the hike. See Hike 28 - Cabane de Moiry for more information.

The Cabane de Moiry (9,268-ft.) sits atop a rocky knoll with dramatic views of the Moiry Glacier and the high peaks towering above the valley to the west including the Pointes de Mourti, Tsa de l'Ano and Pointe de Moiry. Pigne de la Le dominates the view to the south.

From the hut the trail descends from the knoll and then drops down very steep switchbacks on slopes covered with boulders and rocky meadows, losing 800-ft. in half a mile. At 0.7 miles the grades abates as the path descends through scree to the right (east) of the lateral moraine of the Moiry Glacier.

Soon the trail climbs to and then descends along the moraine crest accompanied by fine views of the glacier and the ridge rimming the west side of the valley. Turn right at 1.3 miles when you reach the junction with the Haut Tour du Lac – Chemin 2500 toward the Barrage de Moiry, Sorebois and Zinal. (The trail straight ahead descends to the parking lot at the foot of Moiry Glacier where buses depart for Grimentz and Zinal.)

The Chemin 2500 is an undulating path that contours high above the east side of the valley at around 2,500-meters (8,200-ft.). Before starting on the trail turn around for fine views of the Moiry Glacier flowing down the north face of the Grand Cornier at the head of the valley. The tip of Dent Blanche rises beyond the Grand Cornier. Across the valley the rugged ridge rimming the west side of the valley dominates the view. Below is the small lake at the foot of the glacier.

The path now heads northwest, curving around a ridge extending from the Garde de Bordon (10,860-ft.). At 2.0 miles pass a trail dropping steeply down to the road running along the east side of the lake. This path also connects with the trail traversing the lake's western shore and the road around the eastern shore. Ahead are ever improving views of the Lac de Moiry and Sasseneire (10,675-ft.) and Diablon (10,016-ft.) rising to the northwest above the head of the lake.

At 2.6 miles the path rounds the end of the Bordon ridge and we lose our views of the Moiry Glacier. Instead we now look down the full length of the lake and enjoy fine views of the peaks rising to the west/northwest.

At 2.8 miles the trail briefly climbs up a hillside, crosses a rugged stream bed and then drops down a gully beside the stream to avoid a steep, eroded section of the hillside. At 3.1 miles the descent ends and the path resumes its undulating traverse along the hillside.

After a half mile of easy walking the path begins to descend on moderate grades, reaching a junction at 4.4 miles. Here a path, branching left, zig-zags down the hillside to the road at the foot of the Moiry Lake. A short distance beyond is a cafe and bus stop adjacent to the dam at the foot of the lake. In the summer regularly scheduled buses leave from the dam to Grimentz and Zinal.

We turn right at the junction, climbing over 1,500-ft. up steep switchbacks to the Col de Sorebois (9,374-ft.) at 5.8 miles. The pass, located on the ridge separating the Val de Moiry from the Val de Zinal, enjoys fine views of the Weisshorn, Zinalrothorn and Ober Gabelhorn to the southeast. To the southwest, the Bouquetins, Aiguille de la Tsa, Dents de Veisivi, Pigne d'Arolla, Mont Blanc de Cheillon, Grand Combin and Aiguilles Rouges d'Arolla rise beyond the ridge separating the Val de Moiry from Val de Herens. Below the Col, Lac de Moiry sprawls along the floor of the Val de Moiry. Sasseneire, Sex de Marinda and Bec de Bosson fill the skyline to the west. Garde de Bordon rises along the ridge to the south of the Col. Unfortunately views of the peaks towering above the head of the Val de Moiry are mostly blocked by a ridge of the Garde de Bordon.

Hikers with the time and energy can make the short side trip to the summit of the Corne de Sorebois (9,501-ft.), which features terrific 360-degree views that include the Bernese Alps to the north.

When you are done taking in the views descend from the Col on steep to moderately steep grades through pastures on a combination of ski services roads and trails. (The trails cutoff meanders along the road.) The pastures unfortunately are marred by ski apparatus.

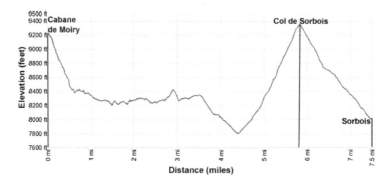

Ignore the ski area and instead focus on the stunning views of the glacier-clad summits of the Weisshorn, Zinalrothorn, Besso and Ober Gabelhorn soaring above the east side of the valley. Garde de Bordon rises above the west side of the Zinal Valley. A segment of the road/trail drops down the east ridge of the Corne de Sorebois. Here we enjoy views that stretch north up the Val d'Anniviers to the Rhone Valley.

If you are not watching it is easy to miss some of the cutoff trails. This is hardly a big deal and does not make a substantial difference in the overall mileage.

Reach Sorebois at 7.5 miles. Here you will find a restaurant, bathrooms and a gondola descending to Zinal. If you wish to walk to Zinal, head south from the lift station on a signed road toward Zinal. After 0.2 miles watch for a trail, signed for Zinal, branching left. The path descends steep switchbacks, losing 2,700-ft. in 2.4 miles for a 9.9 mile walk from the Cabane de Moiry to Zinal. If you miss the turn you can follow the road down. The road is longer and not as steep but shared with mountain bikes. If your budget allows, my advice is to take lift down, saving your knees and energy for tomorrow's walk.

Trailhead Directions

From the Sorebois Cable Car to Zinal / Grimentz: Take the cable car from Sorebois to Zinal. At the bottom station of the Zinal Telepherique, Cable Car station, walk south along the main street for a short distance. Just past the post office you will find grocery stores, restaurants and various types of accommodations.If traveling to Grimentz, catch the direct bus at the Zinal post to Grimentz. Otherwise, take the Vissoie Bus to Vissoie and then change for a bus heading to Grimentz. The direct buses take about 15 minutes. If you need to change in Vissoie the ride will take 58 minutes.

From the Moiry Barrage to Grimentz or Zinal: If you hit bad weather it might make sense to take the bus to Zinal or Grimentz instead of trying to cross the Col. At the glacier parking lot or the dam at the foot of the lake, board a bus headed toward Zinal or Vissoie. There are several stops in Grimentz, about a 20 minute ride from the dam. If you are headed to Zinal, the best bet is to catch a bus heading directly to Zinal. Otherwise, take the Vissoie Bus to Vissoie where you will need to change for a bus going up valley to Zinal. The direct buses take a little over a half hour. If you need to change the ride will take an hour and 15 minute or more, depending on the time of day.

Bus schedules are posted at the bus stops in Zinal, Grimentz and at the dam and are also available online at the SBB website or the SBB app.

Map: Zinal, St. Luc, Gruben and St. Niklaus

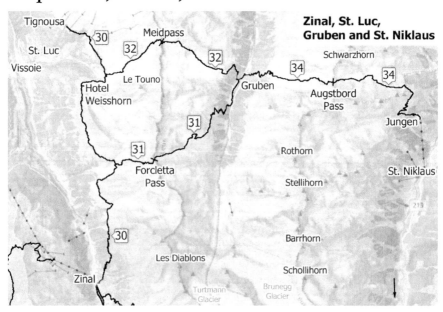

30. St. Luc to Zinal ★★★★★
Distance: 9.7 miles (one way)
Near Zinal in the Valais

Highlights of this scenic walk between St. Luc and Zinal include magnificent views of the high peaks and glaciers gracing the skyline at the head of the Zinal Valley and panoramic views of the rugged summits towering above the Rhone and Anniviers Valleys.

Distance: 9.7 miles (one way)
Elevation: 7,145-ft. at St. Luc
High Point: 7,975-ft.
Elevation Gain: 830-ft./-2,325-ft.
Difficulty: moderate-strenuous

Basecamp: Zinal
Zinal, St. Luc, Gruben and St. Niklaus Map: See page 144
Online Map/Photos: www.hikingwalking.com/stluc-zinal

Why Hike from St. Luc to Zinal

This high traverse above the Anniviers Valley is one of my favorite hikes in the Zinal area. The trail features almost nonstop, breathtaking views of the massive glacier-clad peaks rimming the cirque at the head of the Zinal Valley and the summits towering above the Anniviers and Rhone valleys.

The day starts with a ride up the St. Luc funicular to Tignousa (7,145-ft.) where we get an introduction to the coming attractions. Just outside the upper funicular station views extend south to the Matterhorn rising above the high peaks at the head of the Zinal Valley. To the west a rugged ridge rims the Anniviers valley with vistas stretching to the summits rising above Grimentz to the southwest.

An easy walk, traveling through meadows and trees along the Path of the Planets, soon leads to a trail ascending to the Hotel Weisshorn. This Victorian gem, set atop a grassy knoll, features wide-ranging views of the high peaks towering above the Rhone and Anniviers valleys.

From the hotel the path ascends along the east side of the Anniviers Valley. As you climb views slowly unfold to the magnificent cirque of jagged peaks, clad in glistening glaciers, ringing the head of the Zinal Valley. The distinctively-shaped summit of the Matterhorn rises beyond the cirque. For the remainder of the hike these views evolve and improve as we approach the Zinal Valley.

Beyond the trail's high point, the path gradually descends, contouring around side valleys as it heads south toward Zinal. Along the way the trail traverses meadows sprinkled with wildflowers, passes hillsides cloaked in heather and travels by small Alps (farms).

With 1.5 miles left to go the trail starts the steep descent to Zinal, dropping through trees and intermittent meadows providing our last views of the high peaks. The trail ends above the east side of Zinal, where signs lead down through the village to the shops, hotels and the bus station.

This trail can be hiked in either direction. I strongly advise walking from St. Luc to Zinal so that the amazing views are right in front of you. Some parties choose the hike the trail starting in Zinal and then spending a night at the Hotel Weisshorn before crossing Meidpass to Gruben (Hike 32). If you do walk in reverse, be sure to stop frequently and turn around so you don't miss the great views.

Whatever way you walk pick a day full of promise and get an early start so you can spend a leisurely day enjoying the amazing vistas on this great hike.

St. Luc to Zinal

In St. Luc, take the funicular to Tignousa (7,145-ft.). (See trailhead directions below.) Outside the station find the trail signs and start hiking along the broad track heading southeast toward the Hotel Weisshorn and Zinal.

As you walk ignore the nearby ski lifts and pistes and instead focus on the great views to the south where the distinctively shape summit of the Matterhorn (14,692-ft.) towers above the peaks at the head of the Zinal Valley. To the southeast Les Diablons (11,840-ft.), the Bishorn (13,625-ft.) and the Weisshorn (14,783-ft.) rise above the ridge separating the Anniviers and Turtmann valleys. Below the trail vistas stretch southwest to Grimentz at the foot of the Moiry Valley.

The path, known as the Planets trail, travels through meadows and forest around a shallow side valley, passing short spur paths leading to sculptures of the sun and the planets. The meadows offer fine views of the ridge rimming the west side of the Anniviers valley and Les Diablerets, a flat topped peak, rising above the north side of the Rhone Valley. The white building setting atop a knoll across the valley is the Hotel Weisshorn.

At 0.8 miles pass a side trail at Chalet Blanc. A short distance beyond ignore trails branching right and dropping down to St. Luc. Soon you will start seeing rocks painted with the letter "Z" in yellow. These markers, in additional to the trail signs pointing toward Zinal, will help keep you on track.

Reach the Alp at Touno and a junction at 1.9 miles. Bear right on the trail toward the Hotel Weisshorn and Zinal. The path climbs through rocky meadows on moderate grades, reaching the Weisshorn at 2.9 miles. The circa 1880's Victorian Hotel set atop a grassy knoll features panoramic views of the high peaks towering above the Rhone and Anniviers Valleys.

Behind the hotel is the continuation of the trail to Zinal. The undulating path ascends along meadow-clad slopes beneath the rugged Points de Nava ridge with more fine views. Depending on the time of year, patches of heather and clusters of fireweed enliven the scene.

Near the high point on the hike views slowly unfold to the magnificent cirque at the head of the Zinal Valley, formed by Dent Blanche (14,294-ft.), Pointe de Zinal (12,431-ft.), Mont Durand (12,182-ft.), the Ober Gabelhorn (13,330-ft.) and Le Besso (12,001-ft.). The summit of the Matterhorn rises beyond the head of the cirque. Glaciers cling to the high peaks and the Zinal Glacier spills down the valley beneath the cirque.

Reach the high point (7,975-ft.) on the trail at 4.3 miles. The path now descends on easy grades with ever evolving and expanding views of the high peaks at the head of the valley. Soon the Zinalrothorn (13,848-ft.) and Blanc de Moming (11,936-ft.), along with the Moming Glacier, join the scene.

At 4.5 miles the trail briefly travels along a farm road before branching right onto the continuation of the trail. A large rock painted with the word Zinal and red/white slashes mark the trail.

The meadows along this section of the trail are a great place to stop and take a break to enjoy the magnificent views. Below us the Anniviers Valley splits into two branches; the Zinal Valley to the southeast and the Moiry Valley to the southwest. Grimentz lies at the foot of the Moiry Valley, beneath the rugged Becs de Besson (10,328-ft). The Zinal Valley, to southeast, is ringed by photogenic peaks clad in glistening glaciers. The Corne de Sorebois (9,501-ft.) rises above the confluence of the two valleys.

The path now continues its gentle descent, slowly curving to the left (southeast) as it follows the contours of a shallow side valley beneath the Montagne de Nava. At 4.9 miles reach the junction at Bella Le (7,874-ft.) where a trail branches left toward Forcletta and Gruben (Hike 31). Another path heads right, dropping down to Ayer on the valley floor. We stay on the path toward Barneuza and Zinal.

Gradually we lose our views as the path nears the head of the side valley. At 5.5 miles the trail crosses a steam on a wood bridge and then turns right, descending around the head of the valley on moderate grades. Along the way pass a second junction with a trail climbing to Forcletta and Gruben at 5.6 miles. A short distance beyond the path crosses a second stream on a bridge near an old building and then curves to the right (southwest), descending on easy grades.

At 6.4 miles the path leaves the side valley as it curves to the left (south/southeast), crosses a low ridge and emerges high above the Zinal Valley. Here breathtaking views reopen to the peaks towering above the head of the valley. The town of Zinal is visible on the valley floor. This area is another great place to take a break.

The trail now descends through meadows and then scree covered slopes before curving left into the Barneuza Valley. Travel through pastures and then around the small alp of Sierra Zinal, ignoring the signed trail branching right and dropping down to Ayer on the valley floor.

Beyond the alp the path descends to cross a stream draining the Barneuza valley and then passes a few cement buildings, part of a hydroelectric project. Soon the trail emerges from the side valley and begins a descent on easy to moderate grades through meadows and clusters of tree. Below are views of a large settling pond in Mottec, another part of the hydro system powering the Zinal and Anniviers Valleys.

At 8.2 miles reach a junction with the Promenade des Arolles branching left. We bear right on the trail to Lirec and Zinal that descends on moderate to moderately-steep grades through trees to a wood gate at 8.7 miles. Go through the gate and continue the descent on very steep grades, passing through the alp at Lirec. Here an old two-track road and braided trails drop through the pastures. Both the trail and the road are very steep. Pick the route that looks best to you. Take a break as you descend to appreciate the fine views toward the head of the Zinal Valley.

Below the pastures the trail plunges back into the trees and goes through a second gate before continuing its relentless descent on switchbacks. The grade briefly abates at 9.25 miles as the path crosses a gully, passes a few buildings and then traverses an avalanche chute. Beyond the chute the path travels through a tunnel built beneath an avalanche control barrier.

The final steep descent ends at the parking lot of the Arellaz condo complex along the east side of Zinal. Walk to the road in front of the complex. Here signs direct you to the center of the village where you will find grocery stores, bakeries, outdoor stores, hotels and the bus station.

Trailhead Directions

From Zinal to St Luc, Bella Tola: From the post office in Zinal, board Bus #453 bound for Vissoie. At Vissoie Post, change to Bus #454 to Chandolin, Poste. Get off the bus in St. Luc at the Bella Tola stop. The bus ride from Zinal to St. Luc takes 48 minutes.

From Grimentz to St Luc, Bella Tola: From one of the several bus stops in Grimentz, board Bus #452 bound for Vissoie Poste. At Vissoie Poste change to Bus #454 to Chandolin, Poste. Get off the bus in St. Luc at the Bella Tola stop. The bus ride takes 46-53 minutes.

From the Bella Tola bus stop walk southeast (in the direction the bus is traveling) along the main road. Soon you will reach a hairpin curve. Exit the main road and follow the Route Vieux Village toward the funicular. You will see blue signs for the funicular marking the route. At the next intersection bear left (funicular signs mark the turn). Pass a small side street on the left, the Rue du Cervin. At the next street bear left and in a short distance turn the right onto the Route de Funiculaire. Again, all of these turns are marked with signs. Walk up the road (Route de Funiculaire) to the funicular station on your left. The walk should take about 9 minutes.

See the SBB website or download the app for the current schedule. See the Val Anniviers website for more information about the St. Luc Funicular schedule.

If Walking the Trail in Reverse

Directions to the Trailhead from Zinal: From the Pam Supermarket on the main street in Zinal (just south of the bus station), cross the street and take the steps leading up to the Poste Hotel. At the top of the stairs turn right (south), walk up the street past the Thrift Hotel and then turn left (east) on the next street. Follow this street as it passes a church (on your right) and a large hotel complex (on your left).

At the east end of the hotel take the path branching to the left (northeast) through the grass. The track climbs to meet a road near an intersection. Cross the street and head up the road directly in front of you. There is a sign post along the left side of the road pointing straight ahead (northeast) toward Lirec, Barneuza Alpage and Hotel Weisshorn. Walk in the direction indicated by the sign.

The road ascends between two large apartment complexes, Les Erables and Les Arellaz. Follow the road as it curves to the left behind Les Erables to meet a dirt road ascending the hill. This is the way to the Hotel Weisshorn, Forcletta Pass and St. Luc. (On the first part of this walk, follow the signs pointing toward Lirec, Barneuza Alpage and Hotel Weisshorn.)

31. Zinal to Gruben via Forcletta Pass ★★★★★
Distance: 10.9 miles (one way)
Near Zinal in the Valais

This scenic route between the Val d'Anniviers and Gruben crosses Forcletta Pass and features panoramic views of the high peaks towering above the head of the Zinal and Turtmann Valleys.

Distance: 5.9 miles (one way)/11.8 miles (round-trip) to Forcletta Pass 10.9 miles (one way) to Gruben
Elevation: 5,488-ft. at Trailhead 9,424-ft. at Forcletta Pass 5,988-ft. at Gruben
Elevation Gain: 3,936-ft. to Forcletta Pass -3,436-ft. to Gruben

Difficulty: strenuous
Basecamp: Zinal
Zinal, St. Luc, Gruben and St. Niklaus Map: See page 144
Online Map/Photos: www.hikingwalking.com/forcletta

Why Hike from Zinal to Gruben via Forcletta Pass

Most hikers traveling on the Walker's Haute Route use Meidpass (Hike 32) to cross from the Val d'Anniviers to Gruben in the Turtmanntal (Turtmann Valley). In my opinion the trail from Zinal over the Col de la Forcletta (Forcletta Pass) to Gruben is the more scenic option, although it is longer and more strenuous.

From Zinal a steep climb through forest and pastures leads to a high traverse along a narrow shelf on the east side of the Val de Zinal with wonderful views of the high peaks, including Besso, Mont Durand, Pointe de Zinal, Dent Blanche and Grand Cornier, forming the glacial cirque at the head of the Zinal valley. On a clear day the tip of the Matterhorn can be seen peeking above the cirque.

Near the foot of the valley the trail turns east as lovely views open to the peaks rising above Grimentz to the west. Soon the trail ascends pastures to

Alp Tsahelet and then travels through meadows before the final short, steep climb to Forcletta Pass.

The pass, on the boundary between the French-speaking Valais and the German-speaking Wallis, enjoys good views of the Bernese Alps to the north and the summits towering above Grimentz to the west. Dominating the skyline to the east is a wall of summits rising above the Turtmann Valley.

From the pass the trail drops steeply down scree covered slopes of the Bluomattalli Valley before turning northeast toward Chalte Berg. As you descend wonderful views of the peaks soaring above the head of the Turtmanntal are gradually revealed.

Below Chalte Berg stunning views open to the Brunegghorn, Bishorn and Tete de Milon rising along the glacial cirque at the head of the valley. The tip of the Weisshorn towers above the cirque. The Turtmann and Brunegg Glaciers, along with several waterfalls, spill down the flanks of the peaks.

After enjoying the spectacle, follow the trail as it descends switchbacks through meadows and then forest to the valley floor. Here the trail turns north, traveling through lovely pastures along the west side of a river to the small, tranquil village of Gruben, nestled beneath the Schwarzhorn.

Note there are no places to purchase food or drink along the trail. Pack a lunch and take plenty of water. Get an early start for the best views. Clouds often obscure the high peaks in the afternoon.

The Hotel Schwarzhorn is a busy little place with a nice restaurant and large backyard for relaxing with a cold beer after a long hike. If is best to have advanced reservations if you plan to spend the night here.

This trail can easily be walked in reverse – from Gruben to Zinal. The hike to Forcletta Pass can also be done as a very steep 11.8 mile (round-trip) day hike from Zinal or a 10 mile (round-trip) hike from Gruben

Zinal to Forcletta Pass

- **Distance from Trailhead:** 5.9 miles (one way)
- **Elevation at Forcletta Pass:** 9,424-ft.
- **Elevation Gain:** 3,936-ft.

Note: Trail mileage for this hike assumes you start near the Pam Supermarket on the main street in Zinal. The Pam is a short distance to the south of the bus station. (See trailhead directions below.)

From the Pam Supermarket, cross the main street and take the steps leading up to the Poste Hotel. At the top of the stairs turn right (south) on a paved street. Walk up the street past the Thrift Hotel and then turn left (east) on the next street. Follow this street as it passes a church (on your right) and a large hotel complex (on your left).

At the east end of the hotel take the path branching to the left (northeast) through the grass. The path climbs to meet a road near an intersection. Cross the street and head up the road directly in front of you.

There is a sign post along the left side of the road near a group of garages pointing straight ahead (northeast) toward Lirec, Barneuza Alpage and Hotel Weisshorn. (On the first segment of the hike follow signs pointing toward Lirec and the Hotel Weisshorn.)

The road ascends between the Les Erables and Les Arellaz apartment buildings. Behind the Erables the road curves to the left and turns into a seldom used dirt road.

Follow the dirt road as is climbs steeply uphill. At 0.4 miles pass through a large culvert, providing a route under a large earthen dike, that is part of the town's avalanche and flood control system. Continue along the road as it crosses a stream and passes a chalet.

At 0.5 miles reach a "Y" intersection. The trail to the right leads to Arolec. We bear left, heading north/northeast, on the road toward Lirec, Barneusa (Barneuza) and Hotel Weisshorn.

Cross a small stream and then ascend steep switchbacks up a forested hillside. As you climb watch for places where trails shortcut long hairpin curves in the road. Signs or red and white blazes will mark the shortcuts.

Soon the road breaks out of the trees and climbs steeply through open meadows. Take occasional breaks from the climb to enjoy the views behind you (to the south) of Besso, Pointe de Zinal, Dent Blanche and Grand Cornier towering above Val de Zinal (Zinal Valley).

Just below Lirec, a small chalet perched high above the valley, leave the road for good by taking the trail branching right that heads straight up hill through meadows toward the chalet.

Reach Lirec at 1.1 miles. The trail skirts the right (east) side of the chalet, climbs a hill and then passes through a gate. Signs along the way point toward the Hotel Weisshorn.

Beyond the gate the trail ascends on moderate grades through a larch and pine forest along the valley's east wall. To your left (west), the hillside drops steeply to the Zinal Valley. Segments of the trail with some exposure are fenced or lined with ropes for added safety. The trail should not present any problems unless it is icy. Breaks in the trees offer nice views of the Garde de Bordon on the west side of the valley.

At 1.7 miles, about an hour from Zinal, the grade abates at a small meadow. Ignore the trail branching right toward Promenade des Arolles. We continue straight ahead (north) toward Barneuza Alpage and the Hotel Weisshorn.

The trail now traverses a narrow shelf on easy grades with nice views of the Garde de Bordon and the Corne de Sorebois across the valley. Behind you are magnificent views of the high peaks forming the glacial cirque at the head of the Zinal Valley.

Pass two cement structures (on your right) housing hydro equipment and then curve around the foot of the Barneuza Valley to Barneuza Alpage (7,254-ft.), a small alp at 3.0 miles. From this vantage point the tip of Matterhorn is seen peeking above the cirque at the head of the Zinal Valley.

Signs at the alp point left to a path dropping to Ayer and Mottec on the valley floor. We bear right on the trail toward Belle Le (50-min) and Hotel Weisshorn (1-rh 40-min), which ascends on moderate grades through pretty meadows and small boulder fields as it curves around the end of a ridge.

At 3.6 miles the trail curves to the right and enters a side valley. A small grassy knoll just before the turn is a good place for a quick break to take in the stunning views of the Zinal Valley.

Follow the trail as it ascends on moderate grades heading east along the southern slopes of the side valley. Behind you, to the west, views open to Grimentz and the peaks towering above the resort at the foot of the Val de Moiry. Soon the trail crosses a stream and curves to the left (north/northwest) above an old building, reaching a trail junction (7,677-ft.) at 4.3 miles. Here we leave the trail bound for the Hotel Weisshorn and turn right (east) toward Forcletta (1-hr 45-min) and Gruben (4-hr 30-min).

The narrow trail ascends steeply through lush and sometimes boggy pastures. Keep an eye out for red and white blazed rocks to keep you on track. Soon the path becomes easier to follow as it curves around the south side of a large bowl before the final steep climb to alp Tsahelet (8,278-ft.) at 4.7 miles.

As you approach the alp the trail fades. To keep on track head for the milking barn, staying to the left of the large cross atop a rock outcropping. A sign behind the cross points toward Forclettaz (Forcletta Pass).

Turn right when you reach the alp road and walk to the end of the barn. Here a trail skirts the south side of the barn and then takes a sharp left, climbing steeply up the hill behind the barn. Signs along the path point toward the pass. A few large flat rocks along the trail offer nice spots to take a break and enjoy the views of the peaks towering above Grimentz.

Soon the path tops a rise and briefly travels through rolling pastures to a small tarn at the base of a steep hill at 5.2 miles. As you cross the pasture note the saddle (low point) on the ridge at the top of the hill, this is the pass.

Just beyond the tarn is a trail junction. The path to the left (northwest) heads toward the Hotel Weisshorn and St. Luc. The trail branching to the right climbs steeply through rocky meadows and small rock slides on switchbacks to Forcletta Pass (9,430-ft.), the boundary between the French-speaking Valais and the German-speaking Wallis, at 5.9 miles. Here signs point east toward Meidan-Gruben (2-hr 20-min).

From the pass views extend north to the Bernese Alps. Nearer at hand the Pointe de la Forcletta rises along the rugged ridge to the north of the pass. The Corne de Sorebois and the peaks towering above the Val d'Anniviers fill the horizon to the west. The top of Dent Blanche and Grand Cornier poke above a dark ridge to the south. Dominating the skyline to the east is a wall of summits rising above the Turtmanntal (Turtmann Valley). Unfortunately views of the peaks at the head of the valley are blocked by a ridge. Great views of these peaks will gradually unfold as you descend from the pass toward Gruben.

Forcletta Pass to Gruben

- **Segment Stat:** 5.0 miles (one-way) from Forcletta Pass to Gruben
- **Total Distance:** 10.9 miles (one way)
- **Ending Elevation:** 5,988-ft.
- **Elevation Gain/Loss:** -3,436-ft.

To continue to Gruben, follow the trail as it drops steeply down the east side of the pass, traversing scree covered slopes along the left (north) side of the Bluomattalli valley. Along the way, cross two small streams draining the slopes to the north of the trail.

At 6.8 miles the trail curves to the northeast as it heads around the end of a ridge. The grade abates as the trail travels through beautiful rolling alpine meadows sprinkled with wildflowers. A small peak, Le Boudri, rises to the west. With each step enjoy every-improving views of the peaks towering above the head of the Turtmanntal.

After a brief uphill stint the trail traverses above and then drops down to Chalte Berg (8,000-ft.) at 7.4 miles. Here a muddy trail, heading toward Gruben (1-hr 30-min), descends between the Alp buildings. The trail is not always easy to follow. When you reach a dirt road on the east side of the alp there are two ways to continue. The easiest is to follow the farm road down.

Alternatively look to your left (east) and downhill. You should see a faint, boot-beaten path through the grass. This trail descends steeply through pasture to join the farm road. There are a few red and white blazed rocks along the way. When you reach the farm road, turn left (north) on the road.

Whichever way you go, find a nice spot to stop and enjoy the spectacular views of the Brunegghorn, Bishorn and Tete de Milon that form the massive glacial cirque at the head of the valley. The top of the Weisshorn towers above the cirque. The Turtmann and Brunegg glaciers, along with several waterfalls, spill down the flanks of the peaks. A man-made lake catches the meltwater near the edge of a hanging valley.

Travel along the road for a short distance, if you descended on the trail from the alp, or follow the farm road for 0.6 miles from the alp. Soon you will see a sign to the right (east), slightly below the road, point toward Gruben. Drop down to the trail and turn left (north) toward Gruben.

Travel along the trail as it parallels the road for about 0.3 miles. It is a pretty walk through meadows sprinkled with flowers and low-lying shrubs. In the distance to the north are views of the Bernese Alps. Gruben is now visible on the valley floor.

At 8.5 miles the trail curves to the right (east) and descends through pastures, shortcutting long switchbacks on the road. Soon the trail rejoins the road and follows it around two hairpin curves. Beyond the second hairpin turn watch for a rock on the right (west) side of the road with a red/white arrow pointing downhill. Past the rock look for a post on the left side of the road at 8.8 miles that marks a trail branching to the left. Turn left (east/southeast) on the trail.

Follow the trail as it descends through meadows and then forested hillsides on moderately-steep switchbacks. At 9.8 miles the trail passes along the right (south) side of a group of buildings to a road. Look up valley for a different perspective of the peaks and glaciers towering above the head of the valley.

At the road signs points right (southwest) toward Stausee and the Turtmann Hut. We turn left (northeast) on the road toward Gruben. Follow the macadam road for a short distance along the left (west) side of the river. Just before the road crosses the river you will see trail signs on your left. Take the trail branching left (north) from the road toward Gruben. Do not cross the bridge over the river.

The trail parallels a wooden fence for a short distance, crosses a stream and then travels through meadows on easy grades, passing a small hamlet on the left. Along the way views open to the Schwarzhorn looming over the small village of Gruben. The historic Hotel Schwarzhorn, a stone building with red shutters, is easy to spot

Pass to the right (east) of a house and reach trail signs at 10.5 miles. Bear right (northeast) on the trail toward Gruben, which crosses the river on a good bridge. When you reach the road on the other side of the river turn left (north). You are now in Gruben (5,988-ft.). Walk a short distance north along the road to the Hotel Schwarzhorn at 10.8 miles.

Note there is no places to purchase food or drink along the trail. Pack a lunch and take plenty of water. Get an early start for the best views. Clouds often obscure the high peaks in the afternoon.

The Hotel Schwarzhorn is a busy little place with a nice restaurant and large backyard for relaxing with a cold beer after a long hike. If is best to have advanced reservations if you plan to spend the night here.

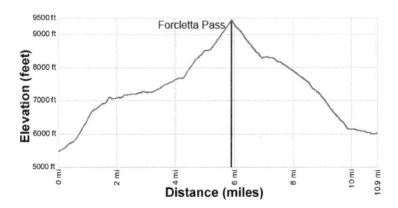

Trailhead Directions

Directions to the trailhead from Zinal: From the Pam Supermarket on the main street in Zinal (just south of the bus station), cross the street and take the steps leading up to the Poste Hotel. At the top of the stairs turn right (south), walk up the street past the Thrift Hotel and then turn left (east) on the next street. Follow this street as it passes a church (on your right) and a large hotel complex (on your left).

At the east end of the hotel take the path branching to the left (northeast) through the grass. The track climbs to meet a road near an intersection. Cross the street and head up the road directly in front of you. There is a sign post along the left side of the road pointing straight ahead (northeast) toward Lirec, Barneuza Alpage and Hotel Weisshorn. Walk in the direction indicated by the sign.

The road ascends between two large apartment complexes, Les Erables and Les Arellaz. Follow the road as it curves to the left behind Les Erables to meet a dirt road ascending the hill. This is the way to the Hotel Weisshorn and Forcletta Pass. (On the first part of this walk, follow the signs pointing toward Lirec, Barneuza Alpage and Hotel Weisshorn.)

Direction to the trailhead from Gruben if walking the route in reverse: From the Hotel Schwarzhorn, walk south along the road for 0.2 miles to a "Y" intersection and take the minor road branching right (southwest), which crosses a bridge over the river. From here follow the directions above in reverse, always looking for signs directing you toward Forcletta Pass and Zinal. (On the west side of the pass you will see large yellow "Z's" painted on rocks directing you toward Zinal.)

32. St. Luc / Hotel Weisshorn to Gruben via Meidpass ★★★★☆

Distance: 6.8 - 7.8 miles (one way)

Near Zinal in the Valais

Meidpass features splendid views of the glacier clad peaks of the Turtmann Valley, the summits towering above the Rhone, Anniviers and Moiry Valleys along with distant views of Grand Combin and Mont Blanc, rising to the southwest beyond the Anniviers Valley.

Distance: 6.8 - 7.8 miles (one way)
Elevation: 7,145-ft. at St. Luc. /
7,667-ft. at Hotel Weisshorn
9,154-ft. at Meidpass
Elevation Gain: 2,009-ft. from St. Luc.
1,487-ft. from the Hotel Weisshorn

Difficulty: moderate-strenuous
Basecamp: Zinal
Zinal, St. Luc, Gruben and St. Niklaus Map: See page 144
Online Map/Photos: www.hikingwalking.com/meidpass

Why Hike from St. Luc / Hotel Weisshorn to Gruben via Meidpass

Two scenic options are available to hikers on the Haute Route crossing from the Anniviers Valley to the Turtmann Valley; Meidpass or Forcletta Pass (Hike 31). Meidpass is the well-traveled path that is lower, less strenuous and easily accessible from the Hotel Weisshorn or St. Luc. The trail over Meidpass is straight forward, ascending and descending through pastures with good views of the surrounding landscape.

The trail to Forcletta, starting in Zinal, is steeper, longer and more challenging. The path travels through rugged, wild terrain, including the gorgeous Bluomattalli valley. See the information on Hike 31 - Zinal to Gruben via Forcletta Pass for a detailed description.

Both trails feature terrific scenery. Hikers crossing Meidpass are treated to expansive, albeit more distant views from the pass. Views along the

Forcletta trail, especially of the high peak of the Turtmanntal, are closer with the best views revealed as you descend from the pass to Chalte Berg area.

So which to choose? It really depends on your time, energy level and where you are based. Meidpass is the logical alternative if your itinerary includes hiking to the Hotel Weisshorn. If you are based in Zinal and up to a challenging ascent then choose Forcletta. (Otherwise take the bus to St. Luc and funicular to Tignousa and then hike to Meidpass.)

If you are tired from the previous days walking or facing questionable weather, Meidpass is the better choice since it is shorter and easier. Opt for Forcletta is you prefer a less traveled route with a longer day. No matter what pass you choose you will have an extremely enjoyable and scenic walk between the two valleys.

So why hike Meidpass? The scenic hike to Meidpass, starting from either St. Luc or the Hotel Weisshorn, ascends through meadows and then scree covered slopes with fine views of the high peaks rimming the west side of the Val Anniviers and Val de Moiry. As the path nears the pass views expand to include a sea of peaks towering above the Rhone Valley and the high summits, including Grand Combin and Mont Blanc, to the southwest.

As you crest the pass impressive views open to Brunegghorn, Bishorn and the Weisshorn soaring above craggy peaks in the Turtmanntal Valley. The summit of the Dom and Taschhorn, located in the Mattertal valley, rise above the ridge rimming the east side of the Turtmann Valley.

The views become partially blocked by intervening low ridges as you descend to the Meidsee, a scenic tarn, and then drop down through meadows to Gruben. Toward the end of the hike beautiful vistas reopen to the Turtmann Glacier spilling down the slopes between Les Diablons, Tete de Milon and the Bishorn at the head of the valley.

Note: Meidpass marks the boundary between the French-speaking Valais and the German-speaking Wallis. Try to remember to switch your greetings to German when you arrive in Gruben.

There are no places to purchase food or drink along the trail. There is a small shop in the Hotel Schwarzhorn in Gruben but it is not a good option for lunch supplies. My advice is the pack lunch for two days before leaving Zinal or Grimentz (the day over Meidpass and then next day over Augstbord) and carry plenty of water. Get an early start for the best views. Clouds often obscure the high peaks in the afternoon.

The Hotel Schwarzhorn in Gruben is a busy little place with a nice restaurant and large backyard for relaxing with a cold beer after a long hike. If is best to have advanced reservations if you plan to spend the night here.

This trail can be walked in reverse – from Gruben to St. Luc/Hotel Weisshorn but involves a 3,000-ft. ascent.

To Gruben via Meidpass

Information from St. Luc:

- **Distance:** 7.8 miles (one way)
- **Trailhead Elevation:** 7,145-ft.
- **High Point at Meidpass:** 9,154-ft.
- **Ending Elevation at Gruben:** 5,964-ft.
- **Net Gain/Loss:** 2,009-ft. / -3,190-ft.

Information from Hotel Weisshorn:

- **Distance:** 6.8 miles (one way)
- **Trailhead Elevation:** 7,667-ft.
- **High Point at Meidpass:** 9,154-ft.
- **Ending Elevation at Gruben:** 5,964-ft.
- **Net Gain/Loss:** 1,487-ft. / - 3,190-ft.

The hike to Meidpass starts at either Tignousa, located at the top of the funicular station in St. Luc, or the Hotel Weisshorn, a circa 1880's Victorian Hotel with panoramic views of the high peaks towering above the Rhone Valley and the Val Anniviers. Note: If you are unable to get into the Weisshorn or opt to skip that day on the Haute Route, you can stay either in Grimentz or Zinal and easily take a bus to St. Luc. (See trailhead directions below.)

Starting from St. Luc

In St. Luc, take the funicular to Tignousa (7,145-ft.). Outside the station find the trail signs and start hiking along the broad track heading southeast toward Meidpass and Gruben.

As you walk ignore the nearby ski lifts and pistes and instead focus on the great views to the south where the distinctively shape summit of the Matterhorn (14,692-ft.) towers above the peaks at the head of the Zinal Valley. To the southeast Les Diablons (11,840-ft.), the Bishorn (13,625-ft.) and the Weisshorn (14,783-ft.) rise above the ridge separating the Anniviers and Turtmanntal (Turtmann) valleys. Below the trail vistas stretch southwest to Grimentz at the foot of the Moiry Valley.

The path, known as the Planets trail, travels through meadows and forest around a shallow side valley, passing short spur paths leading to sculptures of the sun and the planets. The meadows offer fine views of the ridge rimming the west side of the Anniviers Valley and Les Diablerets, a flat topped peak, rising above the north side of the Rhone Valley. The white building setting atop a knoll across the valley is the Hotel Weisshorn.

At 0.8 miles pass a side trail at Chalet Blanc. A short distance beyond ignore trails branching right and dropping down to St. Luc. Reach the alp at

Touno and a junction at 1.9 miles. Here we turn left toward Meidpass and Gruben.

Starting from the Hotel Weisshorn

Behind the Hotel Weisshorn find the signs pointing to Meidpass. The trail heads east, descending on easy grades through meadows. After 0.7 miles the trail curves to the north and soon reaches the alp at Touno and a junction at 0.9 miles. Here we turn right toward Meidpass and Gruben. For the remainder of this description the first number listed in the mileage is the distance is from the Hotel Weisshorn while the second number is the distance from Tignousa (the top of the funicular in St. Luc).

Touno to Gruben via Meidpass

The trail briefly ascends north past an alp building and then turns right (east/northeast), ascending steeply through pastures. The trail soon passes a hut and then continues climbing. At 1.5/2.5 miles the trail veers left and crosses a stream. Le Touno (9,898-ft.) rises above the trail to the south.

At 1.6/2.6 miles the grade eases a bit as the trail travels through an undulating landscape of meadows and low knolls, reaching a junction at 1.7/2.7 miles. Here a short spur trail branches right toward the Lac de Combavert (8,005-ft.). We continue toward Meidpass.

Soon views open left (north/northwest) to the jagged ridge of peaks rising above the north side of the Rhone valley. The ridge forms a lovely backdrop for a small tarn in the meadows a short distance from the trail. Ahead are views of the craggy ridge separating the Anniviers and Turtmann Valleys.

At 2.0/3.0 miles the ascent steepens and the landscape becomes more rugged as the path climbs through rocky meadows toward the ridge. The obvious saddle on the ridge is Meidpass. As you gain elevation the views continue to improve. Le Touno and the Point de Tourtemagne (10,138-ft.) rise to the south. To the north are the peaks rimming the Rhone Valley. Turn around periodically for panoramic views of Sasseneire (10,675-ft.) and Bes de Bosson (10,330-ft.) towering above the Val de Moiry and Grimentz.

At 2.7/3.7 miles reach a junction with a trail branching toward Lac de l'Armina. We bear right toward Meidpass. The trail now climbs steeply up scree covered slopes and rocky meadows. Switchbacks facilitate the ascent. Turn around for panoramic views to the southwest. On a clear day you should be able the see the summits stretching from the Grand Combin (14,154-ft.) to Mont Blanc (15,777-ft.).

Reach Meidpass (9,154-ft.) at 3.2/4.2 miles. As you top the pass views unfold southeast to the glacier-clad Brunegghorn (12,575-ft.), Bishorn (13,625-ft.) and Weisshorn (14,783-ft.) soaring above the intervening ridge of craggy peaks. The Dom (14,911-ft.) and the Taschhorn (14,734-ft.), located in the Mattetal Valley to the east, rise above the ridge rimming the east side of the Turtmann Valley.

Turn around for more amazing view of the high peaks, including the Grand Combin and Mont Blanc, rising beyond the western ridges rimming the Moiry and Anniviers valleys. To the north/northwest a sea of peaks fills the skyline above the Rhone Valley. Rugged crags rise along the ridge above the pass, Aiguilles du Meiden (9,629-ft.) (aka Meidspitz), to the north, and the Pigne de Combavert (9,419-ft.), to the south.

On a beautiful day it is difficult to pull yourself away from this scenic pass. To continue to Gruben, descend the east side of the pass on steep grades, traveling through scree covered slopes and rocky meadows. At 3.5/4.5 miles the grade abates as the path crosses the bowl beneath the Aiguilles du Meiden and Rotighorn (9,708-ft.).

At 3.8/4.8 miles the trail veers right (southeast), skirting the slopes above the west side of the Meidsee (8,730-ft.). This tarn, set in a rocky bowl, is a favorite spot for hikers to take a break, especially if it is windy at the pass.

At 4.0/5.0 miles the trail starts a steep descent down the east side of the Turtmann Valley dropping through meadows and then pastures. At 4.4/5.4 miles the grade moderates before resuming its steep descent at 4.9/5.9 miles.

At 5.25/6.25 miles pass through Meiden Oberstafel and reach a junction. We bear left on the trail toward Gruben. The turn is marked with a small stones painted with red and white slashes. The wide track/road to the right heads toward the Stausee and the Turtmannhutte at the head of the valley.

The trail now descends through pastures with terrific views of the Turtmann Glacier spilling down the slopes between Les Diablons, Tete de Milon and the Bishorn at the head of the valley. The spike rising behind the Bishorn is the Weisshorn.

At 5.4/6.4 miles the trail crosses the road above Mittelstafel, a group of alp buildings seen below the trail. Continue straight ahead on the trail toward Gruben, which descends through meadows, passes through Mittelstafel and then turns left (northeast) at 5.5/6.5 miles, dropping through meadows that give way to trees.

At 5.7/6.7 miles the trail curves to the right (south/southeast), descending through viewless forest to the main road through Gruben at 6.5/7.5 miles. Turn left on the road and walk by summer homes. Ahead you will see a multi-story stone building. This is the Hotel Schwarzhorn. A road on a diagonal veers off the main road and ascends to the hotel at 6.8/7.8 miles. Total elevation loss from the pass to Gruben is 3,190-ft.

The quiet little Turtmann valley feels like a place where time has stood still, harkening back to the days before upscale ski resorts littered the mountain regions of Switzerland. There is a small shop in the Hotel Schwarzhorn where you can buy snacks. My advice is stock up on all needed supplies before leaving the Anniviers Valley.

Transportation in and out of Gruben is very limited. A van runs between the Hotel Schwarzhorn and the Silbahn (Cable car) in Oberems.

From the bottom station of the cable car it is a 10 minute walk to the Turtmann train station, a local stop in the Rhone Valley with connections to Visp in the east and Sion in the west. This is the best escape route if the weather is too bad to proceed over Augstbord Pass.

The time table for the bus and cable car are available on the SBB site. (See the SBB website or download the app for the current schedules.) Note: There are two towns called Gruben in Switzerland. When using the SBB site choose Gruben (VS) as the destination.

The Hotel Schwarzhorn, only open in the summer and early fall, includes 15 private rooms and dormitory accommodations. Meals, snacks and drinks are available in the hotel's cafe.

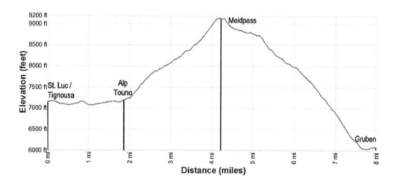

Trailhead Directions

From Zinal to St Luc, Bella Tola: From the post office in Zinal, board bus #453 bound for Vissoie. At Vissoie Post, change to Bus 454 to Chandolin, Poste. Get off the buss in St. Luc at the Bella Tola stop. The bus ride takes 48 minutes.

From Grimentz to St Luc, Bella Tola: From the post office in Grimentz, board bus #452 bound for Vissoie Poste. At Vissoie Post, change to Bus 454 to Chandolin, Poste. Get off the buss in St. Luc at the Bella Tola stop. The bus ride takes 46-53 minutes.

Walk south from the Bella Tola bus stop (in the direction the bus is traveling) along the main road. Soon you will reach a hairpin curve. Exit the main road and follow the Route Vieux Village toward the funicular. You will see blue signs for the funicular marking the route. At the next intersection bear left, continuing to follow the signs. Pass a small side street on the left, the Rue du Cervin. At the next street bear left and in a short distance turn right on the Route de Funiculaire. Again, all of these turns are marked with signs. Walk up the road (Route de Funiculaire) to the funicular station on your left. The walk should take about 9 minutes.

See the SBB website or download the app for the current schedules. See the Val Anniviers website for more information about the St. Luc Funicular schedule.

33. Other Trails in Zinal
Near Zinal in the Valais

33a) Sorebois to Cabane du Petite Mountet

This route boasts jaw-dropping views of high peaks towering above the east side of Zinal and the cirque at the head of the Zinal Valley. Over the years rock slides and avalanches have made a mess of upper section of the trail, turning a great hike into a route. The route portion of the hike is narrow, exposed and travels through avalanche/landslide areas with unstable/shifting rocks. Only experience, surefooted hikers comfortable on expose trails crossing very steep slopes should consider the trail. Before setting out it is imperative that you check on current conditions with the Zinal Tourist Office. At times the trail is closed due to rockfalls or other unsafe conditions.

- **Distance:** 8.2 - 8.9 miles (round-trip)
- **Elevation:** 8,000-ft. at Sorebois
  8,485-ft. at the High Point
  7,028-ft. at Cabane de Petite Mountet
  5,450-ft. at Zinal
- **Elevation Gain / Loss:** 485-ft. / -3,035-ft.
- **Difficulty:** moderately-strenuous to strenuous (depending on direction)
- **Base camp:** Zinal
- **See the Zinal Map:** Page 113

Start the day by riding the cable car to Sorebois. Find the trail signpost behind the lift station and then walk south on a broad track toward the Petite Mountet. Note this is a blue sign meaning that it is a route and not a trail.

At 0.5 miles bear right on a narrow track marked by a red arrow on a rock. Across the valley are grand views of Les Diablons, the cirque formed by the Weisshorn, Schalihorn, Zinalrothorn and Le Besso, and the Ober Gabelhorn. The Moming Glacier spills down the slopes of the Zinalrothorn and Schalihorn. These views will improve and evolve as you continue along the route.

Soon the path starts climbing through rocky meadows. At 1.4 miles the route crosses a stream carrying meltwater from snowfields above the trail. The path crosses a gully at 1.9 miles where chains attached to the rock face provide a level of security.

At 2.0 and 2.5 miles the route passes through slide areas with unstable and shifting rocks. The condition of these areas change based on the year, the time of season and recent rain events. ALWAYS check with the Zinal Tourism office to determine the current condition of the trail. At times this route is closed for unsafe conditions.

While crossing the second slide area the route reaches the high point of the hike. Beyond the last slide the trail descends through meadows and soon reaches a bench where the grade eases and terrific views open to the cirque at the head of the Zinal Valley. The respite is brief. A short distance beyond the path again descends on steep grades. This pattern is repeated two more times as the trail drops down the west side of the valley toward the Petite Mountet.

At 4.8 miles the trail reaches the lateral moraine of the Zinal Glacier. Here the path turns left, climbs the moraine and then turns left (north), reaching the Cabane du Petite Mountet at 4.9 miles.

There are two ways to return to Zinal from the Petite Mountet resulting in an 8.2 or 8.9 mile hike. See Hike 23 - Petite Mountet hike for more information. See the Hike 27 - Sorebois to Lac de Moiry hike for directions to the Sorebois cable car.

33b) Lac de Moiry Circuit

This scenic hike circumnavigates the Lac de Moiry with fine views of the peak rimming the Moiry Valley and the stunning glacier-clad cirque towering above the head of the valley. The path, which can be walked in either direction, travels along trails and paved roads. Parties looking for a longer hike can visit Lac de Chateaupre at the foot of the Moiry Glacier or climb to the Cabane de Moiry.

- **Distance:** 4.5 miles (loop) Moiry Lake Circuit
  5.5 miles (loop plus extension) Moiry Circuit plus side trip to the foot of the Moiry Glacier
  8.9 miles (loop plus extension) Moiry Circuit plus round trip hike to the Cabane de Moiry
- **Elevation:** 7,380-ft. at the Moiry Barrage
  7,723-ft. at the foot of the Moiry Glacier
  9,300-ft. at Cabane de Moiry
- **Elevation Gain:** 500-ft. Circuit
  770-ft. Circuit plus side trip to the foot of the Moiry Glacier
  2,362-ft. Circuit plus round trip hike to the Cabane de Moiry
- **Difficulty:** easy to strenuous depending on the side trips
- **Base camp:** Zinal
- **See the Zinal Map:** Page 113

Take the bus to the Moiry Barrage (dam). At the dam panoramic views stretch south up the length of the lake to the Moiry Glacier spilling down the slopes of the Grand Cornier and Pointe de Zinal. A ridge, punctuated by 9,000-ft. peaks, defines the west side of the Moiry Valley.

Walk west across the dam on a wide paved road to the west end of the dam at 0.4 miles. Here signs point to a trail branching right and dropping down to Grimentz. We bear left and ascend on a road. Follow the road as it curves to the right (south) at a hairpin turn and then reaches a junction at a second hairpin turn at 0.5 miles. At the junction leave the road and take the path straight ahead. The path briefly rises to meet the road and then descends to the trail along the west side of the lake.

From the path enjoy great views of the peaks towering above the head of the valley. Here Dent Blanche joins the scene, rising behind the Grand Cornier. The path now travels through meadows along the lakeshore to the end of the lake at 2.0 miles. Stay on the trail and hike past the end of the lake, crossing a metal bridge to the east side of the inlet stream at 2.3 miles.

At 2.5 mile reach a signed junction. The trail straight ahead continues to the Moiry Glacier area and links to trails climbing to the Cabane de Moiry (Hike 28) and the Haute 2500 route (Hike 29). We make a sharp left toward Gros Liapec, Moiry Barrage and the Tour du Lac 2500.

The path now climbs to meet the road along the east side of the lake at 2.7 miles. Turn left and follow the road back to the dam at 4.5 miles.

Extend the hike by continuing straight ahead at 2.5 miles towards the Moiry Glacier. The path ascends along the east side of the inlet stream, climbs to the road, passes through a parking area and then reaches tiny Lac de Chateaupre near the foot of the glacier. Add 1.0 mile (round trip) to the circuit to visit the area at the base of the glacier.

Alternatively, walk to Lac de Chateaupre and then climb to the Cabane de Moiry (Hike 28), a 4.4 mile (round-trip) extension. Finally, if you wish to shorten the hike, simply walk 0.5 miles to the Lac de Chateaupre. After viewing the area around the foot of the glacier turn around and walk back to the parking lot for a 3.0 mile hike. At the parking area catch a bus back to Grimentz or Zinal. See Hike 28 - the Cabane de Moiry hike for information on the buses going to the dam and the foot of the glacier.

33c) Lac de Moiry to the Col de Torrent

The accent from the Lac de Moiry to the Col de Torrent is accompanied by fine vistas of the cirque at the head of the Moiry Valley and the rugged peaks rimming the east side of the valley. As the trail crest the pass views unfold to the high summits towering above the Val d'Herens and the Val d' Arolla to the southwest. On a clear day views extend to the Grand Combin, Mont Blanc de Cheilon and beyond.

- **Distance:** 7.2 mile (round-trip)
- **Elevation:** 7,193-ft.at Moiry Barrage (Dam)
  9,576-ft. at Col de Torrent
- **Elevation Gain/Loss:** 2,196-ft.
- **Difficulty:** moderately-strenuous
- **Base camp:** Zinal
- **See the Zinal Map:** Page 113

Take the bus from either Zinal or Grimentz to Lac de Moiry Barrage (dam). Walk to the east end of the dam where panoramic views stretch south up the length of the lake to Moiry Glacier spilling down the slopes of the Grand Cornier and Pointe de Zinal. A ridge, punctuated by 9,000-ft. peaks, defines the western slopes of the Moiry Valley.

Walk west across the dam on a wide paved road. Reach the west end of the dam at 0.4 miles. Here signs point to a trail branching right and dropping down to Grimentz. We bear left and ascend switchback up an alp road.

Reach a junction at 0.8 miles. Turn right on a trail that climbs switchbacks to the alp (farm) at the Alpage de Torrent at 1.7 miles. (Alternatively stay on the road, which is not quite as steep, and reach the alp at 1.8 miles.)

Pass the north side of the alp buildings and reach a junction. Here we continue straight ahead (west) on a trail climbing steeply through meadows toward Lac des Autannes (40-min) and the Col de Torrent (1h 30-min). Along the way views toward the head of the Moiry Valley expand and improve.

After 0.5 miles the grade moderates as the trail continues ascending to the Lac des Autannes at 2.7 miles. The lake is a popular picnic spot with splendid views of Dent Blanche, the Grand Cornier and the Glacier de Moiry spilling down the cirque at the head of the Moiry Valley along with the peaks rising above the valley to the east.

The path now travels above the lake's north shore before resuming its ascent on moderately-steep to steep grades through rocky meadows and scree covered slopes. A final stiff climb propels hikers to the Col de Torrent (9,576-ft.), a saddle on the ridge separating the Val de Moiry and Val d'Herens, at 3.6 miles.

From the pass a magnificent panorama of high peaks, including the Grande Dent De Veisivi, Mont Brule, Pigne d'Arolla, Les Aiguilles Rouges d'Arolla, Mont Blanc de Cheilon and the Grand Combin, dominate the view to the southwest. Dent d'Herens peeks above the Glacier de Ferpecle and Glacier du Mont Mine flowing down the flanks of the Tete Blanche at the head of the Val d'Herens. To the east the Weisshorn looms above the low ridges lining the east wall of the Moiry Valley. Below the east side of the pass Lac de Autannes glistens in the sun.

The trail over the pass continues to La Sage Villaz and Les Hauderes is part of the Walker's Haute Route (see Hike 35 - Les Hauderes to Lac de Moiry over the Col de Torrent). After enjoying the views turn around and retrace our step to the Lac de Moiry for a 7.2 mile (round-trip) hike.

Gruben
Location: The Turtmanntal Valley in the Valais

Gruben, aka Meiden, is a tiny village in the Turtmanntal (Turtmann Valley) located between the Mattertal and the Val d'Anniviers. The area, only occupied during the summer season, is happily devoid of any ski apparatus or tourist developments. Instead it remains serenely bucolic with one hotel, the Schwarzhorn (www.hotelschwarzhorn.ch), and a small collection of summer homes and farms.

Most hikers visit the valley as part of the Walker's Haute Route. From the Val d'Anniviers there are two passes: Meidpass (Hike 32) and Forcletta (Hike 31), used by hikers starting in Zinal, Grimentz, St. Luc or the Hotel Weisshorn to reach Gruben. From Gruben walkers climb over Augstbord Pass to Jungen and St. Niklaus (Hike 34) in the Mattertal. The valley is also popular with climbers seeking to summit the valley's high peaks.

The passes and other walks in the valley offer fine views of the summits rimming the valley along with Les Diablons, Tete de Milon, the Brunegghorn, Bishorn and Weisshorn anchoring the impressive cirque at the head of the valley. The Turtmann and Brunegg glaciers spill down the rugged slopes of the cirque. Waterfalls, fed by glacial meltwater, cascade down the sheer walls below the ice sheets.

Getting to Gruben

Take the train to Turtmann, a local stop on the Rhone Valley rail line. From the railway station follow the signs to the cable car to Oberems, about a 20 minute walk. Ride the cable car to Oberems where a minibus will take you to the Hotel Schwarzhorn. Note, when looking for transportation options to Gruben make sure you specify "Gruben, VS" (for Valais) so you get the correct town, schedule and prices.

Good Things to Know about Gruben

- Gruben is in the German part of the Valais. People working at the Schwarzhorn typically speak German, French and English.
- The Schwarzhorn now manages another property a slight distance to the north of the hotel. Advanced reservations are strongly advised. The half pension is a good deal and a recommended option when stay at the hotel.
- Gruben does not have a grocery. The Schwarzhorn does sell a few snacks. Anyone hiking the Haute Route is advised to carry enough food for two lunches; the day you walk to Gruben and the day you leave Gruben.
- There is one hut at the head of the valley, the Turtmann Hut, managed by the SAC.

34. Gruben to Jungen via Augstbord Pass

★★★★★

Distance: 8.2 miles (one way)

Distance: 2.25 miles (one-way)

One of my favorite hikes in the Valais is the steep, scenic climb over Augstbord Pass leading to an overlook with stunning, panoramic views of the Bernese Alps and the high peaks towering above the Mattertal from Stalden to Zermatt.

Distance 3.6 miles to Augstbord
8.2 miles (one way) to Jungen from Gruben via Augstbord Pass
Elevation: 5,988-ft. at Gruben
9,495-ft. at Augstbord
6,562-ft. at Jungen
3,684-ft. at St. Niklaus
Elevation Gain: 3,507-ft. to Augstbord
-2,933-ft. to Jungen
-5,811-ft. to St. Niklaus

Difficulty: strenuous
Basecamp: Gruben
Zinal, St. Luc, Gruben and St. Niklaus Map: See page 144
Online Map/Photos:
www.hikingwalking.com/gruben

Why Hike from Gruben to Jungen via Augstbord Pass

The trail crossing Augstbord Pass between the Turtmanntal (Turtmann Valley) and the Mattertal (Matter Valley) is one of my favorite hikes in the Valais. The trail travels through diverse landscapes with splendid views, crosses a rugged pass and then descends through a rocky moonscape to one of the most stunning viewpoints in the Swiss Alps.

Starting at the Hotel Schwarzhorn in Gruben, a steep climb through forest, pastures and rocky meadows leads to the inner recesses of the untamed Gruobutalli Valley. At the head of the valley the trail ascends through an austere, rocky landscape to Augstbord Pass where fine views encompass the summits towering above the Saas Valley to the east and the Turtmann Valley to the west.

From the pass, the trail drops steeply down scree covered slopes to a rock-strewn valley beneath the flanks of the Schwarzhorn. Soon the trail crosses to the south side of the valley where it traverses a long boulder field before rounding the end of the valley's south ridge to a grassy knoll with breathtaking views.

From the knoll enjoy a panorama of peaks adorn with glaciers. The Bernese Alps fill the skyline to the north. To the east/southeast the peaks of the Mischabel range, including the Nadelhorn, Lenzspitze and the Dom, rise above the Mattertal while the Weisshorn, Bishorn and Brunegghorn dominate to view to the southwest. Monte Rosa, Lyskamm and the Breithorn massifs tower above the head of the Mattertal valley to the south. In the distance to the east are the peaks flanking the east side of the Saas Valley.

From the overlook the trail drops down steep slopes to Jungen, nestled in a hanging valley perched high above the floor of the Mattertal. Here a small cable car whisks hikers down to St. Nicklaus where trains depart for Zermatt or Visp and a bus heads to Grachen.

The trail, while steep is not overly difficult thanks to well-engineered switchbacks facilitating the climb to the pass. There is no place for refreshments between Gruben and Jungen, so pack a lunch and take plenty of water.

This trail can easily be walked in reverse. Check the weather forecast before setting out. Sections of the trail are very difficult to follow in thick fog and the high exposed slopes should be avoided during thunderstorms.

Gruben to Augstbord Pass

- **Distance from Trailhead:** 3.6 miles (one way) /7.2 miles (round-trip)
- **Elevation at Augstbord Pass:** 9,495-ft.
- **Elevation Gain:** 3,507-ft.

At the trailhead, starting behind (south side) of the Schwarzhorn Hotel in Gruben (5,988-ft.), signs point east toward Augstbordpass (3-hr) and St Niklaus (6-hr 40-min). The trail ascends steeply up a broad grassy track, crossing a wood bridge over a stream at 0.2 miles.

Beyond the stream a series of steep switchbacks climb through larch and pine forest. Openings in the trees offer views across the valley to the Meidhorn and the ridge running along the west side of the Turtmanntal (Turtmann Valley). As you ascend, the trees give way to shrub filled meadows with views of the Bernese Alps rising to the north of the Rhone Valley.

Reach a trail junction with a track going left (north) for Chanzibodu. Continue straight ahead following the signs for Augstbordpass (2-hr 10-min), Jungen (4-hr 50-min) and St Niklaus (6-hr 10-min). As the trail gains altitude views open to Les Diablons, towering above the head of the Turtmanntal, and Meidpass (Meid Pass) across the valley.

At 1.4 miles arrive at the junction (7,448-ft.) with the trail branching right (south) to the Turtmannhutte (Turtmann Hut 2-hr 55-min). Bear left on the main trail to Augstbordpass (2-hr). To the north are distant views of Altels and the Balmhorn rising above the head of the Leukerbad Valley.

The trail continues its ascent up steep switchbacks and then crosses a rocky meadow, passing a few old stone buildings. At 1.7 miles reach a second junction (8,907-ft.) with a trail branching right (south) toward the Turtmannhutte (2-hr 40-min). Our trail proceeds straight ahead, ascending through meadows along the left (north) side of the Gruobutalli Valley and a small creek.

At 2.0 miles the trail curves to the right, crosses the creek and then climbs a low knoll, hoping over a stream along the way. From the top of the knoll enjoy great views of Meidpass and the peaks rising along the west side of the Turtmanntal. Rugged slopes with talus aprons line the south side of the Gruobutalli valley.

Re-cross the stream at 2.4 miles and then ascend steeply up rocky meadows along the north side of the valley to the base of a bluff. A rocky trail now ascends the west face of the bluff on very tight, steep switchbacks. Use care if there is ice or snow on the trail.

Reach the top of the bluff at 3.1 miles. Ahead you will see Augstbord Pass, the low saddle on the ridge. Turn around for great views across the Turtmann Valley to the west. Below the trail, to the south, meltwater flows down a rocky gorge.

The trail now ascends grassy meadows atop the bluff. At 3.2 miles follow the trail as it drops into a bowl and curves around the right (south) side of a small tarn nestled beneath the pass. At the east end of the tarn the trail turns left (northeast) and ascends on a diagonal across a boulder field. Rock cairns mark the route. If the boulder field is snow covered, aim for the grassy slopes below the pass.

Beyond the boulder field the trail reaches a grassy slope and turns right (east), climbing steep switchbacks to Augstbord Pass (9,495-ft.) at 3.6 miles. Here distant views extend east toward the peaks towering over the Saastal (Saas Valley) including the Boshorn, Senggchuppa and the Fletschhorn. The Schwarzhorn (10,501-ft.) rises to the north of the pass. The peaks and ridges rising above the Turtmanntal fill the skyline to the west.

(Note: The best views of this hike are not at the pass but atop a grassy knoll overlooking the Mattertal (Matter Valley) at 6.3 miles. I recommend taking a short rest stop at the pass and saving your lunch break for the Mattertal viewpoint.)

Augstbord to Jungen

- **Segment Stat:** 4.6 miles (one-way) from Augstbord Pass to Jungen
- **Total Distance to Jungun:** 8.2 miles (one way)
- **Ending Elevation:** 6,562-ft.
- **Elevation Gain/Loss for Augstbord Pass:** -2,933-ft.

To continue to Jungen (2-hr 45-min) and St Niklaus, follow the trail as it descends from the pass on steep, scree-covered slopes beneath the south facing slopes of the Schwarzhorn. After walking a half mile the grade moderates as the path wanders through boulder-strewn meadows, crossing a few rockslides along the way.

Soon the trail curves to the right (south) and passes through a narrow gap in the rocks at 4.5 miles (0.9 miles from the pass). Beyond the gap the grade steepens as the trail curves to the left, descending through rocky meadows along the north side of the valley.

Reach a "Y" intersection at 4.7 miles where signs point left (northeast) to Embd and Moosealp. Take the trail branching right (east) for Jungen and St Niklaus. (The transportation links from Jungen to either Grachen or Zermatt are more frequent than the buses from Embd and Moosealp.)

The trail soon turns to the right (south), descending to cross a gully to the south side of the valley. Here the path begins to ascend on easy to moderate grades, heading southeast on a well-laid path through a long boulder field.

Reach the top of the boulder field at 5.9 miles. Turn around for nice views of Augstbord Pass to the west. Continue climbing for a short distance to a small shoulder jutting from the ridge at 6.0 miles. Here marvelous views open to the confluence of the Matter and Saas valleys and the surrounding peaks.

Beyond the shoulder the narrow trail clings to the hillside, following a roller coaster course through rocky meadows. There is a feeling of exposure along this section of the route, which may make some members of your party uncomfortable.

Reach a grassy knoll with stunning, panoramic vistas at 6.3 miles. The knoll is a great place for a picnic or to take a break while admiring the views. The Bernese Alps fill the skyline to the north. The peaks of the Mischabel range, including the Nadelhorn, Lenzspitze and the Dom, rise above the east side of the Mattertal while the Weisshorn, Bishorn and Brunegghorn dominate to view to the southwest. Monte Rosa, Lyskamm and the Breithorn tower above the head of the Mattertal valley to the south. In the distance are the peaks flanking the east side of the Saas Valley.

Continue the hike by following the trail as it descends southeast on moderate grades. Turn left toward Jungen at a signed junction at 6.5 miles and follow the trail as it drops steeply down a series of switchbacks through meadows and clusters of larch trees.

Reach a somewhat confusing intersection at 7.0 miles. Here signs point straight ahead toward Juntal. We turn left on the unmarked trail that heads downhill on switchbacks toward Jungen. (Don't take the trail toward Juntal.) At the next signed junction turn right toward Jungen (Jungu 35-min and St. Niklaus). The rest of the way Jungen (Jungu) is on a good, well-marked trail.

At Jungen (6,562-ft.) follow the signed path toward the Luftseilbahn (10-min) passing a small lake along the way. Reach the small cable car descending to St Niklaus at 8.2 miles. You can either take the lift from Jungen to St. Niklaus or walk down to St. Niklaus on a series of very steep, knee-jarring switchbacks. The lift is the recommended option. Note: The 4 person lift takes an extended lunch break. Do not be disheartened if a large group of people are waiting for the lift. Once started, the lift runs continuously until everyone is down.

While the trail between Gruben and Jungen is quite steep, is not overly difficult thanks to well-engineered switchbacks facilitating the climb to the pass. There is no place for refreshments along the way, so pack a lunch and take plenty of water.

This trail can easily be walked in reverse. Frequent trains run between Zermatt and St. Niklaus. At St. Niklaus catch the cable car to Jungen. (See the Jungen Luftseilbahn (Jungen cable car) schedule for more information.) Hikers staying in Grachen can take the bus from Grachen to the St. Niklaus Bahnhof (train station) and then the lift to Jungen. In Jungen, follow the trail signs to Augstbord Pass.

Check the weather forecast before setting out from Gruben. Sections of the trail are very difficult to follow in thick fog and the high exposed slopes should be avoided during thunderstorms.

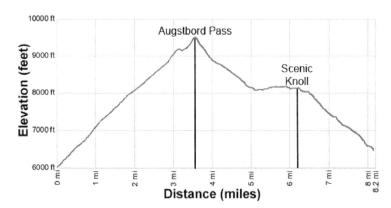

Trailhead Directions

Directions from the Hotel Schwarzhorn in Gruben: This trail starts behind (south side) of the Schwarzhorn Hotel in Gruben

From Zermatt to Jungen: If walking the trail in reverse, take the train from Zermatt to St. Niklaus. In the height of the summer trains depart every half hour. The ride takes about 35 minutes. In St. Niklaus, walk to the southwest end of the train stations (in the direction of Zermatt) and turn right (west) on the first street beyond the train station, which drops down to an underpass beneath the main Visp-Zermatt highway. On the other side of the underpass turn right (northeast) and walk up the road to the Jungen Cable Car station (the Jungen Luftseilbahn).

Les Hauderes and Arolla
Location: The Val d'Herens in the Valais

Val d'Herens (Herens Valley) heads southeast from Sion in the Rhone Valley into the Pennine Alps. At the village of Les Hauderes, the Val d'Arolla (Arolla Valley) splits off to the right (southwest) while the Val d'Herens continues its southeasterly course ending in a scenic cirque, formed by the Grand Cornier, Dent Blanche, Tete Blanche and the ridge of peaks rising to the north of the Aiguille de la Tsa along the Swiss-Italian border. Two long rivers of ice: the Mont Mine and Ferpecle glaciers, separated by a ridge running north from Tete Blanche to Mont Mine, spill down the slopes at the head of the cirque.

The road up the Arolla Valley ends at the village of Arolla, situated beneath a spectacle of rock and ice, anchored by Mont Collon. The Aiguille de la Tsa and Dents de Bertol rim the valley to the west while Aiguilles Rouges d'Arolla and Pigne d'Arolla rise to the east. Monte Brule, L'Eveque and the Petit Mont Collon grace the skyline beyond Mont Collon.

Les Hauderes, set beneath the Dents de Veisivi at the confluence of the Val d'Herens and the Val d'Arolla, is a traditional village with an interesting collection of old wood Valaisian homes decorated with colorful flower boxes in the summer. A stay here gives visitors a taste of what Switzerland was like before the onslaught of the ski industry.

The main part of the quaint village, along the east side of the Valley's main road, includes hotels, bed and breakfasts and restaurants in old chalet style buildings. There are also some vacation rentals. A Denner grocery, the Butcher Les Hauderes and cheese shop, along with two sporting goods stores, are situated along the main road. A good bakery is found across from the main bus stop in the center of the village. Camping Molignon is located just north of the village along the river.

Arolla, nestled beneath the foot of Mont Collon and the Pigne d'Arolla, is known as a mountaineering center. The small hamlet includes two basic groceries, a few hotels and restaurants, an outdoor store, post office and Tourist Information office located around the main square. Here you will also find the bus stop. Camping Arolla is located along the valley floor on the east side of the river before the village.

Both villages are popular stops on the Walker's Haute Route. They also make fine base camps for hikers interested in exploring these quiet valleys off the main tourist track. The hikes on the Walker's Haute Route, including the Col de Reidmatten (Hike 38), the Pas de Chavres (Hike 39) and the Col de Torrent (Hike 35), make for great out-and-back day hikes. Walk from Arolla to Pra Gra (Hike (Hike 40a) with terrific views of the high peaks rimming the head of the Arolla Valley. Extend the day by continuing to the Cabane des Aiguilles Rouges (Hike 40b) and Lac Bleu. For an easier day simply walk between Arolla and Les Hauderes via Lac Bleu and la Gouille (Hike 40c). Staying in the valley also offers the opportunity to visit Bricola (Hike 37), a lovely overlook with front row seat to the Ferpecle Glacier and the high peaks ringing the head of the Val d'Herens. Regularly scheduled buses facilitate travel between Arolla and Les Hauderes as well as other locations in the Val d'Herens.

Getting to Les Hauderes and Arolla

Take the train to Sion Gare (train station), a stop on the main line along the Rhone Valley. On the northwest side of the station is a bus depot. Board a bus bound for Les Hauderes center. The ride takes 47 minutes. To reach Arolla take the bus to Les Hauderes and then change to the bus headed to Arolla (five minute connection). The total time from Sion to Arolla is one hour and 17 minutes.

Nearby Attractions & Rainy Day Activities

There is a lot to do on a rainy day in **Sion** (sion.ch), an easy trip from Les Hauderes or Arolla. The Chateau de Tourbillon, a castle built in the 1300's for the Bishop of Sion, and the Valere Basilica, a 13th century church are set atop two adjacent hills on the east side of the city. The town is also home to interesting art, history and nature museums. Another enjoyable option is to walk around the old town. See the Sion Tourism Site for more options.

Good Things to Know about Les Hauderes and Arolla

- Les Hauderes and Arolla are in the French part of the Valais. People in the hotels typically speak French, German and English.
- La Sage/Villaz, a small hamlet located up the road to the northeast of Les Hauderes, also includes lodging primarily used by hikers on the Haute Route.
- Don't expect high speed internet connections or TV's with excellent cable access. These are simply villages where the emphasis is on outdoor activities and interaction with family and friends.
- There are five huts and mountain refuges in the Val d'Herens and Val de Arolla. Access to some the huts require crossing glaciers and are only recommended for experienced, properly equipped parties.

Maps: Les Hauderes, Lac de Moiry and Bricola

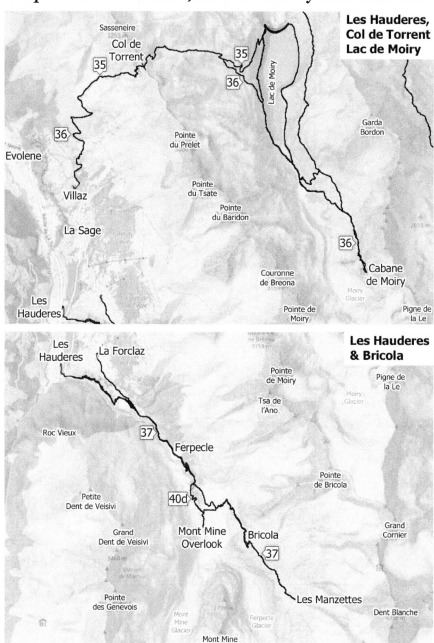

35. Col de Torrent: Les Hauderes to Lac de Moiry ☆☆☆☆☆

Distance: 7.3 miles (one way)

Near Les Hauderes in the Valais

Hikers making the steep climb over the Col de Torrent from La Sage, Villaz to Lac de Moiry are rewarded with splendid views of the high peaks and glaciers towering above the Val d' Herens, Val d' Arolla and the Val de Moiry.

Distance: 3.7 miles (one way) / 7.4 miles (round-trip) to Col Torrent 7.3 miles (one way) to Lac de Moiry from Les Hauderes via Col Torrent
Elevation: 5,716-ft. at Trailhead 9,576-ft. at Col Torrent 7,381-ft. at Lac de Moiry
Elevation Gain: 3,860-ft. - Col Torrent -2,190-ft. to Lac de Moiry

Difficulty: strenuous
Basecamp: Les Hauderes, Arolla
Les Hauderes North Map: See page 175
Online Map/Photos: www.hikingwalking.com/col-torrent

Why Hike from Les Hauderes to Lac de Moiry via the Col de Torrent

One of the most scenic legs of the Walker's Haute Route is trail from Les Hauderes over the Col de Torrent to the Lac de Moiry. The hike, featuring stunning views of three glacial valleys, travels through pretty meadows, crosses a panoramic pass and then visits a shimmering lake with the Moiry Glacier as a backdrop.

The hike starts with a short bus ride from Les Hauderes to La Sage Villaz, which save considerable time and eliminates a 900-ft. climb. From Le Sage, the trail ascends steeply through lovely meadows along the east side of the Val d' Herens. Views soon open to Dent Blanche, Dent d' Herens and the massive glacier field at the head of the valley.

176

Towering above Les Hauderes is the Grande Dent De Veisivi, situated at the end of the long ridge separating the Val d' Herens from Val d' Arolla. To the southwest the Pigne d' Arolla dominates the view at the head of the Arolla Valley. To the north Diablerets rises above the Rhone Valley. As you climb to the Col (pass), views of the high peaks and glaciers expand and improve.

From the Col de Torrent the Grande Dent De Veisivi, Pigne d'Arolla, Les Aiguilles Rouges d'Arolla, Mont Blanc de Cheilon and the Grand Combin dominate the magnificent view to the southwest. Dent d'Herens rises above the glaciers cascading down the flanks of the Tete Blanche to the south. To the east, the Weisshorn looms above the ridges lining the eastern wall of the Moiry Valley.

Beyond the pass the trail drops steeply from the ridge and then passes lovely Lac des Autannes with wonderful views of Dent Blanche, the Grand Cornier and the Glacier de Moiry spilling down the flanks of the peaks encircling the head of the Val de Moiry. The rest of the hike enjoys fine views of the Moiry Valley as it drops to the dam at the head of the Lac de Moiry.

The hike can be extended by hiking down to Grimentz from the dam and/or walking up from Les Hauderes to La Sage, Villaz. Another option is to hike to the Cabane de Moiry (Moiry Hut). This strenuous route splits off from the farm of the Alpage de Torrent and then drops down to the head of the Lac de Moiry before climbing to the Cabane for a 9.5 mile hike that gains an additional 1,800-ft. The climb to the hut can be quite tiring at the end of a long day. See Hike 35 - Les Hauderes to the Cabane de Moiry via the Col de Torrent for more information.

La Sage, Villaz to Col Torrent

- **Distance from Trailhead:** 3.7 miles (one way)
- **Elevation at Col de Torrent:** 9,576-ft.
- **Elevation Gain:** 3,860-ft.

The trail from Les Hauderes to the Col de Torrent is 5.9 miles and gains of almost 4,800-feet. If you are a purist and wish to walk the entire way – go for it. Otherwise, I strongly recommend taking the bus from the Les Hauderes Post to La Sage, Villaz. The six minute ride reduced the distance by 2.2 miles and eliminates 900-ft. from the climb. It also allows you to get to the pass earlier in the day, always a good idea for the best views and to beat the clouds that typically build in the afternoons. (See trailhead directions below.)

From the bus stop in the small village of La Sage Villaz, walk back down the main road about 150-feet and turn left (northeast) on a road with hiking signs pointing toward Mayens de Cotter (50-min), Col de Torrent (3-hr 15-min) and Moiry Barrage (dam) (4-hr 45-min). At the next intersection turn right in the direction of Col de Torrent and Grimentz. Shorty beyond the turn the road curves to the left (northeast) and starts climbing steeply through pastures. As you ascend views open to Pigne d' Arolla (12,454-ft.) at the head of the Arolla Valley to the southwest.

Soon the road curves to the right (northwest) and changes to a dirt track. At 0.4 miles reach a junction where you continue straight ahead on a road ascending along the right (southeast) side of a small stream. (Do not turn left on the road crossing the stream).

Where the road makes a hairpin curve to the right, we bear slightly left on a trail that continues ascending alongside the creek. A wood sign at the junctions points toward the Col de Torrent and Cotter.

Soon the trail crosses the creek on a wood bridge and then curves to the right (north/northeast) zig-zagging steeply up the hillside through pretty pastures. Views open southeast to Dent Blanche and the massive glacier field at the head of the Val d'Herens.

Pass a junction with a minor trail branching to the left (north) toward Cotter and Volovron at 0.6 miles. Continue on the main trail ascending toward the Col de Torrent.

At 0.8 miles turn right (east) onto a gravel road and travel a short distance along the road as it skirts the north side of a stone house. Past the house, where the road curves to the left, a signed trail branches left toward the Col de Torrent. Follow the trail as it climbs on moderate grades through pastures, cutting off a long switchback on the road. As you climb, enjoy stunning views of the high peaks and glaciers at the head of the Val d'Herens and the Arolla Valley to the south.

Reach Mayens de Cotter, a small hamlet, and the continuation of the road at 1.1 miles. Turn left on the road in the direction of Cotter (5-min), Beplan (1-hr 15-min) and the Col de Torrent (2-hr 15-min). Pass two houses on the left (south) side of the road. Just before reaching a house on the right (north) side of the road, take the trail branching to the right (northwest) signed for the Beplan, Col de Torrent and Moiry Barrage (dam).

The trail now climbs through pastures in a northerly direction on long, steep switchbacks. As you ascend, splendid views open to Les Aiguilles Rouges d'Arolla, a ridge of jagged peaks along the west side of the Arolla Valley. To the north Les Diablerets rises above the Rhone Valley.

At 1.9 miles arrows on a rock insure your follow the trail as it curves to the left (northwest). The grade now eases a bit as the path continues its ascent up the east side of the valley. Ahead is a cross mounted on a rock outcropping. Soon views open to the ridge separating the Val d'Herens and the Val de Moiry. The peak rising to the north on the ridge is Sasseneire. The saddle of the ridge to the southeast of Sasseneire is the Col de Torrent.

The trail curves to the right at 2.3 miles, heading northeast toward the ridge. Reach a small pond at Beplan (8,320-ft.) at 2.6 miles. Follow the trail as it skirts the east side of the pond and soon curves to the right (northeast), ascending steeply toward the pass. At 3.3 miles start the final steep climb to the pass on a series of tight switchbacks ascending through rocky meadows and scree covered slopes.

Reach the Col de Torrent (9,576-ft.) at 3.7 miles. Here a magnificent panorama of high peaks, including the Grande Dent De Veisivi, Mont Brule, Pigne d'Arolla, Les Aiguilles Rouges d'Arolla, Mont Blanc de Cheilon and the Grand Combin, dominate the view to the southwest. Dent d'Herens peeks above the Glacier de Ferpecle and Glacier du Mont Mine flowing down the flanks of the Tete Blanche at the head of the Val d' Herens. To the east the Weisshorn looms above the low ridges lining the eastern wall of the Moiry Valley. Below the east side of the pass Lac de Autannes glistens in the sun.

Col Torrent to the Lac de Moiry

- **Segment Stat:** 3.6 miles (one-way) from Col Torrent to Lac de Moiry
- **Total Distance:** 7.3 miles (one way) from La Sage to Lac de Moiry
- **Ending Elevation:** 7,381-ft.
- **Elevation Gain/Loss:** -2,190-ft.

When you are ready to continue the hike, follow the trail as it drops steeply down the east side of the pass. Soon views open to the peaks and glaciers on the ridge rimming the east side of the Moiry Valley and, beyond the ridge, the Val de Zinal. At 4.4 miles the grade eases as the trail passes to the north of the Lac des Autannes. The lake enjoys wonderful views of Dent Blanche, the Grand Cornier and the Glacier de Moiry spilling down the cirque at the head of the Val de Moiry. The lake is a popular picnic spot and a great place to take a break.

Beyond the lake the views toward the head of the valley continue to expand and improve. At 5.0 miles the grade steepens as the trail drops through pretty meadows and passes a small stone house. Reach the farm of the Alpage de Torrent at 5.5 miles. Here a trail splits off the right (south/southeast) toward the head of the Lac de Moiry, the Moiry Glacier and the Cabane de Moiry. We continue straight ahead toward the Moiry Barrage (50-min) and Grimentz (2-hr 20-min).

Soon the trail joins a farm road descending on moderate grades toward the Lac de Moiry. At 5.8 miles the road swings to the left (northeast), and continues its descent to the dam at the foot of the lake. Reach the western end of the Barrage de Moiry (7,381-ft.) at 6.8 miles. Here signs point north to a trail dropping steeply down to Grimentz (1-hr 40-min), losing over 2,250-ft. in 3.8 miles.

We turn right (east) and cross the top of the dam on a wide paved road. Reach the cafe and bus stop at the eastern end of the barrage at 7.2 miles. During the summer regularly scheduled buses depart for Grimentz, Zinal and the head of Lac Moiry.

The hike can be extended by hiking down to Grimentz from the dam and/or walking up from Les Hauderes to La Sage, Villaz. Another option is to hike to the Cabane de Moiry (Moiry Hut). This strenuous route splits off from the farm (Alpage de Torrent) and then drops down to the head of the Lac de Moiry before climbing to the Cabane for a 9.59 mile hike that gains an additional 1,800-ft. on the climb to the hut. The climb to the hut can be quite tiring at the end of a long day. See Hike 36 - Les Hauderes to the Cabane de Moiry via the Col de Torrent for more information.

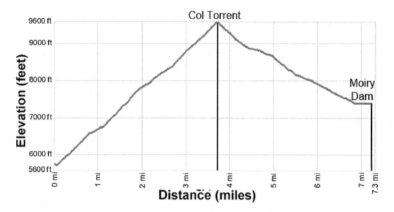

Trailhead Directions

From Les Hauderes Centre: Take Bus 383 in the direction of La Forclaz and get off at La Sage, Villaz. From the bus stop in the small village of La Sage, Villaz, walk back down the main road for about 150-feet and turn left (east) on a road with hiking signs pointing toward Mayens de Cotter (50-min), Col de Torrent (3-hr 15-min) and Moiry Barrage (dam) (4-hr 45-min). The ride to La Sage, Villaz from the Les Hauderes takes 6 minutes and saves almost 900-ft. of altitude gain. Schedules are posted at the bus stop at the square in the center of Les Hauderes, online at the SBB website and on the SBB app.

From the Moiry Barrage to Grimentz or Zinal: At the dam, board a bus headed toward Zinal or Vissoie. There are several stops in Grimentz, about a 20 minute ride from the dam. If you are headed to Zinal, the best bet is to catch a bus headed directly to Zinal. Otherwise, take the Vissoie Bus to Vissoie where you need to change to a bus headed up valley to Zinal. The direct buses take a little over a half hour. If you need to change in Vissoie the ride will take an hour and 15 minute or more depending on the time of day. Schedules are posted at the bus stop by the dam, online at the SBB website and on the SBB app.

36. Col de Torrent: Les Hauderes to Cabane de Moiry ☆☆☆☆☆

Distance: 9.5 miles (one way)

Near Les Hauderes in the Valais

A strenuous day hiking over the Col de Torrent followed by a climb to the Cabane de Moiry features amazing views of the glacier-clad summits towering above the Val d'Herens, the Val d'Arolla and the Val de Moiry. The challenging climb to the hut features breathtaking view of the Moiry Glacier.

Distance: 3.7 miles (one way) to Col Torrent	**Difficulty:** difficult
9.5 miles (one way) to Cabane de Moiry	**Basecamp:** Les Hauderes, Arolla
Elevation: 5,716-ft. at Trailhead	**Les Hauderes North Map:**
9,576-ft. at Col Torrent	See page 175
9,268-ft. at Cabane de Moiry	**Online Map/Photos:**
Elevation Gain: 3,860-ft. - Col Torrent	www.hikingwalking.com/
5,726-ft. / -2,174-ft. to Cabane de Moiry	torrent-moiry

Why Hike from Les Hauderes to Cabane de Moiry via the Col de Torrent

The hike over the Col de Torrent to the Cabane de Moiry is considered one of the most scenic legs on the Walker's Haute route and also one of the most strenuous. Hikers are well compensated for their efforts with grand views of three magnificent glacial valleys, panoramic vistas from the Col de Torrent and dramatic, up-close views of the Moiry Glacier.

I strongly recommend starting the hike by taking the bus from Les Hauderes to La Sage Villaz, which saves time and eliminates a 900-ft. climb. From La Sage the trail ascends through beautiful meadows and then scree covered slopes along the east side of the Val d'Herens to the Col de Torrent. Breathtaking views accompanying the hike extend to the head of the Val d'Herens where a cirque of the 11,000 to 14,000-ft. peaks soar above a massive ice sheet spilling down the valley that separates into two separate flows, the Glacier de Ferpecle and Glacier du Mont Mine. To the north Diablerets rises above the Rhone Valley.

As you gain elevation views expand, stretching southwest to the summits, clad in glistening glaciers, towering over the Arolla Valley. On a clear day vistas extend beyond Arolla to Mont Blanc de Cheilon and the Grand Combin.

As you crest the pass views open east to the Weisshorn towering above the ridge rimming the eastern wall of the Moiry Valley. From the pass the trails drops steeply from the ridge and then passes the lovely Lac des Autannes, with wonderful views of Dent Blanche, the Grand Cornier and the Glacier de Moiry flowing down the flanks of the peaks encircling the head of the Val de Moiry.

Above the alp at Montagne de Torrent (Alpage de Torrent) our path splits from the main route dropping down to the dam at the foot of the Lac de Moiry. Here we bear right on a trail descending southeast that soon joins the trail along the lake shore leading to the head of the lake. Along the way the high peaks towering above the Val de Moiry and the Moiry Glacier grow in stature.

Beyond the lake the trail ascends to a road that connects with the path climbing to the Cabane de Moiry. The 1.8 mile hike to the Cabane gains an additional 1,800-ft. This is a tough ascent at the end of a long day but the amazing views of the Moiry Glacier, a river of ice spilling down the north face of the Grand Cornier, will help take you mind off the stiff climb.

Overall, the 9.5 mile hike from La Sage Villaz to the Cabane gains over 5,700-ft. If you prefer an easier day, hike over the Col and drop down to the dam at the head of the Lac de Moiry. Here you can either descend to Grimentz or take the bus to Grimentz or Zinal. (See Hike 35 - Col de Torrent: Les Hauderes to Lac de Moiry for more information on this option.)

La Sage Villaz to Col Torrent

- **Distance from Trailhead:** 3.7 miles (one way)
- **Elevation at the Col Torrent:** 9,576-ft.
- **Elevation Gain:** 3,860-ft.

The trail from Les Hauderes to the Col de Torrent is 5.9 miles and gains of almost 4,800-feet. If you are a purist and wish to walk the entire way – go for it. Otherwise, I strongly recommend taking the bus from the Les Hauderes Post to La Sage, Villaz. The six minute ride reduced the distance by 2.2 miles and eliminates 900-ft. from the climb. It also allows you to get to the pass earlier in the day, always a good idea for the best views and to beat the clouds that typically build in the afternoons. (See trailhead directions below.)

From the bus stop in the small village of La Sage Villaz, walk back down the main road about 150-feet and turn left (northeast) on a road with hiking signs pointing toward Mayens de Cotter (50-min), Col de Torrent (3-hr 15-min) and Moiry Barrage (dam) (4-hr 45-min). The trail now climbs to the Col de Torrent. For a detailed description of this section of the trail see the first segment of Hike 35 - Les Hauderes to the Lac de Moiry Barrage.

Col Torrent to Cabane de Moiry

- **Segment Stat:** 5.8 miles (one-way) - Col Torrent to Cabane de Moiry
- **Total Distance to the Cabane de Moiry:** 9.5 miles (one way)
- **Elevation at the Cabane de Moiry:** 9,256-ft.
- **Elevation Gain/Loss to the Cabane de Moiry:** 1,866-ft./-2,174-ft.

When you are ready to continue the hike, follow the trail as it drops steeply down the east side of the pass. Soon views open to the peaks on the ridge rimming the east side of the Moiry Valley and the summits rising beyond the ridge in the Zinal Valley. At 4.4 miles the grade eases as the trail passes to the north of the Lac des Autannes. The lake enjoys wonderful views of Dent Blanche, the Grand Cornier and the Glacier de Moiry spilling down the cirque at the head of the Val de Moiry. The lake is a popular picnic spot and a great place to take a break.

Beyond the lake the views toward the head of the valley continues to expand and improve. At 5.0 miles the grade steepens as the trail drops through pretty meadows. Reach a junction just past an interesting stone building (and before reaching the Alpage de Torrent). Here we turn right (south/southeast) on the trail toward the head of the Lac de Moiry, the Moiry Glacier and the Cabane de Moiry. The path straight ahead leads to the Moiry Barrage (Dam) (50-min) and Grimentz (2-hr 20-min).

The trail now descends steeply through meadows to the path circling the Lac de Moiry at 6.1 miles. Ahead are terrific views of the high peaks and glaciers at the head of the Val de Moiry. Turn right (south) on the trail paralleling the lake shore and head toward the Cabane de Moiry. At the head of the lake the trail continues south/southeast, traveling through meadows on easy grades and then crossing a metal bridge over the lake's inlet stream at 6.9 miles. Beyond the stream the trail ascends to join the road at 7.4 miles.

Walk south along the road for a short distance, passing through a parking lot toward Lac de Chateaupre, a meltwater pond at the foot of the Moiry Glacier. Soon you will see signs pointing left (southeast) toward a broad track heading to the Cabane de Moiry (1-hr 25-min). Follow the trail as it skirts the north side of the Lac de Chateaupre, ascending through rocky meadows on easy grades. Views extend southeast to the Moiry Glacier. The Pointe de Mourti and Pointe de Moiry rise to the west above the river of ice.

At 7.8 miles the grade steepens as the path climbs the hillside along the east side of the glacier. Pass a junction at 8.1 miles with a trail, the Haute

Tour de Lac 2500m (Hike 29), branching left toward the Barrage de Moiry, Sorebois and Zinal. We continue straight ahead toward the Moiry Hut.

Beyond the junction the grade eases as the trail ascends atop the lateral moraine running along the east side of the glacier. At 8.3 miles the trail curves to the south, dops off the moraine crest and then travels up a rocky gully to the left (east) of the moraine. Use trails split off from the main track and climb to viewpoints along the moraine.

At 8.7 miles the trail starts climbing a series of very steep switchbacks up a rocky hillside, gaining 800-ft. in a half mile. Turn around and look northwest for nice views of the Pointe du Tsate and Sasseneire rising above the west side of the Lac de Moiry. Directly across the valley is the Couronne de Breona.

The grade abates at 9.3 miles and soon reaches the Cabane de Moiry (9,268-ft.) (Hike 28), an old stone hut with a modern copper-clad addition. at 9.4 miles. From the hut enjoy splendid, bird's-eye-views of the Moiry glacier.

For the best views follow a use trail that travels around the east side of the hut and then climbs to a rocky overlook (9,300-ft.) at 9.5 miles. To the north the glacier, covered with a morass of seracs and crevasses, spills down a steep incline. Pointe de Mourti, Tsa de l'Ano and Points de Moiry tower above the valley to the west. Pigne de la Le dominates the view to the south.

Note: There is a bus that runs from the Moiry Glacier parking lot to Grimentz and Zinal that is helpful if you run into bad weather or member of your party are unable to reach the hut. See the trailhead directions (below) for more information.

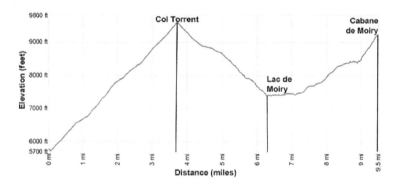

Trailhead Directions

From Les Ha;deres Centre: See Hike 35.

From the Moiry Glacier to Grimentz or Zinal: At the parking lot below the Moiry Glacier, board a bus headed toward Zinal or Vissoie. There are several stops in Grimentz, about a 28 minute ride from the dam. If you are headed to Zinal, the best bet is to catch a bus headed directly to Zinal. Otherwise, take the Vissoie Bus to Vissoie where you need to change for a bus headed up valley to Zinal. The direct buses take a little over 45 minutes.

If you need to change at Vissoie the ride will take an hour and 45 minutes or more, depending on the time of day. Schedules are posted at the bus stop, online at the SBB website and on the SBB app.

37. Bricola ☆☆☆☆☆
Distance: 6.0 - 13.0 miles (round trip)
Near Les Hauderes in the Valais

Two rivers of ice, surrounded by towering peaks, flow down the head of the Val d'Herens. This hike ascends the peaceful valley to the stunning viewpoint at Bricola, a high alp overlooking this spectacle of rock and ice. Extend the hike to Les Manzettes for even better views.

Distance: 10.0 miles (round trip) from La Forclaz to Bricola
12.8 miles (round trip) from La Forclaz to Les Manzettes
13.0 miles (round trip) La Forclaz - Les Manzettes - Les Hauderes
Elevation: 5,670-ft. at Trailhead (La Forclaz)
7,923-ft. at Bricola
8,972-ft. at Les Manzettes
4,835-ft. at Les Hauderes

Elevation Gain: 2,253-ft. to Bricola
3,162-ft. to Les Manzettes
-4,137-ft. to Les Hauderes
Difficulty: strenuous
Basecamp: Les Hauderes, Arolla
Les Hauderes and Bricola Map: See page 175
Online Map/Photos: www.hikingwalking.com/bricola

Why Hike to Bricola

This off-the-beaten path hike ascends to the beautiful meadows of the Bricola alp with dramatic views of two massive glaciers, separated by Mont Mine, at the head of the Val d'Herens. To the east of Mont Mine the Ferpecle Glacier tumbles steeply down the cirque rimmed by Tete Blanche, the Wandfluehorn and Dent Blanche. To the west of Mont Mine, Tete

Blanche, Dents de Bertol and the Aiguille de la Tsa tower above the Mont Mine Glacier.

Along the way the scenic trail travels through small alps and bucolic pastures before climbing steeply to Bricola. Fine views of the Ferpecle and Mont Mine Glacier accompany the hike.

Extend the day by ascending to the terminal moraine along the north side of Les Manzettes Glacier for more stunning views of Dent Blanche and the high peaks towering above the Ferpecle Glacier. On the return leg of the hike a short detour takes you to the foot of the Mont Mine Glacier with more great views of the rugged peaks towering above the river of ice.

Post buses can be used to shorten the hike and reduce the elevation gain. The buses are infrequent and best used at the start of the hike. On the return leg hikers should plan on walking back to Les Hauderes to avoid a long wait or miss the last bus of the day.

From La Forclaz to Bricola

- **Distance from Trailhead:** 10.0 miles (round trip)
- **Elevation at Bricola:** 7,923-ft.
- **Elevation Gain:** 2,253-ft

There are three option for starting this hike; Les Hauderes, La Forclaz and Ferpecle/Salay. This description assumes you take the early bus to La Forclaz. Subtract 2.0 miles (one-way) if you catch the later bus to Ferpecle/Salay. Add 0.8 miles (one way) and 635-ft. in elevation gain if walking from Les Hauderes. I recommend taking the bus to La Forclaz or Ferpecle/Salay and walking back to Les Hauderes.

Starting in Les Hauderes:
Distance: Les Hauderes (4,835-ft.) to Bricola (7,923-ft.): 5.2 miles
Les Hauderes (4,835-ft.) to Les Manzettes (8,972-ft.): 6.6 miles
Elevation gain: To Bricola: 3,088-ft.
To Les Manzettes: 4,137-ft.

Starting in La Forclaz:
Distance: La Forclaz (5,670-ft.) to Bricola (7,923-ft.): 5.0 miles
La Forclaz (5,670-ft.) to Les Manzettes (8,972-ft.): 6.4 miles
Elevation gain: To Bricola: 2,253-ft.
To Les Manzettes: 3,302-ft.

Starting in Ferpecle/Salay:
Distance: Ferpecle (5,810-ft.) to Bricola (7,923-ft.): 3.0 miles
Ferpecle (5,810-ft.) to Les Manzettes (8,972-ft.): 4.4 miles
Elevation gain: To Bricola: 2,113-ft.
To Les Manzettes: 3,162-ft.

Alternate Return Option
From Bricola to Mont Mine Overlook to Les Hauderes: 6.0 miles

From the bus stop at La Forclaz (see trailhead directions) walk southeast on the Route de Ferpecle toward Salay, Ferpecle and Bricola. Signs at the bus stop point the way. In the morning there is little traffic on the road. Ahead are fine views of Dent Blanche (14,291-ft.) and the Ferpecle and Mont Mine Glaciers at the head of the valley. Grand Dent de Veisivi (11,214-ft.) rises to the west.

The paved road descends on easy grades past houses which soon give way to pastures scattered with trees and alp buildings. At 1.0 mile reach an intersection were a yellow trail sign points to the right (south). Turn right on a two-track that descends through a cluster of trees. In 250-ft. turn left on the signed trail toward Salay, Ferpecle and Bricola.

Make note of this intersection. The track continuing to the right descends to Seppec and Les Hauderes. We will make use of this track on the return leg of the hike.

Soon the trail starts ascending on moderate grades through pastures sprinkled with wildflowers and trees, passing a few old wooden alp buildings along the way. The Borgne de Ferpecle, a lovely stream or rushing torrent, depending on the time of year, tumbles down the valley floor below the trail. Yellow diamonds, outlined in black, painted on buildings and rocks will help keep you on track.

At 1.6 miles the valley narrows and the trail rejoins the road. Follow the pave road as it ascends to the tiny hamlet of Le Salay at 2.0 miles. Head through the village on the paved road and soon pass the Le Salay/Ferpecle bus stop on the left side of the road.

Beyond the village the road crosses a creek on a bridge and then climbs through forest, ascending two switchbacks. Parking spaces along the lower switchback are for people visiting the Le Petite Paradis, a small café.

The road soon passes the cafe and then crosses a spillway for the Torrent de Rosses at 2.9 miles. At 3.0 miles reach Ferpecle. Turn left here on a signed trail toward Bricola. The continuation of the road crosses a bridge over the creek and then heads toward the Glacier du Mont Mine. A variation of the route back from Bricola uses this trail. See below for more information.

Note: Cars are not allowed beyond the turn off to Bricola. If you are driving, find a spot to park in the small lot along the right side of the road.

The grade now steepens as the trail climbs a wooded hillside. Intermittent meadows offer views of Mont Mine (9,560-ft.) and the Mont Mine Glacier. Dent de Veisivi and Pointe de Genevois (12,064-ft.) tower above the west side of the valley. You will also see a spillway for the dam, hidden by dense foliage below the trail. Turn around for views that extend down the Val d'Herens to the high peaks rising above the Rhone Valley.

At 3.4 miles the trees thin and the trail curves left, ascending a few switchbacks on easy grades through rocky meadows scattered with small larches and shrubs. To the south views open to Mont Mine rising between the Ferpecle and Mont Mine Glaciers. Dent de Bertol (11,890-ft.) and Bouquetines (12,592-ft.) rise above the head of the Mont Mine Glacier.

Reach a junction at 3.6 miles. Here a trail turns right, descending toward the Mont Mine Glacier. The sign for this trail simply says "Glacier". This is an alternate route for the return leg of the hike. For now, we bear left on the continuation of our trail to Bricola and the Bivouac Col de la Dent Blanche.

Our path ascends east and then southeast on steep grades up grassy slopes littered with rock outcroppings beneath the west facing flanks of the Pointe de Bricola (12,001-ft.). As you climb, views of the glaciers and jagged peaks rimming the head of the valley improve and evolve.

At 4.7 miles the grade abates and the trail now ascends on moderate to easy grades toward the stone buildings at Bricola, set against a scenic backdrop of peaks and glistening glaciers. At 4.8 miles reach Bricola, a meadow-clad bench with a large, three-story stone building and wood cross. Smaller stone sheds and other out buildings are located above the trail. To the southeast, the summit of Dent Blanche soars above the alp.

Pass between the buildings and soon reach an unmarked trail junction. Turn right on the boot beaten path that passes a few more building as it ascends through meadows to an overlook at the south end of the bench at 5.0 miles. Here stunning, panoramic views encompass the massive Ferpecle Glacier, tumbling steeply down the valley beneath the cirque rimmed by Mont Mine, Tete Blanche, the Wandfluehorn and Dent Blanche. Smaller glaciers; cling to the slopes beneath Dent Blanche.

To the west Mont Mine, Dents de Bertol, Aiguille de la Tsa, Pointe de Genevois and Veisivi tower above the deep trench carved by the Mont Mine Glacier. The leading edge of the Mont Mine Glacier lies beneath Bertol. Behind you views stretch down the Val d'Herens to the Rhone Valley. On a beautiful day the overlook is a great place for a picnic or just to take a break before continuing the hike.

At this point you have several choices.

- Turn around and retrace your steps back to La Forclaz and then take the bus back to Les Hauderes
- Turn around and walk back to Les Hauderes
- Continue beyond Bricola to a viewpoint along the terminal moraine beneath the Manzettes Glacier. This option follows the initial segment of the trail/route heading toward the Cabane de la Dent Blanche.

On the return journey you also have an option of taking the detour to the Mont Mine Glacier viewpoint.

To Les Manzettes

- **Segment Stat:** 2.8 miles (round-trip) from Bricola to Les Manzettes
- **Total Distance:** 12.8 miles (round trip) from La Forclaz

- **Maximum Elevation:** 8,972-ft.
- **Elevation Gain/Loss:** 3,162-ft.

From the overlook, return to the junction and turn right on the trail toward the head of the valley. The path climbs a switchback and then continues ascending on moderately to moderately steep grades up rocky meadows. Use care when crossing the streams at 5.2, 5.4 and 5.9 miles. (The second is typically dry later in the season.) The ascent enjoys terrific views of the Ferpecle Glacier and Dent Blanche.

As you climb the landscape become more rugged with meadows scattered with boulders. Just before crossing the second stream you will see signs pointing left to the route climbing to the Cabane Rossier. Above the trail we get glimpses of the summit of the Grand Cornier and the unnamed peaks towering above the east side of the valley.

At 6.0 miles the grade steepens and views open to the lateral moraine along the north side of the Les Manzettes Glacier. Follow the trail as it climbs switchbacks to the top of moraine at 6.2 miles. After a brief stint atop the moraine crest the trail continues its ascent along the moraine's rocky south facing slopes, eventually reaching the foot of the Manzettes glacier.

Only properly equipped parties should cross the glacier. Hikers should stop at 6.4 miles and find a place to enjoy the fabulous views of the Manzettes Glacier clinging to the rugged slopes beneath Dent Blanche. Mont Mine and the snow clad summit of Tete Blanche rise above the Ferpecle Glacier. The high peaks rimming the west side of the valley, along with the Mine Glacier, are seen beyond the Mont Mine ridge.

When you are done enjoying the views retrace your steps to Bricola.

Return Options to Les Hauderes

- **Total Distance:** 13.0 miles (round trip) from La Forclaz
- **Maximum Elevation:** 4,835-ft.
- **Elevation Gain/Loss:** -4,137-ft.

To walk back to Les Hauderes, simply retrace your steps for 3.7 miles from Bricola or 5.0 miles from Manzettes, back to the junction with the two-track and the trail described earlier. Here you will find signs pointing toward Seppec/Les Hauderes. Bear left toward Les Hauderes on the two track.

The two-track road descends on easy grades to the hamlet of Seppac and then turns left, dropping through pastures before turning right in half a mile and traveling along a trail that parallels the east/northeast side of the Borgne de Ferpecle (stream). This trail descends on moderate to steep grades through meadows and forest back to Les Hauderes. Total mileage for the return journey is 5.2 miles from Bricola or 6.6 miles from the Manzettes viewpoint.

Return to Les Hauderes with Side Trip to the Mont Mine Viewpoint

On the return leg of the hike a short detour will take you to the Mont Mine Glacier Viewpoint. From Bricola, retrace your steps for 1.5 miles to the junction with the "Glacier" sign. Turn left in the direction of the "Glacier." The path now descends through meadows scatter with trees, passing a small building constructed with cinder blocks.

Reach a bridge over the Borgne de Ferpecle at 1.7 miles. Rocks beside the raging torrent offer great views stretching south to Dents de Bertol and Mont Mine rising above the Mine Glacier. Cross the bridge, turn left and then walk 0.2 miles to the end of the trail and the Mont Mine Glacier Viewpoint for more fine vistas of the river of ice spilling down to the valley floor.

When you are done viewing the glacier follow the road along the west side of the stream back to Ferpecle and then retrace your steps to La Forclaz or walk back to Les Hauderes, following the directions above. The detour to the glacier viewpoint adds about 0.7 miles to the hike.

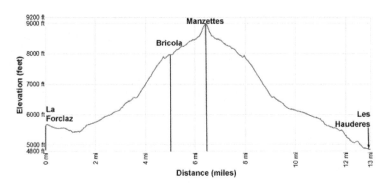

Trailhead Directions

From Les Hauderes: From the main bus stop in Les Hauderes, take Bus 383 to La Forclaz. The bus stop is located in the large square across from the Hotel des Hauderes. There are about five buses a day and the ride takes 16 minutes. The second bus of the day, leaving later in the morning, typically goes all the way to Ferpecle/Salay. The easy walk from La Forclaz to Ferpecle/Salay is 2.05 miles on a road with very little traffic where you can make great time. See the SBB website or download the SBB app for the appropriate bus schedule. Be sure to select La Forclaz, VS to get the correct route.

Alternatively you can walk all the way from Les Hauderes. Find the trailhead signs in the center of town. Then follow the signs toward Ferpecle and Bricola. The walk from Les Hauderes to Bricola is 5.2 miles and gains 3,088-ft.

190

There are only a few buses in the afternoon from either Ferpecle or La Forclaz back to Les Hauderes. Typically it is easier/faster to walk all the way back Les Hauderes as opposed to walking back to La Forclaz or Ferpecle and waiting for the bus.

Hikers with a car can drive to La Forclaz and then turn left on the Route de Ferpecle, following the road for 3.0 miles to Ferpecle where you will find parking places.

Map: Arolla Area Trails

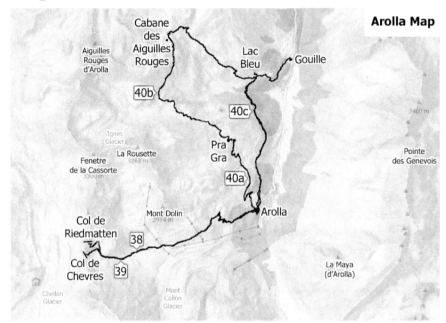

38. Col de Riedmatten ★★★★
Distance: Distance: 7.2 miles (round trip)
Near Les Hauderes in the Valais

This beautiful trail, showcasing the peaks rising along the east and south sides of the Arolla Valley, leads to a pass on a rugged ridge with fine vistas of the Glacier de Cheilon flowing down the Val des Dix, Mont Blanc de Cheilon and Le Pleureur.

Distance: 7.2 miles (round trip)
Elevation: 6,602-ft. at Trailhead
Maximum elevation: 9,679-ft.
Elevation Gain: 3,077-ft.
Difficulty: moderately-strenuous

Basecamp: Les Hauderes, Arolla
Arolla Map: See page 191
Online Map/Photos:
www.hikingwalking.com/reidmatten

Why Hike to the Col de Riedmatten

The walk to the Col de Riedmatten is delightful, traveling through beautiful meadows with splendid views of the glaciers spilling down the slopes of the Pigne d'Arolla. To the east/southeast (behind you), the jagged peaks towering above the east side of the Arolla Valley, including Dent de Perroc, Pointe des Genevois and Aiguille de la Tsa, fill the skyline.

The pass, located on the rugged ridge separating the Val d'Arolla and Val des Dix, enjoys fine views of Mont Blanc de Cheilon rising above the Glacier de Cheilon, a river of ice flowing down the flanks of the peak. To the west, La Luette, Le Pleureur and Le Sale grace the skyline. To the southeast, Mont Collon and the Bouquetins massif dominate the view. On a clear day the top of the Matterhorn joins the scene.

The Col de Riedmatten is within 800-ft. of a second pass on the ridge, the Pas de Chevres, which is 250-ft. lower than Riedmatten. In my opinion the views of Mont Blanc de Cheilon are better from the viewpoint above the Col de Riedmatten while the views to the east of Mont Collon and the Bouquetins massif are slightly better from the Pas de Chevres.

If you are simply doing an out-and-back hike from Arolla I would choose the Col de Riedmatten because of the views of the Val des Dix from the overlook above the pass. The pass also tends to be less crowded.

Pas de Chevres is the best choice for hikers heading to Cabane des Dix (Dix Hut) on the west side of the Cheilon glacier. For more information see Hike 39 - Pas de Chevres.

Note: From the Col de Riedmatten, a very steep trail drops down to the talus slopes above the lateral moraine on the east side of the Cheilon Glacier. Cables and chains along the upper section of the trail provided a level of security down a very steep section with loose, unstable rock. The trail then heads northwest, descending along the moraine and then crosses to the west side valley along the bed of the retreating glacier. Note: Rockfall is also an issue on the descent during inclement weather. Before setting out, check current condition in Arolla.

Arolla to Col de Riedmatten

In the the small village of Arolla, find the hiking signs on the west side of the town square (across from the bus stop). Walk southwest toward Pas de Chevres (2-hr 30-min) and Col de Riedmatten (2-hr 40-min).

At the first hairpin curve in the road, about 100 yards from the signpost, leave the road and continue along a track heading south/southwest. Follow the track as it switchbacks up a wooded hillside on moderate grades. At 0.3 miles pass a sign for the trail to Pra Gra and the Aiguilles Rouges branching to the right (north/northwest). Our trail goes left (southwest) toward the Pas de Chevres and Col de Riedmatten.

Follow the trail as it passes a few building and then skirts the north side of the Grand Hotel Kurhaus. Beyond the hotel the trail curves to the left, ascending west/southwest on moderately-steep grades up the Montagne d'Arolla valley. Openings in the trees offer intermittent views of the glaciers spilling down the rugged slopes of the Pigne d'Arolla to the south.

Ignore the trail at 0.6 miles branching left (south) toward the Cabane Vignettes. At 0.75 miles our trail turns left (southwest) on a road. After traveling a short distance along the road reach a trail junction near a restaurant. Turn right (west) toward Col de Riedmatten and Pas de Chevres.

The trail now climbs moderately steep switchbacks through meadows with grand views of Pigne d'Arolla. Mont Colon towers above the head of the Arolla Valley to the southeast. At 1.3 miles the trail curves to the left (southwest) and ascends steeply to meet a dirt road at the signed junction of Remointse d'Arolla at 1.5 miles.

Cross the road and continue traveling southwest on a trail that pass to the right (north) of the photogenic ruins of a few old stone buildings. Signs near the ruins point to Pas de Chevre (1-hr 35-min), Col de Riedmatten (1-hr 30-min) and Barrage Dix (Dix Dam: 4-hr 35-min).

Beyond the ruins the trail heads west/southwest on moderately-easy grades through rocky meadows sprinkled with wildflowers along the base of

Mont Collon and the rugged crags to the north of the trail. Red and white blazes on rocks keep you on track. To the east (behind you) the jagged peaks towering above the east side of the Arolla Valley, including Dent d'Perroc, Pointe des Genevois and Aiguille de la Tsa, fill the skyline. To the south are splendid views of the glaciers cascading down the flanks of the Pigne d'Arolla massif.

Cross a wood bridge over the creek draining the cirque to the north at 2.5 miles. Soon the grade steepens as the trail starts ascending along the north side of the valley. As the path curves to the right (north), views open to the Pas de Chevres, a saddle on the ridge at the head of the valley.

Reach a junction at 3.2 miles. Here the trail to Pas de Chevres splits off to the left (west). We continue heading north climbing very steeply up rocky meadows toward the Col de Riedmatten. Soon the trail curves to the west, crosses a scree covered slope and then ascends very steep switchbacks to the Col de Riedmatten (9,577-ft.) at 3.6 miles. As you climb watch for chamoix, a goat-like antelope, grazing in the meadows around the pass.

The pass is really just a notch in the ridge. For the best views, climb the ridge to the north of the pass to a knoll. Here panoramic vistas extend south to Mont Blanc de Cheilon rising above the Glacier de Cheilon, a river of ice flowing the flanks of the peak. To the west, La Luette, Le Pleureur and Le Sale fill the skyline. Look carefully across the Cheilon Glacier to see the Cabane des Dix (hut) sitting atop a rocky knob. To the southeast, Mont Collon and the Bouquetins massif dominate the view. On a clear day the top of the Matterhorn graces the horizon.

From the Col de Riedmatten, a narrow, very steep trail drops down to the talus slopes above the lateral moraine along the east side of the Cheilon Glacier. Cables and chains along the upper section of the trail provided a level of security down a very steep slope with poor footing. After the steep drop the trail heads northwest, descending along the moraine and then crosses to the west side of the valley along the bed of the retreating glacier. Note: Rockfall can be an issue on the descent during inclement weather. Before setting out, check current condition in Arolla.

When you are done enjoying the views from the pass/overlook, retrace your steps back to Arolla. Along the way enjoy the wonderful views of the Pigne d' Arolla and the peaks rising along the east side of the Val de Arolla.

Note: Hikers looking for a challenge might want to consider the lollipop loop that visits the Col de Riedmatten and the Pas de Chevres. The clockwise loop descends ladders from the Pas de Chevres to the moraine above the Cheilon Glacier, crosses a boulder field atop the moraine and the climbs to the Col de Riedmatten. For more information see Hike 39 - Pas de Chevres.

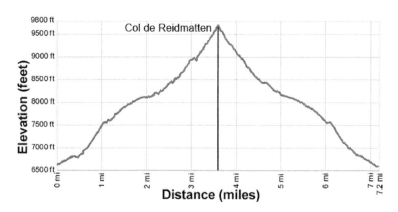

Trailhead Directions

From Les Hauderes: From the large parking area in front of the Les Hauderes Post, take the bus bound for Arolla and get off at the Arolla Post, the last stop on the bus. The ride takes about 25 minutes.

39. Pas de Chevres ☆☆☆☆
Distance: 7.2 miles (round trip)
Near Les Hauderes in the Valais

This scenic trail up the beautiful Montagne d'Arolla valley heads to the Pas de Chevres on a rugged ridge with views of the Glacier de Cheilon, Mont Blanc de Cheilon, Le Pleureur and the peaks rising along the east side of the Arolla Valley.

Distance: 7.2 miles (round trip)
Elevation: 6,602-ft. at Arolla
Maximum elevation: 9,387-ft.
Elevation Gain: 2,785-ft.
Difficulty: smoderate-trenuous

Basecamp: Les Hauderes, Arolla
Arolla Map: See page 191
Online Map/Photos:
www.hikingwalking.com/chevres

Why Hike to the Pas de Chevres

The hike to the Pas de Chevres travels through lovely meadows with great views of the glaciers spilling down the slopes of the Pigne d'Arolla. To the east/southeast (behind you), the jagged peaks towering above the east side of the Arolla Valley, including Dent de Perroc, Pointe des Genevois and Aiguille de la Tsa, fill the skyline

The pass, located on the rugged ridge separating the Val d' Arolla and Val des Dix, enjoys fine views of Mont Blanc de Cheilon rising above the Glacier de Cheilon, a river of ice flowing down the flanks of the peak. To the west, La Luette, Le Pleureur and Le Sale grace the skyline. Look carefully across the Cheilon Glacier to see the Cabane des Dix (Dix Hut) sitting atop a rocky knob. To the southeast, Mont Collon and the Bouquetins massif dominate the view. On a clear day the top of the Matterhorn joins the scene.

The Pas de Chevres is within 800-ft. of a second pass on the ridge, the Col de Riedmatten, which is 250-ft. higher than Chevres. In my opinion the views of Mont Blanc de Cheilon are better from the viewpoint above the Col de Riedmatten while the views to the east of Mont Collon and the Bouquetins massif to the east are slightly better from the Pas de Chevres.

If you are simply doing an out-and-back hike from Arolla I would choose the Col de Reidmatten because of the views of the Val des Dix from the overlook above the pass. The pass also tends to be less crowded. For more information see Hike 38 - Col de Riedmatten. If you have already been to the Col de Riedmatten then check out the Pas de Chevres. It is interesting to see the ladders descending the west side of the pass.

Pas de Chevres is the best choice for hikers heading to Cabane des Dix (Dix Hut) on the west side of the Cheilon Glacier. From the pass ladders drop to the talus slopes above the lateral moraine along the east side of the Cheilon Glacier. From there a rocky trail descends the lateral moraine along the east side of the valley and then crosses the bed of the retreating glacier to the west side of the valley. New ladders and catwalks installed in 2014 now make the descent/climb to the pass easier and safer. Please note the ladders are dangerous when the rungs are wet or icy. Before setting out, check current condition in Arolla.

Some people are very uncomfortable climbing up and down ladders. If this is the case, consider using the Col de Riedmatten trail (Hike 38). Check in Arolla for the current condition. The path down the west side of the path is very steep on loose, unstable rock.

Arolla to Pas de Chevres

In the the small village of Arolla, find the hiking signs on the west side of the town square (across from the bus stop). Walk southwest toward Pas de Chevres (2-hr 30-min) and Col de Riedmatten (2-hr 40-min).

Follow the directions for Hike 38 - Col de Riedmatten Hike to the junction at 3.2 miles. Here the trail to the Col de Riedmatten splits off to the right (north). We turn left (west) climbing steeply up rocky slopes toward the Pas de Chevres. Soon the trail curves to the left (southwest) ascending steeply through rocky meadows and scree covered slopes. At 3.5 miles the trail turns right (west) and climbs very steep, tight switchbacks to the Pas de Chevres (9,465-ft.) at 3.6 miles. As you climb watch for chamoix, a goat-like antelope, grazing in the meadows around the pass.

The pass enjoys somewhat restricted views of Mont Blanc de Cheilon rising above the Glacier de Cheilon, a river of ice flowing down the flanks of the peak. (Climb above the pass for a better view.) To the west, La Luette, Le Pleureur and Le Sale fill the skyline. Look carefully across the Cheilon Glacier to see the Cabane des Dix (Dix Hut) sitting atop a rocky knob. To the southeast, Mont Collon and the Bouquetins massif dominate the view. On a clear day the top of the Matterhorn graces the horizon.

From the Pas de Chevres, ladders descend about 65-ft. to talus slopes above the lateral moraine along the east side of the Glacier de Cheilon. From there a rocky trail descends the valley along the moraine and then crosses the bed of the retreating glacier to the Cabane des Dix (hut) on the west side of the valley. New ladders and catwalks installed in 2014 now make the descent/climb to the pass easier and safer. Please note the ladders are dangerous when the rungs are wet or icy. Before setting out, check current conditions in Arolla.

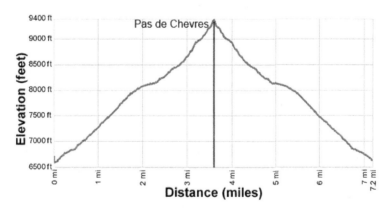

Some people are very uncomfortable climbing up and down ladders. If this is the case, consider using the Col de Riedmatten (Hike 38). Be sure to ask about the current condition of the trail descending from the Col de Riedmatten in Arolla before starting the hike. The descent down the west side of the pass is very steep on loose, unstable rock.

For out-and-back hikers, when you are done enjoying the view from the Pas de Chevres retrace your steps to Arolla. Along the way enjoy the great views of the Pigne d' Arolla and the view of the peaks rising along the east side of the Val de Arolla.

Note: Hikers looking for a challenge might want to consider the lollipop loop that visits the Col de Riedmatten and the Pas de Chevres. The clockwise loop descends ladders from the Pas de Chevres to the moraine above the Cheilon glacier, crosses a boulder field and the climbs the Col de Riedmatten. For more information see Hike 38 - Col de Riedmatten.

Trailhead Directions

From Les Hauderes: From the large parking area in front of the Les Hauderes Post, take the bus bound for Arolla and get off at the Arolla Post, the last stop on the bus. The ride takes about 25 minutes.

40. Other Trails in Les Hauderes and Arolla
Near Les Hauderes and Arolla in the Valais

40a) Arolla to Pra Gra

This trail climbs to an old alp set amid pretty meadow with stunning views of Mont Collon, L'Eveque, Pigne d'Arolla and the Mont Collon Glacier.

- **Distance:** 3.7-4.0 miles (round-trip)
- **Elevation:** 6,602-ft. at Arolla
  8,133-ft. at Pra Gra
- **Elevation Gain / Loss:** 1,531-ft.
- **Difficulty:** moderately-strenuous
- **Base camp:** Arolla, Les Hauderes
- **Arolla Map:** See page 191

In the the small village of Arolla find the hiking signs along the west side of the town square (across from the post bus stop). Climb switchbacks up the paved road toward the Cabane des Aiguilles Rouges. At the fourth hairpin curve take the trail heading northwest that ascends moderately steep to steep grades through trees and then meadows toward Pra Gra and the hut.

Along the way secondary trails shortcut a few of the switchbacks. At 1.8 miles reach a grassy shelf where we see Pra Gra, a collection of photogenic chalets and barns with stone roofs, a short distance to the left. To the south Mont Collon, L'Eveque and the Pigne d'Arolla tower above the head of the valley. Glaciers cling to the flanks of the mountains and spill down the steep valleys between the peaks. To the east a jagged wall of summits, including the Grand Dent de Veisivi, Dent du Perroc, Point des Genevois and the Aiguille de la Tsa, rise above the Arolla valley.

When you are done taking in the views retrace your steps to the trailhead. If starting in Les Hauderes, take one of the regularly scheduled buses from Les Hauderes Center to Arolla.

40b) Arolla to Cabane des Aiguilles Rouges

Dramatic views of the Aiguille Rouges d'Arolla, the summits towering above the head of the Arolla Valley and the peaks rimming the valley to the east are the highlight of this strenuous hike to the Cabane des Aiguille Rouges. A very steep descent leads to Lac Bleu where trails head to Gouille or back to Arolla. This trail is not recommended for anyone uncomfortable on exposed slopes or hikers wishing to avoid very steep descents.

- **Distance:** 6.9 miles (one-way) Arolla - Cabane des Aiguilles Rouges - Lac Bleu - La Gouille
  8.3 mile (loop) Arolla - Cabane des Aiguilles Rouges - Lac Bleu - Arolla
- **Elevation:** 6,602-ft. at Arolla
  9,219-ft. at Cabane des Aiguilles Rouges
  6,857-ft. at Lac Bleu
  6,050-ft. at La Gouille
- **Elevation Gain:** 2,693-ft. to high point
  -2,438-ft. to La Bleu
  -807-ft. to La Gouille
- **Difficulty:** strenuous
- **Base camp:** Arolla, Les Hauderes
- **Arolla Map:** See page 191

Follow Hike 40a to Pra Gra. At Pra Gra bear right (northwest) on the continuation of the trail to the Cabane des Aiguilles Rouges. The path ascends on moderate grades through meadows to the end of the shelf at 2.2 miles. Here the trail curves to the left and crosses the rugged north facing slopes beneath La Roussette, passing through areas of rocky meadows, scree, boulders and streams.

At 3.1 miles the trail curves to the right (north) and ascends on moderate to moderately steep grades through scree covered slopes and rocky meadows along the steep flanks of the Aiguilles Rouges d'Arolla. Fixed chains facilitate the passage along an exposed section of the trail. This area is typically not a problem unless the path is covered with slick snow and ice.

A final stiff climb leads to the cabane (hut) at 4.0 miles. Here panoramic views stretch from Pigne d'Arolla and Mont Collon in the south to the jagged ridge of peaks anchored by Aiguille de la Tsa, Dent du Perroc and the Grand Dent de Veisivi in the east. The glacier-clad Grand Cornier and Dent Blanche rise in the distance to the east. The Aiguille Rouges d'Arolla tower above the hut to the west. Mont de l'Etoile dominates the view to the north.

From the Cabane, the trail ascends briefly to a high point and then curves to the right (northeast), descending on very steep grades across a stream and then scree covered slopes. At 4.3 miles the path swings to the right (southeast) continuing its very steep descent down scree and then rocky meadows, accompanied by fine views of the surrounding peaks.

Reach Lac Bleu, a small clear lake, at 6.2 miles. Twin waterfalls tumble down meadows into the west end of the lake. The lake is a popular destination with families and anyone looking for an easy walk from La Gouille.

To complete the hike, cross the lake's outlet stream on a bridge and then descend through meadows and trees past the hamlet of Louche to La Gouille at 6.9 miles. Here you can catch a post bus to Arolla or Les Hauderes.

Alternatively, complete the loop by turning right (south) at the lake and follow an undulating trail through meadows and trees back to Arolla at 8.3 miles.

40c) Arolla to Lac Bleu and la Gouille/Les Hauderes

This moderate hike traverses the slopes along the west side of the Arolla valley to Lac Bleu. Complete the hike by retracing your steps to Arolla, descending to La Gouille, taking the bus back to Arolla / Les Hauderes or walking back to Les Hauderes.

- **Distance:** 4.2 miles (round-trip) to Lac Bleu
  2.8 - 3.1 miles (one way) to La Gouille
  5.4 miles (one way) to Les Hauderes
- **Elevation:** 6,602-ft. at Arolla
  6,857-ft. at Lac Bleu
  6,050-ft. at La Gouille
  4,835-ft. at Les Hauderes
- **Difficulty:** moderate
- **Base camp:** Arolla, Les Hauderes
- **Arolla Map:** See page 191

In the the small village of Arolla find the hiking signs along the west side of the town square (across from the post bus stop). Ascend switchbacks up the paved road toward the Cabane des Aiguilles Rouges. At the second hairpin curve, near the Center Alpin, is a sign for the trail to Lac Bleu. Alternatively, from Arolla's main square walk northeast up a side road toward the Hotel du Glacier. Before you reach the hotel watch for a steep path on your left that climbs to the Center Alpin, travels between the buildings and then connects with the Lac Blue trail.

The Lac Bleu trail ascends through trees and soon reaches a junction. Bear left on the upper path toward Lac Bleu. As you ascend the trees thin and you reach a second junction. Bear right on an undulating trail traversing through meadows and clusters of trees above the west side of the valley.

At 1.5 miles the path curves to the left and descends to cross a stream on a bridge and then ascends to Lac Bleu, a small clear lake, at 2.1 miles. Twin waterfalls tumble down meadows into the west end of the lake. The lake is a popular destination with families and anyone looking for an easy walk from La Gouille.

When you are ready to move on, either retrace your steps to Arolla or crossing the lake's outlet stream on a bridge and then descend through meadows and trees past the hamlet of Louche to La Gouille at 2.9 - 3.1 miles (depending on the route). In Gouille catch a post bus to Arolla or Les Hauderes.

Hikers with the time and energy can also walk from La Gouille to Les Hauderes. The path briefly travels north (down valley) along the side the road. Soon you cross the road and drop below the right (east) side of the road heading north/northeast through meadows and clusters of trees. As you near Les Hauderes the path rejoins the road. Almost immediately the road crosses a bridge and then descends to Les Hauderes Center at 5.4 miles.

40d) Les Hauderes to Mont Mine Glacier Overlook

This trail travels up a beautiful bucolic valley to Ferpecle and then ascends along to the west of the Ferpecle stream to the Mont Mine Glacier Overlook. Along the way enjoy fine views of the high peaks at the head of the Val d'Herens and the Ferpecle and Mont Mine Glaciers.

- **Distance:** 3.4 - 7.4 miles (round-trip)
- **Elevation:** 5,670-ft. at La Forclaz
  5,810-ft. at Le Salay, Ferpecle
  6,450-ft. at Mont Mine Glacier Overlook
- **Elevation Gain/Loss:** 780-ft. from La Forclaz to Overlook
  640-ft. from Le Salay to Overlook
- **Difficulty:** moderate
- **Base camp:** Les Hauderes
- **Les Hauderes South Map:** See page 175

Follow Hike 37 - Bricola to Ferpecle for 3.0 miles from La Forclaz and 1.0 miles from Le Salay, Ferpecle. Instead of turning left toward Bricola, continue straight ahead on the paved road toward the Glacier du Mont Mine. The road crosses a bridge over the Ferpecle stream and reaches a junction. Turn left on a dirt/gravel road toward the Glacier. At the next junction turn right on a gravel path that ascends switchbacks through trees and meadows. Soon the trees thin and views open to the Ferpecle stream and the peaks rising above the head of the valley. The Mont Mine ridge cleaves the valley in two. Dent Blanche and the Ferpecle Glacier dominate the view to the southeast while straight ahead the Mont Mine Glacier spills down the slopes of Dents de Bertol, the Pointe de Bertol and Mont Mine. The summit of Tete Blanche rises above the ice sheet.

The road now heads up valley on easy grades toward to the foot of the glacier. A path soon breaks off to the left, descending to the stream and a bridged crossing. We continue up valley on the gravel road to the spillway and the first of several settling ponds at 3.8 miles. A use trail continues beyond this point, traveling through the debris left by the retreating glacier along the right (west side) of braided streams meander through gravel beds. Soon you will see a confluence where the meltwater from the Ferpecle and Mont Mine Glaciers meet. Ahead the tongue of the glacier flows down rugged cliffs above the valley floor.

When you are done taking in the views retrace your steps to either Le Salay or La Forclaz and catch a bus back to Les Hauderes. Alternately, walk back to Les Hauderes. See Hike 37 - Bricola for a detailed trail description to/from Ferpecle and information on taking the bus to the trailhead.

41. A Multi-day Hike along the Walker's Haute Route - Les Hauderes to Zermatt or Saas Fee
★★★★★
In the Valais between Les Hauderes and Zermatt or Saas Fee

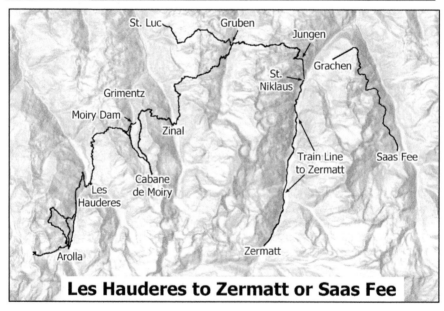

Les Hauderes to Zermatt or Saas Fee

Walking point to point is one of the joys of Swiss hiking. The excellent trail network links huts, villages, towns and resorts allowing avid hikers to fashion multi-day, point-to-point trips accompanied by superb scenery. In the Valais I recommend a shortened and modified version of the Walker's Haute Route between Les Hauderes and Zermatt or Saas Fee. The trip incorporates some of the most scenic segments of the Haute Route, traveling through glorious valleys and crossing panoramic pass with spectacular views of the glacier-clad peaks of the Pennine Alps.

This hike can be accomplished in 4-7 days depending on the route. When possible the route utilizes buses to avoid walking along roads. Cable cars, gondolas, funiculars and chairlifts can be employed to reduce the elevation gain or avoid steep downhill stretches at the end of the day.

The hike can be done nonstop, crossing a pass each day. Alternatively stop in some of the villages along the way for an extra day or so to explore the area on recommended day hikes.

Hikers can choose to stay at simple hotels or more high-end lodging in each of the destinations. The only exception is Gruben where there is only one place to stay. The hike offers the opportunity to sample what it is like to stay in a hut one night and then the next day sleep in a room with a comfy bed and hot shower. For people who wish to avoid huts, the walk provides alternatives for viewing the majestic scenery but staying in more comfortable lodging.

Although the Valais is known for its dry, sunny weather it is still possible to hit days where rain/snow or fog make hiking over a high pass a miserable affair or even dangerous. Public transportation allows you to easily travel to the next valley should you hit bad weather. Typically the transport heads down to a city or town in the Rhone Valley where hikers can tour some of the local sites, enjoy lunch or visit a museum before changing to a train/bus heading to the next destination.

Les Hauderes to Zermatt or Saas Fee

Starting Point: This trip begins in Les Hauderes in the Val d'Herens. To reach Les Hauderes take the bus from the Sion Gare (train station) to Les Hauderes center, a 47 minute trip.

Day 1:

Hike 35 – Les Hauderes to Lac de Moiry via the Col de Torrent:
This classic route to the Val d'Anniviers from Les Hauderes starts with a quick bus ride to La Sage/Villaz, eliminating a 900-ft. climb. From La Sage/Villaz the trail ascends to the Col Torrent and then descends to the Barrage de Moiry (dam) at the foot of Lac de Moiry, a 7.3 mile hike that gains 3,860-ft. Highlights include splendid views of the high peaks and glaciers towering above the Val d'Herens, Val d'Arolla and Val de Moiry. Upon arriving at the dam either walk down to Grimentz (3.5 miles/2 hours) or take the bus to Grimentz or Zinal. I personally prefer staying in Zinal, which allows parties to be well situated for the hike to Gruben on Day 3. Overnight: Zinal or Grimentz.

Note: There is also lodging in La Sage/Villaz at the start of the hike to the Col de Torrent. Reach La Sage/Villaz on a bus from Les Hauderes. This small hamlet has limited services. I recommend staying overnight in Les Hauderes and then taking the bus to La Sage/Villaz on the morning you intend to start the trek.

Extra Days in Les Hauderes: Hikers with the time can spend some extra days in Les Hauderes and/or nearby Arolla. See the Les Hauderes section of this guide for recomended day hikes.

Bad Weather Transport: Take the bus from Les Hauderes to Sion, the train from Sion to Sierre/Siders and then the bus to Zinal or Grimentz. Sion is a great town to explore on a rainy day. See the Les Hauderes section covering nearby attractions and rainy day activities for more information.

Day 1 Alternate Route:

Hike 36 - Les Hauderes to the Cabane de Moiry via the Col de Torrent: From La Sage/Villaz, follow the trail to the Col de Torrent. On the descent from the Col, branch off the main trail on the path to the Cabane de Moiry. This is a very strenuous 9.5 mile day with an altitude gain of 5,726-ft. Overnight: Cabane de Moiry

Day 2:

Hike 28 – Cabane de Moiry: From Grimentz or Zinal take the bus to the Moiry Glacier (the last stop beyond the Moiry Dam) and hike to the Cabane de Moiry. This short 4.0 mile hike, gaining 1,577-ft., features stunning, bird's-eye-views of the Moiry Glacier and the scenic cirque rimming the head of the Val de Moiry. For a longer day get off the bus at the Moiry Barrage (Dam) and then walk the loop around the Lac de Moiry (Hike 33b). At the head of the lake take the 4.0 mile side trip to the Cabane de Moiry. Total distance for this variation is 7.6 miles. Return to your accommodation by taking the bus from Moiry Barrage to either Grimentz or Zinal. (You can also walk up the west side of the lake, visit the hut and then take the bus from the Moiry Glacier back to your accommodations.)

Day 2 Alternate Route:

Hike 29 – Cabane de Moiry to Zinal via the Col de Sorebois: Hikers staying at the Cabane de Moiry can continue on the Walker's Haute Route by descend from the Hut to the Chemin 2500, a high route traveling above the east side of the Lac de Moiry to the Col de Sorebois. At the Col enjoy amazing views of the high summits towering above Zinal and the Lac de Moiry. Cross the col and descend to the ski area at Sorebois where a cable car descends to Zinal. Total distance for this hike is 7.5 miles with 1,574-ft. in elevation gain. Instead of taking the cable car you can walk down to Zinal on a trail losing 2,700-ft. in 2.4 miles for a 9.9 mile day. Overnight: Zinal.

Hikers who overnighted in Zinal or Grimentz can also walk this route. Take the bus to the Moiry Glacier and climb to the Cabane de Moiry (Hike 28). From the Cabane follow the directions above. The distance from this option to the Cabane and then Sorebois is 9.5 miles with a 3,151-ft. elevation gain. Add 2.4 miles if walking all the way down to Zinal.

Extra Days in Zinal: Hikes in the beautiful Zinal Valley features magical views of the soaring peaks and glistening glacier at the head of the Val de Zinal. See the Zinal hikes section of this guide for more information.

Day 3:

Hike 31 – Zinal to Gruben via Forcletta Pass: This terrific hike is accompanied by panoramic views of the high peaks towering above the head of the Zinal and Turtmann Valleys. Total distance is 10.9 miles to Gruben with a 3,936-ft. elevation gain and 3,436-ft. loss. Overnight: Gruben at the Hotel Schwarzhorn.

Bad Weather Transport: From Zinal take the bus to Sierre/Siders train station. At the station purchase a ticket at the machine for Turtmann, a local stop on the Rhone Valley rail line. Catch the next train to Turtmann (you will be heading toward Visp). From the Turtmann station follow the signs to the cable car to Oberems, about a 20 minute walk. Ride the cable car to Oberems where a minibus will take you to the Hotel Schwarzhorn. Note, when looking for transportation options to/from Gruben make sure you specify "Gruben, VS" (for Valais) so you get the correct town, schedule and prices.

Day 3 Alternative:

Hike 32 – St. Luc to Gruben via Meidpass: For an easier day take the bus to St. Luc and then the funicular to Tignousa. From Tignousa it is a 7.8 mile hike with an elevation gain of 2,009-ft. over Meidpass to Gruben. This alternative route features splendid vistas of the glacier-clad peaks at the head of the Turtmann Valley and the Bernese Alps towering above the Rhone Valley. Overnight: Gruben at the Hotel Schwarzhorn.

Day 4:

Hike 35 - Gruben to Jungen via Augstbord Pass: This day heads to one of the best overlooks on the Haute Route, a small meadow-clad bench high above the Mattertal. Here vistas extend from the high peaks towering above Zermatt to the Bernese Alps soaring above the Rhone. The 8.2 mile hike gains 3,507-ft. and then loses 2,933-ft. to Jungen where a cable car descends to St. Niklaus on the floor of the Mattertal. You can skip the cable car and descend a knee crunching trail to St. Niklaus that takes about 2 hours and losses an additional 2,800-ft. in three-plus miles.

On the valley floor either take the train to Zermatt at the head of the Mattertal Valley (35 minutes) or take the bus from St. Niklaus to Grachen on the sunny eastern slopes above the foot of the Mattertal. The trip to Grachen takes 25 minutes. Overnight: Zermatt or Grachen.

Note: Grachen is spelled with an umlaut over the "a". On the SBB website/SBB app enter Graechen. When you see the list of destinations select Grächen, post.

Bad Weather Transport: Take the minibus from the Hotel Schwarzhorn to Oberems where a cable car descends to Turtmann on the valley floor. Follow the signs from the cable car station to the Turtmann train station, a 20 minute walk. Turtmann is a local stop on the Rhone Valley line. At the ticket machine purchase a ticket for Zermatt. Get off the train in Visp, exit the train station and walk a short distance to the separate loading platform for the Matterhorn Gotthard Bahn to Zermatt. The trip from Gruben to Zermatt will take almost three hours.

Alternatively, take the bus to St. Niklaus and then the bus to Grachen. Note: Grachen is spelled with an umlaut over the "a". On the SBB website/SBB app enter Graechen. When you see the list of destinations select Grächen, post.

Extra Days in Zermatt: If time allows, plan a few extra days in Zermatt to enjoy hikes with dramatic views of the Matterhorn along with the largest grouping of 4,000-meter peaks in Switzerland. See the Zermatt section of this guide for more information.

Day 5:

Hike 15 - Grachen to Saas Fee via the Hohenweg Saas Fee: This trail is not part of the Walker's Haute Route but is one of the classic hikes in the Valais. The challenging trail follows a high route along the west side of the Saastal with stunning, nonstop views of the glacier-clad summits towering about the Saas Valley and the Bernese Alps to the north. Overnight: Saas Fee.

Bad Weather Transport: Take the bus from Grachen to the St. Niklaus train station. Board a train heading to Visp and get off at Stalden. At the Stalden train station catch a bus to Saas Fee. (Cross the tracks to the station building. The buses board on the east side of the station. (The bus boarding area contains large yellow squares in the parking area.)

Extra Days in Saas Fee: Saas Fee is set amid the magnificent peaks of the Mischabel Range, to the west, and the Weissmies, to the east. An excellent network of hohenwegs (high routes) and trails showcases this superb mountain scenery. See the Saas Fee section of the guide for details.

Alternate Start: Arolla to Zermatt or Saas Fee

Starting Point: This trip begins in Arolla in the Val d'Arolla. To reach Arolla take the bus from the Sion Gare (train station) to Les Hauderes center and then change to the bus to Arolla (5-minute connection). Total travel time to Arolla is one hour and 17 minutes. (Note: these two days can easily be done from Les Hauderes by taking the bus from Les Hauderes to Arolla, a 30 minute trip.)

Day 1:

Hike 39 - Arolla to Pas de Chevres or Hike 38 – Arolla to the Col de Riedmatten: From Arolla the Walker's Haute Route heads west to two crossing: Pas de Chevres and the Col de Riedmatten, leading to the Val des Dix. A scenic trail to both passes heads up the beautiful Montagne d' Arolla valley with grand views of the glacier spilling down the Pigne d'Arolla. After 3.2 miles the trail splits with the left path climbing to Pas de Chevres and the right to Co de Riedmatten. Vistas from the passes encompass the Glacier de Cheilon flowing down the Val des Dix and the peaks rising to the west. At Riedmatten a very steep trail with poor footing drops to the talus slopes beneath the west side of the pass. At the Pas de Chevres, look down at the 65-ft. of ladders leading to the talus slopes. At both passes you'll be glad you are turning around and walking back to Arolla! Overnight: Arolla.

Day 2:

Hike 40b - Arolla to Les Hauderes via the Cabane des Aiguilles Rouges: There are two choices for walking between the villages of Arolla and Les Hauderes. Hike 40b, the most strenuous trail, ascends to Pra Gra with fabulous views of Mont Collon and the Mont Collon Glacier before climbing to the Cabane des Aiguilles Rouges with dramatic views of the Aiguille Rouges d'Arolla. The trail then descends very steep grades to Lac Bleu and La Gouille, where you can catch the bus to Les Hauderes. The 6.9 mile hike gains 2,693-ft. and loses 3,245-ft.

Hike 40c- Arolla to Lac Bleu and la Gouille/Les Hauderes: Alternatively, take it easy and walk from Arolla to La Bleu and then la Gouille where you can catch a bus to Les Hauderes or walk to Les Hauderes for a 3.1 to 5.4 mile day (respectively).

Days 3 – 7:

Follow days 1 - 5 on the walk from Les Hauderes to Zermatt or Saas Fee.

Luggage Transfers

Dealing with luggage is always an issue when hiking point to point. There are services that will move your luggage but they are VERY expensive. In Switzerland there are two other choices. Hikers with a Half Card (See Discount Cards in Appendix A), can ship luggage between major stations for a small fee. For example, hikers can send a bag from the Sion train station to the Zermatt train station or the Saas Fee Bus Terminal. Alternatively, hikers with a valid ticket can also use the service. So if you don't have a half card it might be worthwhile to purchase a ticket for the trip between Sion and Zermatt (even through you won't use the ticket) and then pay the small fee to ship a bag or two. Read the Luggage section under Appendix A for more information.

The Bernese Alps, Uri Alps and Glarus Alps
Best Hiking Trails between Altdorf and Kandersteg

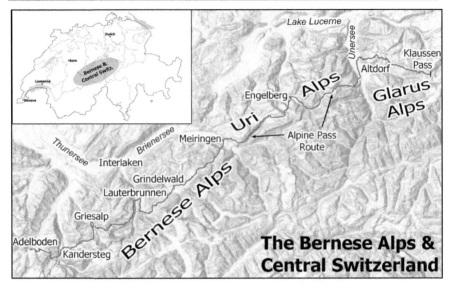

Online Map of the Bernese Alps: www.hikingwalking.com/bernese-map

The Bernese Alps, along with the Uri and Glarus Alps in central Switzerland, are a wonderland of dramatic walls of rock and ice towering above a lush landscape of beautiful forests and meadows sprinkled with wildflowers. Here a profusion of trails wander through verdant valleys, traverse scenic ridges, visit stunning viewpoints and cross panoramic passes. While not as high as the Pennine Alps in the Valais, the Bernese Alps are just as spectacular. The range is best known for a triad of peaks - the Eiger, Monch and Jungfrau, along with splendid mountain scenery.

The spine of the Bernese Alps, running from east to west, defines the boundary between the cantons of the Valais to the south and Bern to the north. From the glacier-clad peaks along the crest the range extends north to Lakes Thun and Brienz. Meltwater from snow and glaciers flows northward to the lakes, cutting a series of scenic valleys rimmed by photogenic summits. These valleys are the home to Meiringen, Grindelwald, Lauterbrunnen, Griesalp and Kandersteg, all excellent base camps for accessing the best trails the region has to offer.

Geographically the Bernese Alps are bounded by the Haslital (Hasli Valley), the home of Meiringen, to the northeast. From a hiker's standpoint the chain continues northeast beyond the Haslital into the Uri and Glarus Alps, often referred to as the Eastern Bernese Alps or the Central Swiss Alps. These lesser known ranges offer terrific options for hikers with some interesting trails well off the tourist circuit. To cover some of the best hikes in central Switzerland this guide includes recommended trails around Engelberg and Altdorf.

The Alpine Pass Route, a popular long distance hiking trail, traverses some of the best scenery the Bernese and Central Swiss Alps have to offer. This guide covers the most beautiful segments of the route between the town of Altdorf and the village of Kandersteg. Each day the route travels through breathtaking landscapes of forests and meadows before climbing over a panoramic pass. Along the way hikers visit Swiss villages, towns and resorts, each with a distinctive character, from the small hamlet of Griesalp to the popular ski resort of Grindelwald.

When trying to decide upon an itinerary in the Swiss Alps the discussion often turns to the weather. The weather in the Bernese and Central Swiss Alps is certainly more unpredictable than the Valais, with more rainy and cloudy days. But the increase in moisture translates into lush meadows and beautiful displays of wildflowers.

Wet/cloudy days usually don't preclude hiking. There are plenty of lower level trails to explore when the high country is shrouded in clouds. Days when the weather changes from good to bad can also create some amazing views, with clouds swirling around the high peaks.

The region offers plenty of rainy day activities. Switzerland is a small country so traveling down to Interlaken and other locations around Lakes Thun, Brienz or Lucerne are good options.

There are also some great attractions closer at hand. In Lauterbrunnen a short walk up the valley leads to Trummelbach Falls, an incredible series of waterfalls thundering down a slot canyon carved in a mountain. A ride up the lifts to the Schilthorn on a cloudy day revealed magical views of the valleys covered in clouds while the summits of the high peaks were bathed in sun.

In short don't let the chance of some rain keep you from visiting this stunning area. Simply be prepared for bad weather and then make the best of any bad days you may encounter. You might be surprised by what you discover.

Grindelwald

Location: The Lutschental (Lutschine Valley) in the Bernese Alps

Grindelwald is a world class ski resort, a popular hiking destination and a base camp for climbers seeking to summit the Eiger and nearby peaks. Visitors from around the world flock to the village to ogle the majestic mountain scenery and ride the Jungfrau Express to the Jungfraujoch (11,362-ft.), situated atop a glacial saddle between the Jungfrau and the Monch with breathtaking views of the Aletsch Glacier and the high peaks of the Bernese Alps.

The resort occupies an idyllic bowl with breathtaking views of some of the most impressive mountains in the Bernese Alps. A magnificent wall of glacier-clad peaks stretching from the Wetterhorn to the Eiger, incised by deep glacial gorges, soars above Grindelwald to the south. Across the valley to the north, slopes cloaked in forest and pastures rise to meadow-clad benches set beneath a rugged ridge of mountains anchored by the Schwarzhorn and the Faulhorn. Grosse Scheidegg sits atop the saddle at the head of the valley to the east while Kleine Scheidegg occupies the pass between the Eiger and the Mannlichen Ridge to the west.

Ascend to the viewpoints above the north side of the Grindelwald and the impressive vistas expand to include the Monch and Jungfrau rising to the southwest beyond the Eiger. Here too the Finsteraarhorn, Fiescherhorn and Schreckhorn join the scene, towering above impressive glaciers spilling down the deep gorges behind the wall formed by the Wetterhorn, Mattenberg and the Eiger.

About Grindelwald

The center of Grindelwald is located along Dorfstrasse, the main street, and the adjacent side streets between the Bahnhof (train station) and the church. Here you will find a wide assortment of lodging, restaurants, bars and shops, including outdoor stores. More lodging, a wide variety of vacation apartments and some restaurants and shops are found on the hillsides above Grindelwald to the north and the slopes below the resort to the south.

The Grindelwald Bahnhof (train station) is located at the west end of the village and includes a platform for the cog railway ascending to Kleine Scheidegg with connections to the cog railroad climbing through tunnels in the mountains to the Jungfraujoch. Directly to the east of the train station is a large Grindelwald Bus (www.grindelwaldbus.ch/en/) stop along the south side of Dorfstrasse. Buses from this location travel along the main street or head to other parts of the resort, including Bussalp, Grosse Scheidegg, Terminal and the Gletscherschlucht, to name a few.

To the east/southeast along Dorfstrasse find the very helpful Grindelwald Tourism (grindelwald.swiss) office on the south side of the street across from the Coop Grocery. A second grocery, the Voi, is located a few blocks beyond on the north side of the street.

The Firstbahn, a multistage gondola to the overlook atop First on the north side of the valley, is located about 0.4 miles from the Bahnhof on a side street off Dorfstrasse across from the vehicle entrance for the Sunstar Hotel. The turn is marked with a sign for the Firstbahn. Walk a short distance up the side street past the Pension Gydisdorf to the ticket booth and entry to the gondola.

There is a gondola to Mannlichen, located along the ridge extending north from Kleine Scheidegg, and a gondola to the Eiger Station, situated beneath the north face of the Eiger. The gondolas can be reached by taking bus 121 to Terminal or bus 123 toward Intramen Egg and getting off at the Terminal stop. Terminal is the home of a new facility for the Mannlichen and Eiger Express gondolas. The Eiger Express is a faster way to reach the cog railway ascending to the Jungfraujoch. You can also take the train from the Grindewald Bahnhof to Terminal. The ride takes 5 minutes. Alternatively, walk to the Terminal Station from the Grindelwald Bahnhof using walkways/roads that descend the hillsides to the south/southwest of the train station. The 0.9 miles walk takes about 20 minutes.

Finally there is a small cable car that ascends to Pfingstegg, situated on a sunny bench beneath the Mattenberg. Take bus 122 toward the Gletscherschlucht and get off at the cable car station or walk to the lift by heading east along Dorfstrasse and then turn right on Grabenstasse, following signs to the Pfingstegg cable car.

During the day the main street of the resort is very crowded with day trippers coming up from Interlaken and visitors traveling to the Jungfraujoch, Firstbahn or visiting the various shops and restaurants. Get an early start to avoid the worst of the crowds. I believe the superb views from the trails more than make up for dealing with the crowds around the popular viewpoints, lifts and the main street.

Hiking around Grindelwald

The high benches above the north side of the valley, as well as the areas around Grosse and Kleine Scheidegg, are laced with scenic trails and overlooks with panoramic views of the magnificent spectacle of rock and ice towering above the south side of the valley. Lifts, trains and buses transport hikers to the high country and the start of these popular hiking trails.

Starting on the west side of the resort, buses and trails climb to Grosse Scheidegg, a fine overlook beneath the north face of the Wetterhorn. From here scenic trails travel to First (Hike 42) and Bussalp (Hike 43) or down the west side of the pass toward Meiringen (Hike 75c).

Take the cable car to First, high above the north side of the valley, for stunning views of the high peaks soaring above the south side of Grindelwald. Great hikes from First travel to the Bachsee (Hike 44) and the Faulhorn (Hike 45). An epic point-to-point hike from First leads to Schynige Platte (Hike 46), accompanied by spectacular views of the Eiger, Monch and Jungfrau, along with the summits towering above the Lauterbrunnen area.

To the east take the Mannlichen gondola to Mannlichen and then walk the aptly named Panoramaweg to Klein Scheidegg (Hike47). The walk can be extended by continuing to the Eiger Glacier Viewpoint. For more jaw-dropping views walk to Wengen (Hike 48) along a segment of the Alpine Pass Route. Several transportation options enable hikers the return to Grindelwald the same day.

The Kleine Scheidegg area can also be reached from Grindelwald via the Cog Railway. From Kleine Scheidegg, visit the Eiger Glacier Viewpoint and/or walk the Eiger Trail (Hike 49) that descends beneath the peak's dramatic north face. A new gondola, the Eiger Express, offers a faster and very scenic ride to the start of the Eiger Trail and the Eiger Glacier area.

Along the south side of the resort walk or take the cable car to Pfingstegg and then hike to the viewpoint at Baregg (Hike 50a) with terrific views of the Fiescherhorn and the Ischmeer Glacier. A route continues beyond the viewpoint to Schreckhorn Hut (Hike 50b).

Getting to Grindelwald

From the Zurich Airport or Zurich Bahnhof (train station) take the train to Interlaken Ost (East). You will need to change trains along the way. In Interlaken, change to the train going to Grindelwald/Lauterbrunnen. Half the cars on the train will be labeled for Grindelwald and the other half for Lauterbrunnen. Make sure you get on a car going to Grindelwald. At Zweilutschinen the train literally splits in half with half the cars going to Grindelwald and the other half heading for Lauterbrunnen. The trip takes about two hours and 40 minutes from Zurich.

From the Geneva Airport or Gare (train station), take the train to Interlaken Ost (East). You will need to change trains along the way. Then follow the directions above. The ride should take about three hours and 50 minutes.

Check the SBB website (sbb.ch/en) /SBB app for directions from other parts of the country.

Nearby Attractions & Rainy Day Activities

The Jungfraujoch, aka Top of Europe, is the top attraction in Grindelwald. The day starts with a cog railroad ride to Kleine Scheidegg or a ride on the Eiger Express gondola to the Eiger Station. At Kleine Scheidegg or the Eiger Station board the Jungfraubahn, a cog railway that climbs through tunnels inside the mountains to the Jungfraujoch, a large facility situated atop a glacier-clad saddle between the Jungfrau and the Monch. It is not only the highest railway station in Europe but also the most expensive to reach. Various viewpoints feature breathtaking vistas of the Aletsch Glacier and the high peaks of the Bernese Alps. The area includes restaurants, an ice cave, a snow park and shops.

The Gletscherschlucht (Glacier Gorge) is a good option if the weather precludes a trip to the high country. Cantilevered walkways twist through a deep gorge, carved by the retreating path of Grindelwald Glacier, channeling the Lutschine River. Children of all ages will like the Spiderweb, a walkable net stretched over the gorge. Information panels explain the geology, glaciers and streams that created this fascinating place. Check at the Tourist Information Center for current hours. From the main street take bus 122 to the entrance of the gorge or walk, following signs along the main street.

The Heimatmuseum, next to the church on Dorfstrasse, is a local history museum with permanent exhibits covering the area's mountaineering, farming and railways along with the development of the village into a world class resort. Check at the Tourist Information Center for current hours.

Schynige Platte, a high overlook atop a ridge at the foot of the Lutschental, can be reached on a long hike from First or by a cog railway from Wilderswil (a train station along the Grindelwald - Interlaken line). At Schynige Platte you will find an interesting alpine botanic garden, great views of the Eiger, Monch and Jungfrau and overlooks featuring terrific vistas of the Bernese Alps, Interlaken, Lake Thun and Lake Brienz. Several short loop trails visit the gardens and lead to more scenic viewpoints.

If you are not planning on traveling to **Lauterbrunnen**, a rainy day is the perfect opportunity to visit this lovely village and take an easy walk up the beautiful Lauterbrunnen Valley (Hike 52). The valley is said to have 72 waterfalls spilling down the sheer cliffs rimming both sides of the vale. I also recommend at trip to Trummelbach Falls, a World Heritage Site showcasing a series of waterfalls thundering down a slot canyon carved into the mountain. See Hike 51 - Lauterbrunnen to Trummelbach Falls for more information.

Another good rainy day option is to take a day trip to **Interlaken**, a 40 minute train ride from Grindelwald. Here you can walk along Lakes Thun and Brienz, take a lake cruise, visit castles along Lake Thun or simply walk along the Hoheweg, the street connecting Lake Brienz to Lake Thun. Visit the Interlaken Tourist site (interlaken.ch/en) for a complete list of options.

Good Things to Know about Grindelwald

- The primary language in Grindelwald is German, although you will hear just about ever language imaginable. The resort is so popular with the Japanese that you will see many signs with German, French, English and Japanese, along with a few other languages.
- There are three campgrounds in Grindelwald: Gletscherdorf at Locherbodenstrasse 29 along the river to the south of the Pfingstegg Lift station, Camping Sand Grindelwald at Wargistalstrasse 8 to the south of the river and Camping Eigernordwand at Bodenstrasse 4 to the south of the train station and river.
- There are three hostels in Grindelwald, the Eiger Lodge, Downtown-Lodge and the Grindelwald Youth Hostel.

Map: Grindelwald Area Trails

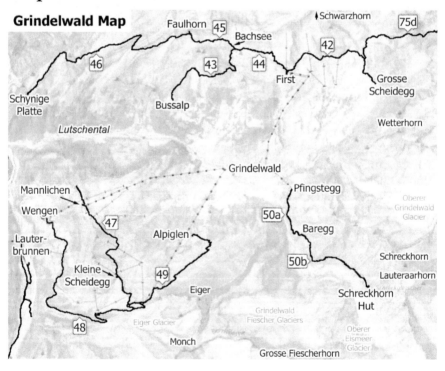

42. Grosse Scheidegg to First ☆☆☆☆☆
Distance: 3.5 miles (One Way)
Near Grindelwald in the Bernese Alps

The trail between Grosse Scheidegg and First follows an undulated path through bucolic meadows with evolving, panoramic views of the massive peaks, adorn with glistening glaciers, towering above the Grindelwald Valley. Along the way waterfalls, wildflowers and small alps add interest to the hike.

Distance: 3.5 miles (one way)
Elevation Gain: 6,452-ft. at Grosse Scheidegg
Maximum elevation: 7,110-ft
Elevation Gain: 658-ft.

Difficulty: moderate
Basecamp: Grindelwald
Grindelwald Map: See page 214
Online Map/Photos:
www.hikingwalking.com/first

Hiking from Grosse Scheidegg to First

Take the bus to Grosse Scheidegg, the saddle on the ridge separating Grindelwald from the Rosenlaui Valley to the northeast. (See trailhead directions below.) Signs at the pass direct walkers to the broad dirt track heading northwest toward Schreckfeld, First and the Faulhorn on the Hohenweg 2400.

Follow the path as it ascends on easy grades along the top of the ridge accompanied by ever improving views of the high peaks, including the Mattenberg, the Monch and the Eiger, rising to the southwest. The Wetterhorn towers above the saddle while below the village of Grindelwald lies cradled in an emerald green basin, bound to the west by the Mannlichen ridge.

At 0.8 miles reach a 3-way junction where signs point right (northeast) to Schwarzwaldalp and Kaltenbrunnen (Chaltenbrunnen). The continuation of the road drops left to Schreckfeld, First and the Faulhorn. We leave the road and continue on the Hohenweg 2400 trail, which ascends above the right side of the road, toward First and the Faulhorn.

The trail curves to the left, traveling through pretty meadows along the base of the Schwarzhorn. At 1.2 miles the path descends on easy grades and soon crosses a wood bridge over a stream cascading down a rocky cleft carved into the hillside.

Reach a junction at 1.8 with a trail branch right (northwest) toward the Schwarzhorn. We continue straight ahead on the Hohenweg 2400 toward First. Before long the trail drops down to and joins a broad dirt track. Views open to the Schreckhorn and Klein Schreckhorn, rising along the ridge above the Mattenberg. To the north are interesting rock formations along the cliffs above the trail.

The track now starts ascending on moderate grades, crossing another stream at 2.1 miles. The grade eases at 2.7 miles where a second trail branches right (north) towards the Schwarzhorn. Here we get our first views of the Fiescherhorn massif towering above the Fiescher Glacier nestled in a bowl behind the Eiger.

Follow the trail as it curves to the left (southwest) and soon joins with a gravel road coming up from Schreckfeld. Beyond the junction the ascent resumes on moderate grades. Watch for a trail branching left from the road at 3.3 miles. Follow this trail, which cuts-off a long switchback on the road, as it climbs steeply to First (7,110-ft.) at 3.5 miles.

First is the highest station for the Firstbahn Gondola, which starts in Grindelwald. The station is situated atop a minor summit with stunning views of the Wetterhorn, Schreckhorn and Eiger. Glaciers spill down the flanks of the massifs into the deep incised gorges between the peaks. Views extend southwest to Klein Scheidegg and the Jungfrau.

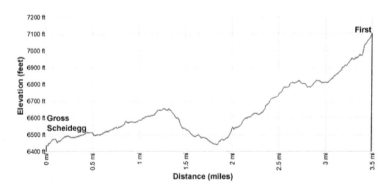

First features a popular restaurant with a sun terrace and a "Cliff Walk", a cantilevered metal walkway bolted to the sheer west face of the First summit that leads to a 150-ft. long viewing platform with panoramic views of the 4,000-meter peaks towering above the south side of the valley. The walkway connects with the restaurant's sun terrace where signs identify the peaks.

When you are done enjoying the views take the First gondola back to Grindelwald. Alternatively, extend the hike with a visit to the Bachsee. The visit to this beautiful lake adds 3.8 miles (round-trip) to the hike with an additional elevation gain of 360-ft. For more information see Hike 44 - First to the Bachsee.

Trailhead Directions

From the Grindelwald Bahnhof (Train Station) to Grosse Scheidegg: Walk east from the train station a short distance along Dorfstasse (the main street in Grindelwald) to the main bus stop (Buswenderplatz) on the south side of the street. Purchase bus tickets at the small ticket booth for Grosse Scheidegg. Take the bus bound for Grosse Scheidegg or Schwarzwaldalp and get off at Grosse Scheidegg. The trip takes 36 minutes.

If you are staying in town, you can also catch the bus at one of several bus stops along the main street. Each stop is named with a sign. Logon to the SBB website or download the app to see the departure times from the stop nearest your accommodations.

From the First to Grindelwald Bahnhof (Train Station): Take the gondola from First to Grindelwald. When you exit the gondola walk down to Grindelwald's main street (Dorfstrasse) and turn right (west). Walk along the main street for 0.4 miles to the Grindelwald Bahnhof (train station).

Note: The First gondola it a multi-stage lift that goes through intermediate stations. At all stations remain seated. The doors will open allowing passengers who wish to get off at the intermediate stations to leave the gondola and then close, continuing the journey to Grindelwald.

43. Grosse Scheidegg to Bussalp ★★★★★
Distance: 3.5 - 8.9 miles (one way)
Near Grindelwald in the Bernese Alps

Panoramic views of the 4,000-meter peaks, glacial cirques and deep gorges to the south of Grindelwald are the highlights of this terrific hike between Grosse Scheidegg and Bussalp.

Distance: 3.5 miles (one way) - First
5.4 miles (one way) to Bachsee
8.9 miles (one way) to Bussalp
Elevation: 6,452-ft. at Grosse
Scheidegg
7,110-ft. at First
7,450-ft. at Bachsee
5,905-ft. at Bussalp

Elevation Gain: 658-ft. to First
998-ft. to Bachsee
-2,001-ft. to Bussalp
Difficulty: moderate-strenuous
Basecamp: Grindelwald
Grindelwald Map: See page 214
Online Map/Photos:
www.hikingwalking.com/bussalp

Why Hike from Grosse Scheidegg to Bussalp

From various viewpoints in Grindelwald, the sheer north faces of the Wetterhorn, Mattenberg and Eiger, split by deep glacial gorges, soar above the south side of the valley. Hidden from this perspective are an amazing set of 4,000-meter peaks, including the Schreckhorn, Fiescherhorn and the Finsteraarhorn.

This scenic hike, traveling from Grosse Scheidegg to Bussalp, features magnificent panoramic views of all these peaks and more from a variety of different angles. Along the way the path passes the photogenic Bachsee, traverses rugged ridges and travels through lovely, wildflower-filled meadows.

Starting in Grosse Scheidegg, hikers are treated to intimate views of the Wetterhorn towering overhead along with side views of the Mattenberg, Monch and Eiger. As the trail traverses the base of the Schwarzhorn views open to the Schreckhorn and Klein Schreckhorn, rising along the ridge above the Mattenberg. Soon the Fiescherhorn massif makes an appearance, towering above Fiescher glacier nestled in a bowl behind the Eiger.

At the First viewpoint we are treated with dazzling views of the Grindelwald Glacier, tumbling in motionless waves down the slopes of the Wetterhorn, Barglistock and Schreckhorn. The Finsteraarhorn rises beyond the glacial cirque formed by the Fiescherhorn, Monch and Eiger.

From First the trail ascends to the Bachsee, where the Wetterhorn and Schreckhorn form the perfect backdrop for this pretty little lake. Our path now turns south and we leave the majority of hikers behind as the trail climbs along the eastern flanks of Reeti to Spitzen, with splendid panoramic views of the Finsteraarhorn soaring above the Obers Ischmeer Glacier.

Soon the trail turns southwest again, crosses Reeti's southeast ridge and then traverses along the peak's south face with terrific views looking directly into the deep glacier carved gorges to the south of Grindelwald. Above the gorges the Grindelwald, Ischmeer and Fiescher Glaciers lie cradled in rugged cirques and spill down the flanks of Grindelwald's high peaks. To the southwest the Jungfrau, Breithorn and Tschingelhorn form the backdrop for Kleine Scheidegg, the saddle on the ridge between the Eiger and Mannlichen. As the trail nears Bussalp the Eiger, Monch and Jungfrau dominate the views to the southwest and we see the Wetterhorn, Schreckhorn and Fiescherhorn from a new angle.

While it is possible to walk to Grosse Scheidegg to start the hike, I strongly recommend taking the bus so you can get an earlier start. Clouds frequently form in the afternoon, obscuring the view of the high peaks.

Beyond First there is no place for refreshments along the trail until you reach Bussalp. Hikers are advised to carry water, lunch and snacks.

Grosse Scheidegg to First

- **Distance from Trailhead:** 3.5 miles (one way)
- **Elevation at First:** 7,110-ft.
- **Elevation Gain:** 658-ft.

Take the bus to Grosse Scheidegg, the saddle on the ridge separating Grindelwald from the Rosenlaui Valley to the northeast. (See trailhead directions below.) Signs at the pass direct walkers to the broad dirt track heading northwest toward Schreckfeld, First and the Faulhorn on the Hohenweg 2400.

The trail now follows the Hohenweg 2400 to First. For a detailed description of this section of the trail see Hike 42 - the Grosse Scheidegg to First Trail.

First to the Bachsee

- **Segment Stat:** 1.9 miles (one way) from First to the Bachsee
- **Total Distance - Grosse Scheidegg to Bachsee:** 5.4 miles (one way)
- **Maximum Elevation:** 7,450-ft.
- **Elevation Gain/Loss:** 998-ft.

Behind the First restaurant and lift station find a signboard. Head northwest toward the Bachalpsee (50-min), Faulhorn (2-hr 20-min) and Schynige Platte (5-hr) on a wide gravel track ascending on moderate grades through meadows. This section of the trail enjoys non-stop views from evolving perspectives. To the southeast the Obere Grindelwald Glacier tumbles in motionless waves down the slopes of the Wetterhorn, Barglistock and Schreckhorn. To the south the Finsteraarhorn rises beyond the glacial cirque formed by the Fiescherhorn, Monch and Eiger. Reeti rises to the west above the bowl cradling the Bachsee (aka Bachalpsee), a popular lake.

After walking about a mile the grade eases as the path continues heading toward the Bachsee. Reach a trail junction at 5.1 miles where a path branches right toward the Hagelsee and Wildgarst. Stay on the main track to the Bachsee. A short distance beyond pass a second junction with a trail heading left (south) toward Waldspitz, Bort and Grindelwald.

At 5.4 miles arrive at a junction at the southeastern end of the Bachsee (7,450-ft.). On a calm day the Schreckhorn is perfectly reflected in the mirror-like surface of the small, unnamed lower lake to the south of the Bachsee. The lake basin is a popular picnic spot and a favorite destination for people looking for an easy hike from First.

If the weather is taking at turn for the worse, I advise turning around at the Bachsee and returning to First where you can catch the gondola down to Grindelwald. The total distance for the Grosse Scheidegg to Bachsee to First hike is 7.3 miles.

Bachsee to Bussalp

- **Segment Stat:** 3.5 miles (one way) from the Bachsee to Bussalp
- **Distance from Grosse Scheidegg to Bussalp:** 8.9 miles (one way)
- **Elevation at Bussalp:** 5,905-ft.
- **Elevation Gain/Loss:** 456-ft. / -2,001-ft.

To continue to Bussalp, return to the trail junction after enjoying the views around the Bachsee. At the junction a path branching right (northwest) skirts the east side of the Bachsee toward the Faulhorn (Hike 45) and Schynige Platte (Hike 46), an excellent hike you should take on another day. Our trail turns left toward Spitzen (20-min), Feld (1-hr) and Bussalp (2-hr), curving to the south as it travels along the north and then west shores of the small lake to the south of the Bachsee.

At 5.6 miles reach the southwestern end of the lake and a trail junction. Here the trail to the left heads to Waldspitz, Bort and Grindelwald. We continue straight ahead on narrow path ascending steeply along the east facing flanks of Reeti. At 6.0 miles the trail crests a minor ridge and then drops into a bowl with a small pond. Beyond the pond a short climbs leads to Spitzen, situated on the ridge extending southeast from Reeti, at 6.1 miles.

Spitzen enjoys splendid, panoramic views of the Finsteraarhorn looming above the Obers Ischmeer Glacier, the Fiescherhorn massif, the Fiescher Glacier, the Schreckhorn and the Eiger. To the southwest the Jungfrau forms the backdrop for Klein Scheidegg, the saddle between the Eiger and the Mannlichen ridge.

The trail, marked with red and white blazes, now climbs steeply up the north side of the ridge, just below the crest. At 6.3 miles the grade abates as the trail crosses the ridge and then climbs a short distance along the south side of the ridge to a small day-use hut and shelter. This is the high point of the hike at 7,906-ft.

Beyond the hut the rocky trail starts a steep descent heading southwest along ridge's southeast face. Rock outcroppings near the hut and large rocks along the trail offer great spots to take a break or eat lunch while gazing at the magnificent scene of 4,000-meter peaks across the valley. The path soon curves to the right (west) as it continues its descent through meadows, now along Reeti's south facing slopes.

At 7.2 miles the grade abates as the trail curves around a grassy ridge to the junction above Feld (7,087-ft.). A path, dropping steeply to the left (south), leads to Feld and Grindelwald. We continue along the trail heading northwest toward Bussalp.

The easy grade ends at 7.5 miles as the path crosses an avalanche chute and then starts descending southwest on moderately steep grades. Turn left at the junction at 7.8 miles on a path descending toward Mittellager and Grindelwald. The trail straight ahead, signed for Bussalp Oberlager, will also get you to Bussalp but is 0.6 miles longer since it takes a circuitous route that travels along a road. As you descend enjoy grand views of the Eiger, Monch and Jungfrau to the southwest. Below the trail, to the south, Bussalp lies nestled in a lovely alpine basin.

Follow the trail as it drops steeply through pastures, crossing a few small streams along the way. Just before reaching Bussalp pass a trail branching right toward the Faulhorn. In Bussalp the trail joins a road. Head south along the road following signs to the Bussalp Restaurant (5,905-ft.). Reach the restaurant and bus stop at 8.9 miles. Here regularly scheduled bus return to Grindelwald.

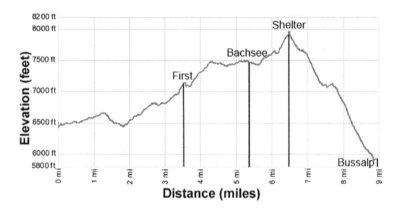

Trailhead Directions

From the Grindelwald Bahnhof (train station) to Grosse Scheidegg: See Hike 42.

From Meiringen to Grosse Scheidegg: Take the bus from the Meiringen Bahnhof to Schwarzwaldalp. At Schwarzwaldalp, change for the bus to Gross Scheidegg. The entire trip takes a little over an hour, including the wait for the connection at Schwarzwaldalp.

Return from Bussalp to Grindelwald: In the tiny hamlet of Bussalp, the postbus leaves from the Bussalp Restaurant. The ride to the Grindelwald Bahnhof (train station) takes 28 minutes.

44. First to the Bachsee ★★★★★
Distance: 3.8 miles (RT)

Near Grindelwald in the Bernese Alps

This very popular hike packs a ton of scenery into a very short distance. Nonstop views encompass Grindalwald's iconic peaks towering above the south side of the valley. These summits form the backdrop for the Bachsee, a gorgeous lake set amid beautiful alpine meadows.

Distance: 3.8 miles (RT)
Elevation: 7,110-ft. at First
7,473-ft. at the Bachsee
Elevation Gain: 363-ft.
Difficulty: easy-moderately

Basecamp: Grindelwald
Grindelwald Map: See page 214
Online Map/Photos:
www.hikingwalking.com/bachsee

Hiking from First to the Bachsee

First (7,110-ft.) is situated atop a minor summit high above the north side of Grindelwald. Overlooks at First feature stunning views of the summits soaring above the Grindelwald Valley, including the Wetterhorn, Schreckhorn and Eiger. Glaciers spill down the flanks of these massifs to deep incised gorges. Views extend southwest to Klein Scheidegg and the Jungfrau and southeast to the peaks rising beyond Grosse Scheidegg.

The facilities around First include a popular restaurant with a sun terrace and a "Cliff Walk", a cantilevered metal walkway bolted to the sheer west face of the First summit that leads to a 150-ft. long viewing platform with panoramic views of Grindelwald's iconic 4,000-meter peaks. The walkway connects with the restaurant's sun terrace where signs identify the mountains.

After enjoying the views at First, start the hike by walking behind the First restaurant and lift station where you will find a trail signboard. Walk northwest toward the Bachalpsee (50-min), Faulhorn (2-hr 20-min) and Schynige Platte (5-hr) on a wide gravel track ascending through meadows on moderate grades. The trail enjoys non-stop, ever evolving views. To the southeast the Grindelwald Glacier tumbles in motionless waves down the slopes of the Wetterhorn, Barglistock and Schreckhorn. To the south the Finsteraarhorn towers beyond the glacial cirque formed by the Fiescherhorn, Monch and Eiger. To the west Reeti rises above the bowl cradling the Bachsee (aka Bachalpsee), the destination for this hike.

After 0.7 miles the grade eases and the trail soon curves to the left (west) through lovely meadows toward the Bachsee. At 1.6 miles the path reaches a junction where a trail branches right toward the Hagelsee and Wildgarst. Stay on the main track to the Bachsee. A short distance beyond pass a second junction with a path heading left (south) toward Waldspitz, Bort and Grindelwald.

At 1.9 miles arrive at a trail junction at the southeastern end of the Bachsee (7,431-ft.). The lake is split in two by a natural dam, with the lower lake located 20-ft. below the upper lake. On a calm day the Schreckhorn is perfectly reflected in the lower-lake's mirror-like surface. Views extend west across the upper lake to the Faulhorn, Esel and Simelihorn rising above the cirque at the head of the valley. The lake basin is a popular picnic spot and a favorite destination for parties looking for an easy hike. Get an early start to avoid the crowds.

When you are done enjoying the lake retrace your steps to the First Gondola for a 3.8 mile hike.

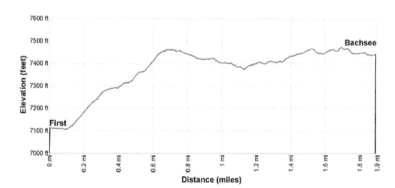

Trailhead Directions

From the Grindelwald Bahnhof (train station) to First Gondola: Walk east along Dorfstrasse, the main street in Grindelwald for 0.4 miles. Turn left on an unnamed street across from the vehicle entrance for the Sunstar Hotel. The turn is marked with a sign for the Firstbahn (First Gondola). (If you pass the Gasthof Steinbock with a pizzeria on the ground floor you have gone too far.) Walk up the street to the First Gondola station, just past the Pension Gydisdorf.

Note: The First gondola it a multi-stage lift that goes through intermediate stations. At all stations remain seated. The doors will open, allowing passengers who wish to get off at the intermediate stations to leave the gondola, and then close before continuing the journey to First.

When purchasing lift tickets it is typically less expensive to purchase a round-trip ticket than two one-way tickets.

45. First to the Faulhorn ☆☆☆☆☆
Distance: 7.2 miles (RT)
Near Grindelwald in the Bernese Alps

Amazing views of the glacier clad peaks towering above Grindelwald and Lauterbrunnen along with views of Lake Brienz and beyond are the highlights of this popular trail climbing to the historic Faulhorn Berghaus and the summit of the Faulhorn.

Distance: 7.2 miles (RT)   **Basecamp:** Grindelwald
Elevation: 7,110-ft. at First   **Grindelwald Map:** See page 214
8,793-ft. at the Faulhorn   **Online Map/Photos:**
Elevation Gain: 1,683-ft.   www.hikingwalking.com/faulhorn
Difficulty: moderate-strenuous

Hiking from First to the Faulhorn

This great hike starts with a scenic gondola ride to First and then travels along the well-trod path to the beautiful Bachsee. Along the way the Wetterhorn, Schreckhorn and the Eiger are the stars of the show, soaring above the Grindelwald Valley.

Beyond the lake the trail climbs to the grassy saddle at Gassenboden (8,373-ft.) where views open to the summits towering above Lauterbrunnen. Our destination, the Faulhorn, is in sight. Beyond the saddle a steep climb leads to the historic Faulhorn Berghotel, situated just below the summit of the Faulhorn. From the hotel and the summit of the Faulhorn enjoy grand views of the Bernese Alps to the south and the Lake Brienz area to the north. The hotel offers rooms and dormitory accommodation along with meals.

An optional extension beyond the Faulhorn junction leads to a stunning overlook with views encompassing the glacier clad peaks soaring above Grindelwald and Lauterbrunnen. On a beautiful day it will be hard to pull yourself away from the stunning views.

First to the Bachsee

The day starts with a gondola ride from Grindelwald to First (7,110-ft.) and then a scenic hike to the Bachsee. For a detailed description of this section of the trail see Hike 44 - First to the Bachsee Trail.

Bachsee to the Faulhorn

After exploring the area around the Bachsee return to the junction. Ignore the trail heading left (southwest) to Spitzen, Feld and Bussalp. Instead turn right (northwest) on the trail toward the Faulhorn (1-hr 30-min), which skirts the right (northeast) shore of the Bachsee.

At the northwest end of the lake the trail curves to the left (west/northwest) and starts a steep ascent through rocky meadows toward a saddle. Switchbacks facilitate the ascent. As you climb turn around for beautiful views of the Wetterhorn and Schreckhorn forming the perfect backdrop for the Bachsee. To the east views open to the Schwarzhorn rising to the north of Grindelwald.

Reach the broad, grassy saddle at Gassenboden (8,373-ft.) at 3.1 miles. Here signs points to a path dropping southwest toward Bussalp. Our trail curves to the right (north) and climbs toward the Faulhorn (25-min), Manndlenen (1-hr 10-min) and Schynige Platte (3-hr 10-min). Panoramic views from the saddle encompass a sea of peaks to the southwest including the Jungfrau, Breithorn and, in the distance, the Bluemlisalp massif. The Faulhorn rises to the north.

Beyond the saddle the trail continues the steep climb, arriving at the Faulhorn junction (8,596-ft.) at 3.4 miles. Turn right (north) on the trail switchbacking up steep, grassy slopes to the Berghaus Faulhorn and the summit of the Faulhorn (8,793-ft.) at 3.6 miles. The stiff climb is rewarded with grand views of the Bernese Alps to the south and the Lake Brienz area to the north. The Faulhorn offers rooms and dormitory accommodations in addition to the restaurant with a deck boasting amazing views of the high peaks to the south.

Overlook Beyond the Faulhorn

If time and energy permit, I strong encourage hikers to descend to the junction below the Faulhorn and then walk 0.4 miles west along the trail toward Manndlenen (1-hr) and Schynige Platte (3-hr). The narrow trail initially drops steeply across the south facing flanks of the Faulhorn. After 0.2 miles the grade eases as the path travels west along a ridge and then climbs a low grassy knoll. Near the top of the knoll watch for red/white blazed rocks marking a turn to the right. (There is no sign.) Here a use-trail continues straight ahead along the top of the knoll to excellent lunch spots with stunning views of the peaks towering above Grindelwald, Lauterbrunnen and beyond. When you are done taking in the views retrace your steps to the Faulhorn junction and then the First gondola. Total round trip distance for this detour is 0.8 miles.

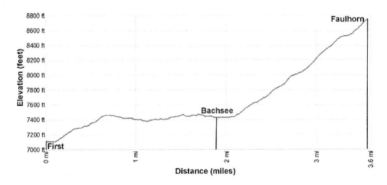

Trailhead Directions

From the Grindelwald Bahnhof (train station) to First Gondola: See Hike 44.

46. First to Schynige Platte ★★★★★
Distance: 10.2 miles (one way)
Near Grindelwald in the Bernese Alps

One of the best hikes in the Grindelwald area features fabulous views of the Bernese Alps stretching from the Wetterhorn, Eiger, Jungfrau and Breithorn, towering above the Grindelwald and Lauterbrunnen Valleys, to the Bluemlisalp massif in the southwest.

Distance: 1.9 miles (one way) to Bachsee
3.8 miles (one way) to Faulhorn Viewpoint
10.2 miles (one way) to Schynige Platte
Elevation: 7,110-ft. at First
7,473-ft. at Bachsee
8,583-ft. at Faulhorn Viewpoint
6,453-ft. at Schynige Platte

Elevation Gain: 363-ft. to Bachsee
1,473-ft. to Faulhorn Viewpoint
-2,130-ft. to Schynige Platte
Difficulty: strenuous
Basecamp: Grindelwald
Grindelwald Map: See page 214
Online Map/Photos:
www.hikingwalking.com/schynige

Why Hike from First to Schynige Platte

There is no shortage of great hikes in the Grindelwald area with fabulous views. My favorite is the trail from First to Schynige Platte, traveling through diverse landscapes with stunning, panoramic views of the Bernese Alps from ever changing perspectives.

The stars of the show are the 4,000-meter peaks soaring above Grindelwald and Lauterbrunnen. Playing a supporting role are two scenic lakes, pretty meadows, glistening glaciers and incredible rock formations. Midway through the hike views of Lake Brienz, later joined by Lake Thun and Interlaken, vie for your attention.

The hike starts with a gondola ride from Grindelwald to First, a panoramic overlook with fabulous views of the Wetterhorn, Schreckhorn, Finsteraarhorn and Eiger. An ascent along the slopes high above the north side of Grindelwald passes the Bachsee and then leads to a saddle where views shift to the Jungfrau, Breithorn and a sea of nearby peaks stretching southwest to the Bluemlisalp massif. Past the saddle the trail traverses a high ridge with dazzling views of the Bernese Alps to the south and Lake Brienz to the north.

At the midpoint of the hike the trail drops down the north side of the ridge where views shift to the amazing rock formations along the south and north faces of the Sagissa ridge. The path then loops around the ridge and descends to the pretty pastures of the Sagistal (Sagis Valley). Here views reopen to the Bernese Alps, now from a different angle, with the austere karst landscape around the Güw area in the foreground.

The last leg of the hike travels along the south and west facing flanks of the Loucherhorn before descending to the pretty meadows above Oberberg with more sensational views of the Bernese Alps. A final short, steep climb leads to Schynige Platte, where a cog railway descends to Wilderswil with connecting trains to Grindelwald, Lauterbrunnen and Interlaken.

Pick a day that promises clear skies and get an early start. The trail is long and quite strenuous, with lots of ups and downs. Hikers should be in good condition and well acclimated. Do not attempt this hike during bad or threatening weather. Most of this hike is along high exposed slopes, not the place to be during a storm.

First to Bachsee

- **Distance from Trailhead:** 1.9 miles (one way)
- **Elevation at the Bachsee:** 7,473-ft.
- **Elevation Gain:** 363-ft.

The day starts with a gondola ride from Grindelwald to First (7,110-ft.) and then a scenic hike to the Bachsee. For a detailed description of this section of the trail see Hike 44 - First to the Bachsee Trail.

Bachsee to the Viewpoint past the Faulhorn Junction

- **Segment Stat:** 1.9 miles (one-way) from the Bachsee to the Knoll/Overlook near the Faulhorn
- **Total Distance:** 3.8 miles (one way)
- **Maximum Elevation:** 8,583-ft.
- **Elevation Gain First to the Viewpoint:** 1,473-ft.

After exploring the area around the Bachsee, return to the junction at the southeast end of the lake. Ignore the trail heading left (southwest) to Spitzen, Feld and Bussalp. Our trail branches right (northwest), skirting the right (northeast) shore of the Bachsee toward Faulhorn (1-hr 30-min) and Schynige Platte (4-hr 15-min).

At the northwest end of the lake the trail curves to the left (west/northwest) and starts a steep ascent through rocky meadows toward a saddle. Switchbacks facilitate the climb. As you ascend turn around for beautiful views of the Wetterhorn and Schreckhorn forming the perfect backdrop for the Bachsee. To the east views open to the Schwarzhorn rising to the north of Grindelwald.

Reach the broad, grassy saddle at Gassenboden (8,373-ft.) at 3.1 miles. Here signs points to a path dropping left (southwest) toward Bussalp. Our trail curves to the right (north) and climbs the toward Faulhorn (25-min), Manndlenen (1-hr 10min) and Schynige Platte (3-hr 10-min). Panoramic views from the saddle encompass a sea of peaks to the southwest including the Jungfrau, Breithorn and, in the distance, the Bluemlisalp massif. The Faulhorn rises to the north.

Beyond the saddle the trail continues the steep climb, arriving at the Faulhorn junction (8,596-ft.) at 3.4 miles. Here a trail heads north, switchbacking up steep grassy slopes to the Berghaus Faulhorn and the summit of the Faulhorn (8,793-ft.). If time and energy permit, a detour to the summit is rewarded with grand views of the Bernese Alps to the south and the Lake Brienz to the north. Add 0.4 mile (round-trip) for the detour.

To continue the hike, turn left (west) at the junction toward Manndlenen (1-hr) and Schynige Platte (3-hr) on a narrow trail that initially drops steeply across the south facing flanks of the Faulhorn. At 3.6 miles the grade eases as the trail travels west along a ridge and then climbs a low grassy knoll. Near the top of the knoll watch for red/white blazed rocks marking a turn to the right at 3.8 miles. (There is no sign.) This is our trail. (A use-trail continues along the top of the knoll to excellent lunch spots with stunning views of the peaks towering above Grindelwald, Lauterbrunnen and beyond.)

Viewpoint to Schynige Platte

- **Segment Stat:** 6.4 miles (one-way) from the Viewpoint to Schynige Platte
- **Total Distance:** 10.2 miles (one way)
- **Ending Elevation:** 6,453-ft.
- **Elevation Gain/Loss:** 2,130-ft.

(Note: There is a lot of elevation gains and losses along this section of the trail making it much more strenuous then indicated by the simple elevation gain/loss between the beginning and end point of the trail segment.)

Turn right (northwest) and descend the blazed trail on a rocky path, following a jog in the ridge. Soon the trail and the ridge curve left (west). The path now descends near the top of the ridge crest to a junction at Pkt. Ignore the trail to the right (north), descending toward Faulegg, Battenalp and Iseltwald along the slopes to the south of Lake Brienz. Our trail curves left (southwest) and follows an undulating course along the south side of the ridge crest with terrific views of the Bernese Alps. These will be your last views of the peaks until you near Schynige Platte.

At 4.6 miles the path crosses to the north side of the ridge where views open to Lake Brienz. Follow the rocky trail as it heads west, descending on moderate grades toward Manndlenen, the location of a small hut and restaurant. Views now encompass the interesting rock formations along the flanks of the Indri-Sagissa, the highpoint on the ridge across the valley. Soon the grade steepens as it path drops down a rocky slope and then swings to the right (northeast), dropping down a very steep trail to Manndlenen (7,690-ft.) at 5.3 miles.

Beyond the restaurant the trail heads northeast, descending limestone ledges on moderate grades along the south face of the Sagissa ridge. Use care along this section of the trail. Some of the rock is quite slick, especially when wet.

At 5.8 miles the trail curves to the left (west/southwest) around the end of the ridge. Below the trail to the north is the Saglistalsee, a small lake, at the foot of the long, narrow Sagistal Valley, a hanging valley nestled between the Roteflue and the Indri-Sagissa.

The path continues descending along the north facing flanks of the Indri-Sagissa, dropping down scree covered slopes and rocky meadows to the pretty pastures at the end of the Sagistal (Sagis Valley) at 6.8 miles. Here the trail descends steeply for a half mile, traveling through the austere karst landscape around the Guw area, and then climbs over a rock outcropping along the east facing flanks of the Loucherhorn.

Along the way views reopen to the Eiger, Monch, Jungfrau and Breithorn towering above the Lauterbrunnen Valley and the peaks lining the south side of the Sefinental valley. To the east are interesting rock formations along the ridges extending southwest from the Indri-Sagissa.

The undulating path now crosses an old rockslide and then curves around a ridge extending southeast from the Loucherhorn, weaving its way through rock outcroppings along the peak's south facing flanks. Soon the trail climbs to and crosses the Loucherhorn's southwest ridge at 8.25 miles. From the ridge enjoy more great views of the Bernese Alps to the south.

After crossing the ridge the trail turns north, descending on easy grades along the west face of the Loucherhorn. Schynige Platte, our destination, is now in view. After a quarter mile the trail curves to the left (southwest) and drops to a junction at Loucheren (6,627-ft.) at 8.6 miles.

Past the junction the descent continue on moderately steep grades through pretty meadows toward Schynige Platte. Short, narrow trails branch right off the main track and climb to the ridge crest where panoramic views open to Lake Brienz, Interlaken and Lake Thun to the north and west. A short detour is recommended to take in the views. Note: Hikers with the time and energy can follow the trails along the ridge crest, taking a longer, circuitous route to the train station at Schynige Platte.

Back on the main trail the grade soon eases as the path weaves its way through pastures, passing above the alp buildings of Oberberg. At 9.7 miles cross a dirt farm road and then climb steeply up a gravel track to Schynige Platte (6,453-ft.) at 10.2 miles.

A cog railway, built in 1893, ferries visitors from Wilderswil to this high overlook with sensational views of the Bernese Alps including the Wetterhorn, Schreckhorn, Finsteraarhorn, Eiger, Monch, Jungfrau and Breithorn. Facility includes a hotel, restaurant and network of nature trails wandering through a botanic garden with over 650 species of plants native to the Swiss Alps.

When you are done exploring the area take the 52 minute ride on the cog railway down to Wilderswil where connecting trains leave for Grindelwald, Lauterbrunnen and Interlaken.

Pick a day that promises clear skies and get an early start. The trail is long and quite strenuous, with lots of ups and downs. Hikers should be in good condition and well acclimated. Do not attempt this hike during bad or threatening weather. Most of this hike is along high, exposed slopes, not the place to be during a storm.

The trail can be hiked from either direction. My preference is to start at First, which is higher than Schynige Platte and closer to the Faulhorn, the high point on the hike. This way you get down from the high point earlier in the day, always a good idea when hiking in the mountains.

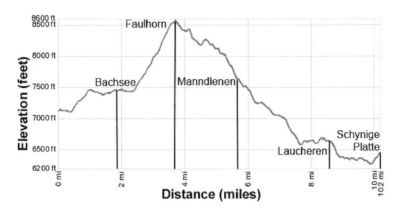

Trailhead Directions

From the Grindelwald Bahnhof (train station) to the First Gondola: Walk east along Dorfstrasse, the main street, in Grindelwald for 0.4 miles. Turn left on an unnamed street across from the vehicle entrance for the Sunstar Hotel. There should be signs for the Firstbahn lift at the turn. (If you pass the Gasthof Steinbock with a pizzeria on the ground floor you have gone too far.) Walk up the street to the First lift station, just past the Pension Gydisdorf.

Note: At the Firstbahn station you can purchase a round-trip ticket that includes the gondola ride to First, a one-way ticket on the cog railway from Schynige Platte to Wilderswil and the train ticket from Wilderswil to Grindelwald. The combined tickets are a better deal than purchasing all the tickets separately. It also saves you from standing in line at Schynige Platte and Wilderswil to purchase tickets.

From the Lauterbrunnen Bahnhof (train station) to the First Gondola: From Lauterbrunnen, take the train bound for Interlaken Ost to Zwelutschinen. In Zwelutschinen board a train bound for Grindelwald. In Grindelwald follow the directions (above) to the First Gondola (Firstbahn).

Returning from Schynige Platte to Grindelwald or Lauterbrunnen: Take the cog railway from Schynige Platte to the Wilderswil Bahnhof (52 minutes). At Wilderswil take the train to Grindelwald / Lauterbrunnen. Half the cars on the train will be labeled for Grindelwald and the other half for Lauterbrunnen. Make sure you get on a car labeled for your destination. At Zweilutschinen the train literally splits in half with half the train going to Grindelwald and the other half heading for Lauterbrunnen. The trip to Grindelwald takes 29 minutes.

There is typically wait time between when the cog train arrives at Wilderswil and when the trains leave for Grindelwald and Lauterbrunnen. Across the street from the train station in Wilderswil is a Migros grocery store, a good place to get a cold drink or a snack while waiting for the connecting train.

47. Panoramaweg: Mannlichen to Kleine Scheidegg ★★★★★
Distance: 2.8 miles (One Way)
Near Grindelwald in the Bernese Alps

The Panoramaweg, between Mannlichen and Kleine Scheidegg, is an easy, popular hike with nonstop views the Eiger, Monch and Jungfrau. Extend the hike with a walk to the Mannlichen summit for more breathtaking views.

Distance: 2.8 miles (one way)
Elevation: 7,293-ft. at Mannlichen
6,762-ft. at Kleine Scheidegg
Elevation Gain: -531-ft.
Difficulty: easy

Basecamp: Grindelwald
Grindelwald Map: See page 214
Online Map/Photos:
www.hikingwalking.com/
panoramaweg

Hiking the Panoramaweg: Mannlichen to Kleine Scheidegg

The day starts by taking a gondola to Mannlichen (7,293-ft.), a small alp situated on a scenic ridge separating the Lutschental and Lauterbrunnental (Grindelwald and Lauterbrunnen Valleys). (See trailhead directions below.) Overlooks atop the ridge near the lift station enjoy great views to the west/southwest up the length of the Lauterbrunnen valley to the Jungfrau, Breithorn and Tschingelhorn along with the peaks lining the Sefinental valley. The Wetterhorn, Schreckhorn, Eiger and Monch dominate the skyline to the east.

Outside the lift station signs point south/southeast to Kleine Scheidegg (1-hr 30-min) along the Hohenweg 2100m. This is one of the themed walks in Grindelwald also known as the Panorama Trail or Panoramaweg. Other signs point north to the Mannlichen viewpoint, reached via the "Royal Walk" themed trail.

To reach Kleine Scheidegg walk to the east side of the lift station and then turn right, south/southeast, on a broad gravel track descending on easy grades through meadows along the base of Mt. Tschuggen (8,270-ft.). In route enjoy wonderful views of the Wetterhorn, Schreckhorn and the massive north wall of the Eiger towering above the Grindelwald valley to the east.

At 1.5 miles the trail curves to the right (south) around a ridge extending from Mt. Tschuggen. A short distance beyond the trail again curves to the right (southwest), crosses under the Honegg chairlift and then descends along the south facing slopes of Mt. Tschuggen. Ahead are fine views of the rugged east wall of the Lauberhorn (8,110-ft.). To the south the Monch and Jungfrau form a beautiful backdrop for the trail descending to Kleine Scheidegg.

Cross the creek draining the slopes between Mt. Tschuggen and the Lauberhorn at 2.1 miles. Beyond the creek the trail turns to the left (southeast) before curving to the right (south) along the base of the Lauberhorn. Ignore the trail branching to the right and climbing toward to Lauberhorn at 2.5 miles. Instead, continue straight ahead toward Kleine Scheidegg.

On a clear day the views of the Eiger, Monch and Jungfrau from this segment of the trail are nothing short of spectacular. Look carefully to see the Jungfraujoch, the highest train station in Europe, housed in a gleaming silver building on the saddle between the Jungfrau and the Monch.

Soon the path reaches the Rotstockli (6,923-ft.), a scenic overlook with terrific views of the Eiger's north wall soaring overhead. From here the trail descends on moderate grades to Kleine Scheidegg (6,762-ft.), located on a saddle between the Lauberhorn and the Eiger, at 2.8 miles.

The railway station at Kleine Scheidegg connects trains from Grindelwald and Lauterbrunnen with trains heading for the Jungfraujoch, a line that partially travels through tunnels dug through the Eiger. The Jungfraujoch (11,371-ft.), or "Top of Europe", is an extremely popular destination with several panoramic restaurants and overlooks. As a result the area around Kleine Scheidegg, including the restaurants, souvenir shops and bathrooms, are often crowded with hordes of tourists.

After you are done exploring the Kleine Scheidegg area, either take the train back to Grindelwald or descend to Grindelwald via Hike 49 – the Eiger Trail.

To the Top of Mannlichen

- **Distance from Trailhead:** 1.2 miles (round trip)
- **Ending/Highest Elevation:** 7,684-ft.
- **Elevation Gain:** 391-ft.

This scenic walk, also starting at the Mannlichen gondola station, leads to the overlook atop Mannlichen, a 7,684-ft. summit at the north end of the Mannlichen ridge. From the Mannlichen lift station, turn north toward the Mannlichen viewpoint, also listed as the Royal Walk on the trail signs. The trail starts out flat but soon starts climbing on moderate to steep grades to the overlook, gaining 400-ft. in 0.6 miles.

This panoramic viewpoint enjoys breathtaking, 360-degree views encompassing the Grindelwald Valley to the east, the high peaks between Schynige Platte and the Schwarzhorn to the north and the summits rimming the Lauterbrunnen Valley to the west. Behind you, to the south, the Wetterhorn, Schreckhorn, Eiger, Monch and Jungfrau dominate the skyline. To the northwest are distant views of the Interlaken area.

When you are done taking in the views, retrace your steps to the Mannlichen lift for a 1.2 mile (round trip) hike. Combine the Royal Walk with the Panoramaweg to Kleine Scheidegg for a 4.0 mile hike.

Trailhead Directions

From the Grindelwald Bahnhof (train station) to Mannlichen: From the Grindelwald train station walk a short distance to the east along the main street to the main bus stop on the south side of the road and catch the #121 bus to Terminal or #123 bus toward Itramen Egg. Get off at the Terminal stop where a new facility includes stations for the Mannlichen and Eiger Express gondolas. The bus rides take 8-12 minutes. You can also take the train from Grindelwald Bahnhof to Grindelwald Terminal (5 minutes).

Alternatively, from the train station follow the yellow signs pointing to the Terminal station for the Mannlichen and Eiger Express gondolas, which is to the northwest of the Grund Station on the Kleine Scheidegg line. The walk descends the hillsides to the south/southwest of the train station, using a combination of walkways and roads to the Terminal Station, a new facility for the Mannlichen and Eiger Express Gondolas. Allocate about 20 minutes for the 0.9 mile walk. The ride up the world's longest passenger-carrying gondola takes about 30 minutes and is quite scenic.

From Lauterbrunnen to Mannlichen: From the train station in Lauterbrunnen, catch the cog railway heading toward Wengen/Kleine Scheidegg and get off in Wengen. (The ride to Wengen takes about 14 minutes.) In Wengen, walk behind the train station to the Dorfstrasse (main street) and turn left (northwest). Soon you will see signs pointing right to a road leading to the cable car station. Along the way pass the Wengen tourism office. Purchase a one-way ticket and take the cable car to Mannlichen. The cable car climbs over 3,000-ft. and takes about 5 minutes. Keep an eye out for chamoix grazing on the grassy slopes beneath the cable car.

From Wengen to Mannlichen: In Wengen, the bottom station for the cable car is located to the north/northeast of the train station (Bahnhof). Walk behind the train station to the Dorfstrasse, the main street, and then turn left (northwest). Soon you will see signs pointing right to the cable car station. Along the way pass the Wengen tourism office. Purchase a one-way ticket and take the cable car to Mannlichen. The cable car climbs over 3,000-ft. and takes about 5 minutes. Keep an eye out for chamoix grazing on the grassy slopes beneath the cable car.

Klein Scheidegg to Grindelwald/Lauterbrunnen: At the Kleine Scheidegg Railway Station, buy a one-way ticket to the Grindelwald or Lauterbrunnen Bahnhof (train station). Trains typically run every 30 minutes.

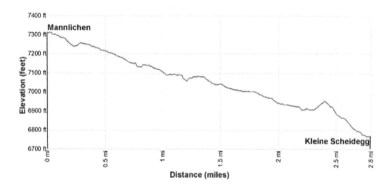

48. Mannlichen to Wengen ★★★★★
Distance: 10.8 miles (one way)
Near Grindelwald in the Bernese Alps

A triad of giants: the Eiger, Monch and Jungfrau, dominate the breathtaking views along this scenic hike from Mannlichen to Wengen.

Distance: 2.8 miles (one way) to Kleine Scheidegg
4.3 miles (one way) to Eiger Glacier Viewpoint
10.8 miles (one way) to Wengen
Elevation: 7,293-ft. at Mannlichen
6,762-ft. at Kleine Scheidegg
7,250-ft. at Eiger Glacier Viewpoint
4,190-ft. at Wengen

Elevation Gain: -531-ft. to Kleine Scheidegg
488-ft. to Eiger Glacier Viewpoint
-3,103-ft. to Wengen
Difficulty: moderate
Basecamp: Grindelwald
Grindelwald Map: See page 214
Online Map/Photos:
www.hikingwalking.com/wengen

Why Hike from Mannlichen to Wengen

Jaw dropping views of the Eiger, Monch and Jungfrau top the list of scenic highlights on this terrific hike between Grindelwald and Wengen. From the top of the gondola at Mannlichen, the route follows a popular trail descending to Klein Scheidegg with panoramic views of the high peaks, including the Wetterhorn, Schreckhorn and the Eiger, towering above the emerald green meadows of Grindelwald.

Beyond Kleine Scheidegg the trail travels to a pretty lake nestled beneath the Eiger's massive north wall and then climbs to an overlook atop a moraine with magnificent views of the Eiger Glacier spilling down the rugged slopes between the Eiger and the Monch. The trail then turns west, descending a valley through lovely meadows with splendid views of the glacier clad slopes of the Monch and Jungfrau. On warm summer afternoons lucky hikers may see icefalls crashing down the rugged cliffs.

As you descend the valley, views open to the Bietenhorn and Schilthorn towering above the Lauterbrunnen Valley. To the south the Gspaltenhorn, rising above the Sefinental Valley, and the Breithorn, at the head of the Lauterbrunnen valley, dominate the view. At the foot of the valley the trail turns north and descends to Wengen. In Wengen trains head down to Lauterbrunnen and climb to Kleine Scheidegg where connecting trains descend to Grindelwald. A cable car also ascends back to Mannlichen.

Walking from village to village is one of the joys of hiking in Switzerland. This trail is a great option if you wish to walk from Grindelwald to Lauterbrunnen, or vice versa.

Mannlichen to Kleine Scheidegg

- **Distance from Trailhead:** 2.8 miles (one way)
- **Elevation:** 7,293-ft. at Mannlichen
  6,762-ft. at Kleine Scheidegg
- **Elevation Gain/Loss:** -531-ft.

The day starts by taking the gondola to Mannlichen (7,293-ft.), a small alp situated on a scenic ridge separating the Lutschental (Grindelwald valley) and Lauterbrunnental (Lauterbrunnen valley). For a detailed description of this section of the trail see Hike 47 - Mannlichen to Klein Scheidegg Trail.

Kleine Scheidegg to Eiger Glacier Viewpoint

- **Segment Stat:** 1.5 miles (one-way) from Kleine Scheidegg to Eiger Glacier Viewpoint
- **Total Distance:** 4.3 miles (one way) from Mannlichen to the Eiger Glacier Viewpoint
- **Maximum Elevation:** 7,250-ft.
- **Elevation Gain/Loss** 488-ft.

From Kleine Scheidegg there are a number of routes to Wengen. The shortest and least scenic descends along the rail line to Wengen. A quick look at a map will show you a variety of possibilities.

My preferred route is a longer and very scenic, visiting the Eiger Glacier before descending to the beautiful alps of Biglenalp and Mettlenalp and then swinging north toward Wengen. Terrific views of the Eiger, Monch, Jungfrau and the high peaks towering above the Sefinental and Lauterbrunnen valleys are your constant companion along much of the trail.

When you are done exploring the Kleine Scheidegg area cross to the south side of the rail tracks and locate the trail signs near the base of the steps leading to the Hotel Bellevue des Alps, an old wood hotel. Follow the signs pointing to the Eigergletscher (Eiger Glacier), directing you to climb the stairs and then turn right, following a broad track ascending on moderate grades above the left (east) side of the train tracks for the Jungfraujoch.

Reach the Fallbodensee, a pretty little lake, at 3.5 miles. On a still day the mirror-like surface of the lake is a photographer's dream with beautiful reflections of the Wetterhorn and Eiger. On the south side of the lake a small building houses an interesting exhibit showing the various routes climbing the Eiger's north wall. It's definitely worth a stop.

At the southeast end of the lake the trail turns right (south) and drops down a gravel track passing through a culvert going under the train tracks. Beyond the culvert the trail resumes its moderate climb, heading south toward the moraine of the Eigergletscher. At 4.0 miles the trail curves to the left (east) as it drops into a shallow bowl and then climbs to an overlook atop the moraine at 4.25 miles. The moraine crest features great views of the glacier tumbling down the rugged slopes between the Eiger and the Monch.

Eiger Glacier Viewpoint to Wengen

- **Segment Stat:** 6.5 miles (one-way) from the Viewpoint to Wengen
- **Total Distance:** 10.8 miles (one way)
- **Ending Elevation:** 4,190-ft.
- **Elevation Gain/Loss:** -3,103-ft.

Signs atop the moraine point left (northeast) toward the Eigergletscher train station and right (southwest) to Biglenalp, Mettlenalp and Wengen. After viewing the glacier, turn right and descend the steep, narrow trail running along the crest of the moraine. Keep an eye out for a small herd of chamoix that graze along the slopes of the moraine wall.

At 4.4 miles travel along the top of the moraine is no longer safe. Here the trail turns right (west), drops off the moraine wall and descends steeply through pretty meadows. The Monch and the Jungfrau tower overhead. To the west views extend to the peaks rising above the Lauterbrunnen Valley.

Reach the junction at Haaregg (6,529-ft) at 4.8 miles and turn left toward Biglenalp (35-min) and Wengen (2-hr 20-min). The trail to the right heads toward Wixi and Wengernalp, a stop on the train going to Wengen and Lauterbrunnen.

Our trail now descends southwest on moderately steep grades along the top of an old moraine. Along the way the meadows give way to low-lying shrubs and small conifers. At 5.3 miles reach an intersection with a trail branching right toward Wengernalp. We turn left on the Bergwanderweg that drops down switchbacks to a trail junction at Weisse Fluh (6,020-ft.) at 5.5 miles. Here we turn left, descending south/southeast toward Biglenalp (15-min) Mettlenalp (50-min) and Wengen (2-hr). The trail to the right leads to the Wengernalp train station.

Follow the trail, covered with roots, as it drops through trees on moderate to moderately-steep grades toward the valley floor. Soon the trees give way to beautiful meadows. A short descent leads to Biglenalp at 6.0 miles, situated along a pretty stream. The meadows around Biglenalp enjoy gorgeous views of the Eiger, Monch and the Eiger Glacier. The Jungfrau looms overhead. Across the valley, waterfalls cascade down clefts in the rugged walls along the base of the Jungfrau. This is a great spot for a picnic or to take a break.

Don't cross the bridges at Biglenalp, instead turn right and descend the along the north side of the stream. Soon the trail curves right away from the stream, traveling through meadows and clusters of trees.

At 6.6 miles the path begins an easy ascent that ends at a junction with a gravel road at Mettlenalp (5,660-ft.) at 7.2 miles. Continue straight ahead on the gravel road in the direction of Stalden (15-min) and Wengen (1-hr 20-min). The road descends on easy grades through open pastures, passing a few farm buildings along the way. This section of the trail enjoys excellent views of the glaciers cascading down the slopes of the Monch and the Jungfrau. On a warm summer afternoon lucky hikers may see an icefall crashing down the rugged cliffs.

Take a detour along the narrow trail branching left at 7.6 miles, to an overlook with breathtaking views of the Eiger, Monch and Jungfrau. The Bietenhorn and Schilthorn fill the skyline above the Lauterbrunnen Valley to the west. The Gspaltenhorn, rising above the Sefinental Valley and the Breithorn, at the head of the Lauterbrunnen valley, dominates the view to the south.

Beyond the overlook follow the signs pointing toward Wengen. The road soon enters the trees as it swings to the right (north/northeast) and climbs over a low hill. Here you get your first distant views of Wengen, nestle in a bowl beneath the west flanks of the ridge separating the Lutschental and Lauterbrunnental. Look carefully along the top of ridge to see the cable car station at Mannlichen.

The trail now starts a long descent on moderate grades heading northeast toward Wengen. Ignore any trails branching left toward Lauterbrunnen. Along the way, pass by Langetrejen, Hannegg and Allmend before the final descent to Wengen. Near Wengen the gravel track turns to a paved road and soon passes under the rail line. Turn left (west) at the next intersection, following the road to the Wengen Bahnhof (train station) at 10.8 miles. Here trains descend to Lauterbrunnen or go up to and over Kleine Scheidegg to Grindelwald. Alternatively you can take the cable car from Wengen back to Mannlichen and then the gondola from Mannlichen down to Grindelwald.

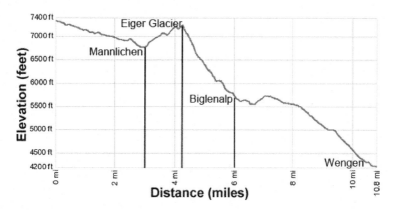

Trailhead Directions

From the Grindelwald Bahnhof (train station) to Mannlichen: See Hike 47.

From Lauterbrunnen to Mannlichen: See Hike 47.

From Wengen to Mannlichen: See Hike 47.

From Wengen to Lauterbrunnen/Grindelwald: From Wengen train station catch the cog railway Lauterbrunnen (14 minutes). To travel to Grindelwald, at the Lauterbrunnen train station take a train heading to Interlaken and get off at Zweilutschinen where you catch a connecting train to Grindelwald.

49. Eiger Trail ★★★★
Distance: 3.8 - 8.5 miles (round trip)
Near Grindelwald in the Bernese Alps

This interesting hike travels along the base of the Eiger with up-close and dramatic views of the iconic peak's sheer north face along with fine views of the Grindelwald Valley and nearby summits. Several options extend the hike, adding to the scenic delights of the day.

Distance: 3.8 - 8.5 miles (round trip)
Elevation: 6,762-ft. at Trailhead
7,612-ft. at High Point
5,243-ft. at Alpiglen
Elevation Gain: 850-ft/-2,369-ft.

Difficulty: moderate
Basecamp: Grindelwald
Grindelwald Map: See page 214
Online Map/Photos:
www.hikingwalking.com/eiger

Why Hike the Eiger Trail

The popular Eiger Trail descends beneath the soaring north face of the Eiger (13,025-ft.) accompanied by panoramic views of the Grindelwald Valley, Kleine Scheidegg and the Lauberhorn. The 3.8 mile trail starts at the Eigergletscher Train Station to the southeast of Kleine Scheidegg, a saddle on the ridge separating the Lauberhorn and the Eiger. (See trailhead directions below).

There are several ways to reach the Eiger Trail. Hikers can take the Eiger Express from the Terminal station in Grindelwald to the Eiger Station. Alternatively, reach the trailhead by taking the train/cog railway from either Grindelwald or Lauterbrunnen to Kleine Scheidegg and then switch to the Jungfrau Railway and get off at the first stop, the Eiger Station.

Kleine Scheidegg is a very busy place, filled with tourists jostling to catch trains to various destinations. If time and energy permit, I strongly suggest walking from Kleine Scheidegg to the start of the Eiger trail, a 1.4 to 1.9 mile hike (described below) resulting in a 5.7 mile point-to-point trip that ends at the Alpiglen rail station.

Hikers looking for a longer day can combine Hike 47 - Panoramaweg: Mannlichen to Kleine Scheidegg trail with the Eiger trail for a highly scenic 8.5 mile point-to-point hike. More information on this alternative is found at the end of the hike description.

The trail can be quite slippery if snow is present, requiring the use of microspikes. Check at the Grindelwald tourist office for current conditions.

The Eiger trail can be walked in either direction. Some parties walk up from Alpiglen to help acclimate and get into condition. The trail is rated as moderately-strenuous if you walk uphill. I personally prefer to walk down so the best scenery it right in front. Whatever way you walk it is a great hike.

Eiger Trail: Eigergletscher to Alpiglen

Note: When riding the train to the Eigergletscher stop you must push the button requesting that the conductor stop at the station. (The stop is what the Swiss refer to as a "Halt on Demand" station.) Announcements will be made in English, along with a few other languages, telling you to request the stop. After the announcement push the halt on demand button and then quickly get off the train when it stops.

At the Eigergletscher train station walk west (toward Kleine Scheidegg) along the tracks, cross to the east side of the tracks at the pedestrian crossing and then follow the signs for the Eiger Trail. The path weaves between buildings and then turns right (east/northeast), ascending along rocky slopes beneath the steep cliffs of the Eiger's west ridge. Along the way the trail passes under a ski lift and then travels by a wall with plaques honoring famous climbers who have attempted to climb the Eiger's north face.

Beyond the plaques the trail descends scree covered slopes on steep grades, crosses a small bowl and then ascends to the top of a low ridge. The

Eiger's north face looms overhead. In the distance are fine views of the Wetterhorn towering above Grosse Scheidegg.

After a brief respite atop the ridge the trail descends scree covered slopes on moderately steep to steep grades. In places the scree gives way to rocky meadows and the footing improves. Depending on the time of year patches of snow and ice still cling to the rugged cliffs above the trail.

Views along the trail continually evolve. To the north a ridge, anchored by the Faulhorn, forms the scenic backdrop for Grindelwald sprawled along the valley floor. The Schwarzhorn, Grosse Scheidegg and the Wetterhorn rim the valley to the northeast. Behind you the Lauberhorn, Tschuggen and Mannlichen fill the skyline. The Eiger's north face soars above the trail.

After 1.6 miles the grade abates. The path now travels through meadows, crossing a few seasonal streams and passing by small waterfalls. Boulders in the meadows offer good perches for taking a break while enjoying the views. After half a mile the trail resumes its descent on moderately-steep to steep grades.

At 2.7 miles the trail reaches a photogenic waterfall. Here the trail curves to the left and drops down a series of switchbacks. The descent is accompanied by good views of a series of waterfalls and deep fissures channeling small streams. Your perspective of the Eiger has now changed so that you have a good view of the top of the peak.

Reach a junction at 3.1 miles. Here the trail to the Gletscherschlucht and Grindelwald (2-hr 25-min) branches to the right. We continue along the trail toward to Alpiglen (25-min).

After one more set of switchback the trail descends on steep to moderately-steep grades through meadows, dropping down some stone steps, to the train station at Alpiglen at 3.8 miles. Here a small station sells return tickets to the Grindelwald Bahnhof.

Kleine Scheidegg to the Eiger Trail

My preferred option is to walk from Kleine Scheidegg to the start of the Eiger Trail at the Eigergletscher Train Station. Upon arriving at Kleine Scheidegg cross to the south side of the rail tracks and locate the trail signs near the base of the steps leading to the Hotel Bellevue des Alps, an old wood hotel. Follow the signs pointing to the Eigergletscher (Eiger Glacier), directing you to climb the stairs and then turn right, following a broad track ascending on moderate grades above the left (east) side of the train tracks for the Jungfraujoch.

Ahead are great views of the glaciers spilling down the slopes of the Jungfrau and the Monch along with the high peaks towering above the Sefinental valley to the west of Lauterbrunnen. The Lauberhorn rises to the northwest.

Reach the Fallbodensee, a pretty little lake, at 0.6 miles. On a still day the mirror-like surface of the lake is a photographer's dream, perfectly reflecting the Wetterhorn and the Eiger. On the south side of the lake a small building houses an interesting exhibit showing the various routes climbing the Eiger's north wall. It's definitely worth a stop.

At the southeast end of the lake the trail turns right (south) and drops down a gravel track, passing through a culvert going under the train tracks. Beyond the culvert the trail heads south/southwest, resuming its ascent on moderate to moderately-steep grades.

Reach at junction at 1.1 miles. To trail to the left (east) heads directly to the Eigergletscher train station and the start of the Eiger trail (the short route – 1.4 miles). The trail straight ahead leads to the moraine of the Eigergletscher and then the train station (the long route – 1.9 miles).

To take the short route turn left (east) and climb switchbacks through pastures, passing over an underground railway tunnel. A short distance to the west of the trail you will see where the trains emerge from the tunnel.

Soon the path climbs above the north side of the train tracks, passes along the backside of the Eigergletscher Railway buildings and reaches the Eiger Trail at 1.4 miles.

The longer route to the train station continues straight ahead at the junction and soon crosses a low ridge. Here the trail curves to the left (southeast) as it drops into a shallow bowl and then climbs to an overlook atop the Eiger Glacier's moraine at 1.4 miles. The overlook features stunning views of Eiger Glacier clinging to the rugged slopes between the Eiger and the Monch.

Walk up the moraine toward the Eigergletscher train station. Progress will be slow as you stop frequently to enjoy the spectacle.

At 1.7 miles turn left on a trail that descends from the moraine and soon arrives at the Eigergletscher train station. Walk west (toward Kleine Scheidegg) a short distance along the tracks to the pedestrian crossing and cross to the east side of the tracks. Here you will find trail signs pointing to the Eiger Trail and Alpiglen. The path travels between the buildings and reaches the start of the trail at 1.9 miles.

Trail Distances:

- **Eiger Trail (Eigergletscher) to Alpiglen:** 3.8 miles
- **Eiger Trail plus the walk from Kleine Scheidegg to the start of the trail:** 5.2 to 5.7 miles
- **Walking from Mannlichen to Kleine Scheidegg** adds 2.8 miles to the day for an 8.0 to 8.5 mile hike. For more information see Hike 47 - Panoramaweg: Mannlichen to Kleine Scheidegg trail description.

Trailhead Directions

From Grindelwald to the Eiger Station via the Eiger Express Gondola: From the Grindelwald train station walk a short distance to the east along the main street to the main bus stop on the south side of the road and catch the #121 bus to Terminal or #123 bus toward Itramen Egg. Get off at the Terminal stop where a new facility includes the valley stations for the Mannlichen and Eiger Express gondolas. The bus rides take about 13 minutes. You can also take the train from Grindelwald Bahnhof to Grindelwald Terminal. The ride takes five minutes. Purchase one-way tickets on the Eiger Express Gondola to the Eiger Station. The ride takes about 20 minutes. Note: Expect the 26-person gondolas to be crowded with people heading to the Jungfraujoch.

Alternatively, from the train station follow the yellow signs pointing to the Terminal station for the Mannlichen and Eiger Express gondolas, which is to the northwest of the Grund Station on the Kleine Scheidegg line. The walk descends the hillsides to the south/southwest of the train station, using a combination of walkways and roads to the Terminal Station. Allocate about 20 minutes for the 0.9 mile walk. Purchase one-way tickets on the Eiger Express Gondola to the Eiger Station. The ride takes about 20 minutes. Note: Expect the 26-person gondolas to be crowded with people heading to the Jungfraujoch.

From Grindelwald to Kleine Scheidegg / Eigergletscher Train Station (2 Trains): Walk to the Grindelwald Bahnhof at the east end of town and take the cog railway to Kleine Scheidegg. In the summer trains generally run every 30 minutes. Get off a Kleine Scheidegg and walk to the south side of the station where you will find the trains heading to the Jungfraujoch. Get on a train heading toward the Jungfraujoch and get off at the Eiger station, the first stop. This is a "Stop on Demand" meaning you need to push the button near the exit door that signals to the conductor that you wish to get off the train. Announcements in English, along with a number of other languages, will tell you when to push the button. The entire ride should take about 50 minutes.

Kleine Scheidegg is a very busy place and boarding the train to the Jungfraujoch can be a tad chaotic. Some cars on the train heading to the Jungfraujoch are reserved for large groups (signs in the windows). Train personnel along the track can direct you to the cars open to the general public.

If you are walking from Kleine Scheidegg to the start of the Eiger Trail, get off the train at Kleine Scheidegg, walk to the south side of the train station and then walk east (toward Grindelwald) to the Hotel des Alpes, a large wood hotel. Here you will find signposts directing to the trail heading to the Eigergletscher train station.

From the Grindelwald Bahnhof (train station) to Mannlichen: See Hike 47.

50. Other Trails in Grindelwald
Near Grindelwald in the Bernese Alps

50a) Pfingstegg to Baregg

The short trail to the Baregg Berghaus travels through trees and then meadows high above the glacial gorge between the Mattenberg and the Eiger with up-close views of the glacier-clad Fiescherhorn, the Mittellegi ridge of the Eiger and the Ischmeer (Eismeer) Glacier. Below the trail are dramatic views of the deep chasm carved by the retreating Lower Grindelwald Glacier.

- **Distance:** 3.4 miles (round-trip)
- **Elevation:** 4,550-ft. at Pfingstegg
  5,817-ft. at Baregg Berghaus
- **Elevation Gain / Loss:** 1,267-ft.
- **Difficulty:** moderately-strenuous
- **Base camp:** Grindelwald
- **Grindelwald Map:** See page 214

Start the trip with a ride up the Pfingstegg cable car to Pfingstegg with fine views of the Wetterhorn, Eiger and the peaks rising above Grindelwald to the north. Hike southwest from the cable car station on a trail intially traveling through trees and intermittent meadows to Baregg. Soon the path curves to the south into the deep gorge created by the retreating Lower Grindelwald Glacier. Fixed cables and fencing provides a level of security along sections of the trail with minor exposure.

After 0.75 miles the trees give way to open meadows as the trail climbs on moderately-steep to steep grades high above the gorge, crossing a stream along the way. At final stiff climb leads to Baregg Berghaus at 1.7 miles. The Berghaus is set atop a grassy knoll with fine views of the Fiescherhorn massif, the east wall and Mittellegi ridge of the Eiger and the Ischmeer

(Eismeer) Glacier spilling down the flanks of the peaks. Meals and dormitory accommodations are available at the Berghaus.

Trailhead Directions: From the Grindelwald Bahnhof, walk east on Dorfstrasse (the main street) for half a mile to Grabenstrasse. Turn right and walk down the street to the bottom station for the Pfingsteggbahn (cable car). Signs along the way will keep you on track.

To walk instead of riding the lift, turn right at the lift station and walk down the road to a bridge crossing the river. There are two paths on the south side of the river ascending to Pfingstegg. The track/alp road to the left, through Auf der Sulz, is longer but not as steep while the trail to the right is shorter but climbs steeply through forest. The walk to Pfingstegg gains over 1,200-ft in elevation and takes 1-hour 20-minute to 1-hour 40-minutes.

50b) Pfingstegg to Schreckhorn Hut

Beyond Baregg a route ascends to the Schreckhorn Hut set against a crag beneath the west face of the Schreckhorn. The hut overlooks a spectacle of rock and ice with front row seats to the Finsteraarhorn towering above the head of the valley and the Fiescherhorn massif rising to the southwest. The Obers Ischmeer (Eismeer) Glacier spills down the flanks of the peaks, coalescing into a massive ice flow streaming down the valley floor.

- **Distance:** 9.4 miles (round-trip)
- **Elevation:** 4,550-ft. at Pfingstegg
  8,290-ft. at Schreckhorn Hut
- **Elevation Gain / Loss:** 3,740-ft.
- **Difficulty:** strenuous
- **Base camp:** Grindelwald
- **Grindelwald Map: See page 214**

Note: This is a challenging, rugged and exposed route. Fixed cables, chains, ladders and pegs facilitate the passage along cliff faces, across streams and traversing exposed sections of the trail. The route in only recommended for experienced, sure-footed hikers with a head for heights.

Follow the directions above to Baregg. The route beyond the Berghaus briefly descends and then contours above the crumbling moraine wall, crossing a few streams along the way. Ahead are fine views of the glacier-clad slopes of the Fiescherhorn massif. As you progress up the valley look back for views of the Monch and the Eiger to the west.

At 2.6 miles the route curves around a ridge and then ascends through meadows with great views of the tongue of the Obers Ischmeer Glacier spilling down a rugged slope. The path soon ascends to the most difficult section of the route where chains, cables, rungs and ladders safeguard the climb up the Rots Gufer cliffs. Below you are the seracs and crevasses of the main icefall.

Past the cliffs the route is easier to folllow as it climbs through rugged meadows, crossing streams along the way. At 4.5 miles the route curves to the left just before reading a moraine and then ascends to the Schreckhorn Hut at 4.7 miles. The hut offers refreshments and dormitory accommodations.

From the hut enjoy grand views of the Obers Ischmeer Glacier spilling down the flanks of the Finsteraarhorn, the highest summit in the Bernese Alps, and Fiescherhorn massif. The various segments of the glacier merge to form a massive ice sheet flowing down the valley floor directly beneath the hut. When you are done taking in the views carefully retrace your steps to Pfingstegg.

Lauterbrunnen
Location: The Lauterbrunnental Valley in the Bernese Alps

The lovely village of Lauterbrunnen, located to the northwest of Grindelwald, lies nestled in emerald green pastures half way up the Lauterbrunnental, a classic glacial valley lined with sheer cliffs and soaring peaks. The valley is known for its splendid waterfalls, of which there are said to be 72. I've not seen that many but the ones I have seen are quite impressive, especially after it rains.

Beautiful Staubbach Falls, the most famous, plunges 975-ft. from a rock overhang at the south end of the village. A short distance up the valley is dramatic Trummelbach Falls, a World Heritage Site, where a series of waterfalls plummet down a slot canyon within a mountain. A walk or drive up the lovely valley passes numerous other falls spilling down the cliffs to the valley floor.

Near the head of the valley the road ends at Stechelberg. Here the valley splits, with the Sefinental (Sefinen Valley) branching to the right (southwest). The rugged summits of the Gspaltenhorn, Butlassa, Hundshore and the Schilthorn rise above this lovely glen. Trails continue south up the Lauterbrunnental to a spectacular glacier-clad cirque, anchored by the

Jungfrau, Gletscherhorn, Abeni Flue, Mittaghorn and the Breithorn, rimming the head of the valley.

About Lauterbrunnen

The center of Lauterbrunnen, located along the main road heading south up the Lauterbrunnental, extends from the Bahnhof (train station) in the north to the church, situated on a curve just before the road crosses to the east side of the Weisse Lutschine River. The main thoroughfare is lined with hotels (some with dormitory accommodations), restaurants, bars, an outdoor store and shops. Additional lodging, including vacation apartments, are located in the area to the east of the river and along the road traveling south up the valley.

The Coop supermarket and the cable car to Grutschalp are located on the west side of the main road across from the train station. The Tourist Information Office (lauterbrunnen.swiss/en/summer/) is a little further up the street.

A sunny shelf along the east side of the Lauterbrunnen Valley is home to the pretty village of Wengen, reached by trails and a cog railway that terminates at Kleine Scheidegg. Murren and Gimmelwald reside on sunny benches along the west side of the valley. The gondola to Grutschalp connects with the railway to Murren. Alternatively, reach Gimmelwald and Murren on the multistage Schilthornbahn traveling to Gimmelwald, Murren, Birg and the summit of the Schilthorn. All three villages are car-free. Murren and Wengen offer a good selection of accommodations, restaurants, shops and tourist services.

My preference is to stay in Lauterbrunnen. It's an easy going, more reasonably priced village that is centrally located to facilitate access to hikes in this guide. Murren and Wengen tend to be more expensive.

Hiking around Lauterbrunnen

Lauterbrunnen is the starting point for some of the great hikes in the Bernese Alps. A short walk up the valley leads to Trummbach Falls (Hike 51). For a longer hike, head up the Lauterbrunnen Valley to Stechelberg (Hike 52), passing some of the valley's photogrenic waterfalls. From Stechelberg scenic trails ascend to Obersteinberg (Hike 53) with splendid vistas of the massive glacier-clad cirque ringing the head of the valley. Ride the gondola to Gimmelwald and then climb the steep trail to Tanzbodeli (Hike 55) for jaw dropping views of the region's most impressive peaks. Other trails lead to the Chilchbalm (Hike 54), a lovely basin beneath the rugged summits of the Sefinental.

Head to Murren and then ascend high above the Sefinental to Sefinenfurgge Pass (Hike 56) on a segment of the Alpine Pass Route that showcases the summits soaring above the Lauterbrunnen, Sefinen and Kiental Valleys. Shorter trails in Murren (Hike 58) lead to various overlooks with panoramic view of the high peaks towering above Lauterbrunnental and beyond.

There are also several walks listed in the Grindelwald section that can easily be done from Lauterbrunnen including:

- First to Schynige Platte (Hike 46)
- Mannlichen to Kleine Scheidegg (Hike 47)
- Mannlichen to Wengen (Hike 48)

Getting to Lauterbrunnen

From the Zurich Airport or Zurich Bahnhof (train station) take the train to Interlaken Ost (East). You will need to change trains along the way. In Interlaken, change to the train going to Grindelwald/Lauterbrunnen. Half the cars on the train will be labeled for Grindelwald and the other half for Lauterbrunnen. Make sure you get on a car labeled for Lauterbrunnen. At Zweilutschinen the train literally splits in half with half the cars going to Grindelwald and the other half heading for Lauterbrunnen. The trip takes about two hours and 25 minutes from Zurich.

From the Geneva Airport or Gare (train station), take the train to Interlaken Ost (East). You will need to change trains along the way. Then follow the directions above. The ride should take about three hours and 25 minutes.

Check the SBB website/SBB app for directions from other parts of the country.

Nearby Attractions & Rainy Day Activities

Visit amazing **Trummelbach Falls**, Europe's largest subterranean waterfalls, that channels meltwater from the Jungfrau glacier down a slot canyon carved deep into the mountain.

Take the **Schilthornbahn**, a multistage cable car, to the summit of the Schilthorn where overlooks feature superb 360-views that encompass the Eiger, Monch and Jungfrau and the high summits of the Bernese Alps. The facility includes a revolving restaurant and a short walk. The facility is somewhat dated with a kitschy James Bond theme but the views are breathtaking.

Schynige Platte, a high overlook atop a ridge at the foot of the Lutschental, can be reached on a long hike from First in Grindelwald or by a cog railway from Wilderswil (along the Lauterbrunnen - Interlaken rail line). At Schynige Platte you will find an interesting alpine botanic garden, great views of the Eiger, Monch and Jungfrau and overlooks featuring terrific vistas of the Bernese Alps, Interlaken, Lake Thun and Lake Brienz. Several short loop trails visit the gardens and lead to more scenic viewpoints.

Tal Museum Lauterbrunnen, located on the main road on the west side of the river, tells the history of the valley. The museum is housed in a well preserved building and includes a large collection of regional artifacts. Hours are limited. Check at the Tourist Office for more information.

A good rainy day option is to take a day trip to **Interlaken**, a 40 minute train ride from Lauterbrunnen. Here you can walk along Lakes Thun and Brienz, take a lake cruise, visit castles along Lake Thun or simply walk along the Hohenweg, the street connecting Lake Brienz to Lake Thun. Visit the Interlaken Tourist Information site for a complete list of options.

Good Things to Know about Lauterbrunnen

- The primary language in Lauterbrunnen is German, although most people also speak French and/or English.
- There are two hostels in Lauterbrunnen. The Valley Hostel is located on the west side of the main street just beyond a small parking lot while the Schutzenbach Backpackers Hostel and Campground is located along the main road on the east side of the river.
- A laundromat (waschsalon) is situated on the west side of the main street in front of the Valley Hostel.
- There are two campgrounds in the valley. The Campground Jungfrau is located at the south end of the village (along the west side of the river). Further up the valley is Schutzenbach Hostel and Campground.

Map: Lauterbrunnen and Griesalp Area Trails

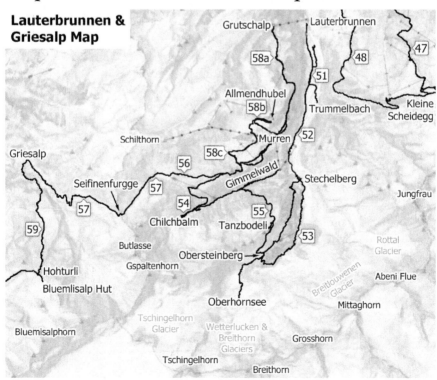

51. Lauterbrunnen to Trummelbach Falls

★★★★☆

Distance: 2.2 miles (one-way) / 4.4 miles (round trip)

Near Lauterbrunnen in the Bernese Alps

This lovely walk up the Lauterbrunnen Valley travels through emerald green meadows and passes photogenic waterfalls on the way to Trummelbach Falls, a World Heritage Site. The dramatic falls are a true natural wonder, showcasing a series of waterfalls thundering down a slot canyon carved into a mountain.

Distance: 2.2 miles (one-way) / 4.4 miles (round-trip)	**Difficulty:** easy
Elevation: 2,610-ft. at Lauterbrunnen 2,720-ft. at Trummelbach Falls	**Basecamp:** Lauterbrunnen
	Lauterbrunnen Map: See page 249
	Online Map/Photos:
Elevation Gain: 110-ft.	www.hikingwalking.com/trummelbach

Why Hike from Lauterbrunnen to Trummelbach Falls

The Lauterbrunnen Valley is said to have 72-waterfalls. I've not seen that many but the number of magnificent waterfalls along the valley is quite impressive. This hike visits two of the most famous falls; Staubbach Falls, located at the southwest end of Lauterbrunnen, and Trummelbach Falls, a World Heritage site and the destination for this hike.

Trummelbach Falls, Europe's largest subterranean waterfalls, channels meltwater from the Jungfrau glacier down a slot canyon carved deep into the mountain. Constant abrasion of glacial debris in the water formed, and continues to shape, the canyon's highly sculpted walls. A funicular, walkways and stairs deep in the mountain permit visitors to access ten viewpoints where waterfalls plummets down chutes, spill through narrow passages and corkscrews down narrow slots. Mist fills the air around the viewpoints.

The falls is definitely worth a visit. Most people take the bus from the Lauterbrunnen Train Station to Trummelbach Falls. My preference is to walk from Lauterbrunnen to Trummelbach, a 2.2 mile hike. The lovely walk heads up the Lauterbrunnen Valley, traveling through pretty pastures and passing small alps. Waterfalls spill down the sheer cliffs along both sides of the valley. If time and energy permit, retrace your steps to Lauterbrunnen for a 4.4 mile hike.

This walk can be done in any weather. On a nice day the brilliant blue skies and emerald green meadows contrast beautifully with the peaks, adorn with glistening glaciers, at the head of the valley. My favorite time to do this hike is on a rainy day. Clouds will probably obscure views of the high peaks but you will see an amazing number of waterfalls in all their glory, pouring from overhangs and splashing down rugged cliff faces.

Lauterbrunnen to Trummelbach Falls

From the train station in Lauterbrunnen, walk south along the main street. At 0.3 miles, just before the street makes a sharp left turn, bear right on a side road. The turn is marked by yellow trail signs on a post pointing toward the Trummelbach Hotel and Stechelberg. There is also a sign pointing toward the Jungfrau campground. As you walk down the road you will pass the Horner Pub and then a large parking lot on your left.

You are now heading up the Lauterbrunnen valley, a classic "U" shaped glaciated valley lined with sheer rock walls. On your right the dramatic 975-ft. Staubbach Falls freefalls down a sheer cliff to the valley floor. At 0.5 miles a short spur trail climbs to the base of the falls, a worthwhile detour for anyone who would like to get an up-close shot of the waterfall.

Past Staubbach Falls you will pass a few houses and then a campground on your left. At all intersections continue heading south on the road. Beyond the campground the trail travels through pastures and small alps with views of more waterfalls tumbling down the walls on both sides of the valley. Straight ahead are fine views of the Breithorn towering above the head of the valley.

Reach Buchen at 1.5 miles and turn left on a signed path for Trummelbach Falls. The trail heads east through pastures and soon crosses a bridge over Weisse Lutschine, the valley's river. Past the bridge the trail turns right (south), paralleling the river. At 1.9 miles the trail turns left (east/southeast) and soon reaches a road. Turn right (south), walk a short distance along the road and then cross the road to the car park for Trummelbach Falls. Walk south through the lot, passing in front of the main building housing a restaurant. (Note: The bus stop is in front of the building.)

Past the main building you will see a sign pointing left to a walkway that leads to the ticket kiosk. After purchasing tickets walk west to the entrance to the falls.

There are a total of ten viewpoints where you will see waterfalls. Most people opt to take a funicular that ascends inside the mountain to the 6th viewpoint. From there you can walk up a series of ramps and stone steps to see viewpoints 7 to 10 and then retrace your steps to the funicular. Here you will find another walkway that descends ramps, stairs and finally an outdoor macadam trail switchbacking past the remaining viewpoints to the ground level. Alternatively, you can walk all the way up and then take the funicular down or walk both directions. The walk is moderately-steep but short.

Note: Mist envelops the areas around the viewpoints. Some of the nearby steps and ramps may be wet and slippery. Be careful.

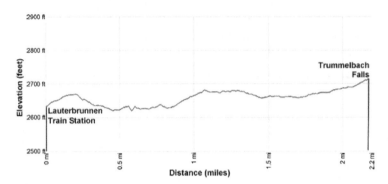

Trailhead Directions

Lauterbrunnen Bahnhof (train station) to Trummelbach Falls: Walk to the Lauterbrunnen Bahnhof bus stop, located at the north end of the train station along the west side of the main road. Catch the #141 bus bound for Stechelberg and get off at the Trummelbach Falls stop. The ride should take about 7-8 minutes. There are a number of stops along the main road through Lauterbrunnen to catch the bus. Check the SBB website or download the SBB app for the current schedule and nearest stop.

From Trummelbach to the Lauterbrunnen Bahnhof (last stop): Walk to the large stone building adjacent to the parking area. In front of the building you will find the Trummelbach Falls bus stop. Catch the #141 bus bound for the Lauterbrunnen Bahnhof. The bus makes a number of stop along the main road through the village. Check the SBB website or download the SBB app for the current schedule and the stop nearest to your destination.

52. Lauterbrunnen to Stechelberg ★★★★☆
Distance: 4.3 miles (one way) / 8.6 miles (round-trip)
Near Lauterbrunnen in the Bernese Alps

This easy hike travels up the enchanting Lauterbrunnen Valley, a classic glacial valley rimmed with sheer cliffs and soaring glacier-clad peaks, passing many beautiful waterfalls on its way to Stechelberg near the head of the valley. Lovely meadows, small alps and the Weisse Lutschine River add to the scenic delights.

Distance: 4.3 miles (one way) /
8.6 miles (round-trip**)**
Elevation: 2,610-ft. at
Lauterbrunnen
3,000-ft. at Stechelberg
Elevation Gain: 390-ft.

Difficulty: easy
Basecamp: Lauterbrunnen
Lauterbrunnen Map: See page 249
Online Map/Photos:
www.hikingwalking.com/stechelberg

Why Hike from Lauterbrunnen to Stechelberg

Lauterbrunnen, which mean "many fountains," is an apt description for the stunning valley said to have over 72 waterfalls. This easy hike follows a broad path up the valley floor, passing many impressive falls freefalling, tumbling and cascading down steep rock walls. Forming the backdrop for this captivating scene is the Breithorn and its neighboring peaks towering above the head of the valley.

This walk can be done in any weather. On a nice day the brilliant blue skies and emerald green meadows contrast beautifully with the peaks, adorn with glistening glaciers, at the head of the valley. My favorite time to do this hike is on a rainy day. Clouds will probably obscure the views of the high peaks but you will see an amazing number of waterfalls in all their glory, pouring from overhangs and splashing down rugged cliff faces.

Extend the hike by retracing your steps from Stechelberg back to Lauterbrunnen for an 8.6 miles round-trip hike.

Lauterbrunnen to Stechelberg

From the train station in Lauterbrunnen, walk south along the main street. At 0.3 miles, just before the street makes a sharp left turn, bear right on a side road. The turn is marked with yellow trail signs at the intersection pointing toward Trummelbach Hotel and Stechelberg. There is also a sign pointing toward the Jungfrau campground. As you walk down the road you'll pass the Horner Pub and then a large parking lot on your left. (This single lane road has little traffic and soon turns into a private road used only by the alps you pass along the way.)

You are now heading up the Lauterbrunnen valley, a classic "U" shaped glaciated valley with sheer rock walls. On your right the dramatic 975-ft. Staubbach Falls freefalls down a sheer cliff to the valley floor. At 0.5 miles a short spur trail climbing to the base of the falls is a worthwhile detour for anyone who would like an up-close shot of the waterfall.

Past the falls the road goes by a few houses and then a campground on your left. At all intersections continue heading south on the road. Beyond the campground the trail travels through pastures and small alps with views of more waterfalls tumbling down the walls on both sides of the valley. Straight ahead are fine views of the Breithorn and the Grosshorn towering above the head of the valley.

Reach Buchen at 1.5 miles. We continue straight ahead. The trail to the left leads to Trummelbach Falls. This 1.4 miles (round-trip) detour is an excellent diversion, leading to a World Heritage site where a series of waterfalls plummet down a slot canyon flowing within a mountain. See the description of the Trummelbach Falls Trail (Hike 51) for more information.

The broad path soon nears the Weiss Lutschine River and then reaches a junction with the road leading across the river to the Breithorn campground and Sandbach at 2.1 miles. The next segment of the walk parallels the pretty river, passing a beautiful falls tumbling down the cliffs below the northern end of Murren, set atop a bench high above the valley floor.

At 2.6 miles reach a junction where the road turns to the left and crosses the river to Stegmatte. We continue along the west side of the river on a gravel path that soon enters the trees. In a short distance views open to a large car park across the river. The lot is for the Schilthornbahn, a multi-stage cable car that ascends to Gimmelwald, Murren, Brig and the Schilthorn. The Schilthorn is a popular viewpoint atop the summit of the Schilthorn with amazing 360-degree views and a revolving restaurant, Piz Gloria, that was featured in the James Bond movie, "On Her Majesty's Secret Service."

At 3.0 miles pass a small park with a picnic area on the right. The park offers views of a gorgeous waterfall cascading down the rugged cliffs beneath the southern end of Murren. Past the picnic area the trail breaks from the trees and soon passes a bridge over the river to the Schilthorn cable car station.

Keep to the west side of the river, admiring the falls seen from the picnic area along with a waterfall spilling down the valley's sheer east wall. Ahead are fine views of the high peaks towering above the head of the valley.

At 3.6 miles pass a junction with a trail branching left toward Matte. Continue along the west side of the river toward the Stechelberg Hotel. More waterfalls are seen cascading down the east side of the valley. At 4.0 miles follow the trail as it turns left, crosses a stream and then travels between two buildings as it heads toward Stechelberg. At the next intersection, by the Alpehof Hotel, turn left toward Stechelberg. Upon reaching the main road turn left again. Walk past the Stechelberg Hotel to the bus stop on the left (west) side of the road 4.3 miles.

There are a number of restaurants in Stechelberg with scenic outdoor terraces where you can relax and get some refreshments before catching the bus to Lauterbrunnen. Alternatively, turn around and walk back to Lauterbrunnen for a 8.6 mile round-trip hike.

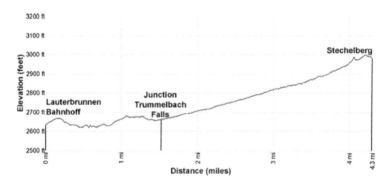

Trailhead Directions

Lauterbrunnen Bahnhof (train station) to the Stechelberg Hotel (last stop): Walk to the Lauterbrunnen Bahnhof bus stop, located at the north end of the station along the west side of the main road. Catch the #141 bus bound for the Stechelberg Hotel. The ride should take about 20 minutes. There are a number of stops along the main road through Lauterbrunnen to catch the bus. Check the SBB website or download the SBB app for the current schedule and nearest stop.

From the Stechelberg Hotel to the Lauterbrunnen Bahnhof (last stop): Walk north past the Stechelberg Hotel to the large parking area and bus stop. Catch the #141 bus bound for the Lauterbrunnen Bahnhof. The ride should take about 20 minutes. The bus makes a number of stop along the main road through the village. Check the SBB website or download the SBB app for the current schedule and the stop nearest to your destination.

53. Obersteinberg Loop ★★★★★
Distance: 6.7 - 10.2 mile (loop)
Near Lauterbrunnen in the Bernese Alps

This loop hike travels to Obersteinberg, a pretty alp with impressive views of the glacier-clad summits rimming the head of the Lauterbrunnen Valley. Views stretch from the Jungfrau in the north to the Breithorn and Tschingelhorn in the south. Extend the hike with a trip to the Oberhornsee, a small lake.

Distance: 3.8 miles (one way) to Obersteinberg
6.7 miles (loop) to Stechelberg
10.2 miles (round trip) to Oberhornsee
Elevation: 2,985-ft. at Stechelberg
5,833-ft. at Obersteinberg
6,775-ft. at Oberhornsee
2,985-ft. at Stechelberg
Elevation Gain: 2,880-ft. to Obersteinberg
940-ft. to Oberhornsee
-2,880-ft. to Stechelberg

Difficulty: strenuous
Basecamp: Lauterbrunnen
Lauterbrunnen Map: See page 249
Online Map/Photos:
www.hikingwalking.com
/obersteinberg

Why Hike the Obersteinberg Loop

Obersteinberg offers a front row seat to a photogenic waterfall, a stunning cirque of summits adorned with glaciers, rugged crags and the pretty meadows at the head of the Lauterbrunnen Valley. Two steep trails travel through forests and meadows to this beautiful overlook. The valley trail, that is a little longer and not quite as steep, is recommended for the trip to Obersteinberg. The high route, which is shorter and steeper but enjoys some great views before it dive bombs to Stechelberg, is suggested for the return leg.

Hikers looking for a longer and more challenging day can extend the hike by visiting the Oberhornsee, a small lake situated in the rocky meadows between the moraines of the Breithorn and Tschingelhorn Glaciers. This side trip adds 3.5 miles (round trip) and 940-ft. of elevation gain to the hike.

Another alternative is to spend the night at the alp at Obersteinberg, which includes a circa 1880 hotel with comfy rooms, dormitory accommodations and a small restaurant with stunning views of the peaks across the valley.

My favorite option is to visit Obersteinberg as part of a trip to Tanzbodeli. This challenging hike, with very steep climbs, rewards hikers with breathtaking scenery. See the trail description for Hike 55 - Tanzbodeli for more information.

Valley Trail from Stechelberg to Obersteinberg

- **Distance from Trailhead:** 3.8 miles (one way)
- **Total Distance Stechelberg to Obersteinberg to Stechelberg:** 7.6 mile (round-trip)
  11.1 miles with side trip to Oberhornsee (see below)
- **Elevation at Stechelberg:** 2,985-ft.
- **Elevation at Obersteinberg:** 5,833-ft.
- **Elevation Gain:** 2,880-ft. / -2,880-ft.

The last stop on the bus from Lauterbrunnen to Stechelberg is just to the north of the Stechelberg Hotel (see trailhead directions below). Walk south (up valley) along the main road past the hotel. At the next two intersections stay to the east of the Weisse Lutschine River on the broad track toward Trachsellauenen, Obersteinberg and Schmadrihutte. Don't cross the bridges over the river.

Past the second junction the trail ascends on moderate grades through pastures and clusters of trees beside the river with views of the high peaks, including the Mittaghorn, Grosshorn and Breithorn, towering above the east side of the valley. At 0.6 miles continue toward Trachsellauenen by crossing a bridge to the west side of the river.

On the west side of the river the trail crosses a broad track (alp road) several times as it ascends on moderately-steep grades through forests and intermittent meadows, cutting off several long switchbacks on the road. Watch for signs that say "Wanderweg" to stay on track. At trail intersections always follow the trail toward Trachsellauenen and Obersteinberg.

Reach the Berghaus Trachsellauenen and then the junction at Trachsellauenen at 1.6 miles. Do not cross the river, instead bear right on the trail toward Bergwerk and Obersteinberg. The grade abates as the path travels beside the river along the base of an avalanche chute. Ahead are fine views of the Breithorn and Grosshorn towering above the head of the valley.

At 1.8 miles the trail enters the trees and reaches a plaque marking the site of the former lead, silver and barite mines at Trachsellauenen. Beyond the mine site the path reaches a somewhat confusing intersection at Bergwerk with signposts pointing in two directions to Obersteinberg. The trail to the right climbs very steeply to the Hotel Tschingelhorn and then Obersteinberg. I recommend the trail to the left toward Schirboden and Obersteinberg that continues up the valley on more reasonable grades and takes the same amount of time.

The trail to the left initially climbs on steep grades that soon moderate as it reaches a second junction. Here a trail branches left to Schmadrihutte. Our trail to Obersteinberg continues its ascent through trees along the west side of the river.

At 2.2 miles views open to an avalanche chute on the slopes of the Mittaghorn. A short distance beyond the trees give way to meadows and views open to high peaks rimming the valley to the southeast. Beautiful Schmadri Falls tumbles down the steep cliffs below the Breithorn. As you climb turn around for fine views of the Jungfrau to the northeast.

At 2.6 miles, pass through the small alp at Schirboden. Ignore the trail branching left to a viewpoint for Holdrifalle (Holdri Falls) and Lager. The grade now steepens and reenters the trees. At 2.8 miles a second detour, again branching left, heads to Talbachfall (Talbach Falls). We keep ascending on the Bergwanderweg (trail) toward Obersteinberg.

A stiff climb soon leads to the junction at Wilde Egg where we bear right toward Obersteinberg. (The trail to the left heads to Tal and the Oberhornsee.) Openings in the trees along the steep ascent offer lovely views of Schmadri Falls and the Grosshorn.

At 3.5 miles the trees give way to meadows and terrific views open to the high peak to the east along with the Breithorn and Tschingelhorn towering above the head of the valley. Reach Obersteinberg (5,833-ft.) and a junction at 3.7 miles. To the left is the trail to the Oberhornsee, a small lake. Turn right and reach the Hotel Obersteinberg at 3.8 miles. The circa 1880 hotel/restaurant offers private rooms and dormitory accommodations.

Obersteinberg is a superb overlook with stunning views of the cirque at the head of the valley and the wall of summits, including the Jungfrau, rimming the valley's east wall. I recommend returning to the junction with the trail to the Oberhornsee and then walking a short distance toward the Oberhornsee to a splendid viewpoint with front row seats for beautiful Schmadri Falls dropping 1,000-ft. from the lip of a hanging valley. The glacial cirque ringing the head of the valley towers above the falls. Visiting the viewpoint adds 0.5 miles (round trip) to the hike.

From Obersteinberg hikers can either retrace their steps to the trailhead for a 7.6 mile round-trip hike or turn the hike into a loop by returning via the west side of the valley (the high route), which is shorter but steeper. My preference is the loop. See the description of the high route below for more information.

Parties with the time and energy can extend the hike with a side trip to the Oberhornsee, a small lake situated in the rocky meadows between the moraines of the Breithorn and Tschingelhorn Glaciers.

Side Trip: Obersteinberg to Oberhornsee

- **Side Trip Distance:** 3.5 miles (round trip) from Obersteinberg to Oberhornsee
- **Elevation at Oberhornsee:** 6,775-ft.
- **Elevation Gain from Obersteinberg to Oberhornsee:** 940-ft.

The trail to the Oberhornsee begins at the "Y" intersection to the south of the Obersteinberg Hotel. Take the trail branching right toward the Oberhorn and Oberhornsee that ascends along the right (west) side of the valley. At 1.0 mile the path crosses a bridge over the Tschingel stream carrying meltwater from the Tschingelfirn glacier. Beyond the bridge the trail climbs steeply to a bench and the Oberhornsee (6,775-ft.), a small lake, gaining 940-ft in 1.75 miles.

The lake enjoys spectacular views of the Breithorn, Tschingelhorn, Gspaltenhorn and the Ellstabhorn anchoring the cirque at the head of the Lauterbrunnen Valley. The Jungfrau dominates the view to the north. After enjoying the lake, retrace your steps to Obersteinberg for a 3.5 mile round trip hike extension.

Obersteinberg to Stechelberg via the High Route

- **Segment Stat:** 2.9 miles (one way) to Stechelberg
- **Total Distance Stechelberg to Obersteinberg (valley route) to Stechelberg (high route):** 6.7 mile (loop)
  10.2 miles with side trip to Oberhornsee
- **Elevation at Obersteinberg:** 5,833-ft.
- **Elevation at Stechelberg:** 2,985-ft.
- **Elevation Gain/Loss:** -2,880-ft.

To take the high route back to Stechelberg, return to the junction at Obersteinberg. Head northeast on the trail toward the Hotel Tschingelhorn and Stechelberg, that travels by the Hotel Obersteinberg and then descends through high meadows on the west side of the valley. Along the way enjoy great views of the glacier-clad peaks across the valley. Initially the trail descends on easy grades but soon the grade steepens.

Pass the Hotel Tschingelhorn at 4.4 miles. Beyond the hotel the trail descends on very steep grades. At 4.9 miles the path enters the trees and loses the views. Reach a junction at 5.9 miles and take the trail headed toward Stechelberg, Gimmelwald and Murren.

Reach a junction at Schwendiwald (3,740-ft.) at 6.1 miles. Turn right (northeast) toward Stechelberg on a trail that drops down a series of steep switchbacks to the valley floor. (The other trail climbs toward Gimmelwald and Murren.) Cross a bridge over the river to the east side of the valley at 6.5 miles and then turn left, following the broad track through the village to the bus stop at the Hotel Stechelberg (2,985-ft./910-meters) at 6.7 miles.

Note: If you return to Stechelberg via the Valley Trail add 0.9 miles to the trail mileage for a 7.6 mile (round-trip) hike or a 11.1 miles hike if you include the optional extension to the Oberhornsee.

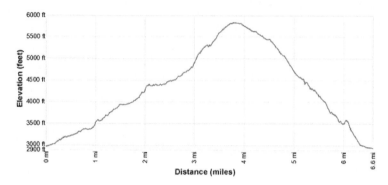

Trailhead Directions

Lauterbrunnen Bahnhof to Stechelberg (last stop): See Hike 52.
From Stechberg to the Lauterbrunnen Bahnhof: See Hike 52.

54. Chilchbalm ★★★★☆
Distance: 5.8 miles (round-trip)
Near Lauterbrunnen in the Bernese Alps

The Chilchbalm, a pretty glacial basin, lies beneath the rugged cirque at the head of the Sefinen Valley. The trail leading to the basin is perfect for anyone looking for a peaceful, relatively easy day hike accompanied by fine views of the Sefinen Lutschine (stream) and the rugged peaks rimming the Sefinen Valley.

Distance: 5.8 miles (round-trip) **Basecamp:** Lauterbrunnen
Elevation: 4,470-ft. at Trailhead **Lauterbrunnen Map:** See page 249
Maximum elevation: 5,040-ft. **Online Map/Photos:**
Elevation Gain: 570-ft. www.hikingwalking.com/chilchbalm
Difficulty: moderate

Why Hike to the Chilchbalm

This is a great trail for a cloudy/rainy day that precludes a trip to higher elevations. It is also a good option for anyone wanting a relaxing hike leading to an off-the-beaten path destination.

The trip can be extended by starting/ending the hike in Stechelberg or returning via Murren. Starting/ends in Stechelberg requires steep ascents/descents. The steep climb on the Murren option is rewarded with great view of the high peaks towering above the Lauterbrunnen Valley and beyond. Information on these options is found at the end of the hike description.

Gimmelwald to the Chilchbalm

The day starts by taking the bus from Lauterbrunnen to the Schilthornbahn and then riding the cable car to Gimmelwald (4,472-ft.), a small village of traditional wood buildings. (See trailhead directions below.) Outside the cable car station in Gimmelwald find the trail signpost and start walking southwest through the village on a paved road toward the Kilchbalm (an alternative spelling of Chilchbalm).

Ignore any trails descending toward Stechelberg. Instead continue heading toward the Kilchbalm. Soon the path curves to the southwest into the Sefinental (Sefinen Valley) where beautiful views open to the Ellstabhorn, Tschingelgrat (Tschingel Ridge), Gspaltenhorn and Butlasse rimming the valley.

At 0.4 miles reach a junction at a hairpin curve. Take the gravel trail, signed for the Kilchbalm, branching right off the paved path. A short distance beyond we leave the last of the houses behind as the broad path descends on moderate grades through meadows along the north side of the Sefinental valley. At 0.6 miles the path crosses a bridge over a stream and then continues descending through trees.

Reach the Sefinental junction on the floor of the Sefinen valley (4,134-ft.) at 1.2 miles. The trail to the left drops down to Stechelberg, an alternative starting location for the hike. (See below for more information.) We continue straight ahead on a path that ascends through pastures on moderate grades, passing a small alp along the way. The cirque, anchored by Butlasse and Gspaltenhorn, fills the skyline at the head of the valley.

Soon the pastures give way to trees and the valley constricts. Our trail now ascends on moderately steep grades beside a rushing stream, passing avalanche chutes and cliffs. At 1.8 miles the path crosses a bridge over a stream tumbling down the steep hillside above the trail.

Reach at junction at 2.0 miles. To the right is a trail heading toward Boganggenalp/Rotstockhutte and Sefinenfurgge, the pass between Lauterbrunnen and Griesalp. We bear left on the trail toward the Chilchbalm.

Beyond the junction the valley briefly widens as the trail travels through meadows with views of the cirque. After a quarter mile the path reenters the trees and crosses a stream on a wood bridge. The valley again constricts as we ascend steeply through trees and intermittent meadows to the Chilchbalm (5,040-ft.) at 2.6 miles.

The pretty glacial basin, clad in rocky meadows and sprinkled with stunted conifers, lies beneath the soaring cirque at the head of the Sefinen Valley. From the basin enjoy fine views of the rugged slopes of Butlasse and the Gspaltenhorn. Small waterfalls, fed by permanent snowfields and small glaciers, spill down the steep cliffs at the head of the valley. Behind you are great views of the Jungfrau rising above the Lauterbrunnen Valley.

As you wander up the basin the trail soon peters out and disappears at 2.9 miles. The upper end of the basin is a great place to take a break and enjoy the scene.

There are several options for the return journey from the basin. The easiest is to simply turn around and walk back to Gimmelwald for a 5.8 miles round trip hike. Alternatively, you could hike all the way back to Stechelberg for a 6.6 mile hike. Hikers looking for a longer, more challenging hike with great views should consider ascending the steep trail to Murren for an 8.9 mile hike.

Chilchbalm to Murren

- **Distance Gimmelwald to Chilchbalm to Murren:** 8.9 miles
- **Elevation at Murren:** 5, 370-ft.
- **Elevation Gain/Loss:** 2,937-ft. / -2,046-ft.
- **Difficulty:** strenuous

To hike to Murren, retrace your steps to the junction with the trail to Sefinenfurgge at 3.8 miles and turn left toward the Sefinenfurgge. The path now climbs long switchbacks up very steep slopes along the north side of the Sefinen Valley, traveling through meadows and clusters of trees.

As you ascend, enjoy ever improving views of the peaks soaring above the Sefinen Valley. The Jungfrau and neighboring peaks tower above the Lauterbrunnen Valley to the east.

At 4.8 miles the grade abates a bit and views open to the Hundshorn and Schilthorn rimming a huge bowl to the west. Rugged cliffs and a photogenic horn rise to the southwest.

The path soon resumes its steep climb and reaches a junction at 5.0 miles. The trail straight ahead leads to the Rotstockhutte and the Sefinenfurgge. We turn right (east) toward Oberberg and Murren.

Past the junction the stiff climbs continues as the trail passes through Oberberg. Beyond the small hamlet the grade moderates as we continue ascending high above the north side of the Sefinen Valley. Ahead are great views of the Eiger, Monch, Jungfrau and nearby peaks rimming the east side of the Lauterbrunnen Valley.

Reach a junction with the Alpine Pass Route and the high point of the trail at 6.2 miles. To the left (west) the Alpine Pass route heads toward the Sefinenfurgge and Griesalp. We turn right toward Spielbodenalp and Murren.

At 6.3 miles ignore the trail to the left climbing to Bryndli and continue toward Murren. The trail now curves around the end of a ridge at the foot of the Sefinen Valley, emerging into the Lauterbrunnen Valley. Here views stretch northeast to the Wetterhorn and the Eiger. Across the valley the high peaks from the Jungfrau to the Breithorn dominate the view to the east/southeast.

At 6.5 mile the trail starts a steep decent down tight switchbacks. Take a break as you descend to enjoy the amazing views of the high peaks across the valley. The grade abates as the trail reaches Spielbodenalp and a junction at 7.0 miles. A restaurant at the alp enjoys fine views of the high peaks.

At the junction continue along the Alpine Pass Route toward Murren. The path descends through pastures, crosses a bridge over the Schiltbach (a small stream) and then ascends to a junction at a gravel road. Turn right on the road toward Murren.

The road descends on moderate to moderately-steep grades through pastures and travels by small alps. Along the way enjoy more fine views of the peaks to the east. At all intersections continue in the direction of Murren.

At 8.3 miles the grade abates as the trail reaches the outskirts of Murren and passes the cable car station with service to Stechelberg. Continue through the town, following the signs for the railway station. Reach the railway station at 8.9 miles. Here a train runs to the cable car that descends to Lauterbrunnen.

For an easier option, reverse the hike and walk from Murren to the Chilchbalm to Gimmelwald.

Starting the Hike at Stechelberg

- **Distance Stechelberg to the Chilchbalm:** 7.6 miles (round trip)
- **Starting Elevation at Stechelberg:** 2,893-ft.
- **Elevation Gain:** 2,147-ft.
- **Difficulty:** moderate

Hikers wishing to forgo the lift can start the hike at Stechelberg. This option requires taking the bus from Lauterbrunnen to the Stechelberg Hotel, the last stop on the line.

From the bus stop walk south through town and watch for a trail signpost marking the turn to the right toward the Chilchbalm. The trail travels through meadows and then begins a steep climb up the south side of the Sefinental valley. At 0.8 miles cross a bridge to the north side of the valley and continue the ascent on easier grades. The path soon reaches a junction with a broad track. Continue straight ahead on the track that ascends through trees along the north side of the creek, reaching the junction at Sefinental at 1.9 miles.

From the Sefinental junction follow the directions above to the Chilchbalm. The hike up from Stechelberg adds 0.8 miles to the hike (one-way) and 1,240-ft. in elevation gain.

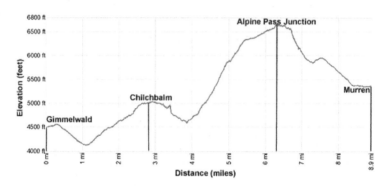

Trailhead Directions

From Lauterbrunnen Bahnhof to Gimmelwald via the Schilthornbahn: From the bus stop near the northern end of the Lauterbrunnen Bahnhof (train station) take the #141 bus bound for Stechelberg and get off at the Schilthornbahn stop, the bottom station for the cable car system to the Schilthorn. The bus ride takes about 14 minutes. Note: There are many bus stops between the train station and the lift station. Check SBB website or download the SBB app for the current schedule and to find the stop near your accommodation.

At the Cable Car station, purchase a ticket for Gimmelwald. Take the cable car to Gimmelwald and exit the cable car station. Note: This is a four stage cable car that goes from bottom station to Gimmelwald and then to Murren, Birg and the Schilthorn, a popular viewpoint.

Lauterbrunnen Bahnhof to Stechelberg Hotel (last stop): See Hike 52.

From Stechelberg Hotel to the Lauterbrunnen Bahnhof (last stop): See Hike 52

From Murren to Lauterbrunnen: Walk to the Murren train station at the north end of the village. Take the train to the Murren Bergbahn, the cable car descending to Lauterbrunnen. The train ride takes 14 minutes and the cable car 4 minutes. The walk from the train to the cable car is short and you should have no problem making the connection.

55. Tanzbodeli ★★★★★
Distance: 7.7 - 8.6 miles (one way)
Near Lauterbrunnen in the Bernese Alps

The best hike in Lauterbrunnen climbs steeply to Tanzbodeli, an overlook atop a grassy plateau with jaw-dropping, panoramic views of the high peaks towering above the Lauterbrunnen and Sefinen Valleys. The return via Obersteinberg is packed with visual delights.

Distance: 3.5 miles (one way) to Tanzbodeli
7.7 - 8.6 miles (one way) to Stechelberg via Obersteinberg
Elevation: 4,480-ft. at Trailhead
7,000-ft. at Tanzbodeli
2,985-ft. at Stechelberg
Elevation Gain: 2,930-ft. to Tanzbodeli
-4,015-ft. to Stechelberg

Difficulty: strenuous
Basecamp: Lauterbrunnen
Lauterbrunnen Map: See page 249
Online Map/Photos:
www.hikingwalking.com/tanzbodeli

Why Hike to Tanzbodeli

This is my favorite hike in Lauterbrunnen with incredible views of the Bernese Alps. The steep trail climbs to Tanzbodeli, "the dance floor", a high grassy plateau on the ridge between the Sefinen and Lauterbrunnen valleys with magnificent, 360-degree views.

Directly across from the plateau the Jungfrau, Gletscherhorn, Abeni Flue and Mittaghorn soar above the east side of the Lauterbrunnen Valley. At the head of the valley a beautiful glacial cirque, formed by the Grosshorn, Breithorn, Tschingelhorn and Ellstabhorn, creates the perfect backdrop for Schmadribachfall (waterfall) plunging down the lip of a hanging valley. To the west/northwest the peaks surrounding the Sefinen Valley, including the Gspaltenhorn and Butlasse, dominate to the view while to the north views extend down the length of the Lauterbrunnen Valley. All around you glaciers, clinging to the flanks of the high peaks, glisten in the sun.

From Tanzbodeli a trail descending on a diagonal high above the Lauterbrunnen Valley, with terrific views of the high peaks, leads to the pretty alp at Obersteinberg. The alp's circa-1880 hotel and restaurant enjoy stunning views of Schmadribachfall plunging 1,000-ft. to the valley floor and the glacial cirque at the head of the valley.

At Obersteinberg, an optional side trip leads to the Oberhornsee, a small lake, situated in the rocky meadows between the moraines of the Breithorn and Tschingelfirn glaciers.

Hikers are presented with two options on the final leg of the hike from Obersteinberg to Stechelberg; a high route and a valley route. The high route is slightly shorter and features more great views of the high peaks before descending steeply through forest. The valley route enjoys fine views of the waterfall as it descends steeply to the valley floor and then wanders down valley beside the Weisse Lutschine River. Both trails end at the Hotel Stechelberg where regularly scheduled buses return to Lauterbrunnen.

This is a strenuous hike that will take longer than the mileage may imply. Pick a day that promises good weather and get an early start so you can enjoy the hike at a leisurely pace and have plenty of time to soak in the views from Tanzbodeli and Obersteinberg.

To Tanzbodeli

- **Distance from Trailhead:** 3.5 miles (one way)/7.5 miles (round trip)
- **Elevation at Tanzbodeli:** 7,000-ft.
- **Elevation Gain:** 2,930-ft.

Take the Schilthorn Cable Car, a multi-stage lift, to the first station in Gimmelwald (4,472-ft.). (See trailhead directions below.) Exit the cable car station and walk southwest toward Busenalp and Obersteinberg on a paved path that travels through the small village of traditional wood houses and small barns. At the first intersection ignore the trail branching left toward Stechelberg, Wasserbrigg and Obersteinberg. Instead continue straight ahead toward Busenalp (2-hr), Obersteinberg (3-hr) and Tanzbodeli (2-hr 45-min).

Soon the path curves to the southwest into the Sefinental (Sefinen Valley) where beautiful views open to the Ellstabhorn, Tschingelgrat (Tschingel Ridge), Gspaltenhorn and Butlasse rising along the valley. Tanzbodeli is seen to the south, the flat plateau to the east of a small horn (the Spitzhorn) on the high ridge rising above a wooded hillside.

At 0.4 miles reach a junction at a hairpin curve. Take the gravel trail branching right off the paved path. The trail now descends west on gentle grades, traveling along the north side of the Sefinen Valley toward Busenalp, Obersteinberg and Tanzbodeli. At 0.6 miles the path crosses a bridge over a stream and then continues descending through trees.

Reach a junction and the floor of the Sefinental valley (4,134-ft.) at 1.2 miles. Ignore the trail continuing straight ahead toward the Kilchbalm, Rotstockhutte and Sefinenfurgge. Instead, follow the gravel path as it makes a sharp left on a hairpin curve toward Busenalp and Obersteinberg. Soon the path reaches a second junction where we turn right toward Tanzbodeli and Obersteinberg. A red arrow on a tree, in addition to signs, marks the turn.

The trail now drops down to and crosses a bridge over the stream draining the Sefinental. Beyond the bridge the trail heads southeast, ascending on very steep grades through forest along the south side of the Sefinental. As you gain altitude openings in the trees offer views of the Lauberhorn and Tschuggen rising along the Mannlichen ridge across the Lauterbrunnen valley to the northeast.

At 2.5 miles the trail curves south into a small valley and the trees give way to pretty meadows. Views open to Tanzbodeli and the Spitzhorn on the ridge towering above the trail to the south.

Reach a "Y" intersection at Untere Busenalp (5,814-ft.) at 2.7 miles. Ignore the trail branching right toward Busenalp. Take the trail to the left toward Tanzbodeli and Obersteinberg. The path now climbs steeply through meadows scattered with trees and low shrubs, heading toward the ridge separating the Sefinen and Lauterbrunnen Valleys. As you gain elevation enjoy great views up the Sefinental Valley to the west. The Jungfrau towers above the Lauterbrunnen Valley to the east.

Crest the ridge and reach Busengrat (6,490-ft.) at 3.1 miles. You are now standing high above the west side of the Lauterbrunnen Valley. Across the valley to the east great views extend from the Jungfrau to the Breithorn.

Turn right at the junction toward Tanzbodeli. The narrow trail climbs very steeply up meadows and rock ledges. At times you may feel the need to use your hands. Reach Tanzbodeli (7,000-ft.), which means the "dance floor", at 3.5 miles. It is fun to watch people arrive at the flat grassy plateau atop the ridge. The first reaction is typically a broad smile, followed by the exclamation -- Wow!

Wow is really the best way to describe the jaw-dropping, 360-degree views from the plateau. The Jungfrau, Gletscherhorn, Abeni Flue and Mittaghorn soar above the east side of the Lauterbrunnen valley. At the head of the valley to the south, the cirque formed by the Grosshorn, Breithorn, Tschingelhorn and Ellstabhorn forms the perfect backdrop for the Schmadribachfall (waterfall) plunging down the lip of a hanging valley. To the west/northwest the peaks surrounding the Sefinental, including the Gspaltenhorn, dominate to the view while to the north views extend down the length of the Lauterbrunnen Valley. All around you glaciers, clinging to the flanks of the high peaks, glisten in the sun.

Tanzbodeli to Obersteinberg to Stechelberg

- **Segment Stat:** 4.2 miles (one-way) from Tanzbodeli to Obersteinberg to Stechelberg
- **Total Distance:** 7.7 - 8.6 miles (one way)
- **Ending Elevation:** 2,985-ft.
- **Elevation Gain/Loss:** -4,015-ft.

On a sunny day it is truly hard to pull yourself away from the amazing Tanzbodeli viewpoint – one of the best in the Bernese Alps. When you are ready to continue hiking, carefully retrace your steps back to the junction at Busengrat and turn south toward Obersteinberg (50-min).

After a short, easy ascent through rocky meadows, the trail curves to the southwest as it descends along the western slopes of the Lauterbrunnen Valley. Across the valley are splendid views extending from the Jungfrau to the Tschingelhorn. The rugged crags of the Ellstabhorn loom above the trail. Soon the buildings of Obersteinberg, nestled on a shelf along the hillside, come into views.

At 4.6 miles the trail curves to the east, descending through bucolic pastures to a junction at Obersteinberg (5,833-ft.) at 4.8 miles. Turn right (south) to visit the pretty alp and the viewpoints just beyond.

The alp includes a circa 1880 hotel, with comfy rooms and dormitory accommodations, and a small restaurant with stunning views of the peaks across the valley. Past the restaurant walk southwest along the trail toward the Oberhornsee for a short distance to a splendid viewpoint with front row seats for beautiful Schmadribachfall, dropping 1,000-ft from the lip of a hanging valley. The stunning glacial cirque ringing the head of the valley towers above the falls. Visiting the viewpoint adds 0.5 miles (round trip) to the hike.

From Obersteinberg hikers are presented with a variety of options. Parties with the time and energy can take a side trip to the Oberhornsee, a small lake, situated in the rocky meadows between the moraines of the Breithorn and Tschingelfirn glaciers.

Side Trip to the Oberhornsee

The trail to the Oberhornsee begins at the "Y" intersection to the south of the Obersteinberg Hotel. Take the trail branch right toward the Oberhorn and Oberhornsee that ascends along the right (west) side of the valley. At 1.0 mile the path crosses a bridge over the Tschingel stream carrying meltwater from the Tschingelfirn Glacier. Beyond the junction the trail climbs steeply to a bench and the Oberhornsee (6,775-ft.), a small lake, after gaining over 940-ft in 1.75 miles.

The lake enjoys spectacular views of the Breithorn, Tschingelhorn, Gspaltenhorn and the Ellstabhorn forming the cirque at the head of the valley. The Jungfrau dominates the view to the north. After enjoy the views, retrace your steps to Obersteinberg. Total round-trip distance for the side trip is 3.5 miles

Trails to Stechelberg

There are two trails from Obersteinberg to Stechelberg, the high route and the valley route. I prefer the high route which is a shorter, steeper and more scenic. The valley route, which is longer and not as steep, enjoys great views of the waterfall, wanders along the west side of the Weisse Lutschine River and passes through Trachsellauenen, the former home to lead, silver and barite mines.

The High Route to Stechelberg

To take the high route, return to the junction to the south of Obersteinberg. Head northeast on the trail toward Hotel Tschingelhorn and Stechelberg, which travels by the Hotel Obersteinberg and then descends through high meadows along the west side of the Lauterbrunnen Valley. Along the way enjoy great views of the peaks across the valley. Initially the trail descends on easy grades but soon the grade steepens.

Pass the Hotel Tschingelhorn at 5.4 miles. Beyond the hotel the trail descends on very steep grades. At 5.9 miles the trail enters the trees and loses the views. Reach a junction at 6.9 miles and take the trail heading toward Stechelberg, Gimmelwald and Murren.

At 7.1 miles reach an intersection at Schwendiwald (3,740-ft.). Turn right (northeast) toward Stechelberg on a trail that drops down a series of steep switchbacks to the valley floor. (The other trail climbs toward Gimmelwald and Murren.) Cross a bridge over the river to the east side of the valley at 7.5 miles and then follow the broad track through the village to the bus stop at the Hotel Stechelberg (2,985-ft.) at 7.7 miles.

The Valley Route to Stechelberg

To take the valley route, walk to the trail junction to the south of the Hotel Obersteinberg. Here a trail signed for Scheuerbode (45-min), Trachsellauenen (1-hr 15-min) and Stechelberg (2-hr) drops down steep switchbacks, traveling through meadows and then scattered trees. Along the way enjoy nice views of Schmadribachfall. Reach Wilde Egg at 5.6 miles, where a trail branches right (south) toward the base of the falls. Continue along the main trail toward Stechelberg, which drops to the valley floor at Schirboden, a bucolic alp set amid pretty meadows.

The trail toward Stechelberg now travels along the west side of the Weiss Lutschine River, passing through meadows and clusters of trees. Behind you are good views of the falls. The peaks along the valley tower overhead. Pass through Bergwerk at 6.7 miles, ignoring the trail that branches left and climbs steeply to the Hotel Tschingelhorn and

Obersteinberg. In a short distance pass Trachsellauenen, a former mining site.

The trail now turns into a broad gravel path which soon joins a gravel alp road. Pass through Im Boden at 7.8 miles where a trail branches right toward Gimmelwald and Murren. We take the trail branching off the road toward Stechelberg (20-min). A good gravel trail drops down to and crosses a wood bridge over the river at 8.0 mile and then travels along the east side of the river. Soon the trail joins with a road through the village, reaching the bus stop at the Hotel Stechelberg (2,985-ft.) at 8.6 mile.

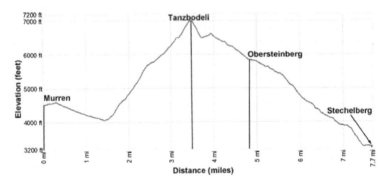

Trailhead Directions

From the Lauterbrunnen Bahnhof to Gimmelwald via the Schilthorn Cable Car system: From the bus stop near the northern end of the Lauterbrunnen Bahnhof (train station), take the #141 bus bound for Stechelberg and get off at the Schilthornbahn, the bottom station for the cable car system to the Schilthorn. The bus ride takes about 14 minutes. Note: There are many bus stops between the train station and the lift station. Check SBB website or download the SBB app for the current schedule and to determine the stop nearest to your accommodation.

At the Cable Car station, purchase a ticket for Gimmelwald. Take the cable car to Gimmelwald and exit the cable car station. Note: This is a four stage cable car which goes from bottom station to Gimmelwald and then to Murren, Birg and the Schilthorn, a popular viewpoint.

Return from Stechelberg to Lauterbrunnen: From the bus stop near the Hotel Stechelberg, catch the bus #141 bound for the Lauterbrunnen Bahnhof. Check the SBB website or download the SBB app for the current schedule.

56. Sefinenfurgge Pass ☆☆☆☆☆
Distance: 8.4 - 12.0 miles (round trip)
Near Lauterbrunnen in the Bernese Alps

This beautiful walk showcases the high peaks soaring above the Lauterbrunnen and Sefinen Valleys. The trail ascends through pretty meadows with nonstop views to Rotstock Hut and then climbs a wild valley to the Sefinenfurgge Pass where vistas open to the Kiental Valley and beyond.

Distance: 8.4 miles (round trip) to Rotstock Hut
12.0 miles (round trip) to Sefinenfurgge Pass
Elevation: 5,374-ft. at Trailhead
6,700-ft. at Rotstock Hut
8,570-ft. at Sefinenfurgge Pass
Elevation Gain: 1,326-ft. to Rotstock Hut
3,196-ft. to Sefinenfurgge Pass

Difficulty: strenuous
Basecamp: Lauterbrunnen
Lauterbrunnen Map: See page 249
Online Map/Photos:
www.hikingwalking.com/sefinen

Why Hike to Sefinenfurgge Pass

The trail to Sefinenfurgge Pass, the second highest pass on the Alpine Pass Route, traverses lovely meadows with breathtaking views of the high peaks towering above the Lauterbrunnen and Sefinen Valleys. The big three, the Eiger, Monch and Jungfrau, are your constant companion through much of the hike.

Along the way the trail crosses a high ridge and enters the Sefinen Valley where the Tschingelspitz, the Gspaltenhorn and Butlasse are the stars of the show. An ascending traverse along the north side of the valley leads to the Rotstock Hut, set atop a grassy knoll with splendid views of the surrounding summits. The hut is a good turnaround point for parties looking for a shorter day (8.4 miles round-trip).

Beyond the hut the trail climbs steeply through rocky meadows and then scree covered slopes to the Sefinenfurgge Pass (8,570-ft.), a small notch on a knife-edge ridge. Here new vistas open to the Armighorn and Dundenhorn rising above the west side of the Kiental Valley. Looking south the Bluemlisalp massif rises above a low ridge. On a sunny day the ridge is a wonderful place to picnic while enjoying the panoramic views before retracing your steps to the trailhead.

The trail continues over the pass toward Griesalp, a stop on the Alpine Pass Route. See Hike 57 - Lauterbrunnen/Murren to Griesalp via the Sefinenfurgge.

To Rotstock Hut

- **Distance from Trailhead:** 8.4 miles (round trip)
- **Elevation at Rotstock Hut:** 6,700-ft.
- **Elevation Gain:** 1,326-ft.

Note: If starting from the Murren mid-station on the Schilthornbahn (cable car), subtract 0.6 miles from the trail distances in this description. (See trailhead directions below.)

The hike to Sefinenfurgge Pass starts by taking the Lauterbrunnen to Murren Bergbahn, which includes a cable car to Grutschalp and then a train ride to Murren. (See trailhead directions below.) From the Murren train station, located at the north end of the village, walk south/southwest along the paved road through the village in the direction of the Schilthornbahn, Rotstockhutte, Sefinenfurgge and Griesalp. The Eiger, Monch and the summit of the Jungfau dominate the view across the Lauterbrunnen Valley to the east.

At 0.6 miles pass the mid station for the Schilthornbahn (cable car) in Murren. Just beyond the station signs point to a road heading southwest toward Spielboden, Rotstockhutte, Sefinenfurgge and Griesalp. Follow the paved track as it ascends on moderate grades through pastures, passing small alps (farms) along the way.

At 1.4 miles pass a trail branching left (south), which drops to Gimmelwald and Stechelberg. A short distance beyond ignore the trail branching right (northwest) toward Blumental, Allmendhubel and the Schilthorn. Views now open to the peaks rising above the Sefinental (Sefinen Valley) to the southwest. Birg and the Schilthorn dominate the view to the west.

Turn left on a trail signed for Spielboden, Sefinenfurgge and Griesalp at 1.7 miles. The trail drops steeply down the hillside, crosses a bridge over the Schilthornbach (Schilthorn stream) and then skirts the north and east sides of the restaurant at Spielbodenalp (5,882-ft.). In front of the restaurant, signs point to a trail heading left (southeast) to Gimmelwald and Murren. We continue along the narrow trail branching right (south) toward Sefinenfurgge and Griesalp.

At 2.0 miles the trail curves to the right (west) and ascends steep, tight switchbacks up the end of the Wasenegg ridge. Reach the top of the switchbacks after gaining over 600-ft. The trail now curves around the head of the ridge and enters the Sefinental. From an overlook at 2.4 miles enjoy terrific views of the Gspaltenhorn, Tschingelspitz and Butlasse towering above the Sefinental. The Monch, Eiger, and Wetterhorn dominate the view to the east while the Grosshorn and Breithorn rise above the head of the Lauterbrunnen valley to the southeast.

Past the viewpoint reach a junction with a trail branching right (north) that climbs steeply to the Bryndi viewpoint atop the ridge. Continue straight ahead (west) on the main trail, contouring along the grassy slopes on the north side of the valley. Views soon open to Sefinenfurgge Pass, the saddle on the ridge at the head of the valley.

Pass a trail on the left (southwest) at 2.7 miles dropping down to Oberberg and Gimmelwald. We stay on the main trail that wanders through pretty pastures with wonderful, bird's-eye views of the cirque formed by Tschingelspitz, the Gspaltenhorn and Butlasse to the southwest. An interesting horn rises at the end of a ridge jutting into the valley. The Schilthorn towers above the high meadows to the northwest. Behind you are terrific views of the peaks lining the east wall of the Lauterbrunnen Valley.

Reach Oberlager (6,729-ft.) at 3.5 miles. Here a trail branches right (northeast) toward Schiltalp and Murren. We continue straight ahead, contouring around a minor ridge and then descending on easy grades toward Rotstockhutte, set atop a grassy knoll.

Near the hut the path curves to the southwest, crosses a stream and soon reaches a junction at Boganggenalp / Rotstockhutte (6,690-ft.) at 4.1 miles. Here a trail branches left (southeast) toward Stechelberg and Gimmelwald.

Cross two more streams and then climb to a junction at 4.2 miles with a trail branching left to the hut. The hut is a good turnaround for parties looking for a shorter day (8.4 miles round-trip) or if the weather is taking a turn for the worse. The hut, which offers refreshments and accommodations, features terrific views of the high peaks soaring above the Lauterbrunnen Valley along with the Schilthorn and summits to the north.

To Sefinenfurgge Pass

- **Segment Distance:** 3.6 miles (round trip) from Rotstock Hut to Sefinenfurgge Pass
- **Total Distance to Sefinenfurgge Pass: 12.0 miles (round trip)**
- **Maximum Elevation: 8,570-ft.**
- **Elevation Gain/Loss: 3,196-ft.**

From the junction at Rotstock Hut, the trail to Sefinenfurgge Pass curves to the right (west) and climbs through rocky pastures on moderate grades. Red and white stakes and blazed rocks help keep you on track. The Schilthorn towers overhead to the north.

At 4.5 miles pass a trail branching right (northwest) toward Rote Hard and the Schilthorn. Our trail curves to the left (southwest), ascending very steep grades up rocky meadows. As you climb, turn around for splendid views of the Eiger, Monch and Jungfrau, along with nearby peaks rising above the east side of the Lauterbrunnen Valley.

Pass a second junction with a trail branching right (north) to Rote Hard and the Schilthorn at 5.0 miles. Just beyond the junction the grade eases as the trail enters a pretty hanging valley, bound to the south by the horn, seen earlier, rising above the end of a low ridge. The trail passes a small pond and then weaves its way through hillocks and high pastures, staying to the right (north) of a stream trickling down the valley floor.

Soon the grade steepens as the trail ascends along the north side of the valley. As you gain height enjoy wonderful views of the Wetterhorn, Eiger, Monch and Jungfrau. Ahead you can see Sefinenfurgge Pass, the notch on the ridge at the head of the valley.

At 5.7 miles the trail briefly drops into a small bowl and then climbs very steep switchbacks through sparse meadows that give way to dark, scree covered slopes. The Hundshorn towers above the trail to the north while behind you are more great views of the high peaks to the east.

A final short, very steep climb propels you to Sefinenfurgge Pass (8,570-ft.) at 6.0 miles. The pass, a notch on a knife-edge ridge, is very narrow. Walk up the ridge to the south of the pass to find a good place to sit and take in the views. Keep an eye out for chamoix often seen grazing on the slopes around the pass.

From the Sefinenfurgge, enjoy great views of the Wetterhorn, Eiger, Monch and Jungfrau. To the west the Armighorn and Dundenhorn fill the skyline above the Kiental Valley. Looking south the Bluemlisalp massif rises above a low ridge. The Hundshorn rises to the north while the Schilthorn dominates the view to the northeast.

When you are done enjoying the views, retrace your steps to the trailhead for a 12.0 mile round-trip hike.

The trail continues over the pass toward Griesalp, a stop on the Alpine Pass Route. See Hike 57 - Lauterbrunnen/Murren to Griesalp via the Sefinenfurgge.

Trailhead Directions

From the Lauterbrunnen Bahnhof: Across the street from the north end of the Lauterbrunnen Bahnhof (train station) find the Lauterbrunnen to Murren Bergbahn. Take the four minute cable car ride to the top station at Grutschalp where you change for the train to Murren, a 14 minute ride. The walk from the cable car to the train is short and you should have no problem making the connection.

The other option is to take the bus from the Lauterbrunnen Bahnhof to the Stechelberg Schilthornbahn. (The destination on the bus will say Stechelberg, which is a few stops beyond the Schilthornbahn.) There are several bus stops in the village, each with a posted timetable. Select the stop that makes sense based on the location of your accommodations.

At the Schilthornbahn station purchase a ticket for Murren, the second stop on the multi-stage cable car trip to the Schilthorn -- a popular viewpoint with a revolving restaurant.

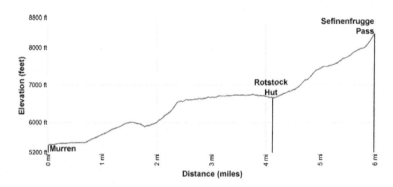

57. Lauterbrunnen (Murren) to Griesalp via Sefinenfurgge Pass ☆☆☆☆☆
Distance: 10.4 miles (one way)
Near Lauterbrunnen in the Bernese Alps

This splendid hike over Sefinenfurgge Pass, the second highest pass on the Alpine Pass Route, enjoys impressive views of the high peaks towering above the Lauterbrunnen, Sefinen and Kiental Valleys.

Distance: 6.0 miles (one way) to
Sefinenfurgge
10.4 miles (one way) to Griesalp
Elevation: 5,380-ft. at Trailhead
8,570-ft. at Sefinenfurgge
4,620-ft. at Griesalp
Elevation Gain: 3,190-ft. to
Sefinenfurgge
-3,950-ft. to Griesalp

Difficulty: strenuous
Basecamp: Lauterbrunnen
Lauterbrunnen Map: See page
249
Online Map/Photos:
www.hikingwalking.com/griesalp

Why Hike from Murren to Griesalp via the Sefinenfurgge

The trail over the Sefinenfurgge, the second highest pass on the Alpine Pass Route, traverses beautiful meadows with breathtaking views of the high peaks towering above the Lauterbrunnen, Sefinen and Kiental Valleys.

After a walk through Murren, set on a sunny shelf high above Lauterbrunnen, the trail ascends through pastures and past small farms on the outskirts of the resort. Great views of the big three, the Eiger, Monch and Jungfrau, are your constant companion. After a short, steep climb up the head of the Wasenegg ridge, the trail enters the Sefinental (Sefinen Valley) where an overlook showcases the Tschingelspitz, Gspaltenhorn and Butlasse towering above the head of the valley.

A beautiful path now contours through pastures along the valley's north slopes to Rotstock Hut. Beyond the hut a steep trail ascends pretty meadows and then scree covered slopes to the Sefinenfurgge Pass (8,570-ft.), a small notch on a knife-edge ridge. Here we enjoy your last views of the Wetterhorn, Eiger, Monch and Jungfrau. To the west new vistas open to the Armighorn and Dundenhorn rising above the west side of the Kiental. Looking south the Bluemlisalp massif rises above a low ridge.

A very steep trail, with the initial section dropping down wood steps with rope handholds, descends to rocky meadows and then drops steeply down to the Kiental Valley floor. Along the way enjoy great views of the Gspaltenhorn, Morgenhorn and Bluemlisalp massif at the head of the valley. An easy trail now travels along the valley floor, passing through small hamlets on its way to Griesalp, a small village with accommodations and a few restaurants.

Be forewarned that the trails on either side of the pass are quite steep. Be especially careful descending the wood stairs dropping down the west side of the pass. The stairs are extremely slick if wet or covered with snow or ice. If in doubt, turn around.

Please note: There are limited accommodations in Griesalp. I strongly recommend making reservations ahead of time during the peak summer hiking season.

Murren to the Sefinenfurgge

- **Distance from Trailhead:** 6.0 miles (one way)
- **Highest Elevation:** 8,570-ft.
- **Elevation Gain:** 8,570-ft.

The hike to Sefinenfurgge Pass starts by taking the Lauterbrunnen to Murren Bergbahn, which includes a cable car to Grutschalp and then a train ride to Murren. (See trailhead directions below.) From the Murren train station, located at the north end of the village, walk south/southwest along the paved road through the village, following the signs to Sefinenefurgge Pass. See Hike 56 - Sefinenfurgge Pass for a detailed description of trail to the pass.

Sefinenfurgge to Griesalp

- **Segment Stat:** 4.4 miles (one-way)
- **Total Distance:** 10.4 miles (one way)
- **Ending Elevation:** 4,620-ft.
- **Elevation Gain/Loss:** -3,950-ft.

To continue to Griesalp, take the trail descending the west side of the pass toward Durrenberg, Bundsteg and Griesalp. Don't take the trail heading south toward Gspaltenhornhutte, Hohturli, Bluemlisalphutte and Griesalp.

A series of wood steps with fixed-rope handholds facilitate the descent down the initial extremely steep section of the trail. After dropping about 100-ft. the steps end and a narrow trail now descends very steep, scree-covered slopes along the north side of the valley. At 6.6 miles the scree gives way to rocky meadows as the trail continues its steep drop down the narrow valley, staying to the right (north) of a stream.

At 7.2 miles the trail curves to the southwest, passes a nice waterfall and then reaches Obere Durrenberg (6,545-ft.) at 7.4 miles. Here the trail joins a gravel track heading toward Burgli, Bundsteg and Griesalp. Soon the track turns to the west and crosses a bridge over the stream.

The track turns south at 7.6 miles and then northwest/west as it drops down steep switchbacks, passing some farm buildings along the way. The Bluemlisalp massif dominates the view to the south.

Reach Burgli (5,305-ft.) at 8.8 miles and turn right (northwest) on the gravel alp road heading toward Steinenberg, Golderli, Bundsteg and Griesalp. The trail to the left (southeast) leads to Bundalp and the Gspaltenhornhutte.

The road descends on easy to moderate grades through pastures and groves of trees with nice views of the Kiental Valley. Be sure to turn around to see the Gspaltenhorn and Morgenhorn rising above the head of the valley.

Reach the small hamlet of Steinenberg (4,823-ft.) at 9.6 miles. Trail signs point straight ahead toward Golderli and Griesalp and also direct you to the various small inns and other types of accommodations in the valley.

At Golderli (4,724-ft.), at 10.1 miles, turn left (southwest) toward Griesalp. The path drops down to and crosses the Gamchibach (Gamchi stream) on a bridge before reaching the center of the small village of Griesalp (4,620-ft.) at 10.4 miles. Here you will find a restaurant, hotels and guest houses along with a postbus stop.

Trailhead Directions

From the Lauterbrunnen Bahnhof: See Hike 56.

58. Other Trails in Lauterbrunnen

Near Lauterbrunnen in the Bernese Alps

58a) Grutschalp to Murren

This short, easy walk along a high bench on the west side of the Lauterbrunnen Valley features terrific views of the big three: the Eiger, Monch and the Jungfrau, along with the Abeni Flue, Mittaghorn and the Grosshorn. The walk is a good option on a day when the weather precludes hikes at higher elevations.

- **Distance:** 2.8 miles (one-way)
- **Elevation:** 4,875-ft. at Grutschalp
  5,374-ft. at Murren
- **Elevation Gain:** 499-ft.
- **Difficulty:** easy
- **Base camp:** Lauterbrunnen
- **Lauterbrunnen Map:** See page 249

Across the street from the northern end of the Lauterbrunnen Bahnhof (train station) find the Lauterbrunnen to Murren Bergbahn. Take the four minute cable car ride to the top station at Grutschalp. (Only purchase a ticket for the cable car and not for the train that continues to Murren.)

Exit the cable car station, cross the train tracks and turn left on the wide track heading to Murren. The trail heads south, traveling above the railway tracks. Below you is the Lauterbrunnen Valley. Directly across the valley is Wengen set beneath the Mannlichen Ridge. A triad of massive peaks; the Jungfrau, Monch and Eiger, dominate the view to the southeast. As you continue along the trail enjoy splendid views of these peaks, along with the summits rimming the east wall of the Lauterbrunnen Valley.

The well maintained trail ascends on easy grades, traveling through meadows and clusters of trees. Reach Winteregg at 1.2 miles with a restaurant and dairy. Beyond Winteregg the path continues south, traveling through a forested area. As you near Murren, enjoy ever improving views of the high peaks towering above the east side of the Lauterbrunnen Valley.

Reach the Murren train station, located at the north end of the village, at 2.8 miles. Extend the hike by walking from Murren to Gimmelwald on a paved alp road with great views of the Jungfrau, Abeni Flue, Mittaghorn, Grosshorn and Breithorn rimming the east side and the head of the Lauterbrunnen Valley. The track descends on moderate grades, losing 832-ft. over 1.7 miles. In Gimmelwald, take the cable car down to the Lauterbrunnen Valley and either ride the bus or walk back to Lauterbrunnen. The easy walk back to Lauterbrunnen adds about 3.0 miles to the day. See Hike 52 -- Lauterbrunnen to Stechelberg for more information.

58b) Murren to Allmendhubel

Ascend through Murren along the Blumental (Flower Valley) to the overlook at Allmendhubel with stunning views of the Eiger, Monch and Jungfrau, the Mannlichen ridge and the summits rising to the west.

- **Distance:** 1.3 - 1.6 miles (one-way) / 2.6 - 3.2 miles (round-trip)
- **Elevation:** 5,374-ft. at Murren
  6,266-ft. at Allmenhubel
- **Elevation Gain / Loss:** 892-ft.
- **Difficulty:** easy to moderate (depending on direction)
- **Base camp:** Lauterbrunnen
- **Lauterbrunnen Map:** See page 249

Take either the Lauterbrunnen to Murren Bergbahn (combination cable car and train) or the Schilthornbahn to Murren (bus to the cable car and then the two-stage cable car to Murren). From the train station walk south/southwest through the village for 0.4 miles and turn right (west/northwest) on a pave track marked for the Blumental and Allmendhubel. If taking the Schilthornbahn cable car, get off in Murren and walk north/northeast for 0.1 miles and turn left toward left (west/northwest) on the paved track toward Allmendhubel.

The trail ascends through pastures, passing chalets and barns. Birg and its neighboring peaks tower above the valley to the west. After walking a half mile the grade eases and you soon reach Pension Sonnenberg at Suppenalp at 0.8 miles from the Schilthornbahn or 1.1 miles from the Murren train station. On the west side of the Pension turn right on the trail ascending to Allmendhubel.

The path soon curves to the right (northeast) as it ascends through meadows and some trees to Allmendhubel at 1.3-1.6 miles. The overlook boasts excellent views of the Eiger, Monch, Jungfrau and Mannlichen Ridge to the east. View extend up the Lauterbrunnen Valley to the Abeni Flue, Mittaghorn and nearby peaks rimming the east side of the valley.

Allmendhubel offers a panoramic restaurant, playground and "flower trail" (a short loop hike above the playground displaying 150 different varieties of alpine flowers) making this a popular spot for families.

Return to Murren by riding the funicular or retrace your steps. Alternatively, follow the Mountain View trail, which passes by Maulerhubel, Dorenhubel and Steinerseggen to Grutschalp where a cable car descends to Lauterbrunnen with grand views of the high peaks to the east. The extended hike adds 3.0 miles to the day.

The hike can be walked in either direction. For an easy hike, take the funicular to Allmendhubel and then walk down. Otherwise the trail is rated moderate.

58c) Northface Trail

Terrific views of the high peaks, flower-filled meadows and charming alps make for a great family walk along the slopes above Murren.

- **Distance:** 4.0 mile (loop)
- **Elevation:** 5,374-ft. at Murren
  6,225-ft. at the high point
  6,266-ft. at Allmendhubel
- **Elevation Gain / Loss:** 1,092-ft.
- **Difficulty:** moderate
- **Base camp:** Lauterbrunnen
- **Lauterbrunnen Map:** See page 249

Start the day by taking the bus to the Schilthornbahn and then the cable car to Murren (two stage trip with a change of cable cars in Gimmelwald). Just beyond the station a blue sign points to the Northface trail which travels south/southwest along a broad path through pastures. Soon the trail curves left, turns to dirt and narrows as it ascends through pastures and clusters of trees, passing small alps as it heads toward Spielbodenalp. The Eiger, Monch and Jungfrau dominate the view across the Lauterbrunnen Valley to the east.

The Abeni Flue, Grosshorn and Breithorn tower above the Lauterbrunnen Valley to the southeast.

After about one mile the trail curves to the right into a side valley and then crosses a bridge over the Schilthornbach (Schilthorn stream). Past the stream the trail ascends to a junction at Spielbodenalp (5,882-ft.) at 1.5 miles. Turn right on the Northface trail that soon recrosses the stream. Past the crossing the path climbs steeply to a broad track at 1.9 miles and turns left, ascending on moderate grades up the track to Schiltalp. Along the way views encompass the Schilthorn towering overhead to the northwest while Birg rises to the north.

At Schiltalp the grade ease as the path travels through meadows beneath Birg. This section of the trail includes 12 signs providing information about the history of the peaks around Murren. Across the valley are amazing views of the Jungfrau, Monch and Eiger. After reaching the high point on the trail at 2.5 miles the path descends on easy grades to cross a tree-covered ridge at 2.9 miles and then descends through trees to a junction at 3.5 miles, just before reaching the Pension Sonnenberg at Suppenalp. Turn left at the junction on the trail ascending to Allmendhubel.

The path soon curves to the right (northeast) as it ascends through meadows and some trees to Allmendhubel at 4.0 miles. The overlook boasts excellent views of the Eiger, Monch, Jungfrau and Mannlichen Ridge to the east. Views extend up the Lauterbrunnen Valley to the Abeni Flue, Mittaghorn and nearby peaks rimming the east side of the valley.

Allmendhubel offers a panoramic restaurant, playground and "flower trail" (a short loop hike above the playground displaying 150 different varieties of alpine flowers) making this a popular spot for families.

Return to Murren by riding the funicular. In Murren walk to the north end of the village and take the train to Grutschalp and then the cable car to Lauterbrunnen. Alternatively, follow the Mountain View trail, which passes by Maulerhubel, Dorenhubel and Steinerseggen to Grutschalp where a cable car descends to Lauterbrunnen with grand views of the high peaks to the east. The extended hike adds 3.0 miles to the day.

Griesalp
Location: The Kiental Valley in the Bernese Alps

Griesalp lies amid pretty meadows at the far end of the Kiental, surrounded by a rugged cirque anchored by Bluemlisalp and the Gspaltenhorn. The tiny hamlet is an important stop on the Alpine Pass route situated between two scenic passes: the Sefinenfurgge and Hohturli, the highest and most challenging pass on the route. Otherwise the peaceful valley is well off the beaten path.

The village, along with nearby Golderli and Pochtenalp, includes a few hotels and pensions, some with dormitory accommodations, and restaurants.

The Griesalp Tourist Information site (www.griesalp.ch/en) provides a list of the valley's accommodations, including mountain huts. In case of bad weather a bus runs from Griesalp to the railway station at Reichenbach. The route travels through the Pochten Gorge on a road said to have the steepest gradient in Europe. Vans are used instead of a standard bus to navigate the tight switchbacks on the road.

Most hikers reach Griesalp on the Alpine Pass Route, starting in either Lauterbrunnen or Kandersteg. This section contains the description of the trail from Griesalp to Kandersteg over Hohturli Pass (Hike 59). The trail from Lauterbrunnen (Murren) to Griesalp via Sefinenfurgge Pass (Hike 57) is found in the Lauterbrunnen section of the guide.

Descriptions of other trails in the area can be found at the Griesalp Tourism Hiking page.

Getting to Griesalp

The Kiental is a side valley branching off of the Kandertal. From either Bern or Brig take the Regio Express on the Lotschberg line to Reichenbach and change for the bus to Griesalp. Look for a minivan instead of a standard bus. Check the SBB website (sbb.ch/en)/SBB app for information on connections to other parts of the country.

59. Griesalp to Kandersteg via Hohturli Pass

★★★★★
Distance: 9.1 miles (one way)
Near Griesalp in the Bernese Alps

The challenging hike over Hohturli Pass features captivating vistas of the high peaks towering above the Kiental and Kandertal valleys, front row seats to the dazzling Bluemlisalp Glacier and stunning views of the rugged cirque soaring above the Oeschinensee, one of the most beautiful lakes in Switzerland.

Distance: 4.1 miles (one way) to
Hohturli and Bluemlisalp Hut
9.1 miles (one way)
Elevation: 4,630-ft. at Griesalp
9,350-ft. at Hohturli and Bluemlisalp
Hut
5,530-ft. at Kandersteg
Elevation Gain: 4,720-ft. to
Hohturli and Bluemlisalp Hut
-3,820-ft. to Kandersteg

Difficulty: strenuous-difficult
Basecamp: Griesalp
Lauterbrunnen and Griesalp
Map: See page 249 and the
Kandersteg and Griesalp Map:
See page 290
Online Map/Photos:
www.hikingwalking.com/hohturli

Why Hike from Griesalp to Kandersteg via the Hohturli Pass

This very strenuous hike over Hohturli Pass, the highest pass on the Alpine Pass Route, features splendid views of the Kiental Valley, the glaciers spilling down the flanks of the Bluemlisalp massif and the Oeschinensee, a stunning lake surrounded by a dramatic cirque.

The hike starts with a steep climb through forests and pastures to Bundalp where the grade steepens as the trail ascends rocky meadows and then scree covered slopes along the southwest side of the Kiental Valley. Views extend from the peaks rising above the head of the valley to Lake Thun in the northwest. Wood steps, fix ropes and chains facilitate the final extremely steep climb to Hohturli Pass (9,114-ft.), where great views encompass the Kiental Valley, the Bluemlisalp glacier, the Oeschinen Valley and beyond.

At the pass take a detour to the Bluemlisalp Hut, perched atop a rocky knoll above the pass. Beyond the hut a use-trail leads to overlooks with wonderful, bird's-eye views of the Bluemlisalp Glacier.

From the pass the trail to Kandersteg plummets down scree-covered slopes, descends along the crest of a moraine wall and then drops down to Ober Bergli, cradled in a lovely hanging valley high above the Oeschinensee. Views along this stage of the trail extend down the Oeschinen Valley to the high peaks rising above Kandersteg.

From Ober Bergli, a spectacular trail contours high above the north side of the breathtaking Oeschinensee with stunning views of the magnificent cirque of rugged peaks, draped with glaciers, towering above the lake's aquamarine waters. Waterfalls, fed by glacial melt water, cascade down the cirque's sheer walls.

The final leg of the trail descends to the lovely meadows near a lift station where a gondola whisks tired but happy hikers down to Kandersteg.

This hike should only be attempted by well-conditioned, acclimated hikers. Do not start the hike during bad weather or if the weather looks threatening. The presence of snow and ice on the trail can turn this hike into a technical climb. Ask about current conditions at the guest houses and inns in Griesalp or talk to other hikers.

Griesalp to Hohturli Pass and Bluemlisalp Hut

- **Distance from Griesalp:** 4.1 miles (one way)
- **Highest Elevation:** 9,350-ft.
- **Elevation Gain:** 4,720-ft.

Find the trail signs across from the Berghaus Griesalp (4,620-ft.), aka the Griesalp Hotelzentrum. Walk south on the trail toward Bundalp (1-hr 15-min), Hohturli/Bluemlisalphutte (4-hr 15-min) and Kandersteg (7-hr 30-min). The trail climbs a hill to a road and then turns left (southeast) on the road toward Hohturli Pass.

At 0.3 miles take the trail branching left off the road toward Hohturli. The trail now enters the forest and crosses a low rise before descending gently through a pasture, passing a trail junction and farm house along the way. At all junctions continue walking toward Hohturli.

Beyond the house the trail crosses a stream at 0.9 miles and then climbs up a forested hillside on a steep rocky path. Soon the forest gives way to pasture as the trail reaches a junction at Untere Bundalp (5,545-ft.). Cross the alp road and continue climbing moderate to steep grades up rocky pastures, shortcutting long switchbacks on the road.

At 1.6 miles the trail crosses the road again and then climbs to the Berghaus-Restaurant Bundalp at Obere Bundalp at 1.7 miles. Here signs direct you along a gravel alp road between two buildings. At the south edge of the alp follow the road as it ascends south through pastures on moderate grades, crossing two streams along the way.

Turn right (south) toward Hohturli on the trail branching off the road at 1.9 miles. The continuation of the route along the road leads to Gspaltenhornhutte and the Sefinenfurgge. Follow the trail as it climbs steeply up undulating, rocky meadows toward the rugged ridge rising to the south. Some sections of the trail are braided and eroded.

At 2.5 miles pass the junction with a trail branching left toward Sefinenfurgge and Gspaltenhornhutte. Continue straight ahead (south) toward Hohturli. The trail now climbs very steep, tight switchbacks along the left side of a gully. Take occasion breaks from the climb to enjoy views of Zahm Andrist, Wild Andrist and the Hundshorn rising across the valley to the north.

At 3.0 miles the meadows give way to scree covered slopes as the trail continues its relentless climb toward a minor ridge extending northeast from the pass. Soon the trail curves to the southeast and climbs through talus and boulders to the ridge crest at 3.3 miles.

The trail quickly crosses the ridge and curves to the southwest, ascending along a narrow bench on the east side of the ridge. Looking up toward the pass you can't help but to wonder how a trail was constructed to scale the extremely steep scree-covered gully running along the east side of the ridge. This is definitely not a trail for anyone with a fear of heights.

Follow the very steep trail, carved into the scree-covered slopes, along the right side of the gully beneath the ridge's sheer rock walls. At 3.5 miles the trail reaches the first of a series of wood steps, some with fix ropes, to facilitate the exceedingly steep climb to the pass. Chains, secured to the rock face along the ridge provide safeguard the final steep haul to the pass.

Reach Hohturli Pass (9,114-ft.) at 3.8 miles and a 4,484-ft. elevation gain. From the pass enjoy great views extending southwest down the length of the Oeschinen Valley to the peaks towering over the west side of Kandersteg. Sefinenfurgge Pass, the notch on the saddle between the Hundshorn and Butlasse, is visible to the east. To the north fine views extend down the Kiental Valley and beyond with Lake Thun in the distance. Nearer at hand are wonderful views of the dazzling glaciers spilling down the flanks of the Bluemlisalp massif to the south.

For even better views of the glacier, turn southeast and climb steep switchbacks leading to Bluemlisalphutte (9,297-ft.). Reach the hut, which offers dormitory accommodations and meals, at 4.0 miles. A use trail, skirting the southwest side of the hut, crosses a large boulder field and then scree-covered slopes on its way to great viewpoints (9,350-ft.) overlooking the Bluemlisalp Glacier at 4.1 miles. Here you have a bird's-eye view of the motionless rivers of ice flowing around the Utem Stock, a horn protruding from the flanks of the Bluemlisalp massif.

From Hohturli to Kandersteg

- **Segment Stat:** 5.0 miles (one-way) from Hohturli to Kandersteg
- **Total Distance:** 9.1 miles (one way)
- **Ending Elevation:** 5,530-ft.
- **Elevation Gain/Loss:** -3,820-ft.

When you are ready to continue to Kandersteg retrace your steps to the pass. From the pass a very steep trails descends west down scree-covered slopes toward Ober Bergli (1-hr 30-min), Oeschinensee (2-hr 14-min) and Kandersteg (3-hr 15-min), losing over 1,000-ft in 0.75 miles. Wood steps and plank bridges facilitate the descent over eroded and extremely steep sections of the trail.

Soon the scree gives way to rocky meadows and the grade eases a bit as the trail curves left (southwest), descending on moderately-steep grades atop the remains of an old moraine wall. Switchbacks help ease the descent down rocky benches. To the south enjoy wonderful views of the tongues of the Bluemlisalp Glacier hanging from a high shelf. Unfortunately the receding glacial tongues are not quite a dramatic as they were 10-15 years ago.

At 5.4 miles the descent steepens as the trail travels along the knife-edge crest of the moraine. Soon the trail drops off the moraine wall, descends very steep switchbacks and then travels through rocky meadows to the pretty pastures above Ober Bergli at 6.4 miles.

Follow the trail as it makes a wide arc around the pastures, avoiding a field strewn with boulders from an old rock slide. The path then crosses a bridge over a stream and soon reaches a trail junction near the farm buildings at Ober Bergli (6,473-ft.) at 6.6 miles. Ober Bergli is located at the foot of a small hanging valley high above the northeast end of the Oeschinensee, in my opinion one of the most beautiful lakes in the Swiss Alps.

From Ober Bergli, there are two trails descending to the Oeschinensee gondola and Kandersteg. The shortest trail branches left (south/southwest) toward the Oeschinensee (45-min) and Kandersteg (1-hr 45-min). This route drops steeply down to Unter Bergli (5,797-ft.) and then descends along the north side of the Oeschinensee to Lager at the foot of the lake. Beyond Lager the trails ascends to the lift station where a gondola whisks hikers down to Kandersteg. Alternatively you can follow a trail from Lager dropping on very steep grades to Kandersteg (3,858-ft.).

A more scenic and slight longer trail contouring high above the north side of the lake branches right (northwest) to Heuber, Lager (1-hr) and Kandersteg (2-hr 10-min). This trail features stunning views of the dramatic cirque of rugged peaks towering above the lake's turquoise waters. On a nice day this is the trail to take. If the weather is threatening or if it is foggy, drop down to the lake.

Assuming it is a nice day, turn right on the high trail. Before long the trail crosses back to the north side of the stream and starts contouring high above the northeast end of the lake. At 6.8 miles great views open to the Doldenhorn towering high above the Oeschinensee. Soon the Frundenhorn joins the scene. Glaciers tumble down the rugged slopes beneath the peaks. Waterfalls, fed by glacial melt water, cascade down the peak's sheer walls to the lake.

The narrow trail now winds through meadows, crosses rockslide and navigates rocky gullies along the valley's steep, sinuous walls, high above the north side of the lake. Caution is required in a few spots with a little bit of exposure.

Turn around for great views that extend up the valley to the pass. The Bluemlisalp Glacier tumbles down the slopes between the Bluemlisalp-Rothorn, Ufem Stock and Wyssi Frau, rugged horns protruding from the flanks of the Bluemlisalp massif.

At 7.7 miles a grassy knoll atop a bench beckons hikers to stop and soak in the sublime views. You now have a great perspective of the amazing sheer walls ringing the Oeschinensee along with the rugged peaks forming the stunning glacial cirque surrounding the lake.

Beyond the knoll the trail descends on steep to moderately-steep grades through meadows and groves of evergreens, crossing a few talus covered slopes along the way. At 8.6 miles the trail reaches a junction with a gravel road. Turn right (west) to take the path toward the Oeschinensee Gondola to Kandersteg. Turn left (east) to walk down to Kandersteg.

I recommend taking the gondola down to Kandersteg. Walk west along the gravel road, following the signs directing you to the bergstation (top of the gondola). Reach the gondola's bergstation (5,530-ft.) at 9.1 miles.

If you prefer to walk all the way to Kandersteg take the trail to the left (east/southeast), which descends to Kandersteg on a steep trail along the Oschibach -- a pleasant stream with nice views of the steep walls lining the south side of the valley. There is also a trail to Kandersteg that starts at the top of the gondola and drops down steep switchbacks beneath the gondola. The trail descending along the Oschibach is the better option.

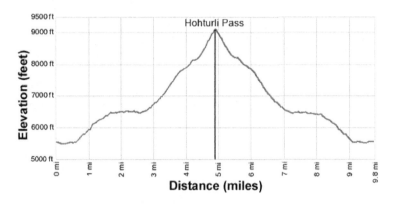

Trailhead Directions

From Griesalp: Find the trail signs near the postbus stop adjacent to the Griesalp Hotelzentrum.

To Griesalp by bus/train: Griesalp is located near the head of the Kiental, a side valley of the Kandertal. Travel on the Bern-Brig Lotschberg railway line to Reischenbach (from Brig or Bern take the Regio Express called "Lotschberger"). At the Reischenbach Bahnhof board the postbus (minibus) to Griesalp. The road to Griesalp travels up very tight hairpin curves on the steepest mountain postal route in Europe. A standard size bus is unable to make the journey. Schedules are available online at the SBB website or download the SBB app.

Kandersteg

Location: The Kandertal (Kander Valley) in the Bernese Alps

The charming village of Kandersteg is set in the Kandertal (Kander Valley), a broad valley rimmed by photogenic peaks. Lake Oeschinen (Oeschinensee), considered to be one of the most beautiful lakes in Switzerland, is the area's most popular attraction. A gondola whisk hikers and tourist to a scenic bench where the stunning lake lies nestled beneath the sheer cliffs of a dramatic cirque of 3,000-meter peaks. The lake is the jumping off point for a loop hike (Hike 60) above the north side of the lake, the trail to Frunden Hut (Hike 61) and the hike to Hohturli Pass (Hike 62), the highest and most challenging crossing on the Alpine Pass Route.

Kandersteg makes a great base camp for hikers to explore not only the Oeschinensee area but also a wide selection of trails in Kandertal and nearby valleys. A cable car ascends to Allmenalp, above the west side of the village, where trails climb to First (Hike 65), the Bunderspitz (Hike 66) and the Bunderchrinde (Hike 68), another crossing on the Alpine Pass Route. Near the head of the valley ride the cable car to Sunnbuel where paths ascend to Gemmi Pass (Hike 63), with far reaching views of the high peaks of the Valais, and Schwarzgratli Pass, a challenging and scenic hike to Adelboden (Hike 64). Additional trails, including the hike to Ammerten Pass and Peak (Hike 67), are found in the Engstligental (Engstligen Valley) to the south of Adelboden and in the nearby Gasternal, a valley branching southeast from the valley station for Sunnbuel.

About Kandersteg

Kandersteg is a traditional village offering a good selection of accommodations, restaurants, an outdoor store and shops along with other traveler services. The village is stretched out along Aussere Dorftstrasse, the main road heading south up the Kandertal. The village center is situated around the intersection of Dorfstrasse and Bahnhofstrasse, a street heading west to the Bahnhof (train station).

The Coop grocery is located on the south side of Bahnhofstrasse. Along the main street to the north of Bahnhofstrasse is a Volg grocery and the Kandersteg Tourist Office (www.kandersteg.ch). The Bakery Tea Room Marmotte and the Restaurant Spycher, with excellent Italian cuisine, are found on the main drag to the south of Bahnhofstrasse.

Buses run from the train station to the Sunnbuel cable car at the south end of the town. You can also walk to Sunnbuel, an easy 1.5 mile walk from the center that takes 30-40 minutes. The Allmenalp cable car is located across the Kander River to the southwest of the train station. The walkway to the Oeschinensee gondola is located along the main street to the north of the Kandersteg Tourist Office and across the street from the Hotel Bernerhof. Head east on the signed pavement traveling through a pretty meadow and then turn left upon reaching a road that soon leads to the gondola station.

Regularly scheduled buses between Kandersteg and Adelboden allow hikers to do point-to-point hikes between the areas and easily return to their accommodations in Kandersteg in the afternoon. For a faster trip, take the train to Frutigen and then change to the bus to Adelboden. Check the SBB website/APP for schedules and ticket prices.

Getting to Kandersteg

From the Zurich Airport or Bahnhof (train station) take the train to Bern and then switch to the train to Kandersteg. The trip takes 2 hours and 11 minutes.

From the Geneva Airport or Geneva Gare (train station) take the train to Brig and then change to the train to Kandersteg. The trip takes 3 hours and 16 minutes.

Kandersteg is on the main train rail line between Bern and Brig. The railway travels through the Lotschberg Tunnel, which starts at the south end of the village and then heads southeast cutting through the Bernese Alps to Goppenstein and Brig in the Valais. The line makes it easy to travel to/from Kandersteg and large Swiss cities such as Thun and Bern, along with a variety of destinations in the Valais. See the SBB website/app for schedules.

Nearby Attractions & Rainy Day Activities

If the weather precludes hiking a good option is to **visit Thun or Bern**. In Thun stroll around the old part of town, exploring the various shops and cafes along with Thun Castle, a 12th century medieval castle. The train trip from Kandersteg takes 50 minutes.

In Bern, walk around the old city -- a Unesco World Heritage Site, go to the Bern Animal Park, explore the Botanic Garden and/or visit the Bern Historical Museum and Einstein Museum. The train ride from Kandersteg to Bern takes an hour and 15 minutes.

The Gasterntal, a side valley branching southeast from the Kandertal, is a recommended excursion from Kandersteg. Reservations are required for the 25 minute bus trip to the Hotel Gasterntal, the last stop in the valley. From the end of the road a beautiful hiking trail ascends over a moraine to the foot of the Alpetli Glacier. I recommend catching the first bus of the day in order to enjoy the hike to the glacier. At the time of this writing the last bus returned to Kandersteg at 6:15 pm.

Good Things to Know about Kandersteg

- The primary language in Kandersteg is German. As with other tourist destinations many people also speak French and/or English.

- The Rendez-Vous is the only campsite in Kandersteg, is locate on the east side of town, just to the south of the gondola to the Oeschinensee. The Rendez-Vous also includes a hostel with rooms, dormitory accommodations and a restaurant.

Map: Kandersteg (East) and Greisalp Trails

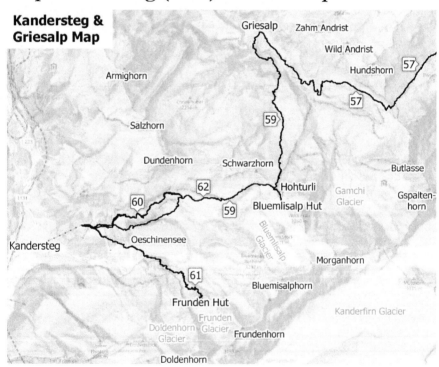

290

60. Oeschinensee Loop ★★★★★
Distance: 5.2 mile (loop)

Near Kandersteg in the Bernese Alps

This terrific loop hike features ever-evolving views of the magnificent glacial cirque towering above the Oeschinensee, one of the most beautiful lakes in the Swiss Alps.

Distance: 2.5 miles (one way) to Ober Bergli
5.2 miles (loop)
Elevation: 5,530-ft. at Trailhead
6,473-ft. at Ober Bergli
6,588-ft. at High Point
Elevation Gain: 943-ft. to Ober Bergli
1,395-ft. to High Point

Difficulty: moderate
Basecamp: Kandersteg
Kandersteg East Map: See page 290
Online Map/Photos:
www.hikingwalking.com/oesch

Why Hike the Oeschinensee Loop

The Oeschinensee, one of the most beautiful lakes in the Swiss Alps, lies nestled beneath the sheer cliffs and rugged flanks of a stunning cirque of 3,000-meter peaks. Glaciers, clinging to the peak's upper slopes, spawn streams coalescing into waterfalls that tumble into the lake. This great loop hike offers wonderful views of the Oeschinensee and the glacial cirque, anchored by the Bluemlisalp, Oeschinenhorn, Frundenhorn and Doldenhorn, from a variety of different perspectives.

The day starts with a scenic gondola ride from Kandersteg to the eastern end of the hanging valley cradling the Oeschinensee. A half-hour walk through pretty meadows and pine forests leads to the lakeshore where great views open to the magnificent wall of peaks encircling the pristine lake.

From the lakeshore, a scenic trail ascends along the north side of the lake, crosses the inlet stream and then climbs steeply to the small alp of Ober Bergli. Views along the way encompass the high peaks towering above the south and east sides of the lake. At the alp the trail turns northwest and then west, contouring high above the north side of the lake.

From the high trail views extend east up the valley to Hohturli pass and the Bluemlisalp massif. The Bluemlisalp glacier tumbles down the slopes between the Bluemlisalp-Rothorn, Ufem Stock and Wyssi Frau, rugged horns protruding from the flanks of the Bluemlisalp massif. To the south the Oeschinenhorn, Frundenhorn and Doldenhorn soar above the Oeschinensee. Glaciers, tumbling down the rugged slopes beneath the peaks, and waterfalls, fed by glacial meltwater, glisten in the sun.

Near the northwest end of the lake the trail drops down to and joins the trail to the gondola station. Hikers can either return to Kandersteg via the gondola or walk down to Kandersteg following a pleasant trail that descends along the Oschibach, the outlet stream for the Oeschinensee.

The trail can be hiked in either direction. I personally prefer walking in the clockwise direction, taking the higher trail first and then returning along the lake shore. Others prefer the counter-clockwise direction as described in the trail detail below. Either option offers amazing views of this stunningly beautiful location.

To Ober Bergli

- **Distance from Trailhead:** 2.5 miles (one way)
- **Elevation at Ober Bergli:** 6,473-ft.
- **Elevation Gain:** 943-ft.

From Kandersteg, take the Kandersteg-Oeschinensee Gondola to the top station (5,530-ft.). (See trailhead directions below.) Exit the gondola station and find the hiking signs at the start of a gravel path heading east. Views from the meadows adjacent to the gondola offer previews of the coming attractions. The Oeschinenhorn, Frundenhorn and Doldenhorn fill the skyline to the east/southeast while the Bunderspitz and the Gross Lohner dominate the view to the southwest.

Walk east along the gravel path toward the Oeschinensee. In a short distance reach a "Y" intersection at Schatthaus (5,479-ft.) and take the trail branching left toward Lager, the Oeschinensee (20-min) and Hohturli (4-hr). Follow the trail as it heads east through meadows and clusters of trees, passing a few minor junctions. In all cases continue along the main trail toward Lager and the Oeschinensee.

Reach a junction at 0.6 miles with a trail branching left toward Heuberg, Ober Bergli, Hohturli and Bluemlisalphutte. This is our return route. We continue straight ahead toward Lager and the Oeschinensee. The trail now descends on easy grades to Lager (5,443-ft.) and a trail junction at 0.9 miles. Turn left at the junction toward the Oeschinensee and Hohturli.

The path soon crosses a stream and then travels through trees above the northwest end of the lake to Chuematti (5,217-ft.) at 1.1 miles. Here a trail drops down to the lake. Take a brief detour to visit the lakeshore and enjoy the great views of the sheer walls and rugged peaks forming the stunning glacial cirque ringing the Oeschinensee. At the eastern end of the lake a waterfall cascades down rock ledges into the lake.

When you are done soaking in the views return to Chuematti and walk east/northeast toward Ober Bergli on a broad gravel track along the north side of the lake. The path ascends on moderately steep grades through clusters of trees and small meadows beneath a rugged hillside, passing a pretty waterfall plunging down a sheer cliff face at 1.3 miles.

At 1.5 miles the grade abates as the trail contours along the base of a cliff with great views of the peaks towering above the east and south sides of the lake, including the Oeschinenhorn, Frundenhorn and Doldenhorn. Waterfalls, fed by glacial meltwater, spill down the steep flanks of the peaks to the lake. Beyond the cliff the trail climbs on easy grades through meadows, crossing two more streams along the way.

Cross a bridge over the stream draining the Bluemlisalp/Hohturli Pass area at 1.9 miles. The trail now curves to the left (northeast), ascending on very steep grades up the rocky meadows beneath the lake's headwall. Ignore any trails branching right toward the buildings of Unter Bergli.

Reach Ober Bergli (6,473-ft.), at the foot of a small hanging valley high above the northeast side of the Oeschinensee, and a trail junction at 2.5 miles. From the alp views extend east/northeast to the Bluemlisalp massif, the Wyssi Frau and the Bluemlisalp Glacier.

At this point you have a few choices. You can wander up valley toward Hohturli Pass, retrace your steps to Lager and the gondola for a 5.0 mile round-trip hike or continue the loop hike. At the junction, continue the loop by turning left (northeast) toward Heuber, Lager (1-hr) and Kandersteg (2-hr 10-min), on a trail contouring high above the north side of the lake.

Completing the Loop

- **Segment Stat:** 2.7 miles (one-way) to the Gondola
- **Total Distance:** 5.2 miles (loop)
- **Highest Elevation:** 6,588-ft.
- **Elevation Gain from the trailhead:** 1,395-ft.

Follow the trail as it crosses to the north side of the stream and starts traversing high above the northeast end of the lake. At 2.7 miles great views reopen to the Doldenhorn towering above the Oeschinensee. Soon the Frundenhorn joins the scene. Glaciers tumble down the rugged slopes beneath the peaks. Waterfalls, fed by glacial melt water, cascade down the peak's sheer walls into the lake.

The narrow trail now winds through meadows, crosses rockslide and navigates rocky gullies along the valley's steep, sinuous walls, high above the north side of the lake. Caution is required in a few exposed areas.

Turn around for great views that extend up the valley to Hohturli pass (Hike 59). The Bluemlisalp Glacier tumbles down the slopes between the

Bluemlisalp-Rothorn, Ufem Stock and Wyssi Frau, rugged horns protruding from the flanks of the Bluemlisalp massif.

At 3.6 miles a grassy knoll with a bench beckons hikers to stop and soak in the sublime views. You now have a great perspective of the amazing sheer walls ringing the Oeschinensee along with the rugged peaks forming the stunning glacial cirque surrounding the lake.

Beyond the knoll the trail descends on steep to moderately-steep grades through meadows and groves of evergreens, crossing a few talus slopes. At 4.6 miles the path reaches the junction with the gravel track leading back to the gondola. Turn right (west) to take the broad track toward the gondola to Kandersteg. Turn left (east) to walk down to Kandersteg.

To take the gondola to Kandersteg, walk west along the gravel track, following signs directing you to the bergstation (top of the gondola). Reach the gondola's bergstation (5,530-ft.) at 5.2 miles.

If you prefer to walk down to Kandersteg take the trail to the left (east/southeast), which descends steeply along the Oschibach, a pleasant stream with nice views of the steep walls lining the south side of the valley. Reach Kandersteg (3,858-ft.) after hiking about 3.0 miles and losing over 1,600-ft. from the junction. Total hiking distance for the loop around the lake, taking the gondola up and walking down to Kandersteg is 7.6 miles.

There is also a trail to Kandersteg that starts at the top of the gondola and drops down steep switchbacks beneath the gondola. The trail that descends along the Oschibach is the better option.

Note: The trail can be hiked in either direction. I personally prefer walking in the clockwise direction, taking the higher trail first and then returning along the lake shore. (Read the first part of the Hohturli Pass hike (Hike 59) to Ober Bergli. From Ober Bergli reverse the directions above and descend to the Oeschinensee.) Others prefer the counter-clockwise direction as described in the trail detail below. Either option offers amazing views of this stunningly beautiful location.

Trailhead Directions

From the Kandersteg Bahnhof (train station) to the Kandersteg-Oeschinensee Gondola: From the front of the train station, walk south a short distance and turn left (east) onto Bahnhofstrasse (Train Station Street). Walk about 700-ft. east on Bahnhofstrasse and turn left (north) on Dorfstrasse (the town's main street). Walk about 650-ft. along Dorfstrasse, passing two streets on the right. Just before the second street you'll go by the Kandersteg Tourism Office on your right, a good place to stop to pickup maps and town information.

A short distance beyond the second street, turn right on a paved walkway heading east through beautiful meadows. The Hotel Bernerhof is directly across from the meadow. Walk a little over 0.3 miles on the pavement to Oschistrasse, passing a pretty little chapel on your right along the way. Turn left on Oschistrasse and walk about 360-ft. to the Kandersteg-

Oeschinensee Gondelbahn (gondola). The gondola ride to the top station takes about nine minutes. See Kandersteg-Oeschinensee Gondelbahn website for the current schedule.

61. Frunden Hut ★★★★★
Distance: 7.8 miles (round-trip)
Near Kandersteg in the Bernese Alps

Frunden Hut is set atop a rock knoll beneath the Frundenhorn and Frunden Glacier, over 3,200-ft. above the Oeschinensee, a beautiful lake. Dramatic views from the overlook encompass the Bluemlisalp massif, adorn with glaciers, along with the high peaks towering above the north side of the lake.

Distance: 7.8 miles (RT)
Elevation: 5,226-ft. at Trailhead
8,399-ft. at Frunden Hut
Elevation Gain: 3,173-ft.
Difficulty: strenuous

Basecamp: Kandersteg
Kandersteg East Map: See page 290
Online Map/Photos:
www.hikingwalking.com/frunden

Why Hike to Frunden Hut

This strenuous hike ascends a very steep, well-constructed trail to Frunden Hut. Excellent views along much of the trail will take your mind off the stiff ascent. Initially the trail features vistas of the Doldenhorn, the Bluemlisalp massif and the Dundenhorn, anchoring the cirque soaring above the Oeschinensee, a gorgeous azure-blue lake. Waterfalls spill down the steep cliffs beneath the peaks, adding to the visual delights.

As the trail gains elevation enjoy ever evolving birds-eye-views of the Oeschinensee and the peaks towering above the north side of this stunning lake. Overhead glaciers tumble down the steep slopes between the Doldenhorn and Bluemlisalphorn while waterfalls cascade down crevasses cut into the cliffs beside the trail.

The hike offers the perfect opportunity to escape the crowds around the Oeschinensee while gaining new perspectives of the impressive mountain scenery. In places fixed cables safeguard sections of the trail that are exposed or may be slippery if wet/icy.

This trail is not recommended for anyone with a fear of heights.

To Frunden Hut

The day starts with a ride up the Oeschinensee Gondola with fine views of the peaks towering above the west side of the Kandersteg valley. (See trailhead directions below.) Upon exiting the gondola station walk east/southeast along a broad track descending on easy grades toward the Oeschinensee. Ahead are lovely views of the high peaks soaring above the lake.

Reach the Schatthaus junction at 0.2 miles and bear right toward Oeschinensee and Frundenhutte. (The trail to the left leads to Hohturli and Bluemlisalphutte.) The path descends through meadows and clusters of trees to the lakeshore and a junction at 0.9 miles. Early in the morning the still waters of the lake reflect the Bluemlisalp massif and its nearby peaks. Photogenic waterfalls spill down the sheer cliffs encircling the lake.

When you are done enjoying the views, return to the junction and turn south on the trail toward Frunden Hut (Frundenhutte). The path travels through meadows above the foot of the lake the then turns left (east), traversing through trees and sections of gravel along the lake's south shore.

At 1.5 miles the path curves away from the lake (southeast) and starts climbing steeply up the slopes beneath the Doldenhorn toward Frunden Hut. Along the way the trail ascends through trees and crosses avalanche chutes. Soon the trees give way to meadows and rock ledges, passing three waterfalls pouring down crevasses etched into the steep cliffs along the trail. Wood bridges cross the streams emanating from the falls.

At 2.5 miles the trail turns south and starts climbing a series of tight, very steep switchbacks straight up a rocky hillside. As you approach a massive rock face the trail curves to the left and zig-zags its way up to a ridge and then continues its stiff climb to the hut. Steps chiseled into the rock and cables secured to the cliff face safeguard this section of the ascent with some exposure.

Reach Frunden Hut (8,399-ft.) at 3.9 miles. Here you efforts are rewarded with superb views of the Frunden Glacier spilling down the north flanks of the Frundenhorn. To the east the Bluemlisalp massif, adorn with glaciers, dominates the views while the Doldenhorn Glacier clings to the slopes beneath its namesake peak.

The overlook, which is 3,200-ft. above the Oeschinensee, features birds-eye-views of the azure blue lake. The Dundenhorn and Bundstock tower above the north side of the lake. Waterfalls tumble down the cliffs beneath Ober Bergli, an alp set atop a grassy knoll.

Roam around the area near the hut to gain different perspectives of the breathtaking scene and to get closer to the Frunden Glacier. There are plenty of great spots to take a break and enjoy the views. After enjoying the scenery walk back to the gondola for a 7.8 miles round-trip hike. Alternatively, instead of taking the gondola to Kandersteg, walk back to town.

To walk back to Kandersteg, return to the junction at the foot of the lake. Here a broad track heads southwest, descending to the village. You can either follow the broad track all the way down or break off from the track and travel along trails for part of the way. The walk back to Kandersteg loses 1,390-ft. and adds 2.4 miles to the day for a 10.2 mile hike.

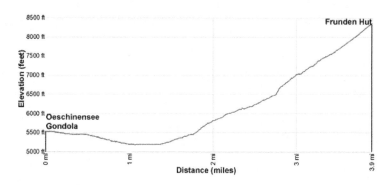

Trailhead Directions

From the Kandersteg Bahnhof (train station) to the Kandersteg-Oeschinensee Gondola: See Hike 60.

62. Hohturli Pass ☆☆☆☆☆
Distance: 9.8 - 10.4 miles (round trip)
Near Kandersteg in the Bernese Alps

Hikers tackling the steep, strenuous ascent to Hohturli Pass are rewarded with stunning vistas of Oeschinensee Lake, marvelous mountain scenery and close-up views of dramatic glaciers.

Distance: 9.8 miles (round trip) to
Hohturli Pass
10.4 miles (round trip) to
Bluemlisalp Hut
Elevation: 5,530-ft. at Trailhead
9,114-ft. at Hohturli Pass
9,297-ft. at Bluemlisalp Hut
Elevation Gain: 3,584-ft. to
Hohturli Pass
3,767-ft. to Bluemlisalp Hut

Difficulty: strenuous
Basecamp: Kandersteg
Kandersteg East Map: See page
290
Online Map/Photos:
www.hikingwalking.com/hohturli-pass

Why Hike to Hohturli Pass

Many hikers visit Hohturli Pass, the highest pass on the Alpine Pass Route, when walking the challenging trail between Griesalp and Kandersteg (Hike 59). Hikers looking for a slightly easier trail to the pass can opt for this highly scenic out-and-back hike from Kandersteg to Hohturli.

The day starts with a quick gondola ride followed by an ascent and then scenic traverse high above the north side of the Oeschinensee, one of the most beautiful lakes in the Swiss Alps. From the trail enjoy splendid views of the magnificent glacial cirque towering above the lake's turquoise waters. After walking a little over 2.5 miles the trail reaches the small alp of Ober Bergli, perched at the foot of a hanging valley high above the lake.

From Ober Bergli the trail climbs steeply through rocky meadows, ascends along the crest of an old moraine and then climbs very steep scree-covered slopes to Hohturli Pass (9,114-ft.). The final climb to the pass is up extremely steep wood steps. Along the way the trail enjoys great views of the tongues of the Bluemlisalp Glacier hanging from a ledge along the trail.

From the pass bird's-eye-views extend southwest to the peaks towering above the west side of Kandersteg. Sefinenfurgge Pass, the notch on the saddle between the Hundshorn and Butlasse, is visible to the east. To the north, vistas stretch down the length of the Kiental Valley to Lake Thun and beyond. To the south, dazzling glaciers spill down the flanks of the Bluemlisalp massif.

An optional side trip climbs from the pass to the Bluemlisalp Hut and an overlook beyond the hut with marvelous views of the Bluemlisalp Glacier and massif.

Be aware that this is a steep, strenuous hike gaining over 3,500-ft. in 4.9 miles. In my opinion the scenic rewards more than compensate for the effort. So pick a day that promises good weather, get an early start and enjoy this beautiful hike to Hohturli Pass and the Bluemlisalp Hut.

To Hohturli Pass

- **Distance from Trailhead:** 9.8 miles (round trip)
- **Highest Elevation:** 9,114-ft,
- **Elevation Gain:** 3,584-ft.

From Kandersteg take the Kandersteg-Oeschinensee Gondola to the top station (5,530-ft.). (See trailhead directions below.) Exit the gondola station and find the hiking signs at the start of a gravel path heading east. Views from the meadows adjacent to the gondola offer previews of the coming attractions. The Oeschinenhorn, Frundenhorn and Doldenhorn fill the skyline to the east/southeast while the Bunderspitz and the Gross Lohner dominate the view to the southwest.

Walk east along the gravel path toward the Oeschinensee. In a short distance reach a "Y" intersection at Schatthaus (5,479-ft.) and take the trail branching left toward Lager, the Oeschinensee (20-min) and Hohturli (4-hr). Follow the trail as it heads east through meadows and clusters of trees, passing a few minor junctions. In all cases continue along the main trail toward Lager and the Oeschinensee.

Reach a junction at 0.6 miles and turn left on the trail toward Heuberg, Ober Bergli, Hohturli and Bluemlisalphutte, which ascends on moderately-steep to steep grades through meadows and trees, crossing a few talus slopes along the way. At 1.4 miles the grade abates as the trail reaches a grassy knoll.

A use trail, heading south, leads to a bench atop the knoll offering a great perspective of the amazing sheer walls ringing the Oeschinensee and the rugged peaks forming the stunning glacial cirque surrounding the lake. Glaciers tumble down the cirque's rugged slopes while waterfalls, fed by glacial melt water, plummet down the sheer walls and into the lake.

Beyond the knoll the trail contours high above the north side of the lake, traveling through meadows, crossing rockslides and navigating rocky gullies along the valley's steep, sinuous walls. Caution is required in a few spots with a little bit of exposure.

The walk is accompanied by glorious views of the Oeschinenhorn, Frundenhorn and Doldenhorn towering high above the south/east side of the Oeschinensee. As you near the head of the lake grand views open up the valley to Hohturli pass. The Bluemlisalp Glacier tumbles down the slopes between the Bluemlisalp-Rothorn, Ufem Stock and Wyssi Frau, rugged horns protruding from the flanks of the Bluemlisalp massif. If you look carefully, you should be able to see the Bluemlisalp Hut perched atop a rocky knoll to the north of the Wyssi Frau.

At 2.3 miles the trail curves to the east, crosses a stream and then curves to the south, reaching the small alp at Ober Bergli (6,473-ft.) and a trail junction at 2.7 miles. Ober Bergli is located at the foot of a hanging valley high above the northeast end of the Oeschinensee.

Turn left at the junction toward Hohturli, Bluemlisalp Hut and Griesalp. The trail to the right, which drops steeply down to Unter Bergli, offers an alternative route back to Kandersteg on return journey.

Soon the trail crosses to the north side of the stream on a metal bridge and starts climbing, making a wide arc around the alp's pastures to avoid a field strewn with boulders from an old rock slide. At 3.0 miles the trail curves to the left (east/northeast) and ascends steeply through rocky meadows along the north side of the valley.

At 3.5 miles the path climbs a series of switchbacks ascending to the knife-edge crest of the eroded moraine of the Bluemlisalp Glacier. To the south enjoy wonderful views of the tongues of the Bluemlisalp glacier hanging from a high shelf. Unfortunately the receding glacial tongues are not quite a dramatic as they were 10-15 years ago.

Follow the trail as it climbs on moderately steep grades along the crest of the moraine. Turn around occasionally for nice views of the peaks, including the Gross Lohner, rising along the west side of Kandersteg. At 3.9 miles the moraine wall ends and the trail now ascends on moderate to moderately-steep grades through meadows and up rock ledges along the north side of the deep trench filled with the rocky remains of the receding glacier. The pass, a notch along ridge at the head of the valley, and the hut, to the right (south) of the pass, are now in sight.

At 4.5 miles the path curves to the east and the rocky meadows give way to scree covered slopes. Follow the trail as it climbs steep to very steep grades toward the pass, gaining over 1,000-ft in 0.75 miles. In places temporary bridges span eroded gullies along the trail. The final push to the pass climbs very steeply up wood steps.

Reach Hohturli Pass (9,114-ft.) at 4.9 miles and a 3,584-ft. elevation gain. From the pass great views extend southwest to the peaks towering above the west side of Kandersteg. Sefinenfurgge Pass, the notch on the saddle between the Hundshorn and Butlasse, is visible to the east. To the north, fine views stretch down the length of the Kiental Valley to Lake Thun and beyond. To the south, dazzling glaciers spill down the flanks of the Bluemlisalp massif.

To Bluemlisalp Hut

- **Segment Stat:** 0.6 miles (round-trip) to Bluemlisalp Hut and Overlook
- **Total Distance:** 10.4 miles (round trip)
- **Maximum Elevation:** 9,350-ft.
- **Elevation Gain/Loss to Bluemlisalp Hut:** 3,820-ft.

For even better views of the glacier, turn southeast and climb steep switchbacks up to Bluemlisalphutte (9,297-ft.). Reach the hut, which offers dormitory accommodations and meals, at 5.1 miles. A use trail, skirting the southwest side of the hut, crosses a large boulder field and then scree-covered slopes on its way to great viewpoints (9,350-ft.) overlooking the Bluemlisalp Glacier at 5.2 miles. Here you have a bird's-eye view of motionless rivers of ice flowing around the Utem Stock, a horn protruding from the flanks of the Bluemlisalp massif.

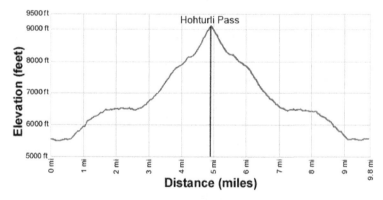

When you are done taking in the views, retrace your steps to the gondola. For variety, you can take an alternate trail from Ober Bergli back to the gondola. At Ober Bergli take the trail branching left (west/southwest) toward the Oeschinensee (45-min) and Kandersteg (1-hr 45-min). This route drops steeply down to Unter Bergli (5,797-ft.) and then follows a descending traverse along the north side of the Oeschinensee to Chuematti and Lager at the foot of the lake. Beyond Lager the trails ascends to the lift station where a gondola whisks hikers down to Kandersteg.

Alternatively if you prefer to walk back to Kandersteg, at Chuematti turn left (east/southeast) on the trail headed toward Kandersteg (1-hr 10-min). The trail descends steeply through meadows and then travels along the Oschibach, a pleasant stream with nice views of the steep walls lining the south side of the valley. Reach Kandersteg (3,858-ft.) after hiking 2.8 miles and losing about 1,400-ft from Chuematti. Total hiking distance to Hohturli, taking the gondola up and walking down is 11.5 miles.

There is also a trail to Kandersteg that starts at the top of the gondola and drops down steep switchbacks beneath the gondola. The trail descending along the Oschibach is the better option.

Trailhead Directions

From the Kandersteg Bahnhof (train station) to the Kandersteg-Oeschinensee Gondola: See Hike 60.

Map: Kandersteg (West) and Adelboden

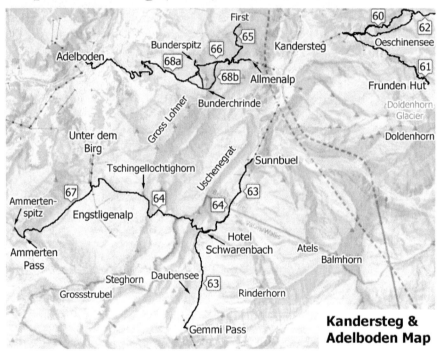

Kandersteg & Adelboden Map

63. Gemmi Pass ★★★★☆
Distance: 10.8 miles (round-trip)

Near Kandersteg in the Bernese Alps

This trail travels up a pretty valley, rimmed by rugged cliffs and soaring peaks, passes the Daubensee, a photogenic lake, and then climbs to Gemmi Pass with panoramic views of the high peaks in the Valais, stretching from Monte Rosa to Dent Blanche and beyond.

Distance: 10.8 miles (round-trip)
Elevation: 6,135-ft. at Trailhead
7,692-ft. at Gemmi Pass
Elevation Gain: 1,557-ft.
Difficulty: moderate

Basecamp: Kandersteg
Kandersteg West Map: See page 302
Online Map/Photos:
www.hikingwalking.com/gemmi

Hiking to Gemmi Pass

Gemmi Pass, situated on a saddle between the Daubenhorn and the Rinderhorn, is a centuries old crossing between the Cantons of Bern to the north and the Valais to the south. From the pass amazing, albeit distant, views encompass the high Pennine Alp in the Valais including Monte Rosa, the Matterhorn, the Weisshorn, Bishorn and Dent Blanche.

This hike, starting to the south of Kandersteg at Sunnbuel, travels through the pretty Spittelmatte Valley and then ascends to and travels along the lakeshore of the Daubensee before the final climb to Gemmi Pass. The hike is relatively easy and features fine views of the high peaks soaring about the east side of the valley and the rugged Uschenegrat Ridge rising to the west.

Start the day by riding the Kandersteg-Sunnbuel cable car to Sunnbuel. (See trailhead directions below.) At Sunnbuel find the trail signpost outside the station and walk southwest on a broad track toward Schwarenbach. The path travels through scattered trees and then descends on moderately easy grades to the Spittelmatte Valley floor.

As you descend enjoy views of Altels and the Rinderhorn towering above the valley to the east while the Uschenegrat, a high ridge, rims the valley to the west. Behind you the Doldenhorn fills the skyline above the Gasterntal Valley to the northeast. Unfortunately large electrical towers run through the valley, slightly marring an otherwise bucolic scene.

Soon we leave the trees behind and travel through pastures on easy grades, reaching a junction at the Spittelmatte alp at 1.0 mile. The broad track continues southwest toward the Schwarenbach (stream), crossing a bridge over a tributary stream and then ascending on easy grades along the west side of the stream. As you head up valley ignore any trails branch off the main track.

At 1.5 miles the grades steepens as the track ascends through a massive rockslide. The slide marks an area destroyed in September 1895 when a part of the glacier along the west facing slopes of Altels broke off and crashed down the hillside, burying part of the valley floor in ice and debris.

At 2.25 miles the grade abates and the trail now curves around a rocky slope and reaches the Hotel Schwarenbach at 2.5 miles. The hotel offers private rooms and dormitory accommodation along with a restaurant with views of the Daubenhorn and nearby peaks rising above valley. Below the hotel is a small lake.

At the west end of the hotel ignore the trail branching right toward Schwarzgratli and Engstligenalp. Instead continue along the broad track toward the Daubensee and Gemmipass. Beyond the hotel the trail curves to the left (south), crosses a bridge over a stream and then starts climbing through rocky meadows on moderate to moderately steep grades toward the Daubensee.

As you ascend enjoy views of the Uschenegrat ridge. Roter Totz and the Steghorn rise above the ridge to the southwest. The Rinderhorn soars above the valley to the east.

At 3.6 miles the climbs ends as the trail crests the bench cradling the Daubensee, the lake beneath Gemmi Pass. Soon the trail reaches the foot of the lake and a stunning viewpoint. Here the Daubenhorn and Rinderhorn rise above the pass, forming the perfect backdrop for this pretty lake. Early in the day the still waters of the lake reflect the high peaks.

A loop trail circles the lake. One leg of this loop branches right, circling around the west side of the lake. We continue on the wide track along the left (east) side of the lake that travels through meadows beside the lake shore accompanied by fine views of the Uschenegrat ridge and the high peaks towering above the pass.

At 4.3 miles ignore the trail branching right, another access point for the loop trail around the lake. Our trail now ascends on easy to moderately-easy grades to a junction just below the Pass at 5.3 miles. The path to the right leads to Gemmi Pass (7,692-ft.) at 5.4 miles and a trail dropping down to Leukerbad. The trail to the left leads to the restaurant, restrooms and the Gemmibahn, a gondola dropping down to Leukerbad, at 5.4 miles.

Overlooks around Gemmi Pass feature breathtaking panoramas of the Pennine Alps in the Valais. On a clear day you can see Monte Rosa, the Matterhorn, the Weisshorn, Bishorn and Dent Blanche, to name a few.

When you are enjoying the views, retrace your steps to the trailhead for a 10.8 mile hike. For variety, you can take the trail around the west side of the lake on the return journey, which adds 0.75 miles to the hike.

Parties looking for a short hike can ride the Gemmibahn down the Leukerbad and then catch a bus to Leuk where a series of trains return to Kandersteg. The ride back to Kandersteg takes about one hour and 40-minutes.

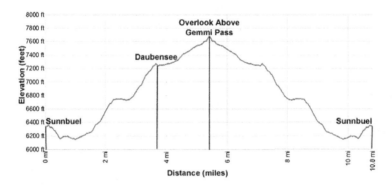

Trailhead Directions

Note: It is possible to walk from Kandersteg to Sunnbuel. The hike adds 3 hours and 2,438-ft. in elevation gain to the day. I strongly recommend taking the cable car. To walk, hike south on the main road through Kandersteg to the Sunnbuel Cable Car Station. Continue on the road past the cable car station. Soon you will see a trail signed for Stock and Sunnbuel. Turn left and follow the trail that climbs steeply to Sunnbuel.

Kandersteg Bahnhof (train station) to Sunnbuel Cable Car:

Walking: From the front (east side) of the train station, walk south a short distance and turn left (east) onto Bahnhofstrasse (Train Station Street). Walk about 700-ft. east on Bahnhofstrasse, passing the Coop Supermarket along the way. When you hit the main road (Dorfstrasse) turn right. Follow the main road to the Luftseilbahn Kandersteg-Sunnbuel (Cable car – Kandersteg to Sunnbuel). The 1.6 mile walk should take about 30-40 minutes.

Bus: Take the #241 bus from the Kandersteg Bahnhof (train station) to the Talstation Luftseilbahn Sunnbuel (valley station for the Sunnbuel Cable Car). The ride should take about 9 minutes. The bus makes a number of stop along the main road through the town. Check the SBB website or download the SBB app for the current schedule and to find the stop nearest to your accommodations.

Gemmi Pass to Kandersteg: From Gemmi Pass ride the Gemmibahn cable car down to Leukerbad. From the valley station, follow signs to the Leukerbad Bahnhof (train station) where you want to take the #471 bus to the Leuk Bahnhof (train station). At the Leuk train station purchase tickets for Kandersteg. You will need to take the train to Gampel-Steg and then switch to the train bound for Goppenstein. At Goppenstein, change to the train to Kandersteg. The entire ride should take about one-hour and 40-minutes. Check the SBB website or download the SBB app for the current schedule and best connections.

64. Kandersteg (Sunnbuel) to Engstligenalp (Adelboden) ☆☆☆☆☆
Distance: 7.3 miles (one way)
Near Kandersteg in the Bernese Alps

This challenging trail features panoramic views of the high peaks towering above the Spittelmatte, Uschene and Engstligenalp Valleys. The path is best suited for sure footed hikers who like demanding trails that cross exposed passes, travel along airy ridges and include steep ascents and descents.

Distance: 3.7 miles (one way) to Schwarzgratli Pass
7.3 miles (one way) to Engstligenalp
Elevation: 6,352-ft. at Trailhead
7,812-ft. at Schwarzgratli Pass
8,723-ft. at Engstligengrat High Point
6,437-ft. at Engstligenalp
Elevation Gain: 1,460-ft. to Schwarzgratli Pass
2,959-ft. to Engstligengrat High Point
-2,286-ft. to Engstligenalp

Difficulty: strenuous
Basecamp: Kandersteg
Kandersteg and Adelboden
Map: See page 302
Online Map/Photos:
www.hikingwalking.com/sunnbuel

Why Hike from Sunnbuel to Adelboden

At the head of the Kandertal (Kander Valley) to the south of Kandersteg lies Spittelmatte, a secluded, hanging valley, easily reached by taking the cable car to Sunnbuel. From Sunnbuel a path descends on easy grades to the pretty valley rimmed by Altels and the Rinderhorn to the east and the Uschenegrat ridge to the west.

A broad track travels through the valley and then ascends an old rockslide to the Hotel Schwarenbach. Here our trail turns west, climbing steeply to Schwarzgratli Pass on the Uschenegrat ridge. Along the way enjoy fine views of the high peaks and the ridge. As you crest the ridge terrific vistas open to the summits towering above the Uschene Valley to the west.

From the pass a steep, exposed, scree-covered trail descends to the Uschene Valley and then ascends an equally steep trail through rocky meadows to the crest of the Engstligengrat, the ridge separating the Uschene and Engstligenalp valleys. Atop the ridge views open to Engstligenalp, a pretty meadow-clad bowl ringed by high peaks.

The path now wanders north and then west along the high, airy ridge with glorious 360-degree views. Ahead the Tschingellochtighorn summit block rises along ridge. Pass to the south of the summit block and then descend steep scree-covered slopes and then meadows to Engstligenalp. At Engstligenalp a cable car whisks hikers down to Unter dem Birg where buses head to Adelboden and/or Kandersteg.

This trail offers an alternative, more demanding crossing to Adelboden than the traditional Alpine Pass Route from Kandersteg to Adelboden via the Bunderchrinde. After leaving the Spittelmatte Valley, you'll be well off the beaten path and find opportunities for short detours and explorations.

If you are uncomfortable with the descent from Schwarzgratli Pass, turn around and follow a trail north along the Uschenegrat ridge to a junction below the Gallihorn. From the junction descend to either Sunnbuel or the Uschene Valley and walk back to Kandersteg. It is also possible to walk back to Kandersteg by taking trails splitting off the Engstligengrat and Artelegrat ridges near the Tschingellochtighorn summit block.

Pick a day full of promise before setting out on this hike. The high ridges and exposed scree slopes should be avoided during thunderstorms, fog or slippery conditions. This trip is only recommended for experience, sure-footed hikers who delight in a challenging day that yields terrific, ever changing views.

Sunnbuel to Schwarzgratli Pass

- **Distance from Trailhead:** 3.7 miles (one way)
- **Elevation at Schwarzgratli Pass:** 7,812-ft.
- **Elevation Gain:** 1,460-ft.

Begin the day by riding the Kandersteg-Sunnbuel cable car to Sunnbuel. (See trailhead directions below.) At Sunnbuel find the trail signpost outside the station and walk southwest on a broad track through scattered trees toward Schwarenbach. The trees give way to pastures as the path descends on moderately easy grades to the Spittelmatte Valley floor.

Along the way enjoy views of Altels and the Rinderhorn towering above the valley to the east while the Uschenegrat, a high ridge, rims the valley to the west. Behind you the Doldenhorn fills the skyline above the intersection of the Kandertal and Gasterntal valleys to the northeast.

On the valley floor the trail travels through pastures on easy grades, reaching a junction at the Spittelmatte alp at 1.0 mile. Bear right on the main track heading up the valley (southwest) toward Schwarenbach.

The track now crosses a bridge over a tributary stream and then ascends on easy grades along the west side of the Schwarzbach stream. As you head up valley ignore any trails branch off the main track.

At 1.5 miles the grades steepens as the track ascends through a massive rockslide. The slide covers an area destroyed in September 1895 when part of the glacier along Altels western slopes broke off and crashed down the hillside, burying the valley floor in ice and debris.

At 2.25 miles the grade abates as the trail curves around a rocky slope, reaching the Hotel Schwarenbach at 2.5 miles. The hotel offers private rooms and dormitory accommodation along with a restaurant with views of the Daubenhorn and nearby peaks rising above valley. Below the hotel is a small lake.

At the far (west) end of the hotel turn right on a narrow trail signed for Schwarzgratli and Engstligenalp. The path ascends steeply up the rocky hillside behind the hotel accompanied by fine views of the Felshore rising along the Uschenegrat ridge.

The path soon turns left and ascends through meadows and rock outcroppings along the east facing slopes of the Uschenegrat ridge. Behind you are great views of the Balmhorn, Altels and, in the distance, the Doldenhorn. The Rinderhorn massif towers above the valley to the east.

At 3.4 miles the grades eases as the trail crests a minor ridge and then ascends along the slopes of a bowl to a signed junction at Schwarzgratli, a pass atop of the Uschenegrat Ridge, at 3.7 miles. Here grand views open northwest to the Tschingellochtighorn and Gross Lohner rising above the Uschene Valley. Turn left at the junction toward Engstligenalp. (The trail to the right heads north along the Uschenegrat Ridge.)

After a brief stint along the ridge crest the trail turns right and descends on a steep, exposed, scree-covered trail traveling along a cliff face. Red and white slashes on the rock will keep you on track. This pass is only recommended for sure footed hikers. Anyone with a fear of heights or discomfort with exposure should not attempt the descent.

Note: If you are not comfortable descending from the Schwarzgratli, turn around and walk back along the ridge to the junction and then walk north along the ridge to the Wyssi Flue. The trail ascends to the summit and then travels along the west facing slopes of the Uschenegrat Ridge to a junction north of the Gallihorn. Here the trail to the left drops down to the Uschene Valley floor and then Kandersteg while the path to the right descends to the Spittelmatte Valley floor near the top station for the Sunnbuel cable car. Either take the cable car or walk back to Kandersteg.

Schwarzgratli Pass to Engstligenalp

- **Segment Stat:** 3.6 miles (one-way) from Schwarzgratli Pass to Engstligenalp
- **Total Distance:** 7.3 miles (one way)
- **Maximum Elevation:** 8,723-ft.
- **Elevation Gain/Loss:** 2,959-ft. / -2,286-ft.

Along the descent from Schwarzgratli Pass reach an intersection with a trail branching right toward the Uschenetal Valley. We continue straight ahead ascending toward Talli and Engstligenalp.

At 4.0 miles the descent ends and the trail now ascends through rocky meadows to a junction at 4.2 miles. The trail to the right drops down to the Uschenetal Valley. We bear left toward the Engstligengrat and Engstligenalp. Behind you are interesting views of the Doldenhorn and the summit of Altels.

Soon we reach a junction at the foot of Talli, a rugged hanging valley sandwiched between the Uschenegrat and Engstligengrat ridges. To the left a trail leads to the Talliseeli, Rot Chumme and Gemmi Pass. We bear right toward Engstligengrat and Engstligenalp on a path that crosses the valley floor and then climbs steeply through meadows and scree along the east facing slopes of the Engstligengrat ridge. Red and white slashes on rocks mark the trail.

Views along the climb stretch east/northeast to the Doldenhorn, Altels and the Rinderhorn. To the south Rote Totz, the Steghorn and Tierhori anchor the cirque at the head of the Talli valley while the Felshore rises to the southeast. The Talliseeli, a meltwater tarn, lies nestled in a rugged bowl below the trail to the south.

Crest the Engstligengrat ridge at 4.9 miles and turn right on the path signed for Engstlingenalp and Kandersteg. The ridge crest enjoys stunning views of the surrounding peaks. In addition of the summits seen on the hike so far, views now open to the cirque, anchored by the Steghorn, Grossstrubel and Ammertenspitz, rimming the Engstligenalp Valley, a large emerald green bowl. The peaks towering above Adelboden dominate the view to the northwest. On a clear day the ice-capped summits of the Weisshorn and Bishorn rise in the distance to the southeast.

The trail now ascends along the ridge toward the rugged summit block of the Tschingellochtighorn. The Gross Lohner massif rises beyond the ridge to the north. At 5.25 miles the trail crosses a minor summit and then follows the ridge as it curves to the left (northwest) toward the Tschingellochtighorn.

Descend on easy grades toward the base of the Tschingellochtighorn's summit block and a junction at 5.4 miles. The trail branching right descends to the Uschenetal and then drops down to Kandersteg. Our trail bears left, traverse beneath the south side of the summit block and then descends very steep scree covered slopes to the Artelegrat Ridge. This section of the trail is exposed and should be avoided by anyone with a fear of heights. It should not be attempted if covered with snow or ice.

Reach the Artelegrat Ridge, extending west/northwest from the Tschingellochtighorn, at 5.6 miles. Here the footing improves but the trail continues its relentless drop down tight switchbacks. Along the way pass another trail, branching right, toward the Uschenetal and Kandersteg.

At 6.1 miles the scree gives way to meadows and the hike gets easier despite the continued steep descent. To the south enjoy fine views of peaks ringing the Engstligenalp valley and the summits towering above the Gils Valley, located to the south of Adelboden. The Gross Lohner dominates the views to the north.

Soon views open to Adelboden to the northwest. At 6.8 miles the grade abates as the trail turns left (south) and descend through pastures to a broad track at 7.2 miles. Turn right (north) and follow the track to the cable car station at Engstligenalp at 7.3 miles. Ride the cable car down to Unter dem Birg and then catch the bus back to Kandersteg or Adelboden. See the trailhead direction below for more information on transportation options.

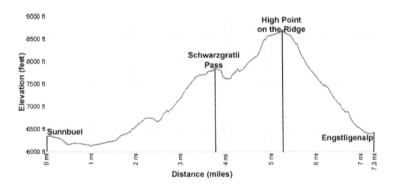

Trailhead Directions

Kandersteg Bahnhof (Train Station) to Sunnbuel Cable Car: See Hike 63

Engstligenalp to Adelboden or the Kandersteg Bahnhof: Take the cable car from Engstligenalp to Unter dem Birg. Exit the cable car and cross the street to the bus stop. Take the #232 bus, which goes all the way to Adelboden. If you wish to return to Kandersteg, get off at Adelboden Oey. Here you need to change to the #230 bus bound for Kandersteg. Walk a short distance north up the road to an intersection, turn right and then walk a short distance to the #230 bus stop. It is very likely that other people will be making this change. If you are confused, ask and people will happily point you in the right direction. Most Swiss speak English.

Parties heading to Kandersteg now have two options. You can stay on the #230 bus all the way to Kandersteg or get off the bus at the Frutigen Train Station and take the train to Kandersteg. The train is faster by 12 minutes. The bus is easier, since you don't have to change. Check the SBB website or download the SBB app for the current schedule. The ride back to Kandersteg takes between one-hour 52-minutes to two hours 4-minutes.

65. Allmenalp to First ☆☆☆☆☆
Distance: 4.0 miles (round-trip)
Near Kandersteg in the Bernese Alps

A very steep climb leads to First, a great overlook high above the west side of Kandersteg, with 360-degree views of the high peaks towering above Oeschinensee, Spittelmatte and the Adelboden (Engstligental) Valleys.

Distance: 4.0 miles (round-trip)
Elevation: 5,653-ft. at Trailhead
8,360-ft. at First
Elevation Gain: 2,707-ft.
Difficulty: difficult

Basecamp: Kandersteg
Kandersteg West Map: See page 302
Online Map/Photos:
www.hikingwalking.com/allmen-first

Why Hike from Allmenalp to First

Some of the best views in the Kandersteg area are from the Bunderspitz and First summits, rising above the west side of the valley. Situated along the ridge between the Kandertal and Engstligental Valleys, First enjoys 360-degree views of the high peaks rimming the east side of the Kandersteg valley as well as the breathtaking cirque soaring above the Oeschinensee. Views extend south to the peaks towering above Gemmi Pass and beyond.

To the west are fine views of the ridge, punctuated by Albristhorn and Gsur, rising above Adelboden to the west.

The path to First is not for the faint of heart. It climbs very steep grades to a knife edge ridge and then to the summit of First. The trail is exposed and not the place to be if the weather is threatening. Fit hikers will like the challenge and dramatic views as the trail gains elevation.

From Allmenalp to First

Take the Allmenalp cable car to the top station at Allmenalp (5,653-ft.). (See trailhead directions below.) Find the signpost outside the station and then follow the steep, broad track heading west toward Obere Allme and First. The path ascends along the north side of the valley, aided by a few switchbacks.

Behind you (across the valley) are grand views of the Doldenhorn, Bluemlisalphorn, Wyssi Frau and Dundehorn anchoring the cirque soaring above the Oeschinensee. At 0.6 miles reach a junction where our trail branches right toward First and Elsigenalp. The trail to the left leads to the Bunderchrinde and Bunderspitz. (See Hike 66 - Bunderspitz.)

Soon the trail curves to the right (northeast) and angles steeply up the slopes beneath the Allmegrat ridge. The grade abates a bit as the trail crosses an avalanche chute and then reaches a small building at Steintal. Here the path turns left on a switchback and then resume the steep climb through rocky meadows.

The grade steepens at 1.3 miles as the trail turns north and heads straight up the slope toward the ridge. Switchbacks facilitate the climb through meadows and scree covered slopes. As you ascend enjoy ever improving views of the summits soaring above the Oeschinensee. Altels and Balmhorn rise to the southeast. To the west/southwest are views of the Ammegrat Ridge, Bunderspitz and Chylne Lohner.

The grade abates a bit at 1.8 miles as the trail swings to the right (northeast) and angles toward the Allmegrat ridge. Reach the ridge crest at 1.9 miles. Here views open to Adelboden, nestled along the valley floor to the west. A ridge of high peaks, anchored by the Albristhorn and Gsur, rim the valley to the west.

The path now ascends along the east side of the knife edge ridge to the summit of First at 2.0 miles. Find a perch atop the summit and take in the stunning 360-degree views. Across the valley are the rugged glacier-clad peaks forming the cirque soaring above the Oeschinensee. The Big Three – the Eiger, Monch and Jungfrau rise beyond the cirque.

To the southeast Altels, the Balmhorn, Rinderhorn, Daubenhorn and Steghorn rim the head of the Kandertal valley. The Bunderspitz and Chlyne Lohner rises beyond the Allmegrat ridge to the south. In the distance, views stretch southwest to the Wildstrubel, the Glacier del la Plaine Morte and beyond. To the west views extend down the length of the Engstligental.

A trail continues beyond the summit, dropping below the west facing slopes of Howang, the summit to the north, and then ascends to the summit of Stand. Here a very steep path drops down to Golitschepass and then to Kandersteg, to the east, or Elsigbach, located to the north of Adelboden. This trail, only recommended for sure-footed hikers with a head for heights, requires some scrambling, is exposed in places and very steep. I recommend turning around at First and returning to the Allmenalp cable car for a 4.0 mile hike.

Trailhead Directions

From Kandersteg to the Valley Station for the Allmenalp Cable Car: From the Kandersteg Bahnhof (train station), walk south along the paved pedestrian walkway paralleling the east side of the tracks. Turn right (west) when you reach Butschelstrasse, the street going under the tracks. Beyond the railway line the road curves to the left (southwest) and soon becomes Allmenbahnstrasse. Signs along the way point to the Allmenalpbahn (cable car). The walk should take about 15 minutes. See the Allmenalp Luftseilbahn for information on the schedule and prices.

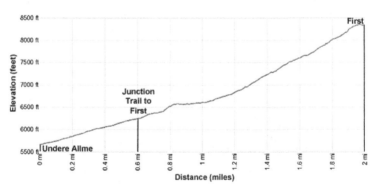

66. Allmenalp to the Bunderspitz ★★★★☆
Distance: 4.4 miles (round-trip)
Near Kandersteg in the Bernese Alps

Hikers completing the very steep climb to the summit of the Bunderspitz are rewarded with amazing views of the cirque soaring above the Oeschinensee along with the high peaks towering above the head of the Kandertal and Adelboden (Engstligental) Valleys.

Distance: 4.4 miles (round-trip)
Elevation: 5,653-ft. at Trailhead
8,353-ft. at the Bunderspitz
Elevation Gain: 2,700-ft.
Difficulty: difficult

Basecamp: Kandersteg
Kandersteg West Map: See page 302
Online Map/Photos:
www.hikingwalking.com/bunderspitz

Why Hike from Allmenalp to Bunderspitz

To say that this hike is steep is an understatement but the panoramic views atop the Bunderspitz are worth the effort. From this airy overlook the Grindelwald triumvirate –the Eiger, Monch and Jungfrau grace the horizon beyond the breathtaking cirque ringing the Oeschinensee. Prominent peaks include the Dundehorn, Bluemlisalphorn, Frundenhorn and Doldenhorn. Further up the Kandertal (Kander Valley) Altels, the Balmhorn and the Rinderhorn punctuate the skyline.

To the west/southwest the peaks and ridges rimming the Adelboden Valley dominate the view while First and the Elsighorn rise along the Allmegrat ridge to the north. To the south the Wildstrubel, Glacier de la Plaine Morte and nearby peaks grace the horizon.

To the Bunderspitz

The day starts with a ride on the Allmenalp Cable Car, which climbs over 1,800-ft. above the valley floor in only 5-minutes, to Allmenalp (5,653-ft.), aka Undere Allme on some maps. (See trailhead directions below.) Exit the station head west on the steep, broad track toward Obere Allme and the Bunderspitz.

The path ascends along the north side of the valley, aided by a few switchbacks. Behind you, across the valley, are grand views of the Doldenhorn, Bluemlisalphorn, Wyssi Frau and Dundehorn, anchoring the cirque soaring above the Oeschinensee.

At 0.6 miles, just before Obere Allme, reach a junction with a trail branching right toward First. (See Hike 65 – Allmenalp to First.) We turn left, staying on the broad track toward Obere Allme and the Bunderspitz.

At 0.8 miles pass Obere Allme, located along a hairpin curve. A short distance beyond you will see a trail branching left. Take this trail, which short-cuts a switchback along the track. The trail quickly rejoins the track and then passes a farm building on the right. A short distance past the building the track gives way to a trail ascending steeply through meadows.

Reach a junction at 1.4 miles. Here the trail to Bunderchrinde branches left. We continue straight ahead toward the Bundergrat ridge and the Bunderspitz.

Soon the grade becomes noticeable steeper as the path climbs through rocky meadows and scree covered slopes on tight switchback. Behind you the views continue to improve and evolve. As you gain elevation the Eiger, Monch and Jungfrau appear beyond the Oeschinensee cirque. Ahead are fine views of Chlyne Loner, the Bundergrat ridge and the Bunderspitz.

The trail, while very steep, is not exposed. As you approach the ridge crest a wire cable, attached to a cliff face, facilitates the climb and adds a level of safety.

Reach the top of the Bundergrat ridge (8,058-ft.) and a junction at 2.0 miles. Here we turn right toward the Bunderspitz. (The trail to the left leads to the Bunderchrinde and Adelboden.) A stiff climb up the west facing slopes just below the ridge crest leads to the summit of the Bunderspitz (8,353-ft.) at 2.2 miles.

The summit enjoys superb views. Without a doubt the stars of the show are the high peaks ringing the Oeschinensee and the summits of the big-three; the Eiger, Monch and Jungfrau, rising beyond Hohturli Pass. Altels, Balmhorn and the Rinderhorn, towering above the east side of the Kandertal valley, appear through a break in the ridge to the south.

The Wildstrubel and the Glacier de la Plaine Morte dominate the views to the south while the Gsur and Albristhorn punctuate the ridge rising above the west side of Adelboden. First, another fine overlook, is seen along the knife edge ridge to the north.

When you are done taking in the views, retrace your steps the trailhead for a 4.4 mile hike.

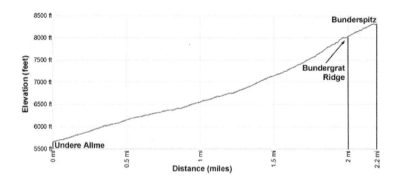

Trailhead Directions

From Kandersteg to the Valley Station for the Allmenalp Cable Car: See Hike 65.

67. Ammerten Pass and the Ammertenspitz

★★★★☆
Distance: 5.5 - 6.5 miles (round trip)
Near Kandersteg in the Bernese Alps

Ascend the beautiful Engstligenalp valley to scenic Ammerten Pass with great views of the peaks surrounding the valley and the mountains rising to the south. From the pass a steep trail leads to the Ammertenspitz summit with panoramic views encompassing the summits towering above Adelboden, Lenk and beyond.

Distance: 5.5 miles (round trip) to
Ammerten Pass
6.5 miles (round trip) to
Ammertenspitz
Elevation: 6,437-ft. at Trailhead
8,015-ft. at Ammerten Pass
8,573-ft. at Ammertenspitz
Elevation Gain: 1,578-ft. to
Ammerten Pass
2,138-ft. to Ammertenspitz

Difficulty: moderately-strenuous
Basecamp: Kandersteg
Kandersteg and Adelboden
Map: See page 302
Online Map/Photos:
www.hikingwalking.com/ammerten

Why Hike to Ammerten Pass and the Ammertenspitz

A trip to Ammerten Pass and the summit of the Ammertenspitz offers a terrific perspective of the high peaks rising above Adelboden and the neighboring valleys. The day starts with an easy walk up the Engstligenalp Valley, a large meadow-clad bowl ringed by rugged peaks and ridges, followed by a moderate to steep climb up the east facing slopes of the Ammertenspitz to the pass. The pass, a broad saddle between the Ammertenspitz and Wildstrubel massif, boasts great views of the Engstligenalp cirque, the summits rising to the south/southwest of the pass as well as the high peaks soaring above Adelboden and Kandersteg.

Hikers with the time and energy will want to continue the hike to the summit of the Ammertenspitz, which adds 1.0 mile (round trip) and 558-ft. of elevation gain to the hike. The summit enjoys birds-eye-views of the summits seen from the pass in addition to vistas extending to the peaks rising around Lenk and the valleys to the west.

Engstligenalp to Ammerten Pass

- **Distance from Trailhead:** 5.5 miles (round trip)
- **Elevation at Ammerten Pass:** 8,015-ft.
- **Elevation Gain:** 1,578-ft.

From Unter dem Birg, ride the cable car to Engstligenalp. (See trailhead directions below.) Outside the station follow the broad track heading south toward Ammertenpass (Ammerten Pass) and Lenk. The trail curves to the right (southwest) as it descends to the valley floor and then crosses bridges over streams at 0.3-miles and 0.4-miles. At all junctions stay on the broad track toward Ammertenpass.

The easy walk up the valley enjoys lovely views of the Engstligenalp valley, a large emerald green bowl ringed by peaks and ridges. Ahead the Steghorn, Grossstrubel and Ammertenspitz tower above the head of the valley. A long ridge, punctuated by the Rotstock and Fitzer, defines the valley to the west while the Engstligengrat and Artelegrat ridges, linked by the Tschingellochtighorn, rim the valley to the east and north.

At 0.7 miles the path crosses a bridge over the Entschlige stream and then ascends to and traverses a bench on the west side of the valley. Turn around and look northeast for great views of Gross Lohner, rising beyond the Artelegrat ridge, and the Tschingellochtighorn. Ahead Ammerten Pass, the saddle on the ridge between the Grossstrubel and Ammertenspitz, is in view.

At 1.5 miles the trail begins climbing through meadows on moderate to moderately-steep grades. At 1.9 miles the grade steepens and the trail now zig-zags up rocky meadows and climbs grassy knolls. Take an occasional break from the stiff climb to enjoy the ever evolving views of the cirque ringing the valley and the high peaks towering above the cirque to the east.

At 2.5 miles the grade briefly abates as the trail swings left (south) into a rocky bowl beneath the pass. Soon the trail resumes its steep climb through rocky meadows and then scree covered slopes to the Ammerten Pass (8,573-ft.) at 2.75 miles. The climb is accompanied by great views of the Ammertenspitz rising to the west.

The broad pass enjoys the terrific views of the cirque ringing the Engstligenalp Valley. In the distance are a host of summits rising beyond the cirque. To the northeast Altels and the Balmhorn tower above the Kandertal valley while the Doldenhorn soars above the Gasteretal valley. On a clear day views stretch to the Bluemlisalphorn and Wyssi Frau, high peaks rising above the Oeschinensee near Kandersteg. To the south the Wildstrubel massif fills the skyline while to the southwest the Wildhorn, the Glacier del la Plaine Morte and tip of the Arpelistock dominate the view.

At this point you can turn around and retrace your steps to the trailhead for a 5.5 mile hike or continue on to the summit of the Ammertenspitz.

Ammerten Pass to Ammertenspitz

- **Segment Stat:** 1.0 miles (round-trip) from Ammerten Pass to Ammertenspitz
- **Total Distance:** 6.5 miles (round trip)
- **Maximum Elevation:** 8,573-ft.
- **Elevation Gain/Loss:** 2,138-ft.

From the pass follow the obvious trail ascending up the ridge crest (northwest) to the summit of the Ammertenspitz. The path steepens as it gains altitude. Tight switchbacks facilitate the final stiff climb to the summit.

Reach the Ammertenspitz (8,753-ft.) at 3.25 miles after gaining 558-ft. in half a mile. Here panoramic, 360-degree views encompass all the peaks previously seen from the pass along with the mountains and ridges rising around Adelboden, to the north, and Lenk area, to the west/southwest.

Signs atop the pass point to a route heading northwest toward Hahnenmoos Pass. (Routes are very challenging trails that involve some scrambling and are only recommended for surefooted hikers.) The route is best walked in the opposite direction, starting at Hahnenmoos Pass.

When you are done taking in the great views return to the trailhead for a 6.5 mile trip.

Trailhead Directions

From Kandersteg to Unter dem Birg and Engstligenalp: There are two options for getting to Unter Dem Birg in Adelboden. The easiest way is to take the #230 bus from the Kandersteg Bahnhof heading to Adelboden Post and get off at the Adelboden Oey stop. At Oey, walk west to the traffic circle, turn left and follow the traffic circle around to Bodenstrasse. Cross Bodenstrasse to the bus stop. (Typically a few other people on the bus are making this connection. If in doubt, tell someone you want to connect to the bus to Unter dem Birg. They can point you in the right direction.)

Catch the #232 bus to Unter dem Birg and the Engstligenalp Cable Car station (the last stop). The bus will stop right in front of the station. After purchasing a round-trip ticket, ride the cable car to Engstligenalp. The entire trip takes about one-hour and 25-minutes. Check the SBB website or download the SBB app for the current schedule and prices.

Alternatively, at the Kandersteg Bahnhof, take the train to Frutigen. At Frutigen, exit the train and then cross the street in front of the station to the bus stop. Here you catch the #230 bus to Adelboden, Oey and then follow the direction above. This option takes one-hour and 10-minutes.

From Adelboden Post to Unter dem Birg and Engstligenalp: Catch the #232 Bus to Unter dem Birg and the Engstligenalp Cable car station (the last stop). The bus stops in front of the cable car station. After purchasing a round-trip ticket, ride the cable car to Engstligenalp.

Engstligenalp to Adelboden or the Kandersteg Bahnhof: See Hike 64.

68. Other Trails in Kandersteg
Near Kandersteg in the Bernese Alps

68a) Kandersteg (Allmenalp) to Adelboden via the Bunderspitz

This scenic crossing climbs steeply from Allmenalp to the Bunderspitz with wide ranging views from the glacier-clad cirque soaring above the Oeschinensee to the summits towering above the head of the Kandersteg valley and Adelboden. A long descent down rocky meadows and pastures leads to Bunderalp and then down the Bunderle valley to Eggetli before the final easy ascent to Adelboden.

- **Distance:** 7.2 miles (one-way)
- **Elevation:** 5,653-ft. at Allmenalp
  8,353-ft. at the Bunderspitz
  4,429-ft. at Adelboden
- **Elevation Gain/Loss:** 2,700-ft./-3,924-ft.
- **Difficulty:** strenuous
- **Base camp:** Kandersteg and Adelboden
- **Kandersteg and Adelboden Map:** See page 302

From Kandersteg, take the cable car to Allmenalp and then follow the directions for Hike 66 - Allmenalp to the Bunderspitz.

From the summit of the Bunderspitz retrace your steps to the junction with the trail dropping down to Allmenalp on the Bundergrat ridge at 2.4 miles. Continue on the trail along the ridge which soon turns right (sign for Bunderchrinde, Bunderchumi, Bunderalp and Adelboden) and starts descending the west side of the ridge toward Adelboden. In a short distance pass a minor junction where a trail branches left to the Bunderchrinde. Here we stay on the trail to Adelboden which drops steeply down the west side of the ridge through scree and rocky meadows to Bunderchumi and a junction at 3.2 miles. This segment of the walk is accompanied by fine views of the Albristhorn and Gsur rising to the west of Adelboden. Adelboden lies nestled along the valley floor.

At the junction the trail connects with the #1 Via Alpina (Alpine Pass Trail) coming down from Bunderchrinde Pass. After a short, very steep descent down tight switchbacks the grades abates as the trail descends through meadows to Bunderalp where you are offer two alternatives to reach Adelboden.

Take the route to the left (Via Alpina) that descends through pastures and woods on a combination of trails and alp roads through the pretty Bunderle Valley to Eggetli. Here we follow the road down to a bridge crossing over the Entschlige River at 6.7 miles. On the west side of the river ascend on easy grades along roads, following the Via Alpina signs to the center of the Adelboden Village.

68b) Kandersteg (Allmenalp) to Adelboden via the Bunderchrinde and Bunderspitz

Here are some alternatives to the traditional Alpine Pass Route between Kandersteg and Adelboden. All involve steep climbs along scree covered slopes with splendid views of the high peaks towering above the Oeschinensee, the head of the Kandersteg Valley, the Gastern Valley and the summits rising to the north of Adelboden and beyond. Check on current trail conditions at the Kandersteg tourist office before setting out on the hikes.

- **Elevation:** 3,858-ft. at Kandersteg
  5,653-ft. at Allmenalp
  8,353-ft. at Bunderspitz
  7,825-ft. at Bunderchrinde
  4,429-ft. at Adelboden
- **Difficulty:** strenuous
- **Base camp:** Kandersteg and Adelboden
- **Kandersteg and Adelboden Map:** See page 302

Option 1: Allmenalp - Bunderspitz - Bunderchrinde - Adelboden
Distance: 7.8 miles (one-way)
Elevation Gain / Loss: 3,015-ft./-4,239-ft.

Follow hike 68a to the summit of the Bunderspitz and then back to the junction with the trail dropping down to Allmenalp. Continue along the ridge to a second junction and bear right on the trail toward the Bunderchrinde, Bunderchumi, Bunderalp and Adelboden. A short distance beyond bear left on the trail to the Bunderchrinde. The trail to right continues its steep decent toward Bunderchumi, Bunderalp and Adelboden. Our trail now descends and then ascends along steep scree slopes under Chlyne Lohner. (Check on the current condition of this segment of the trail at the tourist office in Kandersteg.)

Reach the pass at Bunderchrinde at 3.1 miles, a narrow saddle between rugged rock walls. Here views open east/southeast to the Balmhorn and Doldenhorn towering above the head of the Gasterntal (Gastern Valley). The Albristhorn and Gsur rise above Adelboden, cradled along the valley floor.

After taking in the views, descend the west side of the pass on the #1 Via Alpina Trail (Alpine Pass Route) toward Bunderchumi, Bunderalp and Adelboden. The path drops down very steep, scree covered switchbacks. Soon the trail curves to the right (northwest), descending on a diagonal down more scree before turning left and reaching rocky meadows. The path now drops steeply down the meadows to Bunderchumi at 3.8 miles. From

Bunderchumi follow the direction in Hike 68a to Entschlige River (7.3 miles) and then ascend to Adelboden at 7.8 miles.

Option 2: Allmenalp - Alpschelegrat - Bunderchrinde - Adelboden
Distance: 7.2 miles (one-way)
Elevation Gain / Loss: 2,172-ft./-3,396-ft.

Follow Hike 66 - Allmenalp to Bunderspitz for 1.4 miles to the junction with a trail branching left toward Alpschelegrat and the Bunderchrinde. Turn left and follow the path that ascends steeply along scree covered slopes with some exposure to the Alpschelegrat ridge at 2.0 miles. Fixed cables safeguard a section of the trail. Just below the ridge the footing is not great. Use care through this section. (Check on the current condition of this segment of the trail at the tourist office in Kandersteg.)

Atop the ridge enjoy more fine views of the Oeschinensee area along with Altels, the Balmhorn and the Doldenhorn rising above the Gastern Valley. From the ridge the trail continues ascending steeply through rocky meadows and then more scree to Bunderchrinde Pass, a narrow saddle between rugged rock walls, at 2.5 miles. As you crest the pass views open to the Albristhorn and Gsur rise above Adelboden, cradled along the valley floor.

After taking in the views follow the directions in Option 1 from Bunderchrinde to Bunderchumi at 3.2 miles and Adelboden at 7.2 miles.

Note: From Bunderchrinde you can follow the trail along the western flanks of Chlyne Lohner to the Bunderspitz and then drop down to Adelboden. The detour will add 1.1 miles and 840-ft in elevation gain to the hike.

Option 3: Traditional Alpine Pass Route: Kandersteg - Usser Uschene - Bunderchrinde - Adelboden
Distance: 9.9 miles (one-way)
Elevation Gain / Loss: 3,967-ft./-3,396-ft.

From the Kandersteg Bahnhof (train station) walk south along the paved pedestrian walkway paralleling the east side of the tracks. Turn right (west) when you reach Butschelstrasse, the street going under the tracks. Beyond the railway line the road curves to the left (southwest) and soon becomes Allmenbahnstrasse. Continue heading south (up the valley) past the Allmenalp cable car and then follow the path along the Kander River to the Pfadfinderzentrum (International Scout Camp) at 1.25 miles. At all intersections stay on the #1 Via Alpina toward Uschene and the Bunderchrinde.

Past the camp the trail curves to the right (southwest) and begins ascending through meadows and forest on a combination of tracks, roads and trails. In places the trail shortcuts switchbacks on the road. The ascent steepens as the path climbs along a gorge. Soon the trees give way to beautiful meadows and the grade abates as the trail reaches Aeusser

Ueschinen (alternate spelling) in the Uschenen Valley (Uschenental). The Gross Lohner massif towers above the valley.

The path now ascends on moderate grades, passing beneath the buildings of Usser Uschene, a small alp with a restaurant, and soon reaches a junction at 3.1 miles. Turn right at the junction climbing switchbacks up a track toward Alpschele and the Bunderchrinde. At the top of the switchbacks, just before an alp, take the path to the left that climbs steeply up rocky meadows through a break in a cliff. Cross a stream and some scree along the way. Above the cliff the path curves to the right (northeast) and ascends through rocky meadow on moderate grades to a junction at Alpschele. As you ascend enjoy fine views of the Gasterntal Valley to the southwest. Above you the Bunderchrinde is now in sight.

At the junction bear left toward the Alpschelegrat and Bunderchrinde on a trail that climbs on moderately-steep grades toward the Alpschelegrat ridge. Soon the path swings to the left and reaches a junction at 4.9 miles. The trail to the right heads to the Alpschelegrat ridge. We turn left toward the pass, ascending through scree-covered slopes to the Bunderchrinde (7,825-ft.), a narrow saddle between rugged rock walls, at 5.2 miles.

After enjoying the views from the pass, complete the hike by following the directions in Option 1 from the Bunderchrinde to Adelboden for a 9.9 mile hike.

Reduce the length and elevation gain of the hike by taking the cable car to Allmenalp. Exit the cable car and follow the signs toward Ryharts and Usser Uschene. The path travels along an alp road around the end of the Alpschelegrat ridge to the Alp at Usser Uschene. Reach a junction a short distance beyond the Alp and turn right toward Alp Alpschele and the Bunderchrinde. The track climbs switchback up grassy slopes and then follows a trail through a break in the cliffs to Alpschele before ascending to the Bunderchrinde.

Altdorf and Engelberg

Location: in the Uri and Glarus Alps

Altdorf lies in the lower Reuss Valley to the south of Lake Lucerne. The Reuss Valley marks the boundary between the Uri Alps to the west and the Schwyz and Glarus Alps to the east. Branching east from the Altdorf to Klausen Pass is the Schachental (Schachen Valley), a tributary valley of the Ruess separating the Schwyz Alps to the north from the Glarus Alps to the south. While not as well-known as the Bernese Alps to the west, these ranges lay claim to their fair share of distinctive, glacier-clad peaks, dramatic ridges and lovely valleys accessible from a network of scenic trails.

About Altdorf

Altdorf is a small, attractive town set near the foot of Reuss Valley to the south of the Urnersee, the southern arm of Lake Lucerne. The town, the capitol of the canton of Uri, features a good selection of accommodations, restaurants and shops along with convenient transportation links. Telldenkmal, the square at the center of town, is home to a famous statue of William Tell a Swiss national hero and a local cult figure.

Tellsgasse, Altdorf's main street, runs along the southwest side of Telldenkmal and then curves to the south, turning into Schmiedgasse. These streets, along with adjacent side streets, are the heart of the shopping district. The Uri Tourist Office (uri.swiss) is located along Schutzengrasse, a street branching southeast from Telldenkmal. Further down Schutzengrasse is a good Coop Supermarket. In the same building is the Kley Wascherei, a reliable drop off laundry service. A Spar Supermarket is located on Schmiedgasse and a Migros, at the corner of Gitschenstrasse, a street branching southwest off Schmiedgasse.

Bahnhofstrasse, two blocks to the northwest of Telldenkmal, heads southwest to the Bahnhof (train station) and bus station. The train line runs south/southwest up the Reuss with stops at Amsteg, Andermatt and other jumping off spots to lesser known hiking destinations. Telldenkmal is a meeting point for many of the town's bus lines including the bus to Attinghausen and Klausen Pass, the starting point for hikes in the Altdorf area.

Altdorf makes a great base camp for accessing the area's trails. To the east, the Klausen Pass (Hike 69) segment of the Alpine Pass Route travels down the north side of the Schachental (Schachen Valley) beneath the rugged cliffs and peaks of the Schachentaler Windgallen massif, accompanied by fine views of the Glarus Alps to the south and the Uri Alps to the west. After passing thought Altdorf the Alpine Pass Route then ascends through pretty meadows to Surenen Pass (Hike 72) with splendid view of the Uri Alps, including Titlis – the highest peak in the range to the north of Susten Pass.

Another recommended trail climbs to Hoch Fulen (Hike 70), located in the Glarus Alps along the south side of the Schachental. Here hikers are treated to panoramic views of the high peaks in the Uri, Schwyz and Glarus Alps. A short train ride to the south of Altdorf leads to Amsteg and the Maderanertal, a valley cutting east into the Glarus Alps. The Hohenweg Maderanertal (Hike 71), a high route, loops around the pristine valley surrounded by soaring peaks.

About Engelberg

To the west of Altdorf over Surenen Pass is Engelberg, a mountain resort near the head of the Engelbergertal (Engelberger Valley) in the Uri Alps. The resort is a popular stop for hikers on the Alpine Pass Route and tourist visiting Titlis (10,623-ft.).

Titlis sits to the southwest of an elongated cirque, anchored by the Spannort massif, the Schloss massif, Brunnistock, Wissigstock and Wissberg. Surenen Pass lies nestled in a saddle on the ridge to the southeast of the Brunnistock. From Surenen Pass a scenic trail leads down the Engelbergertal to Blackenalp and then follows the Stierenbach River accompanied by terrific views of Titlis, Grassen, the Grassengrat ridge and the Spannort massif. From Engelberg a segment of the Alpine Pass Route, which at times travels near/below lift lines, ascends to Jochpass. From the pass the trail descends to Engstlenalp and then travels Meiringen on an undulating trail along the north side of the Gantel Valley.

Engelberg, a popular winter ski resort, is centered along the Dorfstrasse between a 12th-century monastery and the area to the west of the Bahnhof (train station), along with the adjacent side streets. As a result of the ski resort, the sprawling village provides plenty of hotels, apartments and other types of lodging options in the summer in addition to restaurants, bars and shops.

The Tourism Office (engelberg.ch/en/) is located on the north side of Dorfstrasse at the intersection with Hinterdorfstrasse. The Migros and Coop grocery stores are situated on opposite sides of Klosterstrasse to the west of Titlisstrasse. To reach the Bahnhof (train station), follow Dorfstrasse to

Bahnhofstrasse and then turn south. The station is in the next block. The cable car to Titlis is located on the south side of the village and the Engelberger River. Signs will direct you to the lift station from various parts of the village.

Getting to Altdorf and Engelberg

To Altdorf: From the Zurich Airport or Zurich Bahnhof (train station) take the train to Altdorf. The direct train takes one hour and 14 minutes. If you need to change it takes one hour and 18 minutes. Frequent, regularly scheduled buses leave from the Bahnhof to Telldenkmal and other stops in Altdorf.

Check the SBB website/SBB app to find the route most convenient to your accommodations and options for reaching Altdorf from other parts of the country.

To Engelberg: From the Zurich Airport or Zurich Bahnhof (train station) take the train to Engelberg. You will need to change in Lucerne. The ride take one our and 45 minutes.

Check the SBB website/SBB app for the current schedule and options for reaching Engelberg from other parts of the country.

Nearby Attractions & Rainy Day Activities

See the Altdorf Tourism website for information about area museums and galleries along with listings for restaurants and shopping.

In Engelberg visit **Mount Titlis**. A gondola and revolving cable car whisk visitors to a glacier atop Kleine Titlis, situate along Titlis' west ridge. Here a panoramic overlook features 360-degree views of the high peaks of the Uri, Bernese and Glarus Alps. The area also includes an Ice Cave, a Cliff Walk with the highest elevation suspension bridge in Europe, shops and restaurants.

On a rainy day in either Altdorf or Engelberg take the train to **Lucerne** and tour the old town, wander though a museum, visit the glass works, learn how to make cheese or take a tour of Lake Lucerne.

Good Things to Know about Altdorf and Engelberg

- The primary language in Altdorf and Engelberg is German. Most people in shops, restaurants and services catering to tourist will also speak French and English.
- The Remo Campground is located in the northern part of Altdorf.
- In Engelberg, Eienwaldli Campsite to the southeast of the center offers camping.
- In Engelberg, the Berghaus Family Hostel offers private rooms and dormitory accommodations. From the train station walk west along Dorfstrasse and then turn right on Acherrainstrasse. Look for the large brown berghaus.

Map: Altdorf Area Trails

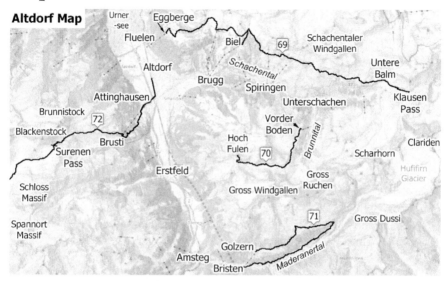

Altdorf Map

Urner -see
Eggberge
Fluelen
Biel
69
Schachentaler Windgallen
Altdorf
Schachental
Untere Balm
Brugg
Spiringen
Attinghausen
Unterschachen
Klausen Pass
Brunnistock
72
Vorder Boden
Blackenstock
Brusti
Hoch Fulen
70
Brunnital
Clariden
Surenen Pass
Scharhorn
Erstfeld
Gross Ruchen
Hufifirn Glacier
Schloss Massif
Gross Windgallen
Spannort Massif
71
Gross Dussi
Golzern
Maderanertal
Amsteg
Bristen

69. Klausen Pass to Eggberge ★★★★★
Distance: 9.5 - 13.9 miles (one way)
Near Altdorf in the the Schwyz Alps

Running between Klausen Pass and Altdorf, the Schachental Hohenweg trail travels high above the north side of the Schachental Valley in the Schwyz Alps with panoramic views of the Glarus Alps to the south and the rugged cliffs of the Schachentaler Windgallen massif towering overhead.

Distance: 9.5 (one way) to Biel
13.9 miles (one way) to Eggberge
Elevation: 6,400-ft. at Trailhead
5,337-ft. at Biel
4,712-ft. at Eggberge
Elevation Gain: -1,063-ft. to Biel
-1,688-ft. to Eggberge

Difficulty: moderate-strenuous
Basecamp: Altdorf
Altdorf Map: See page 327
Online Map/Photos:
www.hikingwalking.com/klausen

Why Hike from Klausen Pass to Eggberge

This lovely walk follows the Schachental Hohenweg, a panoramic trail traveling high above the north side of the Schachental Valley between Klausen Pass and Altdorf. The path is a roller coaster, repeatedly ascending and descending as it crosses ridges and dips into drainage channels. The effort is rewarded with stunning views down the length of the Schachental Valley. The high peaks of the Glarus Alps tower above the valley to the south while rugged ridges of the Schachentaler Windgallen massif rise above the trail.

Klausen Pass (6,400-ft.), a relatively low pass between Linthal and Altdorf, is crossed by a popular road. Regularly scheduled Postbuses climb to the pass facilitating this scenic point-to-point hike that leads from the pass to Biel in 9.5 miles or Eggberge in 13.9 miles walk. Both options use lifts to descend back to the valley floor.

Klausen Pass to Biel

- **Distance from Trailhead:** 9.5 miles (one way)
- **Elevation at Biel:** 5,337-ft.
- **Elevation Gain:** 1,800-ft./-2,800-ft.

Note: There are many ascents and descents along this trail. The actual elevation gain to Eggberge is almost 2,400-ft. while the elevation loss is over 4,000-ft. If you stop at Biel, the elevation gain is about 1,800-ft. while the loss is over 2,800-ft.

The first 1.6 miles of this trail travels along or near the Klausen Pass Road. This description assumes you start at Klausen Pass. You can avoid the walk along the road by taking the bus to Untere Balm, below the west side of Klausen Pass. (See the trailhead directions below.) If you start at Untere Balm subtract 1.6 miles from the mileage in the description below.

From Klausen Pass (6,400-ft.) find the paved path on the south side of the highway, just to the west of the chapel (Kapelle Bruder). Walk south on the path. Soon you will see a signed trail branching right (west) toward Untere Balm, Spiringen and Biel. Turn right and descend through meadows on moderate grades. The trail is marked by white and red posts.

A rugged ridge anchored by the Marcher Stockli towers above north side of the pass. Ahead are distant views of the high peaks, including the Uri Rotstock, Brunnistock and Blackenstock, rising above the west side of Altdorf and the Reuss Valley.

After half a mile the trail ascends to the road and then descends on moderate grades alongside the road to a hairpin curve at Untere Balm at 1.6 miles. Along the way views open to the glacier-clad Scharhorn (10,807-ft.) towering above the emerald green meadows to the south.

At Untere Balm cross the road and then follow the Hohenweg Schachental (Trail #595) toward Biel and Eggberge. (Note: You are also following Trail #1, the Via Alpina or Alpine Pass Route. At 5.1 miles the two trails will diverge.) The broad track now ascends on easy to moderate grades through pastures and meadows beneath rugged cliffs. Across the valley to the south enjoy ever evolving views of the Scharhorn and nearby peaks in the Glarus Range.

At 2.25 miles the path curves around the end of a ridge and then ascends across a shallow valley, echoing the contours of the landscape. Along the way the path passes small farms and a few trails branching off to the right and left. At all intersections continue on the #595 Hohenweg trail.

At 2.9 miles the trail begins a descent that crosses gullies draining the rugged slopes of the Schachentaler Windgallen massif towering overhead. Across the valley to the south Gross Ruchen (10,295-ft.) and Gross Windgallen (10,457-ft.) form the backdrop for the Brunnital Valley, a deep south to north valley that drains into the Schachental. To the southeast the Chammliberg (10,548-ft.) and Clariden (10,718-ft.) are now seen rising along the ridge to the east of the Scharhorn.

Watch for the Alp Stafel junction at 3.5 miles where trail #595 turns right onto a foot path that climbs steeply before descending to meet a broad track at 3.9 miles. Head down the track for 0.2 miles and then turn right on a trail signed for the #595 Hohenweg.

The undulating path now descends through meadows and clusters of trees as it cross a few minor ridges and contours around drainage channels. Reach a junction at Hegerwald at 5.1 miles where trail #1, the Via Alpina, turns lefts and descends steeply downhill. We continue straight ahead on the #595 Hohenweg.

At 5.6 miles the descent ends as the path climbs over an old rock slide and then briefly joins a broad track. Here great views open to the high peaks towering above the foot of the valley above the west side of Altdorf. The Gross Spitzen (7,873-ft.) dominates the view to the south.

At 6.1 miles a small yellow sign with the word "Wanderweg" points to a trail branching right from the track. Bear right on the Wanderweg, which descends on moderate grades, crosses a broad track at Sidenplangg and then joins a farm road at Abneter Wald at 6.5 miles. The descent continues along the road.

Reach a junction of two roads at 6.9 miles. Bear right and start ascending on a broad track that passes the alp of Rietlig. This section of the trail enjoys great views of Altdorf and the high peaks rising to the west/southwest.

At 7.5 miles the broad track curves to the right into a side valley. A short distance beyond the ascent ends and the track now descends on easy grades, reaching the junction with the trail to Biel at 8.6 miles. If you are ready to end the hike, bear left toward Biel on a trail that initially descends and then ascends to the lift station at 9.4 miles. Here a small cable car descends to Brugg on the Klausen Pass road. Otherwise, continue along the #595 trail toward Eggberge.

(At Biel you will also find accommodations, so it is possible to stop here for the night and then continue onto Eggberge and Altdorf. Accommodations are also available at the Edelweiss Skihaus at 9.1 miles.)

To Eggberge

- **Segment Stat:** 4.4 miles (one-way) from Biel to Eggberge
- **Total Distance from Klausen Pass to Eggberge:** 13.9 miles (one way)
- **Ending Elevation:** 4,712-ft.
- **Elevation Gain/Loss:** 2,400-ft./-4,000-ft.

Beyond the Biel junction the trail ascends and soon emerges from the side valley, crossing a second junction with a trail branching left toward Biel at 9.0 miles. A short distance beyond the path curves around the head of a ridge, passing the Edelweiss Skihaus and Restaurant in the small hamlet of Wiltschi at 9.1 miles.

Past the restaurant the undulating path curves to the left and enters a second side valley. Ahead are good views of the rugged ridge rimming the north side of the valley. The trail again exits the side valley, curves around the head of a ridge and enters a third side valley.

At 10.6 miles, near the head of the third side valley, the trail begins ascending on easy to moderate grades. The ascent ends at 11.5 miles as the trail emerges from the side valley, crests a ridges and arrives at the Gross Flesch (aka Fleschsee), a small tarn nestled along the west side of the ridge.

From this point the path descends on moderate grades, losing over 1,200-ft as it drops through trees and pastures to Eggberge at 13.9 miles. The village is set atop a grassy bench at the confluence of the Schachental and Reuss valleys. View stretch northwest to the Urnersee (aka Lake Lucerne), a large lake, and west/southwest to the high peaks towering above the Reuss Valley. At Eggberge a cable car descends to Fluelen, a town near the head of the Urnersee, where buses travel to Altdorf. A nearby train station offers transportation to places farther afield.

The Schachental Hohenweg continues beyond Eggberge, losing 3,320-ft as it drops to Fluelen. Allow 2 hr and 35 minutes for the hike down. I suggest avoiding the knee pounding descent and instead take the cable car.

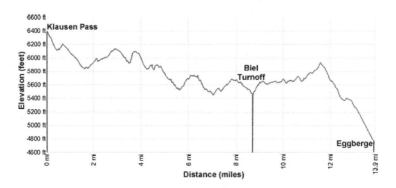

Trailhead Directions

From Altdorf to Klausen Pass: From Altdorf catch the #408 bus at Telldenkmal, the main square in the center of town, to Klausen Passhole (Klausen Pass). If starting from the Altdorf train station take a bus from the train station bound for Brugg and then change at Telldenkmal for the #408 bus to the pass. Check the schedule before setting out. Given the length of this hike it is best to catch an early bus. The ride to the pass takes about 55 minutes.

Bus schedules are posted at the bus stops or are available online at the SBB website or the SBB app. When looking for buses use "Altdorf UR, Telldenkmal", the UR in the name stands for the canton of Uri.

From Altdorf to Untere Balm: From Altdorf catch a bus at Telldenkmal, the main square in the center of town, heading toward Klausen Passhole (Klausen Pass) and get off at Untere Balm. If starting from the Altdorf train station take a bus from the train station bound for Brugg and then change at Telldenkmal for the bus to the pass. Again get off at Untere Balm. Check the schedule before setting out. Given the length of this hike it is best to catch an early bus. The ride to the Untere Balm takes about 47 minutes.

Bus schedules are posted at the bus stops and are available online at the SBB website or the SBB app. When looking for buses use "Altdorf UR, Telldenkmal", the UR in the name stands for the canton of Uri. The stop you want is Unterschachen, Untere Balm.

From Biel Seilbahn/Brugg to Altdorf: From the valley station for the Biel Lift, walk down to the bus stop, located adjacent to a parking lot along the Klausenpass Road. Take the B3 bus bound for Seedorf or the B408 bus bound for Fluelen. Check the bus schedules posted at the bus stops and available online at the SBB website or the SBB app to make sure you are headed in the right direction. When looking for buses use "Altdorf UR, Telldenkmal", the UR in the name stands for the canton of Uri. The ride takes about 17 minutes. See the the Biel to Brugg Seilbahn schedule for more information on the lift (in german).

From Eggberge Luftseilbahn/Flüelen to Altdorf: From the valley station of the Eggberge lift, walk a short distance to the Fluelen/Eggberge bus stop and catch the B408 toward Balm (Klausen) or B1 bus toward Goschenen or Amsteg and get off at Telldenkmal in the center of Altdorf. The ride takes about 9 minutes. Note: The B1 bus heading south lists different end points. Check the bus schedules which are posted at the bus stops and also available online at the SBB website or the SBB app to make sure you are headed in the right direction. When looking for buses use "Altdorf UR, Telldenkmal", the UR in the name stands for the canton of Uri. See the Eggberge Luftseilbahn schedule for more information on the lift.

70. Unterschachen to Hoch Fulen ★★★★★
Distance: 9.6 - 12.0 miles (round trip)
Near Altdorf in the Glarus Alps

This long, challenging hike visits the lovely Brunnital and then ascends a wild, seldom visited valley to Hoch Fulen, a summit with stunning views of the Schachental Mountains, the Glarus Alps and the summits towering above the Reuss Valley to the west.

Distance: 9.6 - 12.0 miles (round trip)
Elevation: 5,305-ft. at Trailhead 8,222-ft. at Hoch Fulen
Elevation Gain: 2,917-ft.
Difficulty: strenuous

Basecamp: Altdorf
Altdorf Map: See page 327
Online Map/Photos: www.hikingwalking.com/hoch-fulen

Why Hike from Unterschachen to Hoch Fulen

Escape the crowds on this strenuous, off-the-beaten path hike climbing to the summit of Hoch Fulen, with breathtaking 360-degree views encompassing the peaks towering above the Schachen, Reuss and Brunni valleys. The hike starts with an easy walk up the Brunnital and then ascends the steep and wild Griess Valley to an airy ridge before the final stiff climb to the top of Hoch Fulen.

The hike, best done by fit, well acclimated hikers, starts with a 1.2 miles (one-way) walk from the Unterschachen bus stop to the Sittlisalp cable car that whisks hikers up 1,700-ft. to a high bench along the west side of the Brunnital. Sections of the hike are very steep, climbing up scree slopes and slabs. Combining the walk to and from the bus with the hike results in a 12.0 mile day with an elevation gain over 3,000-ft.

Before starting the hike check on the status and time table for the Sittlisalp cable car. Be sure to get an early start and pick a day full of promise so that you can enjoy the fabulous views from the summit of Hoch Fulen.

Unterschachen to Hoch Fulen

From the Unterschachen bus stop walk a short distance east (in the direction of Klausen Pass) and then turn right (south) on Bielenhofstrasse (Bielenhof Street) toward the Sittlisalp cable car. Yellow hiking signs at the turn indicate a 20 minute to walk to the lift. (See trailhead directions below.)

The hike passes a few houses, crosses to the west side of the river on a a a bridge and then enters the Brunnital (Brunni Valley). Soon you are walking through a deep valley lined with steep cliffs. Along the way views open to the wall of mountains forming the cirque at the head of the Brunnital.

Just before reaching the cable car station signs for the Sittlisalp Talstation (valley station) direct you to turn left and cross a bridge back to the east side of the river. (Note: Bergstation refers to the upper lift station.) Beyond the bridge turn right on a spur road leading to the car park and cable car station. The total distance from the bus to the Talstation is 1.2 miles.

Take the cable car, which ascends over 1,700-ft., to Sittlisalp Bergstation at Vorder Boden (5,328-ft.). (Note: Sittlisalp is further up the valley.) The bergstation (mountain station) is situated on a broad bench along the west side of the valley. Exit the station and walk a short distance west to a trail signpost and then turn left (south) on the trail toward Hoch Fulen.

Ahead are grand views of Gross Ruchen anchoring the cirque at the head of the valley. To your right (west) the cirque formed by Sittliser, Blinzi and Gross Spitzen rims a large grassy bowl. Behind you the Schachentaler Windgallen towers above the north side of the Schachental.

The hike ascends the valley on easy grades, passing a few alp buildings along the way. At 0.6 miles reach a junction at Sittlisalp Lauwi. Bear right to stay on the main trail heading south up the valley. At 1.25 miles reach Sittlisalp (5,413-ft.). Continue straight ahead toward Hoch Fulen.

Reach Widerflue near the head of the valley at 1.75 miles. Here a trail branches left, descending to Brunni on the valley floor. We continue along the main trail that curves to the right into the Griesstal (Griess Valley) toward Hoch Fulen. Ahead views open to Schwarz Stockli, a peak rising above the south side of the valley. Behind you are ever improving views of the Gross Ruchen and Chli Ruchen.

The trail now ascends steeply for half a mile. Ignore the trail branching right at 2.4 miles and instead continue on the main trail toward Vorder Griesstal and Hoch Fulen. At 2.5 miles the grade eases as the path travels through rocky meadows sprinkled with wildflowers. As you ascend, turnaround occasionally and look east for ever improving views of the Scharhorn. To the south the summit of the Gross Windgallen rises beyond the intervening peaks.

Reach a junction at Vorder Griesstal with a trail branching left toward Seewli at 2.9 miles. Beyond the junction the trail climbs steeply for 0.5 miles to a small bench. As you climb the trail becomes more rugged. Be sure to turn around for fine views of Gross Ruchen and the Scharhorn to the south.

The grade briefly eases as the trail passes the ruins of a building at 3.6 miles. Soon the climb resumes on very steep grades up rock meadows that give way to scree-covered slopes and limestone outcroppings. Red and white slashes on the rocks will keep you on track.

At 4.3 miles the trail reaches the top of a ridge and a junction. Turn right (north) toward Hoch Fulen, simply listed on the sign as FULEN. The ridge enjoys amazing views stretching west across the Reuss Valley to Kronten, the Spannort massif, the Glatt Glacier and the Schloss massif. To the south are more great views of Gross Ruchen and the Scharhorn.

After a brief ascent along the ridge the trail curves left and soon reaches the ridge leading to Hoch Fulen. A final stiff climb up rocky meadows, scree and rock slabs leads to the summit of Hoch Fulen (8,222-ft.) at 4.8 miles.

Dramatic, 360-degree views encompass Clariden, the Scharhorn and Ruchen massif to the east/southeast and the Gross Windgallen to the south. The Schachental Mountains rise to the north. To the southwest a sea of peak rises along the Reuss Valley while the Spannort and Schloss massifs dominate the view to the west. Nearby peaks include the limestone summit of Balmeten (west), the Rinderstock and Rot Grat (ridge) to the south and the Schwarz Stockli and Wiss Stockli to the southeast.

After enjoying the views retrace your steps to the trailhead for a 9.6 miles round-trip hike. The walk to and from the bus stop adds 2.4 miles for a total hike of 12.0 miles. It is also possible to do a point-to-point hike, descends from the summit of Hoch Fulen to Ober Schwandi where a cable car descends to Erstfeld. From Erstfeld take the train to Altdorf. This is a very steep trail that loses over 4,570-ft. Check at the Altdorf Tourist office to determine if the Ober Schwandi lift is running and the condition of the trail before selecting this option.

Trailhead Directions

From Altdorf to Unterschachen and Sittlisalp Seilbahn: From Altdorf catch the #408 bus at Telldenkmal, the main square in the center of town, heading toward Klausen Pass and get off at Unterschachen Post. If starting from the Altdorf train station take a bus from the train station bound for Brugg and then change at Telldenkmal for the #408 bus heading to Klausen Pass. Check the schedule before setting out. Given the length of this hike it is best to catch an early bus. The ride to Unterschachen Post takes about 27 minutes from Telldenkmal.

From the Unterschachen Post bus stop walk east along the Klausen Pass Road to Bielenhofstrasse (Bielenhof Street) and turn right (south) into the Brunnital (Brunni Valley). Walk 1.2 miles to a large car park and the valley station for the Sittlisalp Seilbahn (cable car).

Bus schedules are posted at the bus stops and are available online at the SBB website or the SBB app. When looking for buses use "Altdorf UR, Telldenkmal", the UR in the name stands for the canton of Uri. See the Alp Sittlis site for the cable car timetable.

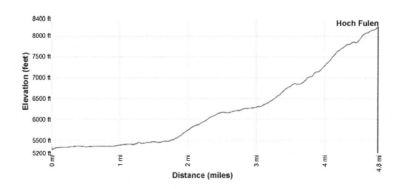

71. Golzern - Hohenweg Maderanertal ⭐⭐⭐⭐⭐
Distance: 5.0 - 9.8 miles (loop)
Near Altdorf in the Glarus Alps

This is another of Switzerland's wonderful high routes with almost nonstop views. The trail loops around the Maderanertal, a pristine valley surrounds by soaring mountains, visiting the Windgallen Hut along the way. Waterfalls, wildflowers and small hamlets add interest to the hike.

Distance: 2.5 miles (one way) to
Windgallen Hut
9.8 miles (loop) to Bristen
Elevation: 4,577-ft. at Trailhead
6,667-ft. at Windgallen Hut
2,730-ft. at Bristen
Elevation Gain: 2,099-ft. to
Windgallen Hut
-3,937-ft. to Bristen

Difficulty: moderate-strenuous
Basecamp: Altdorf
Altdorf Map: See page 327
Online Map/Photos:
www.hikingwalking.com/golzern

Why Hike Golzern - Hohenweg Maderanertal

This enjoyable loop explores the beautiful Maderanertal (Maderaner Valley), the valley south of the Schachental. At Bristen a cable car carries hikers to Golzern and the start of the hike. After passing the Golzerensee, a pretty lake, the trail climbs above the timberline to Windgallen Hut with terrific views of the high peak rimming the valley. The path then descends toward the head of the valley to Tritt with more glorious views of the high peaks and several photogenic waterfalls.

At Tritt, the trail heads back, dropping down to the valley floor at Balmenegg before following the Charstelenbach River back to Bristen. This section of the trail travels through lovely meadows and clusters of trees with fine views stretching up and down the valley. Along the way the path passes delightful waterfalls cascading down steep, rock cliffs and visits a few small hamlets.

The beautiful Maderanertal is not on any tourist circuit, offering a degree of solitude not found on many trails in Switzerland. The area is also devoid of ski lifts, remaining relatively unspoiled and wild in it upper reaches.

From Altdorf it is an hour and 20 minute ride on two buses and a cable car with good connections to the start of the hike. Don't let the length of the ride deter you. Pick a day full of promise and take your time hiking this lovely circuit.

Golzern to Windgallen Hut

- **Distance from Trailhead:** 2.5 miles (one way)/5.0 miles (round-trip)
- **Highest Elevation:** 6,667-ft.
- **Elevation Gain:** 2,099-ft.

Upon arriving at the village of Bristen take the cable car to Golzern. (See trailhead directions below.) Take a few minutes outside the cable car station at Golzern to view Bristen (10,082-ft.), towering above the head of the valley to the southwest. From the trail signpost near the station start walking east on the broad track toward the Golzerensee and Windgallen Hut. The path passes some house as it travels through meadows and scatter trees on easy grades. At the next sign post you will see your trail listed as Trail 590 - the Hohenweg Maderanertal (hohenweg: high route).

At 0.7 miles the trail passes through the village of Seewen and reaches a junction. Straight ahead is a path leading to the Golzerensee, a pretty little lake. We bear left on the Hohenweg 590 toward Windgallen Hut.

The trail now climbs on steep grades through meadows and clusters of trees. The Oberalpstock (10,915-ft.), towering about the south side of the valley, forms a nice backdrop for the Golzerensee, nestled in a tree lined bowl below the trail.

At 1.3 miles, bear left at a junction to stay on the trail to Windgallen Hut. The trail climbs a switchback and then continues ascending northeast toward the hut. The Witenalpstock, Oberalpstock and Grosse Dussi (10,682-ft.) dominate the view across the valley.

The path soon climbs above the timberline, traveling through rocky meadows scattered with rock outcroppings. Ahead views open to the Gross Ruchen (10,292-ft.) and Chli Ruchen soaring above the trail.

Reach a junction at 2.2 miles and bear left on the Hohenweg 590 toward Windgallen Hut. The trail straight ahead, leading to Ofeli and Trift, bypasses the hut but continues along the high route toward the head of the valley. I call this trail the Ofeli Shortcut. I recommend continuing to the hut.

The trail now climbs steeply through rocky meadows, crossing a stream along the way, to reach the hut at 2.5 miles. The hut is set atop a bench amid alpine meadows with breathtaking views of the surrounding peaks. Gross Windgallen (10,456-ft.) and Gross Ruchen punctuate the ridge above the hut to the north. The Witenalpstock and Oberalpstock fill the skyline across the valley to the south while the Tschingelstock, adorned with the Tschingelfirn Glacier, rises to the southwest. At the head of the Maderanertal, to the east, Chli Ruchen and Gross Dussi frame the snout of the Hufifirn Glacier.

The hut is a good turnaround point for parties looking for a shorter hike (5.0 miles round-trip).

Completing the Loop

- **Segment Stat:** 7.3 miles (one-way) to complete the loop from Wingallen Hut to Bristen
- **Total Distance:** 9.8 miles (loop)
- **Maximum Elevation:** 2,730-ft.
- **Elevation Loss to Bristen:** -3,937-ft.

After you are done taking in the views around Windgallen Hut, descend from the hut toward Ofeli. The path drops steeply for 0.25 miles and then moderates.

At 2.8 miles the trail passes through the hamlet of Stafel and soon reaches the junction with the Ofeli Shortcut trail at 3.0 miles. Here we bear left on the Hohenweg 590 toward Tritt. The path now descends on moderate grades through beautiful meadows, crossing several streams along the way. Soon the meadows give way to heather, shrubs and stunted trees.

Across the valley Gross Dussi dominates the view while the Ruchen massif soars overhead.

At 3.5 miles ignore a trail branching left toward Alp Gnof and Tritt. We stay on the main trail toward Tritt and Hufihutte. Reach Ofeli and a junction at 3.6 miles. Here a trail branches right toward Balmenschachen. This is a good shortcut if the weather is taking a turn for the worse. Otherwise continue straight ahead toward Tritt. Across the valley views open to a waterfall spilling from a hanging valley.

The trail crosses a series of metal walkways below a waterfall at 3.8 miles. A small landslide has made a mess of the trail, requiring the detour. A short distance beyond the trail passes another pretty waterfall cascading down a rugged cliff.

Reach Tritt at 4.2 miles. Beyond the alp the trail starts descending on steep switchbacks to the valley floor. Along the way enjoy fine views of Gross Dussi and the snout of the Hufifirn Glacier. Waterfalls spill down the steep cliffs nearby.

At 4.5 miles an unmarked trail branches left. We continue on the main trail, which now turns to the southwest toward Balmenegg and Bristen. Lovely views stretch down the length of the valley to Mount Bristen. Waterfalls tumble down steep cliffs on both sides of the valley.

The switchbacks end as you reach Sassalp and a junction at 5.0 miles. Ignore trails branching left toward Hufihutte. Continue on Hohenweg 590 toward Bristen. The trail now drops on a diagonal down to the valley floor, descending on moderate to moderately-steep grades through meadows and clusters of trees. Along the way we pass several delightful waterfalls and enjoy views of Dussi and Mount Bristen.

Reach Balmenegg at 5.8 miles and a trail junction at 5.9 miles. Ignore the bike trail that heads left. Instead, stay on the Hohenweg 590 toward Bristen.

At 6.6 miles the trail descends to Balmenschachen, crosses the Charstelenbach River on a bridge and then passes through Alp Stossi. The Hohenweg 590 now travels along the valley floor, crossing the river two more times before ending at Bristen near the cable car station at 9.8 miles. From there it is a short walk back to the bus stop.

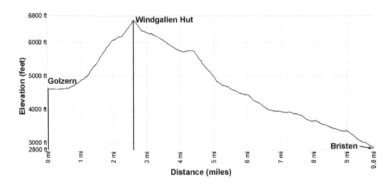

Trailhead Directions

From Altdorf to Golzern: From Altdorf take the #1 bus (Stand B) at Telldenkmal, the main square in the center of town, in the direction of Goschenen. Get off at Amsteg Post and catch the bus to Golzern Talstation Seilbahn (valley station for the cable car) in Bristen. It's a short walk from the bus stop to the cable car. Ride the cable car to Golzern. Check the schedule before setting out. Given the length of this hike it is best to catch an early bus. The two bus rides take about 43 minutes and the cable car takes 36 minutes.

Bus schedules are posted at the bus stops and are available online at the SBB website or the SBB app. When looking for buses use "Altdorf UR, Telldenkmal", the UR in the name stands for the canton of Uri. The schedule and pricing for the cable car is found on the Luftseilbahn Golzern website.

Map: Engelberg Area Trails

Engelberg Map

72. Altdorf to Engelberg via Surenen Pass

★★★★★
Distance: 8.9 - 13.0 miles (one way)
Near Altdorf in the Uri Alps

The Alpine Pass Route from Altdorf to Engelberg ascends through meadows framed by rugged peaks to Surenen Pass where Titlis and the Schloss and Spannort massifs dominate the view. The scenic descent to Engelberg features views of towering, jagged peaks adorn with waterfalls and a dramatic cirque.

Distance: 3.6 miles (one way) to
Surenen Pass
13.0 miles (one way) to Engelberg
Elevation: 5,003-ft. at Trailhead
7,516-ft. at Surenen Pass
3,287-ft. at Engelberg
Elevation Gain: 2,513-ft. to
Surenen Pass
-4,229-ft. to Engelberg

Difficulty: strenuous
Basecamp: Altdorf
Engelberg Map: See page 339
Online Map/Photos:
www.hikingwalking.com/surenen

Why Hike from Altdorf to Engelberg via Surenen Pass

This beautiful hike ascends along a high ridge beneath the steep cliffs of the Brunnistock and Blackenstock before climbing rocky alpine meadows and scree covered slopes to Surenen Pass, a panoramic saddle where snow-capped Titlis (10,623-ft.) is the star of the show. The scenic descent from the pass, through meadows and pastures, enjoys amazing views of the cirque towering above Blackenalp and the waterfalls spilling down the glacier-clad Schloss and Spannort massifs rimming the south side of the Surenen Valley.

The trail is part of the Alpine Pass Route between Altdorf to Engelberg. This description shortens the hike to a more manageable day by taking the cable car from Attinghausen, west of Altdorf, to Brusti and then climbing to

Surenen Pass. Various options are also available to reduce the mileage and eliminate the final segment of the walk along roads to Engelberg.

To Surenen Pass

- **Distance from Trailhead:** 3.6 miles (one way)
- **Elevation at Surenen Pass:** 7,516-ft.
- **Elevation Gain:** 2,513-ft.

Purist may want to hike all the way from Altdorf to Engelberg, a 17.2 mile hike with over 6,000-ft. of elevation gain. My advice is to take advantage of transportation at the beginning and end of the walk so that you have more time to savor the beautiful scenery the area has to offer.

Start the day by taking the bus from Altdorf to Attinghausen where a two-stage cable-car ascends to Brusti. This combination reduces the elevation gain by over 3,500-ft. and cuts the distance by 4.2 miles.

An alternative stopping point at Furenalp employs a cable car and bus to reach Engelberg, eliminating a long walk along roads. See the trailhead directions below for more information on transportation alternatives at the beginning and end of the hike.

Altdorf to Brusti

(Note: regularly scheduled buses travel from central Altdorf and the Altdorf train station to the Attinghausen-Brusti cable car. See the trailhead directions below.)

Walk south from the Altdorf train station along the road paralleling the train line. After 0.7 miles turn right on a road that goes under the railway and highway and then crosses a bridge over the Reuss River. Signs for the Via Alpina (Alpine Pass Route), Surenen Pass and Attinghausen mark the turn.

In Attinghausen, on the west side of the river, continue west/southwest on Burgstrasse (Burg Street) and then bear slightly right onto Kummetstrasse (Kummet Street). Soon you will see the bottom station for the two-stage Attinghausen-Brusti cable car on your left (south) at 1.2 miles.

To take the cable car, walk into the unmanned station and push the signal button on the wall. Wait until you hear the operator's voice answer the call and then reply, "Bergfahrt, bitte." Your party should then enter the cable car, close the door and then push the button inside the cable car to signal to the operator that he can start the cable car. (Payment for the cable car is collected by the operator at the middle station.)

For those walking to Brusti, locate the Via Alpina (Alpine Pass Route) signs outside the cable car station. The path initially ascends along the north side of the Chummetbach stream to the middle cable car station. Here the path crosses to the south side of the stream and briefly climbs along roads before turning right and ascending very steeply through pastures and viewless forest to the top station for the cable car at 4.2 miles. Signs along the way for Brusti and Surenen Pass will keep you on track.

Brusti to Surenen Pass

(Mileage for this section of the description assumes you take the cable car to Brusti. Add 4.2 miles to the trail distances if walking from Altdorf.)

Outside the top station for the cable car at Brusti find a signed track heading west toward Surenenpass and Engelberg. At the first intersection turn left on the broad track toward Surenen Pass.

The trail ascends past houses and then climbs an undulating path along a ridge, traveling through stunted trees, bushes and intermittent meadows. Hand rails offer a level of security along sections of the path with steep drop-offs. Along the way the trail pass through Chraienhoreli where a path branches right to the small alp at Chaserli. We continue toward Surenen Pass. After 0.8 miles the trees give way to low shrubs and meadows where views open east/northeast to Altdorf and the high peaks rimming the Schachental (Schachen Valley).

At 1.1 miles reach Grat where signs point right toward a small alp building and Seedorf. We bear left toward Surenen Pass on the Via Alpina (Alpine Pass Route) trail that climbs through beautiful, wildflower-filled meadows to the ridge separating the Waldnacht Valley to the south from the Gitschital to the north. The path now ascends along or near the ridge crest accompanied by fine views of the Gitschenhoreli, Brunnistock and Blackenstock towering above the head of the valley. Surenen Pass, the saddle to the left (south) of Blackenstock, is now in view. To the northeast you can see a small section of the Urnersee, an arm of the Vierwaldstattersee (Lake Lucerne). To the south a ridge punctuated by rugged peaks rims the Waldnacht Valley.

At 1.6 miles the grade briefly abates as the trail wanders along the ridge and then resumes its climb at 2.0 miles. Soon the grade steepens as the trail ascends to Angistock at 2.5 miles, located near the head of the ridge. Ahead Surenen Pass is now in view.

At Angistock a faint path branches right, crossing steep, scree covered slopes before rejoining the main trail below the pass. Periodic rockslides have made this trail a dicey proposition and warnings painted on nearby rocks indicate that the path is no longer recommended. Instead bear left on the main Via Alpina trail toward Langschnee and Surenen Pass. The trail descends into a bowl, passes the junction at Langschnee, crosses a snowfield that lasts well into the summer and then climbs steeply to the pass at 3.6 miles.

As you crest the pass snow-capped Titlis springs into view, soaring above the Schloss and Spannort massifs rimming the south side of the Surenen Valley. A few small tarns lie below the pass. The rugged crags of Blackenstock rise above the pass to the north. Behind you views stretch east down the Brusti side of the pass. On a nice day the grassy pass is a great place to take a break and enjoy the views.

To Engelberg

- **Segment Stat:** 5.3 - 9.4 miles (one-way) from Surenen Pass to Engelberg
- **Total Distance:** 8.9 - 13.0 miles (one way) to Engelberg
- **Ending Elevation:** 3,287-ft.
- **Elevation Gain/Loss:** -4,229-ft.

The trail on the west side of the pass descends through meadows on steep to moderately steep grades, passing Schutzhutte, an emergency shelter, and then a wooden cross, which seems to be a favorite resting place for a herd of cows. Accompanying the descent are terrific views of Titlis and the wall of high peaks rimming the south side of the Surenen Valley.

Reach Blankenalp at 5.5 miles. This scenic spot, standing at the foot of a massive cirque formed by the Schuflen, Wissigstock, Schlossstock and Blackenstock, includes a restaurant and dormitory accommodations. A short distance past the alp the trail passes a pretty white chapel on a hill and then crosses a bridge over the Stierenbach, the stream draining the valley.

The descent now continues on moderate grades to a second bridge over the Stierenbach and a junction at Stauber at 6.7 miles. Here the trail splits, with the Via Alpina branching left toward Engelberg. The trail to the right heads to Furenalp.

The scenic trail to Furenenalp, a high route gaining about 900-ft. in 2.2 miles, ends at the alp where a cable car descends to the Engelbergertal (Engelberger Valley). Here you can either walk or take a bus to Engelberg. The traditional route, which also includes good views, descends more gradually along the valley floor beside the river, losing over 2,300-ft in 6.5 miles to Engelberg.

Stauber to Engelberg

The traditional valley route to Engelberg descends down the valley along the north side of the river beneath the towering cliffs and jagged peaks of the Spannort massif. Waterfalls, fed by snowmelt and glaciers, cascade down the slopes. Pass a the cable car station at Stafeli at 7.4 miles and the bottom station for the Furenalp cable car at Herrenrutiboden at 10.3 miles. Here the trail joins a macadam road that leads to a popular restaurant near a waterfall at 10.6 miles. (You can catch the bus back to Engelberg at either Herrenrutiboden or the waterfall.)

Hikers wanting to walk the entire way can follow a combination of roads and paths, passing through Vorder Stalden and Holzkapelle to the center of Engelberg for a 17.2 mile hike, if you walked all the way from Altdorf, or a 13.0 mile hike, if you walked from Brusti. At all turns follow the signs toward Engelberg and not the blue Alpine Route signs you may see along the way.

Stauber to Furenalp

The trail to Furenalp ascends on easy to moderate grades up the wildflower-filled meadows beneath the Wissberg. Across the valley enjoy great views of Gross Spannort, Chli Spannort and the Grassengrat ridge. Glaciers adorn the upper slopes of the peaks. Waterfalls cascade down the steep slopes beneath the glaciers.

At 7.6 miles reach a junction at Usser Aebnet. Continue on the main trail to Furenalp. Behind you are terrific views of Blackenstock rising above Surenen Pass. Across the valley to the south the views of the Spannort massif continue to evolve as you head west. At 7.8 miles the grade steepens and soon starts climbing switchbacks. The ascent ends at 8.4 miles. The trail now traverses a grassy bench awash in wildflowers along the south facing slopes of the Wissberg, reaching the cable car station at Furenalp at 8.9 miles.

Take the cable car down to the valley station at Herrenrutiboden. Here you can catch a bus to Engelberg or walk to Engelberg following the directions above.

Trailhead Directions

From Altdorf to Attinghausen/Brusti: From the Altdorf train station catch a #2 bus at Stand B to the Attinghausen Seilbahn. If starting from Telldenkmal, the main square in the center of Altdorf, take the #2 bus from Stand C to the Attinghausen Seilbahn. There are a variety of other bus combinations that work. Bus schedules are posted at the bus stops and are available online at the SBB website or on the SBB app. When looking for buses use "Altdorf UR, Telldenkmal" or "Altdorf UR, Bahnhof", the UR in the name stands for the canton of Uri.

The schedule for the two-stage cable car from Attinghausen to Brusti is available at the Attinghausen Tourism site. The lift typically runs from 7am to 7pm in the summer with a break for lunch. Check the website for the current schedule.

From Furenalp to Engelberg: Take the Furenalp Luftseilbahn to the valley station at Herrenrutiboden where shuttle buses run to Engelberg. The lift typically runs from 8am to 6pm in the summer. You can also walk eight minutes west from the valley station to the bus stop at the Wasserfall (Waterfall) and catch the #10 Bus to Engelberg. Bus schedules are posted at the bus stops and are available online at the SBB website or on the SBB app.

73. Other Trails in Altdorf and Engelberg
Near Engelberg in the Uri Alps

73a) Engelberg to Engstlenalp via Jochpass

This trail, part of the Alpine Pass Route, features some nice views of the peaks rising to the north of Engelberg, the Trubsee, glacier-clad Titlis and the Jochstock. But slopes along the way are littered with ski lifts marring the views on sections of the path. A series of lifts, starting in Engelberg, take visitors all the way up to Jochpass and then down to the meadows just above the Engstlensee. Sections of the trail travel below or near the lifts, detracting from the hike. Note: The areas around the Trubsee and the various lifts stations can be quite crowded.

- **Distance:** 7.8 miles (one-way)
- **Elevation:** 3,271-ft. at Engelberg
  5,892-ft. at Trubsee Hotel
  7,241-ft. at Jochpass
  6,017-ft. at Engstlenalp
- **Elevation Gain/Loss:** 3,970-ft./-1,224-ft.
- **Difficulty:** strenuous
- **Base camp:** Engelberg or Engstlenalp
- **Engelberg Map:** See page 339

From the Engelberg Bahnhof (train station) follow the signs pointing south/southeast toward Banklialp, Trubsee and Jochpass. After following roads for a short distance the route traverses a path on a diagonal through a field before turning right on Banklialpweg and crossing a bridge over the river. At the Banklialp Restaurant we leave the paved road and ascend steeply through trees. At 1.3 miles the trees give way to pastures and the grade abates as the trails continues to Gerschnialp at 1.7 miles.

Past Gerschnialp the path ascends through pastures with fine views of the peaks rising to the north of Engelberg and then climbs more steeply through trees beneath lift lines to the Trubsee Hotel and a cable car station at 3.6 miles. This area is popular with tourist visiting the hotel complex, which includes a restaurant and shops, and the nearby lake. A number of lift lines converge at Trubsee including the cable car route ascending to Titlis.

The trail to Jochpass descends from the cable car station to the Trubsee, a shallow lake, at 3.8 miles and then travels along the southeast end of the lake beneath a chairlift. To the southeast views open to the glacier clad slopes of Titlis. The Graustock, Schafberg and Jochstock rim the valley to the south/southwest.

After crossing a bridge over the lake's inlet stream take the trail branching left and then right (south/southwest) toward Jochpass. (Note: There is another path that climbs to Jochpass that continues along the lakeshore and then climbs to the pass beneath the lift running from Alpstubli to Jochpass. I don't recommend this option.)

Our path now travels through meadows and crosses a broad track at 4.2 miles. Beyond the track the trail climbs steep switchbacks through meadows accompanied by fine views of the Trubsee and the peaks rising to the north of Engelberg. Reach Jochpass, the Berghaus Jochpass and the Jochpass lift station at 5.4 miles. A small pond lies nestled atop the pass near the Berghaus.

At Jochpass we cross the border into the canton of Bern. Here views open to the peaks towering above the northwest side of the Gental valley, the Engstlensee and Engstlenalp, our destination. On the west side of the pass the trail descends through rocky meadows beneath the chairlift to the Engstlensee and then travels above the lake's north shore. Alternatively, at 5.8 miles take the trail branching right that moves away from the lift lines and stays higher above the north side of the valley before rejoining the main trail just before the lake. On both trails views encompass the ridge anchored by the Wendestock massif, Pfaffenhuot and Maren rimming the southeast side of the valley.

Past the lake the trail travels through meadows to Engstlenalp and the Hotel Engstlenalp at 7.8 miles. The hotel offers rooms, dormitory accommodations and meals. Regularly scheduled buses travel from Engstlenalp to Innertkirchen and then Meiringen. See Hike 74 - Engstlenalp to Meiringen for information on the bus to Meiringen.

Note: Hikers that wish to combine the trails from Engelberg to Engstlenalp and Engstlenalp to Meiringen into a single day typically skip most of the first section from Engelberg to Engstlenalp segment by taking one or both of the lifts from Engelberg to the Trubsee and from the Trubsee to Jochpass. From the pass it is an easy walk down to Engstlenalp and the continuation of the Alpine Pass Route to Meiringen (Hike 74 - from Engstlenalp to Meiringen).

Meiringen
Location: The Haslital between the Bernese and Uri Alps

Meiringen lies cradled near the foot of the Haslital (Hasli Valley) amidst the high peaks of the Bernese Alps to the west and the Uri Alps to the east. The valley and the town serves as a crossroads for several mountain passes; Brunig Pass leading to Lucerne, Susten Pass crossing to the Reuss Valley and Grimsel Pass linking to the Rhone Valley in the Valais. Brienz and the Brienzsee (Lake Brienz) are situated at the foot of the Haslital, to the west.

The Reichenbachtal (Reichenbach Valley), branching southwest from the Meiringen, connects the town to Grosse Scheidegg, the pass leading to Grindelwald. Up valley from Meiringen the Gadmental (Gadmen Valley) extends east into the Uri Alps. A short distance up the Gadmental a tributary valley, the Gental, splits off to the northeast to Jochpass, linking Meiringen to Engelberg. Both Grosse Scheidegg and Jochpass are important crossings on the Alpine Pass Route.

The Haslital and its tributary valleys rimmed by rugged ridges and high peaks offer great opportunities for hikers wishing to explore the area. From Jochpass (Hike 73a) in the Gental the Alpine Pass Route descends to Engstlenalp and then travels along the steep slopes and high ridges on the northwest side of the Gental to Planplatten (Hike 74), a panoramic overlook with vistas of the summits towering above five valleys. From Planplatten gondolas/cable cars and trails drop to Meiringen.

After crossing Meiringen on the valley floor, the traditional Alpine Pass Route ascends the Reichenbachtal to Gross Scheidegg (Hike 75c). An alternate, more scenic route departs from the Alpine Pass Route above Schwarzwaldalp (Hike 75d), climbing above the north side of the Reichenbach Valley to the ridge extending north from Grosse Scheidegg. Here hikers can choose to continue to First, a lofty viewpoint above Grindelwald, or head south to Grosse Scheidegg.

A trail through the Rosenlaui Glacier Gorge (Hike 75a), a UNESCO World Heritage site, ascends along the dramatic gorge carved by the Weissenbach River. The trail can be done as a standalone hike or a side trip on a longer hike up the Reichenbach Valley. Hochmoor (Hike 75b), the highest protected moor in Europe, is accessible from Kaltenbrunnen in the Reichenbach Valley. The trail loops high about the southwest side of Meiringen through a beautiful landscape of forest, meadows, bogs and small ponds. At the end of the trail hikers can detour to Reichenbach Falls, the site where Sir Arthur Conan Doyle's character Sherlock Holmes had his famous fight with Moriarty.

About Meiringen

Meiringen is a traditional Swiss town popular with hikers, skiers and tourists visiting sites in the Haslital. The town includes a good selection of accommodations, restaurants, bars and shops to serve the needs of just about any visitor. The town center is along Bahnhofstrasse (called Hauptstrasse to the west and Bundnez to the east) and its adjacent side streets. The Bahnhof (train station) and Tourist Office are located one block south of the main street on Bahnhofplatz. Buses leave from the south side of the train station for a variety of locations, including the Reichenbachtal, Engstlenalp, Susten Pass and Grimsel Pass. The cable car to Hasliberg-Reuti is at the end of Alpbachhalle on the northeast side of the town. This service connects with the series of gondolas to the Alpen Tower at Planplatten.

The Migros Supermarket is located on the north side of Bahnhofstrasse while a Coop is found on Alpwegern, a street branch southwest off Haupstrasse. Meiringen is the home of Swiss meringues. The recommended place to sample this delicacy is the Frutal Bakery and Tea Room at 18 Bahnhofstrasse.

Getting to Meiringen

From the Zurich Airport or Zurich Bahnhof (train station), take the train to Meiringen. You will need to change trains along the way. Ask for an itinerary when making your reservations that includes the required changes and the length of time allowed for the connection. The trip takes about two hours and 10 minutes from Zurich.

From the Geneva Airport or Gare (train station), take the train to Meiringen. You will need to change trains at Bern and Interlaken Ost (East). The trip should take about 3 hours and 40 minutes.

Check the SBB website/SBB app for directions from other parts of the country.

Nearby Attractions & Rainy Day Activities

Reichenbach Falls showcases a series of beautiful waterfalls made famous by author Sir Authur Conan Doyle as the place where the fictitious detective Sherlock Holmes plunged to his death. From the base of the waterfall a trail leads up to the various stages of the falls with viewpoints featuring great vistas of the Haslital.

Aare Gorge (aka Aareschlucht) - Over time the Aare Gorge, a 0.9 mile long chasm that is over 650-ft. deep, has been sculpted by the erosional force of meltwater from glaciers and snow in the Haslital and its side valleys flowing into the Aare River. A series of paths, cantilevered walkways and tunnels offers access to this amazing natural wonder.

The **Sherlock Holmes Museum** includes memorabilia of Sir Arthur Conan Doyle and his fictional character Sherlock Holmes along with a replica of the detective's Victorian parlor at 221b Baker Street in London.

The Restiturm, a ruin of a 13th century castle situated at the foot of the Hasliberges, features nice views of Reichenbach Falls across the valley. The ruins are in the northeast part of the town, about a 20 minute walk from the Bahnhof.

The **Rosenlaui Glacier Gorge**, a UNESCO World Heritage site, ascends through a deep dramatic gorge carved by the Weissenbach River, passing pretty pools, waterfalls, grottoes and sculpted rock formations. See Hike 75a - the Rosenlaui Glacier Gorge for more information

A good rainy day option is to take a day trip to **Interlaken**, a 40 minute train ride from Meiringen. Here you can walk along Lakes Thun and Brienz, take a lake cruise, visit castles along Lake Thun or simply walk along the Hohenweg, the street connecting Lake Brienz to Lake Thun. Visit the Interlaken Tourist Information site for a complete list of options.

Good Things to Know about Meiringen

- The primary language in Meiringen is German although people who deal with tourist will also speak French and/or English.
- There are two campgrounds in Meiringen: Campground Balmweid located on the south side of the Aare River at Blamwiedstrasse 22 and Alpen Camping at Brunigstrasse 47 at the northwest end of Meiringen.
- There is one hostel in Meiringen, the Familienhotel Tourist at Grimselstrasse 82.

Map: Meiringen Area Trails

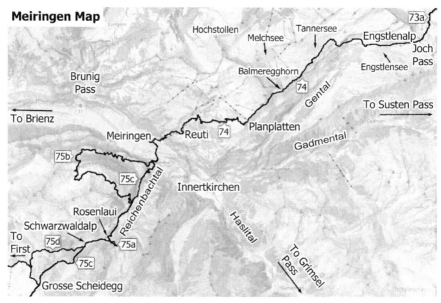

74. Engstlenalp to Meiringen ★★★★★
Distance: 6.4 - 11.0 miles (one way)
Near Meiringen in the Bernese Alps

The beautiful hike from Engstlenalp to Planplatten visits the scenic Tannersee, enjoys terrific views atop the Balmeregghorn and then travels to the overlook at Planplatten with panoramic vistas of the high peaks towering above four valleys.

Distance: 4.5 miles (one way) to Balmeregghorn
6.4 miles (one way) to Planplatten
11.0 miles (one way) to Reuti (Meiringen)
Elevation: 6,017-ft. at Trailhead
7,398-ft. at Balmeregghorn
7,365-ft. at Planplatten
3,491-ft. at Reuti (Meiringen)

Elevation Gain: 1,382-ft. to Balmeregghorn
-567-ft. to Planplatten
-3,874-ft. to Reuti (Meiringen)
Difficulty: moderate-strenuous
Basecamp: Meiringen
Meiringen Map: See page 349
Online Map/Photos:
www.hikingwalking.com/engstlenalp

Why Hike from Engstlenalp to Meiringen

This scenic hike with nonstop views follows the Alpine Pass route between Engstlenalp and Meiringen, traveling along the steep slopes and high ridges on the northwest side of the Gental Valley. Along the way the signature peaks of the Bernese Alps soaring above Reichenbach and Grindelwald Valleys dominate the view to the southwest. The Wendenstocke, Tallistock and the rugged intervening ridge fills the skyline across the Gental Valley while the Jochstock and Titlis rise to the east.

From Engstlenalp the trail climbs the Spycherflue to Tannalp. Here the Rothorn, Glogghus and Hochstollen, towering along the rugged ridge rimming the southwest side of the Melchsee Valley, form the perfect backdrop for the Tannersee, a pretty lake nestled in the pastures of Tannalp.

After skirting the southeast side of the Tannersee the trail climbs atop a ridge with impressive views in all directions. The trail now travels along the ridge crest, ascending to the Balmeregghorn with more splendid views. Here the Dammastock, rising above the glistening Trift Glacier on the south side of the Gadmertal Valley, joins the scene.

Beyond the Balmeregghorn the trail follows an undulating course along the rugged southeast flanks of the Rothorn and the Lauber and then traverses a ridge crest to the overlook at Planplatten. The overlook, at the convergence of four valleys, showcases an amazing panorama of the area's peaks and glaciers.

From Planplatten a combination of gondolas and a cable car whisk hikers to Meiringen. Alternatively, take the trail from Planplatten to Reuti and then ride the cable car to Meiringen or walk the entire way to Meiringen.

Engstlenalp to Balmeregghorn

- **Distance from Trailhead:** 4.5 miles (one way)
- **Highest Elevation:** 7,398-ft.
- **Elevation Gain:** 1,382-ft.

Find the trail signposts in front of the Hotel Engstlenalp in Engstlenalp (6,017-ft.). (See trailhead directions below). Follow the broad track heading northwest toward Tannalp (45-min), Balmeregghorn (2-hr 30-min) and Planplatten (3-hr 45-min) as it travels through pastures and passes the houses and barns of Engstlenalp. In the distance the high peaks towering above Reichenbach and Grindelwald valleys, including the Wellhorn, Wetterhorn and Schreckhorn, dominate the view to the southwest. The Wendenstocke, Tallistock and the rugged intervening ridge fills the skyline across the Gental Valley while the Jochstock and Titlis rise to the east.

At 0.2 miles the trail curves to the left (west) and soon crosses a stream (0.5 miles) beneath a beautiful waterfall cascading down a rock face above the trail. Beyond the stream the trail ascends on moderate grades up a hillside beneath rugged cliffs toward Tannalp. As you climb, enjoy ever improving views of the peaks and ridges seen from the Hotel Engstlenalp.

At 0.7 miles a trail branches left toward Baumgartenalp, Hasliberg and Reuti. We continue along the main path toward Tannenalp, Balmeregghorn and Planplatten. Fixed ropes along the path facilitate the climb up a rocky section of the trail along the Spycherflue, a 260-ft. tall rock wall. This section of the trail could be problematic if covered with ice or slick snow.

At 1.1 miles the trail curves to the right (northwest) and reaches the ridge crest after a final short, steep climb. The path now continues ascending on moderate grades across the pastures of Tannenalp. Soon views open to the hamlet of Tannalp, situated beneath the rugged ridge extending southwest from the Barglen Schiben.

At 1.4 miles the grade abates as the trail curves around a grassy bowl. As you near the buildings of Tannalp views open to the distinctively shaped Graustock to the northeast. Titlis, the Jochstock and Wendenstocke rise above the grassy slopes to the southeast.

Reach a road junction at Tannalp (6,486-ft.) at 1.6 miles. Turn left (southwest) toward the Tannersee (10-min), Balmeregghorn (1-hr 25-min) and Planplatten (2-hr 35-min) on a paved alp road ascending gently through pastures.

At 2.0 miles reach the eastern end of the Tannersee. Here the road curves to the right (west), along the north shore of the Tannersee toward the Melchsee-Frutt. We take the trail branching left (southwest) that skirts the lake's southeastern shore. To the west, the Rothorn and Glogghus tower above the valley beyond the Tannersee.

Reach a junction at the southeastern end of the lake where another trail branches right toward Melchsee-Frutt on a path winding along the lake's south shore. We bear left on the trail heading for Erzegg, Balmeregghorn and Planplatte (aka Planplatten). The path travels through rolling pastures on easy grades and soon joins a broad track that climbs switchbacks up a grassy slope to a cross atop a ridge.

The scenic ridge enjoys marvelous 360-degree views. To the northeast/east the peaks and ridges rising above the Tannersee and Tannalp dominate the view. To the southeast are great views of the summits towering above Engstlenalp. To the south across the Gental valley, the ridge between the Wendenstocke and Tallistock fills the skyline. To the northwest the Rothorn, Glogghus and Hochstollen punctuate the rugged ridge along the west side of the Melchsee valley while to the southwest the high peaks and glaciers of the Bernese Alps form the backdrop for the Balmeregghorn.

Beyond the cross follow the trail, marked with red and white stakes, heading southwest along an undulating landscape atop the ridge. In places fencing along the southeast side of the ridge keeps livestock and hikers off eroded sections of the ridge crest.

At 3.9 miles the trail makes a short, steep descent to a junction at 4.0 miles where a trail branches to the right (north) to Melchsee-Frutt. We continue along the grassy ridge, following the trail as it climbs steep to moderately-steep grades to an overlook at the summit of the Balmeregghorn (7,398-ft.) at 4.5 miles. This is a great place to take a break and enjoy the splendid panoramic views in all directions.

Balmeregghorn to Planplatten (Meiringen)

- **Segment Stat:** 1.9 miles (one-way) from Balmeregghorn to Planplatten
- **Total Distance Engstlenalp to Planplatten:** 6.4 miles (one way)
- **Maximum Elevation:** 7,365-ft.
- **Elevation Gain/Loss:** -567-ft.

After taking in the views atop the Balmeregghorn continue on the trail as it descends along the ridge and soon reaches a signed junction with a path branching right toward Melchsee-Frutt and the top station for a chairlift in the Melchsee valley. We continue along the ridge in the direction of

Planplatten (1-hr 15-min), Reuti (3-hr 50-min) and Meiringen (5-hr). Planplatten is now visible to the southwest.

The trail descends steeply, traveling around a bowl beneath the rugged southeast flanks of the Rothorn. Beyond the bowl ascend on moderate grades up a narrow trail clinging to the Lauber's steep slopes. The trail seems exposed in places but is quite safe.

At 5.4 miles the grade briefly abates as the trail curves around a minor ridge. Beyond the ridge the path descends on moderately-easy grade along steep slopes, crossing several rockslides. The section of the trail is accompanied by great views of the peaks rising above the Gadmertal (Gadmer Valley) to the south.

At 5.8 miles the trail begins an easy traverse along the ridge leading to Planplatten. The trail drops down to and crosses a saddle on the ridge at 6.2 miles where a trail branches left (south) toward Schlafenbielen, Hasliberg and Reuti. Soon a second trail branches right (north) toward Magisalp, Reuti and Meiringen. Ignore both trails and continue along the ridge, climbing moderately steep grades to Planplatten (7,152-ft.) at 6.4 miles.

An overlook along the ridge just beyond Planplatten (7,365-ft.) offers an amazing panorama of the area's peaks and valleys. To the west the aquamarine waters of Lake Brienz lie cradled in a massive bowl at the foot of the Haslital valley. To the east the Sustenhorn towers over Sustenpass at the head of the Gadmertal while the Dammastock rises above the Trift Glacier to the south of the Sustenhorn. To the southwest, the Wetterhorn looms above the green meadows of Grosse Scheidegg while behind you to the northeast the Tallistock and Wendenstocke define the southeast wall of the Gental with Jochpass at its head.

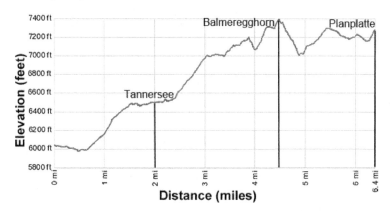

Hikers now have the option of taking the gondola from Planplatten to Reuti, with several changes required at mid stations, or walking down to Reuti. If you plan to hike to Reuti, walk to the viewpoint at Planplatten where signs point straight ahead to Gummenalp (1-hr) and Reuti (2-hr 10-min). The trail drops down the ridge and then turns right, descending on steep switchbacks through meadows and clusters of trees, losing over 3,800-

ft. in 4.6 miles on its way to Reuti. The path is obvious. If you are not sure which way to turn at an intersection, always head toward Reuti and in the direction of the green and blue Via Alpina signs with the number "1". Total hiking distance from Engstlenalp to Reuti is 11.0 miles.

At Reuti a cable car descends to Meiringen. Hiker who wish to walk should follow a well marked trail that drops steeply through pastures and forested hillsides, losing over 1,500-ft. in 2.0 miles on the way to Meiringen.

Trailhead Directions

From Meiringen: Take the bus from the Bahnhof (train station) bound for Engstlenalp. The ride takes about 55 minutes. Note: Check the schedule before departing from the bus stop. Some of the buses go directly to Engstlenalp. Otherwise, take the bus to Innertkirchen and then change to a bus headed for Engstlenalp. Check the SBB website or download the SBB app for the current schedule.

At Planplatten the gondola descends in 3 stages; Alpen Tower (Planplatten) to Magisalp, Magisalp to Bidmi and Bidmi to Reuti. At Reuti a cable car descends to Meiringen. See the Bergbahnen Meiringen-Hasliberg website for the current schedules and prices.

75. Other Trails in Meiringen
Near Meiringen in the Bernese Alps

75a) Rosenlaui Glacier Gorge

The path through the Rosenlaui Glacier Gorge, a UNESCO World Heritage site, ascends along the deep dramatic chasm carved by the Weissenbach River, passing pretty pools, waterfalls, grottoes and sculpted rock formations. The entrance fee is well worth the cost to see this natural wonder.

- **Distance:** 1.3 - 3.3 miles (round-trip)
- **Elevation:** 4,272-ft. at Gschwandtenmad
  4,357-ft. at the Rosenlaui Hotel
  4,990-ft. at High Point in the Gletscherschlucht
- **Elevation Gain:** 633-ft. - 718-ft.
- **Difficulty:** strenuous
- **Base camp:** Meiringen
- **Meiringen Map:** See page 349

Start the day by taking the post bus from the Meiringen Bahnhof (train station) heading toward Schwarzwaldalp and get off at the Rosenlaui Gletscherschlucht. The ride takes about 32 minutes. After paying the entrance fee follow the trail that climbs above the river with fine views of a waterfall. Soon the trail narrows and enters the gorge. The cement path now travels through passages and tunnels blasted out of the gorge's rock walls, climbing steps chiseled into the rock face and visiting overlooks cantilevered over the river. The gorges rugged walls, eroded into fantastical shapes in places, tower overhead.

Along the way the river spills through narrow chutes, plunges down ledges and churns along the riverbed beneath the walkway. Exposed sections ot the hike are safeguarded by metal railings permitting easy passage through the impressive gorge. At the end of the gorge views extend up the steep cliffs carved by the retreating glacier. The snout of the glacier is seen above the cliffs. Dossen looms overhead. When you are done taking in the views follow the return route that descends through forests back to the entry point for a 1.3 mile hike.

The hike can easily be extended by getting off the bus at Gschwandtenmad (27 minute trip) and then walking a mile up the valley to the Glacier Gorge accompanied by views of the Wellhorn and the tongue of the Rosenlaui Glacier. From the bus stop, cross the bridge to the east side of the river and then follow the Via Alpina trail (Alpine Pass Route) that ascends on easy grades alongside the Reichenbach River toward Rosenlaui. The trail initially travels through meadows with views of the surrounding peaks and then enters the forest where we lose the views. At 0.9 miles the trail passes by the Rosenlaui Hotel, a nice place to stop for refreshments, and then ascends more steeply to the Rosenlaui Gletscherschlucht (Glacier Gorge) at 1.0 mile. Total round-trip distance for this option is 3.3 miles.

Alternatively, start at Kaltenbrunnen (23 minute ride from Meiringen) and then ascend to Rosenlaui through Gschwandtenmad. The initial section of this hike travels beside the road. Just before reaching Gschwandtenmad the valley opens up with great views of the Wellhorn and the Rosenlaui Glacier. Starting at Kaltenbrunnen add 2.0 mile (one-way) to the hike. Total round-trip distance is 4.3 miles.

Another option is to incorporate a visit to the Glacier Gorge on the hike to Grosse Scheidegg or First in Grindelwald. See hike 75c and 75d for more information.

75b) Hochmoor

Hochmoor, the highest protected moor in Europe, is located between 4,900-5,900-ft. beneath the northeast face of Tschingel, high above the southwest side of Meiringen. The area, once an Alpine Lake, has silted over and is now a bog with soft soils and vibrant vegetation. Small lakes and ponds lie scattered across the moor, set against a backdrop of granite peaks.

- **Distance:** 6.4 miles (round-trip) or 9.8 miles (semi-loop)
- **Elevation:** 3,985-ft. at Kaltenbrunnen
  6,148-ft. at the high point
  2,034-ft. at Willigen
- **Elevation Gain/Loss:** 2,163-ft./-4,114-ft.

- **Difficulty:** moderately-strenuous
- **Base camp:** Meiringen
- **Meiringen Map:** See page 349

Start the day by taking the post bus from the Meiringen Bahnhof (train station) toward Schwarzwaldalp and get off at the restaurant Kaltenbrunnen. The ride takes about 23 minutes. Walk southwest up the road (toward Rosenlaui and Schwarzwaldalp) a short distance and then turn right on a dirt road toward Obre Stafel (Obrer Stafel) and Waldenalp. The road crosses a bridge over the Reichenbach (river) and then ascends through Torblatz. After a short stretch traveling through forest turn left on a signed trail that climbs on moderately steep grades through meadows sprinkled with wildflowers and clusters of trees. As you climb enjoy views of the Engelhorner massif, the Wellhorn, Dossen, the Wetterhorn and the Rosenlaui Glacier to the south/southeast.

At 0.9 miles pass through Undre Stafel (Undere Stafel). Here we see the first signs for Hochmoor. The path now ascends west/northwest, passing through Obre Stafel at 2.1 miles. A short distance beyond the small hamlet the grade abates and you enter the beautiful moors of the nature reserve. The floor beneath your feet is soft and spongy. Small lakes and ponds are scattered across the area adorn in bog plants. The Engelhorner massif and the peaks rising to the north above Meiringen provide a stunning backdrop to the scene.

Reach the high point (6,148-ft.) of the hike at 3.2 miles. Hikers looking for a shorter/easier day can turn around here and return to Kaltenbrunnen. Otherwise we leave the moors behind as we continue along the trail toward Obersten Wandel. The path now descends steeply into a lovely meadow-clad bowl beneath the the Wandelhorn and the distinctive jagged point of Garzen. Reach the small alp at Obersten Wandel at 3.7 miles. A short distance beyond the trail curves to the right (north) and continues descending to Mittlesten (middle) Wandel, Untersten Wandel and Isetwald. As you descend views open to Lake Lungern to the north. The descent uses a combination of alp tracks and trails.

At Isetwald we bear right (east) on a trail descending through pastures. Soon the way continues on paved roads toward Falcheren. The final descend is along a forest path to Willigen at 9.8 miles. From Willigen either catch a bus or walk back to Meiringen.

If time and energy permit, take a detour or Reichenbachfall (Rychenbachfall), the site where Sir Arthur Conan Doyle's famous character, Sherlock Holmes, and his nemesis Moriarty plunged over the falls.

75c) Meiringen to Grosse Scheidegg

From Meiringen, a long climb up the Reichenbach Valley on the Via Alpina (Alpine Pass Route) leads to Grosse Scheidegg. The best views start after Gschwantemad, where meadows offer vistas of the Engelhorner massif, the Wellhorn, Dossen and the Rosenlaui Glacier. As the trail gains elevation the Wetterhorn, towering over Grosse Scheidegg, dominates the views. Along the way the trail ascends along the Reichenbach River, travels through forests, passes bucolic alps and traverses pretty meadows.

Portions of the path travel along or near the road ascending the valley. Thankfully this road is closed to private traffic so you will only see post buses and bikes. The trip can be shortened by taking the post bus up the valley to Kaltenbrunnen, Gschwandtenmad, Rosenlaui, Schwarzwaldalp or any other intermediate stop of the bus route.

- **Distance:** 5.6 miles from Kaltenbrunnen to Grosse Scheidegg (one-way)

  8.7 miles from Meiringen to Grosse Scheidegg (one-way)
- **Elevation:** 1,952-ft. at Meiringen

  4,000-ft. at Kaltenbrunnen

  4,272-ft. at Gschwandtenmad

  4,357-ft. at the Rosenlaui

  4,774-ft. at Schwarzwaldalp

  6,452-ft. at Grosse Scheidegg
- **Elevation Gain:** 2,452-ft. Kaltenbrunnen to Grosse Scheidegg

  4,500-ft. Mieringen to Grosse Scheidegg
- **Difficulty:** strenuous
- **Base camp:** Meiringen or Grindelwald
- **Meiringen Map:** See page 349

From the Meiringen Bahnhof (train station), follow signs to Rosenlaui and Grosse Scheidegg that lead to the main street. Turn right and head southeast through town. The road will curve to the right and become Alpbachstrasse. You will see #1 Via Alpina (Alpine Pass Route) signs along the way.

At 0.6 miles cross a bridge over the Aare River and then follow a walkway that leads through Willigen. Soon you will see a signpost that point right to a road ascending between houses. Follow the road and then a path that climbs steeply through meadows and trees into the Reichenbach Valley. The trail shortcuts long switchbacks along the road. Occasionally crossing the road and briefly following the road. Along the way pass the restaurant at Schwendi and the buildings in Zwirgi. Keep on track by following the signs pointing toward Grosse Scheidegg.

At 2.3 miles the grade abates as the path travels above or along the road. Here we get our first views of the high peaks ahead. A short distance beyond we reach the restaurant at Kaltenbrunnen at 3.1 miles. A short stint along the road leads to a trail that ascends on comfortable grades through trees near the river, occasionally crossing the road. As you near Gschwantenmad wonderful views open to the Wellhorn, Dossen, the Wetterhorn and the Rosenlaui Glacier.

Pass the tiny hamlet of Gschwantenmad at 4.1 miles. Soon the path reenters the trees, reaching the Rosenlaui hotel and restaurant at 5.0 miles. The trail now curves to the left and soon reaches the Gletscherschlucht (Rosenlaui Glacier Gorge). See hike 75a (above) for more information.

At the glacier gorge our route swings to the right and continues up the valley, passing Broch before arriving at the signpost at Schwarzwaldalp at 6.2 miles. This section of the trail offers fine views of the Wetterhorn. Beyond Schwarzwaldalp the trail moves away from the road and ascends on steeper grades along the east side of the Reichenbach Valley to Teiffenmatten, where the trail turns right (west), crosses the river and soon reaches the road. The path crosses the road and then turns left, ascending up the valley. Soon the path crosses the road again at post bus stop in Alpiglen at 7.5 miles.

The road now climbs a series of switchbacks up to Grosse Scheidegg. Our path ascends on moderately steep grades on a path that takes a more direct route shortcutting the switchbacks on the road. The final push to the pass is accompanied by fine views down the Reichenbach valley and great views of rugged slopes of the Wellhorn and glacier-clad Wetterhorn towering above the trail to the east/southeast.

Reach the hotel and restaurant at Grosse Scheidegg at 8.7 miles. Walk a short distance northwest along the ridge to enjoy the panoramic views of the Bernese Alps. The Mattenberg, Monch and the Eiger dominate the views to the southwest. The Wetterhorn towers above the saddle while below the village of Grindelwald lies cradled in an emerald green basin, bound to the west by the Mannlichen ridge. Behind you are fine views down the Reichenbach Valley toward Meiringen.

From the pass you can follow the Alpine Pass Route descending to Grindelwald, take a bus to Meiringen or Grindelwald or follow the highly scenic trail to First. I recommend the trail to First. See Hike 42 - Grosse Scheidegg to First for more information.

75d) Rosenlaui or Schwarzwaldalp to Grosse Scheidegg or First

This scenic trail to Grosse Scheidegg, an alternative to the Alpine Pass Route, eliminates the initial climb from Meiringen to Rosenlaui. At Schwarzwaldalp, the path climbs above the north side of the Reichenbach Valley with great views of the Wetterhorn and neighboring peaks. The day can easily be extends by continuing the hike to First with breathtaking views of the glacier-clad peaks towering above Grindelwald. Get an early start and include a trip up the dramatic Rosenlaui Glacier Gorge.

- **Distance:** 3.6 - 6.6 miles (one-way)
- **Elevation:** 4,357-ft. at the Rosenlaui
  4,774-ft. at Schwarzwaldalp
  6,592-ft. at High Point on the Grosse Scheidegg Ridge

6,452-ft. at Grosse Scheidegg
7,110-ft. at First

- **Elevation Gain:** 1,818-ft. - 2,753-ft.
- **Difficulty:** moderate
- **Base camp:** Meiringen or Grindelwald
- **Meiringen Map:** See page 349

The Alpine Pass Route between Meiringen and Rosenlaui climbs predominantly through forest near or along the road traveling up the Reichenbach Valley. Beyond Rosenlaui the trail ascends through forests and meadows along the valley floor. Open areas offer fine views of the high peaks rimming the valley as the trail climbs to Grosse Scheidegg. A better alternative is to take the post bus to either Rosenlaui or Schwarzwaldalp and then walk to Grosse Scheidegg or First via Scheidegg-Oberlager. This option ascends along the north slopes of the valley with great views of the glacier-clad Wetterhorn, the Wellhorn and the Engelhorner massif.

Start the day by boarding the bus at the Meiringen Bahnhof bound for Schwarzwaldalp and get off at Rosenlaui Hotel (31 minute ride). For a shorter hike continue on the bus to Schwarzwaldalp (40 minutes). For this description we will start at Rosenlaui. If starting from Schwarzwaldalp subtract 1.2 miles from the mileage listed in this description.

The Rosenlaui Hotel is a circa 1771 Victorian hotel and restaurant restored to its original grandeur. From the hotel, follow the #1 Via Alpina (Alpine Pass Route) toward Grosse Scheidegg. The path heads south for short distance to the Gletscherschlucht (Rosenlaui Glacier Gorge). If time and energy allow, I recommend paying the fee and taking the 1.3 mile walk up of the dramatic gorge carved by meltwater from the Rosenlaui Glacier. See hike 75a (above) for more details.

At the Gorge follow the Alpine Pass trail that curves to the right and continues up the valley, passing Broch before arriving at the signpost at Schwarzwaldalp at 1.2 miles. This section of the trail offers fine views of the Wetterhorn. Turn right (north) at the junction, leaving the Alpine Pass Route, and head to the road going up the valley. At the road turn left and then walk up the road a short distance to a junction with the path to Oberlager at 1.5 miles. Turn right (northwest) toward Oberlager. A good path now ascends through trees. At 2.1 miles the trees give way to pretty meadow beneath the east facing slopes of the Schwarzhorn. To the south the Wetterhorn and Wellhorn soar above the valley while the Hengsteren Glacier lies cradled in a bowl beneath the peaks.

The path now ascends across the meadows and then climbs on moderately steep grades through scattered trees and then meadows to Scheidegg-Oberlager at 3.25 miles. Along the way the trail crosses a creek and enjoys more fine views of the summits towering above the south side of the valley. Vistas extend down the Reichenbach Valley to the Engelhorner massif and beyond.

At Oberlager the grade abates and the trail ascends on gentle grades up an alp road to a junction on the ridge extending northwest from Grosse Scheidegg at 4.0 miles. Here stunning views open to the Wetterhorn, Mattenberg and Eiger towering above the Grindelwald Valley. Grindelwald lies nestled along the valley floor. The Mannlichen Ridge rises to the west. Behind you are sublime views stretching down the length of the Reichenbach Valley.

At the junction a wide track heads left (south/southeast) on easy grades to Grosse Scheidegg at 4.8 miles where buses and a trail descend to Grindelwald. To the right a track drops to Schreckfeld, First and the Faulhorn. To continue the hike we turn right on the Hohenweg 2400 trail, which ascends above the right side of the road toward First and the Faulhorn. The trail now travels through meadows high above the Grindelwald Valley with splendid, nonstop views of the 4,000-meter peaks, glacial cirques and deep gorges to the south of Grindelwald. The going will be slow along this segment of the trail as you will stop often to soak in the scene.

The path reaches First (7,110-ft.) at 6.6 miles. First features a popular restaurant with a sun terrace and a "Cliff Walk", a cantilevered metal walkway bolted to the sheer west face of the First summit that leads to a 150-ft. long viewing platform with panoramic views of the peaks towering above the south side of the valley. The walkway connects with the restaurant's sun terrace where signs identify the peaks. At First, take the multistage gondola down to Grindelwald. See Hike 42 - Grosse Scheidegg to First for more information. There is also a trail that loses over 3,700-ft. as it descends from First to Grindelwald.

76. A Multi-day Hike on the Alpine Pass Route - Altdorf to Kandersteg ★★★★★
In the Bernese Alps and the Central Swiss Alps

The Alpine Pass Route (aka Via Alpina) is the quintessential long distance hike in Switzerland, traveling through some of the finest scenery in the Bernese Alps. This shortened, modified version of the walk between Altdorf and Kandersteg encompasses the most spectacular segments of the trip.

Each day the walk crosses a panoramic pass with far reaching vistas. Trails to the passes travel through magical landscapes of lush meadows, verdant forests, soaring peaks and glistening glaciers, accompanied by a soundtrack of cowbells, birdsong and cascading streams.

The hike can be accomplished nonstop in 7 to 8 days or done in smaller segments. Alternatively, stop in some of the villages along the way for an extra day or two to rest or explore recommended day hikes in the area.

When possible, the route utilizes buses to avoid walking along roads. Cable cars, gondolas and chairlifts can be employed to reduce the elevation gain or avoid steep downhill stretches at the end of the day.

Every day starts and ends in an interesting village, small town or resort along a valley floor. Hikers can choose from a range of lodging options at the destinations. Most offer a variety of restaurants, bakeries, groceries and shops. Alternatively hikers can decide to stay at one of the many huts or berghotels (mountain hotels) along the trail, spending the night in an intimate setting surrounds by spectacular scenery.

It does rain, and occasionally snow, in the Bernese Alps so be prepared with the proper clothing and equipment. As with any mountain area, the weather can get bad enough to make hiking over a high pass a miserable affair or even dangerous. Public transportation allows you to easily travel to the next valley should you hit bad weather. These "escape routes" are described for each segment of the trip.

For an overview map of the route see the Bernese Alps and Central Switzerland Map on page 208.

The Alpine Pass Route (Via Alpina) from Altdorf to Kandersteg

Starting Point: This trip begins in Altdorf near the foot of the Reuss Valley, to the south of Lake Lucerne. From Zurich purchase a train ticket to Altdorf. Depending on the departure time, there are direct trains to Altdorf or you may need to change in Zug. The trip takes about one hour and 20 minutes.

Day 1:

Hike 69 - Klausen Pass to Biel or Eggberge (Altdorf): This is a good warmup hike for the days ahead. Take the bus from Altdorf to Klausen Pass. From the pass the Alpine Pass Route (#1 Via Alpina on trail signs) travels high above the north side of the Schachental Valley with panoramic views of the Glarus Alps to the south and the rugged cliffs of the Schachentaler Windgallen massif overhead.

Our route deviates from the standard Alpine Pass Route by staying high above the valley floor. End the day at Biel, a 9.5 mile hike, or Eggberge, a 13.9 mile walk. At both Biel and Eggberge cable cars descend to the valley floor and connect with buses back to Altdorf. I recommend ending the day at Biel. Some turn this into a two-day walk, staying at the Berggasthaus Biel (rooms and dormitories), the Berggasthaus Eggberge (rooms and dormitories) or other small inns on route. Overnight: Altdorf

Extra Days in Altdorf: There are several scenic day hikes in the Altdorf area. See the Altdorf section of the guide for details.

Day 2:

Hike 72 - Altdorf to Engelberg over Surenen Pass: This day starts with a bus ride to Attinghausen and then a cable car ride to Brusti. The Alpine Pass Trail ascends through forest and then pretty meadows framed by rugged peaks to Surenen Pass, where Titlis and the Schloss and Spannort massifs dominate the view. The descent to Engelberg features more fine views of the high peaks towering above the Surenen Valley.

Starting the hike in Brusti, by using available transport, results in an 8.9 mile day with a 2,513-ft. elevation gain and 4,229-ft. loss. To walk the entire route is 17.2 miles. Accommodations along the route include the Brusti Berggasthaus (rooms and dormitories), Alpbeizli Blackenalp (dormitories) and the Berggasthaus Stafelialp (dormitories). Overnight: Engelberg (small resort with a full complement of accommodations, restaurants and services.)

Bad Weather Transport: At the Altdorf train station purchase a ticket for Engelberg. Trains travel from Altdorf to Lucerne where you will need to change for the train to Altdorf. During certain times of day there may be an additional change in Arth-Goldau. The ride takes two hours and 16 minutes. Luzerne is an interesting place to spend a few hours before traveling to Engelberg.

Day 3:

Hike 73a - Engelberg to Engstlenalp over Jochpass (7.8 miles) and Hike 74 – Engstlenalp to Meirgingen (6.4 – 11.0 miles): Many take 2 days to do this segment of the walk, hiking over Jochpass to the Engstlenalp, overnighting at the Hotel Engstlenalp and then walking to Meiringen following the directions in Hike 74.

The Alpine Pass Route to Jochpass features some nice views of the Trubsee, glacier-clad Titlis and the surrounding peaks but sections of the trail travel beneath or near ski lifts. I recommend taking one day to do this segment by taking the lifts to the Trubsee and then hiking to Jochpass, Engstlenalp and Meiringen for an 11.4 mile day. Mileage on this day can be reduced by taking the lift systems all the way to Jochpass and then walking to Meiringen for an 8.8 mile day.

The beautiful hike from Engstlenalp to Planplatten or Meiringen is not to be missed. The trail travels along steep slopes and high ridges above the northwest side of the Gental Valley with amazing views of the summits lining the Gental Valley and the Bernese Alps. Overnight: Meiringen.

Bad Weather Transport: Purchase a ticket from Engelberg to Meiringen. The route requires a change of trains in Lucerne, an interesting place to spend a few hours before traveling on to Meiringen.

Day 4:

Hike 75c - Meiringen to Grosse Scheidegg: This is another day with route choices. Large portions of this segment of the Alpine Pass Route travels along or near the road ascending the Reichenbach Valley to Grosse

Scheidegg and then descend along or near the road down the Lutschine Valley to Grindelwald.

These roads are not busy, since they are only used by post buses and bikes. Views on the 8.7 milehike to Grosse Scheidegg begin half way up the trail. The entire walk to Grindelwald is 14.3 miles. This is a long day you might want to break into two by staying at Schwarzwaldalp (private rooms and dormitories), 6.2 miles from Meiringen. Hikers splitting the route into two days should consider including Hike 75a –the Rosenlaui Glacier Gorge on the first day.

Unless you are a purist my recommended alternative for this portion of the Alpine Pass Route is to take a bus to Rosenlaui or Schwarzwaldalp in the Reichenbah Valley. Beyond Schwarzwaldalp follow Hike 75d - Rosenlaui (Meiringen) to Grindelwald, which branches off from the main Alpine Pass Route and travels high above the north side of the Reichenbach Valley with better views of the Wetterhorn and neighboring peaks than the traditional route that stays near the valley floor and road.

The trail crosses the ridge to the northwest of Gross Scheidegg, the traditional crossing to Grindelwald. As the trail crests the ridge great views open to the spectacular wall of peaks and glistening glaciers towering above the south side of Grindelwald. From here the path follows a high route to First accompanied by breathtaking views of the glacier-clad peaks soaring above Grindelwald. This 6.6 mile hike from Rosenlaui gains 2,753-ft. With an early start hikers can also visit the Rosenlaui Glacier Gorge (Hike 75a). From First a series of gondolas descend to Grindelwald. Overnight: Grindelwald.

Alternatively, you can take the bus all the way to Grosse Scheidegg and follow Hike 43 - Grosse Scheidegg to Bussalp: a highly scenic walk with panoramic views of the 4,000-meter peaks, glacial cirques and deep gorges to the south side of Grindelwald. From Bussalp regularly scheduled buses descend to Grindelwald. Overnight: Grindelwald.

Extra Days in Grindelwald: There are several terrific hikes in the Grindelwald area. If time and energy permit I suggest taking Hike 46 – First to Schynige Platte, one of best day hikes in area. See the Grindelwald section of the guide for more information.

Bad Weather Transport: At the Meiringen Bahnhof (train station) purchase a ticket to Grindelwald Bahnhof (train station). Take the train from Grindelwald to Interlaken Ost and then change to the train to Grindelwald. Half the cars on the train will be labeled for Grindelwald and the other half for Lauterbrunnen. Make sure you get on a car labeled for your destination. At Zweilutschinen the train literally splits in half with half the train going to Grindelwald and the other half heading for Lauterbrunnen. Interlaken is an interesting place to spend a few hours before traveling on to Grindelwald. The ride takes one hour and 21 minutes.

Day 5:

Hike 48 – Mannlichen (Grindelwald) to Wengen (Lauterbrunnen) over Kleine Scheidegg: The triad of giants: the Eiger, Monch and Jungfrau are the stars of the show on this stunning hike. The traditional Alpine Pass Route basically follows the course of the cog railway from Grindelwald to Kleine Scheidegg. This Mannlichen to Wengen variation is more scenic, incorporating the Panoramaweg from Mannlichen (accessible via a gondola) to Kleine Scheidegg. The route also deviates from the traditional route from Kleine Scheidegg to Wengen that descends along or near the cog railway to Wengen by first visiting the Eiger Glacier Viewpoint and then traveling through Biglenalp, with stunning, close-up views of the Eiger and the Monch. Save you knees for the next day by taking the cog railway from Murren to Lauterbrunnen, which eliminates 1,580-ft. elevation loss. Overnight: Lauterbrunnen.

Note: Hikers who have already done the traditional Alpine Pass Route from Grindelwald to Murren should consider replacing the walk with Hike 46 – First to Schynige Platte. Fit hikers can do this walk in one day. Others might want to break the walk into two days by spending the a night at the Faulhorn (private rooms and dormitories) featuring superb views of the peaks rising above Grindelwald and Lauterbrunnen.

Extra Days in Lauterbrunnen: There is a lot of great day hiking in Lauterbrunnen. See the Lauterbrunnen section of the guide for more information.

Bad Weather Transport: Take the train from Grindelwald to Zweilutschinen and then change to the train to Lauterbrunnen. The ride takes 41 minutes. You can also take the train to Interlaken Ost, tour around for the day and then take the train from Interlaken Ost to Lauterbrunnen.

Day 6

Hike 57 - (Lauterbrunnen) Murren to Griesalp over Sefinenfurgge: This splendid hike, crossing the second highest pass on the Alpine Pass Route, features impressive views of the Eiger, Monch and Jungfrau along with the high peaks towering above the Lauterbrunnen, Sefinen and Kiental Valleys. Overnight: Griesalp.

Bad Weather Transport: The train trip from Lauterbrunnen to Griesalp requires three changes. From Lauterbrunnen travel to Interlaken Ost and then change to a train to Spiez. In Speiz, change to a train going to Reichenbach. In Reichenbach, board a mini bus to Griesalp and get off at the last stop.

Day 7:

Hike 59 - Griesalp to Kandersteg over Hohturli Pass: This hike crossing Hohturli Pass, the highest pass on the Alpine Pass Route, is the most challenging day on the trip. The 9.1 mile hike gaining 4,790-ft. in elevation includes captivating vistas of the high peaks towering above the Kiental and Kandertal Valleys. The hike can be broken into two days by staying at the Bluemlisalp Hut (4.1 miles from Griesalp), set atop a rock knoll above the Hohturli Pass with terrific views of the Bluemlisalp Glacier and the high peaks in the surrounding valleys. Overnight: Kandersteg.

Extra Days in Kandersteg: There are plenty of terrific day hikes in Kandersteg, including the walks to Adelboden (below), which can easily be done from Kandersteg with a return in the afternoon to your lodging. See the Kandersteg section of the guide for more information.

Bad Weather Transport: From Griesalp take the minibus to the Reichenbach train station. At the station board a train to Kandersteg. The ride should take two hours.

Day 8: (Optional)

Hike 68b - Kandersteg to Adelboden over the Bunderchrinde: This is the traditional Alpine Pass Route to Adelboden with fine views of the glacier-clad cirque towering above the Oeschinensee area, the Gastern Valley and the summits rising above Adelboden. The 7.2 mile hike, using the cable car to Allmenalp, gains 2,700-ft. and loses 3,924-ft. Walking up to Allmenalp increases the elevation gain to 3,642-ft.

A demanding and very scenic alternative to the Alpine Pass Route is Hike 64 – Sunnbuel (Kandersteg) to Engstligenalp (Adelboden). This challenging day features panoramic views of the high peaks towering above the Spittelmatte, Uschene and Engstligenalp Valleys. The path is best suited for sure footed hikers who like demanding trails that cross exposed passes, travel along airy ridges and include steep ascents and descents. A cable car to Sunnbuel and then a cable car and bus from Engstligenalp to Adelboden (or back to Kandersteg) reduce the mileage and elevation gain on the hike.

Discount Cards

Look into getting a Swiss Travel Pass or a Swiss Half Card if you plan to take advantage of the buses and lifts along the Alpine Pass Route. It could save you money. See Appendix A for more information.

Luggage Transfers

Dealing with luggage is always an issue when hiking point to point. There are services that will move your luggage but they are VERY expensive. In Switzerland there are two other choices. Hikers with a Half Card (See Discount Cards in Appendix A), can ship luggage between major stations for a small fee. For example, hikers can send a bag from the Altdorf train station to the Grindelwald train station. Alternatively, hikers with a valid ticket can also use the service. So if you don't have a half card it might be worthwhile to purchase a ticket for the trip between Altdorf and Grindelwald (even through you won't use the ticket) and then pay the small fee to ship a bag or two. Read the Luggage section in Appendix A for more information.

The Engadine and Davos

Best Hiking Trails near St. Moritz, Scuol and Davos

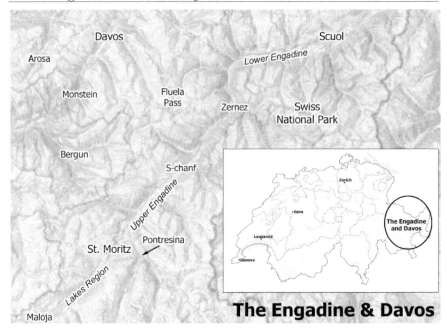

Davos
Arosa
Lower Engadine
Scuol
Monstein
Fluela Pass
Zernez
Swiss National Park
Bergun
S-chanf
Upper Engadine
St. Moritz
Pontresina
Lakes Region
Maloja

Zurich
•Bern
Lausanne
•Geneva
The Engadine and Davos

The Engadine & Davos

Online Engadine/Davos Map: www.hikingwalking.com/engadine-davos

The Engadine, the valley of the River Inn, is located in the Graubunden canton in eastern Switzerland. The valley offers a multitude of great hiking trails from easy walks along beautiful lakes to the moderate jaunts between rustic villages. Strenuous hikes climb over scenic passes with stunning views of glacier-clad peaks and travel up tranquil valleys amid rugged summits. Home to the country's only national park along with the jet-set ski-resort of St. Moritz, the Engadine offers a little something for everyone.

The Engadine is divided into the Upper Engadine and the Lower Engadine. This guide covers the Upper Engadine Lakes District from its headwaters above Maloja to St. Moritz. Also included is the beautiful Bernina Valley, extending southeast from its confluence with the Upper Engadine to Bernina Pass above Lake Bianco, along with Bernina's major side valleys.

The great hikes in the Lower Engadine are located between Lavin and Sur En with the town of Scuol as the recommended base camp. Adjacent side valleys: Tuoi, Tasna and S-charl, along with areas in the Swiss National Park, are home to additional scenic hikes that link with the trail systems in the main valley.

Davos, also in the canton of Graubunden, is located in the Landwasser Valley to the west of the Engadine. The resort is set amid the peaks of the

Plessur, Albula and the Silvretta ranges. A network of splendid hikes crisscross the region, traversing high routes, ascending stunning valleys clad in beautiful meadows and crossing panoramic pass with breathtaking views. Three side valleys: Fluela, Dischma and Sertig, extending east/southeast from the Landwasser Valley, feature some of the most beautiful hikes in the area.

German and Romansh are the primary languages in the Engadine and Davos. In Davos and St. Moritz most people managing accommodations, running restaurants or providing other tourist services also speak English. The Lower Engadine is off the tourist circuit so you may encounter situations where English is not spoken.

The Lower Engadine is a haven for the Romansh language, Switzerland's fourth official language in addition to German, French and Italian. Romansh, a native language derived from Latin, is actively fostered in the Lower Engadine. Here the language is spoken at home, taught in schools and used in signage on shops, businesses and trails.

The Engadine is also special because of its architecture. Many of the charming villages in the Engadine have well preserved traditional homes decorated with Sgraffiti, an artisanal craft that paints and/or etches designs into wet plaster. The best preserved homes are found in Lower Engadine villages of Guarda, Ardez and the center of Scuol.

St. Moritz
Location: In the Canton of Graubunden in the Upper Engadine Valley

Mention St. Moritz and what comes to mind is a luxury resort catering to the rich and famous. But anyone who has visited the St. Moritz area in the summer will tell you the area's real wealth lies in the its majestic mountains, shimmering lakes and glorious forests and meadows.

St Moritz sprawls along the south facing slopes of Piz Nair and around Lake St. Moritz near the foot of the Upper Engadine Lakes District. The Lake District is composed of four gorgeous lakes linked by the River Inn between Maloja, the village the head of the valley, and St. Moritz. The Bernina Alps tower above the valley to the southeast while the Albula Alps fill the skyline to the northwest. Small villages lie amid pretty meadows along the valley floor.

Down valley (northeast) from St. Moritz a broad floodplain between the villages of Celerina and Samedan marks the confluence of the Upper Engadine with Val Bernina (Bernina Valley). The impressive Bernina Valley stretches southeast from the confluence to Bernina Pass. On the southwest side of the valley two stunning side valleys: Roseg and Morteratsch, rimmed by magnificent glacier-clad peaks, extend south into the Bernina Alps. A rugged wall of summits, anchored by Piz Muragl and Piz Languard, towers above the valley to the northeast.

The Upper Engadine and Val Bernina are a hiker's paradise with plenty of excellent trails ranging from easy strolls along the beautiful lakes to moderate jaunts ascending through tranquil valleys to strenuous hikes climbing to scenic huts and crossing panoramic passes with see forever views. Funiculars, cable cars, chairlifts and gondolas transport hikers high above the valley floor, facilitating walks through this magical landscape. Buses and train lines link the resort and villages in the two valleys with the various lifts and trailheads.

About St. Moritz

St. Moritz is composed of two areas: St. Moritz Dorf located on the hillside above the northwest side of Lake St. Moritz and St. Moritz Bad situated around the south end of Lake St. Moritz. Developments between the two areas have created a sprawling resort with a wide assortment of accommodations, restaurants, bars and shops along with every conceivable service a tourist could require. Bad is the place to look for less expensive accommodations.

The Bahnhof (train station) and the adjacent Engadine Bus station (https://engadinbus.ch/linienplan), with lines linking almost every corner of the Upper Engadine and Val Bernina, is situated along the valley floor on the north side of Lake St. Moritz. The center of St. Moritz Dorf is found on the hillside above the station and is linked to the valley floor by a series of escalators accessible from an indoor car park to the west of the train station. From the train station the #1 and #9 buses climb switchbacks up Via Serlas to a traffic circle in Dorf and then head to Schulhausplatz, another major transfer point for buses lines to various locations in the village and the valley.

From the traffic circle and Schulhausplatz streets and walkways spin off in all directions. From Schulhausplatz, Plazza da Scoula heads northeast to Via Maistra, home to high end hotels, boutiques and expensive shops. Via dal Bagn branches southwest from the traffic circle, descending to the valley floor and St. Moritz Bad at the south end of the lake. On the valley floor a pretty walkway around Lake St. Moritz links the train station to St. Moritz Bad.

The Tourist Office (stmoritz.com/en/) at the train station is a good place to get maps and other information. A second tourist office is located in Dorf at Via Maistra 12. There are two Coop Supermarkets in the resort, one in Dorf on Plazza da Scoula to the northeast of Schulhausplatz and a second larger Coop Supermarket Bellevue near the southwest end of the lake at Via dal Bagn 18. Smaller stores include a Denner Express near the Coop Bellevue and a Migrolino at the train station. The Backerei-Konditorei Bad, to the south of the Coop Bellevue at Via dal Bagn 4, is recommended for bread and confections.

In addition to St. Moritz, the charming villages of Sils Maria and Maloja, up valley from St, Moritz, offer hotels, pensions, guesthouses and vacation apartment as do the areas at the base of the lifts, such as Surlej. There are either small groceries or convenience stores in the villages. Buses link the villages to St. Moritz, the train station and lines servicing Val Bernina. Down valley Celerina and Samedan offer more reasonably priced lodging. There is a Coop and Volg grocery in Celerina and a Coop and Avec in Samedan. These two villages are linked to St. Moritz via trains and buses.

In the summer lifts operating in the Upper Engadine Lakes District include Surlej-Corvatsch, which climbs to Murtel where a trail ascends to Fuorcla Surlej (Surlej Pass). A second cable car takes sightseers to the Corvatsch overlook. The Sils-Furtschellas cable car at Sils Maria ascends to the Furtschellas Station where a network of trails travels to various points along the southeast side of the Upper Engadine Valley. Lifts from St. Moritz take mountain bikers to a series of bike friendly trails in the Piz Nair/Corviglia area. (The Piz Nair area is not covered in this guide.)

Pontresina, a resort located near the foot of Val Bernina, is laid-back alternative to St. Moritz. The resort, nestled along the sunny slopes on the northeast side of the valley, is centered along Via Maistra and its adjacent side streets. Here you will find some luxury hotels but also a good number of less costly hotels, pensions, guesthouses and vacation apartments along with restaurants and shops. A Coop Supermarket is situated at Via da Mulin at the south end of the village.

The Pontresina Bahnhof (train station) with trains to St. Moritz and other destinations in the Bernina Valley is located across the valley. Via Da la Staziun links the train station to the village. A bus stop is situated on the northeast side of the station. Buses routes travel along the resort's main street and then head to St. Moritz and other locations in the Upper Engadine Valley.

Near the foot of Val Bernina is the Funicular to Muottas Muragl that connects with trails along the northeast side of valley. A chairlift from Pontresina ascends to Alp Languard and the trail network from Muottas Muragl. Further up Val Bernina the Bernina Diavolezza Cable Car whisks tourist to the scenic overlook atop Diavolezza.

Hikers staying for more that one night in the St. Moritz / Pontresina area should check into the Free Mountain Railway pass offered by participating hotels and holiday apartments during the summer. Visitors staying at accommodations that don't offer the pass can purchase a discounted pass. The pass only makes sense for hikers that will be riding lifts daily and using some of the more expensive lifts, such as cable cars going to Covatsch and Diavolezza.

Hiking around St. Moritz, the Upper Engadine and Val Bernina

The delightful walk along Lake Silvaplana and Lake Sils (Hike 77), located to the southwest of St. Moritz, features lovely views of the high peaks towering above the Upper Engadine Valley. Along the southeast side of the valley the cable car from Surlej to Murtel connects with the trail crossing panoramic Fuorcla Surlej (Hike 78) that links with paths to Coaz Huts and beautiful Roseg Valley (Hike 78). Further up the valley take the cable car to Furtschellas for a scenic hike to Lake Sgrischus and Piz Chuern (Hike 79).

A great point to point hike from the Julier Pass area (on the road leading west from Silvaplana) crosses Grevasalvas Pass (Hike 80), a saddle high above the northwest side of the Upper Engadine. From the pass a trail descends into the Upper Engadine Valley and visits Lake Lunghin and/or drops down to destinations along Lake Sils including Maloja, Plaun da Lej or Sils-Baselgia. Reverse the directions to ascend the northwest side of the Upper Engadine Valley to the hamlet of Grevasalvas, Lake Lunghin and/or Fuorcla Grevasalvas.

In Val Bernina the Muottas Muragl Funicular links to trails heading to Segantini Hut (Hike 81) and the high trails above Alp Languard (Hike 82), all with superb views of the high peaks of the Bernina and Upper Engadine Valleys. Peak baggers will want to ride the Alp Languard chairlift to facilitate the hike to the summit of Piz Languard (Hike 83) with breathtaking 360-degree views of the high peaks in Eastern Switzerland. Alternatively, get off the beaten path with a hike to Fuorcla Pischa (Hike 84).

Other terrific trails in Val Bernina climb the Morteratsch Valley to Boval Hut (Hike 85). Reverse the directions in the hike to Fuorcla Surlej to ascend Val Roseg for a pleasant ramble to the Hotel Roseg Glacier or a harder hike to Fuorcla Surlej or the Coaz Hut (Hike 78).

Getting to St. Moritz

From the Zurich Airport or Zurich Bahnhof (train station) take the train to St. Moritz. The most efficient route requires a change of trains in Chur. The trip takes about three hours and 26 minutes from Zurich.

The train trip from the Geneva Airport or Gare (train station) goes through Zurich and Chur before arriving in St. Moritz. It is a long ride taking over six hours.

Check the SBB website (sbb.ch/en) /SBB app for directions from other parts of the country.

Nearby Attractions & Rainy Day Activities

On a rainy day visitors to the Upper Engadine and Bernina Valleys can explore one or more of the **20 museums** in the area. Check out the list on the St. Moritz Tourism Site.

Lifts around the St. Moritz areas whisk sightseers to overlooks with incredible views of the Bernina Alps, Albula Alps and beyond. Overlooks to consider include **Diavolezza** in Val Bernina and **Corvatsch** and **Piz Nair** in the Upper Engadine.

Take a walk or a bike ride from Sils-Maria up **Val Fex**. The valley is a protected landscape free of lifts, power lines and holiday homes. The walk ascends through forests, pastures and meadows, visiting a few idyllic hamlets along the way. A road, only open to alp vehicles, ascends the valley to Alp Muot Selvas, an off the beaten path destination with a restaurant and fine views of the valley.

A stroll around the **lakes in the Upper Engadine Valley** is the perfect way to spend a day off. Lake St. Moritz is know for its sailboats while Lake Silvaplana is a favorite spot to watch wind surfers. Each lake has its own personality and offers a variety of beautiful spots for a picnic or simply to stop and laze along the lakeshore. Early in the morning the lakes are a photographer's delight, perfectly reflecting the surrounding peaks.

Other great options for a day off include taking a stroll around Sils-Maria, Pontresina or St. Moritz.

Visit **Chur**, the oldest city in Switzerland, on a rainy day. The city is located two hours by train from St. Moritz. While there explore the old town, a car free section of the city, with a variety of museums, galleries, old churches, restaurants and bars to keep you entertained.

Good Things to Know about St. Moritz

- The main languages in St. Moritz are German and Romansh. Visitors from all over the world visit St. Moritz so you will find anyone dealing with tourists able to speak a variety of languages including English and French.
- There are three campgrounds in the Upper Engadine Lakes District: TSC Camping St. Moritz between St. Moritz Bad and Lake Champfer, Camping Silvaplana at the northwest end of the Lake Silvaplana and Camping Maloja at the southeast end of Lake Sils. Down valley Camping Gravatscha at the north end of Samedan includes 9 bungalows while TSC Camping Samedan is located at the confluence of the Upper Engadine with Val Bernina. In the Bernina Valley Camping Morteratsch is located a short distance down valley from the Morteratsch Bahnhof (train station).

- There are two youth hostels in St. Moritz. The Swiss Youth Hostel in St. Moritz Bad is located at Via Surpont 60 (to the south of Lake St. Moritz) and offers private rooms and four person dorms. The nearest bus stop is St. Moritz Bad, Sonne. From the stop walk south to the corner and then turn left on Via Surpont. The Hostel by Randolins, located on the south facing slopes to the west of St. Moritz at Via Curtins 2, provides private rooms and dormitory accommodations. They offer pickup service from the train station. The Somplaz bus stop is a 17 minute walk from the hostel.
- The Swiss Youth Hostel in Pontresina is situated across from the Pontresina Bahnhof (train station) on the west side of Val Bernina. The facility offers both private and shared rooms.
- There are numerous huts and mountain lodges in the Engadine. Note: This list includes huts down valley from St. Moritz. Reservations are recommended.

Map: Upper Engadine Valley Trails

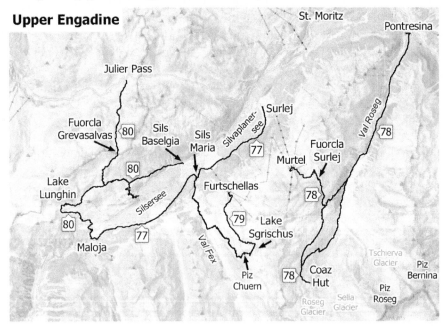

77. Lakes Trail: Silvaplana to Maloja ★★★★★
Distance: 3.3 - 7.9 miles (one-way)

Near St. Moritz in the Upper Engadine

This delightful walk traverses the eastern shores of Lake Silvaplana (Silvaplanersee) and Lake Sils (Silsersee) with lovely views stretching across the lakes to the high peaks towering above the Upper Engadine Valley.

Distance: 3.3 - 7.9 miles
Elevation: 5,870-ft. at Trailhead
6,060-ft. at the Highest Point
Elevation Gain: 190-ft.
Difficulty: easy

Basecamp: St. Moritz
Upper Engadine Map: See page 372
Online Map/Photos:
www.hikingwalking.com/silvaplana

Why Hike the Lakes Trail: Silvaplana to Maloja

This easy hike follows a section of the Senda Segantini (Segantini Trail), passing scenes painted by Giovanni Segantini, a famous 19th century landscape artist. After your walk visit the Segantini Museum in St. Moritz to see his paintings of the shimmering Engadine lakes and rugged peaks.

Families and parties with hikers of mixed abilities will love this scenic ramble. The hike is also a good option if the weather precludes hiking in the high country.

The hike can be walked in either direction, although I prefer walking up valley. You can also shorten the day by stopping or starting the hike in Sils/Segl Maria, a village situated between the two lakes.

Note: Piz in Romansh, a language spoken by some in the Swiss Engadine, means peak and lej, leg and lai means lake. So Piz Lagrev is Lagrev Peak and Lej Segl is Lake Segl, or in German: Silsersee. On trail signs you will often see two different names (one in Romansh and one in German) or different spellings for a destination. For example Sils: German and Segl: Romansh.

Walking the Lakes Trail

Take the bus to Surlej Brucke, located on the east side of the bridge between Lej Suot (Lake Suot) and Lake Silvaplana (Silvaplanersee / Lej da Silvaplauna). (See trailhead directions below.) Walk east (away from the bridge) a short distance to a broad track heading south. Turn right and walk along the track toward Sils/Segl Maria. The path is also signed for trail #25, the Senda Segantini (Segantini Trail).

To your right (west) pass the Castle Crap da Sass, built in 1906 by the German General Count von der Lippe. Views extend up the length of Lake Silvaplana to Piz de la Margna and Piz Lunghin rising above Maloja Pass.

The path now travels through meadows with views of the lake and high peaks from Piz Julier to Piz Lagrev towering above the northwest side of the Upper Engadine Valley. On a still day the high peaks are reflected in the lake's mirror like surface. The village of Silvaplana-Surlej lies along the valley floor at the northeast end of the lake.

At 0.7 miles the path comes abreast of the lakeshore and enters a forest of larch trees. The undulating trail traverses along the shore, passing a waterfall spilling down the slopes above the path. Ignore any trails branching left and ascending to the Alp Sulej and Furtschellas. Instead, stay on the #25 trail to Sils/Segl Maria.

As you approach the head of the lake views open to village of Sils/Segl Maria and the high peaks, including Piz Materdell, Piz Grevasalvas and Piz Lunghin, rising to the west of the Piz Lagrev massif.

Reach the head of the Lake Silvaplana at 2.4 miles and bear left on trail #25 toward Sils/Segl Maria and the Furtschellas lift station. The trail now travels through fields, passing the station for the Furtschellas cable car at 2.8 miles. At the cable car station the trail joins a paved road.

Note: If you wish to cut the hike short you can catch buses returning to St. Moritz at the Furtschellas cable car station and the Sils/Segl Maria Post along the main street (see below).

Continue along the road, bearing left at a "Y" junction. Reach the main road (Chesa Alva or Alvetern depending on your map) through the village of Sils/Segl Maria at 3.2 miles. Turn left at the road and walk along the sidewalk through town, passing several hotels, restaurants, the post office and shops. At the south end of town turn right (northwest) on Via de Marias. (If you start climbing up a hill on a road you have gone too far, turn around and turn left onto Via de Marias.) Signs along the way will point toward trail #25, Isola and Maloja.

Walk along the road, passing the Alpenrose Restaurant on the left. Turn left (west) on the next road, Chesa Cadisch, signed for Isola and Maloja. The path now travels west/southwest through fields with great views of the high peaks rimming the northwest side of the Upper Engadine Valley. Ignore any trails branching left or right off the main trail.

At 4.1 miles reach the foot of Lake Sils (Silsersee/Lej da Segl), the largest of the Engadine lakes. Beautiful views stretch up the length of the lake to Piz Duan rising beyond Maloja Pass. The high peaks from Piz Lagrev to Piz Lunghin dominate the view across the lake to the west/northwest. The Chaste Peninsula extends into the north end of the lake while the wooded island of Chaviolas lies a short distance off the shore.

Past the foot of the lake the undulating trail starts ascending through larches above the lakeshore to a high point at 4.7 miles. Here you are above the northeast end of a large delta jutting into the lake at the foot of Val Fedoz (Fedoz Valley).

The trail now descends through trees and scattered meadows with views of the delta. Soon views open to the Aua da Fedoz, the river draining the Fedoz Valley, flowing across the delta. The rugged crags of Piz Lagrev dominate the views across the lake.

At 5.3 miles cross a bridge over the Aua da Fedoz and enter the small village of Isola, located on the delta. Follow the broad track along the southeast side of the village toward Maloja, passing a restaurant on the way.

Soon we leave the houses behind and continue through pastures to the end of the delta. Beyond the delta the broad track traverse through meadows and trees along the lakeshore.

At 6.0 miles the trail to Maloja branches right off the broad track. Alternative, continue along the broad track to Maloja. I recommend the trail, which traverses beside the lakeshore and is more scenic.

At 6.9 miles pass the entrance to a campsite and a small boat dock along the lake. Signs now point to the bus stop at Maloja Post. For the remainder of the hike we follow the signs to the bus station at the post office.

Reach the head of the lake and a junction at 7.2 miles. Bear left away from the lakeshore toward Maloja Post. (The trail to the right travels along the shore above the head of the lake.) Our path now passes houses as it heads toward the center of town.

At 7.6 miles reach a junction and turn right toward the Maloja bus stop. (The Senda Segantini branches left.) At 7.8 miles reach a "T" intersection and the main street through the town. Turn right and walk north along the road to the post office and bus stop, located on the left (west) side of the street at 7.9 miles.

Trailhead Directions

From St. Moritz Bahnhof (train station) to Surlej, Brucke: From the St. Moritz train station, take either a #1 or #6 bus heading toward Corvatschbahn (Corvatsch cable car) and get off a Surlej Brucke. This stop is located on the east side of the bridge between Lej Suot (Lake Suot) and the Silvaplanersee (Lake Silvaplana). Bus schedules are posted at the bus stops and are available online at the SBB website or on the SBB app.

From Maloja Post to St. Moritz Bahnhof (train station): From the post office in Maloja, board a #4 bus bound for St. Moritz Bahnhof or a #2 bus bound for Pontresina Bahnhof. If you take the #2 bus you need to change at Silvaplana, Freisel Mitte for a #1 bus to St. Moritz Bahnhof. The ride takes 30 minutes on the #4 bus or 40 minutes if you have to change using the #2 and #1 buses. Bus schedules are posted at the bus stops and are available online at the SBB website or on the SBB app.

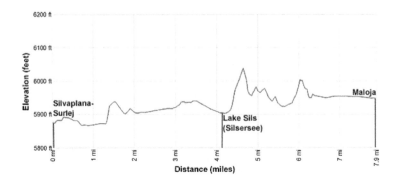

78. Fuorcla Surlej to Pontresina via Coaz Hut

★★★★★
Distance: 3.0 (round-trip) - 12.3 miles (one way)
Near St. Moritz in the Upper Engadine

Glorious, panoramic views of Piz Bernina and Piz Roseg from Fuorcla Surlej, front row seats to an incredible spectacle of rock and ice from Coaz Hut and a lovely walk through the beautiful meadows and forests of Val Roseg make this one of my favorite hikes in the St. Moritz area.

Distance: 3.0 miles (round trip) to Fuorcla Surlej
4.1 miles (one way) to Viewpoint
11.4 miles (round trip) to Coaz Hut
12.3 miles (one way) to Pontresina
Elevation 8,855-ft. at Trailhead
9,039-ft. at Fuorcla Surlej
8,710-ft. at Viewpoint
8,563-ft. at Coaz Hut
5,830-ft. at Pontresina

Elevation Gain: 327-ft. to Fuorcla Surlej
766-ft. to Viewpoint
826-ft./-207-ft. to Coaz Hut
-2,880-ft. to Pontresina
Difficulty: moderate-strenuous
Basecamp: St. Moritz
Upper Engadine Map: See page 372
Online Map/Photos:
www.hikingwalking.com/coaz-hut

Why Hike from Fuorcla Surlej to Pontresina or Coaz Hut

This great hike ascends to Fuorcla Surlej where dramatic views open to Piz Bernina and Piz Roseg and then travels high above Val Roseg (Roseg Valley) toward Coaz Hut accompanied by stunning views of the Bernina Range. Hikers can opt to visit the hut, set amid a glacial wonderland, or walk down the scenic valley to Pontresina.

This hike starts at the Murtel middle station of the Corvatsch cable car. Here hikers are greeted with terrific views of the Upper Engadine lakes plateau. From Mutel a good trail climbs to Fuorcla Surlej (Surlej Pass), renowned for its magnificent views of the Piz Bernina, Piz Roseg and the Tschierva Glacier. In the background, impressive glaciers spill down the slopes of the Sella massif.

Beyond the pass the trail curves south, traveling through pretty meadows sprinkled with wildflowers high above the west side of the Val Roseg. With every step the views of the Bernina range get better and better. Straight ahead are splendid vistas of the peaks forming the valley's glacier-clad head wall, including Piz Sella and Piz Gluschaint, Piz Bernina and Piz Roseg rise directly across the valley. The milky glacial waters of Lej da Vadret (Lake Vadret) lie cradled on the valley floor.

Hikers can either find a scenic lunch spot along the high trail to take in the views or walk to all the way to the Coaz Hut at the head of the valley. The hut, perched on a rocky knob, enjoys awesome, up-close views of the massive Roseg and Sella glaciers tumbling down the valley's head wall. From the high trail two paths descend to the floor of the Val Roseg and then head down valley through pretty meadows and forests to Pontresina.

It is too long for most hikers to go over the pass, visit the hut and then walk down to Pontresina in one day. This trip is best done by spending a night at the Coaz Hut. Day hikers can visit the pass and the hut on an out-and-back hike from Murtel or go part way to the Coaz Hut, stopping at a scenic overlook, before walking down Val Roseg to Pontresina.

Pick a nice day for this hike. A good segment of the trail travels along open, exposed slopes -- not a good place to be if the weather is threatening.

Trailhead to Fuorcla Surlej

- **Distance from Trailhead:** 3.0 miles (round trip)
- **Elevation at seg1:** 9,039-ft.
- **Elevation Gain:** 327-ft.
- **Difficulty:** easy-moderate

Take the bus to Surlej, a small village to the southwest of St. Moritz, and then ride the Corvatsch cable car to the Murtel middle station (8,855-ft.). (See trailhead directions below). From Murtel enjoy splendid views of the Upper Engadine lakes plateau. To the west, Piz d'Emmat Dadaint, Piz Lagrev, Piz Polaschin and the Piz Julier tower above Lake Silvaplana (Silvaplanersee) and Lake Sils (Silsersee), nestled along the valley floor.

At Murtel find the hiking signs outside the lift station and walk in the direction of Fuorcla Surlej (1-hr), Chamanna Coaz (Coaz Hut) (3-hr) and Val Roseg (Roseg Valley) (2-hr 15-min). Follow the trail as it heads southeast, descending gently through an undulating landscape of talus slopes and rocky meadows along the north facing slopes of Piz Murtel. Fuorcla Surlej (Surlej Pass) is visible on the ridge to the east. The top of Piz Tschierva and Piz Boval rise beyond ridge.

At 0.5 miles the trail climbs over the terminal moraine of the Corvatsch Glacier and crosses a few small streams carrying meltwater from the rapidly receding ice sheet. Here views open to the top station for the Corvatsch cable car, situated atop a minor summit overlooking the Corvatsch Glacier. Soon the trail curves to the left (north) and starts climbing on moderate grades toward Fuorcla Surlej. As you ascend, enjoy nice views of the peaks rising along the west side of the Upper Engadine valley.

Reach Fuorcla Surlej at 1.5 miles. Here stunning views of Piz Bernina (13,280-ft.) and Piz Roseg (12,916-ft.), soaring above the east side of Val Roseg, burst onto the scene. The Tschierva Glacier cascades down the west face of the peaks. Piz Sella and Piz Gluschaint tower above the head of the valley blanketed by the Sella and Roseg glaciers. Berghaus Fuorcla Surlej, a restaurant, is located at the pass along with a small photogenic lake. The pass is a great destination for parties looking for a short, highly scenic hike.

Fuorcla Surlej to the Viewpoint or Coaz Hut

- **Segment Stat:** 2.6 miles (one-way) from Fuorcla Surlej to Viewpoint
  4.2 miles from Fuorcla Surlej to Coaz Hut
- **Total Distance:** 4.1 miles (one way) from Murtel to Viewpoint
  5.7 miles (one-way)/ 11.4 miles (round trip) from Murtel to Coaz Hut
- **Maximum Elevation:** 8,710-ft. at Viewpoint
  8,563-ft. at Coaz Hut

- **Elevation Gain:** 766-ft. to Viewpoint
826-ft./-207-ft. to Coaz Hut

When you are done soaking in the views, hike southeast on the trail toward Chamanna Coaz (Coaz Hut), Val Roseg and Puntraschigna (the Romansh spelling of Pontresina). The path descends on moderate grades along the west side of Val Roseg, passing a junction at 1.7 miles with a trail branching left (northeast) toward Pontresina. Our trail bears right toward Coaz Hut, traveling through pretty meadows with every improving views of the valley's high peaks and glaciers. After crossing a pretty stream at 2.4 miles the trail curves to the south and climbs briefly before continuing its descent on moderate to moderately steep grades.

Soon the trail crosses another small stream below a lovely waterfall and then begins a traverse across a broad avalanche chute. At 2.7 miles rocks block the continuation of the trail. Turn left here, following a detour on a trail that switchbacks down the hillside along the north side a stream for 0.1 miles to a junction. Ignore the trail branching left toward Alp Ota and Pontresina. Instead turn right toward Coaz Hut on a path that crosses a wood bridge over the stream.

Past the bridge the detour climbs steeply up the hillside for a short distance and turns left, rejoining the original trail at 3.0 miles. The path now ascends on easy grades along the west side of the valley. At 3.4 miles pass a junction with a closed trail branching left.

Beyond the junction our trail curves to the southwest as it travels through pretty meadows with splendid views of the Bernina peaks, including Piz Sella and Piz Gluschaint anchoring the glacier-clad cirque at the head of the valley. Piz Bernina and Piz Roseg rise directly across the valley. The milky glacial waters of Lej da Vadret (Lake Vadret) lie cradled on the valley floor.

Beyond this point hikers need to make a decision to go all the way to Coaz Hut on an out-and-back hike or continue to Pontresina by heading down the Roseg Valley. Visiting the hut and then continuing to Pontresina is too long for most hikers to accomplish in a day. (We advise a two day trip with an overnight stay at the hut.)

Out-and-Back Hike to Coaz Hut

To visit the hut on an out-and-back hike, continue ascending along the trail on moderate grades. At 4.5 miles the trail starts descending on easy grades. As the path nears the head of the valley at 5.3 miles it curves to the left (southeast), traveling through rocky meadows that give way to scree covered slopes strewn with large boulders.

Soon the trail drops through a landscape of rock slabs, reaching Coaz Hut (8,563-ft.) at 5.7 miles. The hut, situated on a rocky knob beneath the Roseg Glacier, enjoys amazing views of the Roseg and Stella glaciers tumbling down the valley's head wall. To the north views extend down the length of Val Roseg. Behind the hut a use trail climbs a moraine wall for a bird's-eye-views of the hut and the glaciers.

When you are ready to head back, retrace your steps to Murtel for an 11.4 mile round-trip hike and then take the cable car down to Surlej.

Hiking to the Viewpoint

Hikers preferring to return via Val Roseg to Pontresina should not attempt to reach the hut but instead find a comfortable perch along the trail. My favorite spot is at 4.1 miles where the grade abates as the trail traverses a grassy bench. Large, flat rocks offer great perches for enjoying a picnic lunch while soaking in the dramatic views of the glacier-clad cirque at the head of Val Roseg. Across the valley Piz Bernina and Piz Roseg dominate the view.

Viewpoint to Pontresina

- **Segment Stat:** 8.2 miles (one-way)
- **Total Distance from Murtel to Pontresina:** 12.3 miles (one way)
- **Ending Elevation:** 5,830-ft.
- **Elevation Gain/Loss:** -2,880-ft.

To continue to Pontresina via Val Roseg, turn around and follow the trail as it descends on easy grades, passing the blocked junction at 4.8 miles. Bear right at the detour at 5.2 miles. Follow the trail for 0.2 miles as it descends on steep grades and then crosses the wood bridge over the stream. At the trail junction beyond the bridge take the trail branching right toward Alp Ota, Roseg and Puntraschigna (Pontresina). (The trail to the left climbs to Fuorcla Surlej and back to Murtel (the middle station on the Corvatsch cable car) in 2.8 miles for an 8.2 mile round-trip hike.

The trail to Pontresina descends on steep switchbacks to the valley floor and a junction at 7.0 miles, accompanied by great views of the high peaks. Along the way pass the buildings of Alp Surovel at 6.2 miles.

At the junction a trail ascends south along the valley floor toward Coaz Hut. Our trail heads northeast, descending on easy grades along the west side of Val Roseg toward Roseg and Puntraschigna. The Ova da Roseg (Roseg River) flows down the valley to your right. Be sure to turn around for lovely views of peaks, cloaked in glaciers, towering above the head of the valley.

Pass the Hotel Roseggletscher (Hotel Roseg Glacier) (6,558-ft.) at 7.8 miles. Beyond the hotel take the broad path branching right toward Puntraschigna (1-hr 45-min). (The trail to the left climbs to Fuorcla Surlej.)

At 8.0 miles cross a bridge over the Ova da Roseg (stream). On the east side of the valley the path turns left (northeast) and briefly travels along a dirt road shared by walkers, horse carriages and bikes. At 8.5 miles leave the road by taking the trail designated for walkers branching right.

The walker's trail down the valley is lovely, traveling through meadows and clusters of larch and pine trees on the right (east) side of the valley. Along the way follow the signs to the Pontresina train station.

At 10 miles the trail enters the trees. Turn left (west) when you reach a paved road at 12 miles and walk a quarter mile to the Pontresina Train Station (5,830-ft.) where you can catch a train or a bus back to St. Moritz. (See directions below). The village of Pontresina is located across the Flax River on the north side of the Bernina Valley. Total distance for the hike is 12.3 miles.

Note: From Coaz Hut there is an alternative trail that heads down the Roseg Valley. From the hut follow the trail toward Fuorcla Surlej for 0.7 miles to a junction with a trail that drops steeply down to the Lej da Vadret. The trail then travels along the west side of the lake and eventually joins with the main trail heading toward Hotel Roseg. Total distance from Coaz Hut to Pontresina via this route is 9.4 miles.

In my opinion the high trail back to Pontresina, accessed after the detour, is more scenic. Hiker choosing to do an out and back hike to Coaz Hut from Pontresina will want to take the high route out and the low route back for variety. The length of this trip will require an overnight stay in the hut. Total distance for the loop is 19 miles.

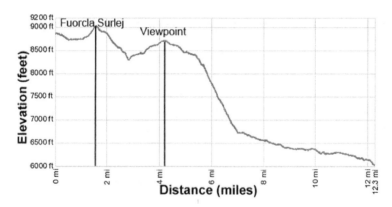

Trailhead Directions

St. Moritz to Corvatsch Cable Car in Surlej: In St. Moritz board a #6 bus bound for Sils/Segl Maria, Posta or a #1 bus for Surlej, Corvatschbahn and get off at the Corvatschbahn (Corvatsch Cable Car) station in Surlej. (Visit the St. Moritz tourism office to get a bus map, the Engadin Bus site for route maps/schedules or the SBB Website/SBB App to determine the stop closest to your accommodations.) The bus ride will take between 20-40 minutes depending on the connections. (Note: You may need to change buses.) At Corvatsch, purchase a ticket to Murtel, the middle station for the cable way.

Pontresina Bahnhof (train station) to St. Moritz: At the train station, take the train to St. Moritz, a 12 minute ride, or take the #1 bus in the direction of Surlej, Corvatschbahn and get off at the stop in St. Moritz that is closest to your accommodation. The ride to the center of St. Moritz takes about 13 minutes. See the SBB Website or the SBB App for the current train and bus schedules.

79. Lej Sgrischus and Piz Chuern ★★★★★
Distance: 6.4 - 7.6 miles (round trip)
Near St. Moritz in the Upper Engadine

Skip the crowds on this great hike that travels through Alp Munt, visits lovely Lake Sgrischus and then climbs to a panoramic overlook atop Piz Chuern with views of the Corvatsch massif and the high peaks towering above the Fex, Fedoz and Upper Engadine valleys.

Distance: 6.4 miles (round trip) to Piz Chuern
7.6 miles (one-way) to Sils/Segl Maria
Elevation: 7,589-ft. at Trailhead
8,806-ft. at Piz Chuern
5,935-ft. at Sils/Segl Maria
Elevation Gain: 1,460-ft. to Piz Chuern
-2,871-ft. to Sils/Segl Maria

Difficulty: moderate
Basecamp: St. Moritz
Upper Engadine Map: See page 372
Online Map/Photos: www.hikingwalking.com/piz-chuern

Why Hike to Lej Sgrischus and Piz Chuern

Most people riding the Furtschellas cable car hike the Wasserweg (Water Trail), a loop that passes through rocky meadows and small tarns amid ski pistes and lifts. I instead recommend taking the path less traveled and head to Lej Sgrischus (Lake Sgrischus), a pretty lake nestled beneath Piz Corvatsch's south ridge. From the lake it is an easy climb to the top to Piz Chuern where terrific, 360-degree views extending to the peaks rising above Lake Sils (Silsersee/Lej da Segl) in the Upper Engadine Valley. To the west/southwest are the summits rimming the Fex and Fedoz valleys while to the east the Piz Corvatsch massif fills the skyline above Lej Sgrischus.

The trail initially travels along the west facing flanks of Piz Corvatsch to Alp Munt, a high pasture set atop a bench overlooking Val Fex. From the Alp a steep trail climbs to the lake accompanied by great views of the surrounding peaks. From there it is an easy ascent to Piz Chuern.

From the overlook atop Piz Chuern either retrace your steps to the Furtschellas cable car or extend the day by descending the steep trail to Val Fex and then walk back to Sils/Segl Maria. Whatever your choice it is a great day out with terrific, nonstop views.

Furtschellas to Lej Sgrischus and Piz Chuern

Note: Piz in Romansh, a language spoken by some in the Swiss Engadine, means peak and lej means lake. So Piz Corvatsch is Corvatsch Peak and Lej Segl is Lake Segl, or in German the Silsersee. On trail signs you will often see two different names (one in Romansh and one in German) or different spellings for a destination. For example Sils: German and Segl: Romansh.

From Sils/Segl Maria, take the Furtschellas cable car to the middle station. (See trailhead directions below.) Outside the station find the trail signpost and starting ascending on moderate to moderately-steep switchbacks through rocky meadows toward Alp Munt, Lej Sgrischus and Piz Chuern. At all intersections continue toward Alp Munt and Lej Sgrischus. As you ascend enjoy great views extending west/northwest to the high peaks rising above Lake Sils (Silsersee/ Lej da Segl) and Lake Silvaplana (Silvaplanersee/Lej Silvaplauna). The Piz Julier massif and nearby summits dominate the view to the north.

At 0.6 miles the grade abates as the trail passes an intersection where the Wasserweg trail turns left. We bear right, curving around the end of a ridge extending west from the Piz Corvatsch massif.

At 0.8 mile reach a high point on the ridge. The undulating path now curves to the south/southeast around the ridge, descending through meadows scattered with rocky knolls high above the east side of Val Fex. Ahead views open to the ridge separating the Fex and Fedoz Valleys. Piz Salatschina, Piz Led, Piz Guz and Piz Flora punctuate the ridge while Piz da la Margna and Piz Fedoz rise along the ridge above the west side of Val Fedoz. Soon the summits at the head of the Fex Valley, Il Chaputschin and Piz Tremoggia join the scene.

At 1.0 mile pass a junction with a trail branching left and ascending steeply to Grialetsch and Lej Sgrischus. (This is a longer, steeper and more rugged route to the lake.) We continue straight ahead toward Alp Munt and Leg Sgrischus.

A short, steep decent followed by an undulating path through meadows leads to a junction at the north end of Alp Munt at 1.5 miles. Here a trail branching northwest descends to Marmore and Sils/Segl Maria. (Hikers wishing to walk up instead of taking the cable car will join the trail to Lej Sgrischus here.) We continue through the rocky pastures of Alp Munt, passing the building at Munt Sura at 1.7 miles. Ahead are fine views of Piz Chuern and Il Chaputschin. A waterfall tumbles down the steep slopes at the head of the Alp.

Reach a junction and the south end of Alp Munt at 2.0 miles. The trail to the right drops down the east side of Fex Valley toward Sils/Segl Maria. We bear left on the trail to Lej Sgrischus that climbs switchbacks up a steep hillside beside a stream. Take a break as you climb to enjoy the great views of Lake Sils and the high peaks rimming the northwest side of the Upper Engadine Valley.

Soon the trail crosses the stream and views open to a pond nestled beneath rugged cliffs of Piz Chuern. This is not Lej Sgrischus. Continue climbing up the steep slopes to the north of the tarn.

At 2.4 miles the grade abates a bit and soon passes the other end of the Grialetsch trail. Beyond the junction the path ascends to a bench and reaches the north end of Lej Sgrischus at 2.6 miles. The lake lies cradled in meadows beneath Piz Corvatsch and the Crasta dal Lej-Sgrischus (Lake Sgrischus ridge). Views stretch south/southeast across the lake to Il Chaputschin and Piz Fora. Piz Chuern is seen to the southwest.

Cross the lake's outlet stream and arrive at a signed junction with a trail heading southwest toward Piz Chuern, Val Fex and Sils/Segl Maria. Initially the trail ascends on easy grades above the lake's western shore. Ahead are views of the cirque at the head of the Fex valley and the summits rising above Lake Sils. Near the south end of the lake the grades steepens as the trail swings to the west and climbs to the broad, meadow-clad summit of Piz Chuern (8,806-ft.) at 3.2 miles.

From the summit panoramic views encompass the rugged peaks towering above Lake Sils and the Upper Engadine Valley. The summits rising above the Fez and Fedoz valleys dominate the view to the west while the cirque at the head of Val Fez fills the skyline to the southwest. Behind us, to the southeast, the rugged Piz Corvatsch massif towers above Lake Sgrischus. Below our birds-eye-roost are the emerald green meadows of Val Fez.

From Piz Chuern you have two choices for the return. The easiest option is to retrace your steps the Furtschellas cable car and take the lift down to Sils/Segl Maria. Alternatively, follow the trail dropping off the west side of Piz Chuern toward Sils/Segl Maria. The path descends steeply down the peak's west facing flanks and then curves to the northwest at 3.6 miles, continuing its descent through meadows high above the east side of Val Fex.

After crossing two streams the grade moderates at 4.4 miles. At 4.7 the descent again steepens as the path drops down to a junction at 5.1 miles. Here you have two choices. Turn left (up valley) on a trail that angles down to the valley floor (longer and less steep) or continue straight head on the path that descend tight, steep switchback to the valley floor.

Take the latter option and reach the valley floor at 5.5 miles. Turn right and head down valley on easy grades following the signs back to Sils/Segl Maria post. Along the way pass the villages of Fez-Crasta and Fez-Platta where you can find refreshments. Reach Sils/Segl Maria post at 7.6 miles after losing 2,871-ft. in elevation. Here you can catch a bus back to St. Moritz.

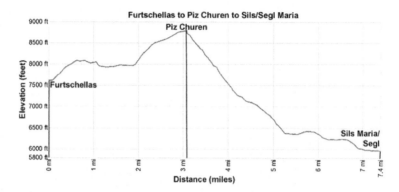

Trailhead Directions

From the St. Moritz Bahnhof (train station) to Furtschellasbahn (Furtschellas Cable Car): At the St. Moritz Train Station board a #6 bus heading toward Corvatschbahn. Get off at Silvaplana Kreisel Mitte and change to the #6 bus to Sils/Segl Maria, Furtschellasbahn. Ride the Furtschellas Cable Car to the Mittelstation (middle station) where the hike starts.

Get bus information from the local tourist office, visit the Engadine Bus Routes page or go to SBB website / SBB app to find the closest stop to your accommodations. Check the Current News section of the Corvatsch-Furtschellas website for a current Sils/Segl to Furtschellas cable car schedule and prices.

Hikers preferring to walk instead of taking the Furtschellas cable car should take the #6 bus to Sils Maria Post and then follow signs to Marmore and Alp Munt. Walking from Sils/Segl Maria will add over 1,500-ft. and 2.2 miles (one-way) to the day.

80. Julier Pass to Fuorcla Grevasalvas to Maloja

★★★★☆

Distance: 5.2 - 8.4 miles (one way)

Near St. Moritz in the Upper Engadine

Two pretty lakes, a panoramic pass and lovely views of the Albula and Bernina Alps are the scenic rewards of this hike crossing the rugged range between Julier Pass and the Upper Engadine Lakes plateau.

Distance: 2.6 miles (one way)/ 5.2 miles (round-trip) to Fuorcla Grevasalvas
8.4 miles (one way) to Maloja
Elevation: 7,330-ft. at Trailhead
8,819-ft. at Fuorcla Grevasalvas
5,950-ft. at Maloja
Elevation Gain: 1,490-ft. to Fuorcla Grevasalvas
-3,542-ft. to Maloja

Difficulty: moderate-strenuous
Basecamp: St. Moritz
Upper Engadine Map: See page 372
Online Map/Photos:
www.hikingwalking.com/julier

Why Hike Julier Pass to Fuorcla Grevasalvas to Maloja

This great hike travels up a beautiful valley, crosses the scenic Fuorcla Grevasalvas (Grevasalvas Pass) and then traverses high above the north side of the Upper Engadine valley before dropping down to Maloja. Along the way the hike visits two idyllic lakes and enjoys splendid views of the Albula and Bernina Alps.

The day starts with a postbus ride to a stop just west of Julier Pass. From the bus stop head south on a trail climbing steeply to a hanging valley cradling pretty Lake Grevasalvas beneath the rugged slopes of Piz Lagrev. Beyond the lake the trail travels through lovely meadows, crosses a boulder field and then climbs talus slopes to Fuorcla Grevasalvas. Here panoramic views encompass the peaks of the Albula range, located to the north of the Engadine Lakes plateau, and the Bernina peaks to the south. The glacier-clad slopes of Piz Gluschaint to Piz Fora dominate the views to the south of Lake Sils (Silsersee/Lej da Segl) while the Monte Sissone massif fills the skyline above Maloja to the southwest.

From the pass a rocky trail descends along the south facing slopes of Piz d'Emmat Dadaint and then turns south, dropping steeply to the pretty pastures of the Plaun Grand were it turns west toward Lake Lunghin. A climb through rocky meadows and along talus slopes leads to the hanging valley where Lake Lunghin lies nestled in a rocky bowl.

From the lake a trail descends steeply to Maloja, with grand views of the Bernina Range and the Upper Engadine Lakes. In Maloja, hikers can catch a postbus back to St. Moritz.

Note: This hike travels through several boulder fields and includes a steep descent to Maloja. Alternatively, the hike can be shortened and made easier by dropping down from the pass to Plaun de Lej, for a 6.25 mile hike, or traversing above Lake Sils to Sils/Segl Baselgia, for a 6.9 mile hike.

Trailhead to Fuorcla Grevasalvas

- **Distance from Trailhead:** 2.6 miles (one way)/5.2 miles (round-trip)
- **Highest Elevation:** 8,819-ft.
- **Elevation Gain:** 1,490-ft.

Note: Piz in Romansh, a language spoken by some in the Swiss Engadine, means peak, Fuorcla means pass and lej means lake. So Piz Lagrev is Lagrev Peak, Fuorcla Grevasalvas is Grevasalvas Pass and Lej Segl is Lake Segl, or in German the Silsersee. On trail signs you will often see two different names (one in Romansh and one in German) or different spellings for a destination. For example Sils: German and Segl: Romansh.

From St. Moritz, take a bus to Julier, La Veduta. This is the first bus stop after Julier Pass (to the west of the pass). (See trailhead directions below.) Carefully cross to the south side of the road and find the trail signpost near a small pond. Head south/southwest toward Lej Grevasalvas (Lake Grevasalvas), Fuorcla Grevasalvas and Maloja on a trail climbing a grassy hillside on moderate to steep grades. Along the way enjoy great views of the peaks in the Albula ranges rising to the north of the highway. Piz Julier towers beyond the pass to the northeast.

After 0.75 miles the trail crests a grassy knoll and views open to idyllic Lake Grevasalvas (9,613-ft.) cradled in a meadows beneath Piz Lagrev. Piz d'Emmat Dadora and Piz d'Emmat Dadaint rise to the southwest. The pretty aquamarine lake is a popular with people looking for an easy day and a great picnic spot.

From the knoll, a rocky trail drops down to and crosses the outlet stream at the foot of the lake. The path then heads up the Grevasalvas Valley on gentle grades, making a wide arc around the west side of the lake. Along the way the trail crosses a stream draining unseen lakes to the west/southwest of the trail.

Past the stream crossing the path briefly travels atop an old moraine wall before dropping down to cross a creek, typically dry after the snow has melted. Beyond the crossing the trail climbs steeply up rocky ledges along the west side of the narrow valley.

At 1.8 miles the grade abates as the trail travels through an undulating landscape of rocky meadows. Views open to the pass (Fuorcla Grevasalvas), the saddle on the ridge at the head of the valley.

At 2.1 miles the trail starts climbing steeply up rocky meadows. The meadows soon give way to scree-covered slopes and boulder fields. Red/white blazed rocks mark the trail through the boulders. The final push to the pass involves a short, very steep climb up scree covered slopes.

Reach Fuorcla Grevasalvas (8,819-ft.), located on the ridge between Piz Lagrev and Piz d'Emmat Dadaint, at 2.6 miles. Here stunning views open to the glacier-clad, 3,000-meter peaks of the Bernina range towering above the Upper Engadine Valley to the south. Maloja and Lake Sils (Silsersee/Lej da Segl) lies nestled along the valley floor. To the south of Maloja the Forno Glacier spills down a dramatic cirque anchored by Monte Sissone, Torrone and Cima di Castello. Behind you, to the north, the Albula Range fills the skyline.

Fuorcla Grevasalvas to Maloja

- **Segment Stat:** 5.8 miles (one-way) from Fuorcla Grevasalvas to Maloja
- **Total Distance:** 8.4 miles (one way)
- **Ending Elevation:** 5,950-ft.
- **Elevation Gain/Loss:** -3,542-ft.

After taking a break and enjoying the views, head down the south side of the pass toward Grevasalvas and Maloja. The trail initially drops steeply through talus before leveling out and traveling through boulder fields and then rocky meadows along the south facing slopes of Piz d' Emmat Dadaint. Pay attention to the red and white markers on the rocks to stay on track through the boulders.

At 3.1 miles the trail begins a very steep descent through pretty meadows with great views of the Bernina peaks towering above Lake Sils. To the west views open to Piz Grevasalvas. Soon the trail turns south as it continues dropping steeply through rocky meadows.

The grade moderates at 3.7 miles as the path descends through rolling pastures and reaches a "T" intersection at Plaun Grand at 4.0 miles. Here hikers have the option of turning left (east) on a trail descending to Plaun da Lej for a 6.3 miles hike or Sils/Segl-Baselgia for a 6.9 miles hike. At Plaun da Lej and Segl/Baseglia hikers can catch a postbus back to St. Moritz. (See below for more information on these alternatives.)

If time, energy and the weather are on your side, I recommend turning right (west) toward Lagh dal Lunghin (Lake Lunghin). The trail to the lake ascends through meadows on easy to moderate grades and soon reaches a junction near a pretty stream. Ignore the trail branching right to Lej Nair, a small lake, and Piz Grevasalvas. Continue on the main trail that now curves to the southwest as it ascending along the right (north) side of a small stream.

At 4.7 miles the trail crosses the stream and then climbs the grassy slopes of a ridge extending southeast from Piz Grevasalvas. As you climb, enjoy great views of the Bernina peaks, Lake Sils and Maloja.

Cross the ridge at 5.2 miles. The narrow trail now curves northwest, contouring along a steep hillside on the west side of the ridge. Use care as the trail crosses several long boulder fields as it ascends on easy grades toward the lake. Soon the trail curves to the left (west) and climbs to the hanging valley where Lagh dal Lunghin (8,169-ft.) lies in a rocky basin beneath Piz Grevasalvas at 5.8 miles. Piz Lunghin rises to the south.

Cross the wood bridge over the outlet stream and then walk along the dam to a trail skirting the south side of the lake. Rocky knolls along the lake shore beckon hikers to sit and take a break.

Soon you will reach a junction. Here a sign points to a path branching right (west) toward Pass Lunghin. We will need to leave that hike for another day. We turn left (south) on the trail descending to Maloja.

Our trail drops on very steep grades from the hanging valley, traveling through rocky meadows with lovely views of the peaks to the south. The grade abates briefly as the trail crosses a wood bridge over the outlet stream for Lake Lunghin at 6.5 miles. Beyond the bridge the trail continues its relentless descent, facilitated by a series of switchbacks.

Reach a junction at Plan di Zoch at 7.5 miles and turn right (south) toward Pila and Maloja. Descend steep switchbacks with great views of Lake Sils and Maloja. At 7.75 miles the grade abates as the trail curves to the right (southwest) and climbs through trees over a low rise, passing the small hamlet of Pila. At Pila the trail joins a broad track that descends to the highway at 8.1 miles.

Cross the highway and turn right (southwest), walking along the sidewalk toward Maloja. The bus stop at Post office in Maloja (5,950-ft.) is located on the west side of the street at 8.4 miles. Here you can catch a bus back to St. Moritz.

Alternate Return via Plaun de Lej or Sils/Segl- Baselgia

For a shorter and easier day, avoid the climb to Lake Lunghin and instead descend from the pass to Plaun de Leg or Sils/Segl-Baselgia. At the "T" intersection at Plaun Grand at 4.0 miles, turn left (east) toward Grevasalvas and Sils/Segl-Baselgia. The path now descends on moderately-steep to steep grades through meadows with more fine views of the peaks rising above Lake Sils. The village of Grevasalvas lies in a meadow-clad bowl below.

At 4.9 mile reach a junction with the Via Engadina trail to Sils/Segl-Baselgia. Here you need to make a choice to bear right toward Grevasalvas or turn left on the Via Engadina trail. The path to Grevasalvas descends through pastures and soon turns right, passing through the pretty little village. Restaurants in the village are popular lunch spots.

At the west end of the village turn left on the broad track dropping down moderate switchbacks to Plaun de Lej (5,900-ft.) at 6.25 miles. Here you can catch a bus back to St. Moritz.

The walk to Sils/Segl-Baselgia is longer but quite pretty, traversing the slopes above the northwest shore of Lake Sils. To reach Sils/Segl-Baselgia, turn left at the junction at 4.9 miles and follow the Via Engadine trail northeast. The path descends through meadows beneath the steep slopes of Piz Lagrev. After passing through a small valley the trail emerges on open slopes with fine views of Lake Sils.

At 5.9 miles the path travels through scattered larches along a rocky hillside. The trail builders did an excellent job laying large, flat slabs along the path to facilitate passage through this area.

Reach at junction at 6.6 miles. Bear right toward Sils/Segl-Baselgia. The path branching left continues along the Via Engadina to Silvaplana. Our path now descends to a "T" intersection along the main highway in the Upper Engadine Valley. Carefully cross the highway and then head south/southeast along a side road into Sils/Segl-Baselgia (5,900-ft.). Look for the bus stop on the left (west) side of the road about 250-ft. from the intersection at 6.9 miles. Here you can catch a bus back to St. Moritz. (See directions below.)

Total elevation loss for the alternate return from the Grevasalvas Pass to Plaun de Lej or Sils/Segl-Baselgia is 2,919-ft.

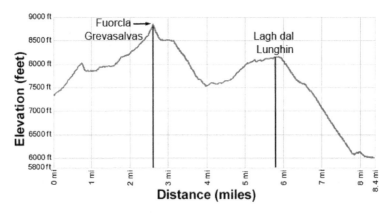

Trailhead Directions

From St. Moritz Bahnhof to Julier, La Veduta: From the St. Moritz Bahnhof (train station) purchase a ticket for Julier, La Veduta and board bus 182 to Chur. Get off the bus at La Veduta, the first stop after the bus goes over Julier Pass. The ride takes about 30 minutes. (There is a restaurant at this stop called the Ospizio La Veduta.) Carefully cross to the south side of the road where you will find a trail signpost.

From Maloja, Plaun de Lej and Sils/Segl Baselgia to St. Moritz: At the Maloja Post, board a #4 Postbus to St. Moritz Bahnhof (train station). The ride takes about 41 minutes. Note the bus makes a number of stops in St. Moritz on the way to the train station. Check the SBB website or the SBB app to determine the stop nearest to your accommodations.

You can also take a #2 Postbus headed to Pontresina. This option requires you to change to a #1 bus at Silvaplana Post bound for the Samedan Bahnhof. Get off the bus at the St. Moritz Bahnhof or whatever stop is most convenient to your accommodations. The ride takes about 43 minutes.

The #4 and #2 buses also stop at Plaun de Lej and Sils/Segl Baselgia. If you catch the #2 bus, follow the directions above for changing at Silvaplana.

Map: Val Bernina Area Trails

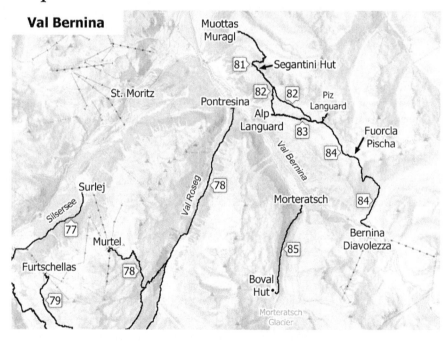

81. Segantini Hut ☆☆☆☆☆

Distance: 4.5 miles (RT)

Near St. Moritz in the Upper Engadine / Val Bernina

The Segantini Hut, high above Pontresina in the Bernina Valley, offers birds-eye-views of the summits soaring above the Roseg, Morteratsch and Upper Engadine Valleys.

Distance: 4.5 miles (RT)
Elevation: 8,050-ft. at Trailhead
8,960-ft. at the Hut
Elevation Gain: 910-ft.
Difficulty: moderate

Basecamp: St. Moritz
Val Bernina Map: See page 391
Online Map/Photos:
www.hikingwalking.com/segantini

Why Hike to the Segantini Hut

This short, popular hike features scenic views of the Muragl Valley and panoramic vistas from the historic Segantini Hut, perched atop a ridge high above the northeast side of the Bernina Valley. From the hut, views stretch south up Val Roseg to the Roseg, Sella and Tschierva glaciers spilling down a dramatic cirque rimmed by 3,000-meter peaks. Piz Bernina soars above the head of the ridge separating the Roseg Valley from the Morteratsch Valley to the east.

Competing for your attention are the rugged peaks of the Albula Alps towering above the Upper Engadine Valley to the west/northwest. St. Moritz and its namesake lake lie along the valley floor beneath the towering summits.

Sections of the trail are steep but manageable for most hikers. The hut, now a restaurant, offers refreshments. Alternatively, pack lunch and continue along the ridge a short distance beyond the hut to find a picnic spot with front row seats to the stunning views.

Hikers comfortable with narrow, rugged trails with some exposure can continue beyond the hut on an airy trail with more spectacular views of the

Bernina Valley. See Hike 82 - Muottas Muragl to Alp Languard hike for more information.

Hiking to the Segantini Hut

Take the Muottas Muragl Funicular from the Punt Muragl Talstation (bottom station) to Muottas Muragl (8,051-ft.). (See trailhead directions below). Overlooks near the exit of the funicular station offer stunning views of the Albula Alps, dominated by Piz Julier and Piz Ot, towering above the northwest side of the Upper Engadine Valley. St. Moritz, Celerina and Samedan lie nestled along the valley floor.

To the south views extend up Val Roseg to the high peaks of the Bernina Alps, including Piz Bernina, Piz Scerscen, Piz Roseg and Piz Gluschaint, to name a few. To the east/southeast, Piz Vadret and Piz Muragl fill the skyline above the Val Muragl (Muragl Valley).

After enjoying the views find the trail signpost behind the funicular station and head southeast toward Chamanna Segantini (Segantini Hut). The trail descends on moderate grades through pastures, passing Alp Muottas along the way. At 0.9 miles the grade abates as the path reaches the floor of Val Muragl and passes a small building. Ignore the trail to the right that drops to Punt Muragl and Samedan.

Just before reaching a stream pass a trail branching left at 1.1 miles toward Lej Muragl (Lake Muragl) and Fcla. Muragl (Muragl Pass). Continue straight ahead crossing the wood bridge over the stream draining Val Muragl.

On the other side of the bridge pass a trail branching right (west) and descending to Unterer Schafberg, Alp Languard and Puntraschinga (a Romansh derivation of Pontresina). Our trail toward Chamanna Segantini now climbs a series of steep switchbacks up to the ridge extending northwest from Munt da la Bes-cha. At 1.6 miles the switchbacks end and the trail curves to right, continuing its steep climb toward the ridge crest.

As you ascend enjoy ever improving views of Piz Ot and the peaks lining the head of the Val Saluver to the west of Celerina. To the north, Piz Kesch, Piz Cotschen and nearby peaks form the backdrop for Muottas Muragl.

At 1.9 miles the trail curves to the left (southwest) and climbs to the ridge crest at Munt de la Bes-cha (8,683-ft.). Here glorious views encompass Piz Ot, Piz Julier and the high peaks of the Albula range rising above the northwest side of the Upper Engadine Valley. Beneath the overlook, Celerina and Samedan lie on either side of the flood plain marking the confluence of Val Bernina with the Upper Engadine valley. Views extend up the Upper Engadine valley to St. Moritz, Lake St. Moritz, Lake Silvaplana and, in the distance, Lake Sils.

To south are wonderful views of Piz Roseg, Piz Scerscen, Piz Sella and Piz Gluschaint rising above the head of Val Roseg. Piz Bernina, Piz Zupo and Piz Palu soar above the Morteratsch Valley to the east of Val Roseg.

The trail now climbs steeply up the broad ridge crest to the Segantini Hut (8,960-ft.) at 2.1 miles. The hut, now a restaurant, is named after a famous artist that painted and died here in 1899. From the hut and surrounding area enjoy breathtaking views of the Bernina massif, Val Roseg, the Upper Engadine Valley and the Albula Alps. Beyond the hut the path travels on easy grades along the ridge, passing some nice places to sit and take in the views at 2.25 miles.

The trail continues beyond the ridge crest to Alp Languard. Sections of this trail are very narrow and exposed. Fix cables safeguard problematic sections of the path. See Hike 82 - Muottas Muragl to Alp Languard for more information on the trail beyond the Segantini Hut.

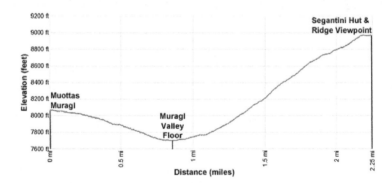

Trailhead Directions

From St. Moritz: From the St. Moritz Bahnhof, take the #1 bus toward Samedan, which stops at Punt Muragl (the bottom station of the Muottas Muragl Funicular), located in Val Bernina to the northwest of Pontresina. There are other bus routes that stop at Punt Muragl leaving from St. Moritz, St. Moritz Bad and Pontresina. Get bus information from the local tourist office, the Engadine Bus Routes page or the SBB website/SBB app to find the closest stop to your accommodations.

82. Muottas Muragl to Alp Languard ★★★★★
Distance: 4.0 - 6.0 miles (one way)
Near St. Moritz in the Upper Engadine / Val Bernina

A short hike that is long on panoramic views of the high peak towering above the Roseg, Morteratsch and Upper Engadine valleys. Extend the hike with a high traverse beneath the ridge anchored by Piz Muragl and Piz Languard for great views of the Bernina massif.

Distance: 4.0 miles (one way) to Alp Languard (short)
6.0 miles (one way) to Alp Languard (long)
Elevation: 8,050-ft. at Trailhead
8,970-ft. at Alp Languard (short)
9,020-ft. at Alp Languard (long)
Elevation Gain: 1,270-ft. to Alp Languard (short)
1,556-ft. to Alp Languard (long)

Difficulty: moderate-strenuous
Basecamp: St. Moritz
Val Bernina Map: See page 391
Online Map/Photos:
www.hikingwalking.com/alp-languard

Why Hike from Muottas Muragl to Alp Languard

The impressive Bernina Valley stretches southeast from its confluence with the Upper Engadine Valley to the Italian border. Along the southwest side of the Bernina are two impressive side valleys; Roseg and Morteratsch, rimmed by magnificent glacier-clad peaks. A massive wall of summits, anchored by Piz Muragl and Piz Languard, towers above the northeast side of the valley.

The Muottas Muragl to Alp Languard hike starts above the northeast side of Val Bernina near its confluence with the Upper Engadine. From Punt Muragl ride the funicular to the top station at Muottas Muragl. Here splendid views encompass Piz Julier and Piz Ot towering above the Upper Engadine Valley to the west/northwest. The high peaks of the Bernina Alps soaring above the Roseg and Morteratsch valleys fill the skyline to the south while Piz Vadret and Piz Muragl rise above the Muragl valley to the east.

From the funicular station the trail descends to and crosses the Muragl Valley and then ascends steeply to a scenic overlook atop the ridge extending northwest from Munt da la Bes-cha. From here every step of the hike is packed with stunning views of the Bernina massif and the peaks rimming the Roseg and Morteratsch valleys along with the summits towering above the Upper Engadine Valley.

A brief ascent along the ridge leads to the Segantini Hut and more great views. From the hut the trail descends briefly before beginning a traverse beneath the rugged peaks and ridges lining the northeast side of the Bernina Valley. At 3.0 miles the path reaches the first of two junctions where a trail drops steeply to Alp Languard. The "short" version of the hike (4.0 miles) turns right at the first junction and descends to Alp Languard along the themed Climate Trail, which includes eighteen information panels explaining how climate change is impacting the alpine environment.

Alternatively, extend the hike by continuing straight ahead toward Piz Languard. The trail now curves around the west facing flanks of Muot da Barba Peider and then, after a short ascent, traverses beneath the ridge anchored by Piz Muragl and Piz Languard. This section of the trail travels through boulder fields and rocky meadows, climbs around a few obstacles and boasts spectacular views of the Roseg and Morteratsch valleys, the Bernina massif and nearby summits. At a junction below Piz Languard a second trail drops down the chairlift at Alp Languard for a 6.0 mile hike.

This trail should not present any problems for most hikers up to the Segantini Hut. Beyond the hut short sections of the trail, especially on the longer option, are narrow and exposed. Fix chains bolted to the rock safeguard these segments of the path. There are also a few places where you may need to use your hands to negotiate short, steep descents. Both trails dropping down to Alp Languard are quite steep.

Pick a beautiful day so you can take your time and soak in the views on this scenic hike. Get an early start to avoid the clouds that typically move in as the day progresses and obscure the views.

Short Version of the Hike to Alp Languard

- **Distance from Trailhead:** 4.0 miles (one way)
- **Highest Elevation:** 8,970-ft.
- **Elevation Gain:** 1,270-ft.

Take the Muottas Muragl Funicular from the Punt Muragl Talstation (bottom station) to Muottas Muragl (8,051-ft.). (See trailhead directions below). Overlooks near the exit of the funicular station offer stunning views of the Albula Alps, dominated by Piz Julier and Piz Ot, towering above the northwest side of the Upper Engadine Valley. St. Moritz, Celerina and Samedan lie nestled along the valley floor.

To the south views extend up Val Roseg to the high peaks of the Bernina Alps, including Piz Bernina, Piz Scerscen, Piz Roseg and Piz Gluschaint, to name a few. To the east/southeast, Piz Vadret and Piz Muragl fill the skyline above the Val Muragl (Muragl Valley).

When you are done enjoying the views, find the trail signpost behind the funicular station and head southeast toward Chana Segantini (Segantini Hut). For a detailed description of this section of the trail see Hike 81 - the Segantini Hut Trail.

From the Segantini Hut and surrounding area enjoy breathtaking views of the Bernina massif, Val Roseg, the Upper Engadine Valley and the Albula Alps. Beyond the hut the path travels on easy grades along the ridge, passing some nice places to sit and take in the views.

Hikers not comfortable with narrow, exposed trails should turn around here and return to Muottas Muragl for a 4.5 mile hike. Otherwise, pass a junction at 2.25 miles with a trail branching left and climbing to the summit of Las Sours. Our trail, branching right, drops steeply through meadows along the southwest face of the ridge.

Reach a trail junction at 2.5 miles. The trail to the right descends very steep switchbacks to Unterer Schafberg and Pontresina. We take the trail straight ahead toward the Bergstation Languard and Piz Languard. You are now on the Climate Trail, which features eighteen information panels explaining how climate change is impacting the alpine environment.

Follow the trail as it traverses southeast along the extremely steep flanks of Las Sours, passing through an area of rock walls constructed as avalanche barriers. Fixed chains provide a level of security along narrow, exposed section of the path. Along the way enjoy stunning, non-stop views of the Bernina massif, Piz Zupo and Piz Palu and the Morteratsch Glacier.

Reach a "Y" intersection at 3.0 miles. Here a decision needs to be made. For the short version of the hike take the trail branching right toward the Bergstation Languard and Puntraschinga (alternative spelling of Pontresina). This path descends steeply on a diagonal along the slopes beneath Piz Muragl to a junction at 3.9 miles. Turn right at the junction toward toward Bergstation Languard, which is now in sight, and Pontresina. Reach the chairlift at Alp Languard (7,631-ft.) at 4.0 miles. A six minute chairlift ride whisks hikers down to Pontresina. Alternatively, a trail drops steeply down the hillside to Pontresina, losing over 1,600-ft. in 1.8 miles.

Long Version of the Hike to Alp Languard

- **Segment Stat:** 2.0 miles (one-way) for the longer version of the hike
- **Total Distance for seg2:** 6.0 miles (one way)
- **Highest Elevation:** 9,020-ft.
- **Elevation Gain/Loss:** 1,556-ft.

For the longer version of the walk, at the "Y" junction at 3.0 miles take the trail branching left toward Piz Languard. This rocky, undulating trail curves around the slopes beneath Muot da Barba Peider, a minor peak on the ridge extending southwest from Piz Muragl, passing through an area with more avalanche barriers. Here great views open to Lake Languard nestled in meadows beneath Piz Albris near the head of the Languard Valley.

At 3.25 miles the trail ascends on moderate to moderately-steep grades up scree-covered slopes. The grade abates as 3.6 miles. The path now traverses through scree and rocky meadows beneath the ridge anchored by Piz Muragl and Piz Languard. Views extend south up the Morteratsch Valley to the Morteratsch Glacier flowing down the cirque defined by Piz Bernina, Piz Argient, Piz Zupo and the Bellavista ridge. Piz Palu towers above the Pers Glacier.

At 4.0 miles the rocky slopes give way to meadows and the hiking gets easier. Piz Languard now dominates the view above the trail. Great views extend up the length of the Languard valley to Fuorcla Pischa, the pass at the head of the valley.

At 4.6 miles reach a junction with the second trail branching right toward Piz Languard. The trail to the left ascends steeply toward Piz Languard and Fuorcla Pischa. Parties with the time, energy and good weather can opt to climb Piz Languard before descending to Alp Languard. The very strenuous climb gains over 1,700-ft. in 1.2 miles. For more information see Hike 83 - Piz Languard.

Turn right (west) at the junction and descend steeply toward Alp Languard and the Languard chairlift. Pass a junction with a trail branching southeast toward Lake Languard and Chamana Paradis (Paradis Hut) at 5.1 miles.

The descent to Alp Languard is accompanied by fine views of the peaks rising above the Upper Engadine Valley, Piz Albris towering above the Languard Valley and the Bernina massif rising beyond the Paradis ridge lining the south side of the Languard Valley. At 5.8 pass a second trail heading southeast toward Lake Languard and the Paradis Hut. Ahead our destination, Alp Languard and the lift down to Pontresina are in sight.

Reach Alp Languard (7,631-ft.) and the Languard chairlift at 6.0 miles. Here you will also find trails dropping down to Pontresina (spelled Puntraschigna in Romansh). The knee crunching descent to town loses over 1,600-ft. in 1.8 miles. My advice is the save your knees and take the chairlift, which carries you down to the village in just 6 minutes.

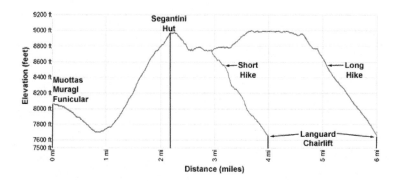

Trailhead Directions

From St. Moritz: From the St. Moritz Bahnhof, take the #1 bus toward Samedan, which stops at Punt Muragl (the bottom station of the Muottas Muragl Funicular), located in Val Bernina to the northwest of Pontresina. There are other bus routes that stop at Punt Muragl leaving from St. Moritz, St. Moritz Bad and Pontresina. Get bus information from the local tourist office, the Engadine Bus Routes page or the SBB website/SBB app to find the closest stop to your accommodations.

From Alp Languard to St. Moritz: Take the chairlift from Alp Languard to the bottom station in Pontresina. Exit the chair lift and walk down the street. Take a right (northwest) on Via Cruscheda. Follow Crusheda down to Via Maistra, the main street in Pontresina. Continue straight ahead on Maistra (northwest) to the Pontresina Rondo bus stop. Catch the #1 bus in the direction of Surlej, Corvatschbahn and get off at the stop in St. Moritz closest to your accommodations. The ride takes 45 minutes. Get bus information from the local tourist office, the Engadine Bus Routes page or the SBB website/SBB app to find the closest stop to your accommodations.

Other options require a bus change or a long walk. For example, you can walk to the Pontresina, Punt Ota Sur bus stop. (To find the Punt Ota Sur stop, continue along Via Miastra and turn left on Via Da la Staziun. Follow this street for a short distance to the Punta Ota Sur bus stop.) At this stop, get on a #2 bus bounds for Silvaplana post. Change to the #1 bus (headed to the St. Moritz Bahnhof) at the Punt Muragl Talstation (valley station).

You can also follow Via Da la Staziun as it drops down the hill, crosses the River Flax on a bridge and then curves around to the Pontresina train station. At the train station get on a train headed for St. Moritz. The walk to the train station takes about 20 minutes.

83. Piz Languard ★★★★★

Distance: 5.0 miles (round-trip)

Near St. Moritz in the Upper Engadine / Val Bernina

Breathtaking views of the summits towering above the Upper Engadine and Bernina Valleys reward hikers completing the very steep climb to the summit of Piz Languard. This summit is one of the easier 3,000-meter peaks to scale, with a good, albeit rugged, trail going to the top.

Distance: 5.0 miles (round-trip)
Elevation: 7,631-ft. at Trailhead
10,699-ft. at the Summit
Elevation Gain: 3,068-ft.
Difficulty: difficult

Basecamp: St. Moritz
Val Bernina Map: See page 391
Online Map/Photos:
www.hikingwalking.com/piz-languard

Why Hike to Piz Languard

The trail to the summit of Piz Languard is popular, and deservedly so, with stunning vistas in all directions. Undoubtedly, the star of the show is the Bernina massif and its shimmering glaciers across the valley to the south. To the west views extend to the summits towering above the Upper Engadine Valley while the peaks rising above the Upper Bernina Valley and the Italian border fill the skyline to the east/southeast. On a clear day distant views stretch southwest to Monte Rosa and northwest to Todi.

This trail is best suit to sure footed hikers with a head for heights. The trail up to the Georgy Hut is steep but should not present any problems unless covered by snow and/or ice. Beyond the hut section of the trail have some exposure. Happily fixed cables safeguard the climb up airy sections of the path.

Pick a beautiful day for this hike and get an early start. The climb to the top will take longer than you expect. You can walk all the way up to the summit from Pontresina but I recommend taking the chairlift to Alp Languard. Using the chairlift will speed the trip to the top, helping your to beat the clouds that typically move in during the afternoon and obscure the great views.

After completing the climb you can then either walk back to Alp Languard or Pontresina, extend the day with a hike to Fuorcla Pischa (Pischa Pass) or visit Lake Languard on the loop trail around the Languard Valley.

Hiking to Piz Languard

In Pontresina, ride the Languard chairlift to Alp Languard. (See trailhead directions below.) Outside the lift station find the trail signpost and start waking east toward Piz Languard and Fuorcla Pischa.

The trail angles up the northeast side of Val Languard (Languard Valley), along the southwest facing slopes of the ridge between Piz Muragl and Piz Languard, accompanied by fine views of Piz Cambrena, Palu and Bernina to the south. At 0.2 miles the trail splits with the path to the right (southeast) heading toward Chamanna Paradis (Paradis Hut) and Lej Languard (Lake Languard). We bear left toward Piz Languard and Fuorcla Pischa.

The trail now climbs steeply through meadows. Ahead are fine views of Piz Languard, the Languard ridge and Piz Albris. To the west the high peaks rimming the Upper Engadine Valley form the backdrop for St. Moritz sprawled along the valley floor. The rugged ridge between Piz Muragl and Piz Languard rises to the north. As you gain elevation views expand to the Morteratsch Glacier flowing down the deep valley beneath Piz Bernina.

Pass a second trail branching right toward Chamanna Paradis and Lej Languard at 0.9 miles and then at 1.3 miles a trail branching left to Chamanna Segantini (Segantini Hut). We continue toward Piz Languard and Fuorcla Pischa.

The path now ascends steep switchbacks beneath the south facing slopes of Piz Languard, passing a third trail to Lej Languard at 1.6 miles. Another series of steep switchbacks lead to the junction with a trail to the summit of Piz Languard, branching left, at 1.8 miles. The trail to the right heads toward Fuorcla Pischa and Bernina Suot.

Turn left toward the summit. The rocky path steepens and becomes more rugged as it switchbacks up the south ridge of Piz Languard to the Chamanna Georgy (Georgy Hut) (10,463-ft.) at 2.25 miles.

The hut, sitting atop a small bench along the south ridge, boasts breathtaking views of the Bernina massif, the Upper Engadine valley and the Bernina Pass area. It's a great place to take a break, catch your breath and/or purchase some refreshments before the final stiff climb to the summit.

For those interested in sunset or sunrise views, the hut offers dormitory accommodations (reservations required) and meals. A herd of ibex is often seen roaming around the area.

Beyond the hut the airy trail winds through very steep, rocky terrain up the south ridge of Piz Languard, gaining over 230-ft. to the summit. Cables affixed to the rock safeguard the climb up exposed sections of the trail.

Reach the summit of Piz Languard (10,699-ft.) at 2.5 miles. The jaw-dropping, spectacular views make all the hard work worthwhile. To the south the Bernina massif dominates the view. The Morteratsch Glacier, a massive river of ice flows downs the slopes beneath Piz Morteratsch, Piz Bernina, Piz Argient, Piz Zupo and the Bellavista Ridge, while the Pers Glacier adorns the slopes of Piz Palu and Piz Cambrena.

To the east/southeast views extend to the Bernina Pass region and the high peaks along the Swiss-Italian border. Closer at hand is the Fuorcla Pischa area, where Piz Pischa rises above Lake Pruna and Lake Pischa nestled in rocky bowls. To the north are the summits rimming the Pruna and Chamuera Valleys. To the west the high peaks towering above the Upper Engadine Valley and beyond fill the skyline. St. Moritz and the Lake St. Moritz lie along the valley floor. On a clear day distant views stretch southwest to Monte Rosa and northwest to Todi.

When you are done taking in the views retrace your steps to Alp Languard and the chairlift down to Pontresina for a 5.0 mile hike. Walking up from the Pontresina will add 1.8 miles and over 1,600-ft in elevation gain (one-way) to the hike. If you wish to extend the day, I suggest taking the trail to Fuorcla Pischa (Hike 84) or descending to Lake Languard before returning to Alp Languard.

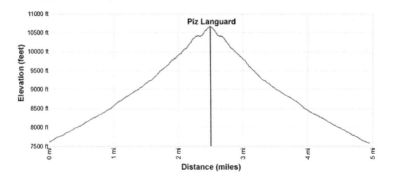

Trailhead Directions

From St. Moritz to Alp Languard: At the St. Moritz Bahnhof, board a #1 bus in the direction of the Samedan Bahnhof. Get off at the Punt Muragl Talstation and change to a #2 bus bound for Pontresina Bahnhof. Ride the #2 bus to the Pontresina Rondo stop. Get bus information from the local tourist office, the Engadine Bus Routes website or the SBB website/SBB app to find the closest stop to your accommodations.

From the Pontresina Rondo, walk southeast on Via Maistra, the main street in Pontresina, for one block to Via da Scoula. Here you will see a street branching left off Via Maistra called Via Cruscheda. Walk up Cruscheda and then turn left to reach the bottom station for the Sesselbahn Languard (Languard Chairlift) to Alp Languard. Signs will mark the turn to the chairlift. The bus ride and the walk should take 20-25 minutes depending on connections.

You can also take the train from St. Moritz bound for Tirano and get off at Pontresina Bahnhof. Exit the train station and turn right, walking along the road which turns into Via da la Staziun. The road soon crosses a river. Beyond the crossing turn right at the "Y" intersection and ascend to cross the highway and then the River Flax. Continue up the road a short distance and cross Via Da Mulin. Just beyond turn right on a walkway (La Senda) that climbs to Via Maistra, the main street in Pontresina. Turn left (northeast) and walk up Via Maistra. Soon you will pass the Hotel Schweizerhof, a peach colored building on the right. At the north end of the hotel turn right (east/northeast) and climb the steps. At the top of the stairs, cross the street and continue heading east/northeast on the side street, past the car park to the bottom station of the Languard chairlift. Trains schedules are available at the SBB website/SBB app.

Check the St. Moritz Mountain Adventure website for information on the Alp Languard Chairlift operating dates and hours.

84. Alp Languard to Fuorcla Pischa ★★★★★
Distance: 6.7 miles (one way)
Near St. Moritz in the Upper Engadine / Val Bernina

Get off the beaten path with this scenic hike climbing to Fuorcla Pischa, a high pass at the head of Val Languard. The hike enjoys great views of the glacier clad Bernina massif, Piz Languard and the stark basin, sprinkled with tarns, below Pischa Pass.

Distance: 6.7 miles (one way)
Elevation: 7,631-ft. at Trailhead
9,600-ft. at Fuorcla Pischa
Elevation Gain: 1,965-ft.
Difficulty: moderate-strenuous

Basecamp: St. Moritz
Val Bernina Map: See page 391
Online Map/Photos:
www.hikingwalking.com/pischa

Why Hike from Alp Languard to Fuorcla Pischa

This varied and beautiful hike climbs along the southwest facing slopes between Piz Muragl and Piz Languard to the junction with the trail to Piz Languard. Beyond the junction the path traverses below the Crasta Languard (Languard ridge) to Fuorcla Pischa (9,341-ft.), an alpine pass overlooking a rocky basin dotted with tarns. Piz Albris, Piz Pischa and Piz dal Fain rise above the basin. From the pass the trail descends steeply to the Val da Fain and then travels down the valley to Alp Bernina and Bernina Suot.

The hike offers a degree of solitude not found on many of the trails in the St. Moritz area. After passing the junction with the trail to Piz Languard you will have the path mostly to yourself. The remainder of the hike travels through an untamed moonscape of rock and small tarns and then a wild valley where ibex seem to outnumber hikers. Only after dropping into the Val da Fain will you start seeing hikers and bikers.

Pick a nice day for this hike. Long sections of the trail are above timberline on exposed slopes, not the place to be during a thunderstorm. Snowfields linger into mid-July around the pass making the crossing problematic early in the season.

Hiking to Fuorcla Pischa and Bernina Suot

Note: Piz in Romansh, a language spoken in the Swiss Engadine, means peak, fuorcla means pass and chamanna is hut. So Piz Languard is Languard Peak, Fuorcla Pischa is Pischa Pass and Chamanna Segantini is Segantini Hut.

In Pontresina, ride the Languard chairlift to Alp Languard. (See trailhead directions below.) Outside the lift station find the trail signpost and start waking east toward Piz Languard and Fuorcla Pischa.

The trail angles up the northeast side of Val Languard on the southwest facing slopes between Piz Muragl and Piz Languard, accompanied by fine views of Piz Cambrena, Palu and Bernina in the distance to the south. At 0.2 miles the trail splits with the path to the right (southeast) heading toward Chamanna Paradis (Paradis Hut) and Lej Languard (Lake Languard). We bear left toward Piz Languard and Fuorcla Pischa.

The trail now climbs steeply through meadows. Ahead are fine views of Piz Languard, the Languard ridge and Piz Albris. To the west the high peaks rimming the Upper Engadine Valley form the backdrop for St. Moritz sprawled along the valley floor. The rugged ridge between Piz Muragl and Piz Languard rises to the north. As you gain elevation views expand to the Morteratsch Glacier flowing down the deep valley beneath Piz Bernina.

Pass a second trail branching right (southeast) toward Chamanna Paradis and Lej Languard at 0.9 miles and then at 1.3 miles a trail branching left to Chamanna Segantini (Segantini Hut). We continue toward Piz Languard and Fuorcla Pischa.

The path now ascends steep switchbacks beneath the south facing slopes of Piz Languard, passing a third trail to Lej Languard at 1.6 miles. Another series of steep switchbacks lead to the high point (9,600-ft.) of the hike and a junction at 1.8 miles with a trail branching left to the summit of Piz Languard. (See Hike 83 - Piz Languard for more information.) We bear right toward Fuorcla Pischa and Bernina Suot.

The path now descends gently along scree covered slopes beneath the Crasta Languard (Languard ridge). Ahead Piz Albris rises above the head of the Languard valley, a rocky landscape dotted with small tarns. The Bernina massif, adorn with glaciers, rises beyond the Paradis ridge rimming the valley to the south.

At 2.5 miles pass the last trail descending to Lej Languard and Chamanna Paradis before the pass. For those walking to the pass and back this trail offers an alternative return to the Alp Languard chairlift.

The trail now ascends on easy grades through a rocky moonscape toward the pass. Turn around as you climb for incredible views of Piz Languard, Crasta Languard and the peaks of the Upper Engadine Valley towering above St. Moritz.

Reach Fuorcla Pischa (9,341-ft.) at 3.1 miles. Piz Albris towers above the pass to the south. Piz Pischa and Piz dal Fain dominate the view to the east. Lej da Pischa (Pischa Lake) and smaller tarns lie amid rock knolls and scree slopes below the peaks. Piz Alv and Piz Minor rise above the southeast side of the Val da Fain. In the distance are the peaks rimming the Swiss-Italian border.

You can turn around at the pass and return to Alp Languard for a 6.2 miles round-trip hike. I personally prefer to cover new ground, so I recommend continuing the hike over the pass to Bernina Suot. Note the descent from the pass to Bernina Suot loses over 2,700-ft.

The path descends the east side of Fuorcla Pischa and soon reaches a junction. We bear right toward Bernina Suot. The trail to the left leads to Lake Pischa and the route to Fuorcla Tschuffer.

Beyond the intersection the trail descends on moderate to moderately steep grades for 0.3 miles and then traverses along a bench through a starkly beautiful landscape of rock outcroppings, boulder fields and small tarns. Look down to see small flower growing amid the rocks beside the trail.

At 3.7 miles the bench abruptly ends and views open to the Val da Fain, a deep, emerald green valley rimmed by granite peaks. The trail now descends steeply beneath the east facing slopes of Piz Albris. Ahead are lovely views of Piz Cambrena, Piz Palu, Piz Zupo, and Piz Bernina soaring above the Diavolezza area. Lago Bianco, a large reservoir at Bernina Pass, dominates the view to the southeast. Behind you a waterfall on the outlet stream for Lake Pischa cascades down steep cliffs into the Val da Fain.

At 4.2 miles the trail turns left (northeast) at a sharp hairpin curve. A short distance beyond the path turns right (southeast), descending a series of tight, steep switchbacks down grassy slopes to the west of Lake Pischa's outlet stream. The switchbacks end at 5.1 miles and the grade abates as the path curves to the right (south). The trail now descends to a wide track along the valley floor at 5.4 miles. Here we turn right (down valley) toward Bernina Suot. (Note: bikes are allowed on this trail.)

The track descends on easy to moderate grades down the Val da Fain above the west side of the Fain River. At 6.1 miles pass a trail branching left to Alp Bernina. At 6.4 miles the track exits the mouth of the valley and crosses a bridge over the Bernina River. On the south side of the bridge turn left at the junction. Soon the trail reaches the highway. Carefully cross the highway and enter the car park for the Diavolezza cable car, train station and bus stop. Reach the trail station/bus stop at 6.7 miles. It is also possible to turn right after crossing the highway and follow a trail to the Bernina Suot train station. Diavolezza is closer.

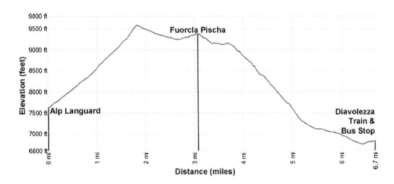

Trailhead Directions

There are several options to get to the Languard chairlift at the start of the hike and back to St. Moritz from Bernina Diavolezza. Check the current schedules to determine which options will be faster. Schedules are posted at the train stations/bus stops and on the SBB website/SBB app.

From St. Moritz to Alp Languard: See Hike 83.

From Bernina Diavolezza to St. Moritz: The best options are to take the train directly to St. Moritz or catch the #705 bus to St. Moritz Bahnhof. Another option is to get on the #701 bus bound for the Pontresina Bahnhof and get off at Pontresina Post. Wait at the stop for the next bus heading toward Surlej/Corvatschbahn and get off at the St. Moritz train station or another stop convenient to your accommodations. Check the SBB website/SBB app for current schedules and see which option is fastest.

85. Morteratsch Glacier and Boval Hut ★★★★★
Distance: 6.7 - 8.0 miles (round trip)
Near St. Moritz in the Upper Engadine / Val Bernina

The hike to the Boval Hut enjoys breathtaking views of the dramatic glacial cirque at the head of the Morteratsch Valley, dominated by the Piz Palu and Bernina massifs along with the Morteratsch and Pers Glaciers.

Distance: 6.7-8.0 miles (round trip)
Elevation: 6,220-ft. at Trailhead
8,225-ft. at the Hut
Elevation Gain: 2,005-ft.
Difficulty: moderate-strenuous

Basecamp: St. Moritz
Val Bernina Map: See page 391
Online Map/Photos:
www.hikingwalking.com/boval-hut

Why Hike to the Morteratsch Glacier and Boval Hut

The trail to the Boval Hut features fabulous views of the magnificent glacial cirque at the head of the Morteratsch Valley and should be on everyone's short list when visiting the St. Moritz area.

From the train station at Morteratsch, the trail climbs the valley's western wall and then ascends along/atop the western lateral moraine of the Morteratsch Glacier. Here grand views open to Piz Palu, the Bellavista ridge, Piz Bernina, Piz Morteratsch and nearby peaks, forming the valley's spectacular head wall. The Morteratsch glacier spills down from the slopes between the Bellavista ridge and Piz Bernina to the valley floor where it is joined by the Pers glacier, tumbling down the flanks of the Piz Palu massif.

The hike ends at the Boval Hut (8,186-ft.), sitting atop a bench beneath Piz Boval. The hut and areas around the hut feature awesome views of the glacier clad peaks towering above the head of the valley. A motionless river of ice, formed by the combined glaciers, flows along the valley floor.

The hike can be extended by descending from the Boval Hut trail to the Morteratsch Glacier trail and then hiking to the foot of the glacier.

Note: Fix chains are provided along a section of the trail that climbs steep switchbacks with some minor exposure.

To the Boval Hut

Take the train to Morteratsch (6,220-ft.), located in the Bernina Valley. (See below). Walk east from the station past the Hotel Morteratsch. Turn right on the first road that crosses the train tracks. Across the tracks are hiking signs. Walk south on the trail toward the Vadret de Morteratsch (Morteratsch Glacier) (50-min) and Chamanna de Boval (Boval Hut) (2-hr). In less than 0.1 miles reach a junction. Turn right on the trail toward the Boval Hut. The broad trail straight ahead leads to the foot of the glacier.

Soon the trail starts ascending on moderately-steep grades up the west side of the valley through a forest of larch and pine trees. Switchbacks facilitate the climb. Openings in the trees offer tantalizing views of the high peaks and glaciers at the head of the valley.

At 0.6 miles pass a trail, branching right, to Pontresina (Puntraschigna is the Romansh spelling). A short distance beyond a second trail branches right to the Chunetta viewpoint (6,834-ft.). The short 5 minute detour to the viewpoint rewards hikers with great views of the glacier-clad peaks at the head of the valley. To be honest, these are the same views you will see soon along the main trail. Still it is a nice diversion and a good destination for parties short on time or who can't make it all the way to the Boval Hut.

Past the viewpoint ignore the trail branching left (southeast) at 0.8 miles and dropping steeply down to the Morteratsch Glacier trail on the valley floor trail. We continue straight ahead toward the Boval Hut.

Beyond the junction the trees thin and terrific views open to the incredible glacial cirque at the head of the valley. Cross a wood bridge over a stream at 1.3 miles. Past the bridge the trail climbs to the crest of the lateral moraine along the west side of the Morteratsch glacier. The trail now travels either atop the moraine or in the trough below the moraine. Large sections of the moraine are eroded and unstable. The trail builders are in a constant battle to strike a balance between offering hikers great views of the valley while keeping parties off potentially dangerous parts of the moraine wall.

Views continue to improve as you head up valley. A wall of mountains, including Piz Palu, the Bellavista ridge, Crast' Aguzza, Piz Bernina and Piz Morteratsch, form the valley's spectacular head wall. The Morteratsch glacier spills down from the slopes between the Bellavista ridge and Piz Bernina to the valley floor where it is joined by the Pers glacier, tumbling down the flanks of the Piz Palu massif.

At 2.1 miles views open to beautiful waterfalls, fed by glacial meltwater, cascading down the steep slopes above the trail. Munt Pers (Pers Mountain) rises above the east side of the valley. The rapidly receding Morteratsch glacier is now seen flowing along the valley floor. Across the valley the Pers glacier barely reaches the valley floor.

The grade steepens as the trail continues up the valley. Ahead a knoll protruding into the valley partially blocks the view up the valley. At 2.7 miles the moraine wall has collapsed and the trail is forced to climb switchbacks up the flanks of the rugged hillside. Fix chains safeguard steep, partially exposed sections of the trail. The grade eases at the top of the switchbacks and the path now ascends along the valley's steep western slopes high above the glacier flowing down the valley floor.

At 3.1 miles the trail rounds the knoll and views reopen to the valley's glacier-clad head wall. Piz Trovat, Piz d'Arlas and Piz Cambrena now join the scene, rising to the northeast of the Piz Palu massif. Soon the trail curves left (southwest/west) as it climbs switchbacks up rocky meadows to the Boval Hut (8,186-ft.) at 3.3 miles. The hut, sitting in rugged meadows atop a bench, offers refreshments and accommodations. Breathtaking views from the hut encompass the Bernina massif and the Morteratsch Glacier.

A use trail climbs the rocky hillside above the hut to great viewpoints with panoramic vistas of the valley's head wall. Here you have a front row seat to the amazing spectacle of rock and ice. Piz Morteratsch, Piz Bernina, the Bellavista ridge, Piz Palu and Piz Cambrena dominate the dramatic glacial cirque at the head of the valley. The Morteratsch and Pers glaciers flow in motionless waves down the flanks of the peaks. Piz Boval towers above the hut to the west while to the east Piz Trovat, Piz d'Arlas and Piz Cambrena form an arc around a massive bowl cradling the Pers glacier.

When you are done taking in the views retrace your steps to the Morteratsch train station. Ambitious hikers can drop down to the Morteratsch Glacier trail on the valley floor (passed on the way to Boval Hut), losing about 300-ft. in 0.3 miles, and then walk up the valley for one mile to the foot of the glacier. The return trip to the Morteratsch train station from the glacier is 1.8 miles. Total hiking distance to visit the hut and the foot of the glacier is 8.0 miles.

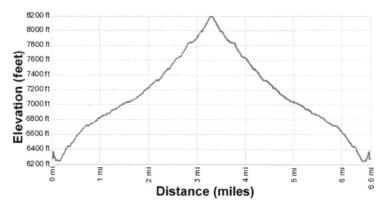

Trailhead Directions

From St. Moritz to Morteratsch: Take the train from the St. Moritz Bahnhof to Morteratsch. Depending on the time of day the ride will take 24 to 28 minutes. Check the SBB website/app for the current train schedule.

Scuol

Location: In the Canton of Graubunden in the Lower Engadine Valley

The beautiful Lower Engadine region of Switzerland is recommended for hikers seeking an off the beaten path destination with terrific trails. The Silvretta Range towers above the valley to the north while the Engadine Dolomites rise to the south. Each range is cut by deep valleys rimmed by rugged peaks and stunning cirques. Water flows down the tributary valleys into the River Inn rushing along the valley floor.

Here you will not find massive 4,000-meter mountains draped with glaciers. Instead this is a landscape of gray jagged peaks rising above dense forests and beautiful meadows. It's a peaceful, beguiling landscape that will entice you to explore its hidden delights.

The landscape forms the backdrop for an interesting culture with a distinct language, architecture and traditions. In the valley's villages you will hear and see signs in Romansh, a native language derived from Latin. People will greet you by saying, "Allegra," meaning, "joy to you."

The charming villages, spread along the hillsides and the valley floor, are filled with traditional houses arranged along cobbled streets. Facades are decorated with Sgraffiti, a technique popular during the 17th and mid-18th century that paints and/or etches designs into wet plaster. Architectural features include arched doors, thick walls and deep set windows. Many homes are built with large entrance halls. Others are designed with barns on the bottom floor. Visit Guarda, Ardez, Ftan and the center of Scuol to see the best examples of these architectural gems.

An excellent network of trails crisscrosses the region catering to hikers of varying interests and abilities. Outings range from lovely strolls between quaint villages to paths ascending through meadows to superb overlooks. Avid, fit hikers will love the challenging trails climbing to spectacular pass.

A lakes basin above the south side of Lavin and the S-charl valley, branching south from the Lower Engadine at Scuol, are home to the Swiss National Park, the country's largest nature reserve. The park is dedicated to preserving the wild, pristine landscape and the region's flora and fauna. Strict rules govern visiting the park. Biking and camping are not allowed and hikers are required to follow strict rules including staying on the designated trails and only eating in specific rest areas.

About Scuol and the Nearby Villages

Scuol, the largest village in the valley, is the recommended base camp for the region with good transportation links to trailheads. There are plenty of hotels, guesthouses, vacation apartments and other types of lodging in Scuol along with restaurants, bars and shops to meet a hiker's needs.

The center of the village is located along the Stradun, the main street through the middle of the village, and is bounded to the north by valley's main highway and to the south by the River Inn (En in Romansh). The Bahnhof (staziun in Romansh) is situated at the west end of the village across the main highway. At the southeast end of the station is a bus hub. Another bus hub is located in front of the Post Office on the south side of the Stradun. A Tourist Office (scuol-zernez.engadin.com) and a Coop Supermarket are situated in the complex to the west of the Post Office. At the east end of the Stradun is a Volg Grocery.

During the summer participating hotels offer free travel passes on the Scuol - Muotta Naluns gondola and the Ftan Chairlift, which whisk hikers to trail systems around the Muotta Naluns ski area and Prui (at the top of the chairlift). The local buses and train line between Scuol and Zernez are also free with the pass.

Lodging is also available in Ftan, Zernez, Guarda, Ardez and some of the smaller villages in the valley. Shopping and other services are somewhat limited and the transportation to trailheads, especially those in the S-charl Valley, is more time consuming.

Hiking around Scuol and the Lower Engadine Valley

The hike between Guarda and Scuol (Hike 86), a scenic traverse along the north side of the Lower Engadine Valley, offers a good introduction to the region that combines superb views of the valley's high peaks with lovely strolls through the traditional villages. The hike to Alp Laret and Piz Clunas (Hike 87), also on the north side of the valley, visits the scenic overlooks at Mout da l'Hom and the summit of Piz Clunas with panoramic views of the Engadine Dolomite range to the south.

From Guarda a long, challenging trail ascends to the Tuoi Hut and then crosses Furcletta Pass, visiting three beautiful valleys on its way to Ardez. The Guarda to Ardez hike (Hike 88) can be shorten and made easier by simply doing an out-and-back hike to the Tuoi Hut.

From Lavin, to the west of Guarda, a trail ascends the Zeznina Valley to the gorgeous Macun Lakes (Hike 89) in the Swiss National Park. Other National Park hikes are found along the S-charl road. Take the bus from Scuol to S-charl and get off at the Mingerbrucke stop to hike up Val Minger.

(Hike 90) The trail ascends lovely Val Minger to Sur il Foss, a scenic pass with superb views of Val Minger, Val Plavna and beyond. Extend the day by walking to Tarasp or taking the demanding trail over the Fuorcla da Botsch. Alternatively, get off the bus at S-charl and walk up the beautiful S-charl Valley to the Fuorcla Funtuna da S-charl (Hike 92), a broad pass overlooking the Mustair Valley and then continue to Ofenpass where a combination of a bus and train will return you to Scuol.

While not in the park the trail to Val Sesvenna and Sesvenna Pass (Hike 91), also starting at S-charl, climbs to a meadow-clad bowl with fine views of the peaks towering above S-charl. Extend the hike with a strenuous climb to the pass on the Swiss-Italian border.

Other options include visiting the Uina Gorge (Hike 93), a narrow chasm between two sheer rock walls, on the long hike up the Val d'Uina. For an easy day walk to Tarasp (Hike 94) and visit the Tarasp Castle. There are several routes allowing you to turn the hike into a longer loop. For a shorter day, take the bus to Tarasp and then walk back.

Getting to Scuol

From the Zurich Airport or Zurich Bahnhof (train station) take the train to Scuol-Tarasp Staziun. You will need to changes trains in Landquart. The trip takes about two and 38 minutes from Zurich.

From the Geneva Airport or Gare (train station) take the train to Scuol-Tarasp Staziun. The trip requires changing trains in Zurich and Landquart. This is a very long ride that takes five hours and 44 minutes.

Check the SBB website/app for directions from other locations.

Nearby Attractions & Rainy Day Activities

The **Museum of the Lower Engadin**e in Scuol is located in the lower plaza (south of the Stradun) in an historic home built around 1700. Rooms in the house contain furniture and artifacts showing how people lived during the period. There is also an exhibit displaying prehistoric finds in the Lower Engadine region.

Take a guided tour of the **Castle of Tarasp**, located in the small village of Tarasp to the southwest of Scuol. Built in 1040, the Castle was restored in the summer of 1900 to its original state. Ernst Ludwig von Hessen inherited the castle in 1916. Today the castle is owned by a private foundation and houses a collection of antiques and modern and contemporary art.

The ruins of the **Castle Steinsberg in Ardez**, built in 1209, are set atop a rocky knoll with grand views of the Lower Engadine Valley and the village of Ardez. The site includes the ruins of the St. Luzius chapel.

Take a walk through the villages of Guarda, Ardez and Scuol to views the architecture, visit the shops and sample the local cuisine. It is easy to walk between the villages (See Hike 86 - Guarda to Scuol) or take the train. This is a good option for a rainy day.

Good Things to Know about Scuol and the Lower Engadine

- In the Lower Engadine people speak German and Romansh. Typically people will speak some English but that is not the case everywhere. The Romansh language is spoken, lived and fostered in Lower Engadine. There is a law stating that the signage on shops and businesses must be in Romansh. School children are taught exclusively in Romansh until grade three. After that, German is the first foreign language introduced, followed by French and English (from grade five) or Italian.

- There is one campground in Scuol, the Swiss Campground at Gurlina, located along the south side of the River Inn. There is a second campground in Sur En situated to the east (up valley) from Scuol on the south side of the River Inn.

- The Scuol Youth Hostel, on Via da la Staziun to the southeast of the train station, offers private and shared rooms.

Map: Scuol and the Lower Engadine Valley

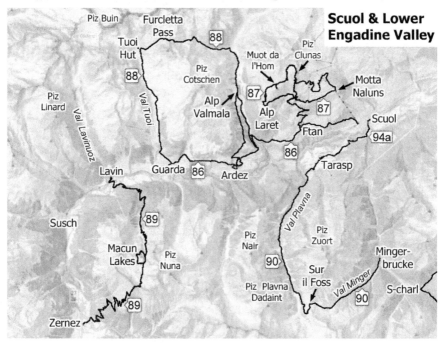

86. Guarda to Scuol ★★★★☆
Distance: 6.8 - 9.4 miles (one-way)
Near Scuol in the Lower Engadine

This scenic traverse along the north side of the Lower Engadine Valley combines great views of the valley's high peaks with lovely rambles through pretty villages with traditional Engadine homes decorated with sgraffiti.

Distance: 6.8 - 9.4 miles (one-way)
Elevation: 5,427-ft. at Trailhead
4,219-ft. at Scuol
Elevation Gain/Loss: 1,500-ft./2,200-ft.
Difficulty: moderate

Basecamp: Scuol
Scuol and Lower Engadine
Map: See page 413
Online Map/Photos:
www.hikingwalking.com/guarda-scuol

Why Hike from Guarda to Scuol

This interesting walk travels along sunny benches and gentles slopes high above the north side of the River Inn (En in Romansh) in the Lower Engadine Valley. The path follows farm tracks and trails through meadows and forests, passing through charming villages with traditional houses decorated with sgraffiti (plural of Sgraffito), a decorative art form popular during the 17th and mid-18th centuries.

The hike, passing through Guarda, Bos-cha, Ardez and Ftan before reaching Scuol, can be done in either direction and is easily shortened by starting/ending the hike in Ardez or Ftan. The trail is a great option for anyone looking for an easy day or if the weather precludes hiking at higher elevations.

Plan on more time than the mileage implies. Hikers will be tempted to explore the villages to see the wide variety of sgraffiti, browse through some of the interesting shops and enjoy one of the restaurants before continuing to the next destination.

There is a lot of up and down along the hike, more than the net difference between the high and low point in the trail statistics. Over the length of the hike the trail gains over 1,500-ft. and loses more than 2,200-ft. Except for the final 1,190-ft. drop to Scuol, the elevation gains/losses are on easy to moderate grades.

Walking from Guarda to Scuol

The day starts with a train and bus ride to the village of Guarda. (See trailhead directions below.) The well preserved village is filled with beautiful, traditional Engadine houses adorn with sgraffiti, a technique where the top layer of plaster is scratched or incised with a design, revealing a lower layer of plaster in a contrasting color.

Walk east along the main road through the village toward Bos-cha and Ardez on the Via son Giachen (Route #43). Signs at the bus stop will help get you started. As you wander through the town enjoy the wide range of sgraffiti designs on the homes lining the street.

At 0.25 miles reach a junction at the east end of the village. Bear left on the road, signed for Route 43, toward Bos-cha and Ardez. Ahead are views of the small village of Bos-cha set against a backdrop of rugged peaks rising above the south side of the River Inn in the Lower Engadine Valley.

The path now travels through pastures and scattered trees. At all intersections stay on Route 43. As you walk views open south across the valley to Piz Macun, Piz Nuna and Piz Sursass rimming the head of Val Nuna (Nuna Valley).

Reach the small village of Bos-cha at 1.1 miles. To the west the high peaks rising along the Fluela Pass Road dominate the views. At the east end of the village signs now point toward Ardez and Ftan.

Beyond Bos-cha the path descends on moderate to easy grades through pastures and scattered trees with views up Val Nuna. Piz Nair, Piz Zuort, Piz Minger and a host of rugged peaks fill the skyline to the southeast. Soon views open to Ardez and the ruins of the Steinsberg Castle.

Reach Ardez at 2.7 miles. The path now winds through the village, passing many traditional homes decorated with sgraffiti. One very interesting structure is adorned with an elaborate mural of Adam and Eve in the Garden of Eden.

Ignore a sign telling you to turn left and instead continue along the road. At 3.0 miles reach a fountain in the middle of a square situated right below the castle ruins. Here a path branches right and climbs to the ruins set atop a knoll. The ruins include the 4-story castle keep (tower) and an interesting smaller ruin. The knoll boasts fine vistas stretching up and down the Lower Engadine Valley along with birds-eye-views of Ardez.

Ardez is a convenient spot to cut the hike short. Simply walk south through the village to the train station located on the valley floor. Here trains head east to Scuol and west toward Landquart and Pontresina (St. Moritz).

When you are done exploring the ruins, return to the square with the fountain and follow the road heading northeast. Soon you will see a path, marked for Ftan, branching left (north) and ascending through pastures.

Reach a junction at 3.5 miles and bear right (northeast) on the path toward Ftan, Alp Valmala and Route #43. Turn around for views of the castle set against a backdrop of the peaks lining Val Sampuoir across the valley.

At 4.0 miles reach Ruina Chanoua, the ruins of an old tavern. Beyond the ruins the trail curves to the left (north) and soon joins a road. Follow the road as it travels up the west side of Val Tasna (Tasna Valley).

At 4.7 miles the road crosses the Tasnan River on a bridge. On the east side of the river we turn left (up the Tasna Valley) on a track signed for Alp Valmala, Ftan and Route #43. A short distance beyond exit the track by turning right (east) on a trail signed for Ftan and Route #43. Ftan is painted in red and white letters on a large rock at the intersection. (The track continues up the valley to Alp Valmala.)

Our path climbs through trees, heading south/southeast. Soon the trail exits the trees and curves to the left, leaving the Tasna Valley. We now head east/southeast, traveling through pastures and scattered trees toward Ftan. To the south views open to Piz Minger and the summit towering above the west side of the S-charl valley, a tributary valley branching south from the River Inn.

At 6.1 miles the trail reaches a paved road. Turn right, following the road for a short distance before turning left on a secondary road that continues east/northeast toward Ftan. None of these roads have much if any traffic.

This section of the route enjoys great views of the Piz Minger massif and the high peaks rising above the south side of the Lower Engadine Valley. As you progress up the road you will start passing houses and soon reach the old section of Ftan called Ftan-Grond at 6.8 miles. (Ftan is composed of two connected villages; Ftan-Grond and Ftan-Pitschen to the east.)

Take some time to explore this pretty village set atop a sun drenched terrace. Of particular note is the church tower, separated from the main church building, and the large houses with the barns on the bottom floor.

Ftan is another spot to cut the hike short. The bus stop is located in the center of the village adjacent to the Post Office. Regularly scheduled buses head to the Scuol Train Station and then make a number of stops along the main road through Scuol.

When you are done exploring the village, return to the village center and head northeast, following the signs pointing toward Scuol/Route #43. Reach Ftan-Pitschen at 7.25 miles. From the village views stretch south to the Tarasp Castle, set atop a hill along the valley floor on the south side of the River Inn. Piz Minger, Piz Zuort, Piz Pisoc and Piz Lavetscha tower above the castle to the south. Piz Plavna Dadaint, Piz Plattas and Piz Nair rise above Val Plavna (Plavna Valley).

Exit the village on a broad track that descends on easy to moderate grades through pastures with panoramic vistas of the peaks to the south. Along the way views open to Scuol sprawled along the valley floor.

At 8.2 miles the grade steepens as the track drops off the terrace. Turn right at 8.7 miles on a signed trail that descends steeply to Scuol. Near the end of the descent the path passes the Motta Naluns cable car station and then turns right, dropping down to the Scuol-Tarasp train station at 9.4 miles. Here you can follow the Via da le Staziun down to an intersection (traffic circle) with the main highway through the valley. Carefully cross the intersection and continue along Via da le Staziun, which passes through the center of Scuol.

Scuol, the capital of the Lower Engadine region, is a delightful place to explore. It includes a wide selection of restaurant and shops along with beautifully preserved traditional homes and a pretty church set atop a scenic knoll.

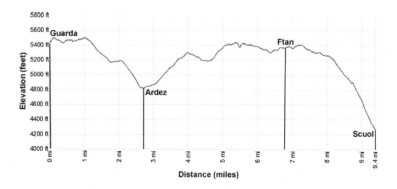

Trailhead Directions

From Scuol to Guarda: Take the train from Scuol in the direction of Pontresina or Landquart and get off at Guarda staziun (station). The ride takes about 12 minutes. Note: Guarda is a "stop on demand" station. Listen for the conductor to announce the stop. He/she will tell you it is a stop on demand. You must then push the "Stop on Demand" button, typically located near the door, to signal to the conductor that you wish to get off the train in Guarda.

Guarda sits atop a bench high above the north side of the Lower Engadine Valley. At the Guarda staziun change to the minibus that climbs to the village in 8 minutes. Depending on the time of day, you will either need to wait for 5 minutes or 18 minutes to catch the bus.

You can also walk to the village up a very steep trail climbing through pastures or ascend on the road. (Follow the signs behind the train station.) I recommend taking the bus, which eliminates a 1.7 mile walk that gains over 700-ft. in elevation.

Consult the SBB Website/SBB app for the current schedule and wait times. Note: When searching for schedules note that Guarda, cumun is the name of the bus stop in the village while Guarda, staziun is the name of the train station on the valley floor.

From Ftan to Scuol: From Ftan, Cumun post bus stop, located in the center of the village adjacent to the Post Office, board a bus bound for Scuol. The ride will take 12 minutes to the Scuol Train Station. The bus continues beyond the train station, making a number of stops in Scuol. Consult the SBB Website/SBB app to find the stop nearest your accommodation.

87. Alp Laret and Piz Clunas ☆☆☆☆☆
Distance: 7.3 - 9.2 miles (loop)
Near Scuol in the Lower Engadine

This loop hike ascends thorough lovely meadows to the overlook at Mout da l'Hom and then the summit of Piz Clunas with panoramic views of the high peaks towering above the Lower Engadine Valley and beyond.

Distance: 3.1 miles (one way) to Alp Laret
5.9 miles (one way) to Piz Clunas
9.2 miles (loop) to Motta Naluns
Elevation: 7,008-ft. at Trailhead
7,238-ft. at Alp Laret
9,160-ft. at Piz Clunas
7,008-ft. at Motta Naluns
Elevation Gain: 570-ft. to Alp Laret
1,922-ft. to Piz Clunas
-2,152-ft. to Motta Naluns

Difficulty: moderate-strenuous
Basecamp: Scuol
Scuol and Lower Engadine Map: See page 413
Online Map/Photos:
www.hikingwalking.com/piz-clunas

Why Hike to Alp Laret and Piz Clunas

This hike, starting in either Ftan or Scuol, uses ski lifts to reach the slopes high above the north side of the Lower Engadine Valley and then travels along scenic paths to pretty Alp Laret. Here the trail ascends to Muot da l'Hom, a panoramic overlook with wonderful views of the high peaks towering above the River Inn (En in Romansh) and the tributary valleys to the south and west. From the viewpoint the trail climbs Piz Clunas with superb, 360-degree views of the Lower Engadine Valley and beyond.

A steep descent down the south facing slopes of Piz Clunas leads to trail dropping steeply down to Prui and Ftan or a more gentle descent through meadows and ski slopes to the top of the Motta Naluns lift that descends to Scuol. The hike can be extended by eliminating the lifts at either the start or end of the hike.

Note: The trails along this hike, with the exception of the paths ascending and descending Piz Clunas, are open to mountain bikes. Much of this hike travels above the timberline and is not recommended during bad weather or if thunderstorms are threatening.

Motta Naluns to Prui and Alp Laret

- **Distance from Trailhead:** 3.1 miles (one way)
- **Highest Elevation:** 7,238-ft.
- **Elevation Gain:** 570-ft.

This description assumes you start the day by taking the cable car from Scuol to Motta Naluns. To shorten the hike, take a bus to Ftan and then ride the chairlift to Prui. If starting in Prui, subtract 1.2-miles from the trail mileage in this description. (See trailhead directions below.)

Outside the Motta Naluns lift station find the trail signpost and start walking west/southwest on a wide track toward Prui and Alp Laret. The trail initially travels on level grades and then descends on moderate to easy grades through wildflower-filled meadows and scattered trees to Prui at 1.2 miles.

Along the way enjoy great views to the south across the Lower Engadine Valley of Piz Lavetscha, Piz Pisoc and Piz Zuort rising above the Zuort Valley and Piz Plavna, Piz Plattas and Piz Nair towering above the west side of the Plavna Valley. The high peaks soaring above the Macun Lakes and Susch are seen in the distance to the southwest.

At Prui (aka Nateas/S-Chabaellera on the trail sign), bear right (northwest) on a two-track toward Alp Laret. The path travels through pretty meadows and then ascends steeply through a forest of larch and pine trees to a gravel road and trail junction at 1.7 miles. Turn left (west) on the road towards Alp Laret and Munt da l'Hom on the Via Engiadina trail. To the north views open to meadows, awash in wildflowers, and avalanche fencing high on the south facing slopes of Piz Clunas.

Walk a short distance on the road to an intersection and turn right (north) on a lesser used gravel road towards Alp Laret. Soon we bear right on a trail marked for the Via Engiadina that ascends a short distance uphill to another set of signs at 1.9 miles. Bear left toward Alp Laret. The trail to the right, signed for Piz Clunas, will be used on the return journey.

The undulating path climbs on easy to moderate grades through meadows sprinkled with wildflowers, offering great views of the peaks towering above the south side of the valley. Soon the trail crosses a creek on a wood bridge and then ascends through rocky meadows, cresting a ridge to a meadow clad bench at 2.7 miles.

Descend on easy grades across the bench toward Alp Laret. Soon views open west to Piz Cotschen rising above the Tasna Valley. Reach Alp Laret at 3.1 miles. The inn and restaurant, composed of three lovely old stone buildings, boasts superb views of high peaks of the Lower Engadine Valley.

Al Laret to Piz Clunas

- **Segment Stat:** 2.8 miles (one-way) from Al Laret to Piz Clunas
- **Total Distance:** 5.9 miles (one way)
- **Maximum Elevation:** 9,160-ft.
- **Elevation Gain/Loss:** 1,922-ft.

Walk behind the Alp buildings to a junction where signs point left toward a path dropping down to Ftan and the continuation of the Via Engiadina up the Tasna Valley to Alp Valmala and Ardez. We turn right on the trail toward Piz Clunas (1-hr 45-min), Muot da l'Hom (1-hr) and Alp Clunas (1-hr 15-min).

The trail widens as it ascends the hill behind the Alp, passing an old water trough. Soon you will come to a steep track breaking off to the left. Either trail you are on (the main trail) or the one to the left works. The steeper path to the left has better views.

For this description we take the track to the left. As you proceed uphill the trail deteriorates, becoming eroded and braided as it ascends on moderately-steep to steep grades. The climb is accompanied by fine views of Piz Cotschen and the summits rising above the d'Urezzas and Urschai Valleys to the northwest.

Soon the trail heads for and then curves around the left side of a small knoll. This portion of the trail is poorly marked. Keep an eye out for red and white markers on rocks and stakes to keep on track.

Past the knoll our path reconnects with the main trail. The combined trail narrows as it climbs through open meadows. Views of the mountains rimming the Tasna, d'Urezzas and Urschai Valleys, to the west/northwest, along with the peaks rising above of the Lower Engadine Valley, to the south, continue to improve as you gain elevation.

At 3.7 miles the trail curves to the right (northeast), ascending steeply toward a saddle and Muot da l'Hom. Ahead views open to Minschun Pitschen and Piz la Greala to the north.

At 4.2 miles the trail crests a saddle and reaches a junction with a trail branching right to the Muot da l'Hom overlook. The path straight ahead leads to Piz Clunas and Alp Clunas. I recommend taking the 0.3 miles detour (round-trip) to the overlook for stunning, 360-degree views of the surrounding peaks before continuing to Piz Clunas. In addition to the peaks soaring above the the Lower Engadine Valley and rimming the Tasna, d'Urezzas and Urschai Valleys, the vantage point includes great views of Piz Minschun and Piz Clunas to the north/northeast.

Beyond the overlook the trail soon descends on easy grades to meet a gravel road. Follow the road to a sign pointing to the left toward Piz Clunas at 4.9 miles. There appears to be no trail at the marker. You can angle northwest across the meadows, cross a creek and soon meet the trail to Piz Clunas.

The easier option is to continue a short distance along the road and cross a stream. Past the stream, look left (north) for a narrow trail heading uphill. This is the trail to Piz Clunas. The trail become more distinct as it climbs steeply above the right (east) side of the stream and then curves to the right (northeast) through meadows. Soon we pass above Lac da Minschun, a small lake nestled in a bowl beneath the craggy slopes of Piz Minschun.

The path now climbs very steeply up the rocky hillside to the top of the ridge extending north from Piz Clunas. A stiff climb up the narrow ridge crest leads to the summit of Piz Clunas (9,160-ft.) at 5.9 miles. From the summit enjoy breathtaking, panoramic views. The mountains rimming the Tasna, d'Urezzas and Urschai Valleys dominate the view to west/northeast. The summits towering above the Lower Engadine Valley fill the skyline to the south. Vistas extend southeast to the peaks rising above the S-charl valley and southwest to the mountains soaring above Susch. The rugged summit of Piz Minschun rises above Piz Clunas to the north. Below the overlook distinctive Tarasp Castle is seen along the valley floor to the south of the River Inn.

Piz Clunas to Prui/Ftan or Motta Naluns/Scuol

- **Segment Stat:** 3.3 miles (one-way) to Complete the Hike
- **Total Distance:** 9.2 miles (loop)
- **Ending Elevation:** 7,008-ft.
- **Elevation Gain/Loss:** -2,152-ft.

When you are done taking in the views, follow the trail descending very steeply down the south facing slopes of Piz Clunas. Soon the path reaches switchbacks and the grade moderates a bit as it drops down to a gravel road and the Alp Clunas junction at 6.8 miles. Here hikers have a choice. Straight ahead a sign points across the road to a trail descending to Prui (50-min) and Ftan (1-hr 45-min). Alternative, turn left (east) and follow the road toward Chamanna Naluns (Naluns Hut/35-min) and Motta Naluns (1-hr 30-min).

To Prui and Ftan

To return to Prui and Ftan, cross the road and descend steeply through meadows with fine views to the south. A series of short switchbacks facilitate the descent. At 7.8 miles reach the junction we pass earlier in the day (at 1.7 miles). Now reverse the remainder of the walk to return to the chair lift at 8.5 miles (7.3 miles if starting at Prui).

Alternatively, you can walk all the way down to Ftan. To walk back to Ftan, at the junction at 6.8 miles, instead of turning left toward Prui turn right (west) and follow the signs back to Ftan at 10.6 miles (9.4 miles if starting the hike from Prui). The descent, losing over 1,500-ft., travels through meadows and forest with nice views of the high peaks to the south.

Whether you take the chairlift or walk down to Ftan, return to Scuol by bus. It is also possible to walk from Ftan to Scuol. The 2.6 mile walk loses 1,175-ft. on its way to Scuol.

To Motta Naluns

To return to Motta Naluns, turn left at the junction toward Chamanna Naluns (Naluns Hut) and Motta Naluns. Follow the road as it descends on easy grades to a junction at 7.1 miles. Here we bear left on a trail that crosses an old landslide and then descends through ski slopes to a junction below a man-made pond at 8.0 miles. This segment of the trail enjoys great views to the south. Along the way vistas open Piz Nair, Fuorcla Campatsch and Piz Campatsch to the north.

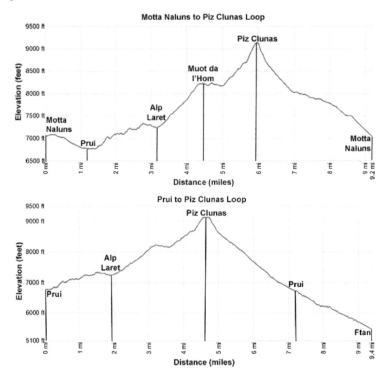

Turn left at the junction, following the trail signs back to Motta Naluns at 9.2 miles. At Motta Naluns ride the gondola down to Scuol.

422

Note: The trails along this hike, with the exception of the paths ascending and descending Piz Clunas, are open to mountain bikes. Typically there are few bikes on the trail. Much of this trail travels above the timberline and is not recommended during bad weather or if thunderstorms are threatening.

Trailhead Directions

From Scuol to Motta Naluns: From the Scuol Train Station walk northeast to the valley station for the gondola to Motta Naluns. The walk should take about 5 minutes. The ride to Motta Naluns takes about 12 minutes. See the Bergbahnen-Scuol Website for the gondola schedule. Depending on where you are staying in Scuol, you may wish to ride the bus to the train station. Consult the SBB Website/SBB app to find the bus stop nearest your accommodation. The train station is listed as Scuol-Tarasp on the SBB site.

Scuol to Ftan/Prui: From the Scuol Train Station, board the #921 but to Ftan and get off in the Cumun stop, located next to the Post Office in the center of town. From here, follow the signs to Ftan Fionas and the bottom station of the chairlift to Prui. The bus ride takes 11 minutes and the walk to the lift station takes about 10 minutes.

Consult the SBB Website/SBB app to find the bus stop nearest your accommodation. See the Bergbahnen-Scuol Website for the chairlift schedule. Note the lift shuts down for one hour at lunch time.

88. Guarda to Ardez via Furcletta Pass
Distance: 9.0 - 13.5 miles (one way)
Near Scuol in the Lower Engadine

This long, demanding hike visits three scenic valleys and crosses a panoramic pass with splendid views of the high peaks of the Silveretta and Engadine Dolomite Alps.

Distance: 9.0 miles (round trip) to
Tuoi Hut
11.4 miles (round trip) to Furcletta Pass
13.5 miles (one way) to Ardez
Elevation: 5,424-ft. at Trailhead
7,382-ft. at Tuoi Hut
8,973-ft. at Furcletta Pass
4,708-ft. at Ardez
Elevation Gain: 1,958-ft. to Tuoi Hut
3,549-ft. to Furcletta Pass
-4,265-ft. to Ardez.

Difficulty: strenuous
Basecamp: Scuol
Scuol and Lower Engadine
Map: See page 413
Online Map/Photos:
www.hikingwalking.com/
guarda-ardez

Why Hike from Guarda to Ardez via Furcletta Pass

Serious hikers will love this long, strenuous walk with knockout views of the high peaks of the Silveretta and Dolomite Engadine Alps. The hike starts with a beautiful walk up the Tuoi Valley, traveling through flower filled meadows to Chamanna Tuoi (Tuoi Hut). From the hut enjoy fine views of Piz Fliana rising above the west side of the valley while Piz Buin, Piz Jeramias and the Dreilanderspitz, straddling the Swiss-Austrian border, tower above the valley.

From the hut the trail turns east and ascends steeply through meadows where views open to the Tuoi Glacier, cradled in a bowl beneath the Dreilanderspitz, Hinter Jamspitz and Piz Tuoi. The path then climbs steeply through scree, boulders and snow fields to Furcletta Pass, with dramatic views of the jagged peaks rising above the west side of the Tuoi valley and beyond. To the east, fine views extend down the Val d'Urezzas to Piz Minschun towering about the east side of the Val Tasna.

Beyond the pass the trail drops steeply down scree-covered slopes that give way to pretty meadows beneath a beautiful cirque towering above the north side of the Urezzas valley. The trail then descends along the north side of the valley to the head of Val Tasna. Here the path turns south and descends through meadows and forests accompanied by superb views of the Dolomite Engadine range rising above the south side of the Lower Engadine Valley.

This is a very long and strenuous hike gaining over 3,500-ft. on the climb to the pass and then dropping over 4,200-ft. to Ardez. Get an early start and allocate 7-8 hours to complete the walk, depending on you pace and the number of stops along the way.

An out-and-back hike to the Tuoi Hut offers hikers a shorter and less strenuous day while still enjoying the scenic delights of the Tuoi Valley.

Trailhead to Tuoi Hut

- **Distance from Trailhead:** 4.5 miles (one-way) / 9.0 miles (round trip)
- **Elevation at the Hut:** 7,382-ft.
- **Elevation Gain:** 1,958-ft.

The day starts with a train and bus ride to the village of Guarda. (See trailhead directions below.) The well preserved village is filled with beautiful, traditional Engadine houses adorn with sgraffiti, a technique where the top layer of plaster is scratched or incised with a design, revealing a lower layer of plaster in a contrasting color.

From the bus stop in the village, walk a short distance (about 700-ft.) east/northeast along the main street to a fountain in front of a house. Look for a sign on the east side of the house pointing left (north) toward Alp Sura and Chamanna Tuoi (Tuoi Hut). Turn left and follow the paved lane between houses. The road surface turns to gravel as the track ascends northwest on easy to moderate grades through pastures toward Val Tuoi (Tuoi Valley). As you head uphill enjoy views of the Engadine Dolomite range rising above the Lower Engadine Valley to the south and the summits towering above Susch to the west.

At 0.7 miles the trail curves to the right (north) into the Tuoi valley, ascending at a steady pace through flower-filled meadows and cluster of larch and pine trees along the east side of the valley. Ignore any trails branching right or left. Instead keep to the gravel road, following the signs to the Tuoi Hut.

At 1.3 miles the grade eases as the trail skirts a forested hillside. Soon the trees give way to meadows and views opens to the cirque at the head of the valley, dominated by Piz Buin. The buildings of Alp Suot are seen along the valley floor in the distance.

The track splits at 2.5 miles, shortly before reaching Alp Suot. Take the dirt/gravel road branching right toward the Tuoi Hut, Alp Sura and Lai Blau, which climbs on moderately-steep grades up a hill. The road straight ahead goes to Alp Suot.

Part way up the hill the trail passes Via Braja (6,742-ft.) where a trail branches right toward Alp Sura and Ardez. We continue along the main trail climbing toward Lai Blau and the Tuoi Hut. As you ascend the hill, turn around for great views of the peaks rising above the Lower Engadine Valley to the south.

Reach a "Y" intersection at 3.0 miles. The trail to the right heads to Lai Blau. We bear left toward the Tuoi Hut on a wide track that descends to and then gently climbs along the right (east) side of the stream.

The trail veers away from the stream as it nears a small wood building and then ascends on moderate grades toward the head of the valley. Across the valley, to the west, a pretty waterfall tumbles down the craggy slopes.

Reach Chamanna Tuoi (7,382-ft.) at 4.5 miles. The stone structure, offering dormitory accommodations and meals, enjoys great views of nearby peaks. Piz Buin, Piz Jeramias and the Dreilanderspitz, along the Swiss-Austrian border, tower above the head of the valley while Piz Fliana dominates the view to the west.

At this point you can turn around and retrace your steps to Guarda (9.0 mile round-trip hike), climb to Furcletta Pass to enjoy the views (11.4 mile round-trip hike) or cross the pass and then head down the Tasna Valley to Ardez (13.5 mile point-to-point hike).

Tuoi Hut to Furcletta Pass

- **Segment Stat:** 1.2 miles (one-way) to from the Hut to Furcletta Pass
- **Total Distance:** 5.7 miles (one-way) / 11.4 miles (round trip)
- **Maximum Elevation:** 8,973-ft.
- **Elevation Gain/Loss:** 3,549-ft.

To continue the hike to Furcletta Pass and Ardez, go around the left (west) side of the hut and follow the trail as it curves to the right (east/northeast) and climbs very steeply through rocky meadows toward Furcletta Pass and Urezzas, staying to the right (south) of a stream. Along the way pass a trail branching right toward Lai Blau. As you ascend, enjoy ever expanding views of the peaks to the north and west. Soon great views open to the Tuoi Glacier, cradled in a bowl beneath the cirque formed by the Dreilanderspitz, Hinter Jamspitz and Piz Tuoi.

At 5.1 miles the path begins a steep ascent along a rocky gully, staying to the left (north) of a small stream. Soon the trail crosses the stream, climbs out of the gully and skirts the right (east) side of a small tarn. Before reaching the end of the tarn the trail curves to the right (northeast) and climbs another rocky gully. Red and white blazed rocks help keep you on track.

The final ascent to the pass climbs very steeply up a boulder field, marked by red and white blazed rocks and stakes. Sections of the route are often covered in snow. If this is the case, located the sign at the top of the pass and pick a route through the snow, following the footsteps of others uphill. As you ascend, enjoy splendid views of the peaks rising along the north and west sides of the valley.

Reach Furcletta Pass (8,973-ft.) at 5.7 miles. The pass, a saddle on the ridge between Piz Furcletta and Piz da las Cavigliadas, enjoys magnificent views west to Piz Fliana, Piz Buin and beyond to the Verstanclahorn. To the east views extend down the Val d'Urezzas to Piz Minschun towering about the east side of Val Tasna. Piz Chaschlogna dominates the view along the north side of the Urezzas valley.

From the pass you can either return to Guarda for an 11.4 mile round trip hike or continue the hike over Furcletta pass to Ardez for a 13.5 mile point-to-point hike. I recommend heading toward Ardez (3-hr 14-min) via the scenic Urezzas and Tasna Valleys.

Furcletta Pass to Ardez

- **Segment Stat:** 7.8 miles (one-way) from the the Pass to Ardez
- **Total Distance:** 13.5 miles (one way)
- **Ending Elevation:** 4,708-ft.
- **Elevation Gain/Loss:** -4,265-ft.

To walk to Ardez, follow the trail as it drops steeply down the east side of the pass through scree, boulders and, at times, snow fields. Use caution if the route is covered in snow and turn around if you don't feel comfortable descending the slick slopes.

Cross the stream draining snowmelt from the pass at 6.2 miles and 6.3 miles and then a small side stream. Beyond the crossings the trail drops down very steep switchbacks. As you descend, rocky slopes give way to flower-speckled meadows and views open to a beautiful cirque towering above the north side of the trail.

At 7.1 miles the grade abates as the trail crosses a braided stream carrying meltwater from the Urezzas Glacier, nestled in the cirque on the north side of the valley. Depending on the time of year, crossing the streams may involve simple rock hopping or getting your feet wet. In places, wooden planks help to keep your feet dry.

Across the stream are the remains of old stone alp buildings at Marangun d'Urezzas. Past the alp the path keeps to the north (left side) of the Urezzas stream.

Reach the alp buildings at Urezzas (6,926-ft.) and a trail junction at 8.0 miles. Bear right (east/southeast) on the trail heading toward Alp Valmala (25-min) and Ardez (2-hr 15-min). The trail to the left (northeast) leads to the Jamtal Hut and Pass Futschol.

The trail to Alp Valmala crosses a bridge to the south side of the Urezzas stream and then travels through pastures, curving to the right (south) as it enters the Val Tasna (Tasna Valley). Ignore the trail crossing a bridge to a dirt road on the the east side of the Tasnan River. Instead continue heading south down the west side of Val Tasna beside the rushing waters of the Tasnan River.

Reach Alp Valmala (6,493-ft.) and a trail junction at 8.9 miles. The trail to the left crosses the Tasnan River and then heads toward Alp Laret and Ftan. We continue straight ahead toward Ardez (1-hr 45-min) on a trail skirting the right (west) side of the alp buildings. Beyond the alp the trail descends on easy grades, passing through pastures with nice views of the peaks rising above the Lower Engadine Valley to the south. Behind you are nice views up Val Tasna.

At 9.9 miles a junction offers two options for returning to Ardez, a high route and a low route. Both are the same length. The high route or Via

Engiadina trail, branching right toward Ardez and Munt, is the more scenic option but involves some ups and downs as it crosses minor drainages high above the west side of the valley. The low route, branching left, drops down to and then travels along the west side of the river before turning southwest toward Ardez.

I prefer the high route which travels through lovely wildflower-filled pastures with expansive views to the south. Beyond the meadows the trail passes though clusters of larch and pine trees as it dips in and out of minor drainages. At 11.7 miles the path reaches a large meadow at the foot of the valley with spectacular views of the Engadine Dolomite peaks towering above the Lower Engadine valley.

Beyond the meadow the trail drops down to meet a broad track above Ardez. Turn left (east) and follow a broad path for 0.3 miles to a junction where the signs point right (south) to a track descending steeply to Ardez. The train station is located on the south side of the village near the highway at 13.5 miles. Signs along the way will keep you on track.

Note: This is a very long and strenuous hike, gaining over 3,500-ft. on the climb to the pass and then dropping over 4,200-ft. to Ardez. Get an early start and allocate 7-8 hours to complete the walk, depending on you pace and the number of stops along the way.

An out-and-back hike to the Tuoi Huts offers hikers a shorter and less strenuous day while still enjoying the scenic delights of the Tuoi Valley.

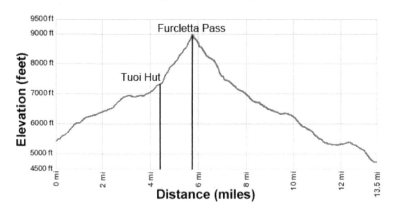

Trailhead Directions

From Scuol to Guarda: See Hike 86

From Ardez to Scuol: Take the train from Ardez to Scuol. The ride takes about 10 minutes.

89. Macun Lakes ★★★★★
Distance: 12.0 - 12.7 miles (round-trip)
Near Scuol in the Lower Engadine

This trail ascends the Zeznina Valley to the gorgeous Macun Lakes in the Swiss National Park. The glacial lake basin lies nestled beneath a rugged cirque high above the Lower Engadine Valley. Extend the hike with a challenging climb to the Baselgia Ridge and a very steep descent to Zernez.

Distance: 12.0 - 12.7 miles (round-trip)
Elevation: 4,698-ft. at Trailhead
8,583-ft. at the Lakes Basin
Elevation Gain: 3,885-ft.
Difficulty: strenuous

Basecamp: Scuol
Scuol and Lower Engadine
Map: See page 413
Online Map/Photos:
www.hikingwalking.com/macun

Why Hike to the Macun Lakes

The Macun Lakes were added to the Swiss National Park in 2000. Hikers making the steep climb up the Zeznina Valley to the basin will immediately understand why this unique area merited National Park status. Over 20 lakes and tarns lie cradled in a beautiful glacial basin beneath a rugged cirque of 10,000-ft. peaks.

The hike to the basin is accompanied by fine views of the high peaks towering above the north side of the Lower Engadine Valley. Upon reaching the basin, a loop trail travels by the three largest lakes before rejoining the main trail back to Lavin.

Fit, surefooted hikers up for a challenge can extend the hike by climbing to the Fuorcletta da Barcli (9,347-ft.), a saddle on the Baselgia Ridge. As you ascend the summits of the Engadine Valley form the backdrop for magnificent views of the basin. At the pass, vistas open to the high peaks to the west/southwest of Zernez.

From the saddle, climb to a high point on the ridge (9,662-ft.) with views that now include the peaks gracing the skyline to the west. Leave the

National Park as you drop off the ridge and descend on very steep to moderately-steep grades down the flanks of Munt Baselgia to Zernez.

The hike along the ridge and initial descent to Zernez is not recommended for anyone with a fear of heights. Keep in mind this hike gains over 4,900-ft. to the high point and the ridge and then loses more than 4,800-ft. on the descent to Zernez.

Don't attempt the climb to the ridge under snowy or icy conditions unless properly equipped. Pick a day full of promise and turn around if the weather takes a turn for the worse. The ridge is not the place to be during a thunderstorm.

Lavin to the Macun Lakes

Take the train from Scuol to Lavin (see trailhead directions below). Exit the train station and turn right (southwest) on Pra-San Jorg Strasse (street). Follow the street until it ends at Via Maistra. Turn right (southwest) on Via Maistra. The road soon crosses the Lavinuoz River on a bridge. Turn left on Plaz Strasse, the first street after the bridge. Walk one block and then bear left on Tanter/Auas, which crosses the river again on a bridge and soon become Suot Roven Strasse.

Ahead you will see a covered bridge over the River Inn (En in Romansh). Turn right and cross the River Inn using the covered bridge. On the east side of the river turn right on a broad gravel track signed for Alp Zeznina Dadaint, Macun and Zernez.

The track passes barns and a home and then becomes a two-track. Soon you will see trail signs on the left (east) pointing to Alp Zeznina Dadaint, Macun and Zernez. Turn left and ascend wooded slopes on moderate grades. At all intersections continue toward Alp Zeznina Dadaint and Macun.

At 1.9 miles crosses the Aua da Zeznina (Zeznina stream) on a wood bridge. On the east side of the river the trail turns right (south) and starts climbing moderately-steep to steep switchbacks through a larch/pine forest up the east side of the Zeznina Valley to Alp Zeznina Dadoura at 2.8 miles.

Past the Alp the path ascends on moderate grades through forests and intermittent meadows. At 3.4 miles the trees give way to meadows and we reach the stone cottage of Alp Zeznina Dadaint at 3.6 miles. Turn around here for fine views stretching north across the Lower Engadine Valley to the high peaks, including the glacier-clad Piz Buin, rising above the Tuoi and Lavinuoz Valleys.

The trail now climbs steeply up pastures and rocky meadows. At 4.1 miles the path starts ascending a series of switchbacks, passing a trail branching left toward Murtera at 4.7 miles. Beyond the junction the switchbacks continue climbing up rocky meadows and scree covered slopes.

At 5.5 miles the trail crosses the stream and then ascends on easy grades across a narrow bench, passing a small tarn along the way. Reach a junction on the bench at 5.7 miles. Here a boot beaten path, branching right, travels by the tarn and then ascends to the Macun Lakes (35-min).

I recommend continuing up the main trail toward the Macun Lakes (10-min), Fuorcletta da Barcli (1-hr) and Zernez (4-hr 15-min). The trail ascends along the west side of the stream and enters the Swiss National Park. Ahead views open to the gorgeous Macun Lakes basin, composed of more than 20 lakes and tarns nestled beneath a rugged cirque of 10,000-ft. peaks.

Reach a junction at 6.0 miles along the north shore of beautiful Lai d'Immez, one of the larger lakes in the basin. Here a trail branches right, traveling along the north shore of Lake Immez and then curves to the right (north), passing along the east shores of Lai da La Messa Gluna and Lai dal Dragun. Beyond Dragun the path descends to the small tarn and the junction we passed at 5.7 miles. After looping around the lakes retrace your steps down the Zeznina Valley to Lavin for a 12.7 miles round-trip hike.

To Fuorcletta da Barcli and Zernez

- **Distance:** 13.2 miles (one-way)
- **Maximum Elevation:** 9,662-ft.
- **Elevation at Zernez** 4,826-ft.
- **Elevation Gain/Loss:** 4,964-ft. /-4,836-ft.
- **Difficulty:** Very Strenuous

To continue to Fuorcletta da Barcli (Barcli Pass) and Zernez, cross Lake Immez's outlet stream on a bridge and then climb steeply up rocky meadows and scree slopes to Fuorcletta da Barcli (9,347-ft.), a saddle on the Baselgia Ridge, at 6.8 miles. The climb is accompanied by splendid views of the Macun Lakes basin. From the saddle, the summits of the Silvretta range towering beyond the Lower Engadine Valley fill the skyline to the north. To the south Piz Quattervals and the high peaks rising above the Cluozza and Spol Valleys dominate the view.

At the saddle, turn right (west) and ascend along the rocky ridge. The trail is marked with red and white slashes on the rocks. Reach the high point (9,662-ft.) of the hike at 7.0 miles. This is truly an amazing overlook with views extending southwest to the high peaks towering above the Fluela Valley. Glacier-clad Piz Sarsura is easy to pick-out on the skyline. To the north are more great views of the Macun Lakes Basin and the peaks rising above the Lower Engadine Valley.

When you are done enjoying the views, follow the trail as it turns left (southwest), exits the Park and then descends on very steep grades through scree and rocky meadows to a saddle on the ridge to the north of Munt Baselgia's summit at 7.5 miles. Descend from the saddle on steep switchbacks down rocky meadows along Munt Baselgia's west facing slopes.

At 8.9 miles the grade abates a bit as the descent continues down switchbacks through meadows that give way to forested slopes. At all junctions follow the signs to the Zernez train station. Pass under electric lines at 11.6 miles and then drop through forest and then pastures to the eastern edge of Zernez at 12.6 miles. Signs now point the way through the village to the train station at 13.2 miles.

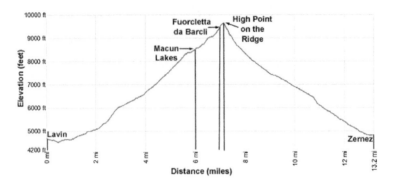

Trailhead Directions

From Scuol to Lavin: Take the train from Scuol toward Pontresina or Landquart and get off at Lavin. The ride takes about 20 minutes. Consult the SBB Website/SBB app for the current schedule.

From Zernez to Scuol: Take the train from Zernez to Scuol. The ride should take about 36 minutes. Consult the SBB Website/SBB app for the current schedule.

90. Val Minger ★★★★☆
Distance: 6.8 - 10.4 miles (one way)
Near Scuol in the Lower Engadine

Panoramic views of rugged peaks, two beautiful valleys and a chance to see wildlife are the scenic rewards of this great hike, one of the best in the Swiss National Park, visiting Val Minger and Val Plavna.

432

Distance: 6.8 miles (round trip) to Sur il Foss

10.4 miles (one way) to Tarasp

Elevation: 5,428-ft. at Trailhead

7,664-ft. at Sur il Foss

4,616-ft. at Tarasp

Elevation Gain: 2,236-ft. to Sur il Foss

-3,408-ft. to Tarasp

Difficulty: moderate-strenuous

Basecamp: Scuol

Scuol and Lower Engadine Map: See page 413

Online Map/Photos: www.hikingwalking.com/val-minger

Why Hike Val Minger

This beautiful hike, my favorite in the Swiss National Park, ascends Val Minger to the beautiful meadows of Alp Minger with panoramic views of Piz Minger, Piz Foraz and Piz Plavna Dadaint. From the alp the trail climbs to Sur il Foss, a saddle on the ridge between Piz Minger and Piz Foraz, and then ascends along the scenic ridge. Magnificent, 360-degree views from the ridge encompass the peaks ringing the Plavna and Minger valleys along with the Sesvenna Lischana range to the east and the wall of peaks rising above the Lower Engadine Valley to the north.

From the ridge the trail drops down to the bucolic meadows of Alp Plavna and then descends along Val Plavna's extensive flood plain, lined with rugged peaks. The final leg of the hike drops through meadows and forests to the village of Tarasp, with intermittent views of the high peaks rising above Ftan and Scuol.

Hikers looking for a more challenging day will want to continue the hike from Sur il Foss over Fuorcla Val dal Botsch to Il Fuorn. This leg of the hike is very strenuous and includes steep ascents and descents.

From the Trailhead to Sur il Foss

- **Distance from Trailhead:** 3.4 miles (one-way) / 6.8 miles (round trip)
- **Highest Elevation:** 7,664-ft.
- **Elevation Gain:** 2,236-ft.

From the train station at Scuol, take the bus headed for S-charl and get off at the Val Minger (Mingerbrucke) stop. (See trailhead directions below.) The bus stop is located near the parking lot for a small concrete dam and water intake on the Clemgia River.

Cross the dam to the west side of the river and then follow the trail as it climbs southwest on gentle to moderate grades through a forest of larch and pine trees. At 0.3 miles the trail passes through a small meadow containing the ruins of an old stable. Here we get our first tantalizing glimpse of the scenery to come before plunging back into the woods.

Our trail soon leads to the stream draining Val Minger, which will be our constant companion along the initial segment of the hike. As the trees thin the trail passes the confluence of the Val Foraz, a side valley branching to the south at 0.8 miles. Interesting rock formations, caused by erosion of the canyon's glacial gravel walls, are found near the confluence. One of the formations looks like the head of a raven and another like the head of a witch.

Soon views open the rugged peaks and craggy slopes flanking the Minger valley. Turn around for distant views of the peaks of the Sesvenna Lischana range, including Piz Madlain and the Piz San Jon massif, rising above the east side of the S-charl valley.

The trail now ascends at a steady pace, crossing the rocky stream four times over the next 1.25 miles. The trail and steam crossings are marked by red and white stakes. Typically the stream contains little or no water so the crossings should not present any problems.

As the trees thin views open to Piz Foraz rising along the south side of the valley. The triangular top of Piz Plavna Dadaint is seen above the trees to the west. As you climb, keep an eye out for red deer and chamoix on the slopes of Piz Minger and Piz dals Cotschen, looming above the trail to the north.

At 2.2 miles the trees give way to the beautiful open meadows of Alp Minger. Reach the official park rest stop (7,115-ft.), with stunning 360-degree views, at 2.5 miles. Piz Minger towers above the valley to the north while Piz Foraz and its craggy ridges dominate the view to the south. To the west, the pyramid-shaped Piz Plavna Dadaint rises beyond Sur il Foss, the saddle on the ridge between Piz Minger and Piz Foraz at the head of the valley. To the east, the peaks soaring above the east side of the S-charl valley fill the skyline. This is another good spot to look for red deer and chamoix.

The rest area, equipped with benches and tables, is delineated by yellow posts. This is the only place in the valley where hikers are allowed to eat. My recommendation is not to eat lunch here. Instead enjoy the views and then continue to the saddle, which is outside the National Park. At the pass you can sit anywhere you like.

When you are ready to continue follow the path as it heads west, ascending on easy grades through low-lying shrubs. Soon the trail curves to the northwest, climbing through pretty meadows with great views of the peaks surrounding the valley. At 3.0 miles the grade steepens and the path curves to the west and ascends a grassy gully along the left (south) side of a stream.

Reach Sur il Foss (7,602-ft.) at 3.4 miles. The pass, which is outside the park, is situated on a broad, grassy saddle overlooking Val Plavna to the west and Val Minger to the east. The Piz Plavna Dadaint massif dominates the view across the Plavna Valley. Piz Minger towers above the pass to the north while a rugged cirque rims the head of Val Plavna to the south. The Sesvenna Lischana range fills the skyline to the east.

At this point you have three choices. You can either turn around and retrace your steps to the trailhead for a 6.8 mile round trip hike, walk to Tarasp via the Val Plavna (3-hr) or climb to the pass at Fuorcla Val dal

Botsch (1-hr 45-min) and then descend to Il Fuorn (3-hrs). I recommend walking to Tarasp via the Val Plavna. The Fuorcla Val da Botsch extension is quite strenuous and very steep. (See below for more information on this option.)

From Sur il Foss to Tarasp

- **Segment Stat:** 7.0 miles (one-way) from Sur il Foss to Tarasp
- **Total Distance:** 10.4 miles (one way)
- **Ending Elevation:** 4,616-ft.
- **Elevation Gain/Loss:** -3,408-ft.

To walk to the village of Tarasp from Sur il Foss, turn left (south) toward Val Plavna and Fuorcla Val dal Botsch. The wide track travels along the top of the ridge and then traverses beneath a minor summit accompanied by fine views of Piz Plavna Dadaint massif and the glacial cirque ringing the head of Val Plavna.

Reach a junction at 3.8 miles and turn right on the trail descending toward Alp Plavna and Tarasp-Fontana. The trail straight ahead leads to Fuorcla Val dal Botsch and Il Fuorn. If you look carefully, you can see the trail to the right of the head of the valley climbing very steeply up scree-covered slopes to Fuorcla Val dal Botsch, a saddle in the ridge between Piz Murters and Piz dal Botsch.

Our trail drops down steep switchbacks and then turns north/northwest, descending through rocky meadows and then trees on steep to moderately steep grades to Alp Plavna (6,811-ft.) at 4.8 miles. Piz Plavna Dadaint towers above the idyllic little alp to the west.

At the alp the trail joins a jeep road that descends through pretty pastures sprinkled with wildflowers toward Tarasp. The walk enjoys great views of the craggy peaks lining both sides of the valley. Ahead the peaks forming the northern wall of the Lower Engadine Valley fill the skyline.

Soon the trail curves to the northwest, descending on moderate grades along the right (east) side of the Aua da Plavna, the river draining the Plavna Valley. Beyond the alp the meadows give way to trees.

At 5.2 miles the grade eases as the trail descends along a seldom used road through a massive flood plain covered in small white rocks. It appears that at times during the spring melt the stream bed widens to engulf the entire valley floor. Avalanche chutes scar the flanks of the rugged peaks lining both sides of the valley, creating wide talus aprons at the base of the peaks. It is amazing to think about the forces of water and ice that have created this landscape.

At 5.6 miles the road crosses a bridge to the west side of the river and then continues descending on easy grades along the rocky valley floor. At 6.6 miles the flood plain ends and the grade steepens as the trail drops through forest and meadows. From the meadows enjoy nice views of the peaks rising to the north of Ftan and Scuol.

At 7.3 miles the road crosses a stream and reaches a trail junction. The road branching left leads to Alp Laisch, Plaz and Ardez. We bear right on a trail dropping steeply down meadows toward Resgia Plavna and Tarasp-Fontana. Soon the valley narrows and the trail descends steep to moderately-steep grades through meadows and trees along the left (west) side of the rushing river. At 7.9 miles the trail turns into a dirt road.

Reach Resgia Plavna (5,135-ft.) and a junction at 8.7 mile. Continue straight ahead on the dirt road toward Tarasp (40-min), passing a small building with a picnic table and wood carvings of elves. Soon the road crosses a bridge to the east side of the river.

Beyond the bridge the grade abates as the trail descends through trees. Opening in the forest offer views of Ftan, nestled in meadows on a bench along the north side of the Lower Engadine Valley. Pass three more junctions, at each continue on the broad track headed toward Tarasp-Fontana.

At 9.6 miles the descent steepens as the trail curves northeast and drops down to Tarasp. As you reach the town the track turns to pavement and leads to the center of the village where the Schloss (Castle) Tarasp is perched on a high promontory above the town. The bus stop in Tarasp (4,616-ft.) is located near a peach colored building, the former Hotel Tarasp, at 10.4 miles. Before getting on the bus back to Scuol enjoy the views of Piz Lischana, which forms the perfect backdrop for the town's picturesque little lake.

Fuorcla Val da Botsch to Il Fuorn

- **Segment Stat:** 5.6 miles (one-way) to Fuorcla Val da Botsch to Il Fuorn
- **Total Distance:** 9.0 miles (one way)
- **Maximum Elevation:** 8,782-ft.
- **Elevation Gain/Loss:** 3,430-ft./-2,800-ft.

Note: The hike over the Fuorcla Val da Botsch is quite strenuous and includes steep ascents and descents.

To continue the hike over Fuorcla Val da Botsch to Il Fuorn from Sur il Foss, turn left (south) toward Val Plavna and Fuorcla Val dal Botsch. The wide track travels along the top of the ridge and then traverses beneath a minor peak accompanied by fine views of Piz Plavna Dadaint massif and the glacial cirque ringing the head of Val Plavna. Distant views extend north to the peaks rising above the Lower Engadine Valley.

Reach a junction at 3.8 miles. The trail to the right drops steeply to Alp Plavna and Tarasp-Fontana. We continue straight ahead (southeast) toward Fuorcla Val dal Botsch and Il Fuorn. If you look carefully, you can see the trail, located to the right of the head of the valley, climbing steeply up scree-covered slopes to Fuorcla Val dal Botsch, a saddle in the ridge between Piz Murters and Piz dal Botsch.

The trail now descends gently toward the head of Val Plavna, crossing a stream at 4.6 miles. Beyond the stream the trail turns right (southwest), ascending through rocky meadows and then climbing very steep scree covered slopes to the pass at 5.5 miles. The stiff ascent gains over 1,200-ft. in less than a mile.

Fuorcla Val dal Botsch (8,782-ft.) enjoys magnificent views of the sea of peaks to the west, including the distant Bernina Alps. Nearer at hand are great views of the cirque at the head of the Val Plavna and the Piz Plavna Dadaint massif. Piz Minger and the Sesvenna Lischana range dominate the view to the northeast while the peaks towering above the Lower Engadine Valley fill the skyline to the north.

From Fuorcla Val da Botsch, descend on steep grades to Il Fuorn (5,886-ft.), losing over 2,800-ft. in 3.5 miles. The last 0.7 miles of the hike travels along the road to the bus stop. Total hiking distance is 9.0 miles.

To return to Scuol, catch the bus to Zernez and then take the train from Zernez to Scuol. The trip back to Scuol takes 1 hour and 24 minutes.

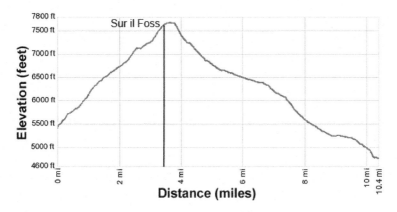

Trailhead Directions

From Scuol to the Val Minger Trailhead: From the train station in Scuol, take the #913 bus headed toward S-charl and get off at the Val Minger (Mingerbrucke) stop. The bus makes several stops in Scuol between the train station and Val Minger. Visit the SBB Website/SBB app to find the stop nearest your accommodations. The ride takes about 26 minutes.

If you are staying in another part of the valley, take the train or the postbus to Scuol and then catch the postbus to Val Minger. Note: This is a very popular route. Get an early start and, if possible, purchase your tickets the night before the hike.

From Tarasp to Scuol: From the Fontana bus stop in Tarasp (near a peach colored building, the former Hotel Tarasp, and across from a small lake), take the #923 bus toward Sent, Sur En and get off at the Scuol train station. The ride takes 11 minutes. The bus makes several stops in Scuol. Consult the SBB website/app to find the stop nearest your lodgings.

Map: Scuol & the Lower Engadine Valley #2

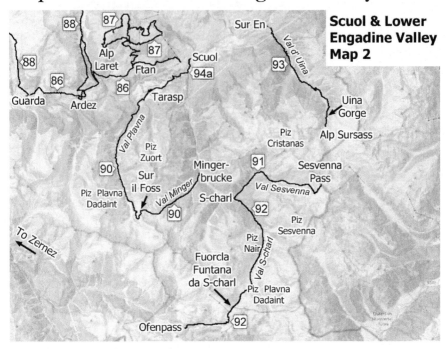

Scuol & Lower Engadine Valley Map 2

91. Val Sesvenna and Fuorcla Sesvenna ★★★★☆
Distance: 8.6 - 10.2 miles (round trip)
Near Scuol in the Lower Engadine

Ascend the Sesvenna Valley to a rocky, meadow-clad bowl accompanied by fine views of the peaks and summits rising to the west. Extend the hike with a very steep climb to Sesvenna Pass with stunning vistas of the rugged Sesvenna cirque and the summits towering above the S-charl Valley, the Swiss-Italian border and beyond.

Distance: 8.6 miles (round trip) to Val Sesvenna

10.2 miles (round trip) to Fuorcla Sesvenna

Elevation: 5,930-ft. at Trailhead

8,071-ft. at Val Sesvenna

9,249-ft. at Fuorcla Sesvenna

Elevation Gain: 2,141-ft. to Val Sesvenna

3,319-ft. to Fuorcla Sesvenna

Difficulty: moderate-strenuous

Basecamp: Scuol

Scuol and Lower Engadine Map #2: See page 438

Online Map/Photos:
www.hikingwalking.com/sesvenna

Why Hike to Val Sesvenna and Fuorcla Sesvenna

This is really two hikes in one. The first segment of the hike ascends to Alp Sesvenna and then travels up a secluded valley with great views of nearby peaks and the summit rising above the S-charl Valley. A meadow-clad bowl beneath a very steep wall near the head of the valley marks the end of this segment and is the turnaround point for many hikers.

The second segment of the hike requires a very steep climb up the wall. The effort is rewarded when the trail crests the wall and views open to Lake Sesvenna nestled in a stark basin beneath a photogenic cirque anchored by Piz Sesvenna. A final climbs leads to Fuorcla Sesvenna, a saddle on a high ridge on the north side of the cirque. From the pass panoramic views encompass the cirque, the peaks towering above the S-charl Valley and the summits rimming the Swiss-Italian border and beyond.

The climb up the wall is very steep and is only recommended for sure-foot hikers. There is a lot of loose rock, so take your time. Trekking poles are highly recommended, especially for the descent on the return leg of the hike.

This trail is shared by mountain bikes but is considered a very difficult bike route due to the climb/descent of the wall. As such, you will probably see few if any bikes along the path.

Trail Ascending Val Sesvenna

- **Distance from Trailhead:** 4.3 miles (one-way) / 8.6 miles (round trip)
- **Highest Elevation:** 8,071-ft.
- **Elevation Gain:** 2,141-ft.

Take the bus from Scuol to S-charl. (See trailhead directions below.) From the S-charl bus stop follow the farm track heading northeast out of the main square up Val Sesvenna (Sesvenna Valley) toward Alp Sesvenna. A trail signpost at the bus stop in S-charl will help get you started.

The track ascends on gentle grades through pastures along the right (southeast) side of the Sesvenna stream (Aua Sesvenna). Soon the track enters the trees. As you ascend views open left (north) to interesting rock formation on the highly eroded slopes of Piz Madlain.

At 0.7 miles the track crosses the stream and the grade steepens. Ahead Piz d'Immez and Piz Cristanas rim the valley to the northeast while behind you vistas extend up the Val Tavru (Tavru Valley) to Piz Tavru.

At 1.1 miles the track crosses a tributary stream and then ascends through trees high above the Aua Sesvenna, crossing two more side streams at 1.3 miles. Beyond the crossings the trail, now a two-track, climbs on moderately-steep grades through meadows.

Reach Alp Sesvenna (6,886-ft.), sitting in large meadow-clad bowl at 1.6 miles. (This is a fine destination for parties looking for a shorter hike.) Here the road ends and the trail swings to the right (east) through open meadows to an intersection at 1.7 miles. Our trail continues straight ahead toward Fuorcla Sesvenna (2-hr 25-min). Ignore the route (blue trail sign), branching left (north/northeast), and ascending steeply up the Fora da l'Aua to Rims (3-hrs) and the Lischana Hut (4-hrs).

The path now traverses through meadows with fine views north to Piz Cotschen, Piz d'Immez and the Fora da l'Aua, a stream spill down the ridge between the two peaks, along with the summits towering above the Tavru Valley to the southwest. At 1.8 miles the path curves to the right (southeast), crosses a stream on logs and then traverses a scree covered slope before passing through a wood gate. Turn around for great views of Piz Madlain.

Beyond the gate the trail ascends on moderate grades up the narrow valley, traveling through trees and intermittent meadows. At 2.4 miles the grade abates as the trees gives way to meadows scattered with shrubs.

At 2.7 miles the climb resumes on moderately-steep to steep grades up rocky meadows and scree covered slopes above the Aua Sesvenna. The stream, punctuated by small waterfalls, tumbles down the valley floor below the trail. As you climb turn around for superb views of Piz Minger, Piz Zuort and Piz Pisoc towering above the west side of the S-charl Valley.

At 3.0 miles the grade abates as the trail reaches a large open valley adorn with a spectacular display of wildflowers at the height of the summer. The unspoiled glen is nestled beneath the craggy, sculpted walls of Piz Cornet, Piz Cristanas and Piz Rims to the north. Piz Plazer and Piz Sesvenna tower above the valley to the south.

Near the head of the valley the trail curves to the left and ascends steeply along the north side of the valley. Soon views open to the summit of the Fernerspitz towering above the head of the valley. Turn around for more great views of Piz Minger, Piz Zuort and Piz Pisoc to the west/northwest.

At 4.2 miles the path curves to the right (southeast) as it crests a bench. Here the grade abates as the trail enters a small bowl. To the right (south) views open to a large moraine spilling down the slopes between Piz Plazer and Piz Sesvenna. Ahead the trail is seen climbing a very steep, rocky slope. The high peaks rising above the S-charl valley fill the skyline to the west.

Reach the foot of the rock wall at 4.3 miles. This is a good turnaround spot, especially if the trail to the pass is covered in snow/ice. Find a nice spot to sit and enjoy the gorgeous views to the west and the rugged peaks rimming the valley. When you are done taking in the views, retrace your steps to the trailhead for a 8.6 miles round-trip hike.

To Fuorcla Sesvenna

- **Segment Stat:** 1.6 miles (round-trip) to Fuorcla Sesvenna
- **Total Distance:** 10.2 miles (round trip)
- **Maximum Elevation:** 9,249-ft.
- **Elevation Gain/Loss:** 3,319-ft.

Note: Continuing to the Sesvenna Pass changes the difficulty rating to very strenuous.

To continue to the Fuorcla Sesvenna (Sesvenna Pass), climb the very steep, rocky wall on a boot beaten track. There is a lot of loose rock, so take your time. Trekking poles are highly recommended, especially for the descent on the return leg of the hike.

Crest the top of the wall (8,694-ft.) at 4.5 miles. Here stunning views open Lai da Sesvenna (Lake Sesvenna) cradled in a rocky bowl beneath the cirque anchored by Piz Sesvenna, Piz Muntpitschen and the Fernerspitz. The Sesvenna Glacier clings to the slopes of the cirque. The path now swings to the left (east/northeast) and climbs steeply through rocky meadows and rock outcroppings to Fuorcla Sesvenna (9,249-ft.) at 5.1 miles.

The pass, a saddle on the ridge between the Schadler and Fernerspitz along the Swiss-Italian border, enjoys fine views of the distinctive Follakopf towering above the Lago Sesvenna to the east. A small tarn lies below the pass. The Rasassspitz and the Vernungkopf rise to the northeast. Behind you are panoramic views of the cirque anchored by Piz Sesvenna and its glacier while distant views stretch west to the Engadine peaks.

When you are done taking the views retrace your steps to S-charl for a 10.2 miles round-trip hike. Along the way enjoy the wildflower-filled meadows and great views of the summits rising above S-charl and the valleys to the west.

It is possible to continue down the east side of the pass to the Sesvenna Hut and then go over Schlinig Pass and down the Val d'Uina to Sur En in the Lower Engadine Valley. This 10-hour hike is best done as a multi-day hike by spending a night at the Sesvenna Hut, which offers meals and dormitory accommodations.

Trailhead Directions

From Scuol to S-charl: From the train station in Scuol, take the #913 bus headed toward S-charl and get off at the last stop in S-charl. The bus makes several stops in Scuol. Visit the SBB Website/SBB app to find the stop nearest your accommodations. The beautiful ride up the Val S-charl takes about 41 minutes.

If you are staying in another part of the valley, take the train or the postbus to Scuol and then catch the postbus to S-charl. Note: This is a very popular route. Get an early start and if possible purchase your tickets the night before the hike.

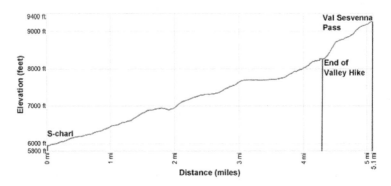

92. S-charl to Ofenpass ★★★★★
Distance: 6.8 - 8.4 miles (one-way)
Near Scuol in the Lower Engadine

Forested slopes, expansive meadows and the pretty Clemgia River, meandering down a scenic valley beneath rugged peaks and rounded mountains, are the hallmarks of this hike up the S-charl Valley to Fuorcla Funtana da S-charl, a broad pass overlooking the S-charl and Mustair Valleys. End the hike by descending into the Mustair Valley to Ofenpass (Pass dal Fuorn in Romansh).

Distance: 6.8 - 8.4 miles (one-way)
Elevation: 5,930-ft. at Trailhead
Maximum elevation: 7,854-ft.
Elevation Gain: 1,924-ft.
Difficulty: moderate

Basecamp: Scuol
Scuol and Lower Engadine
Map: See page 413
Online Map/Photos:
www.hikingwalking.com/ofenpass

Why Hike from S-charl to Ofenpass

This lovely walk up the S-charl Valley beside the Clemgia River leads to the vast meadows of Alp Astras. Here the trail ascends through alpine meadows to Fuorcla Funtana da S-charl with views of the S-charl and Mustair Valleys. End the hike by descend from the pass into the scenic Mustair Valley and then follow the Senda Val Mustair to Ofenpass (Pass dal Fuorn in Romansh).

The walk travels through forests and pretty meadows, passing small Alps along the way. Views encompass the rugged peaks and rounded mountains rimming S-charl and its tributary valleys along with the summits towering above the Mustair Valley. Most of the trail is rated as moderate, except for two short, steep segments ascending to and descending from the Funtana da S-charl pass.

The walk can be shortened by hiking to the turnoff for Alp Praditschol. The resulting 6.8 miles hike, rated as moderately-easy, is a good option for families or if the weather is taking a turn for the worse. You can also avoid the long return trip via bus and train from Ofenpass by simply turning around at Fuorcla Funtana da S-charl and tracing your steps to S-charl for an 11.4 mile round-trip hike.

You will be sharing the trail with bikes but the broad path up the valley facilitates multiple uses. At the end of the trip a bus and train ride returns hikers to Scuol.

To Ofenpass

Start the day with a bus ride from Scuol to S-charl. (See trailhead directions below.) Begin hiking southeast up a broad gravel/dirt track toward Funtana da S-charl and Susom Give. Susom Give is a hotel located at Ofenpass (Pass dal Fuorn in Romansh). Trail signposts at the bus stop will help get you started.

The track ascends on easy to moderate grades through meadows and forest up the beautiful S-charl valley along the north/northeast side of the Clemgia River. Behind you the rugged peaks towering above the north side of the Lower Engadine Valley form a lovely backdrop for the small hamlet. As you proceed up the valley views open southeast to the rounded, green slopes of Mot Falain and the rugged slopes of Piz Murtera.

Pass Plan d'Immez at 1.6 miles. A short distance beyond ignore the trail branching left to Alp Plazer. The board track now curves to the right (south) and crosses a bridge over the stream draining the Plazer Valley at 1.8 miles.

Reach a junction at 2.3 miles with a trail branching left toward Tamangur Dadora and Dadaint. We stay on the trail to Susom Give that crosses to the west side of the Clemgia River on a bridge. This crossing is a good turn around point for families looking for an easy hike.

The track now curves to the right (southwest) and ascends through lovely meadows. To the southeast the cirque anchored by Piz Murtera and the Lorenziberg dominate the view. Below the track the river meanders through emerald green meadows along the valley floor. As you ascend, turnaround for nice views of Piz Plazer and Piz Sesvenna towering above the Plazer Valley to the northeast.

At 3.4 miles pass a track branching right to Alp Praditschol. Ahead views open of the ridge extending east from Piz Vallatscha and the barren, rounded summit of Mot Radond. Alp Astras is now in view. This junction is another possible turnaround point for parties looking for an easy day.

Beyond Alp Praditschol the grade abates and the trail now traverses through meadows to Alp Astras and a trail junction at 4.25 miles. Here a path branches left, heading back toward Tamangur Dadora and S-charl. We bear right (south) on the trail that goes behind the alp to a second junction where we turn right (southwest) toward Funtana da S-charl and Susom Give. The trail to the left leads to the Costainas Pass.

The trail now climbs steeply through meadows with great views of Piz Vallatscha and Piz d'Astras to the west/northwest. Piz Murtera rises above the east side of the S-charl valley while Piz Plazer and Piz Sesvenna dominate the view to the northeast.

At 4.7 miles the grade abates as the trail traverses through the Plan Mattun. A half mile beyond the ascent resumes, now on moderate grades, to Fuorcla Funtana da S-charl (7,848-ft.) at 5.7 miles. In Romansh this translates into the S-charl Spring Pass. Here a sign points south to Alp da Munt and Pass dal Fuorn (the Romansh form of Ofenpass).

Behind you are great view of the peaks rising to the north/northeast above the S-charl and Plazer Valleys. Follow the trail south as it crosses the broad pass. Along the way views open to the peaks rimming the south side of the Mustair Valley from Piz Turettas the pyramid-shaped Piz Daint.

At 5.9 miles the trail begins descending from the pass, reaching a junction at 6.0 miles. We bear right on the trail to Pass dal Fuorn (Ofenpass). (The trail to the left leads to Alp da Munt and Tschierv.) The boot beaten path now drops steeply down the hillside. Soon the path becomes clearer and views open to the Plaun da l'Aua.

At 6.6 miles the grade abates as the trail curves to the west, traveling through meadows with scattered trees to a junction with the Senda Val Mustair at 6.9 miles. We turn right (west) here toward Pass dal Fuorn.

The Senda Val Mustair, a wide gravel track, now descends on easy to moderate grades through the Plaun da l'Aua to a junction at 7.4 miles. Here we bear right toward the Pass Dal Fuorn (Ofenpass). In a short distance the trail enters the trees and traverses above the highway before dropping down to the Pass dal Fuorn (Ofenpass) and the Hotel Susom Give at 8.4 miles.

Trailhead Directions

From Scuol to S-charl: See Hike 90.

Ofenpass to Scuol: The bus stop at Ofenpass is located in the parking lot adjacent to the Hotel Susom Give. Take the #811 bus bound for Zernez, staziun (Zernez Train Station). Get off at the train station and catch a train bound for Scuol-Tarasp. The entire trip will take an hour and 23 minutes. At the Scuol train station you can either walk back to your accommodations or catch a local bus. Visit the SBB Website/SBB app to find the stop nearest your accommodations.

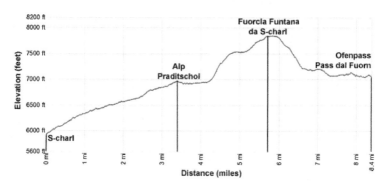

93. Val d' Uina ★★★★★
Distance: 12.4 miles (round-trip)
Near Scuol in the Lower Engadine

This trail, popular with hikers and mountain bikers, ascends through forest and then the meadows of Alp Dadaint before traveling through the dramatic Uina Gorge, a narrow chasm between two sheer rock walls.

Distance: 12.4 miles (round-trip)
Elevation: 3,688-ft. at Trailhead
7,058-ft. at the top of the Gorge
Elevation Gain: 3,370-ft.
Difficulty: moderate-strenuous

Basecamp: Scuol
Scuol and Lower Engadine
Map: See page 413
Online Map/Photos:
www.hikingwalking.com/uina

Why Hike Val d' Uina

The spectacular Uina Gorge, composed of two near vertical rock walls, guards the head of the Uina Valley. When looking toward the gorge it seems impossible that a route could pass through this chasm. But a trail, carved and tunneled through the sheer rock walls, does indeed travel through this amazing gorge accompanied by dramatic views of the gorge and the river tumbling down the ravine beneath the path.

To reach the gorge requires a long hike up a forested track, with limited views, along the floor the Uina Valley. After 4.3 miles the trail breaks from the trees and we get our first views of the narrow cleft at the head of the valley.

The trail through the gorge, while exposed in sections, is secured with railings and fixed cables. People with a fear of heights or uncomfortable on exposed trail will want to avoid the hike.

This trail is very popular with hikers and mountain bikers. Hikers should expect to see bikers pushing and/or carrying their bikes through the gorge. Everyone needs to be cautious and considerate to ensure safe passage along this section of the trail. If you don't like sharing a path with mountain bikes then find another trail.

Hiking Val d' Uina

Take the bus from Scuol to Sur En, a small hamlet located on the south side of the River Inn (En in Romansh) in the Lower Engadine Valley. (See trailhead directions below.) At the bus stop signs point southeast up the road toward Uina Dadaint and Chna Lischana (Lischana Hut).

Walk along the dirt road as it passes through the village and then ascends on moderate grades through forest along the east side of the river. Cross a bridge to the west side of the river at 0.4 miles. As you progress up the narrow valley the road will cross the river several times. All crossings are bridged.

At 2.0 miles the valley widens as the trail crosses a bridge back to the west side of the valley to avoid the remains of a landslide. Here the river has cut a channel through the rock debris deposited along the valley floor. Ahead we get our first glimpse of Piz Rims towering above the west side of the valley. Views of the peak will continue to improve as you ascend the valley.

At 2.5 miles ignore the road branching right to Uina Dadora. A short distance beyond we pass through meadows with views of the summits rising above the Curtinatsch Valley to the south and then cross a bridge to the east side of the river. A short segment of the trail along the east side of the river offers more views of the peaks rising to the west before we plunge back into the trees.

After climbing a few switchbacks the trees give way to the meadows at Alp Uina Dadaint at 4.3 miles. Here views open to Piz Mezdi and Piz da Gliasen rising along the east side of the valley. The path now ascends through the meadows, passing the alp buildings where you can purchase cheese, yogurt and other refreshments.

Past the alp the trail briefly travels through trees before again emerging on meadows with fine views toward the head of the valley. Look closely and you will see where the trail is carved into the sheer rock face.

At 5.0 miles the grade steepens as the trail ascends a rugged hillside through scattered trees. Along the way, cross a makeshift bridge over a stream tumbling down a rocky side canyon. The crossing enjoys great views down the Uina Valley to the peaks rising above the north side of the Lower Engadine Valley.

Beyond the crossing the trail climbs steeply to the entrance of the dramatic Uina Gorge, a narrow chasm between two sheer rock walls, at 5.7 miles. The trail now ascends along a path carved into the gorge's eastern wall, high above the river tumbling down a narrow ravine. At times the trail passes through short tunnels. Handrails and fixed cables safeguard exposed sections of the trail.

Care should be used along this section of the trail. Look ahead and watch for bike riders who must carry or push their bikes through the gorge. Thankfully there are many places along the trail where it is easy to step out of the way.

The trail emerges from the Uina Gorge at 6.0 miles and soon passes a junction with trail branching right toward Rims, the Lischana Hut and the route to Fora da l'Aua at 6.2 miles. We continue toward the Sesvenna Hut on a path ascending on easy grades through the pretty meadows of Alp Sursass beneath Piz Cristanas and Piz d'Immez. The meadows are a great place to take a break and enjoy a picnic lunch before retracing your steps back through the amazing gorge to the trailhead at Sur En.

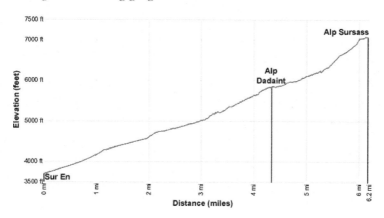

Trailhead Directions

From the Scuol to Sent, Sur En: From the Scuol Train station, board the #923 bus heading toward Sent, Sur En. The bus travels east along the north side of the River Inn (En in Romansh) before crossing to the south side of the river. The first stop on the south side of the river is the Sur En campground. Do not get off here. Instead, continue to the last stop in the small hamlet of Sur En. The ride takes 24 minutes.

On the way to Sur En, the bus travels through the Scuol. Consult the SBB Website/SBB app to find the bus stop nearest your accommodation.

94. Other Trails in Scuol
Near Scuol in the Lower Engadine

94a) Tarasp to Scuol

This pleasant walk travels through forest and alpine meadows, visiting Vulpera, Avrona and Lake Nair before descending to Tarasp. Sections of the walk above Lake Nair feature fine views of Ftan, across the Lower Engadine Valley, Tarasp and the Tarasp Schloss (Castle).

- **Distance:** 3.1 - 5.0 miles (one-way)
- **Elevation:** 3,973-ft. at Scuol
  5,170-ft. at the High Point above Lake Nair
  4,616-ft. at Tarasp
- **Elevation Gain:** 643-ft. - 1,197-ft.
- **Difficulty:** easy-moderate
- **Base camp:** Scuol
- **Scuol and Lower Engadine Map:** See page 413

There are a variety of ways to start this walk. From Scuol, take one of the bridges over the River Inn (En in Romansh) to the south side of the Lower Engadine Valley. Once on the south side of the River Inn follow the signs to Vulpera and Avrona. (If you take the bridge to the west of the Catholic Church you will pass by the ice skating rink and then cross a bridge over the Clemgia River.)

The path to Vulpera ascends through trees to the village, the first site of spa tourism in the Lower Engadine Valley. In Vulpera you have two options. You can take the short route to Tarasp by simply following the trail to Tarasp that travels through Vulpera and then ascends on easy grades through forest and pastures to the village accompanied by fine views of the Lower Engadine Valley. For the longer route follow the signs to Avrona.

The trail to Avrona ascends through trees to the tiny hamlet. In Avrona take the trail signed for Lake Nair that climbs on easy grades through trees and then meadows to the small lake. Alternatively, take a detour by following the signs to Jurada. This longer route heads south through trees and intermittent meadows. Openings offer views to the south/southeast. Soon the path reaches a wooded overlook with views of the Clemgia Gorge and the high peaks rising along the east/southeast side of the S-charl Valley. From the overlook the trail turns north and then swings to the west, traveling through scattered trees and meadows above Lake Nair. Views encompass the high moors around the pretty lake, the village of Ftan set atop a bench on the north side of the Lower Engadine Valley and the Tarasp Schloss (castle).

From the trail above Lake Nair either descend to the lake or continue on the path above the lake to Tarasp Fontana. If you take the trail to Lake Nair, from the lake follow the path that descends along the west side of Motta da Sparsels to Tarasp.

A visit to the Tarasp Schloss (castle) is highly recommended. Return to Scuol by catching the bus 923 toward Sent/Sur En and get off at the Scuol train station or a stop in the village convenient to your accommodations. Alternatively walk back to Scuol via Vulpera for a 6.2 or 8.1 mile hike, depending on the route you took to Tarasp.

Davos

Location: In the Canton of Graubunden in the Landwasser Valley

Davos (5,118-ft.), one of the highest towns in Europe, sits near the head of the Landwasser Valley at the confluence of three major ranges. The Albula Alps fill the skyline to the southeast, the rugged summits of the Plessur range rise to the west while the high peaks of the Silvretta Range soar above the area to the northeast.

At the north end of Davos the beautiful Fluelatal (Fluela Valley) extends south/southeast from the Landwasser, separating the Silvretta Range to the north from the Albula Alps to the south. The Fluela Wisshorn and Schwarzhorn tower above Fluela Pass at the head of the valley.

Two major side valleys: Sertig and Dischma, stretch southeast from the Landwasser, slicing deep into the Albula Alps. These lush, bucolic valleys are rimmed by photogenic peaks and dramatic cirques.

Davos and Klosters, its sister village to the northeast, have transformed this amazing alpine terrain into a winter sports mecca, boasting the largest ski area in Switzerland. The town is also home to the World Economic Forum, an annual winter meeting of global political and business elites.

In the summer briefcases and skis give way to backpacks and hiking boots as residents and visitors flock to the mountains crisscrossed with a network of over 400-miles of hiking trails. A wealth of accommodations, restaurants, bars, shops and a casino provide every service a visitor could need, making the area an excellent base camp. Funiculars, cable cars, gondolas and buses facilitate access to the high areas.

About Davos

Davos is composed of two parts, older Davos Dorf to the northeast and the newer, glitzier Davos Platz to the southwest, each with its own Bahnhof (train station) and adjacent bus station. The center sprawls between the train stations, linked by Promenade Street (one-way heading southwest) and

Talstrasse (one-way heading northeast). The architecture is a hodge-podge of older buildings, high rises and modern, luxury buildings.

The main Tourist Information Office (davos.ch/en) is a Talstrasse 41, adjacent to the Sportzentrum. There is also a smaller tourist information office at the Davos Dorf train station. Guest cards are available for overnight guests in the Davos-Klosters area. The cards provide free transport on local buses and area trains along with discounts on funicular, cable car and gondola tickets. Note: the free bus travel excludes trips to the side valleys of Dischma, Sertig, Monstein and Wiesen. Make sure you read the fine print accompanying the card to understand the current exclusions.

Along Promenade and Talstrasse, in addition to the adjacent side street, are a wide range of hotels, guesthouses, pensions and vacation rentals. A Coop, Aldi, Spars and Migros Supermarkets are located near the Davos Platz train station. A smaller Spar and a Migros Grocery store are situated close to the Davos Dorf station. More groceries of various sizes and specialty food stores are found along Promenade Street. Promenade is also home to numerous shops, boutiques, cafes, restaurants and bars.

The two-stage Parsennbahn (Parsenn funicular) at Promenade 157 climbs to the Weissflujoch towering above the west side of the valley. The Hohenweg middle station on the funicular connects with scenic trails traversing above the west side of Davos. The Schatzalpbahn (Schatzalp Funicular), located on Obere Street off of the Promenade in Davos Platz, transports hikers to Schatzalp, connecting with the Panoramaweg and Davos Alpentour trails. Cable cars also ascend to the Jackobshorn and the slopes beneath the Rinerhorn on the east side of the valley and Pischa ridge located a short distance up the Fluela Pass road.

In Klosters the Gotschnabahn cable car, aka Parsenn Klosters, situated on the west side of the Klosters Bahnhof (train station), ferries visitors to the Gotschnagrat (Gotschna Ridge), the starting point for the Panoramaweg and several other hikes. Klosters is also home to the Madrisa Gondola, located to the north of the Klosters Bahnhof, where you will find more hiking trails, a childrens play area and amusement park.

There are plenty of accommodations and a good selection of shops, groceries and other conveniences in Klosters. Down valley from Davos are several smaller villages, such as Davos Frauenkirch and Davos Glaris that offer some accommodations and limited services. All are linked to Davos by train and/or bus.

Hiking around Davos

On the west side of the Landwasser Valley are two classic traverses. The Davos Panoramaweg (Hike 95) is a very scenic trail traveling between Gotschnagrat and Schatzalp that visits Strela Pass along the way. Extend the hike by walking to Latschuelfurgga, a saddle on the ridge between the Chupfenflue and the Wannengrat. The Davos Alpentour (Hike 96) is a lovely mid-level walk that stays at or near the timberline as it traverses between Glaris and Schatzalp accompanied by fine view of the peaks rising to the east.

The valleys extending east/southeast from the Landwasser Valley are home to some of the area's best hikes. Take the bus up the Sertig Valley to the hamlet of Sertig and then walk a short distance up the bucolic glen to a junction where the trail splits. To the right is the off-the-beaten path trail up the pristine Ducan Valley to scenic Fanezfurgga Pass (Hike 99). To the left a trail climbs the lovely Chuealp Valley to Sertig Pass (Hike 97), with grand views of Piz Kesch and the Ducan Ridge.

Ride the bus up the Dischma Valley to Durrboden where a trail heads up the Furgga Valley to Grialetsch Pass (Hike 101) with panoramic viewpoint of the high peaks towering above the Grialetsch Valley. Extend the hike by climbing to Radont Pass (Hike 101) with terrific views of the Schwarzhorn and the Fluela Pass area. Alternatively, continue up the Dischma Valley to Scaletta Pass (Hike 100) accompanied by vistas of the summits towering above the valley. Fit, energetic hikers will want to walk from Sertig to Durrboden (Hike 98) on a trail the crosses the two panoramic passes; Sertig and Scaletta, and travels through five scenic valleys along the way.

The Fluela Pass road is the gateway to more great hiking. Below the west side of Fluela Pass a trail ascends north to Jorifluela Pass (Hike 104) and then descends into the stunning Joriseen Lakes Basin before dropping down the untamed Jori Valley to the Berghaus Vereina. To the east of Fluela Pass a path climbs steeply to the summit of the Schwarzhorn (Hike 102) with superb, panoramic views of the peaks in Northeastern Graubunden. An epic hike summits the Schwarzhorn and then crosses Radont and Grialetsch passes (Hike 103), ending the day at Durrboden.

Getting to Davos

From the Zurich Airport or Zurich Bahnhof (train station) take the train to Davos Dorf or Davos Platz. The trip will require a change of trains in Landquart. Some schedules will also make you change trains a second time in Klosters Platz. The trip takes about two hours and 13 minutes to Davos Dorf and two hours and 26 minutes to Davos Platz.

The train trip from the Geneva Airport or Gare (train station) goes through Zurich and Landquart before arriving in Davos Dorf or Platz. The long ride takes five hours and 21 minutes to Dorf or five hours and 25 minutes to Platz.

Nearby Attractions & Rainy Day Activities

A stroll around **Lake Davos** is a lovely outing any time of year. The easy path travels through meadows and forest along the lakeshore, accompanied by nice views of the surrounding area. The Lake is located at the northeast end of Davos Dorf, a short walk from the train station. See Hike 105a - Davoser See Loop for more information.

Botanical Garden Alpinum Schatzalp contains over 5,000 different plant species from mountains all over the world. An easy walk leads through the gardens with fine views of the high peaks to the east.

The Kirchner Museum Davos contains the world's largest collection of the expressionist paintings by Ernst Ludwig Krichner.

The Heimat Museum Davos is a local history museum tracing the development of Davos from a farming village to an international tourist destination. Exhibits display the museum's collection of items encompassing the area's customs, handicrafts and everyday life.

Take the **Parsennbahn** (Parsenn funicular) to the top of the Weissfluhjoch for panoramic views of the Davos region and beyond.

The **Gotschnabahn** cable car (aka Parsenn Klosters) from Klosters to Gotschnagrat is another scenic overlook with splendid views of the Silvretta Alps and the Madrissa area.

Take the train to **Klosters** and walk around the village. The Nutli Huschi Folk Museum (Monbielerstrasse 11), housed in a circa 1565 home, allows visitors to experience the traditional way of life for the Walser people. The collection includes furniture, tools and toys from the 16th to 18th centuries. Check the hours before making the trip.

Visit **Chur**, the oldest city in Switzerland, on a rainy day. The city is located two hours by train from Davos. While there explore the old town, a car free section of the city, with a variety of museums, galleries, old churches, restaurants and bars to keep you entertained. Note the train journey from Davos Dorf requires a train changes in Davos Platz. Depending on the schedule you may also need to change again at Filisur.

Good Things to Know about Davos

- The main language in Davos is German. Visitors from all over the world visit Davos so anyone dealing with tourists speaks a variety of languages including English and French.

- There are two campgrounds in the Landwasser Valley: Sunstar Camping Stellplatz Davos at Oberwiessstrasse 3 in Davos Platz and Camping, RinerLodge at Landwasser 64 in Davos Glaris (southwest of Davos).

- There are two youth hostels in the Davos area. The Davos Youth Palace (Jugendherberge Davos) is located at Horlaubenstrasse 27 above the west side of Davos Dorf. The hostel offers both private and shared rooms and is a 14 minute walk from the Davos Dorf train station. The Klosters Youth Hostel Soldanella, located at Talstrasse 73 in Klosters, includes both private and shared rooms and is a 12 minute walk from the Klosters Platz train station.

- There are numerous huts and mountain lodges in the Davos/Klosters area. See the Davos Tourism site for a complete list, which includes nearby valleys. Reservations are recommended.

Maps: Davos Area Trails

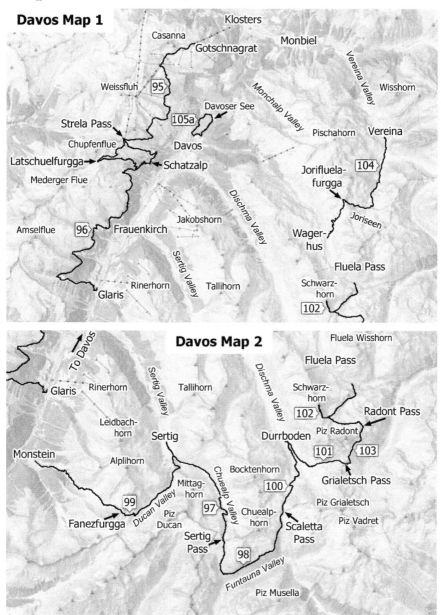

Davos Map 1

Klosters

Casanna

Gotschnagrat

Monbiel

Vereina Valley

Weissfluh 95

Wisshorn

Davoser See

Strela Pass

Monchalp Valley

105a

Pischahorn

Vereina

Chupfenflue

Davos

Latschuelfurgga

Schatzalp

Jorifluela-furgga

104

Mederger Flue

Dischma Valley

Joriseen

Jakobshorn

Amselflue 96

Frauenkirch

Wager-hus

Sertig Valley

Fluela Pass

Rinerhorn

Tallihorn

Schwarz-horn

Glaris

102

Davos Map 2

Fluela Wisshorn

To Davos

Fluela Pass

Rinerhorn

Sertig Valley

Tallihorn

Dischma Valley

Schwarz-horn

Glaris

102

Radont Pass

Leidbach-horn

Sertig

Durrboden

Piz Radont

Monstein

Alplihorn

101

103

Bocktenhorn

Grialetsch Pass

Mittag-horn

Chuealp Valley

100

Piz Grialetsch

99

Chuealp-horn

Piz Vadret

Fanezfurgga

Ducan Valley

Piz Ducan

97

Scaletta Pass

Sertig Pass

98

Funtauna Valley

Piz Musella

453

95. Davos Panoramaweg - Gotschnagrat to Schatzalp ☆☆☆☆☆

Distance: 4.7 - 11.5 miles (one way)

Near Davos in Eastern Switzerland

The Davos Panoramaweg, a classic high traverse above the west side of the Davos Valley, features great views of the high peaks and glacier clad summits towering above the Davos, Klosters, Fluela, Dischma and Sertig valleys.

Distance: 6.4 miles (one way) to Strela Pass
8.5 miles (one way) to Schatzalp
11.5 miles (one way) to Latschuelfurgga and Schatzalp
Elevation: 7,484-ft. at Trailhead
7,700-ft. at Strela Pass
7,963-ft. at Latschuelfurgga
6106-ft. at Schatzalp
Elevation Gain: 390-ft. to Strela Pass
-1,594-ft. to Schatzalp
-1,857-ft. from Latschuelfurgga and Schatzalp

Difficulty: moderate
Basecamp: Davos
Davos West Map: See page 453
Online Map/Photos:
www.hikingwalking.com/davos-panoramaweg

Why Hike the Davos Panoramaweg - Gotschnagrat to Schatzalp

A cable car ride to Gotschnagrat leads to the start of the Davos Panoramaweg, a trail traversing high above the Davos Valley with amazing views of the surrounding peaks. Gotschnagrat, a stunning overlook above the confluence of the Davos and Prattigau valleys, serves up the first great views of the hike, stretching from Madrissa to the north to the glacier-clad Silvrettahorn massif to the east.

From the overlook the trail travels through meadows between 7,500-ft. and 7,600-ft. with unobstructed views of the summits rising above the Davos Valley and three long side valleys extending southeast. Various viewpoints and benches beckon hikers to stop and take in the scenery.

The traditional Panoramaweg trail visits Strela Pass before descending on moderately-steep grades to the funicular at Schatzalp. Alternatively, cut the trail short by descending to the middle station of the Weissfluhjoch funicular or extend the day by hiking to the wind swept Latschuelfurgga saddle before dropping down to Schatzalp.

The Panoramaweg passes through a few ski areas, which mar the otherwise lovely meadows along the trail. Try not to let these eyesores detract from this scenic trip filled with great views of the area's high peaks.

There are a lot of ups and downs along the trail but no real serious climbs. Only on the last trail segment to Schatzalp do we hit some moderately-steep descents. Note: The elevation gains and losses listed on the hike only indicate the net gain or losses and not the total gain and loss.

The hike can be walked in either direction and is shared by bikes. I advise getting an early start. Typically there are not many bikes on the trail early in the morning.

Gotschnagrat to Strela Pass

- **Distance from Trailhead:** 6.4 miles (one way)
- **Elevation at Strela Pass:** 7,700-ft.
- **Elevation Gain:** 390-ft.

Take the Gotschnabahn (Gotschnagrat cable car) from Klosters Platz to Gotschnagrat (7,484-ft.). (See trailhead directions below.) Before starting the hike enjoy the panoramic views from the Gotschnagrat overlook high above the confluence of the Landwasser (where Davos is located) and Prattigau Valleys. Rugged Casanna and the Gruenhorn rise along the ridge to the west of Gotschnagrat. Madrissa and the peaks towering above Klosters fill the skyline to the north/northeast. The Silvrettahorn and its massive glaciers dominate the view to the east. Across the Davos valley views extend up the Monchalp Valley to the Pischahorn.

When you are done taking in the views find the trail sign outside the lift station. Follow the Panoramaweg, a broad track, heading southwest toward Parsennhutte, Parsennfurgga and Strelapass. At all turns stay on the Panoramaweg.

At 0.4 miles reach a junction with a trail labeled "Bergwanderweg" branching right. Take this trail which descends on gentle grades through meadows, contouring beneath the Gruenhorn and Casanna to Parsennhutte at 1.4 miles.

Along the way views open to the Davosersee (Davos Lake), Davos Dorf and the peaks rimming the Dischma and Sertig Valleys, long tributary valleys extending southeast from the main Landwasser Valley. At Parsennhutte the trail rejoins the broad track.

The area around Parsennhutte is littered with ski lifts and buildings. Thankfully you soon leave the ski area behind. At 1.7 miles take the trail branching left to stay on the Panoramaweg. The broad track to the right continues up a side valley to the Totalpsee.

Our trail now ascends on easy grades through rocky meadows and scree covered slopes, traversing beneath the east facing slopes of the Totalphorn. Behind you are good views of the Silvrettahorn, Casanna and the Gotschnagrat area.

At 2.8 miles the path curves around a ridge extending from the Totalphorn and views open to the Salezer Horn at the end of the Mittelgrat (Mittel ridge) extending east from the Weissfluhjoch. The path now descends to cross the Totalpbach stream and then ascends to cross the northeast ridge of the Salezer Horn at 3.5 miles.

The ridge crest is a great spot to stop and take in the views. You are now looking directly up the Dischma Valley to the east. The Fluela Schwarzhorn, Piz Grialetsch, Scalettahorn and Sattelhorn anchor the cirque towering above the head of the valley. To the north the Madrissa massif forms the back drop for the Gotschnagrat area and Casanna. To the northeast the summits of the Silvretta massif and peaks rising above the Monchalp valley fill the skyline.

Beyond the ridge the trail contours through pretty meadows beneath the east and south facing flanks of the Salezer Horn, traveling through a section of avalanche barriers along the way. Views now extend south as far as Piz Ela and the Tinzenhorn towering above the Albula valley. To the southeast, across the Landwasser Valley, the Alplihorn and the peaks rimming the Sertig Valley are now in focus. Ahead the rugged gray crags and summit of the Gross Schiahorn dominate the view.

At 4.2 miles reach a junction with a trail dropping down to Station Hohenweg, the middle station on the Parsenn funicular to the Weissfluhjoch. Hikers looking for a shorter day can turn left here, descend to the station at 4.7 miles and then take the funicular down to Davos Dorf.

Beyond the junction the trail passes under the funicular and then contours around the southeast facing slopes of the Weissfluhjoch (9,331-ft.). At all junctions stay on the Panoramaweg toward Strelapass and Schatzalp.

At 5.0 miles the trail curves to the southeast as it traverses beneath the rugged east ridge of the Schiahorn. Soon the path swings around the end of the ridge, passing through an area of avalanche barriers as it heads west on an undulating trail under the Schiahorn's south facing flanks. Ahead views open to Strelapass, a notch on the ridge. To the southeast are fine views of the peaks rimming the Sertig Valley.

At 6.2 miles a short steep climb leads to Strela Pass (7,700-ft.) at 6.4 miles. Here fine views extend northwest to the high peaks rising above Langwies and Chur. The Weissfluhjoch dominates the view to the north. The Sertig Valley stretches southeast from Davos Platz to the Mittaghorn

(8,970-ft.) where the valley splits into the Chuealp and Ducan Valleys, each rimmed by high summits.

Hikers have a choice after enjoying the views. The standard Panoramaweg hike descends from Strelapass to Schatzalp at 8.5 miles. At Schatzalp a funicular descends to Davos Platz. Alternatively, extend the hike by walking to the Latschuelfurgga and then to Schatzalp, an 11.2 mile hike.

Strelapass to Schatzalp

- **Segment Stat:** 2.1 miles (one-way) from Strelapass to Schatzalp
- **Total Distance:** 8.5 miles (one way)
- **Elevation:** 7,700-ft. at Strela Pass
  6,106-ft. at Schatzalp
- **Elevation Gain/Loss to Schatzalp:** -1,594-ft.

After taking in the views at Strelapass, find the signpost near the Berghaus Strelapass. Head east/southeast toward Strelaalp and Schatzalp, descending on moderately steep grades down a broad grassy ridge above the south side of the Schiatobel Valley. As you descend enjoy views of the Schiahorn, the Sertig Valley and Davos Platz.

At 8.0 miles the path curves sharply to the southwest, descending on moderate grades to the historic Hotel Schatzalp (6,106-ft.) and the Schatzalpbahn, a funicular dropping down to Davos Platz, at 8.5 miles. Elevation loss from the Strelapass to Schatzalp is 1,594-ft.

Strelapass to Latschuelfurgga to Schatzalp

- **Segment Stat:** 5.1 miles (one-way) from Strelapass to Latschuelfurgga to Schatzalp
- **Total Distance:** 11.5 miles (one way)
- **Maximum Elevation:** 7,963-ft.
- **Elevation Gain/Loss:** 260-ft. / -1,857-ft.

Extend the day by continuing the hike to the Latschuelfurgga, a saddle on the ridge between the Chupfenflue and Wannengrat. Not many hikers continue this way so you should now enjoy some solitude.

At a signpost near the Berghaus Strelapass, head south/southwest on a good trail toward Latschuelfurgga. The path travels by the top of the lift at Station Strelapass and then ascends on moderate grades past the Strelasee, a small tarn, to the top of a low ridge. From the ridge enjoy views of the Jakobshorn, across the valley to the southeast, and the high peaks rising above the Sertig, Dischma and Fluela valleys to the east/northeast. Ahead views open to the Latschuelfurgga area.

The path descends on easy grades from the ridge crest to the Latschuelfurgga saddle at 8.2 miles. To the east are distant views of the high peaks towering above Chur and beyond. To the southwest the rugged Mederger Flue and Chorbsch Horn rises above a small, corrugated valley.

A trail drops down the west side of the pass toward Arosa. We take the trail descending east toward Podestatenalp and Schatzalp. Initially the trail descends on moderately easy grades. At 9.3 mile the path steepens as it drops through pastures, passing the small alp at Schonboden. Switchbacks facilitate the stiff descent to the junction at Podestatenalp at 10.5 miles.

At the junction turn left toward Schatzalp. The trail now enters the trees and descends on moderately steep switchbacks. As you near Schatzalp, the path travels through a pretty flower garden and passes signs to the Alpinum, an interesting botanical garden. Beyond the garden the trail leads to Schatzalp and the funicular to Davos Platz at 11.5 miles. Elevation loss from the high point along the ridge crest to Schatzalp is 1,857-ft.

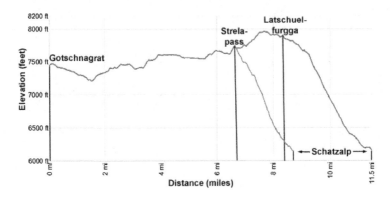

Trailhead Directions

This hike can be done in either direction.

From Davos Dorf Bahnhof to the Gotschnabahn (Gotschnagrat cable car): Take the train from Davos Dorf heading toward Landquart or Klosters Platz and get off at Klosters Platz. On the west side of the platform is the Gotschnabahn (Gotschnagrat cable car/Parsenn Klosters). Purchase a one-way ticket for the cable car. The train ride takes 25 minutes.

From Davos Dorf Bahnhof to Schatzalp: From the Davos Dorf train station, take the #1, 3 or 4 bus heading to Davos Platz Schatzalpbahn (the funicular in Davos Platz climbing to Schatzalp). Get off at the funicular station and purchase a one-way to the Schatzalp. You can check the current bus schedules at the SBB website/SBB app to find the stop nearest to your accommodations.

From Schatzalp to Davos Dorf Bahnhof: Take the funicular from Schatzalp to the bottom station. Catch a #1 or 3 bus headed to Davos Platz or Davos Glaris. Get off the bus at Davos Platz, Postplatz and walk to the Davos Platz train station. At the station take the train to Davos Dorf. You can check the current bus schedules at the SBB website/SBB app to find the stop nearest to your accommodations.

96. Davos Alpentour – Glaris to Schatzalp

★★★★☆

Distance: Up to 10.8 miles (one way)

Near Davos in Eastern Switzerland

This lovely walk traverses above or near the timberline along the west side of the Davos Valley with fine views of the peaks towering above the east side of the valley and the summits rimming the ridge to the west. Alternative destinations allow hikers to easily shorten the walk.

Distance: Up to 10.8 miles (one way)

Elevation: 4,734-ft. at Trailhead 6,670-ft. at Schatzalp

Elevation Gain: 1,926-ft.

Difficulty: moderate-strenuous

Basecamp: Davos

Davos West Map: See page 453

Online Map/Photos: www.hikingwalking.com/alpentour

Why Hike the Davos Alpentour – Glaris to Schatzalp

This mid-level walk, traversing above or near the timberline along the west side of the Landwasser Valley (the valley where Davos is located), features great views of the high peaks towering above the east side of the valley as well as the summits rising above the trail to the west.

After climbing above Glaris the undulating trail heads north staying between 6,100-ft to 6,700-ft. on its way to Schatzalp, where a funicular whisks hikers down to Davos Platz. The path can be walked in either direction. Walking north, as described below, requires a moderate to moderately-steep ascend from the valley floor to the traverse. Walking south is rated as moderate since it utilizes the funicular to reach the traverse and then drops down to Glaris at the end of the hike. I like both directions.

Shorten the hike by using one of the many trails that drop down to bus stops and train stations along the valley floor. The hike can also be shortened by starting the hike at Frauenkirch and climbing to Stafelalp (+1,270-ft.).

The Alpentour is a great option if there is snow at higher elevations or the weather precludes hiking in the high country. Hikers looking for an easier day will also appreciate this scenic path that passes through pretty meadows and visits small villages.

Be forewarned that you will be sharing the trail with mountain bikes. I have not found this generally to be a problem.

Due to the undulating nature of this trail, the elevation gain and loss is greater than the net difference between the high and low points on the hike.

Hiking the Davos Alpentour

From the bus stop at Glaris Ortolfi (see trailhead directions below), walk north (toward Davos) a short distance and turn left on the first street with a bridge over the river. The street is just to the south of the Hotel Post. Here you will find trail signs for the Davoser Alpentour heading toward Barentaler Alp, Stafelalp and Davos Platz. At all junctions stay on the Alpentour toward Stafelalp.

After crossing the river on a bridge, bear left on a road and then follow the trail signs for the Alpentour. The route winds up through Glaris, passing typical Walser farmhouses set amid pastures. At 0.4 miles the road crosses the Baretalbach (stream) on a bridge. Soon signs point left (west/northwest) to a track climbing on moderate to moderately-steep grades up the Baretal Valley along the north side of the stream.

The Baretal Valley is one of the larger tributary valleys that branches off the main Davos Valley in a westerly direction. As you ascend the valley note the profusion of dwarf mountain pines.

At 0.7 miles we leave the roads behind and continue ascending on a trail through trees and intermittent meadows. Openings offer views of Strel, rising along the ridge rimming the west side of the Landwasser Valley. Below the trail the Baretalbach cascades down a rocky creek bed. Behind you (east) the Rinerhorn towers above the east side of the Davos Valley

At 1.6 miles the trees give way to meadows. A short distance beyond the trail curves to the right, rejoining a farm track. Ahead views open to Barentaler Alp. To the east are lovely views of the Rinerhorn and Alplihorn.

Soon we reach a junction at Barentaler Alp. Here the Alpentour turns left on another farm track heading up the valley.

At 2.0 miles turn right (northeast) at a junction toward Chummeralp and Stafelalp. From here until Schatzalp the Alpentour will follow an undulating traverse along the west side of the valley near or above the timberline, curving in and out of side valleys.

The trail now continues its ascent through scattered trees and meadows with fine views of the peaks rimming the east side of the Landwasser Valley. At 2.9 miles reach the first of two high points (6,670-ft.) on the trail, located along the east ridge of the Amselflue. Turn around and look west/southwest for good views of Strel and Valbellahorn.

The path now descends on moderate to moderately-steep grades into the Chummertalli Valley, another tributary valley branching west off the Landwasser Valley. Meadows offer views of the Schwarzhorn and Chummerhureli rising above the north side of the valley. The Amselflue towers above the head of the valley to the west.

At 3.7 miles the path crosses the Chummerbach on a bridge and then ascends on moderate grades up the valley's north slopes accompanied by more good views of the Amselflue. Along the way, signs point to a trail descending to train/bus stops in Frauenkirch and Glaris. These are just the first of several trails where parties looking to cut the hike short can descend to the Landwasser Valley floor and return to Davos.

At 4.6 miles we reach Chummeralp, the location of a hut dating back to the 19th century. The Alp enjoys terrific views of the surrounding peaks. Beyond the alp the trail climbs to the second high point (6,670-ft.) on the Alpentour, located atop the ridge extending east from the Chummerhureli.

The path now descends through pretty meadows, crossing a few small drainages along the way. Signs for the Alpentour point toward Stafelalp, Erbalp, Schatzalp and Davos Platz. Behind you are views of the Chummerhureli, Schwarzhorn and Tiejer Flue.

At 5.6 miles the trail crosses a bridge over the Sutzibach and then drops down to Stafelalp at 6.1 miles. The village contains many traditional houses including the Berghaus Stafelalp, which is around 250-years old. The building now houses a small inn and a restaurant. Stafelalp is another good place to cut the hike short. Here you will find trails descending to Frauenkirch, where buses and trains return to Davos.

Beyond the alp the trail curves around a shallow side valley and then travels through scattered trees and meadows, passing through the small hamlet of Assererb. Reach a junction at 7.4 miles, five-minutes from Erb Alp. The trail branching right descends to Davos Platz, another option for shortening the hike. We continue along the Alpentour, passing through Erb Alp on the way to Gruenialp and Schatzalp.

The path now ascends on moderate grades through meadows. To the east/southeast, views open to the high peaks towering above the Sertig Valley, a tributary valley branching southeast off the Landwasser Valley.

At 8.0 miles the trail crests a low ridge and views open northwest to Strela and the Chupfenflue. After crossing the Bildjibach on a bridge, the path descends on moderately steep grades to Gruenialp at 8.5 miles. Trails branching to the right drop down to Davos Platz.

Beyond Gruenialp, the undulating Alpentour heads toward Schatzalp, traveling through meadows with fine views to the north/northeast of Davos, the Davosee and the high peaks rising above Klosters and the Durrboden Valley. Along the way the trail dips in and out of several minor drainages before cross a tributary of the Albertibach.

At 9.3 miles the trail drops into a rocky gully and crosses the Albertibach on a bridge. As the trail ascends out of the drainage it enters the trees, climbing above a landslide and then descending to a pretty meadows with great views of the Alplihorn, Mittaghorn and Piz Ducan towering above the Sertig Valley.

The views are short lived. Soon the path plunges back into the trees and descends switchbacks to Schatzalp. This segment of the trail crosses the Guggerbach on a bridge and passes trails branching left to the Alpinum (Botanic Garden), which boasts a collection of approximately 5,000 plant species from mountains all around the world.

Walk through the hotel complex to the funicular station and the end of the Alpentour at 10.8 miles. The funicular descends to Davos Platz where buses connect to location in Davos Platz and Davos Dorf.

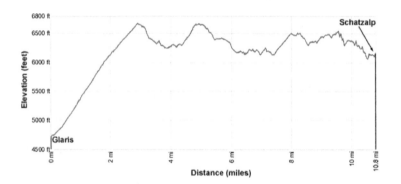

Trailhead Directions

From the Davos Dorf Bahnhof to Glaris Ortolfi: Take the #1 bus heading toward Glaris and get off the Glaris Ortolfi. The ride should take 21 minutes. You can check the current bus schedules at the SBB website/SBB app to find the stop along the #1 route nearest to your accommodations.

From Schatzalp to Davos Dorf Bahnhof: Take the funicular from Schatzalp to the bottom station. Catch a #1 or 3 bus headed to Davos Dorf. Get off the bus at at the Davos Dorf Bahnhof. You can check the current bus schedules at the SBB website/SBB app to find the stop nearest to your accommodations.

If walking the hike in reverse:

From Davos Dorf Bahnhof to Schatzalp: From the Davos Dorf train station, take the #1 or 3 bus heading to Davos Platz and get off at the Davos Platz Schatzalpbahn (the funicular in Davos Platz climbing to Schatzalp). Purchase a one-way ticket to the Schatzalp. You can check the current bus schedules at the SBB website/SBB app to find the stop nearest to your accommodations.

97. Sertig Pass ★★★★★

Distance: 8.4 miles (round trip)

Near Davos in Eastern Switzerland

Ascend a bucolic valley and then scree-covered slopes to scenic Sertig Pass with terrific views of the cirque rimming the Tschuvel Valley. Along the way enjoy fine views of the summits rimming the Ducan and Chuealp Valleys.

Distance: 8.4 miles (round trip)
Elevation: 6,099-ft. at Trailhead
8,986-ft. at Sertig Pass
Elevation Gain: 2,887-ft.
Difficulty: moderate-strenuous

Basecamp: Davos
Davos Map 2: See page 453
Online Map/Photos:
www.hikingwalking.com/sertig

Why Hike to Sertig Pass

The beautiful Sertig Valley, a tributary of the Landwasser Valley, extends southeast through lush pastures with enticing views of the surrounding high peaks. Beyond the last village the valley splits into the Ducan and Chuealp valleys. This scenic hike ascends the Chuealp Valley (Chuealptal), clad in pretty meadows and rimmed by rugged peaks, to Sertig Pass.

From the pass views extend south to the cirque ringing the lovely Tschuvel Valley, anchored by photogenic Piz Kesch and the glistening Porchabella Glacier. The serrated peaks of the Ducan Range dominate the view to the west while the Bocktenhorn and neighboring summits soar above Chuealptal.

The broad pass is a great place for a picnic or simply to take a break to enjoy the views. Watch your time so you don't miss the last bus of the day returning to Davos from Sertig Sand. Energetic hikers with the time and favorable weather will want to extend the hike by continuing over the pass to Durrboden. See Hike 98 - Sertig to Durrboden for more information.

I strongly recommend getting the first bus of the day to trailhead at Sertig Sand. This will allow plenty of time to enjoy this beautiful hike at your leisure.

Sertig to Sertig Pass

Take the bus from Davos to Sertig Sand (see trailhead directions below). The bus stops in front of the Walserhuus Restaurant/Hotel in Sertig Sand (6,099-ft.). Walk south along the road skirting the east side of the restaurant, past the parking lot (left). The trail signpost is just beyond the parking lot. Continue straight ahead on the alp road toward Chuealp, Sertigpass, Scalettapass and Durrboden.

The trail ascends on easy grades through pastures along the east side of the valley. The Sertigbach, a pretty stream, meanders down the idyllic valley beside the trail. Ahead the Mittaghorn, Plattenflue and Piz Duncan, rising along the southeast side of the Ducan Valley, dominate the view.

Reach a "Y" intersection at 0.4 miles and turn left (southeast) up the Chuealp Valley toward Sertig Pass. The trail to the right (south) ascends the Ducan Valley to the Fanezfurgga and Monstein. See Hike 99 - Sertig to Monstein for more information.

Follow the trail as it ascends the dirt road on moderate grades. Behind you the Alplihorn and Leidbachhorn tower above the west side of the Sertig Valley.

At 1.4 miles views open to the rugged Chuealphorn at the head of the Chuealp Valley. The Mittaghorn soars above the trail to the west while the delightful Chuealpbach flows along a rocky streambed to the right (west) of the trail.

Pass a barn/milking station at 1.7 miles and then reach a junction at 2.4 miles near Grunsee (7,208-ft.), a small tarn. Here the road ends. Bear right on the trail crossing a wood bridge over the Chuealpbach. Beyond the bridge the path climbs steeply through pastures along the west side of the valley. A second smaller bridge at 2.4 miles keeps your feet dry while crossing a stream cascading down the steep, grassy slopes above the trail.

The trail now climbs a few switchbacks and then continues on a diagonal up the west side of the valley. As you ascend enjoy ever improving views of the rugged cirque at the head of the valley. Behind you the Bocktenhorn dominates the view to the northeast.

Soon meadows give way to scree-covered slopes. At 3.9 miles views open to Sertig Pass, the saddle on the ridge at the head of the valley. Nestled in a depression below the trail is a small tarn, covered in ice/snow early in the season.

The trail now climbs steeply up the west side of a rocky bowl to Sertig Pass (8,986-ft.) at 4.2 miles. As you crest the pass Piz Kesch (11,214-ft.), the highest peak in the Albula Alps, burst onto the scene to the south. The Porchabella Glacier flows down the flanks of this majestic peak, soaring above the head of the Tschuvel Valley, while Piz Murtelet and Piz Forun rim the valley to the west. The serrated peaks of the Ducan Ridge fill the skyline to the west of the pass.

The pass is a great place to take a break and enjoy the views. Most parties turn around at this point and retrace their steps to Sertig Sand. If you have the time and energy, along with good weather, I highly recommend continuing over the Sertig Pass to Scaletta Pass and Durrboden. See Hike 98 - Sertig to Durrboden hiking for more information.

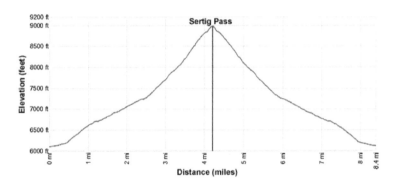

Trailhead Directions

Davos to Sertig: From the Bahnhof (train station) at Davos Platz (the southwest end of town), board the bus to Sertig. Purchase a ticket for Sertig Sand, the last stop on the line. The scenic ride up the Sertig Valley takes about 27 minutes. Regularly scheduled buses return to Davos via the same route. A schedule is posted at the bus stop of Sertig Sand. You can also check the current schedules at the SBB website/SBB app.

Note: Buses and trains travel between Davos Dorf and Davos Platz. The train ride takes three minutes. Buses take a variety of routes through the town. Pick up a bus schedule at the Tourism Office at the Davos Dorf Bahnhof or near the Sportzentrum in the middle of town, or consult the SBB website/SBB app to find the stop closest to your accommodations.

98. Sertig to Durrboden ★★★★★

Distance: 11.0 miles (one way)

Near Davos in Eastern Switzerland

This terrific hike crosses two panoramic passes, Sertig Pass and Scaletta Pass, and travels through five scenic valleys. Along the way hikers enjoy splendid views of Piz Kesch, Piz Vadret, the Ducan Ridge, the Schwarzhorn and the Chuealphorn, to name a few.

Distance: 4.2 miles (one way) - Sertig Pass
8.3 miles (one way) to Scaletta Pass
11.0 miles (one way) to Durrboden
Elevation: 6,099-ft. at Trailhead
8,986-ft. at Sertig Pass
8,550-ft. at Scaletta Pass
6,620-ft. at Durrboden
Elevation Gain: 2,887-ft to Sertig Pass
540-ft. to Scaletta Pass
-1,930-ft. to Durrboden

Difficulty: strenuous
Basecamp: Davos
Davos Map 2: See page 453
Online Map/Photos:
www.hikingwalking.com/
sertig-durrboden

Why Hike from Sertig to Durrboden

This splendid hike crosses two scenic passes linking the German-speaking Davos region with the Romansh Upper Engadine. Along the way the trail traverses five beautiful valleys clad in pretty meadows and ringed by high peaks draped with glaciers.

Starting in Sertig Sand, the hike ascends the beautiful Chuealp Valley to Sertig Pass where views open to Piz Kesch, the highest peak in the Albula Alps, soaring above the Val dal Tschuvel. The serrated peaks of the Ducan Ridge dominate the view to the west.

Beyond the pass the trail drops down the Val Sartiv and then traverses the Val Funtauna beneath the flanks of the Chuealphorn. Fantastic views of the Piz Vadret massif, soon joined by Piz Grialetsch to the northeast, accompany the delightful walk through meadows sprinkled with wildflowers.

As the trail turns into the Val Susauna and climbs toward Scaletta Pass views open of the high peaks towering above the valleys to the southwest. Soon the trail crests Scaletta Pass and the distinctive triangular-shaped Schwarzhorn, the highest peak in the Davos area, bursts onto the scene.

A good trail now descends through rocky meadows and scree-covered slopes to the floor of the Dischma Valley, accompanied by great views of the Raduner Rothorn and Piz Redont. As the trail reaches the valley floor the panorama of peaks, including Scaletta Peak and Piz Grialetsch, along with the Scaletta Glacier, will make you wish you had rear view mirrors. The problem is easily solved by frequently turning around to enjoy the marvelous views.

The hike ends at Durrboden, a small alp with a Berghaus and restaurant. Before returning to Davos by postbus find a nice perch on the restaurant's scenic sun terrace for a much deserved drink and snack.

This is a long hike with a fair amount of up and down. I strongly recommend getting an early start and catching the first postbus of the day to Sertig Sand. This will give you ample time to enjoy the beautiful hike and still arrive in Durrboden in time to catch the last bus back to Davos.

At the time of this writing the postbus between Davos and Durrboden ran seven times a day with the last bus returning to Davos at 6:30pm. These times are subject to change. Check the current schedules at the SBB website/SBB app.

To Sertig Pass

- **Distance from Trailhead:** 4.2 miles (one way)
- **Elevation:** 8,986-ft.
- **Elevation Gain:** 2,887-ft.

Note: This trail can be hiked in either direction. I recommend catching the first bus of the day so you get over the high passes earlier in the day, always a good idea in the mountains. It will also insure you have plenty of time to enjoy the hike while still making the last bus back to Davos from either Sertig of Durrboden.

Take the bus from Davos to Sertig Sand (see trailhead directions below) and then follow the direction in Hike 97 to Sertig Pass. Reach Sertig Pass (8,986-ft.) at 4.2 miles.

As you crest the pass Piz Kesch (11,214-ft.), the highest peak in the Albula Alps, burst onto the scene to the south. The Porchabella Glacier flows down the flanks of this majestic peak, soaring above the head of the Tschuvel Valley, while Piz Murtelet and Piz Forun rim the valley to the west. The serrated peaks of the Ducan Ridge fill the skyline to the west/southwest of the pass.

The pass is a great place to take a break and enjoy the views. Most parties turn around at this point and retrace their steps to Sertig Sand. If you have the time and energy, along with good weather, I highly recommend continuing over the Sertig Pass to Scaletta Pass and Durrboden.

To Scaletta Pass

- **Segment Stat:** 4.1 miles (one-way) from Sertig Pass to Scaletta Pass
- **Total Distance to Scaletta Pass:** 8.3 miles (one way)
- **Maximum Elevation:** 8,550-ft.
- **Elevation Gain/Loss:** -976-ft. / 540-ft.

To continue the hike, follow the trail down the south side of the pass toward Scalettapass (2-hr) and Durrboden (3-hr 15-min). (Ignore the trail heading right (southwest) toward Lai da Ravais, Chants and Bergun.) Red and white blazed rocks mark the path dropping steeply through rocky meadows.

As you descend, views open west to Lake Ravais and Lake Ravais Suot (south) along with Piz Ducan towering above the northeast end of the Ducan Ridge. To the south Piz Kesch commands your attention.

Pass a junction with a trail branching right (northwest) and climbing toward the Ravais Lakes, Chants and Bergun at 5.0 miles. Beyond the intersection the grade eases a bit as the descent continues down the Val Sartiv (Sartiv Valley) to a second junction at 5.2 miles. Here a trail branches right (south) and crosses a creek heading toward the Kesch Hut, Alp Funtauna and Cinuous-chel/Brail. Our trail to Scaletta Pass curves to the left and descends steeply along the left (east) side of the stream.

At 5.3 miles reach an intersection with another trail branching right toward the Kesch Hut and Chants. We turn left (east) toward Scalettapass and Durrboden. Ahead views open to the Piz Vadret massif. Before continuing, turn around for your last good views of Piz Kesch. With binoculars or a zoom lens on a camera you should be able to see the Kesch Hut on a grassy knoll along the right (west) side of the valley.

Our trail now ascends on easy grades through meadows sprinkled with wildflowers along the north side of the Val Funtauna (Funtauna Valley). Soon the trail curves to the left (northeast), traveling beneath the rugged south face of the Chuealphorn. Along the way enjoy terrific views of the Piz Vadret massif, which is soon joined by Piz Grialetsch, to the northeast. Alp Funtauna is seen on the valley floor. Piz Musella rises at the end of the ridge rimming the south side of the valley. At 6.5 miles views open to the Chuealphorn towering above the north side of the trail and the peaks rising above the Engadina Ota (Upper Engadine) Valley to the southeast.

At 7.0 miles the trail curves left (northeast) into the Val Susauna, ascending through meadows on easy to moderate grades toward Scaletta Pass. In three-quarters of a mile our path joins with a trail coming up from the Alp Funtauna. Scaletta Pass, the saddle at the head of the valley, is now in sight.

Follow the path as it ascends on moderate grades, crossing several streams carrying meltwater from glaciers and snowfields on the flanks of the Chuealphorn. Reach Scaletta Pass (8,550-ft.), a crossing on a medieval trade route between Chur, Davos and S-chanf, at 8.3 miles.

The pass is a great place to take a break and enjoy the views. The rugged ridge dominated by the Schwarzhorn, towering above the east side of the Dischma Valley, dominates the views to the north. Behind you, Piz Musella, Piz Viluoch and Piz Griatschouls fill the skyline to the south. The Chuealphorn and its glacier rise above the ridge to the west of the pass and are easiest to see before reaching the pass.

Just below the north side of the pass is a small shelter. In front of the shelter are several large, flat rocks – the perfect place for a picnic or a break.

To Durrboden

- **Segment Stat:** 2.7 miles (one-way) from Scaletta Pass to Durrboden
- **Total Distance to Durrboden:** 11.0 miles (one way)
- **Ending Elevation:** 6,620-ft.
- **Elevation Gain/Loss:** -1,930-ft.

To finish the hike, descend the trail on moderately-steep grades down the north side of the pass toward Durrboden (1-hr 15-min). The path drops through rocky meadows and then scree-covered slopes, crossing a few streams along the way. As you descend views open to the Bocktenhorn rising along the west side of the valley. To the northeast, the Raduner Rothorn and Piz Redont tower above the Furgga Valley.

You are now sharing a trail with mountain bikes. As you descend, watch for bikes coming down from the pass. Thankfully the rocky trail forces them to go slowly.

The scree covered slopes gradually give way to meadows filled with wildflowers during the end of July and beginning of August. At 9.3 miles views open east to the trail climbing to Fuorcla da Grialetsch (Grialetsch Pass) beneath the slopes of the Raduner Rothorn.

Pass a junction with a cutoff trail branching right toward Grialetsch Hut and the Fuorcla da Grialetsch at 9.8 miles. A little further along turn around and look south to see the Scalettahorn and Piz Grialetsch towering above the head of the valley. The Scaletta Glaciers flows down the rugged flanks of the peaks. Views of the peaks and glaciers at the head of the valley will improve as you near Durrboden.

At 10.2 miles the grade eases a bit as the trail travels through pastures between the streams draining the Scaletta Pass area and the Furggasee, a small lake below Grialetsch Pass. Pass through a gate a 10.5 miles. The trail now drops steeply down grassy slopes strewn with boulders. Durrboden, our destination, is now in sight.

As we near the alp the grade eases. Cross a bridge over the Furggabach at 10.9 miles and reach the historic Berghaus at 11.0 miles. The Berghaus includes a nice restaurant with lovely views of the peaks ringing the valley. The bus stop is located in front of the Berghaus.

Note: Since this trail crosses two passes the simple difference between the maximum and minimum elevation for each segment does not accurately reflect the true elevation gain and loss for the hike. The total elevation gain is about 3,430-ft while the total loss is -2,930-ft.

I strongly advise getting an early start if you intend to walk all the way to Durrboden. At the time of this writing the postbus between Davos and Durrboden ran seven times a day with the last bus returning to Davos at 6:30pm. These times are subject to change. Check the current schedules at the SBB website/SBB app for the current schedule.

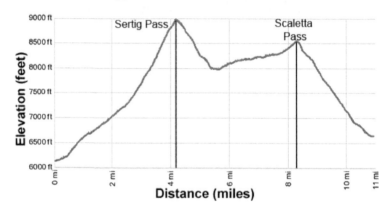

Trailhead Directions

Davos to Sertig: From the Bahnhof (train station) at Davos Platz (the southwest end of town), board the bus to Sertig. Purchase a ticket for Sertig Sand, the last stop on the line. The scenic ride up the Sertig Valley takes about 27 minutes. Regularly scheduled buses return to Davos via the same route. A schedule is posted at the bus stop of Sertig Sand. You can also check the current schedules at the SBB website/SBB app.

Davos to Durrboden: From the Bahnhof (train station) at Davos Dorf (at the northeast end of town), board the bus to Durrboden. Get off at the last stop on the bus. The scenic ride up the Dischma Valley takes about 30 minutes. Regularly scheduled buses return to Davos via the same route. A schedule is posted at the bus stop at Durrboden. You can also check the current schedules at the SBB website/SBB app.

Note: Buses and trains travel between Davos Dorf and Davos Platz. The train ride takes three minutes. Buses take a variety of routes through the town. Pick up a bus schedule at the Tourism Office at the Davos Dorf Bahnhof or near the Sportzentrum in the middle of town, or consult the SBB website/SBB app to find the stop closest to your accommodations.

99. Sertig to Monstein via Fanezfurgga Pass

★★★★☆

Distance: 7.2 - 7.7 miles (one way)

Near Davos in Eastern Switzerland

Get off the beaten path with this great hike ascending the Ducan Valley to Fanezfurgga Pass. Highlights include the Ducan Ridge, Ducan Glacier and the Chrachenhorn towering above the head of the Ducan valley. Finish the hike by descending the pretty Oberalp Valley to Monstein.

Distance: 7.2 miles (one way)	**Basecamp:** Davos
Elevation: 6,099-ft. at Trailhead	**Davos Map 2:** See page 453
8,465-ft. at Fanezfurgga Pass	**Online Map/Photos:**
Elevation Gain: 2,366-ft.	www.hikingwalking.com/sertig-
Difficulty: moderate-strenuous	monstein

Why Hike from Sertig to Monstein via Fanezfurgga Pass

This trail ascends the wild and rugged Ducantal (Ducan Valley), a classic glacial valley rimmed by photogenic summits along Ducan Ridge, and then climbs to Fanezfurgga Pass on the saddle between the Chrachenhorn (9,485-ft.) and the Strel Ridge. Beyond the pass the trail descends through the beautiful meadows of the Oberalp Valley to Monstein.

The hike starts with a short, easy ascent up the Sertig Valley, passing a beautiful waterfall on the Ducanbach. Beyond the falls we leave the last vestiges of civilization behind and climb through an untamed valley clad in rocky meadows and talus slopes beneath soaring peaks and rugged ridges.

The pass enjoys terrific views of the summits rimming the Ducan Valley and, in the distance the Chuealphorn. To the west the high peaks rising above the upper Davos Valley fill the skyline. Closer at hand is the Ducan Glacier, spilling down the slopes of the Ducan Dador, and Ducanfurgga Pass, set against a backdrop of the summits rimming the Stugl Valley.

The remainder of the walk is a scenic, albeit steep descent down the Oberalp Valley to Monstein where buses return to Davos.

The hike can be walked in either direction. I prefer starting in Sertig because there is less elevation to gain and the views are better going up the Ducan Valley.

This is not a good hike to undertake in bad weather or poor visibility. Pick a beautiful day and get the first bus of the day to Sertig where the hike starts, allowing plenty of time to enjoy the hike at a leisurely pace.

Sertig to Fanezfurgga to Monstein

The beautiful Sertig Valley, a tributary of the Landwasser Valley, extends southeast through lush pastures with enticing views of the surrounding high peaks. Beyond the last village the valley splits into the Ducan and Chuealp. This hike takes the trail less traveled, ascending the rugged and unspoiled Ducan Valley to Fanezfurgga Pass. Beyond the pass the trail descends the pretty Oberalp Valley to Monstein.

Take the bus from Davos to Sertig Sand (see trailhead directions below). The bus stops in front of the Walserhuus Restaurant/Hotel in Sertig Sand (6,099-ft.). Walk south along the road skirting the east side of the restaurant to a trail signpost, located just beyond the parking lot on the left side of the road. Continue straight ahead on the alp road toward Fanezfurgga, Oberalp and Monstein.

The trail ascends on easy grades through pastures along the east side of the valley. The Sertigbach, a pretty stream, meanders down the idyllic valley beside the trail. Ahead the Mittaghorn, Plattenflue and Piz Duncan, rising along the southeast side of the Ducan Valley, dominate the view.

Reach a "Y" intersection at 0.4 miles. Here we turn right (south) on the trail climbing toward the Ducan Valley. The path to the left (southeast) ascends the Chuealp Valley toward Sertig Pass, Scaletta Pass and Durrboden. See Hike 97 - Sertig Pass for more information on this trail.

Our trail crosses a bridge over the Chuealpbach and ascends on easy grades along the east side of the Ducanbach, the stream draining the Ducan Valley. Ahead views open to beautiful Sertig Falls, a photogenic waterfall tumbling 200-ft. down a rugged, rocky chasm in three stages.

At 0.7 miles reach a junction where a spur trail to the falls (Wasserfall) branches right. (The 0.5 mile round-trip detour to the falls is recommended to get good views of this dramatic cascade.) We bear left on the trail toward Fanezfurgga.

Our path ascends steeply through a larch forest and intermittent meadows, climbing up the end of an old terminal moraine at to the foot of the Ducan Valley. At 1.2 miles the grade abates. The trail now travels through meadows to a bridge crossing the Ducanbach to the west side of the valley. The Plattenflue and Piz Ducan soar above the east side of the valley.

The rugged, untamed glacial valley is sandwiched between the Strel Ridge to the west and the Duncan Ridge, anchored by Piz Ducan, to the east. The trail now curves to the southwest as it climbs steep to moderately-steep grades through rocky meadows and scree slopes along the west side of the valley.

At 1.9 miles the grade lessens and gorgeous views open up the length of the valley to the Chrachenhorn and Ducan Dador at the head of the valley. The Ducan Glacier clings to the slopes between the Ducan Dador and the Chlein Duncan. The saddle on the ridge between the two peaks is the Ducanfurgga, not our pass. The Fanezfurgga, unseen at this point, is located along the valley's west ridge between the Strel Ridge and Chrachenhorn.

The path now ascends through pretty wildflower-filled meadows on moderately easy grades. At 2.5 miles the grade steepens as the trail angles away from the valley floor and begins climbing the slopes along the west side of the valley. The terrain becomes more rugged as the path ascends through avalanche chutes. Some weird and wonderful rock formations appear along the trail.

Soon the path enters a gully along the base of a lateral moraine and the valley's western slopes. The path ascends steeply to the head of the gully and then curves to the right, climbing steep switchbacks up the valley's west slopes to exit the gully. Beyond the gully the ascent continues with ever improving views of peaks along the Ducan ridge, the Ducan Glacier and the Ducanfurgga. Ahead views open to the Fanezfurgga. The Strel ridge dominates the view to the north.

At 3.3 miles the grade briefly abates as the path crests a bench and then ascends through meadows and rocky outcroppings to a junction at 3.5 miles. Here a trail branches left to the Ducanfurgga, Stuls and Bergun. We bear right on the trail toward Fanezfurgga, Oberalp and Monstein. The path now climbs steeply to the Fanezfurgga Pass (8,465-ft.) at 3.6 miles.

Sublime views from the pass extend south/southeast to the Ducan Glacier clinging to the rugged slopes between Duncan Dador and Chlein Duncan. The high peaks along the Duncan ridge, anchored by Piz Duncan, dominate the view to the east while the summits rising above the Chuealp Valley are seen to the northeast. A sea of peaks towering above the Davos Valley and beyond fill the skyline to the west. The Chrachenhorn soars above the pass to the southwest while the rugged Strel Ridge and the Alplihorn rise to the northeast.

When you are done admiring the views, follow the trail descending steeply through rocky meadows and scree down the west side of the pass toward Oberalp and Monstein. At 4.0 miles the grade briefly abates as the path passes below the Mitteltalli, a side valley, along the southwest facing flanks of the Alplihorn.

At 4.25 miles the grade steepens as the path drops down pretty meadows beneath the rugged slopes of the Alplihorn to the northeast and the Chrachenhorn to the south. As you descend turn around for great views of the Strel Ridge rising above Fanezfurgga Pass. Ahead are ever improving views of the high peaks rimming the west side of the Davos Valley.

You are now descending above the northeast side of the Oberalpbach, the stream draining the Oberalp valley. Initially the stream is composed of several channels that soon consolidate into a one flow.

At 4.8 miles pass the old wood buildings at Fanezmeder. Turn around here for good views of the Chrachenhorn towering above the head of the valley.

The grade briefly steepens as the path drops down switchbacks and crosses a pretty tributary stream carrying snowmelt from the slopes of the Alplihorn. Beyond the stream the path continues descending on moderately-steep grades. Along the way meadows give way to low shrubs and then scattered larches.

At 6.0 miles reach the hamlet at Oberalp. Here the trail turns into a broad track/road. Travel along the track for a quarter of a mile to a junction. At this point you can either continue down the broad track toward Monstein or turn left, cross the Oberalpbach on a bridge and then descends along a trail on the southwest side of the creek. This trail crosses back over the stream and rejoins the road at 6.7 miles.

Soon the track enters the town of Monstein (5,312-ft.) and arrives at the bus stop at 7.2 miles. Eelevation loss from the pass to the village is 3,153-ft.

Monstein is a pretty village, composed of typical Walser timber houses, some still covered with larch tiles. Along the way you will also see the old grain storage buildings set atop stilts. Thirsty hikers will be interested to know that Monstein is home to one of Europe's highest breweries. Stop at one of the local restaurants to sample the brew.

Watch your time so you don't miss your bus back to Davos. Remember that you need to change buses at Glaris on the return to Davos.

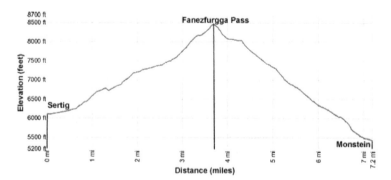

Trailhead Directions

Davos to Sertig: See Hike 97.

From Monstein to Davos: Take the #10 bus from Monstein to the Glaris Bahnhof (train station). At Glaris change for a #1 bus to Davos Postplatz or Davos Dorf Bahnhof. Check the current schedules at the SBB website/app to determine to find the stop nearest you lodging.

100. Durrboden to Scaletta Pass ★★★★★
Distance: 5.2 miles (round-trip)
Near Davos in Eastern Switzerland

The trail to Scaletta Pass ascends through pastures, rocky meadows and then scree covered slopes with ever evolving views of high summits surrounding the photogenic valley. Highlights include the glacier-clad Scalettahorn, the Schwarzhorn massif and the peaks towering above Fuorcla da Grialetsch.

Distance: 5.2 miles (round-trip)
Elevation: 6,575-ft. at Trailhead
8,547-ft. at Scaletta Pass
Elevation Gain: 1,972-ft.
Difficulty: moderate-strenuous

Basecamp: Davos
Davos Map 2: See page 453
Online Map/Photos:
www.hikingwalking.com/scaletta

Why Hike from Durrboden to Scaletta Pass

The lovely Dischma Valley, extending southeast from the Landwasser valley from Davos Dorf, is sprinkled with small villages set amid emerald green meadows beneath rugged peaks. Regularly scheduled buses travel to the Berggasthaus Durrboden, the last settlement near the head of the valley.

Above the Berggasthaus the valley branches into three lobes ringed by high summits. The Furgga Valley, with its lovely lake and the popular Grialetsch hut, lies to the east. The Scaletta Glacier spills down the slopes of the Scalettahorn and Piz Grialetsch in the aptly named Gletschtalli (Glacier Valley) to the southeast. Our trail to Scaletta Pass ascends southwest up the third lobe, the continuation of the Dischma Valley, rimmed by the Bocktenhorn, Leidhorn, Augstenhureli and Chuealphorn to the west and the Peak 2834 to the east.

To Scaletta Pass

Take the post bus from Davos to the Durrboden Restaurant (Berggasthaus Durrboden), the last stop in the Dischma Valley (see trailhead directions below). The historic Berghaus includes a nice restaurant with lovely views of the Scaletta Glacier, Piz Grialetsch, the Scalettahorn and neighboring peaks rising above the of the Gletschtalli. The Raduner Rothorn and Schwarzhorn tower above the valley to the east.

Walk along the east side of the Berghaus to the end of the car park. Here a trail signpost points to a broad track heading southeast through pastures up the Dischma Valley to Scaletta Pass. A short distance beyond the track splits. We bear right on the trail to Scaletta Pass. The trail to the left leads to the Grialetsch Hut, Fuorcla Radont (Radont Pass) and Fluela Ospiz. See Hike 101 - Durrboden to Fuorcla da Grialetsch and Fuorcla Radont for more information.

The trail soon crosses a bridge over the Furggabach (Furgga stream) and then ascends on moderate grades through pretty meadows between the Dischmabach (Dischma stream), to the west, and Furggabach, to the east.

At 0.4 miles go through a gate and then pass a small tarn near Gletschboden. A short distance beyond the grade steepens as the path ascends through rocky meadows scattered with shrubs. Ahead are fine views of the glacier-clad cirque, anchored by the Chilbiritzenspitz, Piz Grialetsch and the Scalettahorn, ringing the Gletschtalli Valley.

At 1.1 miles pass a junction with a trail branching left toward the Grialetsch Hut. Our path to Scaletta Pass now curves to the southwest, climbing through rocky meadows and then scree covered slopes beneath the west facing slopes of the Scalettahorn massif. A few switchbacks facilitate the climb.

Turn around for great views of the Raduner Rothorn and Schwarzhorn to the northeast. The Dischmabach tumbles down a rugged slope strewn with rock outcroppings to the west of the trail.

As you gain elevation views open to the Fuorcla da Grialetsch, the pass at the head of the Furgga Valley to the east. Piz Radont and the Chilbiritzenspitz rise above the pass. The Bocktenhorn, Leidhorn and Augstenhureli rise along the ridge above the west side of the trail. A small tarn at Seeboden lies nestled in the meadows along the valley floor. The Dischmabach cascades down a rugged cliff above the head of the tarn.

At 2.1 miles the grade briefly abates as the trail reaches a bench. Here the path travels through a rocky area. The trail builders having lovingly laid rock slabs along this section of the trail to ease the passage. Soon the climb resumes on moderately-steep grade up rocky meadows and rugged slopes.

At 2.4 miles the trail crosses the stream and then climbs a few steep switchbacks to Scaletta Pass (8,550-ft.) at 2.6 miles. The pass, a crossing on a medieval trade route between Chur, Davos and S-chanf, is a great place to take a break and enjoy the views of the rugged ridge, dominated by the Chlein Schwarzhorn, Schwarzhorn and Raduner Rothorn, towering above the east side of the Dischma Valley. To the south, Piz Musella, Piz Viluoch and Piz Griatschouls fill the skyline. The Chuealphorn and its glacier rise above the ridge to the southwest of the pass. (Walk a short distance down the south side of the pass for better views of the Chuealphorn.)

Just below the north side of the pass is a small shelter. In front of the shelter are several large, flat rocks – the perfect place for a picnic or a short break. When you are done enjoying the views retrace your steps to Durrboden. Alternatively, you can continue over the pass, descend through Alp Funtauna and then cross Sertig Pass to Sertig where buses return to Davos. See Hike 98 - Sertig to Durrboden for more information.

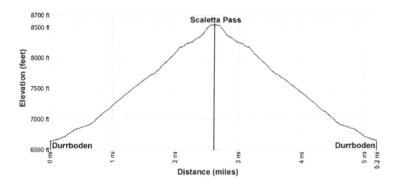

Trailhead Directions

Davos to Durrboden: See Hike 98.

101. Durrboden to Fuorcla da Grialetsch and Fuorcla Radont ★★★★★
Distance: 4.8 - 7.7 miles (round trip)
Near Davos in Eastern Switzerland

Two scenic passes and views of the high peaks towering above four beautiful valleys are the highlights of this trail climbing from Durrboden to Fuorcla da Grialetsch and Fuorcla Radont. Along the way the trail passes by pretty tarns and enjoys fine views of the Scaletta and Grialetsch Glaciers.

Distance: 4.8 - 7.7 miles (round-trip)
Elevation: 6,575-ft. at Trailhead
9,137-ft. at Fuorcla Radont
Elevation Gain: 2,562-ft.
Difficulty: moderate-strenuous

Basecamp: Davos
Davos Map 2: See page 453
Online Map/Photos:
www.hikingwalking.com/radont

Why Hike from Durrboden to Fuorcla da Grialetsch and Fuorcla Radont

This trail packs a lot of scenery into a relatively short distance. Beginning in the Dischma Valley beneath the Schwarzhorn, the path ascends the Furgga Valley to the Grialetsch Pass/Col, a pretty area with two small lakes and fine views of Piz Sarsura massif and the Grialetsch Glacier. The area around the hut is a great place for a picnic or to simply relax in the sun amid the beautiful scenery.

Hikers looking for a longer day will want to continue to the Fuorcla Radont on a trail climbing through rocky meadows, scree covered slopes and a small boulder field. This segment of the path offers splendid views of Piz Grialetsch, Piz Vadret and Piz Sarsura anchoring the cirque at the head of the Grialetsch Valley along with the summits rimming the valley's eastern wall. As you crest Radont Pass great views unfold of the Schwarzhorn towering above Fluela Pass.

Hiking from Durrboden to Fuorcla da Grialetsch and Fuorcla Radont

Start the day with a scenic postbus ride up the Dischma Valley to the Berggasthaus Durrboden, the last settlement near the head of the valley. (See trailhead directions below.) The valley, a southeast trending tributary of the Landwasser Valley, is clad in pretty pastures sprinkled with small villages nestled beneath rugged peaks.

The historic Berghaus includes a nice restaurant with lovely views of the Scaletta Glacier, Piz Grialetsch, the Scalettahorn and neighboring peaks rising above the of the Gletschtalli. The Raduner Rothorn and Schwarzhorn tower above the east side of the valley.

Above the Berggasthaus the valley branches into three lobes ringed by high summits. To the southwest is the main Dischma valley rimmed by the Bocktenhorn, Leidhorn and Augstenhureli to the west and the Peak 2834 (9,298-ft.) to the east. The Scaletta Glacier spills down the slopes of the Scalettahorn and Piz Grialetsch in the aptly named Gletschtalli (Glacier Valley) to the southeast. Our trail ascends the Furgga Valley, with its lovely lake and the popular Grialetsch Hut, to the east.

Walk along the east side of the Berghaus to the end of the car park. Here a trail signpost points to a broad track heading southeast through pastures to

Scaletta Pass (Hike 100), the Grialetsch Hut and Fuorcla Radont. A short distance beyond the track splits. We bear left on the trail to Grialetsch Hut and Fuorcla Radont. The trail to the right leads to Scaletta Pass.

Our trail ascends on moderate grades through meadows to the east of the Furggabach, a stream draining the Furgga Valley. Ahead are nice views of the Scaletta Glacier clinging to the rugged slopes above the Gletschtalli. At 0.6 miles the grade steepens and views open southwest to the Chuealphorn, Augstenhureli and Leidhorn rising above the Scaletta Pass area.

At 1.1 miles the trail curves to the left (east) and reaches a junction with a trail branching right toward Scaletta Pass. We continue on the main trail to the Grialetsch Hut. The path now climbs on steep grades through rocky meadows up the north side of the Furgga Valley. The Furggabach spills down the valley floor beneath the trail. The rugged slopes of the Raduner Rothorn tower overhead.

At 2.0 miles the grade abates as the trail traverses along the south side of the Furggasee (Lake Furgga), a pretty tarn set beneath the south facing slopes of the Raduner Rothorn and Piz Radont. Past the lake the path ascends on gentle grades to Fuorcla da Grialetsch (Grialetsch Col/Pass) (8,320-ft.) and a trail junction at 2.4 miles. Here views open to the Piz Sarsura massif and the Grialetsch Glacier to the east/southeast. To the south the Chilbiritzenspitz towers above the pass while two small tarns lie nestled amid the meadows and rocky slopes.

From the junction a trail wanders south to the Grialetsch Hut with more great views of the Grialetsch Glacier and the Piz Sarsura massif along with the beautiful area around the Fuorcla da Grialetsch. The hut offers dormitory accommodations and refreshments.

The hut is a great turnaround point for hikers looking for a shorter, easier day. Simply find a perch with great views of the tarns and the surrounding summits to enjoy a picnic lunch and then retrace your steps to the trailhead for a 4.8 mile round-trip hike with a 1,745-ft. elevation gain.

For hikers with the time, energy and good weather, I recommend continuing beyond the Fuorcla da Grialetsch to Fuorcla Radont. This segment of the trail features terrific views of the high peaks towering above the Grialetsch Valley. From the pass enjoy stunning views of the Schwarzhorn soaring above the Radont Valley.

To reach Fuorcla Radont, turn left at the junction. The trail ascends steeply through rocky meadows to a bench along the west facing flanks of Piz Radont, high above the west side of the Grialetsch Valley. As you climb turn around for birds-eye-views of the Fuorcla da Grialetsch area along with splendid vistas of Piz Grialetsch, Piz Vadret and Piz Sarsura anchoring the cirque at the head of the Grialetsch Valley. The Grialetsch Glacier clings to the cirque's rugged slopes.

Crest the bench at 2.75 miles. The path now traverses the bench beneath the rugged slopes of Piz Radont. In route pass a small tarn and traverses the scree clad slopes of an avalanche chute.

At 3.2 miles the ascent resumes up rocky meadows and scree covered slopes. A short section of this trail segment entails a somewhat tedious crossing of a boulder field. Red and white slashes on the rock will keep you on track through the boulders.

At 3.7 miles a grassy knoll offers a great spot to take a break and enjoy the views of the high peaks rimming the Grialetsch Valley. Beyond the knoll a moderate climb, passing above two small tarns, leads to Fuorcla Radont (Radont Col/Pass) at 3.85 miles. The pass enjoys fine views of the Schwarzhorn soaring above the Radont Valley along with the Grialetsch cirque. Below the west side of the pass is a rocky moonscape.

You now have two choices. The easiest option is to turn around and enjoy the great views as you head back to Durrboden got a 7.7 mile round-trip hike. Alternatively, you can drop down a very steep, rocky trail to Fluela Pass, losing over 1,300-ft. in 2.2 miles.

The trail over Fuorcla Radont can be combined with a hike to the Schwarzhorn for a challenging and scenic 8.4 miles point to point hike. The pass is served by regularly scheduled buses from Davos. See Hike 103 - Fluela Pass – Schwarzhorn - Durrboden for more information.

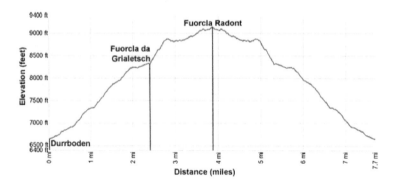

Trailhead Directions

Davos to Durrboden: See Hike 98.

480

102. Fluela Pass to the Schwarzhorn ★★★★★
Distance: 4.6 miles (round-trip)
Near Davos in Eastern Switzerland

Hike to the summit of the Schwarzhorn for splendid, panoramic views of the high peaks in the northeast Graubunden area and beyond. The Schwarzhorn is considered to be one of the easier 3,000-meter peaks to ascend in the Swiss Alps.

Distance: 4.6 miles (round-trip)
Elevation: 7,817-ft. at Trailhead
10,318-ft. at the Schwarzhorn
Elevation Gain: 2,501-ft.
Difficulty: strenuous-difficult

Basecamp: Davos
Davos Map 2: See page 453
Online Map/Photos:
www.hikingwalking.com/schwarzhorn

Why Hike from Fluela Pass to the Schwarzhorn

Far reaching, 360-degree views of the high peaks in the Lower and Upper Engadine Valleys and the summits towering above the Davos area and beyond are the highlights of the hike to the summit of the Schwarzhorn. The steep trail is recommended for hikers with the stamina and conditioning to ascend 2,500-ft. in 2.3 miles. Many consider the summit to be one of the most accessible of the 3,000-meter peaks in the Alps.

The hike, starting near Fluela Pass, climbs up the west side of a beautiful cirque anchored by Piz Radont, the Raduner Rothorn and the Schwarzhorn. The stiff climb travels through meadows, scree covered slopes and then the Schwarzhorn's rugged southeast ridge to the summit. The ridge includes a slightly exposed trail section that soon widens.

Pick a beautiful day and get an early start to enjoy the views. Extend the day by turning the hike into a point-to-point journey to Durrboden in the lovely Dischma Valley. See Hike 103 - Fluela Pass – Schwarzhorn - Durrboden hike for more information.

(Note: The Schwarzhorn in Davos is often referred to as the Fluela Schwarzhorn to distinguish the peak from the Schwarzhorn in the Valais.)

Hiking to the Schwarzhorn

Start the day by taking the bus from Davos to the Schwarzhorn trailhead, located along the Fluelapass (Fluela Pass) road. (See trailhead directions below.) Get off the bus at the first stop after Fluelapass (east side of the pass). The stop and the trailhead are located along the south side of the road.

Note for hikers driving to the trailhead: There is limited parking at the trailhead. If the lot is full, turn around and park at Fluela Pass. A 0.6 mile (one-way) trail, traveling above the north side of the Fluelapass Road, leads to the Schwarzhorn trailhead. Follow the trail signed for the Schwarzhorn, Fuorcla Radont, Grialetschhutte and Durrboden. This description assumes you are starting at the bus stop. If starting at the pass, add 0.6 miles (one-way) to the mileage in the description below.

At the trailhead, walk southeast on the trail signed for Schwarzhorn, Fuorcla Radont, Grialetschhutte and Durrboden. The trail immediately starts climbing on moderately-steep to steep grades through rocky meadows and intermittent scree. Along the way pass a junction with a trail branching left. We continue on the trail to the Schwarzhorn. Behind you (north) the Fluela Wisshorn towers above the Fluelapass road.

At 0.3 miles the trail climbs a few steep switchbacks and then swings to the right (southwest), entering the Radont Valley rimmed with a cirque anchored by Piz Radont, the Raduner Rothorn and the Schwarzhorn. The path now ascends on moderately-steep to steep grades beneath the east facing slopes of the Schwarzhorn accompanied by great views of Piz Radont to the south.

Reach a junction at 0.5 miles with a trail branching left (south) toward Fuorcla Radont and the Grialetschhutte. We continue on the trail to the Schwarzhorn.

Beyond the junction views open to the Raduner Rothorn and Fuorcla Radont (Radont Pass), the saddle on the ridge to the northeast of Piz Radont. Soon the Schwarzhorn (10,318-ft.) joins the scene. Below the trail a stream winds down the valley floor.

At 1.0 mile the path starts climbing switchbacks. Soon the meadows give way to scree covered slopes. Turn around occasionally to appreciate the fine views stretching northeast to Piz Linard and the peaks towering above the Fluelapass Road and the Lower Engadine Valley.

The grade steepens as the path ascends tight switchbacks up the rugged slopes beneath the Schwarzhornfurgga (Schwarzhorn Pass). Here views open to the Schwarzhorn's south ridge, the route to the summit.

At 1.6 miles reach a junction with a trail branching left (east) toward Fuorcla Radont. Large rocks around the junction provide convenient resting places before continuing the ascent.

After taking a break continue straight ahead toward the Schwarzhorn, reaching the Schwarzhornfurgga at 1.75 miles. From the pass views stretch west to the high peaks rimming the Dischma Valley and beyond. Behind you the summits rising above the Lower Engadine valley fill the skyline.

Turn right and follow the trail as it climbs very steep switchbacks up the south ridge to the summit of the Schwarzhorn (10,318-ft.) at 2.3 miles. Initially the trail has some minor exposure but soon the ridge widens and the remainder of the stiff climb to the top is on a good, albeit very steep, trail.

From the summit enjoy breathtaking, panoramic views that extend northwest down the Dischma Valley to Davos. The Fluela Wisshorn towers above Fluela Pass to the north. Piz Linard soars above a sea of peaks rising above the Lower Engadine Valley to the east. The Piz Sarsura massif, Piz Vadret and the Grialetsch Glacier are seen beyond Piz Radont to the south. Piz Kesch, the Porchabella Glacier and the summits rimming the upper Dischma, Funtauna and Tschuvel valleys grace the skyline to the southwest.

When you are done taking in the views retrace your steps to the trailhead for a 4.6 miles round-trip hike. Parties looking for a longer day can return to the junction with the trail to Fuorcla Radont at 3.0 miles. From here you can hike to Fuorcla Radont in 1.25 miles and then take the trail descending the east side of the Radont valley back to the trailhead for a 6.4 mile hike. Alternatively, continue over Fuorcla Radont to Durrboden for an 8.1 mile hike. See Hike 103 - Fluela Pass - Schwarzhorn - Durrboden hike for more information.

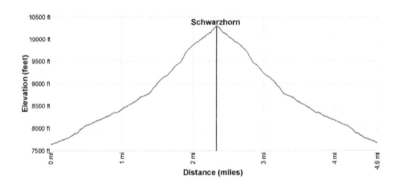

Trailhead Directions

From the Davos Dorf Bahnhof: Take the #331 bus heading toward Susch and get off at Susch, Abzw. Schwarzhorn. (Abzw. is an abbreviation for Abzweigung or junction.) This is the first stop after Fluela Pass (east side of the pass). The trailhead is located on the south side of the highway. The ride takes 24 minutes.

Note: If you are driving, there is limited parking at the trailhead. If the lot is full, turn around and park at Fluela Pass. From the pass, locate the trail at the northeast end of the parking area. The trail traverses the north side of the Schwarzsee, a lake, and then travels along the slopes above the north side of the highway to the Schwarzhorn trailhead in 0.6 miles.

103. Fluela Pass – Schwarzhorn – Durrboden

★★★★★

Distance: 6.4 (loop) - 8.1 miles (one way)

Near Davos in Eastern Switzerland

This epic hike summits the Schwarzhorn, crosses two panoramic passes and visits four scenic valleys in route to Durrboden. Highlights include the high peaks towering above the Lower Engadine, the cirque at the head of the Grialetsch Valley and the summits rimming the Dischma, Funtauna and Tschuvel Valleys.

Distance: 2.3 miles (one way) to Schwarzhorn
4.25 miles (one way) to Fuorcla Radont
8.1 miles (one way) to Durrboden
Elevation: 7,817-ft. at Trailhead
10,318-ft. at Schwarzhorn
9,137-ft. at Fuorcla Radont
6,620-ft. at Durrboden
Elevation Gain: 2,501-ft. to Schwarzhorn
380-ft. to Fuorcla Radont
-2,562-ft. to Durrboden

Difficulty: strenuous-difficult
Basecamp: Davos
Davos Map 2: See page 453
Online Map/Photos:
www.hikingwalking.com/fluela

Why Hike from Fluela Pass – Schwarzhorn - Durrboden

This challenging hike climbs to the summit of the Schwarzhorn with breathtaking, 360-degree views of the high peaks in northeastern Graubunden and beyond. After descending from the summit the trail crosses a rugged bowl beneath the Raduner Rothorn and Piz Radont before ascending to Fuorcla Radont (Radont Pass). Views from the pass encompass the summits rising above the Grialetsch Valley and the splendid cirque at the head of the valley anchored by Piz Sarsura, Piz Vadret and Piz Grialetsch.

The views of the Grialetsch valley continue as the trail descends to Fuorcla da Grialetsch (Grialetsch Pass). This lovely spot, set amid a meadow clad bench with two small tarns, features close-up views of the Grialetsch cirque.

Beyond the pass the trail drops into the Furgga Valley where fine views extend up the Dischma Valley to the Scaletta Pass area. The final leg of the trail descends to Durrboden where the peaks rimming the Gletschtalli Valley and the Scaletta Glacier are the stars of the show.

Pick a day full of promise before attempting this hike. There is a lot of up and down along rugged trails with over 3,000-ft. of elevation gain and more than 5,000-ft. of elevation loss. Keep an eye on the time so you don't miss the last bus from Durrboden back to Davos.

Trailhead to the Summit of the Schwarzhorn

- **Distance from Trailhead:** 2.3 miles (one way)
- **Elevation:** 10,318-ft.
- **Elevation Gain:** 2,501-ft.

(Note: The Schwarzhorn in Davos is often referred to as the Fluela Schwarzhorn to distinguish the peak from the Schwarzhorn in the Valais.)

Start the day by taking the bus from Davos to the Schwarzhorn trailhead, located along the Fluelapass (Fluela Pass) road. (See trailhead directions below.) Get off the bus at the first stop after Fluelapass (east side of the pass). The stop and the trailhead are located along the south side of the road.

Note for hikers driving to the trailhead: There is limited parking at the trailhead. If the lot is full, turn around and park at Fluela Pass. A 0.6 mile (one-way) trail, traveling above the north side of the Fluelapass Road, leads to the Schwarzhorn trailhead. Follow the trail signed for the Schwarzhorn, Fuorcla Radont, Grialetschhutte and Durrboden. This description assumes you are starting at the bus stop. If starting at the pass, add 0.6 miles (one-way) to the mileage in the description below.

Now follow the directions in Hike 102 - Fluela Pass to the Schwarzhorn. From the summit enjoy breathtaking, panoramic views that extend northwest down the Dischma Valley to Davos. The Fluela Wisshorn and nearby peaks tower above Fluela Pass to the north. Piz Linard soars above a sea of peaks rising above the Lower Engadine Valley to the east. The Piz Sarsura massif, Piz Vadret and the Grialetsch Glacier are seen beyond Piz Radont to the south. Piz Kesch, the Porchabella Glacier and the summits rimming the upper Dischma, Funtauna and Tschuvel valleys grace the skyline to the southwest.

To Fuorcla Radont

- **Segment Stat:** 1.95 miles (one-way) from the Schwarzhorn to Fuorcla Radont
- **Total Distance:** 4.25 miles (one way)
- **Maximum Elevation:** 9,137-ft.
- **Elevation Gain/Loss:** 380-ft./-1,560-ft.

When you are done taking in the views atop the Schwarzhorn, descend from the peak and return to the junction with the trail to Fuorcla Radont at 3.0 miles. Turn right (east) at the junction and follow the trail as it descends into the rocky bowl beneath the Raduner Rothorn and Piz Radont.

The path crosses the stark bowl containing the rocky remains from the receding Rothorn Glacier. The remnants of the glacier cling to the slopes beneath Piz Radont. The rugged bowl is strewn with boulders and dotted with small tarns. Red and white slashes on the rock keep you on track.

The hike through the bowl is accompanied by fine views stretching north/northeast from the Fluela Wisshorn to Piz Linard. Behind you, to the west, the Schwarzhorn soars above the bowl. Piz Radont looms above the trail to the south.

At 3.5 miles the trail passes along the south shore of a scenic tarn. Soon the path goes over a small hump and reaches a junction at 4.0 miles. Turn right (southeast) on the trail climbing steeply to Fuorcla Radont (Radont Pass) at 4.25 miles. As you crest the pass great views open to the peaks rimming the east side of the Grialetsch Valley and the splendid cirque at the head of the valley, anchored by Piz Grialetsch, Piz Vadret and Piz Sarsura. The Grialetsch Glacier spills down the slopes of the cirque. Behind you are more fine views of the Schwarzhorn.

From the pass you can drop down the east side of the Radont Valley to Fluela Pass area on a trail losing over 1,300-ft. in just under 2.2 miles for a 6.4 miles loop or continue over the pass to Fuorcla Grialetsch and Durrboden. If time and energy allow, I recommend continuing to Durrboden.

Fuorcla Radont to Fuorcla da Grialetsch to Durrboden

- **Segment Stat:** 3.85 miles (one-way) from Fuorcla Radont to Durrboden
- **Total Distance:** 8.1 miles (round trip)
- **Ending Elevation:** 6,620-ft.
- **Elevation Gain/Loss:** -2,562-ft.

From the Fuorcla Radont the trail descends on easy to moderate grades down the south side of the pass to a grassy knoll with more great views of the Grialetsch cirque. Beyond the knoll the trail soon reaches and crosses a boulder field before dropping down to a bench beneath the east facing slopes of Piz Radont at 4.9 miles.

The grade abates as the path crosses the bowl, reaching the end of the bench at 5.35 miles. Here views open to the Fuorcla da Grialetsch (Grialetsch Pass) area set amid pretty meadows beneath the rugged slopes of the Chilbiritzenspitz. Two lovely tarns lie nestled in the meadows.

The path now descends on steep grades to Fuorcla da Grialetsch (8,320-ft.) and a trail junction at 5.7 miles. To the east are great views of Piz Vadret, the Piz Sarsura massif and the Grialetsch Glacier.

From the junction a trail wanders south to the Grialetsch Hut with more great views of the Grialetsch Glacier and the Piz Sarsura massif along with the beautiful meadows and tarns around the Grialetsch Hut. The hut offers dormitory accommodations and refreshments.

After exploring the area round the hut return to the junction and head west toward Durrboden. The trail descends on gentle grades down the Furgga Valley to the Furggasee (Lake Furgga), a pretty tarn set beneath the south facing slopes of the Raduner Rothorn and Piz Radont at 6.1 miles.

The path traverses the south shore of the lake and then drops steeply down rocky meadows along the north side of the Furgga Valley. The Furggabach (Furgga stream) spills down the valley floor beneath the trail. The rugged slopes of the Raduner Rothorn tower above the trail to the north. Along the way views open southwest to the Chuealphorn, Augstenhureli and Leidhorn rising above the Scaletta Pass area.

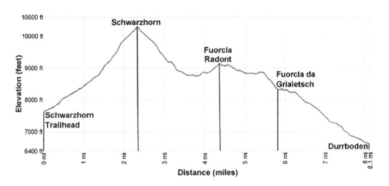

At 7.0 miles the trail curves to the right (northeast) and reaches a junction with a trail branching left toward Scaletta Pass. We continue on the trail descending to Durrboden. Behind you are fine vistas of the Scaletta Glacier clinging to the rugged slopes ringing the Gletschtalli Valley. Ahead views open to a cluster of buildings at Durrboden.

The grade moderates at 7.5 miles as the trail descends through meadows to the east of the Furggabach. Near Durrboden we pass a junction with a trail heading up the Dischma Valley to Scaletta Pass. A short distance beyond we reach the Bergghaus at Durrboden at 8.1 miles.

The historic Berghaus includes a nice restaurant with lovely views of Piz Grialetsch, the Scalettahorn, the Scaletta Glacier and nearby peaks rising above the Gletschtalli. The Raduner Rothorn and Schwarzhorn tower above the east side of the valley. Go around the front of the building to find the bus stop and schedule for the buses returning to Davos.

Trailhead Directions

From the Davos Dorf Bahnhof: See Hike 102.

Durrboden to Davos: Find the bus stop in front of the Berggasthaus at Durrboden. Take the #12 bus bound for Davos Dorf Bahnhof (train station at the northeast end of town) at get off at the train station (the last stop). The ride takes about 32 minutes. A bus schedule is posted at the bus stop of Durrboden. Check the SBB webstie/app for the current schedule.

Note: Buses and trains travel between Davos Dorf and Davos Platz. The train ride takes 3 minutes. Buses take a variety of routes through the town. Pick up a bus schedule at the Tourism Office at the Davos Dorf Bahnhof or near the Sportzentrum in the middle of town, or check the SBB website/app for the current schedules.

104. Wagerhus to Berghaus Vereina via Jorifluelafurgga ★★★★☆
Distance: 6.0 miles (one-way)
Near Davos in Eastern Switzerland

Stunning views of the Joriseen lakes, the Fluela Wisshorn and Jori Glacier await hikers climbing to Jorifluelafurgga. From the pass the trail descends to a beautiful lake basin and then drops down the lovely, untamed Jori Valley, ringed by high peaks, to the Berghaus Vereina.

Distance: 6.0 miles (one-way)
Elevation: 7,238-ft. at Trailhead
8,930-ft. at the Jorifluelafurgga
6,375-ft. at Vereina
Elevation Gain: 1,692-ft./-2,555-ft.

Difficulty: moderate-strenuous
Basecamp: Davos
Davos Map 2: See page 453
Online Map/Photos:
www.hikingwalking.com/vereina

Why Hike from Wagerhus to Berghaus Vereina via Jorifluelafurgga

A stiff climb to the scenic Jorifluelafurgga, a saddle on the ridge to the south of the Jorihorn, is amply rewarded with wonderful views of the photogenic Joriseen lakes and the high peaks towering above the Jori Valley and its tributary glens. From the pass the trail drops down to the lakes basin where hikers can wander among these turquoise-green jewels set against a backdrop of the Fluela Wisshorn and the Jori Glacier.

Finish the hike with a steep descent into the pretty meadows of the wild and pristine Jori Valley. Here lovely views stretching up the Suser Valley to Piz Linard and up the Vernela Valley to the glacier-clad Verstanclahorn.

A short section of the trail dropping down from the pass has some exposure. Fix cables safeguard this segment of the path.

Hiking from Wagerhus to Berghaus Vereina

Start the day with a post bus ride up the Fluela Pass road (Fluelapassstrassa) to the Wagerhus stop. (See trailhead directions below.) Here signs point north/northeast to a trail climbing to the Jorifluelafurgga and Winterlucke. The moderately-steep trail ascends on an angle up the west facing slopes of the ridge between the Jorihorn and Winterlucke. The climb through rocky meadows and intermittent scree enjoys great views of the Schwarzhorn and the Fluela Wisshorn towering above Fluela Pass to the southwest.

At 0.6 miles pass a trail branches right toward Winterlucke Pass. (This trail is very challenging with very steep ascents up slippery, scree covered slopes.) Beyond the junction the trail climbs switchbacks up the Mullersch Talli valley beneath the south facing slopes of the Jorihorn, passing a small lake along the way.

At 1.7 miles the trail curves to the left (north) and ascends the south side of a gully. The path soon swings to the right about the head of the gully and then descends slightly to reach the Jorifluelafurgga, a saddle atop the rugged ridge to the south of the Jorihorn, at 2.1 miles

As you crest the saddle stunning views open to the Joriseen, a group of small lakes nestled in a pretty basin amid meadows and scree slopes. The high peaks rising above the Jori, Suser, Vernela and Vereina valleys fill the skyline to the northeast.

After taking in the views, descend the east side of the craggy ridge on a trail dropping down a series of rocky steps. A short exposed segment of the path is safeguarded with fixed cables. Beyond this section the trail descends through rock and scree covered slopes on steep grades. At 2.5 miles the scree gives way to meadows.

Reach the first of the Joriseen lakes at 2.7 miles. Here the grade abates and the undulating trail now travels southeast along the bench cradling the lakes. The colors of the lakes in the basin vary. The first lake, which is spring fed, is deep blue. The larger lakes are turquoise green, coloring resulting from sunlight reflecting off the glacial slit (also known as rock flour) suspended in the water.

As you cross the bench gorgeous views open to the Jori Glacier clinging to the slopes of the Fluela Wisshorn soaring above the south side of the lakes basin. The Isentallispitz, Gorihorn and Jorihorn tower above the west side of the Jori Valley. The Unghurhorner ridge and the Plattenhorn massif rise above the Suser Valley while the Roggenhorn and Verstanclahorn rim the north side of the Vernela Valley. In the distance the serrated ridges and summits of the Schildflue and Chessler fill the skyline to the north of the Vereina Valley.

At 3.0 miles the trail crosses a metal bridge over the outlet stream for the largest lake. Beyond the bridge the path ascends along a ridge overlooking the Jori Valley to a junction at 3.2 miles. Here we enjoy more great views of the Fluela Wisshorn and the Jori Glacier.

At the junction signs point to trails heading to the Winterlucke Pass, to the south, Joriflesspass, to the east, and Berghaus Vereina, to the north. The side trip to Joriflesspass is recommended it time and energy permit. The 1.8 mile (round-trip) detour takes you by several other lakes and features nice views of the peaks towering above Val Fless.

When you are ready to continue the hike, take the trail towards the Berghaus Vereina, which descend steeply down rugged slopes to the Joribach (Jori stream) at 3.8 miles. The descent continues along the east side of the stream to the valley floor at 4.0 miles. Here the grade eases as the path descends on easy grades through beautiful meadows, crossing a series of streams flowing into the Joribach.

At 4.3 miles the trail drops down a steep slope to the next step along the valley floor. The grade briefly eases but soon resumes its steep descent through meadows to the confluence of the Jori and Suser Valleys at 5.2 miles. During the height of the summer season the slopes above the trail are populated with pretty clusters of heather.

At 5.4 miles the path crosses the Suserbach (Suser stream) on a bridge. Look up the valley to see the summit of Piz Linard peeking over the head of the valley. After a short stint along the east side of the Joribach the trail moves away from the stream and soon reaches the confluence of the Jori and Vernela Valleys. The glacier-clad Verstanclahorn towers above the head of the Vernela Valley.

After crossing the Vernelabach on a bridge at 5.9 mile the trail ends at a broad track. Turn left and walk along the track to the Berghaus Vereina at 6.0 miles. Elevation loss from the Jorifluelafurgga to the Berghaus is 2,555-ft.

The Berghaus Vereina, built in the 1930's, is situation atop a rocky knoll and offers accommodations and refreshments. Contact the Berghaus to arrange accommodations at 081 422 12 16 or check out their website at http://www.berghausvereina.ch.

With advanced planning hikers can take the mini bus from the Berghaus to Klosters. Reservation are required and can be made by contacting Sport Gotschna at 081 422 11 97 or by sending an email to info@gotschnasport.ch.

Otherwise it is a 6.4 miles walk, with a 2,050-ft. elevation loss, down a private road through the Vereina Valley to Monbiel where you can catch a bus to Klosters and then take a train or bus back to Davos.

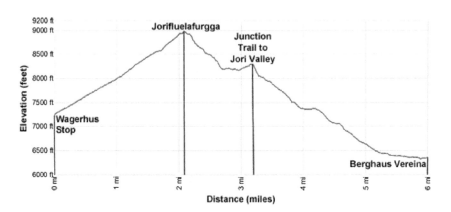

Trailhead Directions

From Davos Dorf, Bahnhof to Wagerhus on the Fluela Pass Road: At the Davos Dorf train station, board the #331 bus heading to either Susch, Staziun or Fluela, Ospiz (Fluela Pass) and get off at the Wagerhus stop. The ride takes about 17 minutes. You can check the current schedules at the SBB website/SBB app. When searching for the stop use Wagerhus/Abzw. Joriseen

From Monbiel to Davos Dorf: From the Monbiel Parkplatz (the large parking lot at the east end of Monbiel), board the #232 bus to Klosters Platz Bahnhof (train station). Get off at the train station and take the train from Klosters Platz to Davos Dorf or Davos Platz, depending on which stop is closest to your accommodations. The trip from Monbiel to Davos should take 39 to 45 minutes depending on connections. You can check the current schedules at the SBB website/SBB app. When searching for the stop in Monbiel use Klosters, Monbiel Parkplatz.

105. Other Trails in Davos

Near Davos in Eastern Switzerland

105a) Davoser See (Lake Davos) Loop

This short, lovely walk around a pretty lake is perfect all year long and a great option if the weather prevents walking in the high country.

- **Distance:** 2.5 mile (loop)
- **Elevation:** 5,112-ft. at Davoser See
- **Elevation Gain:** Essential flat
- **Difficulty:** esay
- **Base camp:** Davos
- **Davos West Map**: See page 453

Lake Davos (Davoser See) is located at the north end of Davos Dorf. The short, easy walk travels on a broad path through meadows and forests along the lakeshore. In the still of the morning the crystal clear waters reflect the surrounding landscape of pastures, forested hills and nearby homes set against a backdrop of the peaks surrounding the Davos area. The north end of the lake offers the best views.

Swimmers, boaters and windsurfers enjoy the lake during the summer. Two restaurants offer refreshments while secluded spots along the lakeshore will appeal to picnickers. The walk is a great option when the weather precludes walking in the high country or for anyone looking for an easy, relaxing stroll. On a clear evening it is a great spot of star gazing.

To reach the lake walk north from the Davos Dorf Bahnhof (train station) along Bahnhofstrasse, the main street through Davos, to the south end of the lake. The walk should take about 8 minutes.

Appendix A: Traveling in Switzerland
Information and tips to faciliate cacation planning

Accommodations

Hotels, Inns and Pensions run the gamut from high-end luxury properties to simple affairs. Star ratings will help you sort through the options. The least expensive hotels offer rooms with sinks and shared baths. Hotel-Garni is a designation to indicate the property only serves breakfast. Other hotels offer half pension (breakfast and dinner) or full pensions (3 meals). Half pensions can be a good deal.

Bed and Breakfasts - Bed and Breakfasts in Switzerland are typically just small hotels and not rooms in private homes. Bed and Breakfast Switzerland (bnb.ch/en) and the Switzerland Tourism site (myswitzerland.com) provide lists of Bed and Breakfasts.

Vacation Rentals - Staying in an apartment and cooking your own meals is a good way to save money while visiting Switzerland. You'll also get a better feel for the villages or towns where you are staying since you will deal with local vendors selling food, baked goods, meat, cheese and other specialties. One quirk in Switzerland is the requirement for a one week stay, typically Saturday to Saturday, for many rentals. You will find some shorter stays in the larger resorts including Zermatt and Grindelwald.

Websites used to find vacation rental apartments in the U.S., such as VRBO and AirBnB, typically include vacation rentals in Switzerland. You can also check out sites such as Interhome (interhome.ch/en), E-domizil (e-domizil.ch/en) and myswitzerland.com. The local tourist sites for each town or village are another good source of listings.

Mountain Inns, Berghotels and Berggasthaus - Typically reached by hiking trails or near the top of lifts, these lovely old lodges are set in scenic locations and usually only open in the summer. They feature simple private rooms and/or dormitory accommodations along with meals. The dining rooms double as shared spaces where people talk, play games or enjoy a drink. Most have shared bathrooms. Some offer hot water and showers. Reservations are recommended. The Hotel Thrift in the Thrift Valley near Zermatt and the Faulhorn above Grindelwald are good examples of berghotels. These simple lodges may seem expensive but remember that prices include meals and all supplies need to be flow in via helicopter or transported on lifts.

Hostels – Most hostels in Switzerland are run by the Swiss Youth Hostels (youthhostel.ch/en), affiliated with Hostels International. Properties offer both private rooms and dormitory accommodations. Sleeping bags are not permitted for fear of bed bugs. Swiss Hostels (swisshostels.com/en) is another good source. Membership is not required and their standards for member properties are not as stringent. There are also private hostels. Note: Hostels in many popular tourist sites are expensive when compared to other destinations.

Camping - Campgrounds are well maintained and typically in good locations. This guide lists the campgrounds near the recommended base camps. More campgrounds can be found at Camping.ch and MyCamper.ch. Campgrounds may include bungalows, private rooms, dormitories and/or a restaurant.

Mountain Huts – The Swiss Alpine Club (sac-cas.ch/en) manages 153 mountain huts. Reservations are recommended and members receive discounts. There are also private huts. Most huts can be booked online or by calling.

Huts typically provide dormitory accommodations, with bunk beds and/or mattress arranged side by side on a platform. Some include private rooms. Meals are served in a cozy communal dining area. (You can bring your own food if you prefer.) Toilets are usually outdoors in separate buildings. Most huts have fantastic views from outdoor patios that serve beer and other refreshments. It is a friendly atmosphere with people sharing stories and experiences.

Here are a few pointers. Remember that each hut has slightly different rules. Typically you must take off your boots in the entryway/boot room (boot racks are provided) before entering the hut. Likewise leave trekking poles, ice axes, etc. in the entry in the allotted spaced. After checking in I recommend finding a mattress or bunk in a far corner of the room, preferable near a window and away from the door. Sleeping bag liners are required (blankets and a pillow are provided).

Take earplugs (very important) and bring a headlamp. Most people staying in huts are respectful of one another, minimizing noise and respecting the lights out time. But dormitories can still be noisy with people snoring, getting up to go to the bathroom at night and setting off early in the morning. There is also an unspoken rule that you should do any packing or rearranging of your backpack outside the dormitory room so you don't disturb others early in the morning.

Finally, research the huts so you can select the best option on your route. All huts are not the same. Some might have better food, more stunning views and a few even have showers. All food, drinks and other supplies are typically delivered to the huts via helicopter. Prices reflect the expense of getting the supplies to the remote location.

Transportation

The Swiss have built one of the world's best transportation systems linking airports, railroads, cities, towns and villages along with providing access to trailheads. Forget renting a car. Trains, buses and lifts (cable cars, gondolas, funiculars and chair lifts) with well-timed connections will whisk you to your destinations. Discount travel cards are available for trips lasting from a weekend to a year.

Trains - The excellent Swiss train system is composed of state run and a few private carriers, such as the railway to Zermatt. The excellent system is typically on time, clean and comfortable with frequent, well timed connections with other trains and the Post bus system. The staff is polite and helpful. Trains usually include first and second class compartments. The second class seating is comfortable. First class compartments are roomier and less crowded but costs much more.

Tickets can be purchased online, at ticket machines or at ticket counters. (Note: ticket purchase can include the entire route, including the final connection via bus if required.) When purchasing tickets at a counter you can ask for an itinerary that will show the connection information including the track for the connecting train or the connecting bus number along with the time allowed for the connection. This information is also available on the SBB website (sbb.ch/en)/App. At the stations you will find schedules listed on yellow signs.

Connections are flexible. It is not a problem if you miss a connection or decide you want to stop for lunch or check out a museum before continuing to your final destination later in the day. Just take the next convenient train/bus.

Buses - Yellow Post Buses supplement and extend the rail system. The buses link areas within towns and between towns with remote villages. Connections are timed so that buses meet incoming trains. Bus stations are conveniently located adjacent to railway stations. The Swiss Rail website (sbb.ch/en) includes train (both state-run and private), bus and lift schedules, allowing you to easily find a schedule to get you to/from anywhere in the country. Tickets can be purchased directly from the bus driver (cash only), on the SBB website/App, from machines at the bus stop or at the service counters of some post offices.

Mountain Rail Systems (lifts) - This class of transportation includes funiculars (seilbahn in German / funiculaire in French), cable cars (luftseilbahn / telepherique), gondolas (gondelbahn / telecabine) and chairlifts (sesselbahn / telesiege). When arriving in a new area it is helpful to stop at the tourist office and get information on the daily start and end times for the various systems. Make sure you know the time for the last ride down. Schedules are also available on online (see the local tourism office sites).

Luggage

Be sure to put your luggage in designated places on trains and buses so that it does not take up a seat or impede passage ways. Trains include overhead storage racks, separate storage shelves and, at times, a place behind the seat. Keep an eye on your luggage. Theft is not common but does occur. Buses have limited room in overhead racks. The driver will stow luggage that does not fit in the overhead compartment in the large compartments accessible from the outside of the bus. Large backpacks, skis and other oversized items should go in these storage areas.

Larger train stations in Switzerland include lockers (fees apply) where you can leave your luggage for up to 24 hours. This is very convenient if you arrive in a city by train and want to tour around for a few hours before heading to your next destination.

Swiss Discount Cards

Swiss Travel Passes offer substantial savings on trains, buses and lifts (cable cars, gondolas, funiculars and chairlifts) along with discounts on some tourist attractions. Passes can be purchased at major train stations. Some passes can also be purchased online ahead of time. Always read the small print to understand the exclusions. URL: sbb.ch/en/leisure-holidays/travel-in-switzerland/international-guests/swiss-travel-pass.html .

Swiss Travel Pass - This card offers unlimited travel by train, bus and boat, discounts of 25%-50% on funiculars, gondolas, chairlifts and cable cars and private railways, free use of public transportation in 90 towns and cities, free admission to over 500 museums along with discounts on other tourist attractions. See the website for the current list of benefits.

Passes can be purchase for stays ranging from three to 15 days. A Swiss Travel Pass Flex offers the same benefits but is valid on 3, 4, 8, or 15 freely selectable days within a one month period. Both cards are offered at 15% discount for people under 26 years of age. Children under 6 travel free when accompanied by a pass holder while children between age 6-16 travel free when accompanied by a parent with a Swiss Family Card. See the website for more details. This discount card can be a great deal for people who are constantly moving between locations.

URL's: Swiss Pass - sbb.ch/en/leisure-holidays/travel-in-switzerland/international-guests/swiss-travel-pass.html

Swiss Half Cards - Half Cards are designed for longer stays in Switzerland. Cards can be purchased for one month or one year. (The one month cards are a special offer for international guests.) A half cards can quickly pays for itself. The card offers a 50% discount on trains, buses, boats and most mountain railways (funiculars, gondolas, cable cars and chair lifts.) The discount does not apply to privately owned mountain railways or trains, such as the train line running to Zermatt. There is also a 50% discount on the use of public transportation in 90 urban areas. A half card also allows you to ship luggage between major stations for a reasonable fee. See the Luggage information on the SBB sites for conditions. Check the station services page to see which stations offer the baggage transfer service.

Children between 6 and 16 years of age accompanied by a parent holding a valid ticket travel free of charge with a complimentary Swiss Family Card. Children under 6 years of age travel free when accompanied by a travel card holder. Cards can be purchased for a one month period or one year, which works well for someone on a long term visit to the country. The one month card can be purchased online. Purchase the one year card at a major train station upon arrival. Note: You must have an address is Switzerland where the card can be mailed. (A hotel will work, just make sure you ask the hotel if they will receive mail for you ahead of time. In the meantime the SBB will issue a temporary card good for 10 days.) See the website for the current list of benefits and rules.

URLs: One month card: sbb.ch/en/leisure-holidays/travel-in-switzerland/international-guests/swiss-halffare-card.html

1 Year Card: sbb.ch/en/travelcards-and-tickets/railpasses/half-fare-travelcard.html

Luggage: sbb.ch/en/station-services/before-your-journey/luggage/luggage/station-to-station.html

Station Services: sbb.ch/en/station-services/at-the-station/railway-stations.html

Gastekarte or Visitor Cards are available in some tourist resorts, towns and villages. The cards may offer free or discounted travel on buses, trains and lifts and/or reduced prices for area museums, swimming pools and other tourist attractions. Cards are typically given out at your accommodation. Check at the local tourist office if you are not staying at a participating accommodation to see if you can purchase a card. Purchasing a card is not always a good deal unless you are planning on riding the most expensive lifts.

Food

The two major grocery store chains: Migros and the Coop, are great places to shop for food in Switzerland. There are several smaller chains: Volg, Denner and Spar, along with private run stores in the smaller towns and villages. Swiss bakeries carry a wide selection of bread, pastries and other confections. There are also specialty cheese and meat stores.

Hikers will find a good selection of nuts, dried fruits, canned fish, cheese and cold cuts in stores for a packed lunch. There is also a good selection of fresh fruit, energy bars and candy to keep you going on the trail.

When hiking always carry water or a water filter. Cows and sheep graze in the high country where ever there is good grass. Assume all the water supplies are unsafe to drink.

Breakfast is buffet style in most hotels and includes items such as bread, jam, butter, cereal, yogurt, cold cuts, hard boiled eggs, juice, coffee and tea. Some buffets are very simple while others have a wide variety of items. In huts breakfast is very simple: bread, butter, jam, coffee and tea.

Lunch at mountain huts will be simple but relatively expensive. Remember everything you purchase at a hut needs to be transported by helicopter, mule or cable car/gondola to the site. This adds to the cost.

Larger Coops and Migros Supermarkets include cafeterias. They offer a great selection of prepared foods at reasonable prices. In the larger cities you will find a good selection of restaurants. The smaller towns and villages will have less variety. Many restaurants, including the Coop and Migros cafes, offer daily meal specials which are good deal for anyone on a budget.

Hiking in Switzerland

Signs - Excellent signage and great maintenance are the hallmarks of Swiss hiking trails. Standard yellow trail signs on metal posts include pointers to destinations with the average expected time for the hike. For example, at the beginning of the Hohbalm trail in Zermatt you will see a yellow sign listing the time as "Hohbalmen 1 Std. 5 Min." (Std is the abbreviation for Stunde which means hour.) Mileage is not listed. Instead the time takes into account the mileage, elevation gain/loss and trail difficulty. The time does not take into account breaks. As you hike the trails you will soon learn if you are hiking at a faster or slower pace than the time listed on the signs. Some signs include white location markers indicating the name of the location and altitude in meters.

Trails can be marked as Wanderwegs (basic hiking trail) or Bergwegs (mountain trails that travel through more rugged terrain). Red and white blazes on rocks supplement the signs, helping you to navigate through potentially confusing terrain, boulder fields and other obstacles.

Blue/White sign designate high alpine routes for fit, experienced hikers. Some scrambling, climbing or glacier travel may be required. Routes can also have some exposure and tricky footing. Routes are not included in this guide.

Pink signs are for winter trails.

Fences and Gates

- When passing through a closed gate always make sure it is closed once you are through. "Bitte Die Tur Schloseen" or "fermez la porte, s.v.p." means please close the fence, in German and French (respectively).
- Electric fences surrounding grazing fields are made of colorful plastic strips typically strung on plastic stakes. If you look carefully you will see the electric wires running through the strips. Most are connected to batteries or solar panels. Gates on electric fences are equipped with a black plastic hand grips with a hook on one end and a spring on the other. To pass through the gate use the hand grip to unhook the fencing. Be sure to re-hook the gate in the same way you found it.

Pack it In/Pack it Out - The trails in Switzerland are typically spotless. Keep them in this condition by carrying out all your garbage. Likewise, bury personal waste and take used toilet paper with you. Carry a small zip lock or other container for this purpose.

Safety

- Hiking and other outdoor recreational activities involve a certain degree of risk and are by their very nature potentially hazardous. It is not within the scope of this guide to allow for disclosure of all potential hazards and risks involved in outdoor activities. All participants in such activities must assume the responsibility of their own actions and safety.
- Check at local tourism office to determine if there are any issues with the trails you plan to hike. Avalanches and rock falls can turn a safe trail into a hazard. The locals are the best people to ask about current conditions.
- Always carry rain gear and warm clothing. A beautiful day can quickly change into a cold, wet affair during a thunderstorm. If you see the weather taking a turn for the worse, turn around and/or get down from exposed areas as quickly as possible. Getting an early start is the best way to avoid storms that tend to occur in the afternoon.
- Don't try to cross a glacier unless properly equipped and with an experienced guide.
- Use your judgment as you would in your home country when walking in the mountains. Don't take unnecessary risks. If you are uncomfortable on a trail, turn around and find another walk for the day.

Websites

- **HikingWalking.com** – is the online adjunct to this guide. Here you will find photo galleries and interactive maps for all the hikes in this guide.

- **Swiss Topo Maps** - Excellent interactive topo maps showing the country's extensive trail system along with towns, roads and other features. They also offer an app and sell hard copy topographic maps at 1:25,000 scale. The maps are generally available in outdoor stores and at tourist offices. (map.geo.admin.ch/?topic=swisstopo)
- **SwitzerlandMobility** – Hiking in Switzerland - maps and information on trails. (schweizmobil.ch/en/wanderland.html)

Hard Copy Maps - Don't depend on having an internet connection in the high country. Carry the appropriate maps. Outdoor stores and tourist offices typically will have a good selection of maps for the surrounding area.

- **Kummerly + Fey** - Good selection of hiking maps at a scale of 1:60,000. (swisstravelcenter.ch/en/outdoor-leisure/hiking/)
- **Swiss Topographic Maps** are available in outdoor stores and bookstore. Excellent hard copy maps at 1:25,000 scale covering the entire country and 1:50,000 scale covering the regions.

Transportation

- **SBB – Swiss Rail System** - excellent site with schedules and prices for buses, trains, lifts and other transportation. (sbb.ch/en)
- Hikes in this guide making use of funiculars, cable cars, gondolas and/or chairlifts. Query the name of the lift or go to the local tourism websites for links to schedules and pricing.

Weather - The best time for hiking in the Swiss Alps is between July and mid to late September. If you go in June you will run into snow in the high country. Likewise, push the trip later in the year and you will find passes blocked by early season snow. Weather changes quickly in the mountains. Make sure you are prepared for sudden temperature drops and/or storms.

The low lying cities and towns can get quite warm during the summer. In the past air conditioning was rarely needed in Switzerland. This is changing. Air condition is not available in many hotels or other types of accommodations although fans are becoming more prevalent. Up in the mountains it cools down at night, so even if you hit a heat wave it will still be comfortable for sleeping.

Hours - When you arrive in a town or village it is a good idea to check on opening hours. Restaurants are typically open for lunch between noon and 2:30 pm and for dinner from 6 pm to 9:30 pm. Stores may be closed for a lunch break and have reduced hours on Saturday. Many businesses are closed Sundays. Some places are closed one or two days during the week. Shops and restaurants in the villages and small towns tend to have more traditional hours while in the larger cities and resorts the opening times are more flexible.

Holidays - During the summer the main holiday to watch for is National Day on August 1st. Make sure you have your accommodations booked for that day or, better yet, the week encompassing the first day of August. It is a period when everyone in Switzerland takes a vacation. Vacation destinations are booked ahead of time and transportation is packed.

Languages - There are four official languages in Switzerland: German, French, Italian and Romansh.

Currency - The Swiss Franc (CHF) is the country's official currency.

Tipping - Tipping is not necessary in Switzerland. Restaurants pay a living wage. Some customers round the bill up to the nearest franc. If you do tip, give the tip directly to the server.

Public Toilet - Public toilets are available in many locations. The facilities are neat and clean. Many toilets will require a small fee of 1 CHF (swiss franc) or 2 CHF. The facilities are referred to as a WC, Toiletten (German), Toilettes (French) or Gabinetti (Italian). Women's rooms are signed for Damen, Frauen, Signore or Femmes while men's rooms are labeled as Herren, Signore, Hommes or Messieurs. Bathrooms are located in most tourist offices, train stations and large supermarkets.

Appendix B. Switzerland on a Budget

Tips for saving money while traveling in Switzerland

"Isn't Switzerland expensive?" This is a questions frequently asked by people planning a trip to the country. The answer is yes, but there are ways to still see this beautiful country on a budget.

- Instead of constantly moving around pick one or two destinations. Moving between destinations means more money spent on transportation and less time for hiking. You can't see it all so choose a few standout destinations and then spend several days or a week at each hiking the trails.
- If your main purpose is hiking then avoid the major cities. Staying in the cities is expensive. If you fly into Zurich on an overnight flight get on a train at the airport and travel either mid-way or all the way to your first hiking destination.
- Staying at a hostel is a good way to save money. The price of hostels and small hotels with shared facilities varies by location.
- Find a place to stay in some of the outlying neighborhoods or nearby towns. For example, instead of staying in Zermatt look for accommodations in Randa or Tasch. Some budget travelers stay in Interlaken or Widerswil and then take the train to Grindelwald and/or Lauterbrunnen. Keep in mind you will need to take a train to your hike, so having a discount card (see Appendix A) might make sense.

- Staying at a vacation apartment and cooking your own meals is another great option for saving money. Budget travelers can find rooms on AirBnB or other apps. Alternatively, look into the couch surfing apps (use caution on this option and research the sites/hosts well). Vacation rentals are my preferred choice when traveling in Switzerland.
- Restaurants are expensive. Instead, purchase food at grocery stores. Many of these stores have a takeout section. Check out the cafes in grocery stores or the meals of the day offered by area restaurants. Pizza and ethnic food such as Thai, Chinese, Indian, Middle Eastern and Kebab shops are great options for lower cost meals.
- Pack your lunch. Eating at huts is expensive. If you want to eat at a hut and are on a budget then try the soup, which typically comes with a side of bread. It is delicious and filling.
- Look into purchasing a Swiss discount card (see Appendix A). Remember you don't need or want to rent a car in Switzerland. Think about the places you will visit and the hikes your wish to take. With this information you can easily look at fares and quickly see if a discount card will save money based on your itinerary. You can also select places to go where the resort or local villages offer Guest Cards. Saas Fee is an excellent example of a place where the Guest Card will save you a lot of money. (Make sure the accommodation where you are staying offers the the local card.)
- There are hiking destinations where many of the trailheads are reachable on foot or by a bus ride, which is considerably less expensive than riding a cable car or other type of lift. Alternatively, fit and conditioned hikers can either forgo the cable car completely or take it one way (up) and walk down. Note: cable cars and other types of lifts save you a lot of time and elevation gain. Half Cards or Swiss Passes can greatly reduce the cost. Guest Cards are another way to reduce or eliminate the cost of lifts and other types of local transport.
- You don't need a hiking guide. Swiss trails are very well marked and your fellow hikers are friendly and always willing to help. Ditto with touring around the cities. Stop at the tourist office, pick-up a map and ask the helpful people at the counter for ideas given your interests. They can help you plan your day.

Printed in Great Britain
by Amazon

83504612R00292